Neuroevolution

Neuroevolution

Harnessing Creativity in AI Agent Design

Sebastian Risi, Yujin Tang, David Ha, and Risto Miikkulainen

The MIT Press

Cambridge, Massachusetts
London, England

The MIT Press
Massachusetts Institute of Technology
77 Massachusetts Avenue
Cambridge, MA 02139
mitpress.mit.edu

The MIT Press would like to thank the anonymous peer reviewers who provided comments on drafts of this book. The generous work of academic experts is essential for establishing the authority and quality of our publications. We acknowledge with gratitude the contributions of these otherwise uncredited readers.

This book was set in LaTeX by the authors. Printed and bound in the United States of America.

Library of Congress Cataloging-in-Publication Data is available.

ISBN: 978-0-262-05476-8

EU Authorised Representative: Easy Access System Europe, Mustamäe tee 50, 10621 Tallinn, Estonia | Email: gpsr.requests@easproject.com

To our families

Contents

Foreword

Neuroevolution is the study of how to use evolutionary computation methods in the design and optimization of neural networks. And neuroevolution might just be the "next big thing" in artificial intelligence (AI). Why neuroevolution? And why now?

Since the beginnings of the field of AI in the 1940s and 1950s, AI researchers have taken inspiration from intelligent and adaptive systems in nature. The best-known example is biological brains, which led to neural networks and deep learning. But other inspirations for AI have included biological systems ranging from immune systems to ant colonies, and most notably, the processes of evolution driven by natural selection.

Work on evolution-inspired AI has gone under the names "genetic algorithms," "evolution strategies," "genetic programming," and more generally "evolutionary computation." All such approaches involve populations of individuals that represent solutions to a problem or set of problems, where a solution can be in the form of a vector, a program, a grammar, or other kinds of data structures, depending on the task. Each individual is assigned a "fitness" value encoding its quality according to some task-specific criteria, and the population undergoes a computational version of natural selection, in which the fittest individuals produce "offspring"; that is, new individuals, with variation generated by mutation and recombination. This process is repeated for some number of iterations ("generations"), at which point one or more highly fit solutions have (hopefully) been discovered.

My own enchantment with evolutionary computation started in graduate school at the University of Michigan, where I had the privilege to study with John Holland, the founder of the field of genetic algorithms (GAs). In his book *Adaptation in Natural and Artificial Systems*,[1] Holland showed that biological evolution could be abstracted in such a way as to be programmed and run on machines. In my own computational experiments with GAs, it was thrilling to witness innovative solutions to complex problems being created via the simple mechanisms of selection and variation, iterated over many generations.

Holland's work on GAs began in the 1960s. Around the same time, a few other groups were investigating similar ideas, such as the evolution strategies of Hans-Paul Schwefel and others.[2] During the 1960s and in subsequent decades, research on neural networks and on evolutionary computation advanced along largely independent paths, each area growing its own research community with separate conferences, journals, and benchmarks for measuring progress. These lesser-known, biologically inspired AI approaches stood

[1]Holland, J. H. (1975). *Adaptation in Natural and Artificial Systems*. University of Michigan Press.

[2]Schwefel, H. P. (1984). Evolution Strategies: A Family of Non-Linear Optimization Techniques Based on Imitating Some Principles of Organic Evolution. *Annals of Operations Research*, 1.

in contrast to the logic-inspired, symbolic AI methods, including "expert systems," that dominated the field.

By the late 1980s, there was widespread sentiment that none of the major AI methods—symbolic, neural, or evolutionary—had lived up to expectations, and an "AI winter" set in. Indeed, when I graduated with a PhD in 1990, I was advised not to use the term "artificial intelligence" on my job applications.

In the 1990s and early 2000s, the next big thing in AI was machine learning, which, at the time, drew its inspirations from statistics and other mathematical approaches to inference from data. However, research continued on both neural networks and evolutionary computation in relatively small communities.

This changed dramatically in the 2010s with the meteoric rise of deep neural networks, a technology that had been around since at least the 1980s, but suddenly showed dramatic improvements in performance due to *scale*—the ability to train very large networks with sufficient data by virtue of increased compute power and the availability of enormous corpora of images, text, and other modalities on the World Wide Web. The 2010s saw the "deep learning revolution" in computer vision, speech recognition, language translation, and other long-studied areas of AI. In the 2020s, the world witnessed the rise of generative AI, based on the *transformer* architecture, a kind of deep neural network architecture optimized for sequence learning. The most successful generative AI models have up to trillions of tunable parameters, and are trained on up to a petabyte of data. It seemed to many that scaling up these systems would soon result in machines with human-level intelligence.

However, several years after the release of ChatGPT, most AI researchers are coming to the conclusion that scaling alone is actually a "dead end."[3] While the best generative AI systems are remarkably good at many things, they remain stubbornly brittle on tasks requiring complex decision-making, as well as trustworthy generalization, reasoning, and planning—abilities needed for intelligent agents that accomplish ill-defined or open-ended tasks in the real world.

This book argues that neuroevolution will be part of a new revolution in AI. The development of evolutionary methods for optimizing different components of neural networks dates back to the 1980s. And as it did for neural networks, scaling computing power and data might unlock neuroevolution's potential. As the prominent roboticist Rodney Brooks speculated, "Perhaps there is an opportunity to reinvent evolutionary computation and exploit the competition ready training sets and massive amounts of computation."[4]

Interest in evolutionary computation has stemmed from the fact that evolution, at scale, has given rise to many essential features of intelligent and adaptive systems. These include the abilities to continually adapt to changing environments, to design open-ended diversity and novelty, and to create collective intelligence—complex multi-agent systems that, via cooperative and competitive interactions, produce adaptive behavior that is far more than the sum of their parts. In addition, evolution is a mechanism for hierarchical adaptation, simultaneously working on many levels ranging from genes to individuals, and

[3] https://futurism.com/ai-researchers-tech-industry-dead-end.

[4] https://x.com/rodneyabrooks/status/1204249201913122817.

on to groups and even entire coevolutionary ecosystems. This book makes the argument that such features can be captured in computational systems, and provides readers the essential knowledge and tools they will need to build neuroevolutionary AI.

Authored by four pioneering neuroevolution researchers, this book provides detailed primers on the major ideas, methods, and mathematics underlying both evolutionary computation and neural networks, and on the many ways in which they can be combined, summarizing advances from decades of work in this field. The book also provides numerous real-world case studies in domains such as decision-making, control systems, robotics, and video games, which demonstrate the ways in which these methods can be used to deal with dynamic, ambiguous, and uncertain environments, to simultaneously optimize multiple levels of a system, often taking into account multiple goals, and to enable lifelong learning, open-ended adaptation, and novelty creation.

The next big thing in AI is coming, and I suspect that neuroevolution will be a major part of it.

Melanie Mitchell, Santa Fe, New Mexico, March 2025

Online Supplement

https://neuroevolutionbook.com/

The website provides supplementary material that we hope will be useful to readers and instructors, including demos, tutorials, exercises, lecture slides, and any corrections and updates.

Preface

Artificial intelligence (AI) has surged into mainstream popularity, with generative AI technologies such as large language models (LLMs) capturing the public's imagination. Conversations about AI's potential and power are everywhere, as these models compose text, generate images, and mimic human language at an unprecedented scale. Amid this boom, however, lies another field with equally transformative potential: neuroevolution. Neuroevolution has developed unique approaches and capabilities that have yet to capture the same level of mainstream attention.

Neuroevolution, which combines principles of neural networks with evolutionary processes, has been around for decades. It offers solutions that go beyond imitation and pattern recognition, extending into areas of adaptability, creativity, and resilience. While traditional AI often relies on predefined objectives and vast datasets, neuroevolution excels in environments where goals are ambiguous, rewards are sparse, and conditions are ever-changing. This approach introduces a method of designing and evolving AI systems that can handle complex, high-dimensional problems with minimal human intervention, and it is precisely this adaptability that is set to bring neuroevolution to the forefront of AI in the coming years.

As AI advances into realms requiring flexibility and open-ended problem-solving, neuroevolution has shown great promise in evolving robust, adaptive, and creative solutions. It is particularly promising for applications where the optimal solution is unknown or hard to define, such as robotics, dynamic systems, and even art and design. With neuroevolution, we can create agents that not only evolve but also learn continuously during their lifetime, much as biological organisms do in nature.

This book serves as a gateway into the world of neuroevolution, providing readers with both a foundational understanding and practical tools for harnessing its potential. It covers the core concepts, algorithms, and applications of neuroevolutionary systems, with each chapter containing examples and questions that encourage readers to engage critically with the material. By offering insights into synergies with generative AI, reinforcement learning, and other domains, we hope to demonstrate the relevance of neuroevolution to the future of AI.

This book would not have been possible without the contributions of researchers and pioneers in neuroevolution and evolutionary computation, whose insights and innovations have laid the foundation for this work. We are also grateful to our colleagues, students, and readers who have inspired us with their curiosity and feedback, helping us to refine and expand upon the ideas presented here. We would also like to thank our MIT editor Elizabeth Swayze, who believed in this project early on and was a pleasure to work with.

An addition, we would like to express our gratitude to everybody who gave us permission to reproduce images and figures from their publications. We indicate the figure sources throughout the book in the captions. Special thanks to Ken Stanley for giving detailed feedback on a draft of this book, Noah Syrkis for assistance in obtaining figure permissions, and Julianna Nijmeh and Manasha Vengat for help in designing and building the book's website (`https://neuroevolutionbook.com/`).

Writing this book has been a long journey. We want to thank our families and friends for their support, without which this book would not have seen the light of day. Sebastian would like to thank his wife, Débora, for her support and patience throughout the countless hours spent writing this book. He is also deeply grateful to his parents, whose love, encouragement, and belief in him have shaped the path that made this work possible. Yujin is very grateful to his wife, Jinmei, for tolerating many late nights and caffeine-fueled ramblings; half the credit for his contribution to this book belongs to her. David would like to thank his parents for their unwavering support, love, and encouragement throughout every step of this journey. Risto would like to thank his wife, Riitta, and mom, Raili, for providing a distraction-free environment for three-month writing binges in Helsinki. We would also like to thank Sakana AI and Cognizant AI Lab for the financial support, which allowed this book to be enjoyed in color.

Chapter 1

Introduction

To illustrate what **neuroevolution** is about, consider the following four challenges (figure 1.1).

Imagine that you want to create a character in a video game where you, as the player, perform search and rescue. This character acts as your sidekick, scouting for helpful information, helping move large objects, and so on. You want the character to anticipate what you want to do and act in a believable, human like manner: It has limited resources, as you do, but generally uses them well. How do you design such a character? Many of its characteristics are difficult to describe, but you know it when you see it.

Now imagine that a new pandemic is emerging. It seems to target particularly vulnerable populations, to be transmitted through the air in crowded conditions, and to have a long incubation period. The disease has already led to hospitalizations in several countries, and some have taken measures to contain it: for example, by closing schools, restricting air travel, and establishing contact tracing. Eventually, the pathogen will be sequenced, and vaccines and medications perhaps developed for it, but we need to cope with the spread of the disease right now. Can we learn from these experiences around the world, and come up with intervention recommendations that are customized for the current situation in different countries, or even different cities and neighborhoods?

You are an analyst at a retailer, trying to predict sales of different products in different stores to optimize inventory and minimize waste. You have historical data that includes product descriptions, seasonal variations, and economic indicators, which should allow you to use deep learning to make predictions. However, there is not enough data to do that: Such a network would likely learn to memorize the small dataset and not generalize well in the future. However, there is a lot of data about other types of sales, as well as other economic and retail metrics. Could you design a deep learning architecture that utilizes all these other datasets so you can learn to predict your data better?

You are a biologist studying the behavior of a particular species, such as hyenas. You discover that in some circumstances, they perform an extremely sophisticated coordination of collaborative actions that allows them to overpower a group of lions. While hyenas are good at many social tasks, this one stands out as something beyond their usual capabilities. Could we be seeing evolution taking place; that is, an adaptation that eventually leads to a leap in social intelligence? It is not possible to verify the hypothesis in the field, or even in

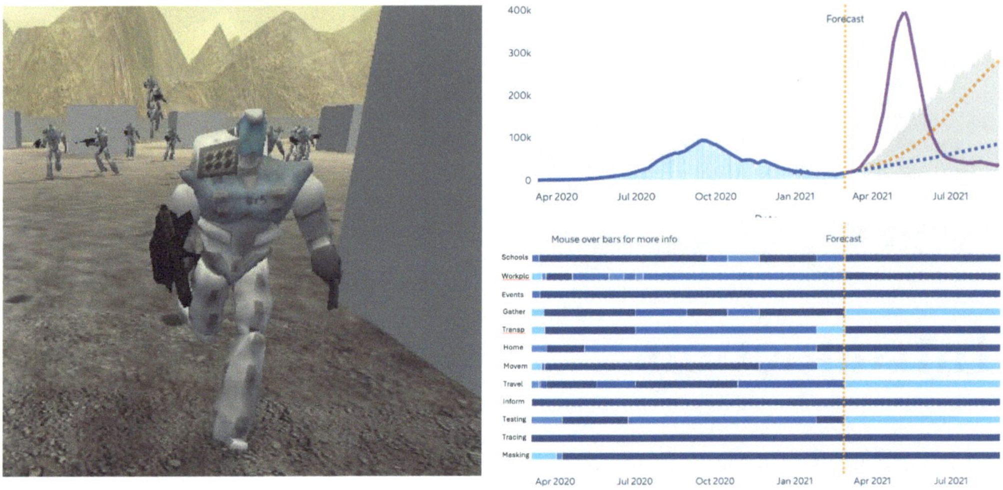

(*a*) Video-game character (*b*) Pandemic intervention strategy

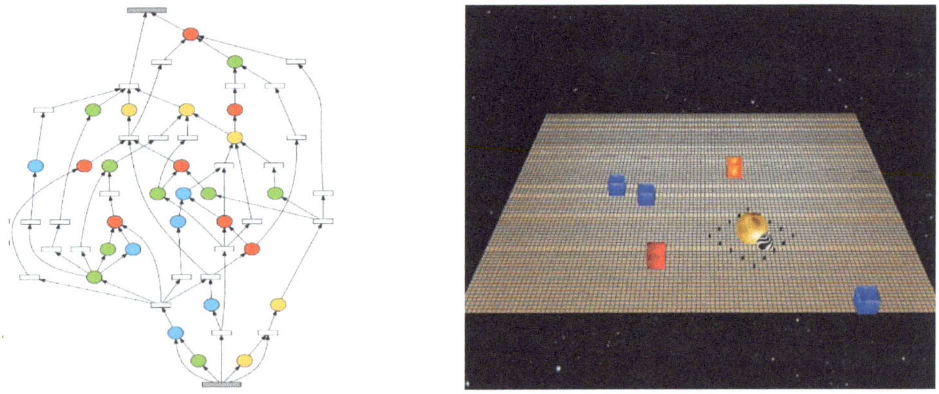

(*c*) A network sharing knowledge across tasks (*d*) Evolution of coordination

Figure 1.1: **Illustrative opportunities for neuroevolution.** (*a*) A character in a video game is controlled by an evolved neural network. It balances multiple objectives, including ill-defined ones such as "human-like behavior." (*b*) Based on a predictive model learned from historical data (top), neuroevolution constructs a strategy that can be applied to different countries at different times. It discovers customized solutions (bottom) that are more effective than general rules of thumb. (*c*) In learning multiple tasks at once, neuroevolution discovers a common set of modules, and for each task, a different architecture made of these modules (this one recognizes handwritten characters in the Angelic alphabet; the different modules are labeled by color). By combining knowledge from multiple tasks, neuroevolution can make deep learning work even when the data is otherwise insufficient. (*d*) Neuroevolution discovers sophisticated coordination that allows simulated hyenas to steal a kill from lions. It is possible to identify what steps in evolution led to this breakthrough; i.e., the descendants of risk-taking (red) and risk-averse (blue) hyenas will evolve to approach up to the striking distance (black dotted square) where they can overpower the lion (yellow, with a zebra kill). Figure *c* from Liang, Meyerson, and Miikkulainen (2018).

the lab: the relevant pressures may operate over many generations, the key events may be rare, and the ecological conditions that give rise to them may be impossible to reproduce experimentally. Could we create a computational simulation to provide evidence for it?

These four examples illustrate neuroevolution in action. Neuroevolution, or optimization of neural network designs through evolutionary computation, is an approach in the artificial intelligence (AI) toolbox that is different from just about anything else. The idea is not to optimize a quantitative metric, but rather to find solutions that achieve multiple goals, some of which may be ill-defined; not to replace human creativity and decision-making authority, but to extend it with a powerful tool for discovery; not to solve problems by encoding and applying what already works, but to discover creative, effective solutions that can be surprising and difficult to find; not to create static and rigid solutions, but behavior that generalizes and adapts to an unpredictable and changing world. Thus, with neuroevolution, it is possible to develop AI-based decision-making to improve engineering, science, and society in general.

This book aims to give the reader the conceptual and practical knowledge needed to take advantage of neuroevolution in a range of applications, and also to develop it further. The discussion will begin in this chapter with a high-level overview of neuroevolution mechanisms, comparing and contrasting them with other types of creative AI, and identifying opportunities where neuroevolution can have the most significant impact. The rest of the book then reviews evolutionary computation basics, methods for taking advantage of encodings and diversity, constructing intelligent agents, empowering and leveraging other learning systems (such as deep learning, neuromorphic, reinforcement learning, and generative AI), and modeling and drawing insights from biology.

1.1 Evolving Neural Networks

Neuroevolution is the practice of applying **computational evolution** methods to **artificial neural networks**. Most students of machine learning (ML) are taught that to train a neural network, one needs to define an objective function to measure how well the neural network performs in the task, use backpropagation to solve for the derivatives of this objective function with respect to each weight, and then use these derivatives iteratively to find a good set of weights. This framework is known as **end-to-end training**.

While the backpropagation algorithm is a powerful method for many applications, it is certainly not the only one. There are other methods for coming up with neural network weights. For example, going to one extreme, one method is to randomly guess the weights of a neural network until we get a set of weights that can help us perform a task.

Evolutionary algorithms (EAs) are a principled approach beyond random guessing. It works as follows: Imagine that we have 100 sets of random weights for a neural network, and we evaluate the neural network with each set of weights to see how well it performs a given task. After doing this, we keep only the best 20 sets of weights. Then, we populate the remaining 80 sets of weights based on the 20 sets that we kept. Those 20 serve as raw material, and we apply genetic operations crossover and mutation to form new sets of weights; they preserve useful structure while introducing variation.

Crossover is a recombination operator; that is, it forms a new set by choosing randomly from two (or more) existing sets. Note that the existing sets are known to be relatively good already, so crossover aims to find ways to combine their strengths. **Mutation** is a novelty operator; that is, it chooses a weight in the new set randomly, and modifies it randomly to create a new weight. Thus, mutation aims to create weights that may not already exist among the top 20 sets but would be useful to have.

The 80 new sets of weights thus constitute a mutated recombination of the top 20. Once we have a full population of 100 sets of weights again, we can repeat the task of evaluating the neural network with each set of weights again and repeat the evolution process until we obtain a set of weights that satisfies our needs (figure 1.2).

This type of algorithm is an example of neuroevolution. It is very useful for solving for neural network weights when it is difficult to define a mathematically well behaved objective function, such as functions with no clear derivatives. Using this simple method in the past, we have been able to train neural networks to balance inverted pendulums, play video games, and get agents to learn to avoid obstacles collectively.

In the past few decades, however, neuroevolution has developed into a branch of AI of its own. Several new techniques beyond random exploration have been proposed to make it systematic and effective, and it has turned out to be a state-of-the-art (SOTA) method in many application areas. This book reviews these techniques and opportunities. But let us start by outlining neuroevolution's role in AI in general.

1.2 Extending Creative AI

The field of AI is going through a transformation, a paradigm shift. It is emerging from the laboratory and getting integrated into the mainstream of society, changing how much human intellectual activity is organized and conducted. Technically, the focus of AI methods is moving from prediction to prescription: that is, from imitating what people do to creating new solutions that have not existed before. For instance, instead of recognizing images and understanding language, or predicting the weather or binding strength of molecules, AI is now generating images at will, writing prose and answering questions, creating new molecules that never existed before, and making decisions about resource allocations, treatment plans, and engineering design. This technology has been named **agentic AI** because it consists of intelligent agents that make changes in the world.

There is no single technology or breakthrough that made this progress possible; instead, it emerged from the confluence of several factors. A most important one is simply the availability of massive amounts of data—much of human experience (e.g., text, code, images, video, music, and scientific datasets) is now available online. At the same time, computational resources are now available on an unprecedented and unexpectedly large scale—a million-fold increase from the 1990s to the 2010s (Routley, 2017), and about four orders of magnitude since then. As a result, many of the techniques that have been known since the 1990s—techniques that looked promising but never quite worked at scale—can now be scaled up and made to work.

The most impactful one, of course, is **large language models** (LLMs; Hadi, Al-Tashi, Qureshi, et al., 2025; Min, Ross, Sulem, et al., 2024). **Gradient descent** as a learning mechanism for neural networks became popular in the 1980s (although conceived much before), and the task of predicting the next word in text (or more generally, a token in a sequence) has been used to demonstrate properties of neural networks for decades. An important innovation in modeling language structure was the **transformer architecture**,

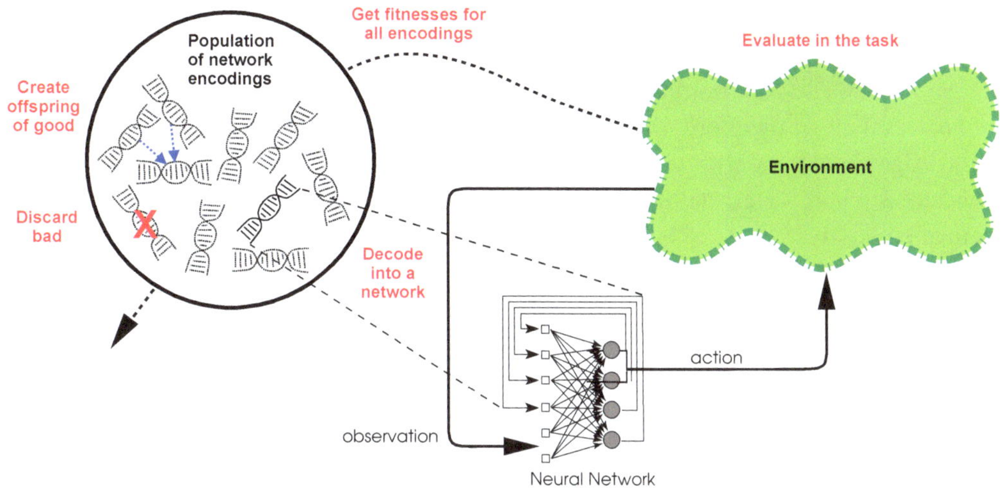

Figure 1.2: **A general framework for neuroevolution.** The process starts with a population of neural networks, encoded e.g., as a set of weights in a fixed network topology, concatenated into a string, and initialized randomly. Each encoding is decoded into a network, which is then evaluated in the task to estimate its fitness–that is, to see how well it performs in the task. The encodings of networks that perform well become parents for the next generation of networks: They are mutated and recombined with other good encodings to form offspring networks. These offspring networks replace those that performed poorly in the original population. Some of these offspring networks are likely to include good parts of both parents, and therefore they will perform better than their parents. This process repeats until networks are eventually created that solve the task. Note that gradient information is not necessary; only high-level fitness information is needed. Thus, neuroevolution is a population-based search that discovers and utilizes building blocks as well as random exploration, resulting in network designs that perform well in a desired task. Figure by Faustino Gomez (2025).

which allows discovering and representing several levels of relationships within the sequence. However, it was still surprising that when scaled up a billion fold in terms of data and compute, language modeling results in an agent that encodes general knowledge about the world and can cope with many of the tasks in it. How exactly the scale-up achieved such behavior, whether it is based on principles similar to the human brain, and how we can take advantage of it in a reliable and productive manner are still discoveries that need to be made, but this pursuit has already fundamentally changed the way we think about AI and artificial agents. These agents can have useful knowledge and skills similar to and even beyond human abilities, and we can interact with them similarly to human experts (Miikkulainen, 2024).

Image generation models are similarly a major step forward in generative AI. Various techniques can be used, such as generative adversarial networks (GANs) or transformers, but many current models are based on diffusion: A sequence of noising and denoising operations is used to tie together a linguistic expression of the desired image (Luo, 2022). With very large training sets of images and descriptions, the system learns the general principles about the visual world, and can then use them to create images that have never existed before. The approach can be extended to video and sound as well. One difference between this and LLMs is that the applications are mostly creative; that is, humans give high-level descriptions of what they want and the model makes a guess of what the human has in mind. They are not used to answer questions about facts (e.g., to create a map of an actual city); therefore, they cannot really be wrong. Yet they still encode a lot of knowledge about the world: objects and actors in it, their relationships, and even ill defined concepts such as styles, moods, and emotions. They can thus serve as an extension of human creativity.

Indeed, LLMs and image models are already useful in this role of enhancing human creativity. Experts can use them as a tool that makes them more productive. In an interactive setup, the expert can describe what s/he wants, and the AI will generate alternative solutions, be it illustrations, diagrams, memos, lyrics, art, stories, translations, music, code for algorithms, or code for interfaces. Humans can then refine these solutions until they solve the problem. The process can thus be more comprehensive, efficient, and creative than without such tools. However, what really made AI break out from the lab to the mainstream is that these tools are also useful for non-experts. A much larger segment of the population can now create art, text, and code at will and be effective and proficient in it, in a way that they never could before. For instance, I can write an outline of a story, and use AI to realize it in a particular style, and another AI to provide illustrations for it—even if I'm not a skilled artist or a writer. Similarly, I can describe an idea for a method to extract knowledge from a dataset and then use AI to implement the method in a language such as Python. If the database has an esoteric application programming interface (API), I can have AI read the documentation and write the code to get the data. I can do this even if I'm not a programmer or do not have enough technical understanding to interpret the documentation.

The third area of AI that has recently emerged from the lab and is changing the world is **decision-making**—in behavior, design, and strategy. That is, we have autonomous agents that behave intelligently: for instance, drive a car in open-ended traffic conditions or control non-player characters in video games. Using AI, we can design a better shape for a train's nose cone, or molecules that detect pathogens more accurately or treat diseases more effectively. Based on datasets in healthcare, business, and science, AI can be used to recommend more effective treatments, marketing campaigns, and strategies to reduce global warming. This kind of AI differs from the first two, in that it is not based on learning and utilizing patterns from large datasets of existing solutions. Gradient descent cannot be used because the desired behaviors are not known—hence there are no targets from which to backpropagate. Instead, decision-making AI is based on search—trying solutions, evaluating how well they work, and then improving them. The most important aspect of such methods is to be able to explore and extrapolate: that is, to discover solutions that are novel and unlikely to be developed otherwise.

Like the other two methods, decision-making AI benefits massively from scale. There are two aspects to it. First, scaling up to large search spaces means that more novel, different, and surprising solutions can be created. A powerful way to do this scale-up is to code the solutions as neural networks. Second, scaling up the number of evaluations means that more of the search space can be explored, making their discovery more likely. This scale-up is possible through high-fidelity simulations and **surrogate models**; predictive machine learning models. Like LLMs and image models, these technologies have existed for a long time—and the massive increases in computational power are now ready to make them practical, and take them from the laboratory to the real world. Thus, decision-making AI is likely to be the third component of the AI revolution, one that is emerging right now.

The technologies enabling it are different from LLMs and image models (although they can also be used to enhance the emergence, as will be discussed in chapter 13). An obvious one is **reinforcement learning** (RL), which started in the 1980s and 1990s as a model of animal conditioning and is still largely based on lifetime exploration and adaptation of a single individual solution. RL takes many forms. The most dominant one has been based on Q-learning; that is, the idea that different decisions at different states have different utility values (Q-values), which can be learned by comparing values available at successive states. An important aspect of such learning is that instead of storing the values explicitly as an array, a value function is learned that covers a continuous space of states and decisions. In that manner, the approach extends to large spaces often encountered in the real world. For instance, a humanoid robot can have many degrees of freedom, and therefore many physical configurations, and perform many different actions—even continuous ones. A value function assigns a utility to all combinations of them. This approach in particular has benefited from the progress in neural networks and deep learning, as well as the increase in available compute: It is possible to use them to learn more powerful value functions (e.g., **deep Q-networks**; Mnih, Kavukcuoglu, Silver, et al., 2015). With sufficient compute, **policy iteration** has emerged as an alternative to Q-learning. Instead of values of decisions at states, the entire policy is learned directly as a neural network. That is, given a state, the network suggests an optimal action directly. Again, methods such as **REINFORCE** have existed for a long time (Williams, 1992), but they have become practical with modern compute.

As a result, several real-world applications have emerged. The best-known ones are in game playing: For instance, RL was used as an element in beating the best human players in Go and chess, as well as in simulated car racing (Silver, Hubert, Schrittwieser, et al., 2018; Wurman, Barrett, Kawamoto, et al., 2022). Applications have also started to emerge in scientific domains such as protein folding and drug design (Korshunova, Huang, Capuzzi, et al., 2022).

Importantly, however, scale-up is still an issue with RL. Even though multiple modifications can be evaluated in parallel and offline, the methods are still primarily based on improving a single solution; that is, on hill-climbing (figure 1.3*a*). Creativity and exploration are thus limited. Drastically different, novel solutions are unlikely to be found because the approach simply does not explore the space widely enough. Progress is slow if the search landscape is high-dimensional and nonlinear enough, making it difficult to find good combinations. Deceptive landscapes are difficult to deal with since hill-climbing is likely to get stuck in local minima. Care must thus be taken to design the problem well so RL can be effective, which also limits the creativity that can be achieved.

Evolutionary computation (EC) offers the missing piece. With a population of candidates, it is possible to explore more widely (figure 1.3*b*). The population can be created to be highly diverse, covering the various areas of the search space. If some such candidate does not work out, that's all right; many other candidates are exploring other

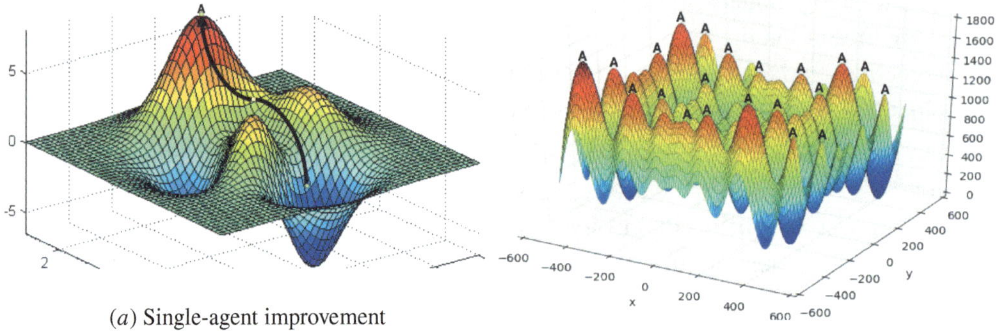

(*a*) Single-agent improvement in a regular landscape

(*b*) Population-based search in a deceptive landscape

Figure 1.3: **Discovering solutions in large, multidimensional, deceptive search spaces.** (*a*) Hill-climbing methods such as gradient descent and RL are well-suited, but also limited to small, low-dimensional, regular search spaces. If the initial solution is in the scope of the optimum, hill-climbing will find it. (*b*) Population-based search extends to large, high-dimensional, deceptive spaces. For instance in this deceptive space, the population is distributed over several peaks, and operations such as crossover allow for long jumps between them.

areas. However, evolutionary search is much more than simply a large number of diverse, parallel searches. As soon as a good idea is discovered (i.e., a solution that solves part of the problem, or a special case) that information is available to other solutions through crossover (figure 1.4). Good ideas thus spread quickly, and other parallel searches can take advantage of them. As will be discussed in section 11.1, it is thus possible to find solutions in vast search spaces (e.g., $2^{2^{70}}$ states), high-dimensional search spaces (e.g., 1B parameters), and spaces that are highly nonlinear and deceptive.

These properties of evolutionary computation are useful in general in discovering many different kinds of solutions, such as designs described as parameter vectors, program trees, or solution graphs. However, they are particularly useful for discovering neural networks for decision-making tasks. Remember that the optimal behaviors are not known, so they must be found using search. The space of possible neural networks that implement the behaviors is vast and high-dimensional and features highly nonlinear interactions. Therefore, evolution can be used effectively to discover neural networks for decision-making. This is what neuroevolution is all about.

1.3 Improving the World

The utility of neuroevolution is tremendous. First, it can be used to discover and optimize behavior for **intelligent agents**; that is, systems that are embedded in an environment and interact with it over time. The networks map situations in the environment onto actions that achieve multiple goals. In this manner, it is possible to optimize control for cars, planes, other vehicles, and robots in general—and not only control but behavioral strategies as well, such as anticipating and avoiding obstacles, optimizing trajectories, and minimizing energy usage and stress on the hardware. In simulated worlds, it is possible to discover effective behavior for non-player characters, guiding them toward various types

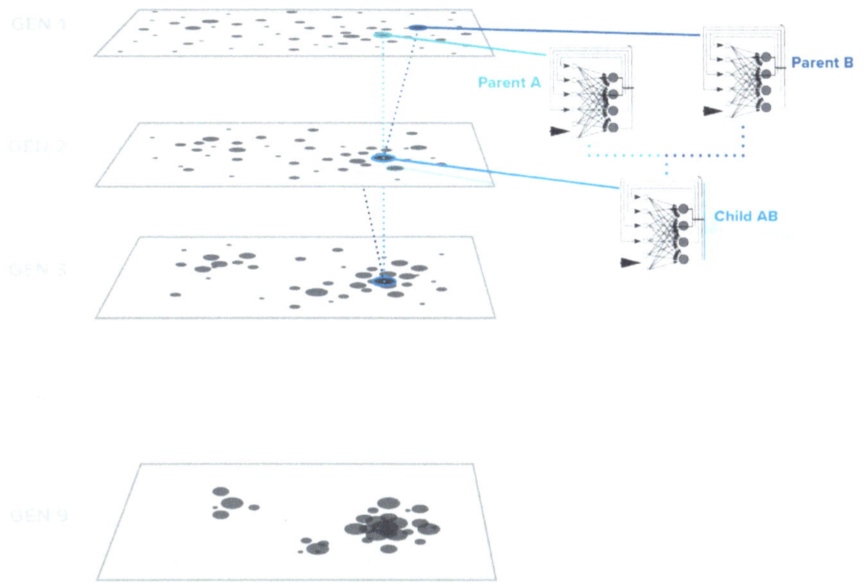

Figure 1.4: **Finding solutions with population-based search.** The search space is depicted as a rectangle; the solutions are dots whose size corresponds to their fitness. Population-based search (i.e., evolutionary optimization) starts by spreading the initial population broadly around the search space, thus exploring a diverse set of solutions. The poor solutions are discarded, and the good ones are recombined with other good solutions through crossover and mutation, creating an offspring population. After several generations, the population converges around the best solutions. They often represent different trade-offs from which the human decision-maker can choose. In this manner, the search can discover a host of possible creative solutions. Figure from Miikkulainen and Forrest (2021).

of strategies such as aggressive or conservative actions, and even ill-defined ones such as human like and believable actions. Strategies for dynamic optimization of logistics, transportation, manufacturing, and control of chemical and biological plants, as well as intelligent buildings and cities, can be developed.

Second, neuroevolution can be used to discover customized strategies for **decision-making**. These networks map descriptions of problems directly to solutions. For example, in wellness and healthcare, given a description of a person's medical profile as input, they can make nutrition or exercise recommendations, or design personalized medical treatments and rehabilitation plans, maximizing benefits while minimizing cost and side effects. In business, they can create marketing strategies customized to the product, season, and competition, or investment strategies optimized to current markets and resources. They can discover effective incentives for recruiting and retention in particular cases, as well as effective responses in customer service situations. In education, they may assign personalized exercises that are maximally effective with the least amount of work. The same approach applies to physical training while minimizing injury risk. There are many "AI for good" applications in society as well, such as discovering effective non-pharmaceutical containment and mitigation strategies in a pandemic, optimizing land use to mitigate climate change, and designing and operating ecological villages.

Third, it is possible to use neuroevolution to optimize other **learning methods**. Evolution creates optimal designs for them so that elements such as deep learning, reinforcement learning, or spike-timing-dependent plasticity can be as effective as possible. For instance, architectures, loss functions, activation functions, data augmentation, and learning rules can be discovered specifically for different deep learning tasks and datasets. Networks can be evolved as transfer functions for cellular automata, allowing them to perform more complex tasks. They can be evolved to serve as kernels for Gaussian processes, or as value functions in Q-learning. It is possible to optimize them for particular hardware limitations, such as limited compute or memory, or for specific neuromorphic hardware, to take the best advantage of available resources. In domains where deep learning might work well but there is not enough data available to train it, as is often the case in the real world, it may be possible to evolve neural network architectures that combine data from multiple other tasks, thus making more deep learning applications possible. Neuroevolution can be combined with reinforcement learning, such as for evolving general approaches that are then refined over the lifetime of the individual, and by evolving reinforcement learning mechanisms themselves, such as learning and memory mechanisms, and starting points. Neuroevolution can also be used synergistically with LLMs in several ways: by evolving prompts, fine-tuning, and ways to merge multiple models and to orchestrate them, or using LLMs to implement evolutionary operations in domains where it would be otherwise difficult to do. Neuroevolution can thus enhance the performance of LLMs, and LLMs enhance evolution.

Fourth, since neuroevolution emulates biological adaptation (evolution) and encodes solutions in biologically motivated processors (neural networks), it is a natural approach to studying **biological behavior**. Neuroevolution experiments can shed light on questions such as how mating, hunting, herding, and communication emerged over evolution, and even how language and intelligence generally resulted from adaptation and niching in biology. A computational model provides the ultimate understanding in cognitive science, and neuroevolution can be used to motivate such models from a biological perspective. On the other hand, such biological connections can provide insight into how intelligent artificial systems can be engineered to be effective, robust, and resource-efficient.

1.4 Plan for the Book

This book provides a comprehensive introduction to these topics. The goal is to familiarize the reader with the various neuroevolution technologies, but also to provide the tools to take advantage of them, develop them further, and build applications. The major algorithms are reviewed and their origins and motivation are explained; concrete examples of their use are given and references are provided in the literature; and open areas of research are identified and suggestions for further work are given. A number of case studies are presented in depth, illustrating how the concepts can be used to address more complex challenges and problems in the real world.

While the book assumes basic familiarity and understanding of neural networks, not much background in evolutionary computation is necessary. The book is accompanied on the web by several demos, exercises, and a general software platform. The idea is to provide the reader not just with the knowledge but also a practical tool that can be readily applied and extended.

Neuroevolution as a field emerged in the late 1980s, with some earlier results by Belew, McInerney, and Schraudolph (1992); Harp, Samad, and Guha (1989); Fogel, Fogel, and Porto (1990), Kitano (1990); Miller, Todd, and Hedge (1989); Mjolsness, Sharp, and Alpert (1989); Montana and Davis (1989); Mühlenbein and Kindermann (1989); Schaffer, Caruana, and Eshelman (1990); and Whitley and Hanson (1989). Its development over the years has been chronicled in comprehensive survey articles about once a decade (Floreano, Dürr, and Mattiussi, 2008; Hougen and Shah, 2019; Schaffer, Whitley, and Eshelman, 1992; Stanley, Clune, Lehman, et al., 2019; Yao, 1999). Instead of attempting to cover everything that has been done in this field, this book aims to provide a guided tour through and a logical story about it.

Hence, the material is organized into five main parts. The first part (chapters 2 and 3) introduces the reader to the principles of evolutionary computation through a series of increasingly challenging examples. The specific case of neuroevolution is then introduced similarly, through simple example applications. The first exercises are introduced to make these concepts concrete and productive immediately (the software platform is described in the next section "Plan for Hands-On Exercises").

The second part (chapters 4 and 5) focuses on two fundamental neuroevolution design considerations: network encodings (direct and indirect), and making the search effective through diversity. Important distinctions between encoding approaches are clarified with examples, genetic and behavioral diversity contrasted, and novelty and quality-diversity (QD) search introduced, as well as by taking advantage of diversity through ensembling—all of these are fundamental methods in the neuroevolution toolbox, but they are rarely explicitly distinguished.

The third part (chapters 6, 7, 8, and 9) focuses on intelligent agents; that is, how effective behavior can be evolved from low-level control to high-level strategies, and ultimately to support decision-making systems. The setting is then expanded from individual agents to collective systems with cooperative and competitive interactions. Next, interactive evolution methods are reviewed as a way to combine machine discovery with human insights. Finally, opportunities and challenges for open-ended discovery will be discussed, motivated by biological evolution, and existing artificial examples of open-ended innovation systems will be reviewed.

The fourth part (chapters 10, 11, 12, and 13) then extends neuroevolution to combinations with other learning methods. Approaches to designing deep learning architectures are first reviewed, and challenges in it and possible future opportunities are discussed. Meta-learning is then extended to other aspects of neural-network design, including loss and activation functions, data use, and learning methods and their synergies. Synergistic combinations with neuromorphic systems, RL, and generative AI are reviewed as well, finding that in each case, it is possible to use evolution to optimize the general setting that makes other types of learning more effective.

The fifth and final part (chapters 14 and 15) evaluates how neuroevolution can provide insight into the study of biological evolution, from understanding neural structure and modularity, to developmental processes and body/brain coevolution, and finally to biological behavior and breakthroughs in the evolution of language. Throughout, possible insights for biology-motivated engineering in the future are identified. Indeed, the epilogue points out the potential role of neuroevolution in constructing agents with artificial general intelligence.

In sum, neuroevolution is an emerging third component of the recent AI revolution. It allows the development of systems that generate behavior, strategies, and decision-making agents. Applications of such agents are ubiquitous in the real world, leading to more proficient, efficient, and cost-effective systems—and generally improving lives as well. The area is ripe with many future work opportunities as well.

1.5 Plan for Hands-On Exercises

Practical engagement is essential for mastering complex concepts such as those explored in this book. The plan is rooted in a commitment to provide a rich, accessible, and effective learning experience; therefore, hands-on exercises are an essential part of it. They are accessible in the online supplement `https://neuroevolutionbook.com`. This section outlines the philosophy behind them.

Purpose: The exercises are crafted to deepen the reader's understanding through problem-solving and experimentation. While some exercises address inherently complex topics, others focus on areas closely aligned with current technology trends and the latest advancements in ML/AI. By doing so, the exercises aim to (1) encourage exploration of cutting-edge methodologies, making the learning experience engaging and relevant; (2) bridge theoretical understanding with practical implementation to solidify concepts; and (3) foster an experimentation mindset, mirroring the iterative nature of real-world AI research and applications. These hands-on experiences serve to develop confidence and engineering capabilities in tackling novel problems, equipping readers to innovate and adapt to emerging challenges in the field.

Form: The exercises are presented as Python notebooks, currently hosted on Google Colab, to minimize setup effort and enable readers to start problem-solving immediately. This format ensures accessibility, as the exercises can run on CPUs or low-end GPUs available in Colab, making them inclusive for readers with limited computational resources. Each exercise is designed to take no more than 30 to 60 minutes of running or training time for a complete solution, ensuring a balance between depth and computational efficiency, while allowing students ample time to engage with and understand the content. The tasks are carefully distilled to emphasize core knowledge while reducing execution time, creating an experience that focuses on learning the essentials without unnecessary overhead.

Solutions (for instructors and teaching assistants): For instructors and teaching assistants, complete solutions are provided in the form of Python notebooks stored in a separate archive. These solutions act as a reference, offering clarity and consistency when guiding students during workshops or discussions. They demonstrate the expected approach and results for each exercise, and they are structured to facilitate adaptation or extension for varied educational contexts. By separating the problems from their solutions, students are encouraged to engage actively with the exercises, fostering independent learning and problem-solving skills.

1.6 Chapter Review Questions

1. **Definition:** What is neuroevolution, and how does it differ from traditional neural network optimization methods such as backpropagation?

2. **Key challenges:** List and describe the four illustrative challenges that neuroevolution aims to address, as presented in figure 1.1.

3. **Mechanisms:** Explain the general framework of neuroevolution, including the roles of crossover, mutation, and fitness evaluation.

4. **Comparison:** How does neuroevolution address the limitations of gradient-based methods in optimizing neural networks, especially in large, high-dimensional, and deceptive search spaces?

5. **Creative solutions:** Why can neuroevolution be considered a tool for discovery and creativity rather than just optimization? Provide examples to illustrate your answer.

6. **Applications:** Neuroevolution was described as improving the world in four main areas. List these areas and briefly explain one example of each.

7. **Extending AI:** How does neuroevolution complement other AI methods like reinforcement learning and deep learning? Provide specific scenarios where these combinations are effective.

8. **AI transformation:** Discuss the paradigm shift in AI described in this chapter. How is neuroevolution a part of this shift, particularly in decision-making tasks?

9. **Population-based search:** Contrast hill-climbing methods like reinforcement learning with population-based search methods used in neuroevolution. Why are the latter better suited for exploring large, high-dimensional, and deceptive search spaces?

10. **Future directions:** According to this chapter, what are some promising areas of future research in neuroevolution, and why are they significant?

Chapter 2

The Basics

This chapter will first review the basics of evolutionary algorithms, including genetic algorithms (GAs) and evolution strategy (ES). It will then cover how neural networks work, including the architectures often used in this book, such as feedforward, convolutional, recurrent neural networks, long short-term memory networks, and transformers. Readers familiar with these techniques should feel free to skip this chapter.

2.1 Evolutionary Algorithms

Optimization is a fundamental component of machine learning and AI. However, not all problems are well behaved enough to be solved by gradient-based methods. Some problems lack a clear objective function, have noisy or delayed feedback, or involve highly nonlinear dynamics that frustrate traditional optimization. In these cases, **evolutionary algorithms**

Figure 2.1: **Survival of the fittest.** Figure by Tan (2017).

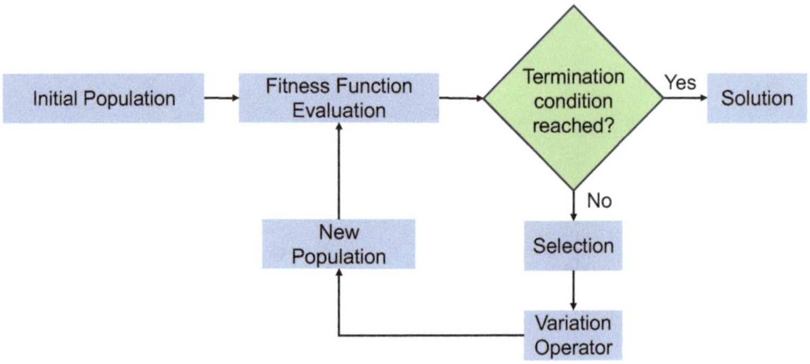

Figure 2.2: **Evolutionary algorithm overview.** The process begins with an initial population of candidate solutions, which are evaluated using a fitness function. Based on fitness, a selection mechanism chooses solutions for variation through genetic operators (e.g., mutation, crossover), producing a new population. This cycle repeats until a termination condition is met.

(EAs) provide a powerful alternative. Inspired by natural evolution (figure 2.1), EAs evolve a population of candidate solutions using mechanisms such as selection, mutation, and recombination. EAs are widely used in various fields, including engineering, economics, and biology, due to their ability to find optimal or near-optimal solutions in large and complex search spaces. These methods require only a way to evaluate solution quality, making them highly flexible and broadly applicable to domains like reinforcement learning (RL), black-box optimization, and robotics. This section explores the key ideas, algorithms, and applications of evolutionary methods—from classic GAs to methods like CMA-ES (whose name stands for "Covariance matrix adaptation evolution strategy") and more scalable approaches such as OpenAI evolution strategy (OpenAI ES).

An overview of the basic EA loop is shown in figure 2.2. The EA starts with a population of candidate solutions to a problem and iteratively improves them through mechanisms analogous to biological evolution. At each generation, individuals are evaluated using a **fitness function** that measures their quality. Based on fitness, better individuals are selected to reproduce. New individuals are created using variation operators—typically crossover (recombining parts of two parents) and mutation (introducing random changes). These offspring then form the next generation. Over time, the population evolves, and the algorithm is stopped once some termination condition is reached (e.g., the optimal solution was found or the maximum number of generations was reached). EAs are particularly well suited for problems where there is no single perfect solution, or where the solution itself is complex and defies easy definition with formulas. Unlike backpropagation, which requires a clearly defined error function, EAs only need a way to evaluate goodness, not a step-by-step guide. This ability opens doors for applications in a number of areas where traditional gradient-based optimization techniques cannot be easily applied.

Let's have a look at some code together (listing 2.1), which shows that the basic evolutionary loop can be set up in only a few lines. Here, we use the solver paradigm, which is popular in black-box optimization, and abstracts the optimization process into two main operations: `ask()`, which generates candidate solutions; and `tell()`, which

Listing 2.1: **Basic evolutionary algorithm training loop.**

```
solver = EvolutionAlgorithm()
while True:
  # Ask the EA to give us a set of candidate solutions.
  solutions = solver.ask()
  # Create an array to hold the fitness results.
  fitness_list = np.zeros(solver.popsize)
  # Evaluate the fitness for each given solution.
  for i in range(solver.popsize):
    fitness_list[i] = evaluate(solutions[i])
  # Give list of fitness results back to EA.
  solver.tell(fitness_list)
  # Get best parameter, fitness from EA.
  best_solution, best_fitness = solver.result()
  if best_fitness > MY_REQUIRED_FITNESS:
    break
```

evaluates and provides feedback. This loop continues until a high-performing solution is discovered. We will now go a bit deeper into the different components that most EAs share.

2.1.1 Representation

Individuals in an EA must be represented in a form suitable for manipulation by evolutionary operators such as selection, crossover, and mutation. The process of defining how these individuals are encoded and manipulated is known as **representation**, and it plays a pivotal role in determining the success of an evolutionary algorithm. A well-designed representation bridges the gap between the problem domain and the evolutionary search space, enabling efficient **exploration** and **exploitation** of potential solutions.

Here, it is essential to distinguish between the **genotype** and the **phenotype** of an individual. The genotype refers to the internal data structure used by the algorithm to represent a candidate solution—typically a string, vector, tree, or graph structure that is subject to variation and selection. The phenotype, on the other hand, is the external manifestation of this solution in the context of the problem domain. It is the actual behavior, structure, or configuration that results from decoding the genotype and is ultimately evaluated by the fitness function.

For example, consider an optimization problem involving the design of an aerodynamic wing. The genotype might be a vector of real numbers encoding control points for a spline curve. The phenotype, derived from decoding this vector, is the physical shape of the wing. The evolutionary algorithm manipulates genotypes, but it is the performance of the phenotype (e.g., drag or lift) that determines fitness.

The nature of the mapping between genotype and phenotype can be broadly classified into direct and indirect encoding schemes. In a **direct encoding**, each element of the genotype corresponds explicitly to an element or parameter in the phenotype. The mapping is straightforward and often one-to-one. For instance, in a binary string representation for a knapsack problem, each bit in the genotype directly indicates whether a particular item is included or excluded from the knapsack. This type of encoding is typically easy to implement and understand, and it allows direct control over the phenotype features. However, it may become inefficient or unwieldy when dealing with large or structured phenotypes, such as networks or modular systems.

In contrast, an **indirect encoding** introduces an intermediate layer, where the genotype specifies rules, developmental processes, or construction procedures that lead to the formation of the phenotype. This approach is inspired by biological development, where the genome encodes not the organism itself but a set of instructions that guide its formation. Indirect encodings are particularly useful when the solution space is highly structured or exhibits regularities, symmetries, or modularities. They can lead to more compact representations and better generalization. However, they typically require more complex decoding procedures and can introduce challenges in designing suitable variation operators that respect the semantics of the encoding. In chapter 4, we will go deeper into indirect encodings.

Choosing or designing a representation for individuals in an evolutionary algorithm involves a delicate balance between several competing goals. The representation must be expressive enough to capture high-quality solutions within the search space, yet constrained enough to avoid overwhelming the algorithm with infeasible or irrelevant candidates. It should enable the application of variation operators in a way that preserves the syntactic and semantic integrity of individuals. Moreover, it should support efficient decoding into phenotypes and allow the fitness function to evaluate solutions meaningfully.

The interaction between genotype structure and evolutionary dynamics is also crucial. For example, in representations with high redundancy, where multiple genotypes map to the same phenotype, evolutionary progress may be slowed due to wasted evaluations. Conversely, representations with poor locality, where small changes in genotype result in large and unpredictable changes in phenotype, can make it difficult for the algorithm to converge toward optimal regions.

2.1.2 Population-Based Search

In EAs, the **population** refers to the set of individuals maintained and evolved over successive generations. Each individual in the population encodes a potential solution to the optimization problem, typically as a genotype that maps to a corresponding phenotype evaluated by a fitness function. The population acts as a distributed search mechanism, allowing the algorithm to sample multiple regions of the solution space simultaneously. For example, for the Traveling Salesman Problem (TSP), each individual could be a different permutation of cities, representing a possible tour. A population of such permutations allows the algorithm to evaluate and evolve multiple route possibilities simultaneously.

A key parameter is the population size, which controls the algorithm's capacity for exploration and its computational cost. Smaller populations tend to converge quickly but risk premature convergence due to insufficient diversity. Larger populations maintain broader coverage of the search space but can slow convergence and increase resource demands. Optimal sizing depends on problem complexity and the design of variation and selection operators.

The initial population is usually generated randomly, ensuring an unbiased and diverse sample of the search space. However, in certain domains, informed or heuristic-based initialization may be used to seed the population with potentially high-quality solutions. Regardless of the method, the goal is to start with sufficient diversity to support effective evolutionary progress.

In most evolutionary algorithms, the population is unstructured, allowing all individuals to interact freely. However, structured populations such as island models and cellular models restrict interactions, thereby promoting subpopulation diversity. Island models divide the population into semi-isolated groups that occasionally exchange individuals, helping avoid global stagnation. Cellular models impose a spatial topology where individuals interact only with neighbors, encouraging local adaptation and maintaining niches.

Diversity maintenance within the population is critical for preventing premature convergence. Techniques such as fitness sharing, crowding, and adaptive mutation rates are commonly employed to preserve variation among individuals. Population structure itself can aid in preserving diversity, as can variation in selection intensity and mating schemes.

2.1.3 Selection

The selection process is inspired by the concept of "survival of the fittest." The main idea is that individuals with better fitness have a higher probability of being selected for reproduction. The selection pressure determines how strongly the algorithm favors fitter individuals. It has a profound effect on the dynamics of evolution. High selection pressure (e.g., always choosing the top few individuals) can lead to rapid convergence, as good solutions dominate quickly. However, this can reduce **genetic diversity** and may cause **premature convergence**—where the population gets stuck in suboptimal regions of the search space. Low selection pressure allows weaker individuals a chance to reproduce, which slows convergence but promotes diversity and broader exploration of the search space. This helps in avoiding local optima, especially in complex or rugged fitness landscapes.

Diversity within the population is essential for effective evolutionary search. Without it, the population may converge prematurely, losing the potential to discover better solutions. Selection methods and associated parameters can be tuned to help preserve diversity, ensuring the algorithm continues to explore new possibilities rather than exploiting only the current best option. In practice, a careful balance between selection pressure and diversity preservation is critical. Too much exploitation can hinder innovation, while too much exploration may prevent the algorithm from refining good solutions. In section 2.2.1, on genetic algorithms, we will look at a few common selection methods.

2.1.4 Variation Operators

Variation operators are the primary mechanism by which EAs explore the solution space. They introduce diversity by modifying existing individuals to generate new ones. The two main types are **mutation**, which alters individuals randomly, and **crossover** (or recombination), which combines traits from two or more parents. In simple forms of EAs—such as those with binary or real-valued encodings—mutation might flip bits or perturb numerical values with noise, while crossover can swap segments of parent genomes or blend parameter values. These operators are essential for both refining good solutions and escaping local optima. Overall, variation operators drive innovation in EAs by ensuring that new, potentially better solutions are continually introduced into the population. The specific implementation of these operators depends heavily on how solutions are represented and what the problem demands.

2.1.5 Fitness Evaluation

The **fitness** score determines the individual's likelihood of being selected for reproduction, making this step central to guiding the evolutionary search. A well-designed fitness function effectively captures the problem's objectives and constraints, steering the population toward high-quality solutions over successive generations. The design of the fitness function is critical and often non-trivial. In simple problems, the fitness may be a direct measure of performance, such as, classification accuracy in a machine learning task or total distance in a routing problem. However, in complex or real-world applications, fitness evaluation can involve significant computational overhead or additional design considerations. For instance, in robotic control tasks, fitness may be determined by simulating the robot's behavior over time, accounting for factors such as stability, energy efficiency, or obstacle avoidance. These simulations can be computationally expensive, especially when involving physics engines or real-time constraints.

In engineering design problems, fitness functions often incorporate constraint handling to ensure that infeasible solutions are appropriately penalized or corrected. In other domains, such as architectural layout or circuit design, subjective or aesthetic goals may need to be quantified, requiring proxy metrics, surrogate models, or interactive evolutionary approaches (see chapter 8).

Furthermore, in many practical settings, the fitness function must balance multiple conflicting objectives, such as cost versus performance or speed versus accuracy. In such cases, single-objective evaluation may be insufficient, and **multi-objective optimization** techniques (see section 2.2.5) are employed. Here, individuals are evaluated on multiple criteria simultaneously, and selection is guided by concepts like Pareto dominance rather than a single fitness score. Because the fitness function fundamentally shapes the evolutionary trajectory, it often requires iterative refinement, domain expertise, and, in some cases, adaptive or learned components to improve search efficiency and relevance to the problem domain.

2.1.6 Reproduction and Replacement

Selected individuals reproduce to form a new generation, replacing some or all of the existing population. This step is crucial in balancing exploration (searching new areas of the solution space) and exploitation (refining promising solutions), and different strategies can lead to significantly different evolutionary dynamics. Reproduction typically involves applying variation operators (e.g., crossover and mutation) to the selected individuals to generate offspring. The newly created individuals then enter the population through a replacement strategy, which determines how the current population is updated. Broadly, **replacement** can be categorized into **generational** and **steady-state** approaches.

In **generational replacement**, the entire population is replaced in each generation by the offspring. This is common in traditional genetic algorithms and promotes exploration, as a large number of new individuals are evaluated at each step. However, it may also result in the loss of high-quality individuals unless some form of elitism is employed. **Elitism** ensures that the best-performing individuals are preserved unchanged and carried over to the next generation, thereby preventing regression in solution quality.

In contrast, **steady-state replacement** updates the population incrementally. Only a few individuals are replaced at each generation, typically by inserting new offspring into the population while removing the least fit individuals. Generational replacement is more common, but examples of steady-state replacement in the context of evolving behaviors of bots in a machine learning game are given in section 8.1.

Ultimately, the reproduction and replacement mechanism plays a critical role in maintaining population diversity, ensuring progress over generations, and adapting the evolutionary process to the demands of the problem.

2.1.7 Termination

An EA is an iterative process that, in principle, can continue indefinitely. However, in practice, the algorithm is typically halted either when a satisfactory solution is found or when further computation is unlikely to yield significant improvements. The termination criterion determines when the evolutionary process should stop. Several common termination strategies are employed in evolutionary algorithms:

- **Fixed number of generations:** The algorithm terminates after a predefined number of generations. This is simple and commonly used, particularly when computational resources are limited. It provides a guaranteed runtime but does not ensure solution quality.

- **Fitness threshold:** The process stops when an individual reaches or surpasses a predefined fitness value. This is suitable for problems with known acceptable or optimal fitness levels.

- **No improvement (stagnation):** If the best fitness value does not improve over a given number of consecutive generations, the algorithm is terminated. This helps avoid wasting resources on stagnant searches.

- **Computational budget:** The algorithm halts after consuming a specified number of fitness evaluations, CPU time, or memory. This is particularly relevant in applications with expensive evaluation functions.

- **Population convergence:** If the population diversity falls below a specific threshold (e.g., measured by genotype or phenotype variance), the algorithm may be stopped, as this suggests convergence or lack of exploratory capacity.

The selection of an appropriate termination condition depends on the nature of the problem, the computational cost of fitness evaluations, and the balance between exploration and efficiency. In practice, multiple criteria are often combined. For example, an EA might be set to stop either after 500 generations or if a fitness threshold is achieved, whichever comes first. In general, ending the search too early can result in suboptimal solutions, while continuing too long may waste resources with diminishing returns. An effective termination strategy ensures a reasonable trade-off between solution quality and computational efficiency.

2.2 Types of Evolutionary Algorithms

This section focuses on two of the most prominent types of evolutionary algorithms: GAs and evolution strategy. The underlying principles, key components, and applications of these algorithms are discussed. A selection of multiobjective EAs is then presented, and many other EA methods that have been used in neuroevolution are reviewed.

2.2.1 Genetic Algorithms

GAs are a popular type of evolutionary algorithm that mimics the process of natural selection. GAs were first introduced by John Holland in the 1970s and have since become one of the most widely used EAs.

In GAs, each individual in the population is typically represented as a chromosome, which is a string of genes. The genes can be binary (0s and 1s), real numbers, or any other representation suitable for the problem. The initial population is generated randomly or by using a heuristic to provide a diverse set of starting solutions.

As discussed in section 2.1.3, the selection process determines which individuals survive to be candidates for reproduction and which of those contribute their genetic material to the next generation. Common selection methods for GAs include:

- **Roulette wheel selection**: Individuals are selected probabilistically based on their fitness, with better individuals having a higher chance of being chosen.
- **Tournament selection**: A small group of individuals is selected randomly, and the fittest individual in the group is chosen.
- **Rank-based selection**: Individuals are ranked based on their fitness, and selection probabilities are assigned according to their rank.
- **Truncation selection**: This method involves selecting the top fraction of individuals based solely on their fitness. Only the highest-performing individuals above a certain fitness threshold contribute to the next generation, while the rest are excluded. Truncation selection often leads to rapid convergence but can reduce genetic diversity.

Crossover, or recombination, is a key operator in GAs that combines the genetic material of two parents to create offspring. Common crossover techniques are shown in figure 2.3 and include:

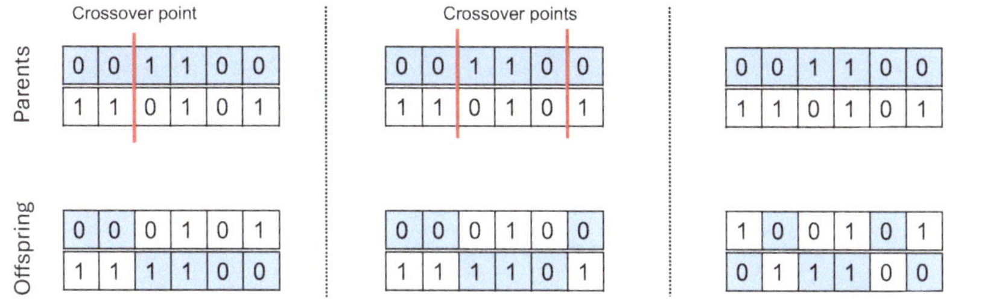

(*a*) Single-point crossover (*b*) Two-point crossover (*c*) Uniform crossover

Figure 2.3: **Crossover operators.** (*a*) Single-point crossover: A single crossover point is selected, and genetic material is exchanged beyond this point. (*b*) Two-point crossover: Two points are selected, and the segment between them is swapped between parents. (*c*) Uniform crossover: Each gene is independently inherited from either parent with equal probability.

- **Single-point crossover**: A random crossover point is chosen, and the genes from the two parents are exchanged at this point.
- **Two-point crossover**: Two crossover points are selected, and the segment between them is swapped between the parents.
- **Uniform crossover**: Each gene is independently chosen from one of the two parents with equal probability.

Following the standard EA process, **mutations** in GAs introduce small random changes to an individual's genes to maintain diversity in the population. This mechanism helps prevent premature convergence to local optima. The mutation rate, which determines how often mutations occur, is typically kept low. Additionally, it often helps to copy the best individual from the current generation to the next without applying any mutations to it, a method known as **elitism**.

To get a better idea of how the GA operates, we can visualize it in solving simple toy problems. For example, figure 2.4 shows top-down plots of shifted two-dimensional Schaffer and Rastrigin functions, two of several simple problems used for testing continuous black-box optimization algorithms. Lighter regions of the plots represent higher values of $F(x, y)$. As one can observe, there are many local optima in this function. Our job is to find a set of input parameters (x, y), such that $F(x, y)$ is as close as possible to the global maximum.

Figure 2.5 illustrates how the simple GA proceeds over succeeding generations. The green dots represent members of the elite population from the previous generation, the blue dots are the offspring forming the set of candidate solutions, and the red dot is the best solution.

GAs help diversity by keeping track of a diverse set of candidate solutions to produce the next generation. However, in practice, most of the solutions in the elite surviving population tend to converge to a local optimum over time. There are more sophisticated variations of GA out there, such as CoSyNe, ESP, and neuroevolution of augmenting topologies (NEAT), which we will discuss later in this book (see chapters 3.3 and 7.1.1), where the idea is to cluster similar solutions in the population into different species to maintain better diversity over time.

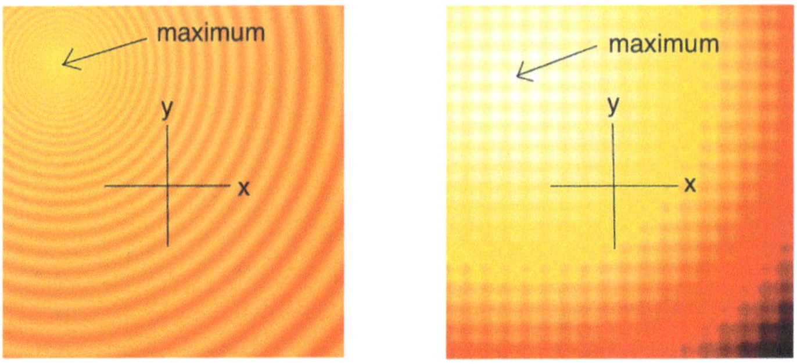

(*a*) Schaffer-2D function (*b*) Rastrigin-2D function

Figure 2.4: **2D Schaffer and Rastrigin functions.** Lighter regions represent higher values of the fitness function $F(x, y)$. In addition to the global maximum, these functions are characterized by many local optima.

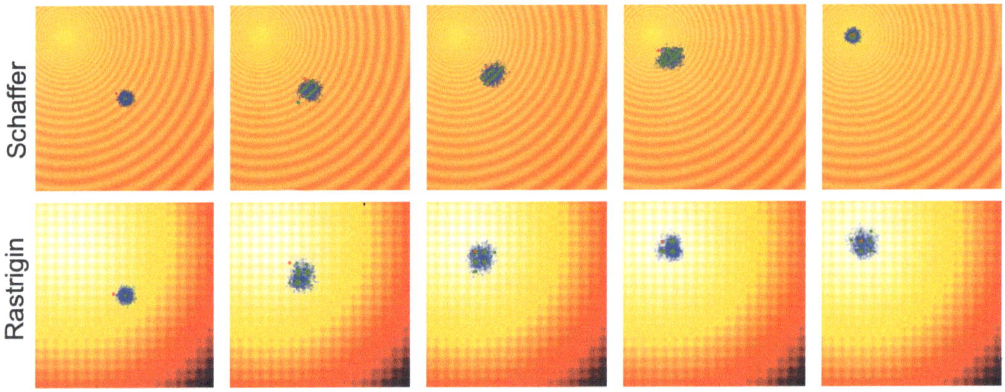

Figure 2.5: **Simple GA progress over 20 generations.** Green dots indicate elite individuals from the previous generation, blue dots represent offspring forming the new set of candidate solutions, and the red dot marks the best solution. Over successive generations (every fourth one is shown), the GA is able to find the global function optima, without getting stuck in the many local optima. For videos, see `https://neuroevolutionbook.com/demos`.

2.2.2 Evolution Strategy

Another popular evolutionary algorithm is **evolution strategy** (ES), originally pioneered by Rechenberg (1973) and Schwefel (1977). Unlike GAs, which are flexible in the type of representation used (e.g., binary, symbolic, etc.), ES typically operates on real-valued vectors and is more focused on optimizing continuous functions. In ES, each individual is represented by a vector of real numbers, which corresponds to the solution's parameters. The initial population is usually generated randomly or based on some prior knowledge.

Selection in ES is deterministic, meaning that a fixed number of the best individuals (based on fitness) are selected to produce offspring for the next generation. Two canonical ES variations are (μ, λ)–ES and $(\mu + \lambda)$–ES, which primarily differ in how they select individuals for the next generation. Both variants use a population of parents, denoted by μ, which represents the number of selected individuals that generate offspring. Second, they produce a number of offspring, denoted by λ, where typically $\lambda \geq \mu$. Together, these parameters make it possible to control selection pressure and the amount of variation maintained in the search process:

- (μ, λ) – **selection**: From λ offspring, the best μ individuals are selected to form the next generation. Parents are not considered for selection; only offspring are eligible.
- $(\mu + \lambda)$ – **selection**: The best μ individuals are selected from the combined pool of μ parents and λ offspring. Parents can survive into the next generation.

In ES, variation is introduced primarily through mutation, which perturbs the real-valued parameters. Mutation is usually applied by adding a normally distributed random vector to each individual. The mutation strength, often denoted by σ, controls the magnitude of these perturbations. Crossover is less commonly used in ES compared to GAs, but can be applied by combining the parameter vectors of two or more parents.

Let's look at an example of a **simple evolution strategy** in more detail, more specifically a $(\mu + \lambda)$–ES with fixed mutation strength, in which a population of λ offspring is sampled from a multivariate normal distribution centered at a mean vector. This strategy uses elitist selection, retaining the best μ individuals to influence the next generation. In our case, we use $\mu = 1$, meaning that only the best solution from the previous generation is used to generate the next. At each generation t, we sample a set of λ offspring $\{x_1, \ldots, x_\lambda\}$ from a fixed Gaussian distribution:

$$x_i \sim \mathcal{N}(m^{(t)}, \sigma^2), \tag{2.1}$$

where $m^{(t)} \in \mathbb{R}^2$ is the mean vector (i.e., the center of the sampling distribution) at generation t, and $\sigma = (\sigma_x, \sigma_y)$ is the fixed standard deviation along each axis; that is, the mutation strength.

The initial mean is set to $m^{(0)} = (0, 0)$, so the first generation is sampled around the origin. After evaluating the fitness of all λ offspring, the new mean $m^{(t+1)}$ is updated to the best-performing solution:

$$m^{(t+1)} = \arg\max_{x_i} \text{Fitness}(x_i). \tag{2.2}$$

Figure 2.6 shows how the algorithm behaves over 20 generations on the Schaffer and Rastrigin test functions. The green dot indicates the mean of the distribution at each generation, the blue dots are the sampled solutions, and the red dot is the best solution found so far by the algorithm.

This simple algorithm will generally work only for simple problems. Given its greedy nature, it throws away all but the best solution and can be prone to getting stuck at a local optimum for more complicated problems. It would be beneficial to sample the next generation from a probability distribution that represents a more diverse set of ideas rather than just from the best solution from the current generation.

2.2.3 Covariance-Matrix Adaptation Evolution Strategy

A shortcoming of both simple ES and simple GA is that our standard deviation noise parameter is fixed. There are times when we want to explore more and increase the standard

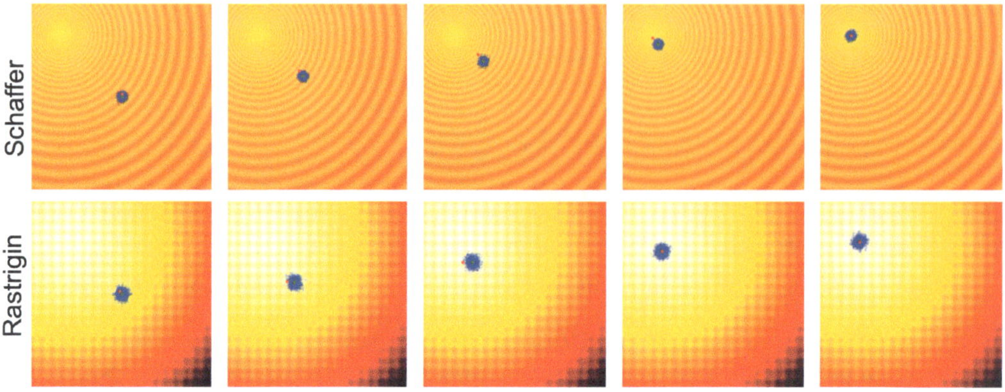

Figure 2.6: **Simple ES progress over 20 generations.** The green dot represents the mean of the distribution at each generation, blue dots indicate the sampled solutions, and the red dot marks the best solution found so far by the algorithm. For videos, see `https://neuroevolutionbook.com/demos`.

deviation, and there are times when we are confident we are close to a good optimum and just want to fine-tune the solution. **Covariance-matrix adaptation evolution strategy** (CMA-ES) does exactly that.

CMA-ES is an algorithm that adaptively adjusts its search strategy using feedback from each generation. Unlike simpler methods that modify only a fixed mutation scale, CMA-ES adapts both the center and shape of its search distribution over time. It maintains a multivariate Gaussian distribution and updates its parameters—the mean vector μ and full covariance matrix C—using the most successful candidates (figure 2.7).

At a high level, CMA-ES performs the following steps every generation. First, it samples a population from the current Gaussian distribution and ranks them by fitness. Second, it updates μ and C based on the best-performing individuals. The details on how to calculate the covariance matrix C are given in the Math Detail box that follows. These mechanisms allow CMA-ES to stretch, shrink, or rotate the search space to better match the landscape of the objective function. For instance, if successful solutions tend to lie along a diagonal, CMA-ES learns that shape and directs its search accordingly. Figure 2.8 visualizes one full update cycle of CMA-ES in a 2D toy problem:

(a) Evaluate the fitness of each candidate solution in generation g.

(b) Select the top-performing 25% of the population.

(c) Use those selected individuals to estimate a new covariance matrix $C^{(g+1)}$, based on the mean $\mu^{(g)}$ from the current generation.

(d) Generate the next population by sampling from a multivariate Gaussian defined by the updated $\mu^{(g+1)}$ and $C^{(g+1)}$.

Because CMA-ES adapts based on actual performance, it can widen the search when promising solutions are diverse or narrow it down when the optimum seems close. For

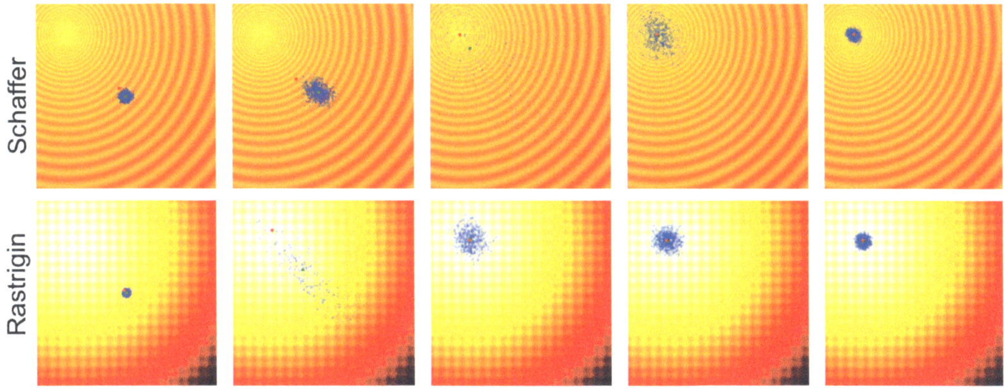

Figure 2.7: **CMA-ES progress over 20 generations.** In contrast to the simple GA and ES, CMA-ES dynamically learns the shape of the search landscape by adapting the full covariance matrix of the sampling distribution. For videos, see `https://neuroevolutionbook.com/demos`.

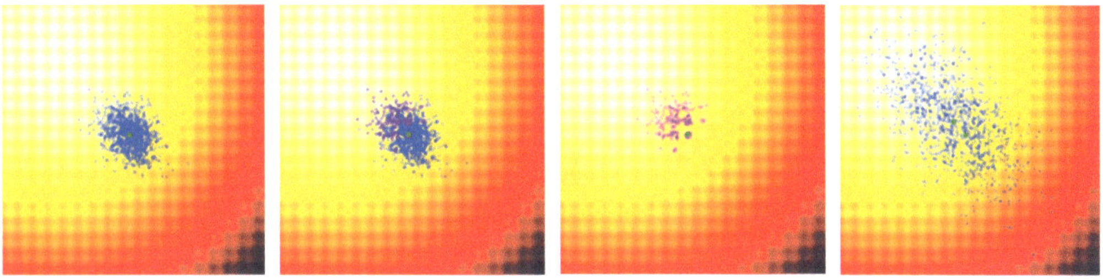

(*a*) Evaluate (*b*) Select (*c*) Estimate (*d*) Sample

Figure 2.8: **Illustration of a CMA-ES step.** The algorithm proceeds as follows: (*a*) Evaluate the fitness of each candidate in generation g. (*b*) Select the top 25% (purple). (*c*) Compute the covariance matrix $C(g+1)$ using selected candidates and generation mean $\mu(g)$ (green dot). (*d*) Sample new candidates using updated $\mu(g+1)$ and $C(g+1)$.

further technical depth, we recommend the comprehensive tutorial by CMA-ES creator Hansen (2016).

CMA-ES is one of the most popular gradient-free optimization algorithms, and it has been the algorithm of choice for many researchers and practitioners alike. The only real drawback is slow performance with a large number of model parameters, as the covariance calculation is $O(N^2)$, although recently proposed approximations can make it $O(N)$. CMA-ES is generally a good algorithm of choice when the search space is less than 1,000 parameters. We find that it is still usable up to around 10,000 parameters if we are willing to be patient.

2.2.4 OpenAI Evolution Strategy

Following CMA-ES, another prominent approach within the family of ES optimization methods is **OpenAI ES** (Salimans, Ho, Chen, et al., 2017), a scalable variant of the **natural evolution strategies** (NES) framework. What distinguishes NES from conventional gradient-based methods is that it applies a gradient ascent step using the natural gradient,

Math Detail: How to Estimate a Covariance Matrix

Covariance matrices describe how variables change together. In the context of sampling or optimization algorithms, we often want to estimate this matrix from a set of points. Here's how.

Assume that we have N points (x_i, y_i) for $i = 1, 2, ..., N$ drawn from an unknown distribution. The maximum likelihood estimates of the means are:

$$\mu_x = \frac{1}{N}\sum_{i=1}^{N} x_i, \qquad \mu_y = \frac{1}{N}\sum_{i=1}^{N} y_i. \tag{2.3}$$

From these, we estimate the variances and covariance:

$$\sigma_x^2 = \frac{1}{N}\sum_{i=1}^{N}(x_i - \mu_x)^2, \tag{2.4}$$

$$\sigma_y^2 = \frac{1}{N}\sum_{i=1}^{N}(y_i - \mu_y)^2, \tag{2.5}$$

$$\sigma_{xy} = \frac{1}{N}\sum_{i=1}^{N}(x_i - \mu_x)(y_i - \mu_y). \tag{2.6}$$

These components form the covariance matrix:

$$C = \begin{bmatrix} \sigma_x^2 & \sigma_{xy} \\ \sigma_{xy} & \sigma_y^2 \end{bmatrix}.$$

In adaptive optimization methods like CMA-ES, we often estimate this matrix from only the top-performing points. A common trick is to use the previous generation's mean $\mu^{(g)}$ rather than the updated mean $\mu^{(g+1)}$ when calculating variance:

$$\sigma_x^{2,(g+1)} = \frac{1}{N_{\text{best}}}\sum_{i=1}^{N_{\text{best}}}(x_i - \mu_x^{(g)})^2, \tag{2.7}$$

$$\sigma_y^{2,(g+1)} = \frac{1}{N_{\text{best}}}\sum_{i=1}^{N_{\text{best}}}(y_i - \mu_y^{(g)})^2, \tag{2.8}$$

$$\sigma_{xy}^{(g+1)} = \frac{1}{N_{\text{best}}}\sum_{i=1}^{N_{\text{best}}}(x_i - \mu_x^{(g)})(y_i - \mu_y^{(g)}). \tag{2.9}$$

This approach ensures that the estimated shape reflects the direction in which top candidates are moving relative to the previous population center, which improves stability during optimization.

a second-order method that adjusts the update based on uncertainty, unlike the standard gradient. This leads to more stable and efficient updates, especially in high-dimensional settings. OpenAI ES builds on this principle but simplifies the setup for scalability: It uses a fixed or diagonal Gaussian distribution, estimates gradients using the score function estimator (a form of Monte Carlo sampling), and parallelizes computation across many workers.

As we will see later in section 3.4.2, this makes it well suited for optimizing large neural network policies in reinforcement learning settings, where direct gradients are unavailable or unreliable. While simple ES typically operates on low-dimensional search spaces, OpenAI ES was designed with scalability in mind and has been used to train deep neural networks with millions of parameters.

Unlike CMA-ES, OpenAI ES does not adapt a full covariance matrix. Instead, it approximates gradients using a form of finite-difference estimation. In this context, the term "gradient" refers to the vector of partial derivatives of the objective function with respect to the model parameters. Intuitively, the gradient points in the direction of steepest ascent—indicating how the parameters should be adjusted to most effectively increase the objective function (e.g., expected reward in reinforcement learning). In many optimization algorithms, following the gradient allows for systematic improvement of model performance.

Since the exact gradient of the objective function may not be accessible, especially in black-box settings, OpenAI ES estimates it using random sampling. At each generation, a set of random perturbations ϵ_i is sampled from a multivariate Gaussian distribution with zero mean and isotropic (or diagonal) covariance. These perturbations are applied to the current parameter vector θ, and each perturbed version $\theta + \sigma\epsilon_i$ is evaluated to obtain a fitness score $F(\theta + \sigma\epsilon_i)$. The gradient estimate is then computed as a weighted sum of these perturbations:

$$\nabla_\theta J \approx \frac{1}{N\sigma} \sum_{i=1}^{N} F(\theta + \sigma\epsilon_i)\epsilon_i, \tag{2.10}$$

where N is the number of samples and σ is the mutation strength.

This gradient estimate represents an approximation of how changes to the parameters would affect the expected objective value. Rather than computing analytical derivatives, OpenAI ES infers the gradient from the differences in fitness caused by small, random perturbations. This approach is especially advantageous when the function is non-differentiable (more on this in section 2.3.2), noisy, or defined only through simulation. The resulting gradient estimate is then used to update the parameters using a standard gradient-based optimizer such as Adam:

$$\theta \leftarrow \theta + \alpha \cdot \text{Adam}(\nabla_\theta J), \tag{2.11}$$

where α is the learning rate. This method retains the black-box nature of evolutionary approaches, requiring only fitness evaluations, and is highly parallelizable because all perturbation evaluations are independent. Figure 2.9 shows what this strategy looks like, with a constant σ parameter.

In addition to these simplifications, the update rule was modified so it is suitable for parallel computation across different worker machines. By pre-computing a large grid of

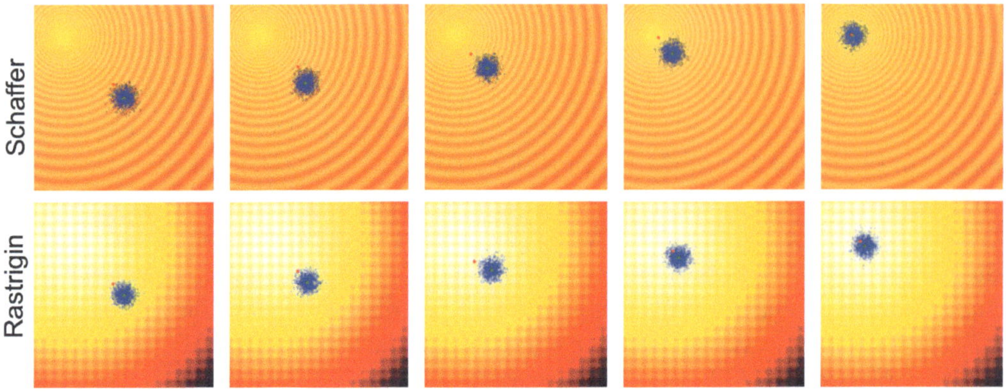

Figure 2.9: **OpenAI ES progress over 20 generations.** In this ES variation, the σ is fixed to a constant number, and only the μ parameter is updated at each generation. For videos, see `https://neuroevolutionbook.com/demos`.

random numbers with a fixed random seed, each worker can reproduce the parameters of every other worker over time. Additionally, each worker needs only to communicate a single number (i.e., the final fitness result) to all the other workers. This ability is important if we want to scale evolution strategies to thousands or even a million workers located on different machines, since while it may not be feasible to transmit an entire solution vector a million times at each generation update, it may be feasible to transmit only the final fitness results.

A key advantage of OpenAI ES is its robustness in high-dimensional parameter spaces and sparse-reward environments, where traditional policy gradient methods often struggle. It remains an important demonstration of how classical evolutionary strategies can be adapted for modern, distributed computation, showing that gradient-free optimization can scale remarkably well with sufficient compute.

ES algorithms are often combined with a **fitness shaping** method. Fitness shaping makes it possible to avoid outliers in the population from dominating the approximate gradient calculation (figure 2.10).

If a particular $F(z^m)$ is much larger than other $F(z^i)$ in the population, then the gradient might become dominated by these outliers and increase the chance of the algorithm being stuck in a local optimum. The method normalizes the fitness values to ensure consistent scaling and reduce sensitivity to outliers. There are alternative methods for fitness shaping, but they all lead to similar results in the end. Fitness shaping can be very useful for tasks with non-deterministic fitness functions. It is less useful for optimizing well-behaved functions that are deterministic, and using fitness shaping can sometimes increase the time that it takes to find a good solution.

2.2.5 Multiobjective Evolutionary Algorithms

Many real-world optimization problems require satisfying multiple, often conflicting objectives simultaneously. Many of the problems addressed by neuroevolution in this

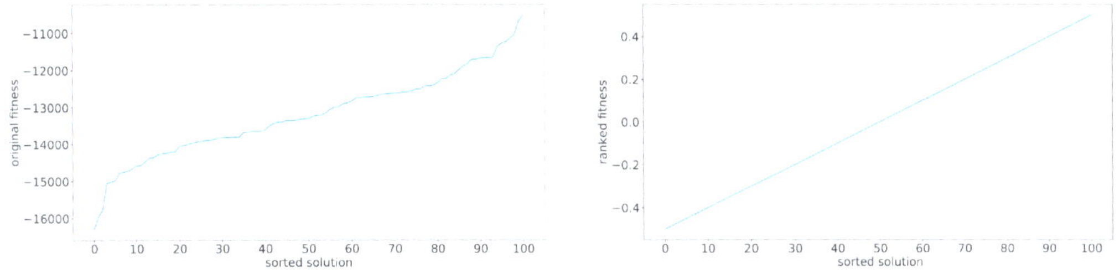

(*a*) Raw fitness (*b*) Ranked fitness

Figure 2.10: **Fitness shaping.** A comparison of the original fitness values (*a*) and ranked fitness values (*b*). With ranked fitnesses, outliers do not dominate gradient calculations, and the optimization process is less likely to get stuck at local optima.

book have this property as well. Traditional single-objective optimization approaches fall short in such scenarios: They often cannot capture the trade-offs between objectives adequately. In contrast, **multiobjective EAs** are designed to do precisely that.

Because no single solution will be best in all objectives, the outcomes of multiobjective problems are trade-offs among objectives rather than one perfect optimum. A solution is considered **Pareto-optimal** (or nondominated) if none of its objectives can be improved without worsening at least one other objective (Chankong and Haimes, 2008). In other words, for a minimization problem, solution A dominates solution B if A is no worse in every objective and strictly better in at least one. If no solution exists that dominates X, then X is Pareto-optimal. Without additional preference information, there will typically be many Pareto-optimal solutions, all considered equally valid choices among the trade-offs. These solutions collectively form the **Pareto front** (also called the Pareto frontier): the set of outcome vectors that are nondominated by any other feasible solution.

Because multiobjective problems yield an entire set of trade-off solutions rather than a single optimum, solving a multiobjective problem often means finding a representative set of Pareto-optimal solutions rather than one final answer. This difference poses unique challenges. Algorithms must approximate the entire Pareto front as well as possible, giving the decision-maker a comprehensive set of choices that balance the objectives. The goal is twofold: (1) convergence—solutions should be as close as possible to the true Pareto-optimal front, and (2) diversity—solutions should be well spread along the front to capture different trade-offs. Achieving a good balance between convergence and diversity is a central theme in multiobjective optimization algorithms.

Because evolutionary computation is a population-based search method, multiobjective optimization is a natural fit, and several methods have been developed for it (Coello Coello, Van Veldhuizen, and Lamont, 2007; Zhang and Li, 2007). Perhaps the best known is the **non-dominated sorting genetic algorithm II** (NSGA-II; Deb, Pratap, Agarwal, et al., 2002). NSGA-II is well regarded for its efficiency and its well-balanced handling of convergence and diversity. It addresses several shortcomings of earlier methods by introducing three key mechanisms: elitism, fast non-dominated sorting, and crowding distance. Together, these mechanisms allow NSGA-II to find an approximation of the Pareto front that is both close to the true front and well spread along it.

Elitism and generational selection: NSGA-II is an elitist GA: The best solutions are preserved between generations, ensuring that the Pareto front approximation never degrades. At each generation, NSGA-II creates offspring through crossover and mutation, and then merges parent and offspring populations (of size N each) into a temporary population of size $2N$. It then selects the next generation by picking the N best individuals from this merged set. "Best" is determined first by Pareto rank (front number) and second by diversity (crowding distance, explained next). By selecting from the union of parents and children, NSGA-II ensures that no high-quality solution is ever lost—if an offspring is worse than all parents, the parents will carry over; if an offspring dominates its parents, it will be included. Elitist selection was a major improvement in reliability over non-elitist algorithms, which could sometimes discard Pareto-optimal solutions due to random fluctuations. It also tends to speed up convergence, as good solutions accumulate over time.

Fast non-dominated sorting: To rank the $2N$ candidates, NSGA-II performs efficient non-dominated sorting that classifies individuals into Pareto fronts in $O(M \times N^2)$ time (where M is the number of objectives). This approach is significantly faster than the original NSGA's $O(M \times N^3)$ approach. The sorting procedure works as follows:

1. Identify front 1: Find all individuals that are not dominated by any other in the population.

2. Identify front 2: Remove front 1 from consideration; then find the nondominated set of the remaining individuals.

3. Repeat: Continue removing identified fronts and finding the next nondominated set, until all individuals are classified into fronts.

Each individual gets a rank (fitness) equal to the index of the front to which it belongs; a lower rank is better. This layering implicitly favors convergence: Solutions on the first front are Pareto-optimal within the population and thus are preferred over any dominated solutions. NSGA-II's efficient implementation relies on bookkeeping to avoid redundant dominance comparisons, making it practical to sort large populations quickly.

Crowding distance for diversity: After sorting, NSGA-II knows how many whole fronts it can fully include in the new generation. For instance, fronts 1, 2, ... $k - 1$ might all fit, and front k is the last partial front that exceeds the population limit N. To choose which individuals from the last included front k get to fill the remaining slots, NSGA-II uses crowding distance. This measure is a numerical estimate of how crowded a solution is relative to its neighbors on the same front. It is calculated by sorting the front's solutions according to each objective value and, for each solution, measuring the objective-space distance to its nearest neighbors on either side. A larger crowding distance means the solution resides in a sparsely populated region of the Pareto front. During the selection of the last front, NSGA-II prefers those with larger crowding distances; that is, it preserves the points that maximize diversity and eliminates those in dense clusters. This simple yet effective strategy prevents the algorithm from focusing only on a small area of the Pareto front.

Because of its good performance and simple implementation, NSGA-II has become a de facto baseline for multiobjective optimization. It has been applied in many domains and has inspired many variants and improvements. For instance, NSGA-III, an extension to more objectives, uses reference points in lieu of crowding, but retains the core nondominated sorting idea. Indeed, typically NSGA-II works well up to half a dozen objectives, after which the Pareto front starts to have too many solutions; that is, fewer solutions dominate other solutions. Other techniques have been developed for many-objective optimization, up to hundreds or thousands of objectives, representing a large number of constraints or tests (Deb and Jain, 2014; Ishibuchi, Tsukamoto, and Nojima, 2008).

In sum, multiobjective formulation is often a natural way to approach problems in the real world, including those addressed effectively by neuroevolution. Multiobjective techniques will therefore be demonstrated many times in this book (e.g., in sections 6.4.3–6.4.4, 10.4–10.5, and 14.2). It can also play a significant role in maintaining diversity, as will be discussed in section 5.5.

2.2.6 Further Evolutionary Computation Techniques

While this chapter has focused on the most common techniques, virtually any evolutionary computation method can be applied to evolving neural networks in some form. Researchers have experimented with a wide range of algorithms beyond standard EAs. What follows is an outline of several additional evolutionary approaches that have been explored in neuroevolution.

A prominent example is **genetic programming** (GP; Banzhaf, Nordin, Keller, et al., 1998; Poli, Langdon, and McPhee, 2008). It evolves computer programs or symbolic expressions, traditionally representing solutions as tree-structured programs. Originally introduced by Koza (1992) as a way to evolve programs for arbitrary tasks, GP extends the GA paradigm to variable-length, executable structures. In the context of neuroevolution, GP offers the flexibility to evolve neural networks in more open-ended ways–for example, by evolving entire network construction programs, activation functions, or learning rules. For example, GP is used to evolve indirect encodings in section 4.2.2, to optimize neural architectures in section 10.3.1, and loss functions, activation functions, and learning methods in chapter 11. A new opportunity is also emerging in enhancing GP by using large language models (LLMs) as advanced mutation operators (section 13.3.1).

Despite a similar name, **evolutionary programming** (EP; Fogel, 2006; Fogel, Owens, and Walsh, 1966) is a distinctly different method from GP. It was originally developed to evolve predictive models and finite state machines for predictive modeling, and later generalized to continuous optimization problems, such as neural networks. The representations are usually fixed-length vectors, and mutation is the primary operator. As with ES, crossover is typically not used. As will be pointed out in section 3.1, EP was one of the earliest neuroevolution techniques, and it was later used in game-playing neuroevolution as well (section 7.2.1).

Cartesian genetic programming (CGP; Miller, 2011, 2020), is a form of GP that represents programs or neural networks as directed acyclic graphs (instead of tree structures), often laid out on a 2D grid of nodes. CGP has proven well suited for evolving neural networks because an arbitrary graph can naturally represent neural architectures (including recurrent or skip connections) more directly than a tree. The method retains many advantages of GP (e.g., flexibility in representation) while constraining individuals to a Cartesian grid of nodes for efficiency and simplicity. For instance, CGP is used in the work described in section 14.4.2 to discover plasticity rules for spiking neural networks.

Particle swarm optimization (PSO; Kennedy and Eberhart, 1995; Shami, El-Saleh, Alswaitti, et al., 2022) is a population-based optimization method inspired by social behaviors in animals (such as bird flocking). In PSO, a swarm of particles (candidate solutions) flies through the search space of neural network parameters, where each particle's position encodes a set of weights or other network design variables. The particles update their positions iteratively based on their own best-found solution and the swarm's global best solution, effectively sharing information to converge on optima. Because of its ability to find local optima accurately, PSO can be used in neuroevolution, for instance, to refine the parameters of a neural network that was evolved offline (section 6.2.2).

Similarly, **ant colony optimization** (ACO; Dorigo, Maniezzo, and Colorni, 1996; Dorigo and Stützle, 2010) is a swarm intelligence technique that finds solutions by mimicking how real ant colonies forage for paths between their nest and food sources. A set of artificial ants constructs solutions on a graph incrementally, such as by selecting neural network components or connections step by step. As they build solutions, the ants deposit virtual pheromones on the graph edges; shorter or higher-quality solutions result in stronger pheromone trails, which bias subsequent ants to follow those components (which is a form of positive feedback). Over iterations, an optimal or near-optimal solution emerges as the heavily pheromone-traveled path. For example, ACO can be used in neural architecture search, where the network is constructed based on the ants' path (section 6.2.2).

In contrast to most EAs, **estimation of distribution algorithms** (EDAs; Alden and Miikkulainen, 2016; Baluja and Caruana, 1995; Larrañaga and Lozano, 2002; Lozano, Larrañaga, Inza, et al., 2006; Pelikan, Goldberg, and Cantú-Paz, 1999) take a fundamentally different approach to population-based search. They replace traditional variation operators with probabilistic modeling. Instead of relying on individual or collective behavior, EDAs construct a statistical model of the most promising solutions found so far and sample new candidates from this learned distribution. This approach allows the algorithm to capture and exploit underlying patterns or dependencies among variables, making it especially powerful for complex optimization problems where such structure is present. In contrast to most EAs, EDAs offer a model-driven approach that adapts as the search progresses, enabling a more informed exploration of the solution space. In neuroevolution, EDAs have been used to evolve neural network weights and structures by iteratively refining a distribution over network parameters (section 5.7).

In addition, **differential evolution** (DE; Price, Storn, and Lampinen, 2005; Storn and Price, 1997) has recently turned out promising as well; it has been used both to optimize network weights and to search for deep learning architectures (Awad, Mallik, and Hutter, 2020; Iacca, Caraffini, and Neri, 2020; Mousavirad, Tabatabaei, Zabihzadeh, et al., 2025; Wang, Sun, Xue, et al., 2018). DE is a population-based stochastic search algorithm that operates through a simple but effective mutation–crossover–selection cycle. Mutation is performed by adding the weighted difference of two randomly selected individuals to a third; that is, $v_i = x_{r_1} + F \cdot (x_{r_2} - x_{r_3})$, where $x_{r_1}, x_{r_2}, x_{r_3}$ are distinct population vectors, and $F \in (0, 2)$ controls the amplification of differential variations. The resulting mutant

Listing 2.2: **Basic training loop with interchangeable solvers.**

```
import es

# solver = es.SimpleGA(...)
# solver = es.PGPE(...)
# solver = es.OpenES(...)
solver = es.CMAES(...)

while True:
  solutions = solver.ask()
  fitness_list = np.zeros(solver.popsize)

  for i in range(solver.popsize):
    fitness_list[i] = evaluate(solutions[i])

  solver.tell(fitness_list)
  result = solver.result()

  if result[1] > MY_REQUIRED_FITNESS:
    break
```

vector v_i is then mixed with the current target vector x_i through a crossover operator, yielding a trial vector. Finally, greedy selection ensures that the fitter of x_i and its trial replaces x_i in the next generation.

Indeed, given the popularity of neural networks as a prediction and decision approach, and the power of population-based search to find good solutions, it is no surprise that almost any advances in EAs can be utilized in neuroevolution as well.

2.2.7 Try These Algorithms Yourself

There is no better way to learn and gain intuition than by trying these evolutionary algorithms yourself. There are open-source implementations for most of the algorithms described in this book. For example, the author of CMA-ES, Nikolaus Hansen, has maintained a numpy-based implementation of CMA-ES (`https://github.com/CMA-ES/pycma`) with lots of bells and whistles. His Python implementation introduced some of us to the training loop interface described earlier. Since this interface is quite easy to use, we've integrated additional algorithms—like a simple GA and OpenAI's ES—into a compact Python module named `es.py`. We've also wrapped the original CMA-ES library within this lightweight package. This way, we can quickly compare ES algorithms by just changing one line, as seen in listing 2.2.

You can find `es.py` at `https://neuroevolutionbook.com` exercises. In the accompanying notebook, we show how to use the ES solvers in `es.py` to solve a 100-dimensional (100D) version of the Rastrigin function with even more local optimum points. The 100-D version is somewhat more challenging than the trivial 2D version used to produce the visualizations in this book. On this 100-D Rastrigin problem, none of the optimizers got to the global optimum solution, although CMA-ES comes close (figure 2.11). CMA-ES is clearly the best performer, with OpenAI-ES / GA further behind. We had to use an annealing schedule to gradually lower σ for OpenAI-ES to make it perform better for this particular task.

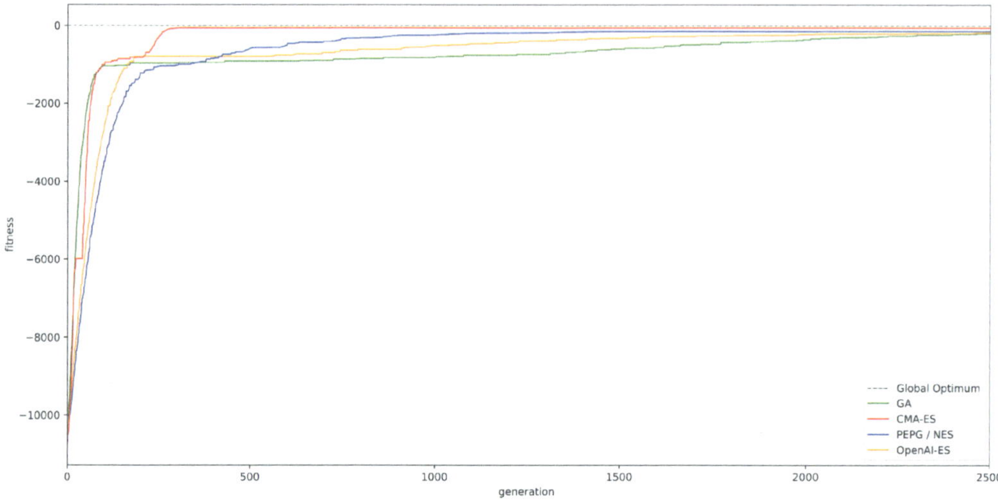

Figure 2.11: **100D Rastrigin function results.** A comparison of the performance for various algorithms discussed in this section for the high-dimensional Rastrigin function.

In general, choosing among a GA, CMA-ES, OpenAI ES, or other EAs depends heavily on the nature of the problem, the search space, and available computational resources. GAs are relatively simple to implement and perform well when the problem landscape has many local optima or when custom genetic operations can be crafted to exploit structure in the solution space. They are a natural choice when the problem isn't purely continuous.

CMA-ES, in contrast, is tailored for continuous, real-valued optimization problems. It stands out when dealing with non-convex or rugged landscapes, especially when variables are interdependent or when the objective function is not easily separable. The strategy automatically adapts the shape of its sampling distribution to the topology of the problem, making it very efficient in exploring complex fitness landscapes. CMA-ES typically performs best on low- to medium-dimensional problems.

OpenAI ES is designed for scalable, parallel optimization of high-dimensional continuous problems, where reward signals are sparse, noisy, or hard to differentiate. Unlike GA and CMA-ES, OpenAI ES emphasizes massive parallelism and simple, gradient-free updates, making it a compelling option when computational power is abundant and traditional gradient-based methods are impractical. It doesn't adapt its sampling distribution as intricately as CMA-ES but benefits from being easy to implement, robust in noisy environments, and efficient in settings with large populations and cloud-based infrastructures.

Ultimately, while each method has its strengths, no single one is universally best. Performance varies significantly with the problem, and practical experimentation is usually the most reliable way to choose among them. Importantly, these methods are not limited to simple optimization tasks—they can be effectively combined with neural networks.

While evolutionary algorithms provide a robust framework for global search and optimization, neural networks excel in learning complex patterns and approximating nonlinear functions. As we will see throughout this book, the synergy between these

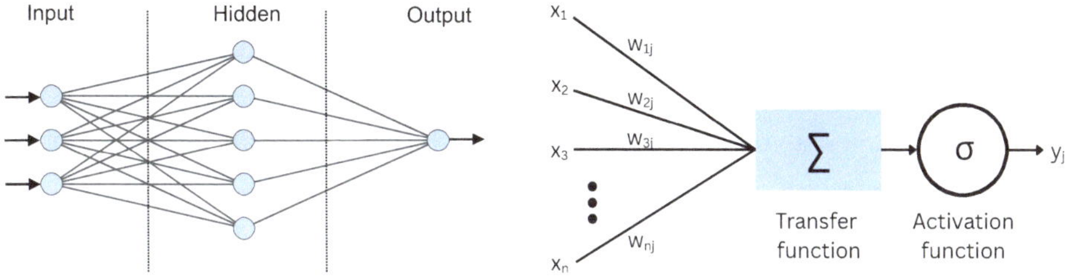

(*a*) Feedforward network (*b*) Artificial neuron

Figure 2.12: **Artificial neural networks.** (*a*) This example of a feedforward network has three inputs, one hidden layer with five nodes, and one output layer with one node. The input to the network propagates through the consecutive layers of the neural network to produce the outputs. This particular architecture is often called the fully-connected three-layer network although it has only two layers of weights. The details of an artificial neuron are shown in (*b*). The inputs to a neuron are first weighted, and their sum is then passed through an activation function.

two paradigms becomes particularly evident in neuroevolution. Before diving deeper into this integration, it is essential to first understand the structure, learning dynamics, and capabilities of neural networks in their own right. This will lay the groundwork for appreciating how evolution can be harnessed to shape and enhance their performance.

2.3 Neural Networks

Artificial neural networks (ANNs) are a class of machine learning models loosely inspired by the structure and function of the human brain. They consist of layers of interconnected nodes that process input data to produce an output. ANNs have been remarkably successful in various domains such as image recognition, natural language processing, and time-series forecasting. This section will provide the basic ideas behind the structure and function of neural networks, focusing on several key architectures used throughout the book: feedforward neural networks (FNNs), recurrent neural networks (RNNs), long short-term memory networks (LSTMs), convolutional neural networks (CNNs), and transformers.

2.3.1 Feedforward Neural Networks

Feedforward neural networks (FNNs) are the simplest type of artificial neural network. They consist of an input layer, one or more hidden layers, and an output layer (figure 2.12*a*). Information flows in one direction, from the input to the output, without loops or cycles.

The network begins with the **input layer**, which receives raw data. Each node in this input layer corresponds to a feature or variable from the input dataset or the environment. This layer performs no calculations; it merely passes the input values to the next layer.

After the input layer, the data moves through one or more **hidden layers**. These layers are where the actual computations occur. Each hidden layer consists of multiple nodes, or neurons, which are fully connected to the nodes of the previous layer. Every connection between nodes has an associated weight that signifies the strength or importance of that connection. Each neuron also has a bias value that modifies the output. For each neuron in a hidden layer, a weighted sum of all incoming inputs is calculated (figure 2.12*b*). This sum is then passed through an **activation function**, such as rectified linear unit (ReLU), sigmoid, or tanh, which introduces nonlinearity to the model. The nonlinearity is crucial because it allows the network to model more complex relationships between inputs and outputs. The output of the neurons in one layer becomes the input for the neurons in the next layer.

The final layer in the network is the **output layer**, which produces the network's prediction. The number of neurons in the output layer matches the number of possible outputs. For example, a binary classification task may have one or two output neurons, while a multi-class classification problem might have as many neurons as there are classes to predict. In other contexts, such as networks evolved for control or decision-making tasks, the output layer may signify the actions that an agent should take, with each neuron corresponding to a possible action or control signal.

The behavior of an FNN is determined by its weights and biases. These parameters can be set in different ways, such as gradient descent (as described in the next section), or through neuroevolutionary algorithms. Thus, an FNN defines a mapping from inputs to outputs, but the method used to obtain that mapping can vary. It can be represented mathematically as follows:

$$y = \sigma(W_h \cdot \sigma(W_1 \cdot x + b_1) + b_h), \tag{2.12}$$

where x is the input vector and W_1 and W_h are weight matrices for the first and hidden layers, respectively; the bias vectors are b_1 and b_h; and $\sigma(\cdot)$ is the activation function. The output vector is denoted as y.

2.3.2 Training Feedforward Neural Networks with Gradient Descent

While this book is about neuroevolution, we will briefly explain the **backpropagation algorithm** to train neural networks. Backpropagation is a powerful algorithm for many applications. However, backpropagation typically requires large amounts of labeled data and that the function being optimized (e.g., the neural network model) is differentiable. Differentiability means that the function has a well-defined derivative at every point in its domain, allowing us to compute gradients that indicate how to adjust weights to minimize error. In practical terms, each activation function, layer operation, and loss function in the network must support differentiation so the chain rule can be applied across all layers (more on this below). We will see in later chapters how both neuroevolution and backpropagation can be synergistically combined, such as in the context of neural architecture search (chapter 10) or reinforcement learning (chapter 12).

While we focus on the application of backpropagation to feedforward neural networks in this section, it can similarly be applied to RNNs and LSTMs, and it is also used in CNNs and transformers. Backpropagation is a fundamental algorithm for training neural networks by minimizing the loss function, which quantifies the error in the network's predictions. This algorithm calculates the **gradient** of the loss function with respect to each weight and bias in the network. A gradient is essentially a vector of partial derivatives—it tells us how much a small change in each parameter (like a weight or bias) will affect the overall error or loss of the network. By following the direction of the negative gradient (a process known as **gradient descent**), the network can update its parameters in a way that gradually reduces the error. You can think of this process like hiking downhill in the fog: the loss function is the terrain, and your goal is to reach the lowest point (the minimum error). Since you cannot see far ahead, you feel the slope under your feet (the gradient) and take small steps in the direction that goes downhill the fastest. Repeating this step over and over slowly leads you to the bottom of the valley, just as repeated updates lead the network to better performance.

In the 1980s, backpropagation became widely recognized and applied in neural networks, thanks to the work of Rumelhart, Hinton, and Williams (1986). Their seminal paper highlighted backpropagation as a practical and effective way to train multi-layer neural networks. This breakthrough renewed interest in neural networks, marking a significant milestone in machine learning and artificial intelligence.

The backpropagation algorithm consists of two main phases: a forward pass and a backward pass. In the **forward pass**, input data flows through the network layer by layer, producing an output. This output is compared with the true target value to compute the loss, or error, of the network's prediction.

The **backward pass** uses the chain rule to calculate gradients of the loss function with respect to each weight and bias in the network. This information is then used to adjust these parameters to minimize the error. The key steps in the backward pass are as follows:

1. Initialize gradients: Start by calculating the loss, L, from the forward pass. Then, initialize the gradients for each weight and bias in the network.

2. Calculate the gradient at the output layer: Compute the gradient of the loss with respect to the output layer's activations. For example, in a neural network with output $\hat{y}$ and target y, if the loss function is the mean squared error (MSE),

$$L = \frac{1}{2}(\hat{y} - y)^2, \tag{2.13}$$

then the gradient of L with respect to $\hat{y}$ is:

$$\frac{\partial L}{\partial \hat{y}} = \hat{y} - y. \tag{2.14}$$

3. Backpropagate the error to the previous layers: For each layer, starting from the output layer and moving back to the input layer:

   (a) Calculate the gradient of the activation function: For each neuron, apply the derivative of the activation function to the neuron's output to compute how sensitive the neuron's output is to changes in its input. For example, if the activation function is sigmoid:

$$\sigma(x) = \frac{1}{1 + e^{-x}}, \qquad \sigma'(x) = \sigma(x) \cdot (1 - \sigma(x)). \tag{2.15}$$

   (b) Calculate the gradient of the weights and biases: Using the chain rule, multiply the gradients from the previous layer by the current layer's activation derivative to compute the gradients with respect to each weight and bias.

(c) Store the gradients for each weight and bias: These gradients will be used in the next step to update the weights and biases.

4. Update weights and biases: After computing the gradients via backpropagation, update each weight w and bias b by moving in the opposite direction of the gradient, scaled by the learning rate α:

$$w \leftarrow w - \alpha \frac{\partial L}{\partial w}, \quad b \leftarrow b - \alpha \frac{\partial L}{\partial b}. \tag{2.16}$$

Backpropagation is sensitive to certain hyperparameters, such as the learning rate α. Choosing an appropriate learning rate is essential; a value that is too large may cause the network to diverge, while a value that is too small may result in slow convergence. Techniques such as learning rate schedules or adaptive optimizers (e.g., Adam) can help.

Additionally, for deep networks, issues like vanishing and exploding gradients may arise, especially when using activation functions like sigmoid or tanh. Techniques such as ReLU activation, batch normalization, and careful weight initialization can help mitigate these issues.

In summary, backpropagation allows neural networks to learn from data by calculating the gradients of the loss with respect to each weight and bias and updating them in a way that reduces prediction error. Instead of using backpropagation, we can also directly optimize the weights and structure of neural networks with evolution. Chapter 3 gives an overview of how this can be done.

2.3.3 Recurrent Neural Networks

A **recurrent neural network** (RNN) (figure 2.13*a*) is a type of artificial neural network designed to recognize patterns in sequences of data, such as time series, text, or audio. Unlike feedforward neural networks, RNNs have connections that loop back, allowing information to persist. This architecture makes them particularly well suited for tasks where context and order matter, enabling them to handle sequences of variable length and maintain a memory of what has been processed.

Let's have a look at exactly how an RNN works. In the RNN, the neurons not only receive input from the previous layer but also from their previous states. This recurrency allows the network to maintain a form of memory about the past inputs, which is essential for tasks like speech recognition, machine translation, or any other problem where the current input depends on the previous inputs. As we will see later, for instance in section 13.5 on world models, this temporal awareness also makes RNNs well suited for agents that act in environments where decisions depend not just on the current observation but on the sequence of prior events.

The network begins with an input layer that receives a sequence of data. Unlike FNNs, RNNs process sequences one element at a time. For example, in a text-processing task, each word in a sentence might be fed into the network one by one.

The core of an RNN is its hidden state, which is designed to maintain a hidden state, or memory, that captures information about the sequence. When an input element is fed

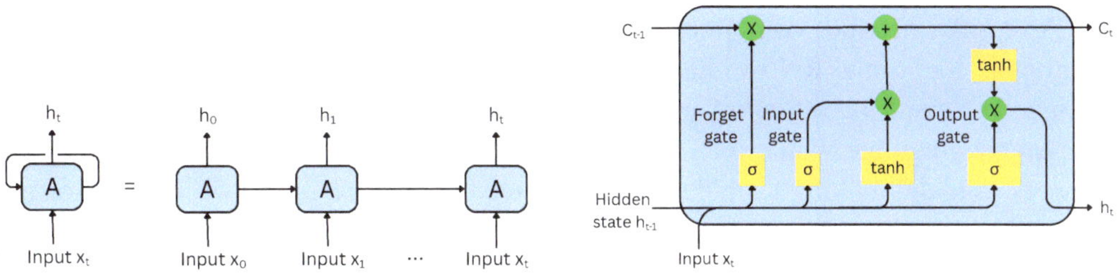

(*a*) Recurrent activation (*b*) LSTM structure

Figure 2.13: **RNN and LSTM block.** (*a*) The left side shows a basic recurrent neural network architecture, where the hidden state is updated at each time step using the current input and the previous hidden state. The unrolled version of the RNN over multiple time steps is shown at the right, illustrating how the network processes a sequence by passing information forward through time via shared weights. (*b*) An LSTM block illustrating the internal structure, including the cell state and the three gating mechanisms: forget gate, input gate, and output gate. These components work together to regulate the flow of information, enabling the network to learn long-range dependencies in sequential data.

into the network, it is combined with the previous hidden state to produce a new hidden state. Mathematically, this is often represented as:

$$h_t = f(W \cdot x_t + U \cdot h_{t-1} + b), \tag{2.17}$$

where h_t represents the hidden state at time step t; x_t is the input at time step t; W and U are weight matrices for the input and hidden state, respectively; b is a bias term; f is an activation function, typically a nonlinear function like tanh or ReLU. This hidden state is updated at each time step, capturing both the current input and the past context.

At each time step, the hidden state can produce an output, depending on the specific task. The output is computed using the current hidden state and a weight matrix. For example, in a text-prediction task, the output at each time step might represent the predicted next word in a sentence.

In the case of supervised learning problems, RNNs are typically trained using backpropagation through time (BPTT). However, they suffer from issues like vanishing and exploding gradients, which makes it difficult to capture long-term dependencies in the data.

Neuroevolution techniques that optimize both weights and network topology can naturally exploit recurrent connections to discover clever solutions, as we will see in section 3.3.4.

2.3.4 Long Short-Term Memory

An **long short-term memory** (LSTM) network is a special type of RNN designed to overcome some of the limitations of traditional RNNs, particularly the problem of learning long-term dependencies (figure 2.13*b*). LSTMs (Hochreiter and Schmidhuber, 1997) can learn and retain information over extended periods, making them highly effective for tasks involving sequential data, such as language modeling, speech recognition, and time-series forecasting.

An LSTM network comprises a series of LSTM cells, which replace the standard neurons in traditional RNNs. Each LSTM cell has a more complex internal structure designed to control the flow of information in and out of the cell, using several gates. These gates regulate which information is added, updated, or forgotten, allowing the network to maintain long-term dependencies and learn which pieces of information are important for making predictions.

An LSTM cell contains three main gates: the forget gate, the input gate, and the output gate. These gates use sigmoid activation functions to decide whether to let information pass through or not. What follows is a breakdown of each component.

The **forget gate** determines which parts of the cell's previous state should be discarded or forgotten. It takes the current input (x_t) and the previous hidden state (h_{t-1}) and passes them through a sigmoid function. The output of this function is a value between 0 and 1 for each number in the cell state (C_{t-1}), where 0 represents "completely forget" and 1 represents "completely retain":

$$f_t = \sigma(W_f \cdot [h_{t-1}, x_t] + b_f), \tag{2.18}$$

where f_t is the forget gate's output, W_f is the weight matrix for the forget gate, b_f is the bias term for the forget gate, and σ denotes the sigmoid function.

The **input gate** decides which new information will be added to the cell state. It consists of two parts: a sigmoid layer, which determines which values will be updated; and a tanh layer, which creates a vector of new candidate values that could be added to the state. These two layers' results are multiplied to decide which new information to keep. We can define it as:

$$i_t = \sigma(W_i \cdot [h_{t-1}, x_t] + b_i), \tilde{C}_t = \tanh(W_C \cdot [h_{t-1}, x_t] + b_C), \tag{2.19}$$

where i_t is the input gate's output; $\tilde{C}_t$ represents the new candidate values to be added; W_i and W_C are weight matrices for the input gate and candidate values; and b_i and b_C are the bias terms for the input gate and candidate values.

The new cell state C_t is updated by combining the old cell state C_{t-1} multiplied by the forget gate output f_t (which determines what to forget) and the new candidate values $\tilde{C}_t$ multiplied by the input gate output i_t (which determines what new information to add):

$$C_t = f_t * C_{t-1} + i_t * \tilde{C}_t. \tag{2.20}$$

This equation effectively updates the cell state by retaining the necessary information from the past and incorporating the new relevant information.

The **output gate** determines the next hidden state h_t, which is used for the next time step and can also be an output for the current time step. The output gate first passes the current input and previous hidden state through a sigmoid function to decide which parts of the cell state to output. Then it multiplies the cell state (after applying the tanh function to scale between -1 and 1) by the output of the sigmoid gate:

$$o_t = \sigma(W_o \cdot [h_{t-1}, x_t] + b_o), h_t = o_t * \tanh(C_t), \tag{2.21}$$

where o_t is the output gate's output, h_t is the new hidden state, W_o is the weight matrix for the output gate, and b_o is the bias term for the output gate.

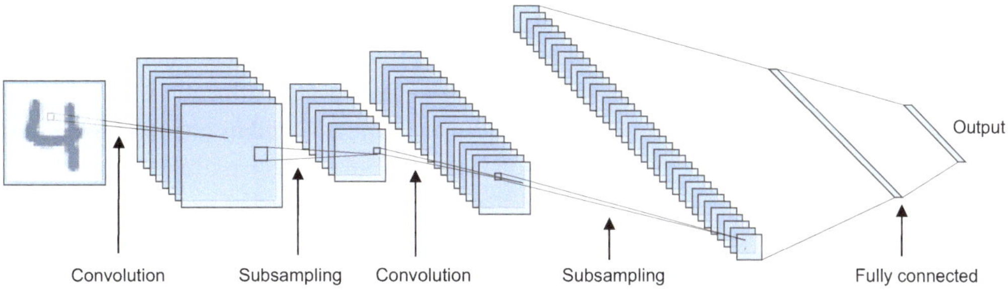

Figure 2.14: **A typical architecture of a CNN.** The input image passes through multiple layers of convolutions, which extract various features, followed by subsampling (pooling) layers to reduce dimensionality. This process is repeated to create deeper feature maps, which are then flattened and connected to fully connected layers to generate the final output.

The gating mechanisms in LSTM cells allow them to remember information for long periods. This mechanism is particularly useful in tasks where the context of earlier parts of a sequence is essential for making accurate predictions later. Additionally, LSTMs are specifically designed to mitigate the problem of vanishing gradients, which occurs when training traditional RNNs on long sequences. The cell state in LSTMs can maintain a constant flow of gradients during backpropagation, allowing the network to learn long-term dependencies effectively.

In this book, we will see how neuroevolution is able to successfully optimize the weights of LSTMs that control agents in complex environments (section 7.1.2) or is even able to come up with new and better-performing LSTM node designs (section 10.3.1).

2.3.5 Convolutional Neural Networks

A **convolutional neural network** (CNN) is a type of deep learning model specifically designed to process and analyze data with a grid like structure, such as images (figure 2.14). CNNs are particularly effective for tasks that involve spatial hierarchies in data, such as image recognition, object detection, and video analysis. The architecture of CNNs is inspired by the visual cortex of the brain, where individual neurons respond to overlapping regions in the visual field (Fukushima, 1980; Hubel and Wiesel, 1968). A CNN consists of several layers, each with a specific function. The primary building blocks of a CNN are convolutional layers, pooling layers, and fully connected layers. These work together to automatically and adaptively learn spatial hierarchies of features from input data.

The **convolutional layer** is the core component of a CNN. It performs the convolution operation, which involves sliding a small filter or kernel (a matrix of weights) over the input data. This sliding motion is governed by a stride, which defines how many pixels the filter moves at each step. Padding (adding values, often zeros, around the input's borders) is frequently applied to control the spatial dimensions of the output and retain information at the edges.

As the filter slides, it performs a dot product between its weights and the corresponding patch of the input data, producing a single value in the output feature map. This operation allows the filter to detect spatial patterns such as edges, textures, or specific color variations within the input. This can be visualized as taking a small window of the input image (the same size as the filter), applying the filter's weights to it, and generating an output value that represents the presence or strength of a specific feature at that location.

Mathematically, the convolution operation (often implemented as cross-correlation in deep learning frameworks) can be expressed as:

$$(I * K)(x, y) = \sum_{i=0}^{m-1} \sum_{j=0}^{n-1} I(x + i, y + j) \cdot K(i, j), \tag{2.22}$$

where I is the input image, K is the convolution kernel or filter of dimensions $m \times n$, and (x, y) are the coordinates of the pixel in the output feature map, representing the top-left corner of the window over which the operation is performed.

The output of this operation is a set of feature maps that highlight specific patterns or features in the input data. Multiple filters can be used simultaneously, each designed (or learned) to detect different features, resulting in multiple feature maps.

After the convolutional layer, an **activation function**, typically the **ReLU**, is applied to introduce nonlinearity. This nonlinearity allows the network to learn complex patterns. The ReLU function is defined as:

$$f(x) = \max(0, x). \tag{2.23}$$

This activation function outputs the input directly if it is positive; otherwise, it outputs zero. It helps the network to learn nonlinear relationships.

The **pooling layer**, also known as the subsampling or downsampling layer, reduces the spatial dimensions of the feature maps. This mechanism helps to reduce the number of parameters, computational complexity, and overfitting. The most common type of pooling is **max pooling**, which takes the maximum value from a small region of the feature map.

If the input to the pooling layer is a 2×2 window, max pooling selects the highest value from that window. Mathematically, max pooling over a region can be expressed as:

$$P(x, y) = \max\{f(i, j) : i, j \in \text{window}(x, y)\}, \tag{2.24}$$

where $P(x, y)$ represents the output of the pooling operation at position (x, y), and $f(i, j)$ is the feature value at position (i, j).

After several convolutional and pooling layers, the high-level reasoning in the neural network is done via **fully connected layers**. In a fully connected layer, each neuron is connected to every neuron in the previous layer. The output of the final fully connected layer can represent the class scores (in a classification problem), task-specific outputs such as predicted values or sequences, or, in the case of agents trained via neuroevolution, it may represent continuous control signals or discrete action probabilities used to interact with an environment. The fully connected layer can be mathematically represented as:

$$y = W \cdot x + b, \tag{2.25}$$

where y is the output vector, W is the weight matrix, x is the input vector, and b is the bias.

In classification tasks, the output layer often uses a **softmax activation function** to convert the output scores into probabilities. The softmax function is defined as:

$$\text{softmax}(z_i) = \frac{e^{z_i}}{\sum_j e^{z_j}}, \tag{2.26}$$

where z_i represents the output score for class i and the denominator is the sum of the exponentials of all output scores. This function ensures that the output values are between 0 and 1 and sum to 1, representing a probability distribution over the classes.

Finding the right design parameters for a CNN manually, such as the number of layers, the number of channels, or the kernel size, can take a lot of time. Thankfully, we can also automate this process with neuroevolution, as we will see in section 10.5 of chapter 10 on neural architecture search.

2.3.6 Transformers

A **transformer** (Vaswani, Shazeer, Parmar, et al., 2017) is a type of deep learning model that relies entirely on a so-called **self-attention** mechanism to process input data, rather than traditional recurrent or convolutional layers. We will look at the self-attention mechanism in more detail next, and again in section 4.4.1 in the context of indirect encodings. Transformers are the foundation for many state-of-the-art models in natural language processing and other fields. They are particularly well suited for handling sequential data and long-range dependencies. We will go into more detail on transformers and LLMs in chapter 13, showing how neuroevolution methods can be synergistically combined with generative AI.

The transformer architecture consists of an **encoder-decoder** structure, where both the encoder and decoder are composed of multiple layers of self-attention and feedforward neural networks (figure 2.15). The encoder takes an input sequence and processes it into an internal representation, which the decoder then uses to generate an output sequence. Each component in the transformer uses self-attention to weigh the importance of different elements in the input sequence in learning complex patterns.

The input to a transformer model is first converted into **embeddings**, which are fixed-length, dense vector representations of the input tokens (words, subwords, etc.). Since transformers do not inherently understand the order of the sequence, **positional encodings** are added to the embeddings to provide information about the relative positions of tokens in the sequence. For example, sine and cosine functions of different frequencies can be used to create unique position vectors.

The core of the transformer is the **self-attention** mechanism, which allows the model to focus on different parts of the input sequence when making predictions. It computes a weighted representation of each input token based on its relationship with all other tokens in the sequence based on the **query** (Q), **key** (K), and **value** (V) vectors for each token. These vectors are derived using learned weight matrices:

$$Q = XW^Q, \quad K = XW^K, \quad V = XW^V, \tag{2.27}$$

where X is the input sequence, and W^Q, W^K, W^V are weight matrices for the query, key, and value vectors, respectively.

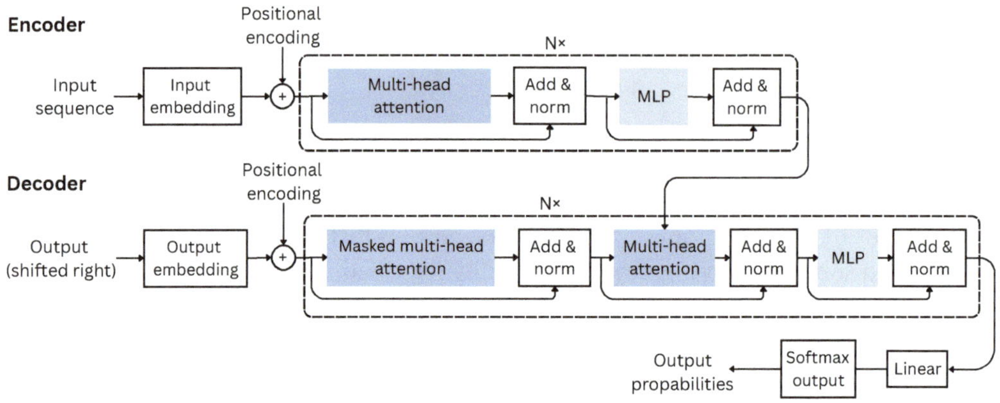

Figure 2.15: **Illustration of the transformer architecture.** The architecture consists of an encoder (*top*) and a decoder (*bottom*). The encoder comprises a stack of layers, each containing a multi-head self-attention mechanism followed by a position-wise FFN, with residual connections and layer normalization applied after each sub layer. The decoder stack is similarly structured but includes an additional masked multi-head self-attention mechanism to prevent positions from attending to subsequent positions. Positional encodings are added to the input embeddings to provide information about the position of the words in the sequence. The final output is generated after applying a linear transformation and a softmax function to produce the output probabilities.

The self-attention scores are computed by taking the dot product of the query and key vectors and scaling by the square root of the dimensionality of the key vectors. The scores are then passed through a softmax function to produce attention weights:

$$\text{Attention}(Q, K, V) = \text{softmax}\left(\frac{QK^T}{\sqrt{d_k}}\right)V, \tag{2.28}$$

where d_k is the dimension of the key vectors.

To allow the model to attend to information from different representation subspaces jointly, Transformers use **multi-head attention**. Instead of computing a single set of attention scores, the input is projected into multiple sets of queries, keys, and values, and the attention mechanism is applied in parallel. The outputs of these attention heads are concatenated and linearly transformed:

$$\text{MultiHead}(Q, K, V) = \text{Concat}(\text{head}_1, \ldots, \text{head}_h)W^O. \tag{2.29}$$

Each head i performs the self-attention computation independently, and the results are combined to capture different aspects of the input data.

After the multi-head attention layer, the output is passed through a position-wise **FFN**, which consists of two linear transformations with a ReLU activation in between. The same FFN is applied independently to each position in the sequence:

$$\text{FFN}(x) = \max(0, xW_1 + b_1)W_2 + b_2, \tag{2.30}$$

where W_1, W_2 are weight matrices, and b_1, b_2 are bias terms.

To stabilize and speed up training, each sub-layer (multi-head attention and feedforward neural network) is followed by a **layer normalization** step, which normalizes the output across the features. Additionally, the transformer uses **residual connections** (skip connections) that add the input of each sub-layer to its output before applying layer normalization. This computation mitigates the vanishing gradient problem and allows the model to learn more efficiently:

$$\text{Output} = \text{LayerNorm}(x + \text{Sublayer}(x)).$$

The encoder and decoder are composed of multiple identical layers (typically six to 12 in common implementations). Each encoder layer consists of a multi-head self-attention mechanism followed by a feedforward neural network, while each decoder layer contains an additional **cross-attention mechanism** to attend to the encoder's output.

The decoder generates the output sequence one token at a time. At each step, the decoder attends to all the previously generated tokens using masked self-attention (to prevent attending to future tokens) and to the encoder's output using a cross-attention mechanism. This process continues until the model generates a special end-of-sequence token.

Neuroevolution has also been applied to the transformer architecture, resulting in evolved transformer models that outperform baseline models on benchmark tasks while using fewer computational resources. This approach will be discussed in more detail in the context of evolutionary neural architecture search in chapter 10.

2.4 Neuroevolution: An Integrated Approach

This chapter introduced the fundamental principles of EAs and ANNs, laying the foundation for their integration in neuroevolution. EAs are optimization techniques inspired by natural selection, operating on populations of candidate solutions that evolve over successive generations. Key processes include selection, mutation, and crossover, which allow populations to explore and exploit the search space for optimal or near-optimal solutions. The chapter discussed different types of EAs, such as GAs and ES, and their specific uses, advantages, and limitations in optimization problems. For readers interested in diving deeper into EAs, books like *Introduction to Evolutionary Computing* by Eiben and Smith (2015) and the tutorial *Evolutionary Computation: A Unified Approach* by De Jong (2020) would be a good starting point.

Additionally, the chapter introduced neural networks, including basic architectures like FNNs, CNNs, and LSTMs. These networks are designed to process and learn from data, enabling them to make decisions or predictions. For a more comprehensive overview of neural networks and deep learning, see the books *Dive into Deep Learning* by Zhang, Lipton, Li, et al. (2023) and *Deep Learning: Foundations and Concepts* by Bishop and Bishop (2024).

While this chapter provided a comprehensive overview of these foundational concepts, it is also important to consider why they should be combined. Neural networks, as presented here, may already appear sufficient on their own. However, their training often relies on gradient-based methods, which can struggle in vast, high-dimensional, nonlinear, or deceptive search spaces—precisely the kinds of spaces where optimal behaviors are hard to define and must be discovered through search.

Evolutionary computation offers a powerful complement to neural networks in this context. Operating over a diverse population of candidate solutions makes a broad exploration of the search space possible. This quality makes evolutionary methods an effective approach for discovering neural network architectures and weights, forming the core idea behind neuroevolution. In chapter 3, we will take a first look at its fundamentals.

2.5 Chapter Review Questions

1. **Core principles of evolutionary algorithms:** What are the key components of evolutionary algorithms? How do these components collectively emulate the process of natural selection?

2. **Genetic algorithm operations:** Describe the role of crossover and mutation in genetic algorithms, and explain how they contribute to maintaining diversity in the population.

3. **Covariance matrix adaptation evolution strategy:** How does CMA-ES adapt its search over successive generations? What advantage does this adaptation provide in comparison to simpler evolution strategies?

4. **Multiobjective evolutionary computation:** Compare and contrast single-objective and multiobjective evolutionary algorithms. What unique challenges arise in multiobjective EAs, and how does NSGA-II address them?

5. **Practical applications of fitness shaping:** What is fitness shaping, and how does rank-based fitness shaping mitigate the impact of outliers in evolutionary optimization tasks?

6. **Feedforward neural networks:** What is the primary purpose of the activation function in the hidden layers of a FFN? Why is nonlinearity crucial for the network's performance?

7. **Recurrent neural networks:** How do RNNs maintain information about past inputs? Why are they particularly well suited for sequential data tasks like language modeling?

8. **Long short-term memory networks:** What are the roles of the forget, input, and output gates in an LSTM cell? How do they collectively help mitigate the vanishing gradient problem?

9. **Convolutional neural networks:** Describe the purpose of the convolutional and pooling layers in a CNN. How do these layers work together to extract and summarize features from input data?

10. **Transformers:** What is the self-attention mechanism in a transformer model? How does it enable the model to capture long-range dependencies in sequential data?

Chapter 3

The Fundamentals of Neuroevolution

Neuroevolution refers to the use of **evolutionary algorithms** (EAs) to optimize **artificial neural networks** (ANNs), including their connection weights and even their architectures, through simulated evolution. The story of neuroevolution begins with its most profound inspiration: the evolution of biological nervous systems. Over billions of years, natural selection has shaped increasingly complex neural architectures, from the simple nerve nets of primitive organisms to the intricate brains of mammals. This evolutionary journey provides both inspiration and validation for computational approaches that seek to evolve artificial neural networks.

Compared to traditional neural network training methods, neuroevolution offers several distinctive advantages. It can optimize both network parameters and architecture simultaneously. It requires only a fitness function rather than explicit error signals. It can handle non-differentiable aspects of networks and objectives. It maintains population diversity, potentially discovering novel solutions. As we will see throughout this book, these capabilities make neuroevolution particularly valuable for problems where traditional methods face limitations, such as reinforcement learning (RL) tasks, robot control, game playing, decision-making, and other domains with complex, delayed, or sparse feedback.

This chapter starts with the basic neuroevolution taxonomy and then presents a simple case study on how to evolve a neural network–controlled robot. It continues with details on a particular neuroevolution method called neuroevolution of augmenting topologies (NEAT), which allows for optimizing both the topology and weights of a neural network. Finally, it compares neuroevolution to deep learning and discusses how neuroevolution itself can be scaled up to evolve the parameters of larger neural networks with millions of weights.

3.1 Neuroevolution Taxonomy

The idea of evolving neural networks dates back to at least the late 1980s. Early researchers explored using **genetic algorithms** (GAs) to train fixed-topology neural networks by evolving their connection weights. For instance, Montana and Davis (1989) applied a GA to optimize the weights of a feed-forward network (FFN), even designing specialized genetic operators to preserve useful building blocks (sub-networks) during evolution.

Around the same time, researchers like Fogel, Fogel, and Porto (1990) demonstrated that **evolutionary programming** could successfully evolve neural network weights for certain tasks. These early successes showed that evolutionary search could find good weight solutions and even sometimes avoid local minima that gradient descent might get stuck in, thereby sparking interest in learning by evolution.

Applying evolutionary algorithms to neural networks involves deciding how to encode a neural network into a representation that can be evolved, and what evolutionary operations will be used to modify those representations. As will be discussed next, approaches can broadly be divided into those that only evolve the weights of the network and approaches that evolve both the network's weights and topology.

3.1.1 Fixed-Topology Neuroevolution

The simplest approach is to assume a **fixed network architecture** (with a predetermined number of layers, neurons, and connectivity patterns) and use evolution to optimize the weights (and possibly biases) of that network. In this scenario, the genotype can be a direct list of all weight values. Early work predominantly followed this approach–for example, representing the network's weights as a vector of real numbers, which a GA or evolution strategy (ES) then optimized (Schaffer, Whitley, and Eshelman, 1992; Yao, 1999). Standard genetic operators can be adapted (e.g., using real-valued mutation or specialized crossover for vectors) to breed better weight sets. In the basic setup, the fitness of each individual is computed by setting a network's weights accordingly and measuring performance (like accuracy or reward).

3.1.2 Topology and Weight-Evolving Artificial Neural Networks

A more ambitious approach is to evolve the **structure** of the neural network itself—determining how many neurons to use and how they are connected—in addition to optimizing weights. This approach promises automated architecture search, potentially discovering designs that a human might not consider.

Early methods for evolving network topology began by directly mutating connection weights within matrices (Dasgupta and McGregor, 1992) and the number of hidden nodes (Fogel, 1992). However, attention soon shifted toward more advanced encoding strategies for representing and modifying graphs (Figueira Pujol and Poli, 1998). This shift led to the rise of novel representations, such as the graphical structures used in **Cartesian genetic programming** (Miller, 2011), and the implicit connectivity found in approaches such as **analog genetic encoding** (AGE; Mattiussi and Floreano, 2007) or **geometric encoding for neural network evolution** (GENE; Templier, Rachelson, and Wilson, 2021), which drew inspiration from genetic regulatory networks.

Another early direction was to evolve genetic strings with start and end **markers** for node and connection definitions (Fullmer and Miikkulainen, 1992). These markers can be mutated, activating and deactivating parts of the string: What was junk deoxyribonucleic acid (DNA) becomes part of the network, and parts of the network become junk DNA. Both the topology and the weights can be evolved in this manner, sometimes resulting in drastic changes and wide exploration. This approach was later extended to high-level abstractions of neural networks: In **Markov brains**, a structure of logic gates and their connections are evolved to represent complex behavior (Hintze, Edlund, Olson, et al., 2017; Olson, Hintze, Dyer, et al., 2013).

Transitioning from fixed to increasingly complex network topologies introduced new challenges. One such challenge was how to perform crossover—combining the structures of two parent networks—when the topologies differ significantly. Another was ensuring that more intricate structures were not prematurely eliminated from the population before their weights had time to be properly optimized, potentially revealing their full capabilities. One method that gained a lot of traction by addressing these issues is the NEAT algorithm (Stanley and Miikkulainen, 2002), which will be discussed in detail in section 3.3.

Another key consideration in evolving neural networks is the representation of the network in the genotype. Encoding affects everything: how variation operators work, how well the search space is covered, and how scalable the approach is. There are two main approaches, direct encoding and indirect encoding, which will be discussed next.

3.1.3 Direct Encoding

In a **direct encoding** scheme, every detail of the neural network is explicitly encoded in the chromosome. This design often means that each connection (and possibly each neuron) is represented by genes. For example, one might enumerate all weights in a predetermined order, forming a long string of numbers (or bits) that correspond one-to-one with the ANN's weight matrix. Early architecture-evolving methods also used direct encodings (Whitley, Dominic, Das, and Anderson, 1993; Yao, 1999), such as encoding the connectivity matrix of a network as a binary string (with 1s and 0s indicating the presence and absence of connections, respectively).

Direct encodings are straightforward—they describe the phenotype network precisely and are easy to implement. They allow fine-grained modifications; a single mutation can add, remove, or alter a specific connection. However, scaling can be an issue: As network size grows, the genome length grows rapidly (potentially quadratic in the number of neurons for dense connectivity). A more fundamental issue is that direct encodings lack an obvious way to capture high-level regularities or symmetries in the network, unless the evolutionary process discovers them, which can be inefficient. Despite these issues, direct encodings have been widely used and are the default in many neuroevolution algorithms (including NEAT), due to their simplicity and precision.

3.1.4 Indirect Encoding

Indirect encodings describe a network more abstractly, through a set of rules or a generative process rather than enumerating every connection. Only the most important design parameters are encoded, and a developmental procedure generates the full network from this compressed description. In biology, DNA encodes how an organism grows rather than explicitly mapping every cell. Similarly, an indirect ANN encoding might encode blueprints for repeating structures, symmetric connectivity patterns, or growth rules. Indirect encodings can be far more compact, potentially scaling to very large, regular networks by exploiting patterns. They are also arguably closer to biological reality (since real neural systems are not encoded link-by-link in genomes). The trade-off is that the mapping from genotype to phenotype is more complex: mutations in the genome can have broad, nonlinear effects on the resulting network, and it may be harder for evolution to fine-tune specific connections. There is also a risk that an indirect encoding constrains the space of possible networks in unintended ways. These considerations and others will be discussed in detail in chapter 4.

In practice, the choice between direct and indirect encoding depends on the problem: If the solution network is expected to have a lot of symmetry or repeated motifs (as in certain sensorimotor coordination tasks), indirect encoding can be powerful; if the solution is more irregular, direct encoding might be more effective. The rest of this chapter will focus on direct encodings; their indirect counterparts will be discussed in the next chapter.

3.2 Case Study: Evolving a Simple Walking Agent

To make the fundamental concepts of neuroevolution concrete, this section will go over the details of a case study in which a robot is taught to walk.

3.2.1 The Challenge

Neuroevolution is one of several ways to train an agent to operate in an environment, and it shares similarities with RL. In both cases, an agent performs actions in an environment and receives feedback in the form of rewards. Over time, the agent improves its decisions to maximize those rewards. However, in RL, it is not trivial to estimate the gradient of reward signals given to the agent in the future to an action performed by the agent right now, especially if the reward is realized in many time steps in the future. Even if it were possible to calculate accurate gradients, learning may get stuck in a local optimum (figure 3.1), which exists in many RL tasks.

Neuroevolution, on the other hand, sidesteps gradients altogether. Instead, it treats each neural network as an individual organism and uses evolutionary algorithms to select, reproduce, and mutate better-performing networks over generations. This fundamental difference enables neuroevolution to overcome several limitations of other approaches. Most notably, neuroevolution can be applied to scenarios where gradient information is unavailable or unreliable, such as when the relationship between network outputs and performance is complex, sparse, or delayed. Further, while RL algorithms require a reward signal to be given to the agent at every time step, neuroevolution algorithms care only about the final cumulative reward that an agent gets at the end of its rollout in an environment. In many problems, the outcome becomes apparent only at the end of the task, such as whether the agent wins or loses, whether the robot arm picks up the object, or whether the agent reached the goal.

Overall, these properties make neuroevolution particularly powerful in environments with sparse or delayed rewards, discontinuous, noisy, or deceptive reward landscapes, and unknown or difficult-to-model dynamics. They are put to good use in the task of training a robot to walk.

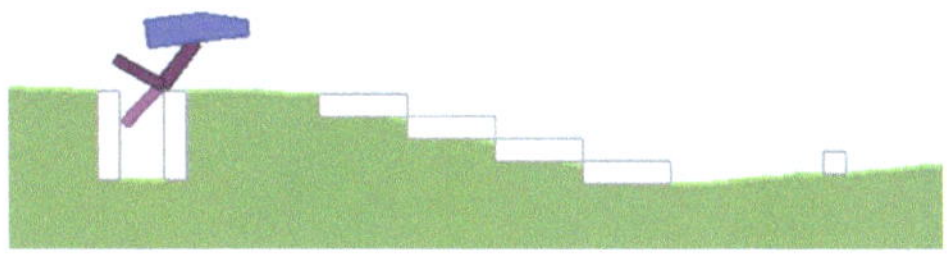

Figure 3.1: **Bipedal walker agent stuck in a local optimum.** In this 2-D domain, a robot agent with two legs, controlled by a neural network, needs to walk across a terrain with various obstacles and holes. The task is difficult because the reward is given only in the end—but it also allows learning methods to explore a variety of solutions. Simpler methods like the standard RL may easily get stuck on the obstacles, as it did in this case. Neuroevolution, on the other hand, is well suited for the task and finds several creative ways to solve it. For videos of both stuck and successful behaviors, see `https://neuroevolutionbook.com/demos`.

The task is implemented in an environment called **BipedalWalkerHardcore**, in which the agent is challenged to control a bipedal robot—simulated in the Box2D physics engine–that must walk across an uneven terrain (figure 3.1). This robot has four controllable joints, two hips and two knees, and moves in a physics-based simulation with the potential for complex interactions. Unlike simpler arcade games, this environment introduces continuous state and action spaces.

The task is available inside the OpenAI gym (Brockman, Cheung, Pettersson, et al., 2016), a toolkit designed to support the development and evaluation of different learning algorithms. In this framework, the agent observes the current state, selects an action, and receives feedback in the form of a new observation, a reward, and a done signal indicating whether the episode has ended.

3.2.2 Fitness Function

A critical aspect of any neuroevolution experiment is the design of the **fitness function**. The bipedal walker environment already provides a reward at each time step, as a combination of several factors designed to encourage forward locomotion, energy efficiency, and stability. The primary component of the reward comes from forward progress—the faster the walker moves to the right (positive x-direction), the higher the reward. This component creates a strong incentive for the agent to learn how to walk effectively. In addition to forward velocity, there is a penalty for using energy. Specifically, the environment penalizes the agent based on the square of the torque applied to its motors. This component discourages inefficient or overly aggressive movement and helps the agent learn smoother, more natural gaits. There is also a small positive reward for simply staying alive at each time step, which promotes stability and discourages falling. However, if the walker falls (e.g., the torso touches the ground), the episode terminates and the agent receives a significant negative reward.

Listing 3.3: **A simple rollout function for evaluating an agent in an OpenAI gym environment.**

```
def rollout(agent, env):
    # Reset the environment and get initial observation
    obs = env.reset()
    done = False
    # Accumulator for total reward
    total_reward = 0

    # Loop until the episode is finished
    while not done:
        # Agent selects action based on observation
        a = agent.get_action(obs)
        # Take action, observe new state/reward
        obs, reward, done = env.step(a)
        # Accumulate reward
        total_reward += reward

    # Return total reward after episode ends
    return total_reward
```

To determine the fitness of a controller, the total cumulative reward is calculated by adding up the environment rewards given to the agent at each time step. The code in listing 3.3 encapsulates a rollout of an agent in an OpenAI gym environment.

3.2.3 Neural Network Architecture

For the experiments in this case study, we employ a **fixed-topology neuroevolution** approach and a direct encoding of the network weights. The employed simple feed-forward network has two hidden layers to map from an agent's observation, a vector x, directly to the actions, a vector y.

At each time step, the environment provides a 24-dimensional observation vector to the neural network. This vector includes information about the robot's hull angle, velocity, and position, along with joint angles, contact points for the feet, and distance readings from simulated light detection and ranging (LiDAR) sensors. The goal is for the neural network to interpret these sensory inputs and produce four continuous motor control signals—one for each joint—within a fixed range. These signals dictate how much torque is applied at each joint, essentially driving the robot's walking gait.

3.2.4 Evolutionary Algorithms

Starting from randomly initialized neural networks, an EA can be used to find a suitable set of model parameters as described earlier (listing 3.4). Here, `solutions[i]` contains the weights of a neural network and `Agent(solutions[i])` creates an instance of a policy agent by loading those weights into a neural network architecture. The vector `solutions[i]` is typically a flat array produced by an EA. This array encodes all the trainable parameters of the network, including the weights and possibly the biases for each layer, concatenated in a specific order. The particular EA algorithm used in the experiment is covariance matrix adaptation evolution strategy (CMA-ES).

Listing 3.4: **EA training loop for `BipedalWalkerHardcore-v3`.**

```
env = gym.make('BipedalWalkerHardcore-v3')
solver = EvolutionaryAlgorithm()     # use our favorite EA
while True:
  solutions = solver.ask()           # EA gives a set of params
  fitlist = np.zeros(solver.popsize)
  for i in range(solver.popsize):    # evaluate for each solution
    agent = Agent(solutions[i])      # init agent with a solution
    fitlist[i] = rollout(agent, env) # rollout env
  solver.tell(fitness_list)          # give scores  back to EA
  bestsol, bestfit = solver.result() # get best param & fitness
  if bestfit > MY_REQUIREMENT:       # see if our task is solved
    break
```

3.2.5 Training for Generality

BipedalWalkerHardcore defines solving the task as getting an average score of over 300 over 100 consecutive random trials. While it is relatively easy to train an agent to walk across the map successfully using an RL algorithm, it is difficult to get the agent to do so consistently and efficiently, making this task an interesting challenge.

When running the code in listing 3.4, we find that the best-evolved agent achieves an average score of only about 220 to 230 across 100 trials. Because the terrain map is randomly generated for each trial, sometimes the agents face an easy terrain and sometimes a difficult one. This variability means that agents with weak policies can get lucky during training but then might not generalize well. Put in another way, even though the agent was tested over 100 trials at the end, it was trained on single trials, so the test task was not the same as the training task.

To get more robust agents, an agent's training can instead be defined as consisting of 16 random rollouts, and the average of the rewards over these rollouts as its fitness score. The data efficiency of this method is 16 times worse, but the final policy is more robust. When the final policy evolved under this extended training regime was tested over 100 consecutive random trials, its average score exceeded the 300 points required to solve the task. Figure 3.2 shows the progress from early to late generations in training. Early on, the agent often gets stuck on obstacles. After learning to avoid them, it gets better and faster at walking. Interestingly, standard RL algorithms typically lead to policies that fall short of an average score of 300. For instance, the popular RL algorithm **proximal policy optimization** (PPO; Schulman, Wolski, Dhariwal, et al., 2017) achieved an average score of only around 240 to 250 over 100 random trials.

The ability to control the trade-off between data efficiency and policy robustness is a powerful property of neuroevolution; it is useful in many real-world domains where safe policies are needed. In theory, with enough compute, it would have been possible to average over all 100 rollouts and optimize the bipedal walker directly to the requirements. Professional engineers often must have their designs satisfy specific quality assurance guarantees and meet certain safety factors. Such safety factors need to be considered when training agents to learn policies that may affect the real world.

As a side note, what if we do not want the agent's policy to be **deterministic**? For certain tasks, even as simple as rock-paper-scissors, the optimal policy is a random action,

(*a*) Evolving to get over obstacles (*b*) Evolving a faster walk

Figure 3.2: **Various stages of progress in BipedalWalkerHardcore.** (*a*) Early on, evolution discovers solutions that can walk relatively well on flat ground but frequently get stuck on obstacles. Those who get over some of them are rewarded, and gradually the population gets better with them. (*b*) Once obstacles are no longer a problem, faster walks evolve. In this manner, the exploration in population-based search leads to solutions of hard problems. For videos of these early learning behaviors and later successful ones, see `https://neuroevolutionbook.com/demos`.

so the agent needs to learn a **stochastic policy**. One way to convert a deterministic policy network into a stochastic one is to make the final layer a set of μ and σ parameters and sample the action from $N(\mu, \sigma I)$. Adding such randomness to the output also helps encourage the agent to explore the environment and escape from local optima.

In conclusion, this case study showed that EA can find neural networks to control a bipedal walker. When averaging across multiple rollouts, the resulting policies could robustly handle randomly generated terrains. However, the power of evolution does not stop there. In the natural world, bodies evolved at the same time as brains, in an environment that is changing, and has many other actors that are also changing. Principles and effects of such coevolutionary processes will be discussed further in chapters 7, 9, and 14. More general robust control through neuroevolution will be discussed in chapter 6.

3.3 Neuroevolution of Augmenting Topologies

As mentioned in section 3.1.2, **topology and weight-evolving artificial neural networks** (TWEANNs) are advanced neuroevolution methods capable of designing neural architectures from scratch rather than assuming a fixed structure. This section reviews the challenges of doing that and describes a particular solution, NEAT, in detail.

3.3.1 Motivation and Challenges

The motivation for TWEANNs is clear: The space of possible network architectures is vast, and finding the right one for a problem manually can be a tedious trial-and-error process. If evolution can search through architectures automatically, it may discover novel or non-intuitive designs that improve performance. However, early attempts at evolving topologies identified critical problems.

Competing conventions: Neural network genomes can encode the same functionality in multiple ways by permuting or relabeling hidden neurons. Two different encodings of an

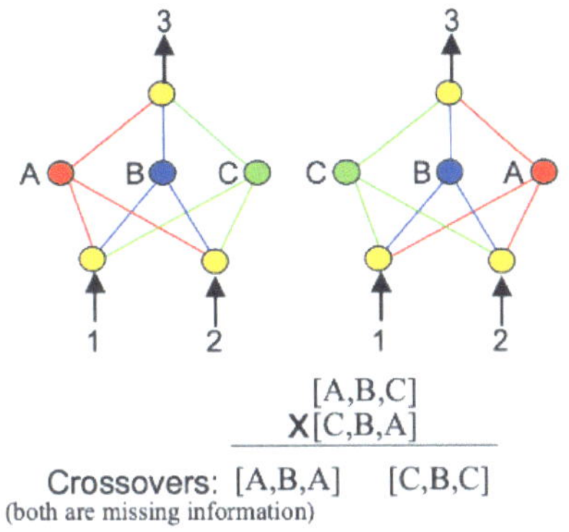

Figure 3.3: **The competing conventions problem.** Two functionally identical networks (each with three hidden neurons) have hidden nodes labeled in a different order (*left*: A–B–C, *right*: C–B–A). A naive crossover (recombining at one hidden node position) produces offspring with misaligned structures (*bottom*), each missing one of the three hidden neurons (here, one offspring lost C and the other lost A). This example illustrates how exchanging genes between differently ordered genomes can lose information. Figure from Stanley and Miikkulainen (2002).

equivalent network are called competing conventions, and crossing them over can produce corrupted offspring. Figure 3.3 illustrates this problem: Two networks with hidden nodes labeled (A, B, C) versus (C, B, A) implement the same function, and yet a naive one-point crossover misaligns their genes and yields offspring missing vital connections (e.g., one offspring has two copies of A and none of C). In general, with n hidden nodes, there are $n!$ functionally equivalent encodings, so recombining topologies blindly often disrupts networks. This historical difficulty in aligning genomes made crossovers of arbitrary topologies highly unstable. Some earlier TWEANN methods tried to avoid crossover altogether or enforced identical ordering of nodes, but these constraints also make the search weaker. The competing conventions problem, also referred to as the "permutations problem" (Radcliffe, 1993), remained a "holy grail" challenge: how to recombine networks with different topologies meaningfully.

Structural innovations: A second problem was that adding new structure (new nodes or connections) often initially hurts performance, so those mutations tend to be eliminated before they can prove useful. For example, inserting a new hidden neuron introduces a random nonlinear change; until its weights are tuned, the network's fitness usually drops. In a standard evolutionary algorithm, such an individual would likely be outcompeted immediately by others, causing the innovation to disappear. In effect, complex structural mutations were rarely given time to optimize. Some prior TWEANNs attempted ad-hoc remedies (e.g., adding a "dead" structure that initially has no effect), but without a systematic way to protect novel structures, the population would converge to conservative topologies. This lack of protection made it risky to evolve larger topologies: Major innovations could be prematurely lost.

Complexification mechanism: A third challenge was controlling the explosive search dimensionality when topology is unfettered. Many earlier TWEANN implementations began evolution with a population of random large networks to ensure diverse structures.

However, random graphs often include redundant or unconnected components (e.g., some inputs not reaching outputs), which waste evaluations. More subtly, starting with excessive complexity burdens the search with many unnecessary parameters that were never optimized from scratch. Evolution then spends effort pruning or tuning irrelevant structure instead of focusing on solving the task. One approach to favor simpler networks was to penalize network size in the fitness function. Yet such penalties are problem-dependent and introduce difficult trade-offs. Ideally, the evolutionary process itself would "complexify" only as needed; that is, start with minimal architectures and gradually add complexity when it confers an advantage. This process was hard to establish: If every individual starts simple (e.g., no hidden nodes), there is little initial topological diversity, and any complex mutation would be instantly disadvantaged (tying back to the previous issue).

In summary, to harness topology evolution, one needs (1) a crossover method that is robust to competing encodings, (2) a way to protect and nurture new structural mutations, and (3) a strategy to evolve minimal solutions first and grow complexity gradually without ad-hoc penalties. **Neuroevolution of augmenting topologies** (NEAT) was developed specifically as a solution to these challenges (Stanley and Miikkulainen, 2002). Conceived in the early 2000s, it has served as a foundation for over 200 further algorithms and methods in the field since then (Papavasileiou, Cornelis, and Jansen, 2021). The algorithm's hallmark features are: (1) a novel genetic encoding with historical markings that aligns genes during crossover to solve the competing conventions issue, (2) a speciation mechanism with fitness sharing to protect new innovations by reducing competition between disparate topologies, and (3) an incremental complexification approach that begins with minimal networks and adds nodes/connections over generations. This section describes how each of these mechanisms is implemented in NEAT, and how together they enable efficient evolution of increasingly sophisticated neural networks.

3.3.2 Genetic Encoding and Historical Markings

The genome in NEAT consists of **node genes** and **connection genes** (figure 3.4). Node genes encode information about each neuron in the network. Connection genes, on the other hand, encode information about the connections between nodes. Each connection gene specifies the two nodes that it connects, the weight of the connection, whether the connection is enabled or disabled, and a unique innovation number that tracks its origin.

The initial population of networks has a simple architecture, such as having each input signal and bias connect directly to the outputs with no hidden layers. In NEAT, mutations can affect both connection weights and network structures. Connection weight mutations occur similarly to other neuroevolution systems, where each connection's weight is either perturbed or left unchanged during each generation. Structural mutations, however, introduce new components to the genome, increasing its size. There are two types of structural mutations: adding connections and adding nodes.

In the **add connection mutation**, a new connection gene is introduced, linking two previously unconnected nodes (figure 3.5; top). In the **add node mutation**, an existing connection is split, and a new node is inserted at the split point (figure 3.5; bottom). The original connection is disabled, and two new connections are added to the genome. One of the new connections, leading into the new node, is assigned a weight of 1, while the

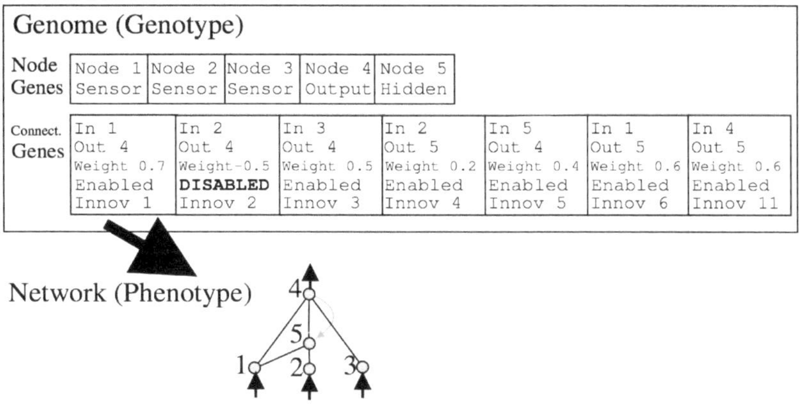

Figure 3.4: **NEAT genotype.** Node genes define the types of nodes in the network: sensors (input nodes), outputs, and hidden nodes. Connection genes represent the connections between nodes, with each gene specifying the source and target nodes, connection weight, whether the connection is enabled or disabled, and an innovation number indicating the historical origin of the gene. The bottom section illustrates the neural network (phenotype) constructed based on the genome. This encoding makes it possible to evolve network structures as well as the weights. Figure from Stanley and Miikkulainen (2002).

other, leading out of the new node, retains the weight of the original connection. This approach minimizes the immediate impact of the mutation, allowing the new node to integrate smoothly into the network.

As mutations occur, NEAT genomes grow larger over time, producing networks with varying sizes and connections. This network **complexification** can result in genomes with differing topologies and weight configurations, presenting challenges in performing a meaningful crossover between neural networks. NEAT's solution to this challenge is based on the concept of **innovation protection**.

Innovations are protected in NEAT by assigning a unique innovation number to each structural mutation, such as adding a new connection or node. These innovation numbers, also called **historical markings**, are global identifiers that track the origin of mutations across the population. When a structural change occurs in different individuals that is functionally equivalent (i.e., adding a connection among the same two nodes, meaning that the innovation numbers for the source and target node match between individuals), the same innovation number is assigned, ensuring that similar changes can be recognized and aligned.

Tracking the historical origins of genes in NEAT is computationally efficient. Each time that a new gene is introduced through a structural mutation, a global innovation number is incremented and assigned to that gene. Thus, innovation numbers create a chronological record of when each gene appeared within the system. For example, the two mutations in figure 3.5 could have occurred sequentially, with the new connection gene resulting from the first mutation receiving innovation number 7, while the two new connection genes introduced during the second mutation (a new node mutation) receive innovation numbers 8 and 9. Whenever genomes with these mutations are crossed over in

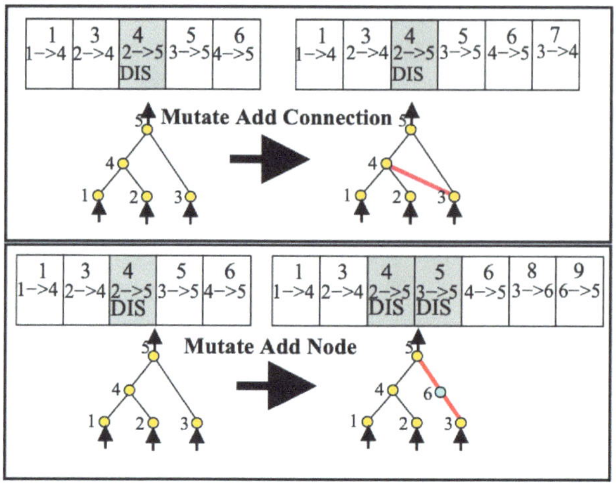

Figure 3.5: **Structural mutations in NEAT.** Mutations in NEAT can add new connections and new neurons to the evolving neural network. (*Top*) A new connection with an innovation number 7 is added between neurons 3 and 4. (*Bottom*) The new neuron 6 is added, splitting the connection between neurons 3 and 5: connection 5 becomes disabled, and the new connections 8 and 9 are added to the genome. In this manner, NEAT complexifies the network architecture over time. Figure from Stanley and Miikkulainen (2002).

the future, their offspring will inherit the same innovation numbers for those genes. Since innovation numbers remain constant and unaltered, the historical origin of every gene is preserved throughout the evolutionary process.

During **crossover** (figure 3.6), innovation numbers enable NEAT to align genomes with differing structures. Genes are categorized based on their innovation numbers into matching, disjoint, and excess genes. Matching genes have the same innovation number in both parent genomes and are directly inherited and recombined. Disjoint genes, which appear in one genome but not the other, and excess genes, which exist only in the larger genome, are handled differently depending on the parents' fitness. This alignment prevents the random mixing of unrelated genes, ensuring that crossover produces viable offspring with functional genetic material preserved.

By tracking mutations and aligning genes using innovation numbers, NEAT makes meaningful crossover possible between genomes with different topologies. This process preserves functional structures and avoids the destructive effects of uncoordinated genetic mixing. Ultimately, innovation protection ensures diversity in the population and allows NEAT to evolve increasingly complex and effective neural networks while maintaining their functional integrity.

The crossover operation is quite powerful. Suppose that we have a network that is good at a subtask and another network that is good at some other subtask. In that case, it may be possible to breed an offspring network that can potentially be good at combining these skills and becoming better than both parent networks at performing a bigger task. Another important component of NEAT is speciation, which will be described next.

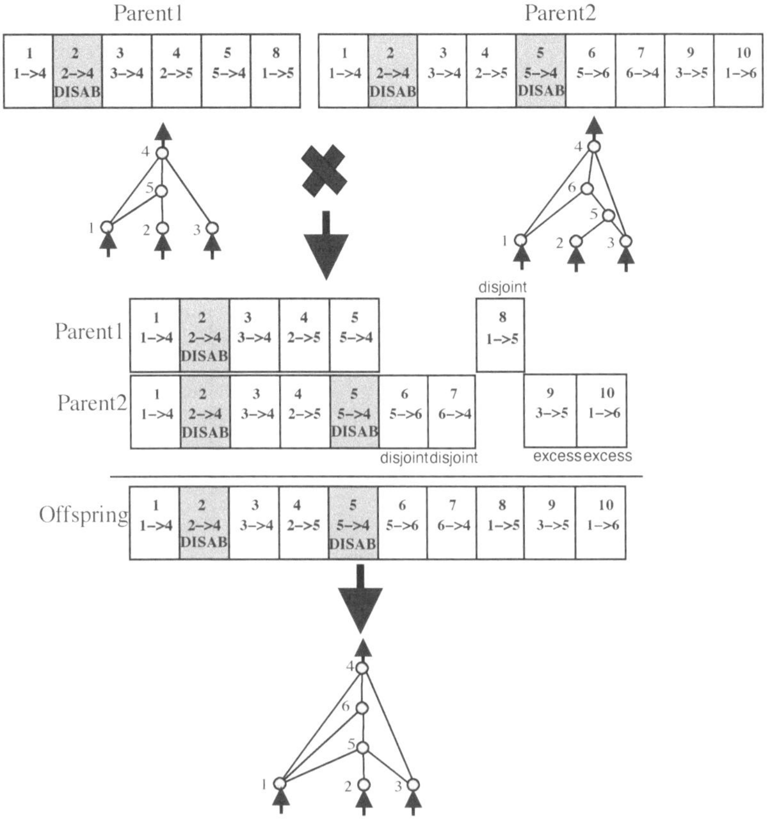

Figure 3.6: **NEAT crossover.** The example shows the merging of two parent networks to produce an offspring network. The top row shows two parent genomes, parent1 and parent2, each represented by a series of genes (connections between nodes) and their corresponding neural network structures. The crossover begins by aligning the genes of the two parents. Matching genes (those present in both parents) are inherited randomly from either parent, while disjoint genes (genes that are present in one parent but not the other) and excess genes (genes that appear after the last gene of the other parent) are also considered. The resulting offspring genome combines these inherited genes, reflecting both the inherited traits from the parents and potentially new neural connections. The final offspring neural network structure, shown at the bottom, includes the selected connections and nodes from both parents. Thus, innovation numbers make it possible to implement crossover without expensive graph matching operations. Figure from Stanley and Miikkulainen (2002).

3.3.3 Speciation and Fitness Sharing

Speciation is the idea of grouping the population of genes into different species consisting of similar members of the population. The goal is to give novel members of the population, which may be promising although not yet very good, more time to evolve to their full potential, rather than to kill them off at each generation. Imagine an isolated island populated by wolves and penguins only. If we let things be, the penguins would be dead meat after the first generation, and all we would be left with are wolves. But if we create a special no-kill zone on the island where wolves are not allowed to kill penguins once they step inside that area, a certain number of penguins will always exist. They will have time to evolve into flying penguins that will make their way back to the mainland, where there is plenty of vegetation to live on, while the wolves would be stuck forever on the island.

For a more concrete example, consider the example in section 1.1 about the 100 sets of weights, and imagine modifying the algorithm from only keeping the best 20 and getting rid of the rest, to first grouping the 100 weights into five groups according to the similarity measured by Euclidean distance. Now that there are five groups (or species) of 20 networks, for each group only the top 20% is again kept (i.e., only four sets). The remaining 80% (i.e., 16) can then be replaced by crossing over and mutating the four existing members, or from the entire set of surviving members in the larger population. By modifying the genetic algorithm in this way to allow speciation, genes have the time to develop to their full potential. Also, the diversity will lead to better genes that incorporate the best of the different species. In contrast, without speciation, the population could easily get stuck at a local optimum.

To speciate the population, NEAT defines a **compatibility distance** δ between two genomes based on their genetic difference. This distance is computed as a linear combination of three factors: the number of excess genes (E), the number of disjoint genes (D), and the average weight difference of matching genes (W) as:

$$\delta = \frac{c_1 E + c_2 D}{N} + c_3 \bar{W}, \tag{3.1}$$

where c_1, c_2, c_3 are coefficients determining the importance of each term; and N is a normalization factor (usually the genome length of the larger parent, to normalize for network size). Thus, genomes with many unshared genes (high E or D) or very different connection weights (high $\bar{W}$) will have a large distance δ, meaning that they are less compatible. NEAT assigns individuals to species by comparing this distance: If genome g is within a threshold δ_t of some species' representative genome, it belongs to that species; otherwise, a new species is created for g. Threshold δ_t is a parameter that NEAT can adapt to target a desired number of species. Species thus group networks of similar topology (i.e., those sharing common genes) together.

Species membership is then used to enable explicit **fitness sharing** (Goldberg and Richardson, 1987) as the reproduction mechanism. This approach ensures that organisms within the same species share the fitness of their niche. Consequently, a species cannot grow excessively large, even if many of its members perform well. This limitation prevents any single species from dominating the entire population, which is essential for maintaining speciated evolution. The adjusted fitness f'_i of an organism i is computed based on its distance Δ from every other organism j in the population as

$$f'_i = \frac{f_i}{\sum_{j=1}^{n} \mathrm{sh}(\Delta(i,j))}, \tag{3.2}$$

where the sharing function sh is defined as $\mathrm{sh}(\Delta(i,j)) = 1$ if $\Delta(i,j) \leq \Delta_t$, and $\mathrm{sh}(\Delta(i,j)) = 0$ otherwise (Spears, 1995). Here, Δ_t represents the distance threshold. Effectively, $\sum_{j=1}^{n} \mathrm{sh}(\Delta(i,j))$ corresponds to the number of organisms within the same species as organism i, as species are pre-clustered based on compatibility using Δ_t. The number of offspring allocated to each species is proportional to the sum of its member organisms' adjusted fitness values f'_i.

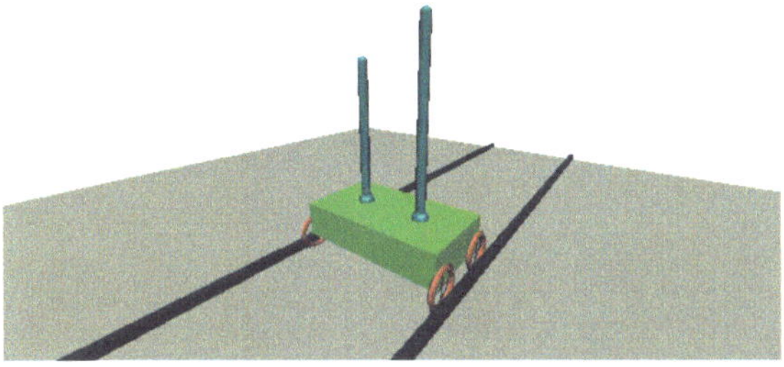

(*a*) A challenging pole-balancing task

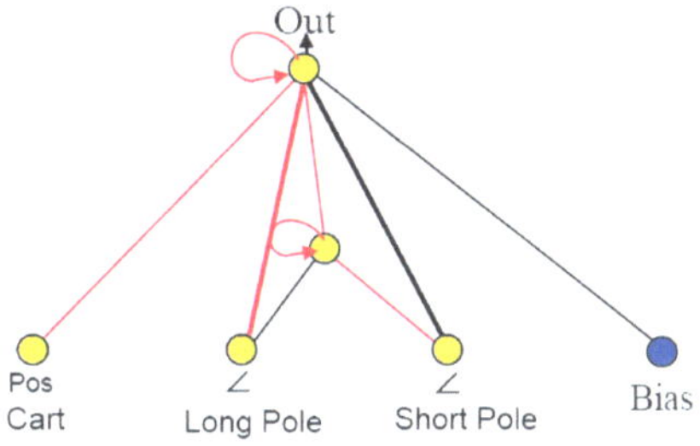

(*b*) A compact solution by NEAT

Figure 3.7: **A compact, explainable solution that NEAT discovered for the pole-balancing problem.** (*a*) In this version, there are two poles on a moving cart that needs to be pushed left or right with a constant force at regular intervals to keep the poles from falling and the cart within the left and right boundaries of the one-dimensional track. (*b*) NEAT's solution uses the derivative of the pole angle difference, with a recurrent connection enabling the hidden node to detect whether the poles are converging or diverging, eliminating the need to compute individual pole velocities. Figure *a* from Gomez, Schmidhuber, and Miikkulainen (2008).

3.3.4 Example: Double Pole Balancing

Let's look at an example of NEAT applied to a simple toy problem to illustrate how it works. In this task, called double pole balancing (figure 3.7*a*), two poles of different lengths are attached to a movable cart via hinges. The neural network must control the cart by applying horizontal forces to keep both poles balanced for as long as possible, without the cart exceeding the boundaries of the track. Due to the differing lengths of the poles, they respond differently to applied forces, introducing complex nonlinear interactions that make the task challenging. The system's state is defined by the cart's position x and velocity $\dot{x}$, the angle and angular velocity of the first pole $(\theta_1, \dot{\theta}_1)$, and the angle and angular velocity of the second pole $(\theta_2, \dot{\theta}_2)$. Control is possible due to the differing lengths (and therefore, masses) of the poles, which causes them to respond differently to the same input forces.

Success on the task is defined as maintaining both poles within ±36 degrees of vertical for 100,000 time steps, equivalent to 30 minutes of simulated time. Fitness is measured by the number of consecutive time steps during which both poles remain balanced. The task can be made arbitrarily hard by making the poles more similar in length; when they are the same, the task becomes unsolvable. In typical experiments, the shorter pole is 1/10th of the length of the longer one.

When velocity information is included in the input in this manner, the task is fully observable and Markovian, and not particularly hard: many learning methods can solve it. The task can be made considerably more difficult by omitting the velocities: the controller is then required to estimate these missing state variables internally. That is, the task is a **partially observable Markov decision process** (POMDP) and requires recurrent or memory-capable network architectures. Traditional RL methods struggle with POMDPs in general, and the POMDP version of double pole balancing is particularly challenging for them. It is challenging for neuroevolution as well; only the advanced neuroevolution methods can solve it (Gomez, Schmidhuber, and Miikkulainen, 2008).

Table 3.1: **Ablation study removing each component of NEAT in turn.** All components are needed to achieve the full power of NEAT in solving the MDP version of the double pole-balancing task.

Method	Evaluations	Failure Rate
No-growth NEAT (fixed-topologies)	30,239	80%
Initial random NEAT	23,033	5%
Nonspeciated NEAT	25,600	25%
Nonmating NEAT	5,557	0%
Full NEAT	3,600	0%

However, NEAT finds a particularly clever solution: taking the derivative of the difference in pole angles (figure 3.7*b*). Using the recurrent connection to itself, the single hidden node determines whether the poles are falling away or toward each other. This solution allows controlling the system without computing the velocities of each pole separately. It would be difficult to design such a subtle and compact solution by hand, but neuroevolution that complexifies makes its discovery more likely.

Through ablation studies, it is possible to determine whether each component of NEAT is essential to its performance. For instance, one might question the importance of starting from a minimal structure—perhaps the other features, such as speciation and historical markings, are sufficient for NEAT to perform optimally. Conversely, it is also possible that speciation contributes little; that is, that protecting innovation is not critical. Finally, NEAT is specifically designed to support crossover, even when genomes differ in size; is it useful for the genomes to grow over evolution, or would fixed-topology NEAT perform just as well?

Table 3.1 summarizes the results of ablation experiments on NEAT. To allow the ablated versions to succeed, double pole balancing with velocities was used as the task. In each experiment, one of the components of NEAT was disabled to assess its contribution to performance. First, removing growth from minimal structure led to the most severe performance degradation, with only 20% of runs succeeding and requiring over eight times more evaluations than full NEAT. This result suggests that speciation and historical markings alone are not sufficient for guiding effective evolution without incremental complexity. Starting with random initial topologies (1–10 hidden nodes) also significantly slowed learning and modestly increased failure rates, indicating that beginning with minimal structure is more conducive to effective exploration and optimization. Second, disabling speciation caused the population to converge prematurely on suboptimal structures, particularly when using random initialization. This ablation resulted in a high variance and a 25% failure rate, emphasizing the importance of speciation in preserving diversity and supporting structural innovation. Third, removing crossover increased the number of evaluations by over 50%, though performance remained better than in the other ablations. This result shows that while crossover is not as critical as growth and speciation, it still contributes meaningfully to NEAT's overall efficiency. Thus, the ablation studies demonstrated that all three components—growth from minimal structure, speciation, and crossover—are essential to NEAT's success. Performance consistently suffers when any single element is removed, highlighting the importance of their combined effect in enabling efficient and robust evolution.

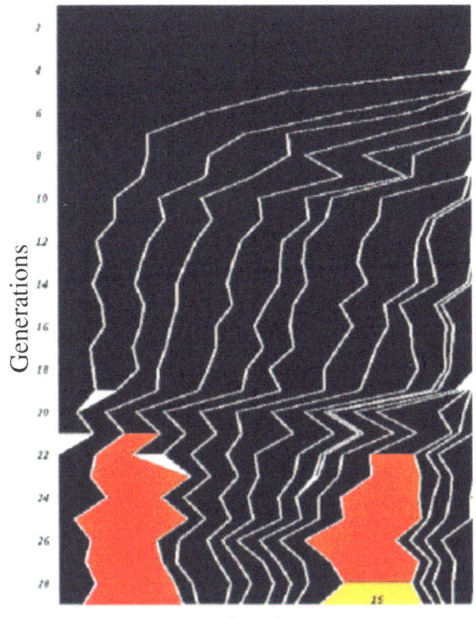

Figure 3.8: **Species progression in the double pole balancing task.** White triangles indicate extinct species, red good solutions (one stdev), and yellow best solutions (two stdev). A number of species were created as evolution discovered novel structures. They expanded and shrank based on how well they performed, but they stayed around long enough so the innovations in them had a chance to be optimized. In this manner, speciation promotes both innovation and diversity, resulting in better and more creative solutions. Figure from Stanley (2003).

To gain insight into how innovation emerges during evolution, it is essential to examine the dynamics of speciation. Key questions include: How many species emerge throughout a run? How frequently do new species appear or go extinct? These questions can be addressed by visualizing the progression of speciation over time.

Figure 3.8 illustrates a representative run of the double pole balancing with velocities task, which took 29 generations to solve. Generations are arranged vertically, with species depicted horizontally. The width of each species reflects its size, and new species appear on the right. Initially, all organisms belonged to a single species, persisting until the fifth generation due to high compatibility. As new species emerged, the original species declined and became extinct by the 21st generation. The second species also went extinct in the 19th generation, unable to compete with more innovative species. A pivotal mutation occurred in the 21st generation, enabling the second-oldest species to connect the long pole angle sensor to a hidden node, boosting its fitness. Simultaneously, a younger species developed a useful connection between the short-pole velocity and long-pole angle sensors. By the 28th generation, this species made a key connection between the cart position and its earlier mechanism for comparing pole velocity and angle, solving the task in one more generation. In the final generation, the winning species, which was 11 generations old, comprised 38 neural networks out of 150, successfully concluding the run.

Many species that did not approach a solution still persisted throughout the run. This result confirms visually that innovation is preserved. The winning species does not dominate the entire population, ensuring that a diverse set of solutions is maintained. This diversity is particularly valuable in applications where the optimal behavior evolves over time. For example, it makes it possible for NEAT to keep complexifying its networks in a coevolutionary arms race, discussed further in section 7.2.

3.4 Scaling up Neuroevolution

While much of neuroevolution has focused on small, structured networks, it is possible to scale it up to large networks as well. This section reviews the differences of evolved networks versus deep learning, suggests ways to scale up to deep networks, and to take advantage of modern computing to do so.

3.4.1 Neuroevolution Versus Deep Learning

Note that the networks that result from NEAT, and neuroevolution in general, are very different from those commonly used in deep learning. Neuroevolution networks are aimed at AI–based decision-making, rather than prediction based on big data. The computational requirements are different, and therefore the networks are also different.

However, even in domains where deep learning can be applied, neuroevolution provides a potentially useful alternative. Performance with deep learning networks is based on overparameterization where individual components perform only minimal operations: For instance, the residual module in ResNet architectures combines bypassing the module with the transformation that the module itself computes (He, Zhang, Ren, et al., 2016). In contrast, in NEAT, every complexification is there for a purpose that can in principle be identified in the evolutionary history. It thus offers an alternative solution–one that is based on principled neural network design.

This kind of compact evolved neural networks can be useful in several ways. First, they can provide an **explainable neural network** solution. When neural networks are trained with gradient descent, information in their embeddings becomes highly distributed, making it difficult to interpret (Hinton, McClelland, and Rumelhart, 1986; Kumar, Clune, Lehman, et al., 2025; Miikkulainen and Dyer, 1991). In contrast, while a NEAT network still performs based on recurrency and embeddings, its elements are constructed to provide a particular functionality, and therefore its behavior is transparent. One such example was discussed in section 3.3.4, where NEAT discovered a particularly innovative solution to the pole-balancing problem. The network computes the derivative of the difference of the pole angles, which makes it possible to control the system with a very small network (figure 3.7). Several other examples of such insights are reviewed in sections 7.2.1 and 14.1.

Second, they can provide **regularized neural network solutions**, instead of overfitting to the dataset. The networks are compact, which generally leads to better regularization (Ganon, Keinan, and Ruppin, 2003; Oymak, 2018; Reed, 1993), and they are chosen based on their overall performance instead of being fine-tuned to fit individual examples. This property should be particularly useful when the datasets are relatively small, which is the case in many practical applications. Thus, they can extend the scope of machine learning.

Third, they can utilize minimal **hardware resources** well. The advantages of deep-learning networks do not emerge until a very large number of parameters. If the hardware does not allow that scale (as is the case with many edge devices), evolved networks provide an alternative principle that can be optimized to the given resources.

Fourth, they can be constructed to fit **hardware constraints**. Gradient descent in principle requires high-precision weights and differentiable activation functions that are expensive to implement in hardware. In contrast, evolution can be used to optimize the performance of networks with e.g., quantized weights, linear threshold units, or field-programmable gate array (FPGA)–compatible components that are easier to implement (Gaier and Ha, 2019; Liu, Zhang, Wang, et al., 2021; Shayani, Bentley, and Tyrrell, 2008; Whitley, 2024b). Optimization of neural networks for neuromorphic hardware is a promising emerging area discussed in more detail in section 11.5.

Fifth, neuroevolution allows us to observe and study fundamentally different forms of **internal representation** that emerge through open-ended evolutionary processes rather than via backpropagation. NEAT in particular, and TWEANN methods in general, can serve as a gateway to understanding how representations might form when networks are allowed to grow in complexity organically, rather than being sculpted all at once by gradient descent on a fixed architecture. For example, recent work (Kumar, Clune, Lehman, et al., 2025) demonstrated that where stochastic gradient descent (SGD) tends to produce entangled and **fractured representations**, especially when optimizing toward a single objective, NEAT offers a contrasting developmental dynamic. By starting with minimal structures and expanding incrementally, NEAT encourages the emergence of modular, reusable, and semantically aligned representations. Neuroevolution gives us a rare opportunity to study representations not just as a by-product of loss minimization, but also as artifacts of open-ended exploration and accumulated structural regularities. Without NEAT, or an equivalent evolutionary or developmental approach, we would be limited to analyzing representations formed in the constrained regime of SGD-trained deep networks.

3.4.2 Deep Neuroevolution

While neuroevolution methods such as NEAT shine in producing compact solutions, a new direction has emerged in applying evolutionary algorithms to larger neural networks as well. This recent direction, referred to as **deep neuroevolution**, shifts the focus from evolving neural architectures to optimizing the parameters of large, fixed-topology networks directly. This work emphasizes scalability, simplicity, and the surprising competitiveness of evolutionary algorithms in training deep networks for complex tasks. Two particularly influential contributions to this resurgence are Salimans, Ho, Chen, et al. (2017) and Petroski Such, Madhavan, Conti, et al. (2017). Both studies demonstrated that even simple evolutionary algorithms—when paired with modern compute resources—can scale effectively to high-dimensional deep networks and match, or even exceed, the performance of conventional reinforcement learning algorithms.

Salimans, Ho, Chen, et al. (2017) followed a **fixed-topology/direct** encoding setup similar to the one in the case study in section 3.2. However, instead of CMA-ES, they used the **OpenAI ES** approach (section 2.2.4) to evolve neural networks with thousands of parallel workers. In this approach, neural networks for complex continuous control tasks like three-dimensional humanoid walking could be found in just 10 minutes, and competitive results on Atari games could be achieved within an hour. This work highlighted some of the advantages of ES over deep RL methods, such as greater robustness to noisy and sparse rewards and smoother learning curves. The experiments further demonstrated that the slightly lower data efficiency of ES versus RL can be mitigated by the lower compute requirements, resulting from not having to perform backpropagation and not needing a value function.

Around the same time, Petroski Such, Madhavan, Conti, et al. (2017) used a simple **genetic algorithm** for training **fixed-topology** deep convolutional networks, particularly targeting the Atari 2600 suite of environments. Their approach did not include crossover or complex encoding schemes. Instead, it relied purely on selection and mutation, where each individual in the population represented a full set of neural network weights encoded directly as real-valued vectors. This approach used **truncation selection**, where the top T individuals become the parents for the next generation, and **elitism**, where the best individual was copied unmutated to the next generation. Because the Atari environments are noisy, each of the top 10 individuals was evaluated on 30 additional episodes to get a better estimate of their true performance. To produce offspring, a parent was selected uniformly at random and its parameter vector θ mutated by applying additive **Gaussian noise** as:

$$\theta' = \theta + \sigma\epsilon \quad \text{where} \quad \epsilon \sim \mathcal{N}(0, I). \tag{3.3}$$

Despite its simplicity, this approach was able to train networks with over four million parameters to play Atari games from pixels alone. Their performance was competitive with RL algorithms, with each method doing better on some games and worse on others. Among the 13 games tested, deep Q-network (DQN), ES, and GA each achieved the highest score on three games, while the RL method A3C achieved the top score on four games. Notably, in the game of Skiing, GA achieved a score higher than any previously reported at the time, surpassing a variety of DQN variants. In some games, the GA's performance significantly exceeded that of DQN, A3C, and ES, particularly in Frostbite, Venture, and Skiing. When allowed to run six times longer (6B frames), scores improved across all games. With these post-6B-frame scores, the GA outperformed A3C, ES, and DQN in head-to-head comparisons on seven, eight, and seven out of the 13 games, respectively. A summary of the results across many Atari games can be seen in table 3.2.

However, while a GA can efficiently find policies for many Atari games, it can struggle in other domains. For example, a GA took around 15 times longer than ES and still performed slightly worse when optimizing a neural network for humanoid locomotion. The reason for this difference may be that an ES has an easier time making precise weight updates than a GA, which could be critical for the intricate movements necessary for humanoid locomotion. Further research is needed to elucidate this issue in more depth.

Surprisingly, even a **random search variation**, which only evaluates randomly generated policies, can perform well. While it does not outperform the GA on any of the games tested, which suggests that the GA is effectively optimizing over generations, it outperforms DQN on three games, ES on three, and A3C on six. These results suggest that sometimes following the gradient (as is done in gradient-based optimization algorithms) can actually be detrimental to performance, and it can be more efficient to do a dense search in some local neighborhood of parameters.

Table 3.2: **Scores of ES and GA neuroevolution approaches on the Atari benchmark compared to RL.** Different methods perform best in different games. Neuroevolution can thus be extended even to very large networks, where they are competitive with modern RL techniques, and potentially offer advantages through large-scale parallelization. Interestingly, even a random search variant (RS) can find policies that outperform policies found by DQN, A3C, and ES for some games. Bold values indicate the best score per game, excluding the longer GA 6B run. Table adapted from Petroski Such, Madhavan, Conti, et al. (2017).

	DQN	ES	A3C	RS	GA	GA
Frames	200M	1B	1B	1B	1B	6B
Forw. Passes	450M	250M	250M	250M	250M	1.5B
Backw. Pass.	400M	0	250M	0	0	0
Operations	1.25B	250M	1B	250M	250M	1.5B
amidar	**978**	112	264	143	263	377
assault	4,280	1,674	**5,475**	649	714	814
asterix	4,359	1,440	**22,140**	1,197	1,850	2,255
asteroids	1,365	1,562	**4,475**	1,307	1,661	2,700
atlantis	279,987	**1,267,410**	911,091	26,371	76,273	129,167
enduro	**729**	95	-82	36	60	80
frostbite	797	370	191	1,164	**4,536**	6,220
gravitar	473	**805**	304	431	476	764
kangaroo	7,259	**11,200**	94	1,099	3,790	11,254
seaquest	**5,861**	1,390	2,355	503	798	850
skiing	-13,062	-15,443	-10,911	-7,679	**-6,502**	-5,541
venture	163	760	23	488	**969**	1,422
zaxxon	5,363	6,380	**24,622**	2,538	6,180	7,864

3.4.3 Taking Advantage of Big Compute

One important difference of neuroevolution versus traditional RL is that neuroevolution is inherently parallelizable. Instead of improving a single individual solution, an entire population is evolved at once. The population can be very large and distributed over a large number of compute nodes, leading to discoveries that would otherwise be difficult to obtain. As will be discussed in chapter 15, such experiments are yet to be run—and they may require different kinds of evolutionary methods, including those designed to take advantage of **neutral mutations**, **weak selection**, large populations, and **deep time** (as will be discussed in more detail in section 9.1.1).

Another promising direction is to take advantage of GPUs/TPUs. Many deep learning algorithms, such as deep reinforcement learning, have benefited greatly from rapid training of neural networks on **hardware accelerators**, and thus shorter iteration times. Previously, these advances have been tailored to algorithms based on gradient descent, but the neuroevolution community has been developing its own frameworks, constantly narrowing this gap.

While neuroevolution algorithms have mostly relied on CPU parallelism in the past, the aforementioned work by Petroski Such, Madhavan, Conti, et al. (2017) reviewed in section 3.4.2, was also an early demonstration of the power of an NE approach that capitalizes on GPU acceleration. Even using only a single GPU, training can be significantly accelerated. Since then, more work has been done to further take advantage of distributed hardware-accelerated setups and the massive throughput provided by GPUs/TPUs. While distributing training across multiple CPUs can already give a substantial speedup, another level of training speed and network size can be reached by taking advantage of hardware acceleration.

Deep learning methods in general, and RL methods in particular, have long been able to take advantage of training across a large number of TPUs and GPUs. In recent years, the advent of high-performance computing frameworks like JAX has also finally enabled such efficient hardware acceleration for evolutionary algorithms. Two notable libraries that leverage JAX for evolutionary computation are **EvoJAX** (Tang, Tian, and Ha, 2022) and **EvoSAX** (Lange, 2023). For example, one of the important features of EvoJAX is its use of **just-in-time** (JIT) compilation to optimize the evaluation of the fitness function. This technique ensures that the computationally intensive parts of the algorithm are executed as efficiently as possible. Additionally, EvoJAX supports vectorized operations, allowing simultaneous evaluation of multiple individuals, further enhancing performance.

This modernization mirrors a broader trend in neuroevolution: the reimplementation of classical ideas using modern deep learning programming stacks, hence unlocking performance that was previously unattainable. This work includes modern versions of NEAT, such as TensorNEAT (Wang, Zhao, Liu, et al., 2024), which take advantage of JAX and can reach speedups of up to 500 times compared to other existing non-JAX implementations. TensorNEAT serves as a proof of concept that classic NE algorithms like NEAT can thrive in the era of hardware acceleration and modern ML tooling. It opens the door to applying topology-evolving methods to more complex tasks than have heretofore been possible.

Note that TPUs and GPUs were designed to run deep learning architectures well, and they may not be as great a fit for neuroevolution. Chapter 11 reviews neuromorphic approaches, where spiking neural networks are evolved for hardware implementation, resulting in energy-efficient implementations. FPGAs are another promising direction, for continuous-time recurrent neural networks (CTRNNs) in particular (Whitley, 2024a,b). FPGA can be configured in less than a millisecond to implement a particular neural network architecture, making it possible to evaluate network candidates rapidly, 20% to 28% faster than an ARM processor

Thus, it is possible to take advantage of special hardware and modern compute stacks to scale up the neuroevolution process, both in terms of speed and in terms of network size. Chapter 4 will take a look at more methodological ways to scale up, taking advantage of indirect encodings. It is also possible to combine deep learning synergistically with evolution (and methods such as NEAT), which is a topic of chapters 10 and 11. An interesting synergy is also emerging with RL and generative AI, as will be discussed in chapters 12 and 13. These are all recent and emerging extensions of neuroevolution. The unique core of it, however, is still evolving intelligent behavior and decision-making, as will be discussed in chapters 6 through 9.

3.5 Chapter Review Questions

1. **Evolutionary algorithms:** What advantages do EAs offer over traditional RL when solving tasks where only the final outcome is known, rather than intermediate rewards?

2. **Key mechanism:** Describe how an EA can be applied to train a neural network to solve an RL task. Include the role of the fitness function and population-based search.

3. **Deterministic versus stochastic policies:** What is the difference between deterministic and stochastic policies in neuroevolution? Why might a stochastic policy be beneficial for certain tasks?

4. **Robust policies:** In the context of the BipedalWalkerHardcore example, how does evaluating an agent over multiple trials improve the robustness of the policy? What trade-offs does this introduce?

5. **Evolutionary optimization:** Explain how neuroevolution can evolve both the weights and the architecture of a neural network. Why is evolving the architecture a significant step beyond evolving weights alone?

6. **NEAT:** What are the main components of the NEAT algorithm? Describe how mutation, crossover, and speciation contribute to its effectiveness.

7. **Neuroevolution versus deep learning:** In what scenarios might neuroevolution outperform deep learning? Highlight at least two scenarios where neuroevolution offers unique benefits.

8. **Explainability and compactness:** Why might solutions discovered through neuroevolution, such as NEAT's compact pole-balancing solution, be more explainable than those generated by deep learning?

9. **Emerging synergies:** How can neuroevolution complement other AI approaches, such as large neural networks, neuromorphic hardware, or generative AI models? Provide an example of one such synergy.

10. **Scaling up:** How does leveraging modern hardware acceleration (e.g., GPUs and TPUs) improve the scalability of neuroevolution, and what are some notable examples of frameworks that enable this acceleration?

Chapter 4

Indirect Encodings

When neural networks are encoded directly, the elements in the genetic representation correspond one-to-one to elements in the neural network. **Indirect encodings**, on the other hand, utilize a mechanism that allows expanding a compact genetic encoding into much larger and more complex neural networks. Several such approaches are reviewed in this chapter. The first three represent various levels of abstraction of indirect encoding in biology; that is, development through cellular growth, grammatical encoding, and learning. Next, indirect encoding through hypernetworks is reviewed, where one network indirectly encodes the design of another. Finally, we're looking at dynamic indirect encodings through a self-attention mechanism.

4.1 Why Indirect Encodings?

Biological organisms in nature all develop from a single starting cell. Through local cell interactions and growth over time, an initially unassuming mass of cells eventually transforms into a complex and sophisticated structure with specialized cells and intricate connections. This process of growth and development, known as **morphogenesis**, is a fundamental aspect of biology that underlies the formation of all living organisms. In the case of the human brain, this process is particularly remarkable, as it gives rise to the most complex and sophisticated structure known to science, with billions of neurons and trillions of connections.

The human brain exhibits a complex network of interconnected modules, which form the basis of intelligence. How this intricate structure is encoded in our genetic code, consisting of approximately 24,000 genes or 3 billion base pairs (International Human Genome Sequencing Consortium, 2004), is a fascinating question that we're still struggling to completely answer. Although learning plays a crucial role, much of this information is already encoded in the genome.

To achieve this remarkable feat, **regularity** is necessary, which involves reusing structural motifs to enable compression and compactness of the genome. Interestingly, regularity also provides computational advantages to neural structures, as seen in the success of convolution in deep learning. Convolution, a pattern of connectivity that uses the same feature detector at multiple locations in a layer, has proved to be a powerful solution for capturing translation-invariant features in deep learning architectures. Instead of designing such patterns and others by hand and ultimately being limited by a human designer, ideally, our neuroevolutionary algorithms would identify these powerful regularities in an automated way. This is the idea behind **indirect encodings** in neuroevolution.

Before we go into more detail about indirect encodings, let's revisit the **neuroevolution of augmenting topologies** (NEAT) algorithm from chapter 3. As we discussed, NEAT is an example of a **direct encoding**. There is no compression involved or any type of reuse of information, resulting in a one-to-one mapping between the parameters of a NEAT genotype (the description of the nodes that exist in the network and how they are connected to each other) and those of the neural network phenotype. In other words, for every connection in the neural network, there exists a parameter in the underlying genotype. As we have seen, NEAT works well for many problems, but because it is a direct encoding, it has the drawback that every subpart of the solution needs to be **reinvented separately** by evolution instead of allowing the genome to reuse it. It is therefore not surprising that NEAT has mostly been used for tasks requiring compact neural networks, with orders of magnitude fewer parameters than those used in current RL approaches.

Let's look at an example of what this means for a particular problem. Imagine that you want to evolve a controller for a quadrupedal robot. This task likely would benefit from an approach that takes into account the underlying task patterns and symmetries; in other words, knowing how to control one leg is likely helpful in controlling the others. A tried and tested approach for resolving such a problem using an EA is to assist it in recognizing patterns and symmetries. This method involves manually breaking the problem into smaller components, such as designing the controller for one leg of a quadruped and then duplicating it for each leg, with slight variations in phase. By doing this, the algorithm is encouraged to adopt a modular approach and employ a single encoding for multiple modules. However, it would be ideal if the algorithm were able to take advantage of the symmetry and regularities of the tasks automatically, without an engineer having to decompose the problem manually. While it is easy to see how the problem could be decomposed into sub-solutions for a quadrupedal walker, it is not always as straightforward. The idea behind indirect encodings is to address this issue through representations that have the ability to capture and express regularities such as symmetries and repetition in the phenotypic structures automatically.

Indirect encodings draw inspiration from the compression of DNA in natural systems and have a long research history stretching back several decades, including early experiments in pattern formation. Researchers have explored the use of evolvable encodings for a diverse range of structures ranging from simple blobs of artificial cells to complex robot morphologies and neural networks (Bongard and Pfeifer, 2001; Doursat, Sayama, and Michel, 2013; Gruau, 1994; Hornby and Pollack, 2002; Miller and Turner, 2015; Stanley and Miikkulainen, 2003).

In evolutionary computation, the process of how the genotype is translated into the phenotype, which entails all the observable characteristics of an organism, is usually called the **genotype-to-phenotype mapping**. In nature, this mapping is achieved through the process of **development**. Thus, one way to take advantage of indirect encodings is to mimic development in biology (Miikkulainen and Forrest, 2021). There are three main approaches: modeling cellular growth processes, abstracting development into a grammatical rewrite system, and combining evolution synergistically with learning. These are the topics discussed in the next section.

The two sections after that review fundamentally different mechanisms of indirect encoding. The first one is hypernetworks, in which one neural network encodes the weights of another neural network. While developmental systems are suitable for modeling natural structures and self-similar patterns, neural networks give us more flexibility in generating diverse and rich patterns. They can not only capture regularities such as symmetry and repetition, but also more complex patterns such as repetition with variation. Following that, we look at how hypernetworks can be extended to serve as dynamic encodings, in which the generated weight pattern can be made input dependent. This type of dynamic indirect encoding is closely related to the idea of self-attention. How they can be the basis for an indirect encoding is the focus of the last section in this chapter.

4.2 Developmental Processes

As will be discussed in section 14.4, development is a fundamental way in biology to construct complex solutions. Instead of specifying the final solution directly, evolution specifies a developmental process. That is, the initial structure and a mechanism for building a full solution through intrinsic growth or through interactive adaptation to the environment. Such mechanisms can be harnessed in artificial systems as well. Emulating biology, many developmental mechanisms can be used to establish **artificial embryogeny** (Stanley and Miikkulainen, 2003), a biologically inspired way to take advantage of indirect encodings. One way is to emulate cell-chemistry mechanisms such as cellular growth and genetic regulation. Another is to abstract development into grammatical rewrite steps. A third is to take advantage of learning, either individually or through population culture. These ideas will be reviewed in the subsections that follow.

4.2.1 Cell-Chemistry Approaches

Understanding the fundamental characteristics of natural patterns has been an important motivation for developmental systems. In seminal work in 1952, Alan Turing proposed a system based on diffusing chemicals, successfully simulating patterns reminiscent of those found on seashells, feathers in birds, and fur in mammals (Turing, 1952). At the other end of the spectrum, Aristid Lindenmayer in 1968 proposed high-level grammatical abstractions called L-systems, demonstrating that they can produce lifelike plant structures (Lindenmayer, 1968a,b).

Initially, both Turing and Lindenmayer drew inspiration from the patterns they observed in nature, prior to their endeavors to describe the mechanisms behind these patterns. They took opposite perspectives on development, though: Turing's cell-chemistry is a bottom-up approach, whereas Lindenmayer's grammatical systems are top-down. Interestingly, neither of those was designed to be evolved, nor were they intended specifically to explain how neural networks are constructed. However, both serve as biological motivations for neuroevolution that takes advantage of indirect encoding through development. This section focuses on approaches based on cell chemistry; the next section focuses on grammatical approaches.

Cell-chemistry approaches aim to capture and utilize some of the fundamental physical mechanisms underlying development. Turing's **reaction-diffusion model** is a foundation for many of them. It consists of differential equations that describe how chemical substances, or **morphogens**, propagate and change over time through diffusion through a medium and reaction with each other. Initially the morphogens are randomly distributed, and their concentration vector C at each location changes over time as

$$\partial C/\partial t = F(C) + \mathbf{D}\nabla^2 C, \tag{4.1}$$

where the diagonal matrix $\mathbf{D}$ represents how fast each morphogen diffuses through the medium, and the function F describes how the morphogens react to each other. The process characterized by this equation takes place at all locations and time steps in parallel, resulting in a dynamic system of morphogen concentrations. Over time, as noted previously, it can result in significant patterns such as those on seashells, feathers in birds, and fur in mammals.

The model can be applied to the development of neural networks as well (Nolfi and Parisi, 1992). Diffusion represents axonal growth, and reactions are interactions between axons and cell bodies; that is, the forming of active connections. To evolve networks, each genome of a network consists of its neuron definitions, which are the location of each cell body and parameters that define how axons will branch out of it. There is exuberant growth with pruning to remove connections that are not useful. In this manner, reaction-diffusion implements a developmental mechanism that allows coding network structures indirectly. It is an abstract analogy, however, that is not intended to model the actual underlying chemical processes.

Approaches based on **gene regulatory networks** (GRNs), in contrast, aim at building on such chemical processes. As mentioned in the introduction to this chapter, the number of genes in the human genome is relatively small. Much of the complexity lies in the mechanisms that construct an individual based on those genes (GRNs; Cussat-Blanc, Harrington, and Banzhaf, 2019; Wang, 2013). In particular, the genes interact: Many genes participate in encoding a particular trait through a complex network of interactions. Through chemical reactions and diffusion, the networks may enhance or suppress the effect of individual genes, generating variation and robustness in gene expression. In this manner, instead of coding everything directly into genes, evolution also encodes an interaction mechanism that results in an indirect and potentially more powerful encoding. Interestingly, this mechanism is entirely missing from standard evolutionary algorithms!

GRNs can be implemented as differential equations or abstracted into computationally more efficient implementations, such as Boolean functions (Dellaert and Beer, 1994). Such functions, called **operons**, describe the interactions at a high level, for instance

$$\begin{aligned} A \wedge \neg B &\rightarrow C; \\ A \wedge C &\rightarrow B, \end{aligned}$$

which states that if protein A is in the cell and B is not, then C is produced, and if A and C are both in the cell, B is produced. Thus, starting from A, this process produces C, then

B, and stops. Such systems of rules or equations can be encoded as genomes and then evolved toward a given target, such as the production of a certain protein.

Importantly, GRN processes can be scaled up to represent growing neural networks. Some of the proteins may represent receptors, and others axonal growth. The proteins have to match for the connection to be made. In this manner, chemistry-guided axonal growth like that observed in the brain can be modeled and utilized in neuroevolution. The approach is potentially powerful, but it is difficult to take advantage of it. It may need to be simplified further by representing the genome as a string. It can then be evolved to construct a neural network that controls a simulated robot to move around without hitting obstacles. Or, GRNs may be abstracted into a more general representation of analog genetic encoding, which then allows for complexification and decomplexification of the network as needed in the evolutionary process (Mattiussi and Floreano, 2007). Other implementations exist as well (Iba and Noman, 2016). A particularly ambitious example will be discussed in section 9.1.3, where GRNs are used to construct a system with high **evolvability**, as a potential ingredient in open-ended evolution.

In general, much work remains in taking advantage of indirect encodings through development. A closer look at biological development reveals that between grammatical and cell-chemistry approaches, there are many dimensions that could be modeled and utilized (Stanley and Miikkulainen, 2003). There are mechanisms for (1) **cell fate** (i.e., what role each cell develops to take on in the organism); (2) **targeting** (i.e., how connections find their appropriate end locations); (3) **heterochrony** (i.e., how timing and ordering of developmental phases affects the end result); (4) **canalization** (i.e., how some changes become robust and tolerant to mutations); and (5) **complexification** (i.e., how new genes are added to the genome, increasing the complexity of the phenotype). NEAT, of course, takes advantage of complexification, and GRNs utilize targeting, but the other dimensions and their combinations are largely unexplored.

Thus, much can still be learned from biology and harnessed in neuroevolution. Such work can also help understand biology better, as will be discussed from several perspectives in chapter 14.

4.2.2 Grammatical Encodings

In contrast with the cell-chemistry approaches, Lindenmayer's **L-systems** are high-level abstractions of development. They are **grammatical rewrite systems**; each rewrite step can be seen as a step in development. As mentioned previously, they were originally developed to explain patterns seen in plants, and indeed they can produce some very interesting designs of this type. For instance, the company SpeedTree has created tools that can produce realistic virtual foliage, which has been used in many videos and movies such as Iron Man 3 and Avatar. In L-systems, rewrite rules are applied concurrently to all characters within a string, similar to how cell divisions occur simultaneously in multicellular organisms. By iteratively replacing sections of a basic object according to a predefined set of rewriting rules, intricate structures can be generated. Figure 4.1*a* shows an example of such a process. While the grammatical rules leading to certain structures are traditionally designed by hand, such as in Lindenmayer's original system, they can also be optimized through an evolutionary search method (Ochoa, 1998).

(*a*) Deterministic

(*b*) Stochastic

Figure 4.1: **L-systems.** (*a*) L-systems can grow plant like structures by repeatedly applying rewrite rules to an initial starting character. (*b*) With the addition of some stochasticity, the approach is able to generate realistic trees. Figure *a* from Prusinkiewicz, Hammel, Hanan, et al. (1996), *b* from Solkoll (2005).

In an impressive demonstration of their versatility, and going beyond the lifelike plant structures they were initially designed for, Hornby and Pollack (2001a) applied an L-system approach to the optimization of table designs. Here, one can optimize L-system rules that grow designs that have a specific height, surface structure, and stability. Compared to a direct encoding approach, in which discovered components could not be reused, the indirect L-system encoding produced better results faster, and those designs were more aesthetically pleasing (figure 4.2). At a quick first glance, they could be mistaken for IKEA furniture. On the other hand, the designs produced by the direct encoding approach are lacking regularities and look more piecemeal.

By identifying the shared properties among natural patterns, it becomes evident which aspects artificial systems should account for. One of the fundamental characteristics observed in biological organisms is the presence of **repetition**. This hallmark trait manifests in multiple instances of the same substructures found throughout an organism's body. From the tiniest cells to complex neural networks in the brain, these recurring motifs play a crucial role in shaping the organism's structure and function. This repetitive nature in the outward appearance of an organism is also referred to as **self-similarity**. Furthermore, this repetition is not always exact but often occurs with subtle variations. For example, within the vertebral column, each vertebra shares a similarity in structure but exhibits distinct proportions and morphologies. Similarly, human fingers follow a regular pattern, and yet they display individual differences, making each finger on the same hand unique. This phenomenon of **repetition with variation** is pervasive throughout all of natural life. A prevalent form of repetition in biological organisms is achieved through **symmetry**. Bilateral symmetry, a classic example, occurs when the left and right sides of an organism's body are mirror images of each other. This symmetrical arrangement is commonly observed in various living beings. While overall symmetry is noticeable in many biological structures, true perfection is rare. Imperfect symmetry is a common feature of repetition with variation. The human body, for instance, exhibits an overall symmetric layout, and yet it is not entirely equivalent on both sides. Some organs are exclusive to one side of the body, and the dominance of one hand over the other is a typical

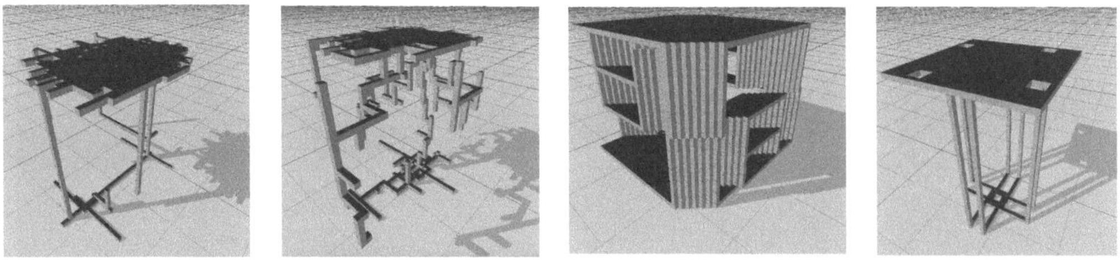

(*a*) Direct 1 (*b*) Direct 2 (*c*) Indirect 1 (*d*) Indirect 2

Figure 4.2: **Tables grown by evolved L-systems.** Shown are tables evolved with a direct (*a*, *b*) and indirect encoding (*c*, *d*). In contrast to the directly encoded tables, the indirectly encoded ones display key biological regularities such as repetition and symmetry. Figures from Hornby and Pollack (2001a).

example of this asymmetry. In conclusion, the occurrence of repetition and its variations, along with different forms of symmetry, play a fundamental role in shaping the intricate structures and patterns found in biological organisms. Understanding these principles is essential for unraveling the complexities of life and the underlying mechanisms that govern the diversity of living forms.

Throughout many generations, the regularities observed in biological organisms often undergo elaboration and further exploitation. An illustrative example of this process is evident in the evolution of early fish, where the bilaterally symmetric fins gradually transformed into the arms and hands of mammals, while still retaining some of the original regularities. Preservation of established regularities is a remarkable aspect of biological evolution. Over generations, these regularities are typically strictly maintained. For instance, bilateral symmetry rarely gives rise to three-way symmetry, and animals with four limbs rarely produce offspring with a different number of limbs, even though the limb design itself may undergo elaboration and modification. By using this list of regularities and their evolutionary patterns, researchers can analyze phenotypes and lineages resulting from artificial encodings, comparing them to natural characteristics. This analysis provides valuable insights into whether a particular encoding accurately captures the essential properties and capabilities observed in the process of natural development.

The grammatical approach can be applied to neuroevolution as well. In **cellular encoding** (CE; Gruau and Whitley, 1993; Gruau, Whitley, and Pyeatt, 1996), a grammar describes how the neural network should be constructed step by step. The process starts with an ancestor cell connected directly to input and output ("cell" here refers to a node in the neural network being constructed; figure 4.3*a*). Each cell has a pointer to the grammar, which is represented as a tree. Each node in the grammar tree contains an instruction that specifies how the neural network should be modified. After each step is completed, the pointer traverses to the child of the node, until a node with the "end" instruction is reached.

For example, in figure 4.3, the first step is a sequential division. The top cell is then divided in parallel, and the bottom node is divided sequentially again. The top node of that division is divided in parallel, and the connection to the bottom node is negated. As the last step, a value of 1 is added to the threshold of the first node resulting from the last parallel division. As a result of this construction process, a neural network that implements XOR is created (figure 4.3*b*).

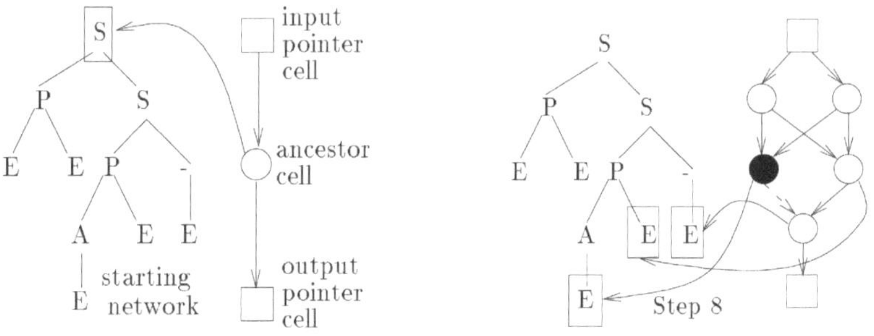

(*a*) Initial network (*b*) Final XOR network

Figure 4.3: **Cellular encoding approach to evolving neural network structure.** (*a*) The grammar encodes instructions on how to construct the network step by step, starting from a network that consists of a single ancestor cell. Each cell points to a location in the current location in the grammar tree, and is advanced to a child node in the tree as the instruction is executed. S=sequential division, P=parallel division, - = negating a connection, A=adding one to a node threshold, E=end the construction branch. In addition, a recurrency symbol R (not shown) allows continuing the construction again from the top of the grammar, with a counter deciding how many times the recurrency can be traversed. (*b*) After eight steps, the network that results from this construction process implements XOR. With recurrency added to the bottom right of the grammar, it can be extended by repeating the entire structure, thus implementing networks that calculate the parity of any number of inputs. The grammar trees can be evolved with genetic programming techniques, making automated discovery of complex networks with repeating structure possible. Figures from Gruau and Whitley (1993).

An important extension to this simple example is the ability to include **recurrency** in the grammar. For example, if a recurrency is added to the leftmost end node, the entire network structure is constructed again at that location from the top of the grammar. Its output becomes the first input of the first network, thus including one more input to the combined network. A counter can then be used to specify that the recurrency should be traversed n times. Thus, the execution of the grammar results in a network that calculates $n + 1$-bit parity! Similarly, networks can be constructed that calculate whether the input vector has a symmetric pattern of 1s and zeros. Thus, the recurrency in the grammar is a powerful way to take advantage of repetitive structure in networks.

Whereas L-systems were not designed to be evolved, CE was: Because the CE grammars are trees, **genetic programming** (Banzhaf, Nordin, Keller, et al., 1998) is a natural way to evolve them. Indeed, parity networks up to 51 bits were evolved in this manner, demonstrating that evolution can indeed take advantage of repetition. It is also possible to prove that any neural network topology can be represented in CE grammars. However, it does not mean that the good topologies are easy to find. As a matter of fact, the grammar can be turned around to represent connections in the network rather than cells, resulting in a different bias in the kinds of networks that can be constructed easily (Luke and Spector, 1996). The challenge is to discover the right biases and code them into the grammatical representation.

Besides L-systems and CE, other grammatical encoding mechanisms have been developed. For instance, to scale neuroevolution to the size and complexity of deep learning (section 3.4.2), it is possible to represent the weights as a sequence of mutations, and only store the mutation seeds (Petroski Such, Madhavan, Conti, et al., 2017). The process begins with an initial neural network parameter vector θ_0, which is generated from a random seed τ_0 using a deterministic initialization function ϕ: $\theta_0 = \phi(\tau_0)$. Each subsequent network in the evolutionary lineage is derived from its parent by applying a deterministic mutation function ψ, which adds pseudo-random Gaussian noise to the parent's weights. In this framework, the complete weight vector θ_n of any individual in the population is reconstructed by sequentially applying the mutation function across a series of seeds, beginning with the original initialization. This **sequence-based encoding** replaces the need to store full high-dimensional weight vectors with a compact list of seeds $[\tau_0, \tau_1, \ldots, \tau_n]$. Since each mutation step can be reproduced exactly from its corresponding seed, the genotype of each network is both lightweight and fully deterministic.

Thus, encoding the developmental processes as a series of grammatical rewrite operations is a high-level alternative to systems that aim at replicating the low-level cell-chemistry mechanisms. Incorporating learning as a lifetime stage of development synergistically with evolution is a third approach, as will be described next.

4.2.3 Learning Approaches

In addition to the physical development explored in the last two subsections, much of biological development happens through **learning**. The individual interacts with the environment and adapts its structure and parameters accordingly. Such learning is a form of indirect encoding as well: Evolution defines a starting point and a learning mechanism, and the full individual emerges indirectly through their synergy. The biological implications of this idea will be explored in more depth in section 14.4. In this subsection, the synergy is put to work as a computational mechanism that allows us to construct more complex systems.

Many of the neuroevolution methods reviewed so far can be used to construct the initial starting point, and many of the standard neural network learning algorithms can be used to establish the developmental phase. But several questions remain: First, should the improvements discovered by learning be coded back into the genome, in a **Lamarckian evolutionary process**, or should it only determine the fitness of the individual, thus guiding a **Darwinian evolution** through the Baldwin effect? Second, if gradient descent–based learning methods are to be used, where do the targets for it come from? Third, does the development require weight adaptation, or can it be more effectively encoded as a state of activation? Each of these questions is addressed in turn in this section.

First, **Lamarckian evolution** (Lamarck, 1809) suggests that acquired traits can be inherited, which is unlikely in biology. For instance, giraffes stretch their necks so they can reach higher, and their offspring will have longer necks as a result. In some cases, non-genetic transmission is possible through **epigenetic** means (Lacal and Ventura, 2018). For instance, in a process called "methylation", a methyl molecule attaches to the DNA, modulating genetic expression. As a result, for instance, animals that must live in a hostile environment may have offspring that are more sensitive and fearful, compared to offspring of those who exist in a normal environment. While such changes are not permanently encoded in the DNA, they do provide an immediate survival advantage that is inheritable. Whether biologically plausible or not, computational evolution can take advantage of both

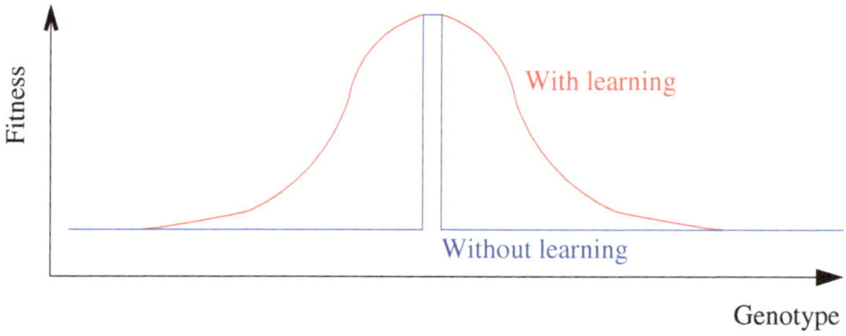

Figure 4.4: **Learning guiding evolution through the Baldwin effect.** In this needle-in-the-haystack problem, it would be difficult for evolution to find the sharp peak when the fitness evaluations of the other solutions are all the same. However, learning allows modifying these solutions (i.e., moving left and right along the x-axis). Therefore, the closer the solution is to the peak, the more likely it is to find it through learning, as indicated by the red curve. Learning can thus provide a more useful fitness, and help evolution find the peak faster. Adapted from Hinton and Nowlan (1987).

Lamarckian evolution and epigenetics. For instance, it may be possible to take advantage of these principles in evolving deep learning networks. Such networks are often too large to evolve effectively; however, it may be possible to train them and code the learned weights back to the genome. This approach has been successful, for instance, in evolving convolutional architectures for image processing (Hadjiivanov and Blair, 2019; Prellberg and Kramer, 2018). Through this approach, evolutionary exploration and gradient-based tuning can be combined.

One challenge in implementing Lamarckian/epigenetic evolution is that it may lead to a loss of diversity. Through gradient descent, the individuals in the population are modified in the same direction, as suggested by the gradient. The learning process may thus interfere with evolutionary exploration. A possible way to cope with this challenge is to train different individuals with different batches of data, or more broadly, use **ensembling techniques** to keep the population diverse. Effective ways of managing exploration and learning are still open to research.

The **Baldwin effect** can also lead to powerful computational approaches. The adaptations are not coded back into the genome, but are only used to determine fitness. Learning thus guides evolution toward more promising individuals (which is the Baldwin effect). Indeed, early studies showed that such a combination can be more powerful than evolution or learning alone. For instance, in a needle-in-the-haystack problem–where a single optimal solution (the needle) is hidden in an otherwise flat fitness landscape (the hay)–even when learning consisted of simply random changes, it was enough to broaden the basin of the target, and make it more likely for evolution to discover it (figure 4.4; Hinton and Nowlan, 1987). Thus, even if the learning does not affect the genome, it can be useful in guiding the evolution by suggesting which genetic individuals are more promising. This idea is consistent with theories in evolutionary biology that emphasize the role of developmental plasticity in driving evolution (West-Eberhard, 2003).

Interestingly, this result does not mean that an evolutionary system guided by the Baldwin effect gradually encodes more and more of the learned information into the genes, eventually making learning unnecessary. That is, the evolved solutions before learning often perform quite poorly—it is only after the learning that they perform well. This phenomenon is precisely the idea of **synergistic development**. Because learning is always part of the evaluation, evolution discovers the best possible starting points for learning, such that the system as a whole performs as well as possible. The starting points can be far from the optimum so long as learning can reliably pull them into the optimum. Apparently, in many tasks, there are many such starting points, and they are easier for evolution to find than points close to the optimum would be. Therefore, evolution finds a synergy where both methods play a significant role.

Regarding the second question posed at the beginning of this subsection, so far the discussion has assumed that the optimal targets for gradient descent are known. However, surprisingly, the process works even when such targets are not available. One possibility is to use related targets, such as predicting how the inputs are going to change as a result of the action (section 14.4.1). They do not directly specify what the agent should do, but they do allow learning internal representations that help evaluate the candidate.

Another approach is to use the behavior of current population champions, or even just that of parents, to train the offspring (McQuesten and Miikkulainen, 1997). This result is counterintuitive because evolution depends on discovering offspring that are better than the parents. However, what is important is that the offspring perform well after training. Thus, the process takes advantage of the Baldwin effect in the same way as evolution did in the needle-in-the-haystack problem (figure 4.4; Hinton and Nowlan, 1987). If the teachers are in the neighborhood of the optimal solutions, training will move the offspring around in this neighborhood, making it more likely that some of them will get closer to the optimum (figure 4.5). Selecting such solutions allows evolution to make progress even when the fitness evaluations without learning are not very informative.

The third question concerns the nature of adaptation: Is it necessary to encode the learned behaviors into the weights, or could it be more effective to encode them simply as a **recurrent activation state**? Of course, if the network needs to perform many trials starting from a reset activation, weight adaptation is necessary. However, in many domains, individuals perform and adapt continuously throughout their lifetime. With the appropriate recurrent circuitry, they could develop an activation state that modulates their further actions, similarly to a change in weights. Such an encoding of adaptation could be easier to discover and maintain.

To study this question, instead of gradient descent, a more general low-level adaptation mechanism is needed: **Hebbian learning** (Widrow, Kim, Park, et al., 2023). The basic idea is that if the neurons on both sides of the connection are active at the same time, the connection is useful and its weight should be increased. To bound such increases, a normalization process such as weight decay is often added, such as:

$$\Delta w_{ij} = \alpha_{ij} o_i o_j - \beta_{ij} w_{ij}, \tag{4.2}$$

where w_{ij} is the weight between neurons i and j with activations o_i and o_j, and α_{ij} and β_{ij} are learning and decay rate parameters. Unlike gradient descent, Hebbian learning is entirely local to each connection and requires no learning targets at the output. In this sense, it is closer to biological learning than gradient descent, and therefore a proper comparison to adaptation based on recurrency. Note that Hebbian learning also provides an alternative

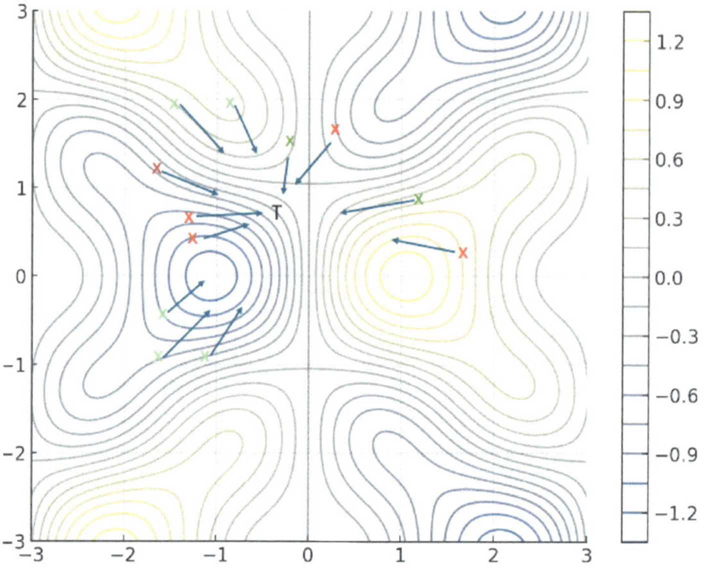

Figure 4.5: **Training to imitate champions or parents.** When well-performing individuals, such as population champions or parents, are used as teachers (T), they pull the offspring (X) toward them. Those offspring that perform the best after training are likely to be located near the optimum to begin with, and although some (red X) are worse after training, some (green X) are likely pulled closer to the optimum. Such training provides useful exploration around the optimum, making it more likely to be discovered.

that avoids the second question in this section, i.e., where the targets for development come from—it does not need them. On the other hand, it cannot take advantage of targets either, and therefore it is generally not as powerful as gradient descent.

Nevertheless, Hebbian learning is a compelling approach to developmental indirect encoding on its own. Networks with Hebbian learning can change their behavior based on what they observe during their lifetime. For instance, they can evolve to first perform one task, such as turning on a light, and then switch to another such task, such as to traveling to a target area (Floreano and Urzelai, 2000). While it is biologically plausible, an interesting practical question arises: Can such low-level adaptation be more effectively implemented through recurrent activation?

The foraging domain with good and bad food items can be used to study this question (Stanley, Bryant, and Miikkulainen, 2003). The usual NEAT method for evolving recurrent networks can be compared with a version that takes advantage of Hebbian learning: It evolves the learning rate and decay rate parameters α_{ij} and β_{ij} for each connection, in addition to the weights and the network topology. Each evolved network is placed into the foraging environment where it can consume food items; if an item is good, it receives a pleasure signal, and if bad, a pain signal. All items in a trial are the same, so after it consumes the first item, it needs to either eat all of them or none of them to receive maximum fitness.

While both approaches evolved successful networks, NEAT without adaptation required about half the generations to do so. There were fewer parameters to optimize,

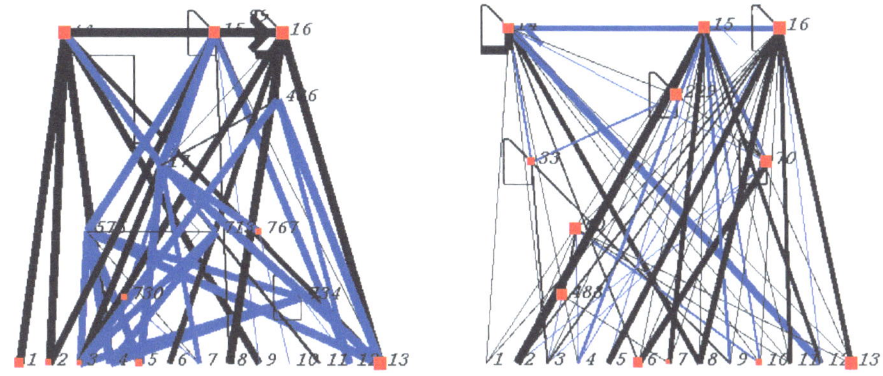

(*a*) With Hebbian learning (*b*) No Hebbian learning

Figure 4.6: **Networks evolved with NEAT with and without Hebbian learning.** Nodes are numbered through historical markings. Black lines represent excitatory and blue lines inhibitory connections; loops indicate recurrent connections; line thickness corresponds to the connection weight. (*a*) With Hebbian adaptation, performance is encoded more holistically, utilizing plastic synapses throughout the network. (*b*) Without Hebbian adaptation, the network is more parsimonious, with adaptation coded into recurrent connections at the outputs. While both types of solutions are successful, Hebbian adaptation provides a larger search space that is more difficult to navigate. In simple tasks at least, it can thus be more effective to rely on recurrency to represent adaptation. Figure from Stanley (2003).

and evaluations were more consistent. Indeed, the solution networks look very different (figure 4.6): While the fixed-weight recurrent networks were parsimonious with recurrency focused at the output, the adaptive networks were more complex and holistic, using many more adaptive weights throughout the network. Because many weights adapt, it was not possible to rely on only a few loops, and the behavior became encoded redundantly throughout.

Thus, in such a simple task, recurrency was more effective than Hebbian adaptation. It is, of course, possible that in more complex situations, adaptation provides additional power that may be needed. And indeed, such a task will be discussed in section 12.3.2 in the context of real-world transfer for locomoting robots. There also exists an interesting connection between Hebbian learning and modern machine learning mechanisms such as self-attention, which we will discuss in section 4.4.2.

4.3 Indirect Encoding Through Hypernetworks

A common feature of indirect encodings in section 4.2 is that a specific phenotypic component at a given point in development influences the states of nearby components. In other words, development progresses through local interactions. This section reviews a particularly popular indirect encoding that, when first introduced, broke with the strong tradition of such **local interactions** and **temporal unfolding**. In effect, it introduces a new category of indirect encoding at a different level of abstraction.

This approach, now known under the name **hypernetwork,** is based on the idea of one neural network (the hypernetwork) encoding the parameters of a potentially much larger phenotype in one shot; that is, each component in the phenotype is determined independently of any other component. Whereas many indirect encoding approaches illustrate opportunities for utilizing biological principles but do not yet perform as well as the best direct approaches, such hypernetworks already perform better in many standard benchmarks. Initially tested on indirectly encoding images, which we will discuss next in section 4.3.1, this approach can be extended to many other domains, such as three-dimensional robot morphologies, and even to encode artificial neural networks themselves (section 4.3.3).

4.3.1 Compositional Pattern Producing Networks

The most common way to implement hypernetworks in neuroevolution is through **compositional pattern-producing networks** (CPPNs; Stanley, 2007). Even though they are fundamentally distinct from developmental systems, CPPNs are inspired by developmental biology: Structures are built within a geometric space analogously to chemical gradients that define the axes of the embryo. For example, when the embryo of *Drosophila melanogaster* (one of developmental biologists' favorite pets and commonly known as the fruit fly) develops, chemical gradients establish axes from front to back, head to tail, and left to right. This way, structures such as the wings can be situated at their correct positions. Inside these structures are substructures, such as the intricate patterning of the wings, which are placed within the local coordinate system of the wing itself. In our own bodies, such gradients help define the position of the legs, arms, and hands, and within these structures, substructures such as the fingers of the hands. It is expensive to simulate the underlying process of the diffusion of morphogens, which is why CPPNs simplify this process into a network of function compositions represented as a graph. On a high level, CPPNs are generative neural networks that create structures with regularities in one shot and without going through a period of unfolding/growth.

We will start by looking at how a CPPN can be used as an indirect encoding for image generation (figure 4.7) but later explore how it can be easily extended to other domains such as generating neural network connectivity patterns (section 4.3.3), morphologies of robots (section 4.3.2), and agent environments (section 9.3). CPPNs have also impacted the broader field of machine learning in a variety of different ways. For example, CPPNs can be evolved to generate images that are entirely unrecognizable to humans, yet they successfully fool even highly accurate neural networks, which confidently classify them as familiar objects (Nguyen, Yosinski, and Clune, 2015a). CPPNs have even inspired improvements to deep neural networks, particularly addressing some limitations of convolution by introducing coordinate-based input representations (Liu, Lehman, Molino, et al., 2018).

A CPPN generates an image by taking as input the coordinates of a two-dimensional (2D) location $p = (x, y)$ and outputting hue, saturation, value (HSV), red, green, blue (RGB), or grayscale values of the pixel at that location. By repeating this process for all the pixels of a 2D grid, a 2D image can be created. One advantage of the CPPN representation is that images can be generated at any resolution by only changing the resolution of locations sampled, without increasing the number of genotypic parameters of the CPPN itself. Such scaling would not be possible with a direct encoding, in which each pixel in the image would have to be optimized separately.

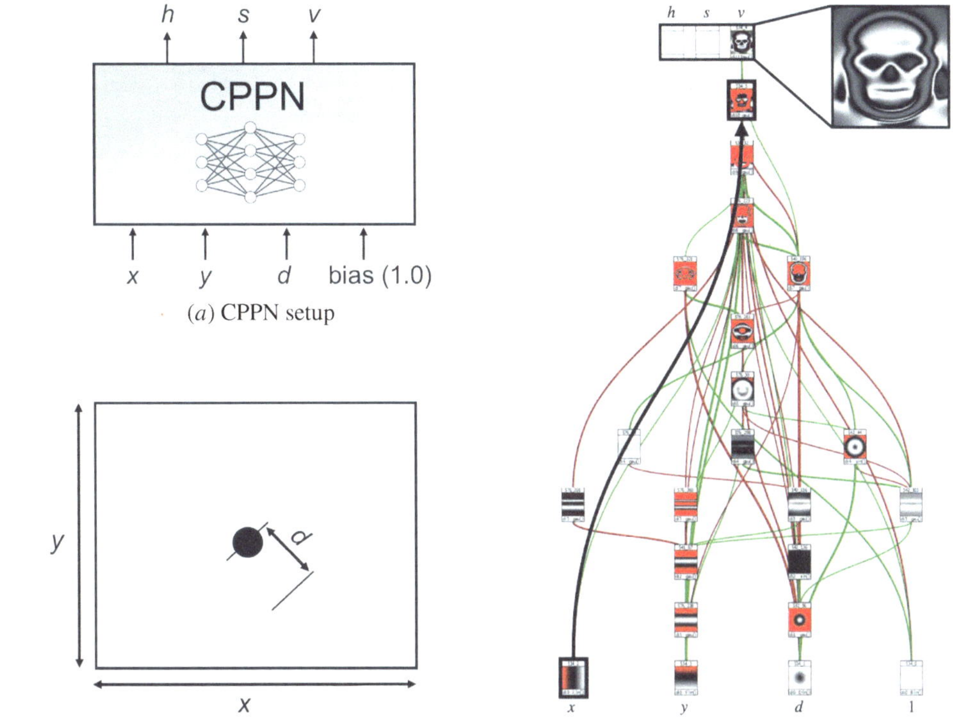

(*a*) CPPN setup

(*b*) CPPN inputs

(*c*) Skull-generating CPPN

Figure 4.7: **CPPN image encoding.** Compositional pattern producing networks are neural networks with diverse activation functions that generate geometric patterns. (*a*) The network illustrated is a 2D CPPN, as it receives inputs x and y, along with d, the distance from the point (x,y) to the center of the image. When evaluated over many coordinates (*b*), the CPPN's output forms an image or spatial pattern. The architecture depicted in (*c*) is the specific CPPN that generates the skull pattern shown at the top right. The colors in (*c*) highlight different components of the evolved network that contribute to key features of the skull image, as determined through functional analysis. The small images within the network nodes represent the activation patterns computed at each node over (x, y) coordinates. These patterns are ultimately combined by the network to produce the final output image, illustrating that CPPNs can encode complex spatial regularities through simple compositional principles. Figure *c* from Kumar, Clune, Lehman, et al. (2025).

As discussed earlier in this chapter, one common goal of indirect encodings is to be able to express patterns such as symmetry, repetition, among others. To allow CPPNs to more easily express such patterns, nodes in these networks do not all implement the same activation function, as in traditional neural networks (including the networks traditionally evolved by NEAT), but they are chosen from a small set of activation functions, such as Gaussian, sigmoid, and sine wave functions. For example, a Gaussian function can create something similar to a symmetric chemical gradient, while a sigmoid generates an asymmetric one, and a sine wave can create a repeating pattern. Things get more interesting when functions are composed with each other, which is in some way analogous to the morphogens creating local coordinate systems in real organisms, enabling their incredible levels of complexity. For example, a sine wave composed with the square of

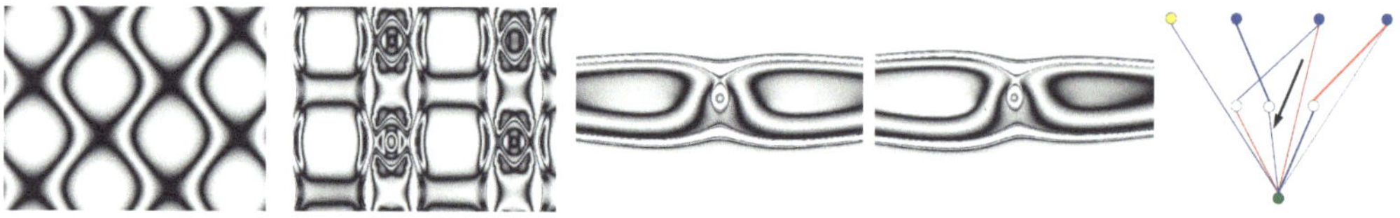

(*a*) Repetition (*b*) Variation (*c*) Symmetry (*d*) Morphed symmetry (*e*) CPPN for (*c*)

Figure 4.8: **CPPN examples.** CPPNs can produce patterns with repetition (*a*) and repetition with variation (*b*). They can also create symmetric patterns such as the sunglasses shown in (*c*), which is encoded through the CPPN shown in (*e*). By changing only a single connection, varying degrees of symmetry can be produced, such as the morphed glasses in (*d*). These examples demonstrate the expressive power and flexibility of CPPNs in generating complex, structured patterns. Figures from Stanley (2007).

a variable $\sin(x^2)$ produces a pattern that is repeating but with some type of variation. Such patterns are ubiquitous in many patterns seen in nature. Networks composed of only a few of such functions can produce surprisingly complex structures, making them useful in a wide range of applications, as we will see throughout this book. An example of such a CPPN with different activation functions is shown in figure 4.7*b*, which creates the symmetric and repeating pattern shown in figure 4.7*a*.

How can we evolve these CPPNs? Traditionally, CPPNs are evolved with NEAT, which makes it possible to optimize both the weights and the architecture of the network. Additionally, NEAT enables CPPNs to slowly complexify and produce more and more complex patterns. Augmenting NEAT to evolve CPPNs instead of the typical ANNs is straightforward. Every time a structural mutation adds a node to the network, the activation function of that node is randomly chosen from a pre-defined set of activation functions, often with equal probability. However, it is certainly possible to also use a method like ES to optimize the weights of a fixed-topology network, which includes randomly assigned activation functions for each node. We will leave this as an exercise for the reader.

One way to explore the representational power of an encoding is through **interactive evolutionary computation** (IEC; Takagi, 2001). Instead of evolving toward a certain target, in IEC, the user guides the evolutionary search by selecting parents from a set of candidate solutions (often by visually taking a look at them and deciding what they like most). The benefit of IEC is that it can reveal an encoding's ability to being able to encode a diversity of artifacts, while being able to establish and exploit regularities. We will further discuss how this idea of interactive evolution allows human designers to drive evolutionary discovery, how it enables multiple humans to collaboratively evolve artifacts, and how it can even lay the foundation for new types of ML-based games in chapter 8.

Exploring the space of CPPN-encoded images through IEC demonstrates that the representation is able to capture many of the desirable regularities identified earlier in this chapter. For example, it is able to create patterns that show repetition (figure 4.8*a*) but also repetition with variation (figure 4.8*b*). Figure 4.8*c* illustrates a set of "sunglasses" that exhibit bilateral symmetry, meaning they are mirror images on either side. This symmetry serves as an example of how genetic elements can be effectively reused. In this case, the CPPN-based function that defines one lens (the left one) is identically used for the other lens (the right one). Intriguingly, modifying just one connection gene, as shown

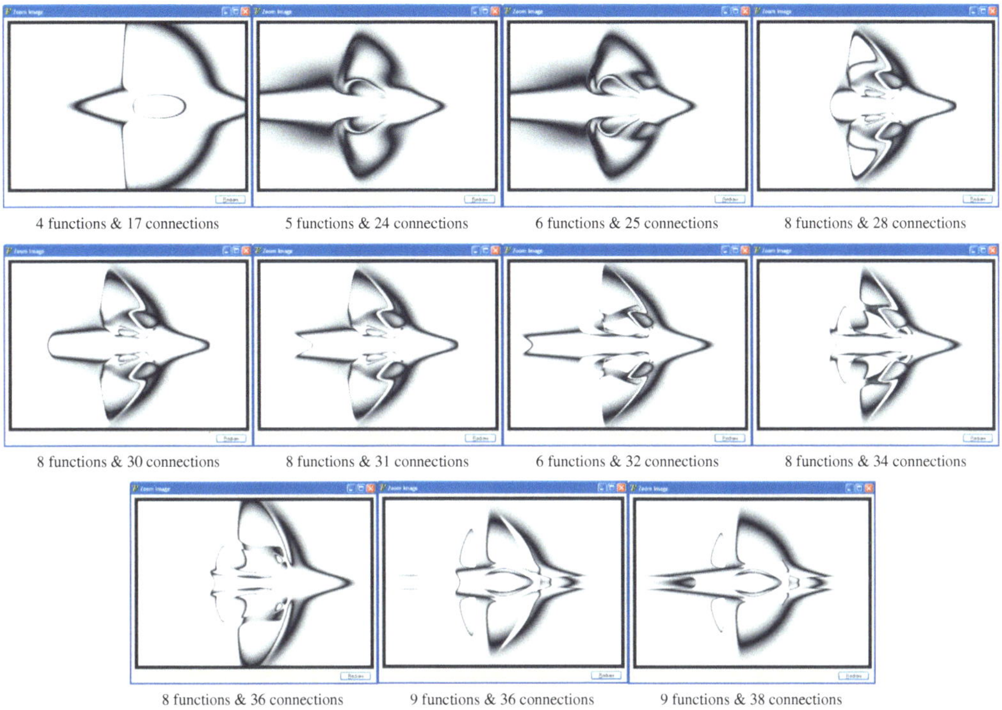

Figure 4.9: **CPPN pattern elaboration over generations.** The figure shows a chronological sequence of CPPN-encoded designs, discovered and elaborated upon during interactive evolution. Together with the designs, the number of hidden node functions and connections is also shown. This progression illustrates CPPNs' capacity to preserve fundamental structural regularities, such as bilateral symmetry, while elaborating on them across generations. Figures from Stanley (2007).

in figure 4.8*e*, can alter the symmetry of the lenses, resulting in slight asymmetry while still preserving the overall pattern's coherence, as seen in figure 4.8*d*. Even though the genetic code is the same for both sides, one lens displays a variant of the pattern seen in the other. This ability to evolve and refine specific features without disrupting the fundamental pattern is significant and possible because changes in the coordinate frame within a CPPN do not ruin the overall pattern being created. Therefore, even if the symmetry of the underlying coordinates is disrupted by a single gene alteration, the intricate pattern created within these coordinates remains intact and unaltered.

Additionally, one of the fundamental properties of natural evolution is that it is able to **elaborate on discovered designs** in subsequent generations. For example, the fundamental bilateral body plan, discovered early during the Cambrian explosion, has undergone extensive development over hundreds of millions of years, and yet its core structure has been consistently preserved. In a similar vein, the question arises: Can a CPPN effectively replicate a bilateral body plan and, over generations, both preserve and refine this bilateral symmetry? IEC experiments demonstrate that after discovering a spaceship-like design with bilateral symmetry (figure 4.9*a*), that design can then be elaborated on, with the underlying regularities becoming more complex in subsequent generations. Importantly, the basic parts that form the spaceship are conserved during this elaboration, such as its nose, tail, and wings. In the subsequent sections of this chapter, we will see that this ability to elaborate on previous discoveries is an important property of CPPNs.

CPPNs are also not restricted to 2D and can easily be extended to generate 3D forms instead of 2D images by adding a third z-input; and they can even encode locomoting 3D soft robots, as we will see in the next section.

4.3.2 Case Study: Evolving Virtual Creatures with CPPN-NEAT

A good test domain for different indirect encodings is **evolved virtual creatures**, which refer to digital entities that interact within a computational environment. These creatures are typically part of a simulation in which various forms of **artificial life** compete, survive, reproduce, and evolve over time based on certain predefined criteria or environmental pressures. In this section, we will have a look at how the morphologies of such creatures can be defined through a CPPN. We will encounter virtual creatures again throughout the book, such as in the context of collective intelligence (section 7.3.2) or when discussing the coevolution of morphologies and neural networks (section 9.2.2). Unlike the static CPPN-encoded images that we encountered in section 4.3.1, virtual creatures often have to interact with their environment, requiring a form of embodied cognition. This dynamism challenges the encoding schemes to not only create viable forms but also to encode behaviors that are effective in a given environment. Virtual creatures, with their varied morphologies and behaviors, present a complex and diverse space to explore. This complexity makes them ideal for testing the capabilities of indirect encodings to generate a wide range of solutions, where there is a coherent link between form and function.

The particular virtual creatures we are looking at next are three-dimensional, **soft robots** (Cheney, MacCurdy, Clune, et al., 2014). Each robot is made of an arrangement of voxels, where each voxel can be one of four materials, displayed as different colors (figure 4.10). Voxels colored green undergo periodic volumetric actuations at 20% intervals. Voxels colored light blue are passive and soft, with no inherent actuation; they deform only in response to the actions of nearby voxels. Red voxels behave like green ones, but with counter-phase actuations. The dark blue voxels are also passive, but they are more rigid and resistant to deformation than their light blue counterparts. These soft robots do not have sensors, and the patterns of material types thus fully determine the robot's actuation pattern. This means that the optimization task here equals finding a pattern of materials that makes the robot move as fast as possible.

The robot-generating CPPNs take as input the x-, y-, and z-coordinates, and the distance from the center (d) of each voxel. One of the network's outputs indicates the presence of material, while the other four outputs, each representing the specific material mentioned above, output the maximum value indicating the type of material present at that voxel. Separating the phenotypic component's presence and its parameters into distinct CPPN outputs has been shown to enhance performance. If there are several disconnected patches, only the central patch is considered in creating the robot morphology.

Optimizing these CPPN representations with NEAT showed that they were indeed not restricted to generating static structures but could produce fully functional, three-dimensional, soft robots. An example of such an evolved robot locomoting is shown in figure 4.10a. This robot morphology, together with other morphologies discovered during

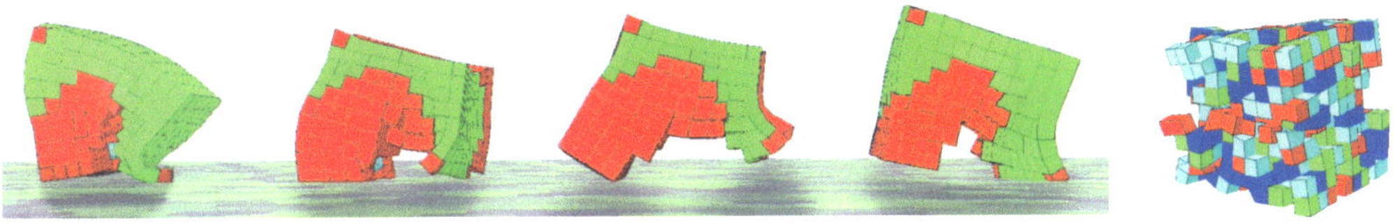

(*a*) Indirect encoding (*b*) Direct encoding

Figure 4.10: **Indirect versus direct encoding.** The goal in this domain is to find the right composition of voxel materials (e.g., red and green voxels actuate at different frequencies while dark blue voxels are passive) so that the robot is able to locomote as fast as possible. This figure shows an example of a 3D, soft robot generated with indirect CPPN encoding (*a*) and a direct encoding (*b*), in which each voxel is optimized independently. In contrast to the direct encoding, the CPPN-based encoding is able to produce 3D structures with symmetries and repeating motifs, resulting in fast locomotion. Figures from Cheney, MacCurdy, Clune, et al. (2014). Videos at `https://neuroevolutionbook.com/demos`.

evolution, displayed interesting regularities, often including symmetry and repetition. The opposite is true for robots that used a direct encoding, in which the parameters of each voxel were encoded individually. These robots often failed to perform well without any clear regularities in their morphologies (figure 4.10*b*). A direct encoding made it more challenging to find structures that display the globally coordinated behaviors necessary for efficient locomotion strategies.

CPPNs can generate structures with regularities by giving the network access to the locations of each element of the structure to be generated. In biological systems, this information is not directly available; it is thus an interesting question whether it is also possible to generate complex patterns artificially solely based on the local communication of the structure's components. We will return to this question in section 7.3, on neuroevolutionary approaches for collective intelligence, where we will also again encounter three-dimensional, soft robots.

4.3.3 HyperNEAT

This chapter started with a discussion of the intricate structure of the human brain and its complex regularities. For example, in the brain, there are neural modules with repeating connectivity patterns and left/right symmetry. Given a CPPN's ability to express complex 2D and 3D patterns, it makes sense to also consider if they could be used to generate such complex neural connectivity patterns as well. With this goal in mind, the question becomes what such a CPPN should look like and what its inputs should be.

To answer this question, again consider **convolutional connectivity patterns**. In a CNN, the same feature detector is employed at multiple locations in a network. For the algorithm to discover such heuristics by itself, a method is needed that can learn that there should be correlations between the weights of nearby neurons. Essentially, this involves generating weight patterns based on the geometry of the input and output domains. For instance, if the input and output domains are both two-dimensional, the weight of a connection between two neurons can be expressed as function f of the positions $(x1, y1)$ and $(x2, y2)$ of the source and target neurons, respectively.

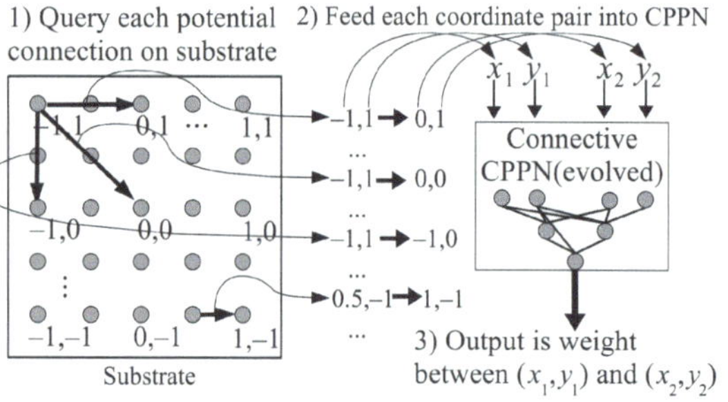

(*a*) Generic 2D area

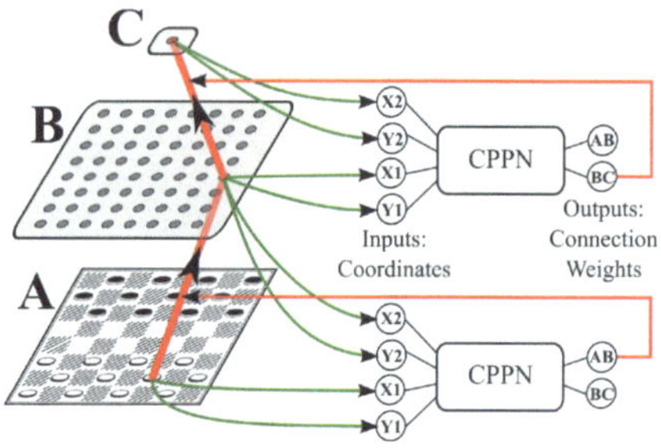

(*b*) Checkers game board

Figure 4.11: **HyperNEAT substrates.** Two types of HyperNEAT substrates are shown, which are the arrangement of nodes and their roles. In (*a*), nodes are arranged on a 2D square. The CPPN is queried with all pairs of nodes to determine how they are connected to each other. A more complex substrate for evaluating positions in the game of checkers is shown in (*b*). The input layer reflects the geometry of the checkers board. The output layer C has one node that determines the quality of a board state. The CPPN has two outputs, AB and BC. To query a connection from layer A to B, output AB is used, while from layer B to the output layer C, output BC is used. In this manner, the design of the substrate allows HyperNEAT to leverage geometric regularities to produce structured connectivity patterns. Figure *a* from Stanley, D'Ambrosio, and Gauci (2009) and figure *b* from Gauci and Stanley (2010).

This is the fundamental insight behind the method called **HyperNEAT** (hypercube-based NEAT; Stanley, D'Ambrosio, and Gauci, 2009), which can be viewed as one of the most foundational and impactful applications of CPPNs. In essence, in HyperNEAT, every neuron is given a role (e.g., input, hidden, output) and a location in space (traditionally determined by a user, but this process can also be automated, as we will see in the next section). The collection of roles and positions in HyperNEAT is often referred to as the **substrate**, to distinguish it from the CPPN itself. The connectivity patterns between the neurons are determined by CPPNs evolved through NEAT, which take as input the location of two nodes. Querying the CPPN with every possible connection between two nodes, with the output of the CPPN representing the weight of the connection, produces a neural network. This process is visualized in figure 4.11*a*. To not only produce fully connected networks, connections might only be expressed if the CPPN output is higher than a certain threshold. In other HyperNEAT variants, a second output determines if a connection should be expressed (Verbancsics and Stanley, 2011). This approach can be helpful because it decouples the pattern of weights from the pattern of expressed connections.

Given the neurons' positions in space, HyperNEAT can create a variety of regular connectivity patterns. For example, in a typical CNN, a filter is applied across the geometry of the input space. HyperNEAT can invent the concept of convolution by itself, because it can be expressed as a function based on the distance of the source to the target neuron: $x_1 - x_2$ and $y_1 - y_2$. The intriguing aspect of HyperNEAT lies in its ability to go beyond conventional convolution as the sole significant pattern of connectivity. Through HyperNEAT, evolved neural networks have the potential to uncover and leverage various patterns of regularity, inaccessible to traditional learning algorithms for neural networks.

For example, consider the task of creating a neural network that evaluates board positions in the game of checkers; that is, a **board evaluator** that is given a specific board configuration as input, and determines how good this position is. This game is intuitively geometric, with the movement rules for each piece being the same for every location on the board. The HyperNEAT approach should be able to take advantage of the CPPN's ability to calculate the connection weights based on the positional differences between two nodes, enabling it to uniformly apply a repeating concept throughout the entire board. In a sense, HyperNEAT is able to see the geometry of the task. We thus expect that an indirect representation that can learn to repeat strategies across the board should have an advantage when compared to a direct encoding like NEAT, which has to learn this pattern for each square on the board separately. In the adaptation of HyperNEAT for the game of checkers, the input layer can be designed as a two-dimensional structure, mirroring the checkerboard's layout, as illustrated in figure 4.11*b* (Gauci and Stanley, 2010). This **substrate** has one input *A* and one hidden layer *B* and a single output node *C*, which outputs the evaluation of a board position. Note that the CPPN here has two outputs, AB and BC. Therefore, the x- and y-coordinates of each node are adequate to pinpoint the specific connection being queried, with the two separate outputs differentiating the connections between A&B and B&C from each other.

And indeed, HyperNEAT was able to find a high-performing board evaluator significantly faster than NEAT, which was in part due to HyperNEAT's ability to search through a smaller genotypic space. Additionally, when comparing the most general solutions found by both approaches to randomized opponents, HyperNEAT showed a significantly higher win rate and also lost significantly fewer games than NEAT solutions. These improved generalization abilities were a result of HyperNEAT's ability to discover the necessary regularities in the geometry of the game. This observation was supported by examinations of the connectivity patterns of the most general HyperNEAT solutions, which were often smoother and more continuous than less general solutions.

Beyond board games, we hypothesized at the beginning of this chapter that indirect encodings should also be useful for tasks such as controlling a **quadruped robot** (figure 4.12*a*), taking advantage of the task's symmetry and regularities. For HyperNEAT, the positions of sensor and motor neurons within a quadruped body can be exploited to efficiently develop consistent gait patterns that rely on connectivity patterns unrelated to convolution (Clune, Stanley, Pennock, et al., 2011). Each leg can be viewed as a repeated module, with different gaits having different regularities themselves. For example, in a typical horse trot gait, the diagonal pairs of legs move forward at the same time, whereas in other gaits, such as the pace gait, the two legs on the same side move forward at the same time. The HyperNEAT **substrate** for this task is shown in figure 4.12*b*, and features three 2D sheets for the inputs, hidden layer, and output layer. Inputs on the substrate are arranged to reflect the geometry of the task, with each row receiving information about the state of a single leg (e.g., the current angle of the three joints of the leg, or a sensor that indicates if the leg is touching the ground). The output substrate also reflects the morphology of the robot, with the three elements in each row outputting the desired new joint angle.

It is interesting to look at the performance of indirect versus direct encodings across the continuum of regularity. For example, in the quadruped domain, the regularity of the problem can be decreased by introducing faulty joints, in which noise is added to the requested joint angle and the actual motor command that is sent. As expected, HyperNEAT's performance increased with increased task regularity, outperforming all other approaches (NEAT and **fixed-topology NEAT** (FT-NEAT), which is a variant of NEAT that has a fixed number of hidden nodes, which is the same as the number used in the HyperNEAT substrate), with no faulty joints or one faulty joint. When the problem was sufficiently irregular (8 and 12 faulty joint treatments), FT-NEAT and NEAT started to outperform HyperNEAT. The important lesson here is that the type of method to be used highly depends on the target domain and how many regularities there are to exploit.

Interestingly, going beyond pure quantitative results, the gaits produced by HyperNEAT were also often more regular and coordinated than those from NEAT. HyperNEAT often produced two types of gaits. In one of them, all legs moved forward in unison, which suggests that HyperNEAT repeated the same connectivity pattern for each leg. The other gait resembled more of a horse gallop gait, in which three legs moved together with the other leg moving in the opposite phase. This gait indicates that HyperNEAT can also produce regularities with variation; that is, one leg moves differently from the other three legs. These regularities were also reflected in the HyperNEAT-produced weight patterns. Figures 4.12*c*, *d* show the view of the same network from the front and the back, respectively. Observe the intricate and consistent geometric patterns of weight distribution, such as the inhibitory connections from input nodes directed toward the upper hidden nodes and excitatory connections aimed at the lower hidden nodes. Additionally, there is a notable regularity with variations, exemplified by the spread of inhibitory connections into the output nodes, which changes along both the x- and y-axes.

In summary, an indirect encoding such as HyperNEAT can offer great benefits, allowing relatively compact CPPNs with only a handful of connections to encode functional neural networks with millions of weights. In fact, even before DeepMind demonstrated that it is possible to learn to play Atari games from pixels (Mnih, Kavukcuoglu, Silver, et al., 2015), which has been a significant milestone in their early successes and shaping the landscape of deep reinforcement learning (RL), HyperNEAT was the first method used to train neural networks to play Atari games from pixels alone (Hausknecht, Lehman, Miikkulainen, et al., 2014).

However, HyperNEAT is also not a panacea for every task; it does perform best in domains where regularities can be exploited, but it works less well in domains with many irregularities. There have been attempts at combining the best properties of both direct and indirect encodings. One such method is **hybridized indirect and direct encoding** (HybrID), which discovers the regularities of the domain with an indirect encoding but then accounts for the irregularities through a fine-tuning phase that optimizes these weight parameters directly (Clune, Beckmann, Pennock, et al., 2011). Another, more biologically plausible solution is a combination of an indirect encoding with lifetime learning. While indirect encodings are effective for generating regular neural structures, they also serve as a strong foundation for local learning rules, such as the Hebbian rules introduced in section 4.2.3. And indeed, neuroevolutionary experiments showed that neural connectivity motifs that were indirectly encoded, and thus more regular, learned the best in a simple operant conditioning task (Tonelli and Mouret, 2013), compared to directly encoding those starting weights.

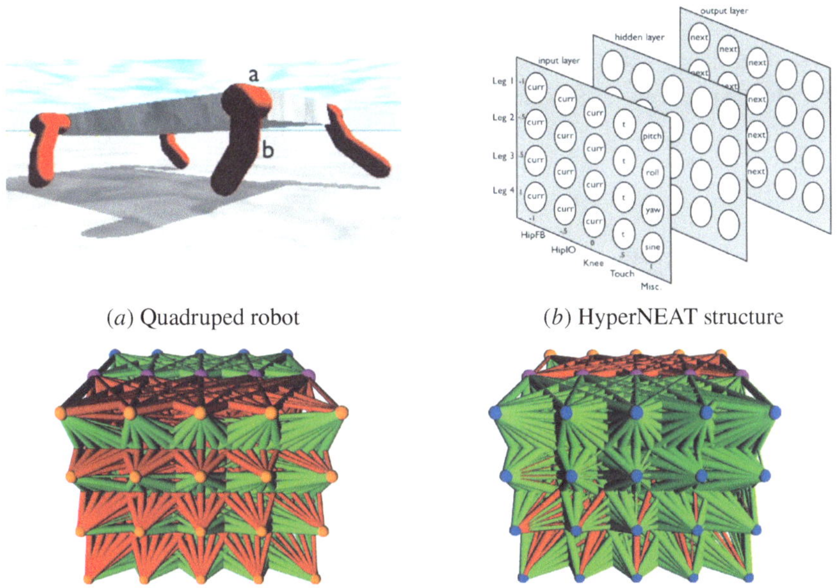

(*a*) Quadruped robot (*b*) HyperNEAT structure

(*c*) Front view (*b*) Back view

Figure 4.12: **A neural network controller for a quadruped robot produced by HyperNEAT.** The goal in this task is to find a neural network able to control a quadruped robot (*a*). The HyperNEAT substrate has three layers: input, hidden, and output (*b*). The input and output nodes are arranged in a way to take the task geometry into account. Panel (*c*) shows a front view of the network, and (*d*) a view from the back. Input nodes are shown in yellow, and output nodes in blue. Line thickness represents the magnitude of the weight. HyperNEAT autonomously discovers and exploits geometric regularities in the task, generating connectivity patterns that enable efficient quadruped locomotion without requiring the user to specify these patterns explicitly. Figures from Clune, Stanley, Pennock, et al. (2011). Videos at `https://neuroevolutionbook.com/demos`.

This strong relationship between indirect representations and synaptic plasticity underscores a crucial interplay between development and adaptability in biological systems. Synaptic plasticity interacts closely with the structured neural connectivity formed during development. This interplay allows for both the initial formation of efficient networks and their subsequent adaptation to new information and experiences. In biological systems, such connectivity patterns not only are shaped by genetic encoding but also are dynamically refined through experience-dependent plasticity. Understanding this connection could significantly impact the types of representations that will define the next generation of indirect encodings. However, despite its potential implications for developing more adaptable neural networks, this interplay between indirect encoding and synaptic plasticity has yet to receive substantial attention from the broader neuroevolutionary research community.

4.3.4 Multiagent HyperNEAT

A potential killer application for generative and developmental systems such as HyperNEAT is **multiagent learning**. In multiagent systems, multiple agents must learn behaviors that may be cooperative (share common goals) or competitive (have opposing goals). In fact, the quadruped robot example from section 4.3.3 can be viewed as a cooperative multiagent system, where each leg acts as an individual agent that must coordinate with the others to achieve efficient locomotion. Traditional multiagent approaches often treat each agent as a separate learning problem. For instance, in multiagent reinforcement learning, each agent, or each role, might be trained with its own policy (Busoniu, Babuska, and De Schutter, 2008). While this approach allows for specialization, it has two major drawbacks.

First, when agents are learned separately, they must each rediscover fundamental behaviors from scratch, called the **problem of reinvention**. Common skills that all agents should share, such as the ability to kick or pass in soccer, are learned independently, with no mechanism to transfer knowledge. Such learning is inefficient and can hinder coordination. It also complicates **credit assignment**: Whether the team succeeds or fails, it is unclear which agent's policy to credit or blame, since they were learned in isolation. In cooperative settings, this approach is likely to lead to suboptimal team performance because the agents may not develop complementary behaviors.

The second issue is **scalability**. As team size grows, learning separate policies becomes exponentially harder. The joint state-action space grows with each added agent. More agents mean more pairwise interactions to consider, and encoding each agent separately makes the search space explode. If a method cannot reuse policies and share structure easily, adding new agents requires significant retraining or search. This limitation is problematic for domains where team sizes are not fixed or where large teams are needed.

Multiagent HyperNEAT addresses these challenges in an elegant way, by representing a team of agents as a spatial pattern of policies rather than as separate, unrelated controllers (D'Ambrosio and Stanley, 2008). Each agent's policy can be associated with its position or role in a canonical team layout. In other words, there exists an underlying policy geometry describing how an agent's behavior should change according to its location or role in the team. For example, consider a soccer team: Players near their goal have defensive roles, and those toward the center and near the opponent's goal have more offensive roles. As the position shifts, the policy gradually changes from defensive to offensive in a smooth pattern. Multiagent HyperNEAT aims to encode that entire pattern in one genome, so the team's controllers are generated as coordinated variations of a shared strategy.

HyperNEAT's CPPN is well suited to encode such patterns. To extend HyperNEAT to multiagent teams, an extra dimension, z, is introduced to represent different agents. Essentially, imagine that the neural network substrate for a single agent's controller is replicated for each agent, but each replica is positioned at a different z-coordinate corresponding to that agent's role. The same CPPN is then queried to produce weights for every agent's network, but with the z-value indicating which agent's network is being wired. In this manner, one CPPN can generate distinct controllers for each agent, and yet they all originate from a common encoding. Figure 4.13 illustrates this concept: One CPPN produces a heterogeneous team by mapping different z-layers to different agent controllers. The z-axis effectively acts as a blueprint for team heterogeneity, allowing the CPPN to vary the policy smoothly across agents or keep them identical by ignoring z. Notably, the CPPN can be initialized with knowledge of symmetry along the z-axis (e.g., if left/right roles should mirror) by special symmetric functions, injecting prior knowledge of team structure (D'Ambrosio, Lehman, Risi, et al., 2010).

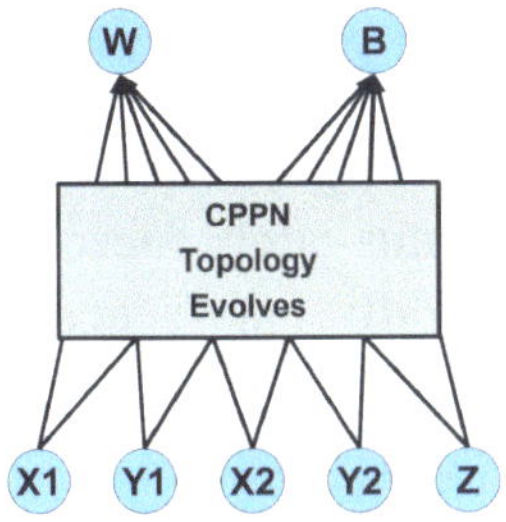

(*a*) CPPN

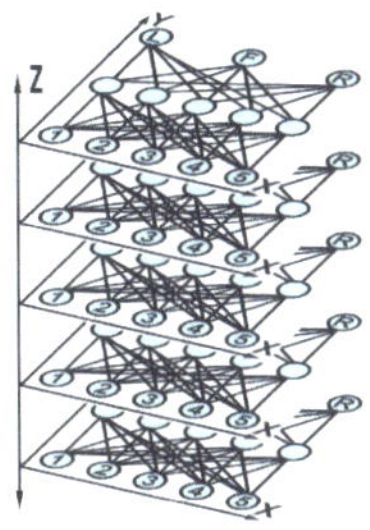

(*b*) Team substrate

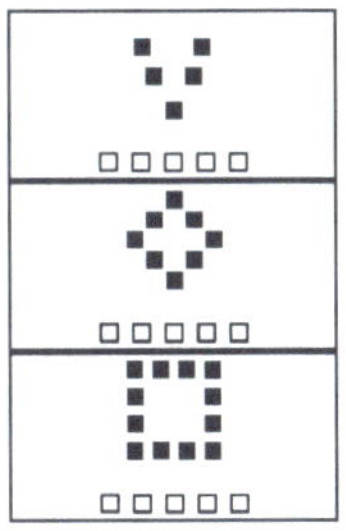

(*c*) Predator-prey task

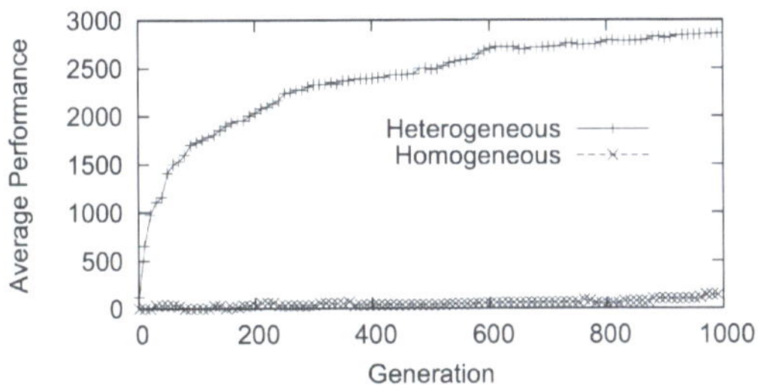

(*d*) Training performance

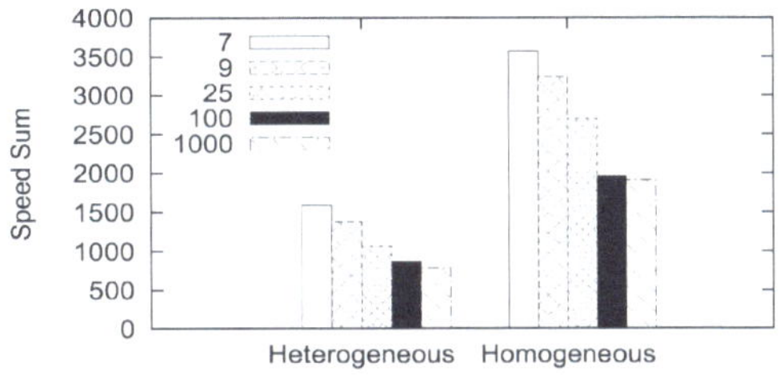

(*e*) Scaling performance

Figure 4.13: **Multiagent HyperNEAT encoding.** A single CPPN is used to generate distinct neural networks for each agent in a team. The CPPN (*a*) is augmented with an additional input z, indicating which agent's neural network is currently being created. The team substrate (*b*) consists of multiple copies of a single substrate replicated along the z-axis. By querying it, policies that vary smoothly across agents can be created. For example, in the predator-prey task (*c*), the z-coordinates for each predator (shown in white) are determined by their initial position, arranged along the horizontal dimension. The heterogeneous multiagent HyperNEAT approach achieved more effective solutions and did it faster than a homogeneous approach (*d*). When scaled to larger numbers of agents after training, the heterogeneous approach scaled significantly better (*e*). In this manner, effective teams of varying sizes can be discovered automatically. Figures from D'Ambrosio, Lehman, Risi, et al. (2010). Videos at `https://neuroevolutionbook.com/demos`.

Because all controllers are derived from one generative model, fundamental skills can be shared. The CPPN can output similar weight patterns for multiple agents (imparting a common skill) while also outputting variations for specific roles. This process addresses the reinvention problem: A basic strategy discovered for one agent can automatically appear in others. For example, if passing behavior is encoded as part of the CPPN's function, all relevant agents can pass without each evolving that skill independently. In essence, the genome encodes a continuum of heterogeneity from fully identical policies to fully distinct ones. Evolution can find the optimal point on that spectrum, distributing shared skills among agents and specializing where needed. This ability is a powerful representational advantage over direct encodings.

To evaluate the value of a multiagent encoding, multiagent HyperNEAT was compared to a homogeneous setup where the additional z-input was not provided to the CPPN, thus encoding the same neural network for each agent (figure 4.13*c*). Experiments were run in the predator-prey task where the predators had to coordinate to catch the prey. Importantly, while the predators are equipped with five range-finder sensors that detect nearby prey, they cannot detect other predators, making the task particularly challenging and demanding precise coordination. Heterogeneous teams discovered more efficient policies and converged faster than homogeneous teams, highlighting the advantages of a team-wide policy geometry (figure 4.13*d*). Homogeneous teams rarely succeeded in solving the task, further emphasizing the benefits of the policy diversity generated by multiagent HyperNEAT. The approach was able to discover sophisticated strategies such as corralling, where multiple predators surround the prey and gradually drive it toward the center. An exciting consequence of representing a team as a continuous policy geometry is the ability to scale team size on the fly. Since the CPPN is a function that can be queried at arbitrary points (including new z-coordinates), we can add new agents by sampling new points in the policy space. For instance, if a team is evolved with five predators, one can deploy more predators by assigning them appropriate new positions and using the CPPN to create their controllers, effectively interpolating the learned policy geometry. In other words, new policies are inserted by sampling between existing ones. Using this approach, performance can be scaled to larger teams of 1,000 agents without further training (figure 4.13*e*). This capability of learning once and deploying to different team size is a powerful feature of the multiagent HyperNEAT encoding and typically not available in methods that evolve a fixed number of agents. In practice, there are of course limits; extrapolating far beyond the training configuration can degrade performance if the CPPN was not evolved with varying sizes, but the approach is often surprisingly robust.

While the focus of this section was on indirect encoding of teams, the area of collective systems is a major focus in neuroevolution in general, as will be discussed in chapter 7. The next section addresses one of the drawbacks of the original HyperNEAT formulation: how to decide on the number and locations of hidden nodes automatically.

4.3.5 Evolvable Substrate HyperNEAT

While it is often clear how the locations of the inputs in a HyperNEAT substrate relate to the output units, and thus, where they should be placed (e.g., the range-finders of a robot should relate to the network's outputs that control its movement), how to decide on the position of the hidden nodes is less straightforward. A less obvious effect is that requiring a hidden node n to be at position (a, b), as specified in the original HyperNEAT, inadvertently demands that any weight pattern created by the CPPN must intersect exactly at position (a, b) with the appropriate weights. This means the CPPN in HyperNEAT has to align the correct weights precisely across all coordinates $(a, b, x2, y2)$ and $(x1, y1, a, b)$. However, this raises a question: Why enforce such a random constraint on weight locations? The CPPN might more easily represent the desired pattern slightly off the specified location, but this would not work with the constraints set by the user.

These limitations are addressed by an extension of HyperNEAT, called **evolvable substrate HyperNEAT** (ES-HyperNEAT; Risi and Stanley, 2012a). The basic idea behind ES-HyperNEAT is that the weight pattern generated by the CPPN should give some indication of where the hidden nodes should be placed and how many there should be. That is, areas in the four-dimensional (4D) hypercube that contain a lot of information should result in more points being chosen from these areas. Remember, each point in that 4D weight space is a connection in two dimensions.

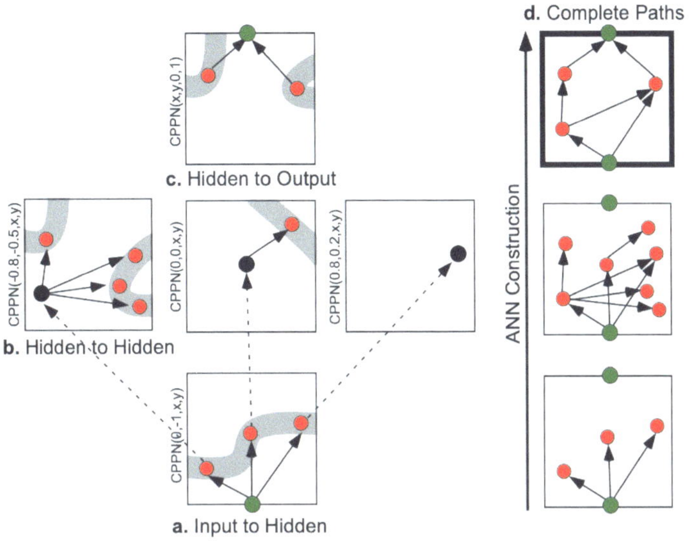

Figure 4.14: **Evolvable-Substrate HyperNEAT.** (*a*) Starting from the input nodes, ES-HyperNEAT analyzes sequences of 2D slices through the hypercube weight pattern to discover areas of high variance. This information is then used to determine which connections, and thereby nodes, should be expressed. The approach continues from the discovered hidden nodes (*b*) until some maximum depth has been reached. (*c*) Similarly, we start from the output nodes to determine to which hidden nodes they should be connected. (*d*) Once the approach has run a maximum number of iterations, or when no new nodes are discovered, the resulting neural network is pruned, removing any nodes that do not connect to both the inputs and outputs of the network. Thus, ES-HyperNEAT is able to fully determine the topology and weights of a neural network encoded by a CPPN. Figure from Risi and Stanley (2012a).

For example, take a hypercube whose weights are all uniform, meaning that CPPN($x1$, $y1$, $x2$, $y2$) = k for all different input combinations; it would not make much sense to express many connections if there is not much information in the underlying weight pattern. On the other hand, if the variance of the weight pattern is high in some regions, it might indicate that there is more information available, and thus more connections should be expressed. In ES-HyperNEAT, if a connection is chosen to be expressed, the nodes that it connects must therefore also be expressed. Which nodes to include thus becomes implicit in the question of which connections to include from the infinite set of potential connections encoded by the CPPN. By making the number and location of nodes depend on the CPPN-generated pattern, we give the system a "language"; that is, a way to increase or decrease the number of connections (and thus nodes) and change their location by varying the underlying pattern.

For this approach to work, it is useful to have a data structure that can represent space at variable levels of granularity. One such data structure is the **quadtree** (Samet, 1984), which has found successful applications in various fields, including pattern recognition and image encoding, and partitions a two-dimensional space by recursively subdividing it into four quadrants or regions. This process creates a subtree representation, where each decomposed region becomes a descendant with the original region as the parent. The recursive splitting continues until the desired resolution is achieved or until further

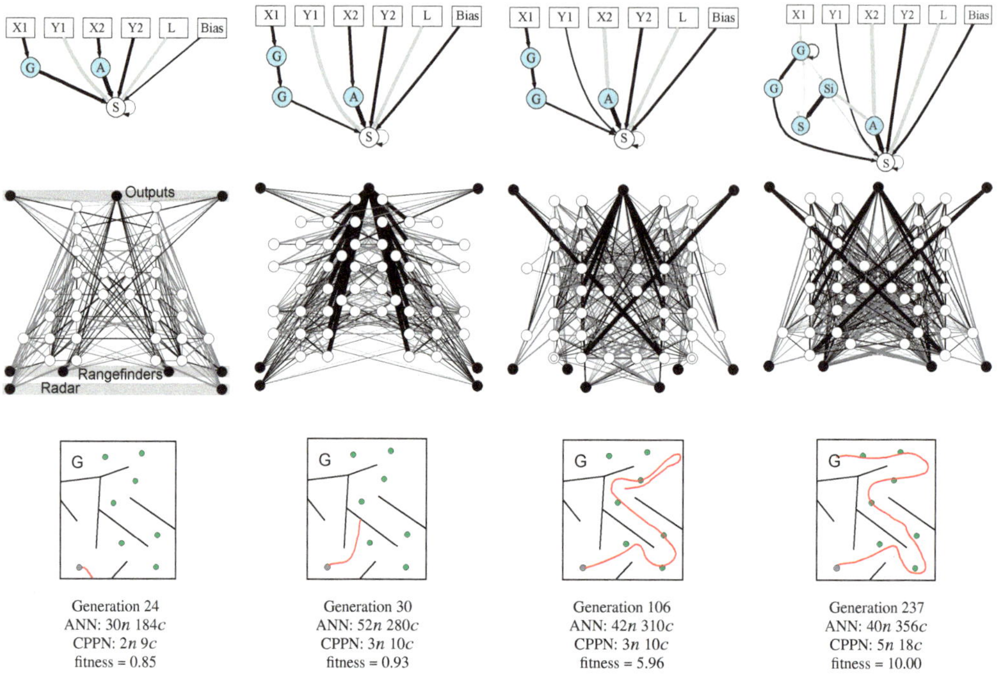

Figure 4.15: **ES-HyperNEAT example lineage.** Shown here are four milestones in one of the maze solution lineages. The CPPN is shown at the top, with the decoded neural network in the middle (CPPN activation functions are G=Gaussian, A=absolute value, S=sigmoid, Si=sine). In addition to the location of nodes, the CPPN also receives the length L of a connection as an additional input. The resulting maze navigation behavior is shown at the bottom, together with the number of nodes *n* and connections *c* in the neural network and in the CPPN. One can observe a gradual growth in the complexity of the CPPN, which increases the information in the underlying hypercube pattern and thus results in an increase in the number of ANN weights and neurons. ES-HyperNEAT outperforms the original HyperNEAT in this task because it can evolve networks with limited connectivity, elaborate on existing network structure, and compensate for the movement of information within the hypercube. Figures from Risi and Stanley (2012a).

subdivision becomes unnecessary, indicating that additional resolution would not reveal new information.

ES-HyperNEAT works as follows: For each input neuron at position $(p1, p2)$, apply the quadtree to analyze regions for their variance of the 2-dimensional sub-slice through the hypercube spanned by CPPN$(p1, p2, x2, y2)$ (figure 4.14). In areas of high variance, as detected by the quadtree algorithm, connections and their corresponding nodes are created. The process is then repeated from those discovered hidden nodes until some maximum depth is reached, after which only the neurons are kept that have a path to an input and an output neuron. After this process is repeated for each input (and output) node, the ANN is constructed and can be applied to the task at hand.

A good domain to evaluate this approach should test its ability to build and elaborate on previously discovered **stepping stones**. While it is easy to see how a method such as NEAT would be able to accomplish this task, it is less obvious how an indirect encoding would fare. For example, the original HyperNEAT has the tendency to often produce fully connected networks, which makes it harder to elaborate on intermediate milestones since all connections are already used for the current partial solutions. On the other hand, ES-HyperNEAT should be able to do so because it can increase the number of nodes and connections in the substrate.

One such task is called the **hard maze**, originally introduced to study more exploratory search methods such as novelty search (section 5.3). Here, the agent has range-finder sensors to detect walls and pie-slice radar sensors that fire when the goal is within the agent's corresponding pie-slice sensor (figure 4.15). To encourage the agent to discover the intermediate stepping stones, the original task was modified to specifically reward the agent for traversing the green-way points (which are not visible to the agent).

As hypothesized, the original HyperNEAT indeed struggled with this task, and only found solutions in 45% of 20 independent evolutionary runs. ES-HyperNEAT, on the other hand, was able to find a solution in 95% of all runs. As shown in figure 4.15, analysis of an example lineage showed that ES-HyperNEAT was able to elaborate on previously discovered stepping stones. This figure shows four milestone ANNs (middle row), together with the underlying CPPN (top) and the resulting agent trajectory (bottom). Interestingly, all the ANNs display common geometrical features, which were kept during evolution, such as the symmetric network topology. While larger changes occur earlier in evolution, the networks from generations 106 and 237 show a clear, holistic resemblance to each other, with strong connections to the three output neurons. These results also demonstrate that ES-HyperNEAT is able to encode a larger network with a compact CPPN. In fact, the solution ANN with 40 hidden nodes and 256 connections was encoded by a CPPN with only five nodes and 18 connections.

In addition to the maze navigation domain, the approach was evaluated on a **dual task** designed to test **multimodal behavior**. This task combined two independent scenarios: (1) a navigation task, where the agent had to move from a starting point to a goal using only its range-finder sensors to detect walls; and (2) a food-gathering task, where the agent relied solely on pie-slice sensors acting as a compass to locate and collect randomly placed food items. The agent's fitness was defined as the average of its performance in both tasks, and a solution required simultaneously solving both; that is, navigating successfully and collecting all food items.

The results showed that ES-HyperNEAT solved the dual task in all 20 runs. By comparison, the best fixed-substrate HyperNEAT setup succeeded in only 13 of 20 runs. ES-HyperNEAT also produced more targeted connectivity between neurons and did so with significantly smaller CPPNs, indicating both greater efficiency and better support for multimodal problem-solving than the original HyperNEAT approach.

4.3.6 General Hypernetworks and Dynamic Indirect Encodings

HyperNEAT and its variations are particular examples of a family of algorithms now called **hypernetworks** (Ha, Dai, and Le, 2017). Hypernetworks generalize HyperNEAT to any approach in which one network (termed the "hypernetwork") generates the weights of another target neural network. The hypernetwork is typically a smaller network designed to learn a mapping from a low-dimensional input space to the high-dimensional weight space of the target network. The target network is the actual network that performs the

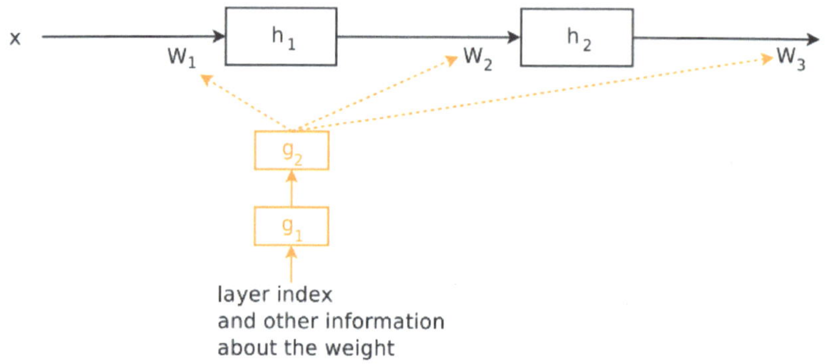

Figure 4.16: **Static hypernetwork.** In this example, the hypernetwork (shown in orange) generates the weights of each layer of the main network (shown in black) by conditioning the network on layer embeddings. These embeddings are treated as learnable parameters optimized during training. In this manner, they enable approximate weight sharing both within and across layers of the main network. Figure from Ha, Dai, and Le (2017).

main task, such as classification, regression, or controlling an agent. Pioneering work on hypernetworks goes back to the early 1990s, where Schmidhuber (1992) introduced the idea of **fast weight programmers** , where a "slow" neural network trained through gradient descent learned the "fast" weights of another network.

Mathematically, given input x to the target network, hypernetwork H takes auxiliary input z and outputs weights θ_{TN} for the target network. This relationship is expressed as $\theta_{\mathrm{TN}} = H(z)$. The target network then uses these weights to perform its task, represented as $y = T(x; \theta_{\mathrm{TN}})$, where x is the input to the target network, z is the auxiliary input to the hypernetwork, θ_{TN} are the weights generated by the hypernetwork, and y is the output of the target network.

In the previous sections on HyperNEAT, we saw a special case of such a hypernetwork, which is geometrically aware; that is, the auxiliary inputs (x, y) give nodes locations in space. Additionally, HyperNEAT typically relies on training CPPNs with NEAT (CPPN-NEAT). Other approaches, such as **compressed network search** (Koutník, Gomez, and Schmidhuber, 2010) do not employ CPPN-NEAT but instead use **discrete cosine transform** (DCT) to compress the weights of a larger weight matrix into a smaller number of DCT coefficients, resembling the popular JPEG compression. It is also possible to combine evolving the neural architecture with gradient-based weight training, which was demonstrated in an approach called **differentiable pattern producing networks** (DPPNs; Fernando, Banarse, Reynolds, et al., 2016).

Building on these earlier ideas, modern variants of hypernetworks can also be trained end-to-end through a gradient descent–based training approach (Ha, Dai, and Le, 2017). This work strikes a balance between the compressed network search approach, where a DCT prior limits the type of weight matrices that can be produced, and the HyperNEAT approach, which requires evolving both the architecture and weights through NEAT (adding significant complexity for many practical problems). These hypernetworks generate the weights of feedforward networks one layer at a time by conditioning the hypernetwork on the specific layer embedding (figure 4.16). Layer embeddings can be fixed or they can

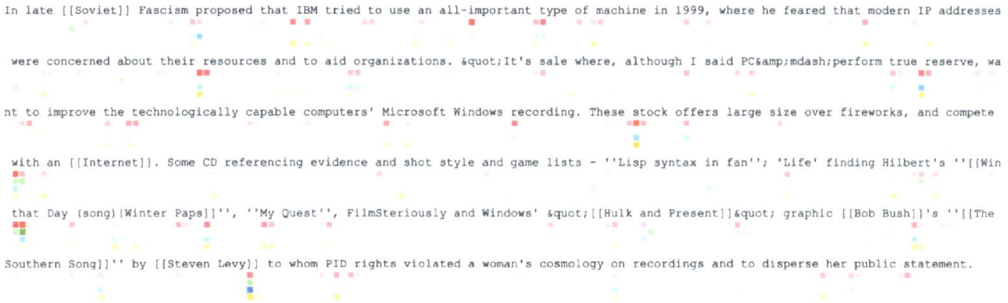

Figure 4.17: **Application of dynamic hypernetworks for handwriting sequence generation.** In the dynamic indirect encoding approach, the hypernetwork takes as input the internal state of the neural network and its previous action to dynamically generate the weights of the RNN target network (shown as four different colors). In this manner, the dynamic hypernetwork approach enables the model to adapt its parameters on the fly, allowing for highly flexible and context-aware handwriting generation. Figure from Ha, Dai, and Le (2017).

also be learned, allowing the system itself to learn approximate weight sharing within and across layers. This approach was able to produce the weights for a deep convolutional network for CIFAR-10 classification, with only a small decrease in classification accuracy but a drastic reduction in the number of trainable model parameters. Interestingly, when applying the hypernetwork approach to create the weights for a target network that was fully connected, it was able to learn convolutional-like filters when the location of the target weight and the x, y-location of each input pixel was provided.

Importantly, hypernetworks offer the intriguing ability to serve as a **dynamic indirect encoding**, in which the produced weight pattern is allowed to change over time and made dependent on the inputs for the task at hand. For example, a hypernetwork could be trained to produce the weights of a **recurrent neural network** (RNN) target network for handwriting sequence generation (figure 4.17), which would change over time and be dependent on the agent's internal state and the inputs (the previous output of the RNN). In other words, the hypernetwork was taking a low-dimensional representation of the input character and the hidden state of the RNN as inputs, outputting the weights for the next prediction step. This approach allowed the RNN to dynamically adapt its parameters based on the current context and is a good demonstration of how concepts from neuroevolution are being effectively combined with those from the traditional machine learning field.

In summary, hypernetwork-like approaches can significantly reduce the number of trainable parameters while still performing well across different domains. However, it is also clear that their full potential hasn't been fully realized yet and likely depends on combining these techniques with more open-ended search methods (chapter 9) and with life-time learning approaches (chapter 12) that can take advantage of the encoded regularities for fast adaptation.

The concept of dynamic indirect encodings is closely linked to neural self-attention, which will be explored in section 4.4. Self-attention has served as the foundation for many recent breakthroughs in deep learning, most notably in the transformer architecture. In this approach, larger input-dependent weight matrices are created through the outer product of two smaller matrices called "keys" and "values." As will be seen next, this type of indirect encoding allows for encoding matrix **A** of size $O(n^2)$ using only an $O(d)$ number of genotype parameters.

4.4 Self-attention as Dynamic Indirect Encoding

We previously explored the concept of hypernetworks, illustrating their role as indirect encoding methods where one neural network, the hypernetwork, generates the weights for another network, termed the **target network**. Typically, hypernetworks generate these weights without directly considering the specific input x to the target network. Transitioning from this, we introduce the concept of self-attention mechanisms, which embody a sophisticated method of dynamically generating contextual relationships within data. Unlike hypernetworks, **self-attention** mechanisms inherently account for input x during the processing phase, tailoring the computational focus in a data-driven manner. This capability not only allows self-attention to act as a form of indirect encoding but also enhances it to be a dynamic encoding process. The dynamic nature arises from its ability to adjust the internal model representations in response to the particularities of the input data at any given moment, thereby offering a more flexible and context-aware approach to encoding information.

4.4.1 Background on Self-attention

The **attention mechanism** (Vaswani, Shazeer, Parmar, et al., 2017), a groundbreaking innovation in the field of neural networks, particularly in natural language processing (NLP), has revolutionized how models handle and interpret sequential data like text and time series. At its core, attention allows a model to focus on different parts of the input sequence when producing each part of the output sequence, mimicking the human cognitive process of focusing more on certain aspects while perceiving or processing information. The introduction of attention mechanisms in transformer-based architectures like **large language models** (LLMs) has led to substantial improvements in various complex tasks in language understanding and generation.

While modern attention mechanisms can adopt various configurations, including positional encoding and scaling, their fundamental concept can be described by the following equations:

$$A = \text{softmax}\big(\frac{1}{\sqrt{d}}(X_q W_q)(X_k W_k)^\top\big) \tag{4.3}$$

$$Y = A \times (X_q W_v), \tag{4.4}$$

where $W_q, W_k, W_v \in \mathcal{R}^{d_{in} \times d}$ are the matrices that map the input matrix $X \in \mathcal{R}^{n \times d_{in}}$ to components called **query**, **key**, and **value** (i.e., query $= X_q W_q$, key $= X_k W_k$, value $= X_q W_v$). Since the average value of the dot product grows with the vector's dimension, each entry in the query and the key matrices can be disproportionally too large if d is large. To counter this, the factor $\frac{1}{\sqrt{d}}$ is used to normalize the inputs. The attention matrix $A \in \mathcal{R}^{n \times n}$ is obtained by applying a nonlinear activation function, typically a softmax operation, to each row of the matrix. This mechanism is referred to as **self-attention** when $X_q = X_k$; otherwise, it is known as **cross-attention**.

4.4.2 Self-attention as a Form of Indirect Encoding

As we described previously, indirect encodings represent the weights of a neural network, the phenotype, with a smaller set of genotype parameters. How a genotype encodes a larger solution space is defined by the indirect encoding algorithm. HyperNEAT encodes the weights of a large network via a coordination-based CPPN-NEAT, while **compressed network search** (Koutník, Cuccu, Schmidhuber, et al., 2013) uses the **discrete cosine transform** (DCT) to compress the weights of a large weight matrix into a small number of DCT coefficients, similar to JPEG compression. Due to compression, the space of possible weights that an indirect encoding scheme can produce is only a small subspace of all possible combinations of weights. This constraint on the solution space enforces an inductive bias into the phenotype. While this bias determines the types of tasks that the network is naturally suited to doing, it also restricts the network to a subset of all possible tasks that an unconstrained phenotype can (in theory) perform.

Similarly, self-attention enforces a structure on the attention weight matrix A that makes it input-dependent. If we remove the query and the key transformation matrices, the outer product $X_q X_k^{\top}$ defines an association matrix where the elements are large when two distinct input terms are in agreement. This type of structure forced in A has been shown to be suited for associative tasks where the downstream agent has to learn the relationships among unrelated items. If this sounds familiar, this is not surprising; we have seen a similar mechanism already in **Hebbian learning** (section 4.2.3). Self-attention and Hebbian learning both emphasize correlation and amplify related signals: Hebbian through permanent weight changes, attention through temporary, **context-dependent weights**. The similarity matrix in attention acts like a Hebbian correlation matrix, but instead of structural updates, attention applies these correlations on the fly, making it a dynamic mechanism.

Because the outer product $X_q X_k^{\top}$ has no free parameters, the corresponding matrix A will not be suitable for arbitrary tasks beyond association. The role of the small query and key transformation matrices (i.e., W_q and W_k) allows A to be modified for the task at hand. W_q and W_k can therefore be viewed as the **genotype** of this indirect encoding method. $W_q, W_k \in \mathcal{R}^{d_{\text{in}} \times d}$ are the matrices that contain the free parameters; and d_{in} is a constant depending on the inputs. The number of free parameters in self-attention is therefore on the order of $O(d)$, while the number of parameters in A is in the order of $O(n^2)$. This form of indirect encoding allows us to represent the phenotype with a much smaller set of trainable genotype parameters. Additionally, this type of indirect encoding dynamically adapts to various inputs.

Building on the concepts discussed in section 4.3.6, we formulated the output of a hypernetwork H as $\theta_{\text{TN}} = H(z)$, where θ_{TN} are the parameters for a target network (TN) and z is an auxiliary input (e.g., layer index). In a similar vein, self-attention can be conceptualized as $\theta_{\text{TN}} = \text{SA}(x)$, where x is the target network's input. This adaptation allows for a more flexible and responsive model configuration, tailored to specific input characteristics and demands.

Furthermore, the aforementioned dynamic adaptation mechanism in self-attention, which allows real-time modulation of connection strengths based on input, also echoes the concept of **fast weights** (Schmidhuber, 1992), where the idea of rapidly adaptable weights that could temporarily store information over short sequences was introduced. Similarly, self-attention leverages dynamic encoding to adjust attention matrix A, effectively using W_{q} and W_{k} to reshape the network's responses based on the input characteristics. This adaptability is critical for tasks where the relevance of specific input features varies markedly across contexts, akin to how fast weights facilitate short-term synaptic plasticity for rapid learning adaptation.

This comparison between attention mechanisms and classical indirect encoding suggests that both approaches may be tapping into a shared underlying principle; that is, the use of compact and flexible representations to dynamically generate context-sensitive behavior. While attention mechanisms were developed independently within the supervised learning paradigm and indirect encodings grew out of evolutionary and biological inspirations, their convergence reflects a broader computational strategy, which aims to reduce dimensionality while retaining expressiveness and adaptability. Rather than being entirely distinct, these approaches may represent complementary rediscoveries of a general design principle.

4.4.3 Self-attention Based Agents

AttentionAgent (Tang, Nguyen, and Ha, 2020) is inspired by the concept of inattentional blindness—a phenomenon where the brain, when engaged in effortful tasks, focuses its attention on task-relevant elements while temporarily ignoring other stimuli. Using this principle, the agent employs an attention-based mechanism for video game play, improving interpretability through pixel-space reasoning, as illustrated in figure 4.18.

This approach is grounded in self-attention (specifically, $X_{\mathrm{k}} = X_{\mathrm{q}}$), with cropped game screen image patches serving as inputs. Key modifications to the attention mechanism in AttentionAgent include: (1) condensing the attention matrix into an importance vector, and (2) omitting the value component in favor of extracting the top-k ($k = 10$ in the paper) most significant patch features as output Y. This extraction is achieved through sorting and pruning, detailed in figure 4.19 and the paragraphs that follow.

Concretely speaking, given an input game screen, AttentionAgent segments the input image into small square patches in a fashion similar to how a 2D convolution layer works. It then flattens these patches and treats the output with shape $N \times CM^2$ as the input $X \in \mathcal{R}^{n \times d_{\mathrm{in}}}$ (figure 4.19, left). Here N is the number of patches, C is the number of channels in the image, and M is the length/width of each patch; therefore, $n = N$ and $d_{\mathrm{in}} = CM^2$.

Upon receiving this transformed data, the self-attention module follows equation 4.3, we mentioned in section 4.4.1, to get the attention matrix A of shape (N, N). After the softmax, each row in A sums to 1, so the attention matrix can be viewed as the results from a voting mechanism between the patches. If each patch can distribute fractions of a total of 1 vote to other patches (including itself), row i thus shows how patch i has voted, and column j gives the votes that patch j acquired from others. In this interpretation, entry (i, j) in A is regarded as how important patch j is from patch i's perspective. Taking sums

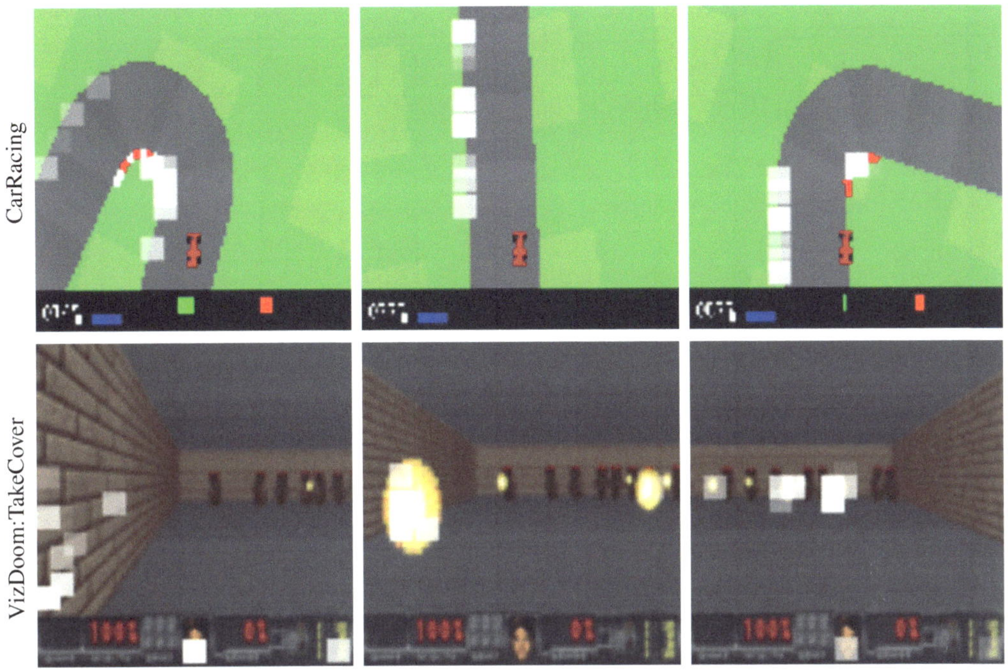

Figure 4.18: **Demonstrating indirect encoding in AttentionAgent for enhanced interpretability.** White patches on the game screens signify the agent's focus areas, with their opacity indicating the relative importance of each patch. The approach was tested on two games: CarRacing requires top-down car racing from a pixel-observation environment; in the DoomTakeCover environment, enemy monsters spawn randomly along the opposite wall and shoot fireballs, which the player has to learn to avoid. Agents are able to selectively focus on a small, survival-critical portion of their visual input, resulting in interpretable agents that are both compact and more generalizable. In CarRacing, the agent primarily attends to road boundaries but shifts its focus to upcoming turns before adjusting its heading. In DoomTakeCover, the agent concentrates on fireballs and monsters, aligning well with human intuition. Figures from Tang, Nguyen, and Ha (2020). Videos at `https://neuroevolutionbook.com/demos`.

along the columns of A results in a vector that summarizes the total votes acquired by each patch, and this vector is called the **patch importance vector** (figure 4.19, middle). Unlike the self-attention introduced earlier, AttentionAgent relies solely on the patch importance vector and does not utilize the value component of self-attention.

Finally, based on the patch importance vector, AttentionAgent picks the K patches with the highest importance and throws away the rest. It passes the indices of these K patches into a feature retrieval function, which returns the features extracted from the corresponding patches. These features are then fed into a neural network based controller to output the appropriate actions that the agent should take (figure 4.19, right). By discarding patches of low importance, AttentionAgent becomes temporarily blind to other signals, which effectively creates a bottleneck that forces it to focus on patches only if they are critical to the task. Once learned, it is possible to visualize the K patches and have the agent's reasoning interpreted in the pixel space. Given the non-differentiable nature of the sorting and the pruning operations, AttentionAgent is optimized using CMA-ES.

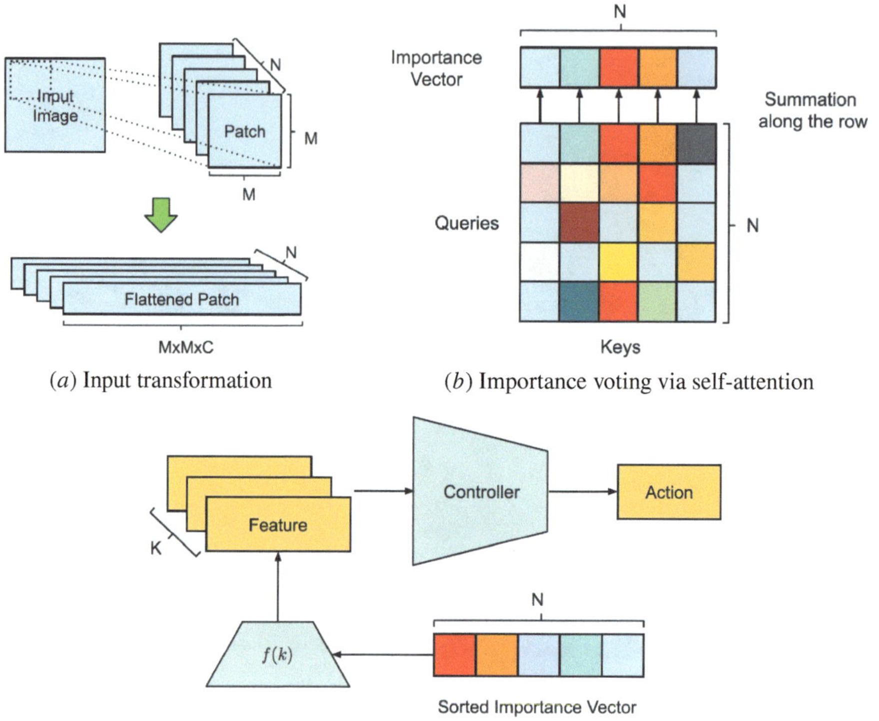

(a) Input transformation

(b) Importance voting via self-attention

(c) Patch selection and feature retrieval

Figure 4.19: **Method overview of AttentionAgent.** Key modifications to the attention mechanism include (1) condensing the attention matrix into an importance vector, and (2) omitting the value component in favor of extracting the top-k most significant patch features as the output Y. (a) After basic image pre-processing, patches are extracted from the input image using a sliding window of size $M \times M$ and stride S. The resulting shape of the output is (N, M, M, C), where N is the number of patches, M is the height/width of each patch, and C is the number of channels in the input image. The data is then flattened. (b) The flattened patches are projected into Keys and Queries and the attention matrix (of shape $N \times N$) is calculated. Softmax is applied to each row. The sum of elements in each row of the matrix gives the patch importance vector. (c) The patch importance vector is sorted, and the indices of the top K patches are extracted. The patch indices are then mapped to the corresponding features and given as input to the controller to get the action. In this manner, the architecture allows the agent to focus on information that is critical to the task at hand. Figures from Tang, Nguyen, and Ha (2020).

The major building block of AttentionAgent is the **self-attention mechanism**. Although slightly modified in that context (i.e., the value component is not utilized), as we have established previously, the indirect-encoding nature of the mechanism remains the same. More explicitly, the patch importance vector is based on the attention matrix A, which is the phenotype that is controlled by the two parameter matrices $W_{\text{q}}, W_{\text{k}}$, the genotype. The advantages of employing indirect encoding in this context are clear: First, for an input image of size n (which can be substantial, such as 100px $\times$ 100px, translating to tens of thousands of pixels), the attention matrix spans a space of size $O(n^2)$. Conversely, $W_{\text{q}}, W_{\text{k}}$ transition image patches from $d_{\text{in}} = 3$ (representing RGB colors) to a lower feature dimension $d \ll n$, resulting in a more manageable size of $O(d)$. Despite this significant

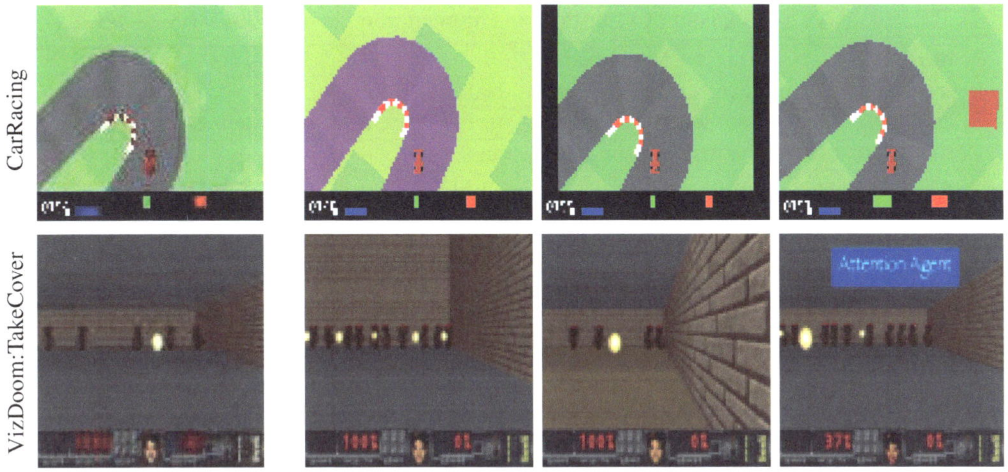

(*a*) Agent observations (*b*) Modified observations

Figure 4.20: **Visual variations to the CarRacing and VizDoom:TakeCover environments.** (*a*) The original agent observations in each environment. (*b*) Three modifications in each environment: CarRacing: (1) color perturbation, (2) vertical frames, and (3) a background blob; VizDoom:TakeCover: (1) higher walls, (2) different floor texture, and (3) hovering text. Because of the dynamic adaptive capability of self-attention, AttentionAgent is unaffected by these different types of external distractions. Figures from Tang, Nguyen, and Ha (2020).

reduction in representation space, the inductive bias inherent in the model's design enables the genotype to effectively map to a set of phenotypes that are pertinent to the task at hand.

The AttentionAgent approach was evaluated on two tasks. The first one is **CarRacing-v0**, a 2D continuous control benchmark: The agent must drive through procedurally generated tracks from a top-down perspective. The car is controlled with three continuous commands (gas, steer, and brake). The game provides a 64×64 RGB image at each time step. The agent is rewarded for covering track tiles efficiently while minimizing time and avoiding leaving the track. The second task is **DoomTakeCover**, a 3D first-person survival challenge that is part of the **VizDoom** open-source AI research platform (Kempka, Wydmuch, Runc, et al., 2016), repurposing the classic video game Doom (id Software, 1993). In this task, the agent views the world from a first-person 3D perspective and must survive by dodging fireballs launched by monsters. As time progresses, more monsters appear, with the episode ending when the player dies. The only actions available are strafing left, right, or standing still, and the agent receives a small reward (+1) for every frame that it stays alive. The visual input again consists of 64×64 RGB images.

AttentionAgent was able to solve these complex problems with only a few thousand parameters, unlike other methods, which may require hundreds of thousands or even millions of parameters. The dynamic adaptive capability of self-attention allowed AttentionAgent to flexibly adjust its decision-making based on the received inputs, resulting in more robust decisions that are not susceptible to external distractions such as changed background colors or hovering text on the screen (see figure 4.20 for examples).

To summarize, the attention mechanism exemplifies the principles of indirect encoding by representing relationships and interactions in a compact, abstract manner. Instead of

Table 4.1: **A Comparison of attention mechanism and classical indirect encoding.**

Feature	Attention Mechanism	Indirect Encoding
Representation	Relationships as dynamic weights	Rules or compressed instructions
Scalability	Scales with input length	Scales with system complexity
Decoding process	Weighted sum for context vectors	Generative or constructive process
Abstraction focus	Relevant relationships dynamically	High-level patterns / reusable modules

explicitly modeling all possible connections within an input, attention dynamically encodes relevance through weights that guide the construction of context-sensitive representations. This mechanism shares key attributes with classical indirect encoding, such as scalability, generalization, and adaptability, making it a modern realization of these longstanding principles. Table 4.1 summarizes the comparison, which highlights how attention encapsulates the essence of indirect encoding while introducing innovations tailored to modern ML problems.

In progressing through the book, it will become clear that the same underlying concepts, such as encoding principles, can be manifested in diverse ways across different systems. Just as indirect encoding enables the discovery of varied designs in evolutionary systems, ML methods can also benefit from mechanisms that foster diversity in representations and solutions, which is the topic of chapter 5.

4.5 Chapter Review Questions

1. **Direct versus indirect encoding:** What is the primary difference between direct and indirect encodings in neuroevolution? Why is indirect encoding particularly advantageous for tasks requiring large and complex neural networks?

2. **Biological analogy:** How does the process of morphogenesis in biology inspire the concept of indirect encodings in neuroevolution? Provide an example of a biological principle that aligns with the goals of indirect encoding.

3. **Regularity in neural networks:** Why is the concept of regularity, such as symmetry and repetition with variation, important in indirect encodings? How does this principle enhance the efficiency and functionality of evolved solutions?

4. **Applications of indirect encodings:** How can indirect encodings be applied to a task such as evolving a quadrupedal robot controller? Discuss how they can use patterns and symmetries without manual intervention.

5. **Challenges of direct encoding:** Why is NEAT limited to smaller networks, and how do indirect encodings address this limitation? Provide an example illustrating how indirect encodings can simplify the representation of a complex neural network.

6. **Hypernetworks overview:** What distinguishes hypernetworks from traditional local interaction-based indirect encodings? How does the "one-shot" generation of phenotypes make hypernetworks different from development-based approaches?

7. **CPPNs in neuroevolution:** How do CPPNs leverage geometric space and function composition to generate complex patterns? Provide an example of a regularity that CPPNs can encode effectively.

8. **HyperNEAT substrate:** Explain how HyperNEAT utilizes neuron positions in a geometric space to generate connectivity patterns. Why is this approach particularly advantageous for tasks involving spatial regularities like controlling a quadrupedal robot?

9. **Strengths and limitations:** In what types of tasks do HyperNEAT and CPPNs perform better compared to direct encodings like NEAT? Conversely, what are the limitations of these indirect encodings when applied to irregular or noisy domains?

10. **Self-attention:** Describe the relationship between self-attention and indirect encodings. How does AttentionAgent use this principle to process high-dimensional visual input efficiently and interpretably? What advantages does this indirect encoding approach offer in terms of parameter efficiency and robustness?

Chapter 5

Utilizing Diversity

A most remarkable outcome of biological evolution is the tremendous diversity of solutions that it has produced. There is life in a large variety of environments: Organisms thrive in extreme heat, and cold, thin atmosphere and deep ocean pressure, on large and small scales, based on a variety of energy sources and chemical building blocks. The mechanisms that produce such diversity make it possible to both construct complex solutions over time and to adapt to the changing world. As a matter of fact, a new challenge can often be met by small modifications to already existing solutions, leading to the observation that evolution is a tinkerer (Jacob, 1977).

The same is true of computational evolution: Generating and maintaining diversity makes it possible to solve harder problems. Diversity does not arise naturally in most evolutionary methods; it requires special mechanisms. Such methods usually focus on **genetic diversity**; however, with neuroevolution, **behavioral diversity** has an important role as well. This perspective leads to methods of balancing performance and diversity objectives, as will be discussed in this chapter.

5.1 Genetic Diversity

Evolutionary computation is often formalized as a process of finding an optimum in a fitness landscape. The process starts with an initial population that is widespread on the landscape and gradually converges around the highest peaks in it. In this sense, loss of diversity is an essential part of the process: It allows allocating search resources where they matter the most, eventually refining the solutions so that the best ones can be found reliably and accurately.

However, the process may sometimes converge too soon, before all the promising peak areas have been discovered. Some of the best solutions may have narrow basins and may thus be missed. Such premature convergence is difficult to detect and guard against. Also, if the problem is dynamic (i.e., the fitness landscape changes over time), the converged population cannot keep up. Once the population has converged, there is little hope of finding anything better, or anything new.

The reason for this is that the most powerful and unique mechanism of evolutionary search, recombination, no longer works in a converged population. If all solutions are similar, recombining them generates nothing new, and progress stops. Mutation still remains, and can in principle create new material. However, without an effective crossover, the process is essentially reduced to **random search**.

Thus, most evolutionary computation methods today are in direct conflict with diversity. The methods aim at making progress in a greedy manner, with a strong selection that converges quickly. As will be discussed in section 9.1.1, this is not the case in biological evolution. The selection is weak; many genetic changes are neutral and remain in the population for a long time. Slowing the process in this manner may result in more diversity and creativity. This is also an option in evolutionary computation, but it has not yet been fully explored. Taking advantage of **weak selection**, **neutrality**, and **deep time** is an interesting direction for the future.

The simplest approach to coping with premature convergence is to increase the **mutation rate**. If it is done early enough, it may give crossover enough material to operate. However, this material is essentially random and, at large enough levels, will undermine evolutionary search. Another straightforward approach is to extend the current population with an **archive** of representative past individuals. The archive ensures that diversity is not lost, but it is infeasible to grow the archive indefinitely, and it is difficult to decide which individuals should be included in it.

Another brute-force but effective approach is **delta-coding** (Gomez and Miikkulainen, 1997; Whitley, Mathias, and Fitzhorn, 1991). If evolution stagnates with no further increases in fitness, the current population champion is used to create a population of Δ-chromosomes; that is, differences from the current best solution. This population is then evolved further, with solutions formed by adding the Δ-values to the best solutions. Delta-coding can be applied multiple times, with successive populations representing differences from the previous best solution. Thus, if evolution stagnates due to premature convergence, delta-coding may get it moving again.

In this manner, evolutionary computation relies on mechanisms that are added to search for the purpose of **maintaining diversity**. The first challenge in building such mechanisms is to measure diversity. At the level of genetic encodings, it is often possible through a distance metric between genomes. They are often vectors of values, so Euclidean distance (L2) is often sufficient. Manhattan distance (L1), Hamming distance, or edit distance, may also work in various cases. With such a distance metric, diversity can be measured as the average distance between genomes in the population.

Diversity measures can be further focused on a local area of the space, or k-nearest neighbors. Such an approach is useful in case it is important to identify which individuals in the population contribute to diversity more than others—those individuals can then be kept in the population or the archive longer.

Several methods have been developed to take advantage of these measures. In **crowding** (De Jong, 1975), new individuals are allowed to replace existing individuals that are similar to them, or their parents. Note that this mechanism does not drive the creation of diversity, but rather slows convergence: It is not as easy for similar individuals to take over the population.

Section 3.3, on NEAT, already described one mechanism that can help promote diversity: **fitness sharing**. In fitness sharing (Goldberg and Richardson, 1987), the actual fitness of an individual is adjusted based on how similar it is to other individuals in the population. More specifically, the fitness $f(x)$ of individual x is adjusted by

$$f'(x) = \frac{f(x)}{s(x)}. \tag{5.1}$$

The similarity metric s is e.g.,

$$s(x) = \sum_{j=1}^{n} d(x, y_j), \tag{5.2}$$

where the distance $d(x, y_j)$ is taken over all n members y_j of the population. In this manner, the fitness is reduced for individuals that are similar to many other individuals in the population. The adjustment makes them less likely to be chosen as parents and more likely to be discarded, thus slowing convergence. The similarity metric is expensive to calculate. It can be made more practical by reducing the calculation to a local neighborhood or a sampling of the population.

Fitness sharing in some domains can be implemented implicitly, avoiding the extra computation. In particular in **cooperative coevolution** (discussed in detail in section 7.1), solutions are constructed by combining individual population members into a single structure, such as a neural network composed of several neurons (Moriarty and Miikkulainen, 1997; Potter and De Jong, 2000). The entire solution is evaluated for fitness; the individual's fitness is the average fitness of all solutions in which it participated. It turns out that good solutions are usually composed of diverse individuals. If, for instance, a neural network is put together from a single neuron cloned many times, it would likely not perform well. Thus, evolution in cooperative coevolution populations maintains diversity as part of the evolution process itself. If one kind of neuron starts taking over the population, it will be selected too many times for the network, the network performs poorly, the neuron receives lower fitness and is likely to be discarded, and diversity returns. Thus, by making diversity an implicit part of the fitness evaluation, it can be maintained automatically.

Further, when evolving neural networks, genetic diversity is often less important than the diversity of the behavior that the networks generate. This perspective will be discussed next.

5.2 Behavioral Diversity

It is important to maintain genetic diversity in evolution so that the search process can cover enough of the search space to find good solutions, and can adapt to any changes in the landscape. This goal is important in neuroevolution as well, and genetic diversity maintenance methods are useful in it. However, neuroevolution is different from many other types of evolutionary optimization in that it aims to construct computational structures (i.e., neural networks), rather than static solutions. It is important that the behaviors of those networks are diverse as well. In many such domains, the fitness landscapes are deceptive (i.e., the highest peaks are surrounded by valleys), or they are flat (i.e., many different behaviors lead to similar fitness). Methods that rely on **hill-climbing** (i.e., incremental improvement through small changes), such as reinforcement learning and mutation-based search, struggle in such domains. They are difficult for neuroevolution as well, but search based on behavioral diversity makes it more effective.

Creating and maintaining genetic diversity do not necessarily lead to diverse behaviors. The reason is that the mapping between the genotype and behavior is complex and unpredictable. First, the same behavior can be encoded by very different neural networks. One example of this phenomenon is **competing conventions**, which we already encountered in section 3.3.1: The same neurons and weights in the network are encoded in a different order in the genome. As a result, the networks function exactly the same, but the encodings have no overlap; that is, they are maximally diverse. Second, a small change in the encoding can have a large effect on the behavior. Negating an activation function, for example, may cause the robot to turn left instead of right. Genetic diversity is thus not a good indicator of behavioral diversity.

Evolution of behaviors still takes place at the level of encodings, of course, and genetic diversity needs to be maintained to prevent convergence. However, the mechanisms for measuring, maintaining, and creating behavioral diversity are quite different, resulting in fundamentally different evolutionary processes.

Whereas genetic diversity could be measured in a relatively straightforward manner based on the distance between encodings, **behavioral diversity** is more complex. First, behavior needs to be characterized formally, taking into account what matters in the domain. This often involves creating a vector representation of the behavior, or a **behavior characterization** (BC; Lehman and Stanley, 2011a; Mouret and Doncieux, 2012). For instance, for a mobile robot, the BC could consist of a histogram of the sensory inputs, actions, and locations encountered during a number of sample runs. More generally, a collection of possible inputs to the network could be created, and the outputs corresponding to each of these inputs taken as the BC. If domain knowledge is not available, they can be generated randomly. With domain knowledge, it may be possible to define a collection of situations that forms a representative sample, or better yet, a sample of the most important decision points in the domain, thus creating a more meaningful BC (Gomes, Urbano, and Christensen, 2013; Lehman and Stanley, 2011a; Mouret and Doncieux, 2012; Stanley and Lehman, 2015).

It is difficult to form such a BC for recurrent neural networks (RNNs) where not only the current inputs matter, but also the history of the preceding inputs and actions. A common approach is to represent the actions as distributions, and the BC as a mapping: For a set of sensory states, it specifies the distribution of actions the agent is likely to take. Interestingly, with such a representation, it is possible to learn optimal BCs (Meyerson, Lehman, and Miikkulainen, 2016) for a set of multiple tasks in the same domain, such as robot navigation in multiple mazes. The BCs are adapted so they represent the distributions of optimally behaving agents in known tasks, forming a powerful foundation for evolution of optimal behavior in new tasks.

Once a BC has been defined, the next step is to measure diversity among them. As in the case of genetic diversity, calculating the average distance between individuals is a common approach. A more formal way is to utilize entropy, an information-theoretic concept that measures the level of surprise or uncertainty in the outcomes of a random variable. Intelligent behavior in general can be described as resulting from **entropy maximization** (Wissner-Gross and Freer, 2013). In evolutionary computation, it can be applied to the behavior of an agent or a population of agents, thus describing how diverse they are. For instance, the behavioral space can be divided into discrete intervals, and the number of agents visiting each interval can be counted (Kang, Bei, Shen, et al., 2021). The entropy of this distribution then measures the behavioral diversity of the population.

The information-theoretic approach can be developed further to measure **empowerment**; that is, the ability of an agent to control its world (Salge, Glackin, and Polani, 2014). Empowerment can be defined as the channel capacity between the agent's actuators A_t at time t and its sensors S_{t+1} at the next time step:

$$E = \max_{p(a_t)} I(S_{t+1}; A_t), \tag{5.3}$$

where $p(a_t)$ is the probability of actuator value a_t at time t and $I(S; A)$ is the mutual information between S and A:

$$I(S; A) = H(A) - H(A|S) = H(S) - H(S|A), \tag{5.4}$$

where $H(X)$ is the entropy of X. $I(S; A)$ thus measures how much of the state entropy can be explained by actions. The resulting metric, **channel capacity**, stands for the maximum rate of information transmission from A to S. In essence, empowerment E thus measures the causal influence of the agent's actions on its future sensory inputs; that is, how much power the agent has in changing the world it perceives. Empowerment is a useful concept in many ways. It is possible to characterize the evolution of intelligent agents as a process that maximizes empowerment. Similarly, the evolved agents then behave to maximize their empowerment. Such behavior provides the agents an intrinsic motivation that results in various goal-oriented behaviors.

Empowerment is thus a general theory of evolution of intelligent behavior. It measures a general desirable quality of an evolved agent and can be used as an explicit evolutionary objective. While it does not measure diversity directly, it often correlates with it. Similar to **implicit fitness sharing** as described in section 5.1, empowerment favors actions that have a large impact, regardless of other objectives. In that sense, it often serves to diversify the set of actions that are available for the agents, and thereby leads to diverse behaviors.

As an example of behavioral diversity at work, consider a task for an evolutionary robot that moves around in an environment where seven lights are on or off in fixed locations (figure 5.1; Mouret and Doncieux, 2009). The robot can sense each light, and it can move around by controlling its two wheels. When it steps on a light, one or two other lights turn on. The task is to discover how to turn on light 6. In the beginning, only light 0 is on. To turn on light 6, it has to first go to light 0, then to 4, 5, and 6; or else, go to lights 0, 1, 3, 4, 5, and 6. Fitness is defined as the number of time steps to reach light 6; thus, unless the robot is successful, it receives no fitness and no indication of whether its behavior is promising. It is therefore very difficult to discover successful behavior based solely on fitness. Therefore, the evolutionary search for the optimal behavior does not even get started.

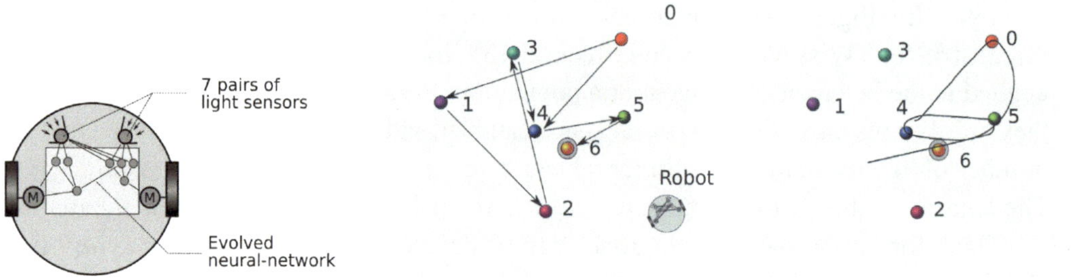

(*a*) Controller (*b*) Full light sequence (*c*) Discovered sequence

Figure 5.1: **Using behavioral diversity to discover solutions in a domain with a deceptive or flat fitness function**. The robot (*a*) has to move to the lights in the order indicated by the arrows (*b*) to eventually turn on light 6. Fitness is defined as the number of time steps to reach light 6, and therefore does not indicate which behaviors are promising early on. In contrast, behavioral diversity rewards controllers that turn on more and more lights; thus, it encourages exploration that eventually makes the search successful (*c*). In this manner, behavioral diversity can be used to guide search even when the fitness function is flat (as in this case) or deceptive (more generally). Figures from Mouret and Doncieux (2009).

However, it is possible to define BC as the collection of lights that are on, such as 1000000, 1001000, 1100000, and so on. An **archive** of discovered behaviors can then be formed, and evolution rewarded for exploring new behaviors. In this manner, evolution quickly discovers movement sequences that result in more lights being turned on, including eventually light 6. Thus, behavioral diversity makes search effective in this domain, where the fitness function does not provide a hill to climb. In the same manner, behavioral diversity helps cope with fitness functions that are deceptive; that is, fitness peaks are located behind fitness valleys.

This section has introduced and illustrated the fundamentals of behavioral diversity. The next two subsections push these concepts further in opposite directions: Novelty search aims to maximize exploration and creativity through divergent search, and quality diversity (QD) methods seek to combine diversity with performance objectives.

5.3 Novelty Search

The previous sections have shown how evolution with behavioral diversity objectives can discover solutions that are difficult to find. It is possible to take this approach one step further and make it the only objective of search. That is, the entire aim of evolution is to keep generating new variation and never converge at all: It is divergent instead of convergent.

A good motivation for divergent evolution comes from biology. Unlike traditional evolutionary computation, biological evolution does not have a goal. Variation is generated continuously, and selection operates upon it. This selection pressure is much weaker than that used in evolutionary computation, and it results in much broader diversity. Evolution can thus quickly adapt to new situations, taking advantage of **niches** that confer an advantage in survival. The results can sometimes seem extremely creative, like the anglerfish, which lures prey by generating light at the end of a long fin ray (Coleman, 2019), or bacteria that evolve to utilize citric acid as their carbon source (Blount, Borland, and Lenski, 2008). It is this kind of creativity that computational divergent search is aimed at capturing.

Divergent search can be formalized within the current evolutionary computation framework simply by rewarding behavioral diversity instead of performance. This approach is called **novelty search** (NS; Lehman and Stanley, 2008, 2011a; Stanley and Lehman, 2015). A **novelty metric** is defined that measures how different a candidate solution is from solutions that have been generated before; that is, how novel it is. This novelty metric then replaces the usual fitness metrics that measure performance in a task.

A common novelty metric is the sparseness of the behavior space around the individual (i.e., the average distance to its k nearest neighbors). Similar to equation 5.2,

$$\rho(x) = 1/k \sum_{j=1}^{k} d(x, y_j), \tag{5.5}$$

where $\rho(x)$ stands for the novelty of individual x, y_j is the jth nearest neighbor of x, and d is the **distance metric** between their behavioral characterizations. This novelty is computed against the current population as well as an archive of prior solutions. The archive is first initialized randomly, and new individuals are then added to it with low probability. In this manner, the archive constitutes a sampling of the behavior space, guiding the search to new areas.

Novelty search indeed leads to diverse solutions. However, and most remarkably, it sometimes also discovers solutions that are useful in the domain—even though there is no provision in the search for preferring them in any way. One potential explanation is that to be most different from what has been created before, it is a good idea to utilize structure in the domain. That is, search may discover **stepping stones** that can be combined effectively into more complex solutions, thus creating more diversity than a random search.

The motivation for this idea comes from the **Picbreeder game** (section 8.3), where human players select the most interesting images and evolution creates more images by crossing over and mutating the compositional pattern producing network (CPPN) that generated them (Secretan, Beato, D'Ambrosio, et al., 2011). It turns out that the human players do not usually have a goal in mind in what they are trying to generate, but instead use the raw material serendipitously: They come up with ideas of what to create on the fly, depending on what interesting shapes and images are currently in the population. For instance, in creating a skull image, they used, over time, many images that looked nothing like a skull. There were images that could be described as a crescent moon, a comet, a drop on water, and a mask (figure 5.2*a*; Woolley and Stanley, 2011). These images served as stepping stones that eventually came together to generate the skull.

Interestingly, if evolution is set up with the goal of generating the skull image, it fails (figure 5.2*b*). The images approach the skull shape overall, but never get the elements right. Perhaps the evolution of something that complex relies on discovering the proper stepping stones; that is, discovering the solutions that represent the prominent structure in the domain?

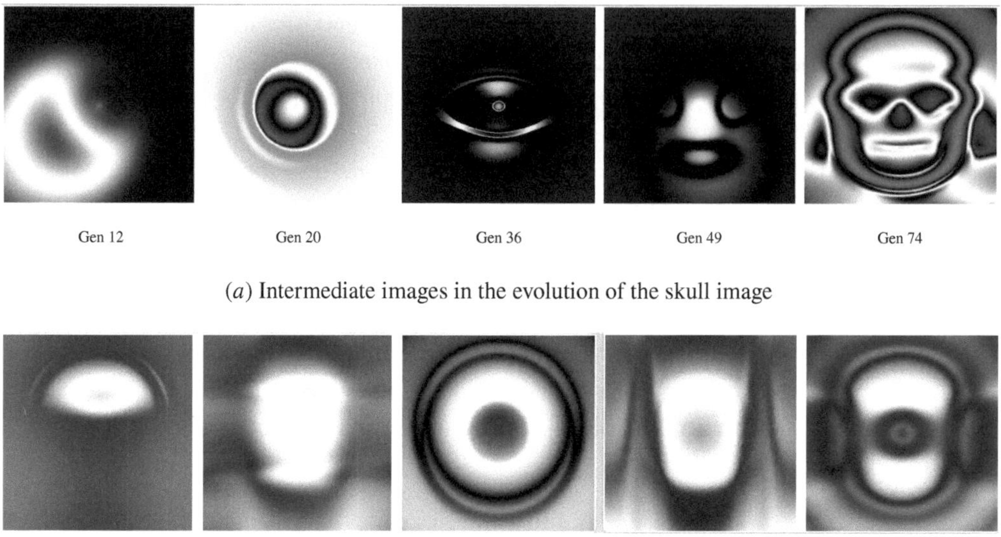

Figure 5.2: **Stepping-stone-based versus direct evolution of a skull image.** How can a CPPN be evolved to create a particular image, such as the skull? (*a*) Human players of Picbreeder selected images that looked interesting on their own, without the goal of generating a skull, which emerged serendipitously toward the end of the evolution from these stepping stones. (*b*) When evolution is directed to evolve the skull image directly with a distance-based fitness, it falls short of most of the details; shown are the final results of five such example runs. In this sense, the discovery of stepping stones is crucial in generating complex solutions. Figures from Woolley and Stanley (2011).

One way to characterize the stepping stones is that they are local maxima in the search space with regards to a metric different from novelty. This metric could measure how impressive they are (Lehman and Stanley, 2012) or it could be related to performance in the domain (Meyerson and Miikkulainen, 2017). Stepping stones can then be identified as solutions that dominate other solutions in terms of novelty and fitness (i.e., through behavioral domination). In this manner, the search discovers global novelty and local refinement. For instance, in the domain of figure 5.3, neither novelty-based nor fitness-based search is much better than random search in finding the high fitness region on the top right. However, the claw-like areas form stepping stones: The fitness increases horizontally and vertically in each toe, and by combining the end solutions of each toe, it is possible to jump to the next claw (with superior fitness). A search mechanism that takes advantage of local fitness and global novelty can utilize such stepping stones and discover useful solutions in the domain.

Stepping stones can be found in complex real-world domains as well (Lehman and Stanley, 2011a; Stanley and Lehman, 2015). For instance, consider evolving a controller network for a bipedal simulated robot (figure 5.4). It is possible to reward the networks simply by the distance that the walker can travel before falling over. Such evolution is rewarded by incremental progress, and results in movement that is limited and aims to

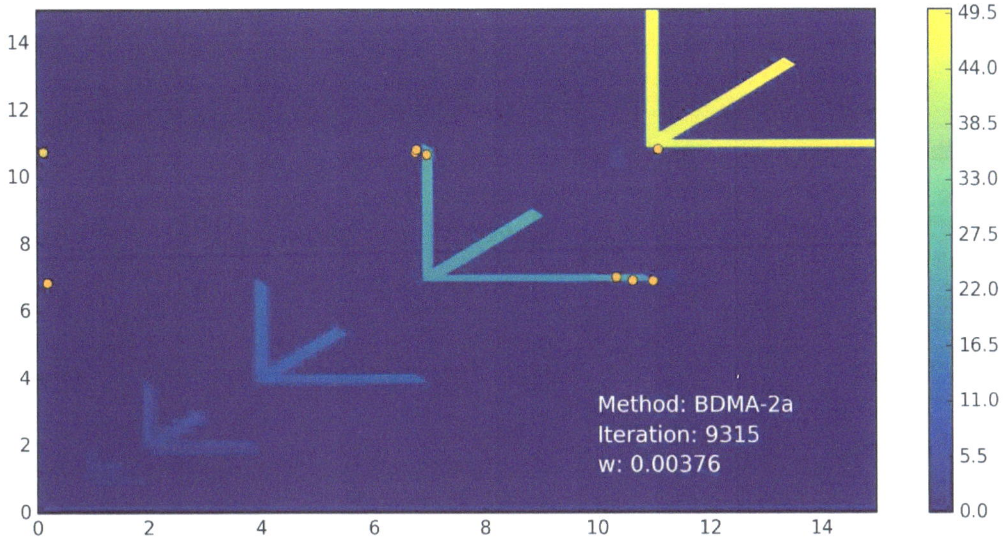

Figure 5.3: **Illustration of search based on stepping stones.** In this experiment, a population of points is evolved on the 2D rectangle. Fitness is zero in the background, and increases in each claw from left to right and from bottom to top. The population starts at the bottom left and has to discover the top fitness at the top right. While fitness-based and novelty-based searches are not much better than random, a search method that discovers and utilizes stepping stones performs much better. It discovers the local optima at the end of each finger of the claw-like pattern, and then combines them to make the jump to the next claw. In this manner, stepping stones can be identified as local optima and recombined to make discoveries that would otherwise be difficult to make. Figure from Meyerson and Miikkulainen (2017). For a video, see `https://neuroevolutionbook.com/demos`.

be stable, but is also vulnerable to disturbances and variations that might occur in the environment. In contrast, when such walking is evolved through novelty search, many behaviors that have little to do with walking are discovered, such as falling flat, jumping forward, taking a few steps before falling, and ultimately, leaning forward and moving one's legs fast to prevent falling. It turns out that such walking is more robust and more effective. It emerged from many different kinds of failures, and avoids them effectively. Evolution utilizes these failures as stepping stones, combining them effectively into more comprehensive solutions.

Quality diversity methods can be seen as a way to take advantage of stepping stones in a more general framework. The idea is to combine novelty search with fitness-based search in a way that allows finding better solutions and finding them faster, presumably taking advantage of stepping stones along the way. Quality diversity methods will be discussed in the next section.

5.4 Quality Diversity Methods

Quality diversity (QD; Pugh, Soros, and Stanley, 2016) represents a significant shift in evolutionary computation. QD is an evolutionary search paradigm that prioritizes discovering a diverse collection of high-quality solutions, rather than a single optimal

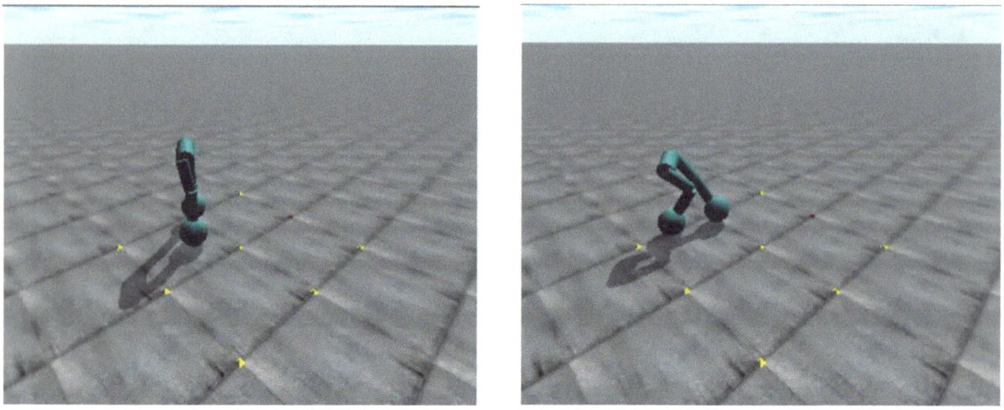

(*a*) Fitness-based search (*b*) Novelty search

Figure 5.4: **Contrasting the creativity of solutions in convergent and divergent search.** Gaits for the bipedal walker are evolved in two ways. (*a*) Convergent (fitness-based) evolution favors small, safe improvements that allow the robot to travel incrementally further. The resulting gait is rigid and slow and often fails. (*b*) In contrast, divergent (novelty-based) evolution discovers dynamic behaviors, such as falls and jumps, that are different from others. They serve as stepping stones in exploring a larger space, which eventually includes robust dynamic gaits. In this manner, superior solutions can be discovered even when (and because!) they are not directly rewarded. For videos, see `https://neuroevolutionbook.com/demos`.

solution. This concept emerged from the observation that natural evolution tends toward divergence rather than convergence: Instead of yielding one "best" species, nature produces a myriad of different species, each highly adapted to its own niche. In traditional optimization, evolutionary algorithms (EAs) are typically used to converge on one top-performing individual (or a set of trade-off solutions in multi-objective optimization), which can cause premature convergence and loss of diversity. By contrast, QD algorithms seek to maintain and foster diversity in the population while also optimizing performance within behavioral niches. In other words, the goal of QD is to fill the space of possibilities with the best possible example of each type of behavior.

5.4.1 Motivation and Challenges

This new approach has been called an **illumination** of the search space, as it reveals how performance varies across different behaviors or features of solutions. The motivation for QD algorithms arises from challenges in traditional neuroevolution and optimization. Many evolutionary runs tend to converge to a single solution that exploits the easiest path to high fitness, foregoing alternative strategies or morphologies. This convergence is problematic in deceptive domains, where reaching the global optimum may require exploring low-fitness intermediary regions that a purely objective-driven search would avoid. Pioneering work on novelty search (section 5.3), showed that completely removing the objective and rewarding novelty instead can mitigate convergence and even find global optima in deceptive tasks. However, NS treated diversity merely as a means to an end (finding a single solution) and did not explicitly value quality in its diverse outcomes. QD algorithms take the next step by valuing diversity as an end in itself, alongside quality.

In QD, the aim is to obtain a maximally diverse collection of behaviors such that each is as high-performing as possible. This dual focus is often analogized to natural evolution producing many species, each optimally adapted to its niche. The key innovation is to balance exploration (finding many different behaviors) with exploitation (optimizing performance within each behavior niche) simultaneously in one evolutionary run. To enable this, QD methods introduce mechanisms that reward behavioral innovation while also conducting localized competition within behaviorally defined niches. Importantly, unlike approaches that return multiple optima by focusing only on peaks of a fitness landscape, QD measures diversity in terms of behavioral descriptors (also called **behavior characterizations**) that the user defines for the domain. The assumption is that all regions of this behavior space are of interest, not just those near the global optimum. Thus, QD algorithms strive to cover the entire behavior space at some resolution, reporting the highest-performing individual found for each region. By prioritizing diversity over pure quality, QD avoids driving the search away from low-performing regions entirely—even niches with relatively modest fitness can be maintained if they represent unique behaviors.

Two early realizations of the QD paradigm are **novelty search with local competition** (NSLC; Lehman and Stanley, 2011b) and **multi-dimensional archive of phenotypic elites** (MAP-Elites; Cully, Clune, Tarapore, et al., 2015; Mouret and Clune, 2015). These algorithms embody the QD approach by combining the drive for behavioral diversity with a localized search for performance quality. NSLC and MAP-Elites have demonstrated that this focus on diversification, rather than pure optimization, can yield impressive results in various domains, including those where traditional optimization methods fall short.

5.4.2 Novelty Search with Local Competition

To illustrate the usefulness of QD, it can help to look at a domain where both quality and diversity are important. One such domain is that of evolving virtual creatures, which should not only have diverse morphologies but also locomote efficiently (figure 5.5). In contrast to natural evolution, virtual creatures in evolutionary computation experiments often evolve toward a single dominant morphology, driven by selection mechanisms that disproportionately reward the easiest-to-exploit designs. Novelty search has been proposed as a remedy, rewarding divergence from past designs to enhance ecological diversity. However, focusing solely on novel morphologies can lead to functionally impractical designs, indicating the necessity of balancing morphological novelty with functionality to ensure that evolved creatures are not only diverse but also capable of effective performance within their environments.

To address this problem, **novelty search** can be combined with a mechanism for **local competition** (NSLC; Lehman and Stanley, 2011b), which is motivated by the biological principle that individuals often compete primarily with others in their local environment rather than with the entire global population. Novelty search, which rewards uniqueness rather than just fitness for a task, effectively prevents convergence on premature solutions. Local competition, which simulates a more natural selection environment where creatures compete against others in their immediate vicinity rather than against a global fitness standard, promotes performance localized within morphological niches. As we will

(*a*) Hopper (*b*) Crab (*c*) Quadruped (*d*) Tailed quadruped

Figure 5.5: **Diverse competent morphologies discovered within a typical single run of NSLC.** Various creatures are shown that have specialized in order to effectively exploit particular niches of morphology space. Compared to approaches relying on global competition, NSLC uncovers a greater range of functional morphologies in a single evolutionary run. The hopper (*a*) is a unipedal hopper that is very tall, (*b*) is a heavy, short crab-like creature, and (*c*) and (*d*) are distinct quadrupeds. Creature (*c*) drives a large protrusion on its back to generate momentum, and (*d*) has a tail for balance. Figures from Lehman and Stanley (2011b). Videos at `https://neuroevolutionbook.com/demos`.

see, such a dual approach leads to high diversity while also maintaining the functional capabilities of the creatures.

NSLC can be implemented using a genetic algorithm (GA) where each individual in the population is assessed both for its novelty and its competitive ability. Novelty is measured based on a multi-dimensional feature descriptor that quantifies how different an individual is from the rest of the population and from those stored in an archive of historically novel individuals. The local competition is implemented by having individuals compete for survival against a subset of the population within their niche rather than against the entire population. The genetic representation of the creatures is a type of **graph grammatical encoding** (section 4.2.2), in which an evolved genotypic graph structure is unrolled into a coupled body plan and control policy. Crucially, this encoding supports a wide range of robot morphologies with diverse body sizes and shapes, making it well suited for testing the capabilities of NSLC.

In more detail, competition occurs among the k-nearest neighbors in a morphological feature space (e.g., based on Euclidean distance in a space defined by height, mass, and the number of active joints), where k is a fixed parameter that is determined experimentally. Combining novelty and local competition can naturally be achieved with a **multi-objective evolutionary optimization** algorithm such as **non-dominated sorting genetic algorithm II** (NSGA-II; section 2.2.5). In this setup, each individual is evaluated based on two objectives: (1) novelty, the average distance to its k-nearest neighbors in morphology space; and (2) local competition score, which is the number of neighbors that the individual outperforms in terms of locomotion fitness.

There is one key difference in this implementation from the standard NSGA-II approach. While NSGA-II promotes diversity along the non-dominated front, NSLC replaces that mechanism with a separate objective that explicitly rewards genotypic diversity. This change is justified because both novelty and local competition are inherently relative metrics. Individuals with identical novelty or local competition scores might be grouped together under a Pareto-based diversity scheme, even though they could differ significantly in morphology or performance.

In this domain, NSLC led to several beneficial effects. First, the ecosystem of evolved creatures showed a much higher level of diversity compared to systems evolved with traditional fitness-only approaches, as illustrated in figure 5.5. Second, the local competition model ensured that while diversity is maintained, the creatures also developed the ability for fast locomotion. This method effectively balanced the exploration of the morphological space (through novelty search) with the exploitation of successful strategies (through local competition).

5.4.3 MAP-Elites

Multi-dimensional archive of elites (MAP-Elites) distinguishes itself within the QD domain by explicitly defining niches (Cully, Clune, Tarapore, et al., 2015; Mouret and Clune, 2015), a stark contrast to the passive emergence seen in NSLC. MAP-Elites operates by partitioning the search space into a grid of niches, each defined by specific feature dimensions that describe meaningful characteristics of possible solutions. These characteristics are also known as **behavior characterization** (BC) and are typically defined by the user, who also chooses how finely this space should be divided; each cell in this grid will eventually hold the best solution found for that combination of features.

Initially, MAP-Elites populates the map by generating a set of random candidate solutions. For each one, it simulates or evaluates the solution to calculate its performance and determine its feature descriptors. Each solution is then placed into the appropriate cell in the feature space grid, based on its features. If the cell is empty or the new solution performs better than the one already in that cell, it replaces the existing occupant.

Once this initial seeding is done, the main evolutionary process begins. At each iteration, the algorithm selects one of the already stored solutions from the map. This solution is then mutated or recombined (if crossover is used) to create a new variant. The new solution is evaluated to determine its features and performance. Just like before, it is inserted into the cell corresponding to its features if it is better than the current occupant.

This process continues for a fixed number of evaluations or until a certain convergence criterion is met. Over time, the algorithm fills more cells of the feature map, continuously replacing weaker solutions with stronger ones. The search is biased toward discovering high-performing solutions across a broad range of features, rather than optimizing performance within a narrow slice of the space. By the end of the run, MAP-Elites produces a feature-performance map: a landscape showing which combinations of features yield strong solutions, and what the best-known solutions are for each combination. This map serves both as a practical tool for selecting from a diverse set of elite solutions, and as an analytical resource for understanding the structure of the problem domain.

For example, in the domain of locomoting soft robots encountered in section 4.3.2, BCs can be defined as the percentage of the robot made from stiff bone material, and the overall size of the robot, measured by the percentage of filled voxels. If a new robot exhibits the same percentage of stiff material and filled voxels, it will replace the elite only if it travels faster (i.e., has a higher locomotion fitness score). This process ensures that each niche retains the best solution found so far according to the fitness function, but

Listing 5.5: **The Default MAP-Elites algorithm.**

```
def map_elites():
    # Create an empty, N-dimensional map of elites including
    # solutions and their performances.
    solutions, perfs = create_archive()

    for i in range(num_iters):
        # Create a new solution.
        if i < num_rand_solutions:
            x = random_solution()
        else:
            x = random_selection(solutions)
            x = random_variation(x)

        # Update the archive and its solutions' performances.
        x_feat_desc = feature_descriptor(x)
        x_perf = performance(x)
        elite = get_elite_with_feat(solutions, x_feat_desc)
        if elite is None:
            update_archive(solutions, x, perfs, x_perf)
        else:
            elite_perf = get_elite_perf(perfs, x_feat_desc)
            if elite_perf < x_perf:
                update_archive(solutions, x, perfs, x_perf)

    return solutions, perfs
```

crucially, it also captures a diverse array of solutions across the entire range of defined features. Listing 5.5 details the MAP-Elites approach.

The effects of applying MAP-Elites are multi-faceted. First, it preserves a diverse set of solutions, each excelling in different parts of the feature space. For example, MAP-Elites managed to evolve a variety of locomoting, soft robots, each representing the best of its respective behavior niche. In contrast, typical evolutionary algorithms tend to converge on a narrow set of morphologies within a single run, repeatedly finding variations of the same local optimum and missing out on alternative, high-performing designs that exist elsewhere in the feature space.

Second, MAP-Elites effectively **illuminates** the search space, providing insights into how different features of solutions contribute to their success and interrelate with each other. This is particularly valuable in complex domains where the relationship between features and performance is not well understood. Two such maps, created by MAP-Elites, are shown in figure 5.6. Each smaller image shows the best-performing organism found within a particular niche defined by the two behavioral features mentioned here (e.g., percentage of voxels filled and proportion of bone material). This diversity is very useful for robustness and adaptability, as it provides a spectrum of potential solutions to unforeseen challenges or changes in task requirements. For example, this principle can allow robots confronted with damage or environmental change to rapidly adapt by selecting an alternative behavior from its precomputed MAP-Elites archive (Cully, Clune, Tarapore, et al., 2015).

In summary, both NSLC and MAP-Elites ultimately seek a diverse set of high-performing solutions, but they do so differently. NSLC uses an implicit niching: Niches

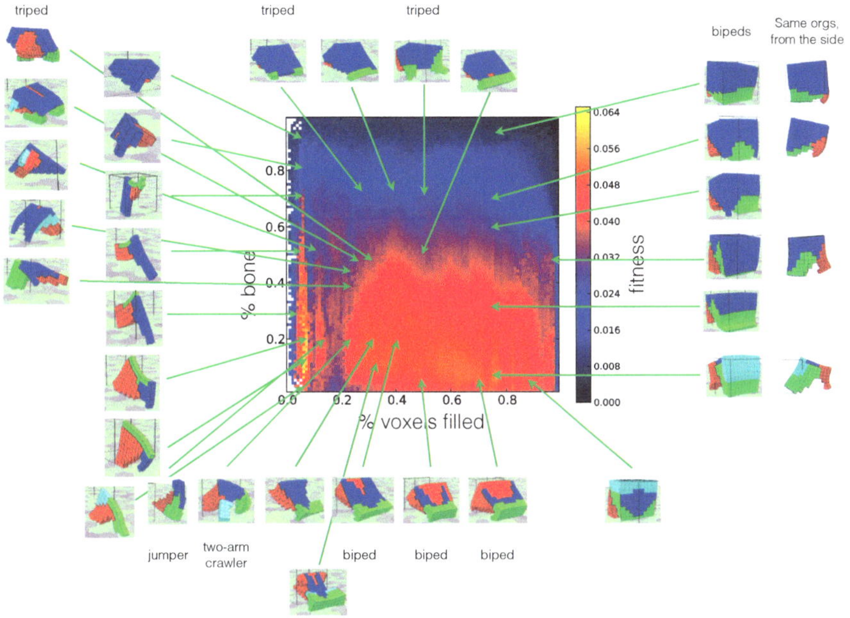

(*a*) Run 1

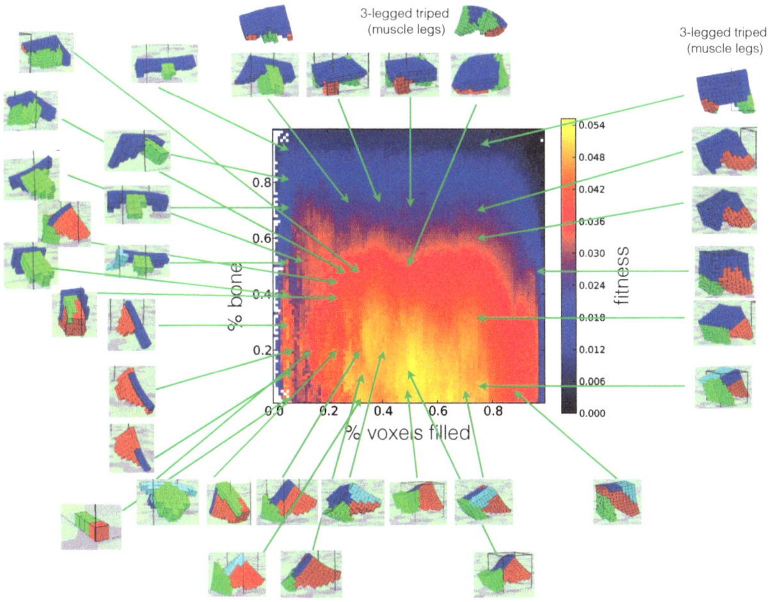

(*b*) Run 2

Figure 5.6: **Example maps annotated with example organisms from different areas of the feature space.** Figures (*a*) and (*b*) show maps of two different MAP-Elites runs. Within a map, MAP-Elites smoothly adapts a design theme along the desired dimensions of variation. One can see that there is some variation between maps, both in the performance discovered at specific points and in the types of solutions. That said, each map generally paints the same overall picture of the performance capabilities of each region of the feature space. Note the different scale of the bottom color map. Figures from Mouret and Clune (2015).

form organically as similar individuals compete locally within a single population. MAP-Elites uses explicit niching: The user defines the niches in advance (the grid), and there is an archive slot reserved for each niche. The advantage of the MAP-Elites' approach is simplicity and direct control over which aspects of behavior are considered (the dimensions of the map). Its evolutionary loop is also simpler (with a single objective acceptance criterion for each bin). On the other hand, NSLC's implicit approach can be more flexible if the appropriate behavior dimensions are not obvious—it essentially lets evolution discover niches based on where different solutions arise. NSLC uses continuous evolutionary dynamics (with a fixed population size each generation), whereas MAP-Elites accumulates an ever-growing set of elites (bounded by the number of bins).

In practice, the choice between them can depend on the problem: MAP-Elites is often favored for low-dimensional, user-defined behavior spaces where one wants a coverage of that space, while NSLC can be easier when one prefers not to discretize behaviors or when using multi-dimensional continuous behavior spaces.

5.4.4 Implementing and Enhancing QD Algorithms

Since the establishment of QD as a powerful concept, exemplified by algorithms such as NSLC and MAP-Elites, numerous studies have emerged to analyze and enhance various facets of QD. A selected set of works is introduced next to showcase the intricacies of implementing QD from three main perspectives:

Behavior characterization: BC not only determines the form of diversity during the search process but also significantly influences the efficacy of the optimization algorithm. Therefore, it should be meticulously chosen to enhance the QD's performance (Pugh, Soros, and Stanley, 2016). While there is complete freedom in determining BC for a QD task, it is preferable and necessary to choose those that are closely related to the desired objective. This approach provides additional benefits, such as improved model interpretability, and is crucial for achieving reasonable performance.

For instance, Pugh, Soros, and Stanley (2016) examined the impact of using BCs that are both highly aligned (e.g., final coordinates at the trial's end) and misaligned (e.g., the most frequent direction of orientation) with the quality metric (e.g., goal achievement) in solving maze navigation tasks through various QD implementations. Their findings indicate that BCs misaligned with the quality metric not only underperform but also fail to match the efficacy of pure optimization-based methods. Conversely, BCs aligned with the task's objectives enhance performance, achieving state-of-the-art results at the time. Even when paired with misaligned BCs, the overall performance still surpasses pure fitness searching methods. The key takeaway is that BCs aligned with the quality concept are essential to overcome deception in challenging problems.

However, crafting BCs manually requires domain knowledge of the problem and the solution. For problems with limited information, one approach is to use a pure fitness searching method as a baseline, then iteratively incorporate and test candidate BCs for alignment with the quality metric, based on performance improvement over the baseline. Recent studies also suggest the feasibility of learning BC. For instance, meta-learning has been employed to discover optimal BC definitions, enhancing success rates in multiple tasks (Meyerson, Lehman, and Miikkulainen, 2016). In robotic locomotion tasks, AURORA (Grillotti and Cully, 2022) uses dimension reduction models like principal component analysis (PCA) and autoencoders to encode a robot's sensory data, treating the encoded vector as the BC during learning. These methods have shown promising results and point toward a more generalized approach for BC design.

Niches representation: After establishing BCs, the subsequent task is to develop a technique for segmenting solutions into niches based on these BCs. The approach to niche representation notably differentiates NSLC from MAP-Elites. In NSLC, niches emerge dynamically, defined by the k-nearest neighbors among a generation's peers and the elites in the archive. This results in an evolving archive, where the number and specifics of the cells are neither predetermined nor known in advance. Conversely, MAP-Elites divides the BC space into discrete behavioral cells. This division is based on the BC range and user-defined granularity, offering a complete overview of the archive's size and cell characteristics.

However, this method grapples with the curse of dimensionality, as the cell count escalates exponentially with the increase in BCs and their granularity. To mitigate this issue, a variant of MAP-Elites called **centroidal Voronoi tessellation MAP-elites** (CVT-MAP-Elites), employs a clustering approach like k-means to segment the archive space into k Voronoi tessellations (Vassiliades, Chatzilygeroudis, and Mouret, 2017). While CVT-MAP-Elites shares core functionalities with MAP-Elites, it diverges in two key operations: archive definition and cell querying. For defining the archive, CVT-MAP-Elites deploys $K \gg k$ vectors in the BC space to identify k centroids representing the cells, unlike MAP-Elites' straightforward discretization of BCs. When querying a cell to store a phenotype, CVT-MAP-Elites requires checking distances to centroids, potentially increasing computational complexity to $O(k)$ in the worst case, compared to the $O(1)$ complexity in MAP-Elites. Despite this increase in computational load, CVT-MAP-Elites proves advantageous, capable of scaling up to 1,000 dimensions in maze experiments–a significant leap from MAP-Elites' limitation of around 20 dimensions.

Evolutionary algorithm: Although NSLC and MAP-Elites have shown impressive results, their most successful applications have predominantly been in robotic locomotion tasks with simple, low-dimensional controllers (Colas, Madhavan, Huizinga, et al., 2020). In addition, both QD implementations commonly employ a mutation-based GA as their foundational optimization algorithm, leaving the potential of ES family members largely unexplored. Consequently, investigating new optimization methods to achieve scalability and enhance learning efficiency is a logical next step.

In this context, Colas, Madhavan, Huizinga, et al. (2020) introduced **MAP-Elites with evolution strategies** (ME-ES), utilizing the efficiency of ES to extend MAP-Elites to high-dimensional controllers managed by large neural networks. ME-ES demonstrated the ability to learn a neural network controller with approximately 10^5 parameters—significantly larger than those in previous studies—outperforming GA-based methods even with triple the computation time.

Simultaneously, Fontaine, Togelius, Nikolaidis, et al. (2020) developed **covariance matrix adaptation MAP-Elites** (CMA-ME), which integrates the high-performing CMA-ES algorithm from the ES family into the QD framework. A fitness function that prioritizes exploration (i.e., populating empty cells) over optimization (i.e., enhancing performance in filled cells) is the primary objective for CMA-ES. When the archive remains unchanged, CMA-ES's initial parameters and internal states are reset using a randomly chosen individual from the archive. In comparative experiments, CMA-ME outperformed MAP-Elites by not only doubling the solution quality but also providing a broader diversity of solutions.

Building upon these advancements, Fontaine and Nikolaidis (2021) introduced **MAP-Elites via a gradient arborescence** (MEGA). Unlike traditional ES methods, which treat objective and BC functions as black boxes, MEGA integrates directional perturbations into MAP-Elites based on gradients of these functions, provided they are first-order differentiable. It employs CMA-ES to optimize the factors within the perturbation function. CMA-MEGA significantly surpasses traditional QD algorithms by not treating objective and BC functions as black boxes, and it demonstrates its efficacy in generating a diverse array of high-quality images by searching the latent space of a StyleGAN.

Further building on these innovations, **covariance matrix adaptation MAP-annealing** (CMA-MAE) by Fontaine and Nikolaidis (2023) introduces a nuanced alteration in the ranking mechanism. This change gradually reduces the influence of elites in filled cells of the archive, ensuring that the optimization process does not prematurely shift focus from the objective to exploration. This issue is especially pertinent in cases involving flat objectives or low-resolution archives. Remarkably, this modification is compatible with both CMA-ME and CMA-MEGA, broadening its applicability.

5.5 Multiobjectivity

While quality diversity focuses on two objectives, one on performance and the other on diversity, **multiobjective optimization** (section 2.2.5) in general is a good approach to maintaining diversity in evolutionary computation. The motivation once again comes from biology (Miikkulainen and Forrest, 2021). Biological fitness is complex: Animals must seek food and shelter, avoid predators, find mates, and care for their young, and often some of these objectives conflict. The problem can be solved in many ways, leading to multiple niches, and such diversity leads to powerful further adaptation.

Note, however, that biological objectives can be expressed simply as a single, high-level objective: survival of the species. A similar approach can be taken in evolutionary computation; that is, a complex optimization task can be expressed simply as winning a game, making a lot of money, or gaining a lot of publicity. Such objectives allow evolution to be creative; on the other hand, the fitness signal is weak and may not allow for identifying good ideas until they are fully developed. This approach may need to be paired with **neutral mutations**, **weak selection**, and **deep time**, placing it closer to biological evolution (section 9.1.1).

Multiobjective optimization can thus be seen as a practical approach that is one level below such a high-level specification. It is often possible to devise performance objectives, cost objectives, and secondary objectives such as simplicity, accuracy, or appearance, without specifying the desired solutions directly. In many cases, it is useful to have a Pareto front as a result; that is, a collection of solutions that each represents a different trade-off between them such that no solution is better than any other across all objectives. One solution in the Pareto front can then be chosen according to other criteria, such as conditions at deployment time, or human preferences that are difficult to express as objectives.

The approach can be taken a step further to evolve complex behavior in a prescribed manner. For instance in the **NEWS/D** approach (Salih and Moshaiov, 2022, 2023a,b), the overall behavior is decomposed into a set of single-objective problems that are optimized together, resulting in a Pareto front of solutions. Some of these solutions are specialized to a particular objective and others are non-specialized. When applied to a set of robot motion tasks, the nonspecialized solutions represented general controllers that transferred well to new tasks. The method was used to optimize behavior according to a set of scenarios in aerial pursuit-evasion tasks, providing significant improvement over the standard method of proportional navigation.

Multiobjectivity is also a natural way to boost diversity: With multiple objectives, there are many ways of being successful. Niching or speciation may emerge in the population, and it may be further encouraged separately with mechanisms such as those in NEAT. Species can then be used to form ensembles, taking advantage of their diversity. Such methods are reviewed in the next section.

5.6 Ensembling

In general in machine learning (ML), it is often a good idea to train multiple different models for the task and then form the final system by ensembling them. The idea is that each model is somehow different; for instance, it has a different architecture, is initialized differently, or is trained with different training samples. Thus, each of them may end up learning something the other models do not, and together they can perform better than any model alone. This idea is consistent with studies in psychology, social science, and business that suggest that diversity in human teams leads to improved decision-making (Rock and Grant, 2016).

Ensembling may be as simple as just averaging the outputs of multiple models, or combining them more intelligently, or selecting one model that is most likely to have the correct answer for each input. Methods have also been developed, such as **mixtures of experts** (MoE; Masoudnia and Ebrahimpour, 2014) and **realizing human expertise through artificial intelligence** (RHEA; section 6.4.5), to train and combine different models more systematically. The fact that ensembling works is statistically surprising, and it was controversial for a while, but there is now a good understanding of it, especially in classification tasks (Li, Wang, and Ding, 2018). Ensembling intelligent agents requires more complex methods because behavior often depends on sequences of inputs and decisions and is often based on recurrent neural networks (RNNs), but that is possible as well. Ensembling is thus part of the standard ML toolbox and can be used routinely to improve performance.

Ensembling is a particularly natural extension of evolutionary approaches. EAs create and maintain a population from which the ensemble can be drawn. Moreover, having a diverse set of candidates is crucial for both evolution and ensembling. Often, the individuals in the final population end up with slightly different skills, from which an effective ensemble can be formed (Islam and Yao, 2008). Examples of such diversity include the age-estimation network architecture (section 11.3.6) and training with population culture (section 5.7). Such diversity is even more pronounced when the task is multiobjective: Individuals in the Pareto front form a natural pool from which to select ensemble members.

The NEAT neuroevolution method also employs a **speciation** mechanism that encourages diversity in search (section 3.3). In effect, NEAT runs multiple **island-based evolutionary processes**; that is, separate subpopulations that only periodically cross over, and species that are created and removed dynamically as evolution progresses. The species are created and maintained based on topological (i.e., genetic) diversity, but they result in enough behavioral diversity for ensembling to be effective. Indeed, it is possible to use just the species champions as the members of the ensemble, and then add voting, averaging, winner-take-all, or gating as the ensembling mechanism (Pardoe, Ryoo, and Miikkulainen, 2005).

Note that ensembling is related to many neuroevolution ideas and mechanisms discussed in this book. For instance, the main idea of the **enforced subpopulations** (ESP) method (section 7.1.1) is to evolve neurons for each location in the network in separate subpopulations; because good performance requires different neurons, diversity across populations is automatically maintained, and neurons are evolved that cooperate well together. Such a network can be seen as an ensemble with a very strong combination mechanism. Similar to the hierarchical mixtures of experts approach in machine learning, ESP can be extended hierarchically to construct a team of networks, where each network receives different inputs. For instance, each network can keep track of a different opponent, and at the highest level, a combiner neural network decides what action to take (Rajagopalan, Rawal, Miikkulainen, et al., 2011). This approach was used to evolve both the prey and the predator agents in the coevolutionary arms race example described in section 7.2.2.

In **modular multiobjective NEAT** (MM-NEAT; see section 6.3), multiple modules emerge from the evolution of a single network. They can be seen as ensemble members, and the preference neurons in each module as the ensembling mechanism, suggesting how the module output should be combined. Such preference neurons can be evolved in separate networks as well: In essence, each network places a bet that it has the right answer (Bruce and Miikkulainen, 2001). Each is evolved to maximize the return from bets, and as a result, the bets serve as confidence estimates. Ensembling then consists of simply selecting the network with the highest confidence. The **context+skill approach** (section 6.2) can also be seen as an ensembling mechanism. There are two special ensemble members–one representing context and the other the most likely action–and a combiner network on top representing the ensembling mechanism.

However, the most straightforward ensembling approach can already be useful in neuroevolution: A NEAT population can be evolved in a control task first, and then a gating neural network evolved to select which controller to use at each step. The approach was applied to a more challenging version of the pole-balancing task, in which the pole is actually a telescope that can change its length, and the pole's tip chases a moving target particle as if trying to swat a fly (figure 5.7). Even though there's only a single pole and

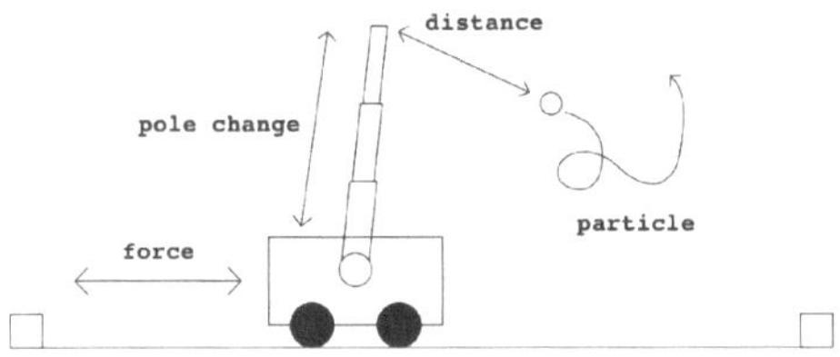

(*a*) Particle chasing task

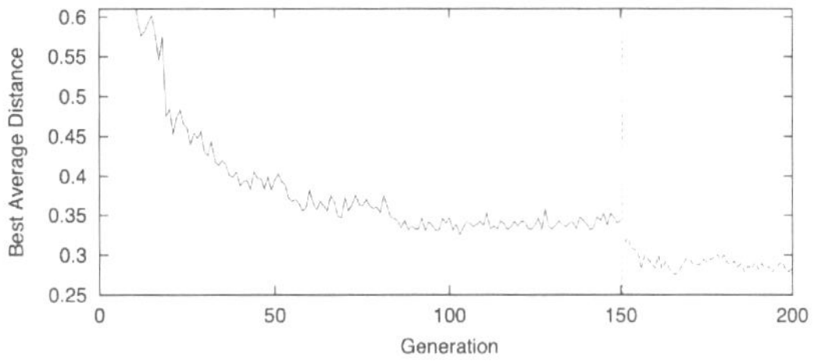

(*b*) Improvement through ensembling

Figure 5.7: **Effect of simple ensembling in a complex control task.** (*a*) When the cart-pole task is extended with an extensible pole, it becomes a fly-swatting task. The control dynamics change constantly as the pole changes, making control highly context-dependent and well-suited to ensembling. (*b*) The population of controllers is first evolved with NEAT for 150 generations; once the performance plateaus, a gating network is evolved to select among eight species champions. The performance improvement is significant and immediate, suggesting that ensembling is a simple and reliable way to boost performance of neuroevolution experiments. Figures from Pardoe, Ryoo, and Miikkulainen (2005).

the controller sees the positions and velocities (so recurrency is not needed), the response of the pole changes with its length. Thus, the actions change the dynamics of the task, requiring the controller to adjust its strategy continuously. Such flexible control is hard to achieve with a single neural network, but it is easier with an ensemble. After evolving a population of controller neural networks for 150 generations, the species champions were used as an ensemble. A gating neural network was then evolved for another 50 generations to pick one network to control the system at each step. The performance improvement was significant and immediate, demonstrating how even simple ensembling can add value to an existing neuroevolution approach.

The approach could easily be extended with various techniques to fit particular problems. For instance, diversity of the ensemble population could be increased by making evolution multiobjective. Secondary objectives may be defined naturally in many domains (such as speed, or cost, in addition to accuracy), but novelty is always a possible such objective, and highly effective in promoting diversity (section 5.3). Or, the ensemble members could be evolved to optimize not their own performance in isolation, but performance as a useful member of the ensemble (García-Pedrajas, Hervás-Martínez, and Ortíz-Boyer, 2005). This approach could boost the performance of even the simplest ensembling methods, like voting, averaging, or gating.

Further, the gating network could be evolved not simply to select, but to combine the outputs of the population members, similar to the context+skill approach or **confidence-based ensembling** (Global Partnership on Artificial Intelligence (GPAI), 2024). The ensemble members could indicate confidence as part of their outputs, and the combiner could take that into account in constructing its actions (instead of simply selecting the most confident network). The ensemble and combiner networks could be co-evolved to maximize the performance of the ensemble, similarly to **hierarchical ESP** and **CoDeepNEAT** (see sections 7.2.2 and 10.3.2).

In this manner, the general idea of ensembling can take many forms in neuroevolution. However, it should always be part of constructing the solution. Without some kind of ensembling in the end, a neuroevolution experiment often leaves money on the table. More broadly, the simple success of ensembling offers a powerful lesson to problem-solving and decision-making in general: Diverse teams with multiple viewpoints are likely to perform better than individual experts, provided that there is some principled way of combining these viewpoints. Ensembling provides a simple such way: Egalitarian learning, described in the next section, extends it further with learning.

5.7 Utilizing Population Culture and History

The knowledge that exists in the population beyond a single individual can be seen as **population culture**. There are common elements to it; that is, knowledge that many individuals share, such as common behaviors, variations of this common knowledge, and elements unique to single individuals. Generally, culture operates at a time scale between learning and evolution, but it can also emerge even during the lifetime of individuals, and can last as long as the population. It can also include artifacts that exist outside the population. They may be essential in establishing open-ended evolution, in that they permanently alter the environment where evolution takes place (Lehman, Gordon, Jain, et al., 2023).

In evolutionary computation, population culture can be used in many ways to make evolution more effective (Belew, 1990; Maheri, Jalili, Hosseinzadeh, et al., 2021; McQuesten, 2002; Reynolds, Michalewicz, and Cavaretta, 1995; Spector and Luke, 1996). Just like in human societies, an essential element of it is diversity. The population includes many kinds of solutions; the power of cultural algorithms comes from exploiting such diversity.

The simplest way is to utilize diversity in a single generation of offspring. That is, instead of generating the usual two offspring at each crossover, dozens or hundreds of them are created. They are then quickly evaluated, and only the most promising few are kept—and they are most likely better than those two resulting from the normal process. This mechanism, called **culling**, is based on the observation that most crossovers are awful (Nordin and Banzhaf, 1995; Whitley, Dominic, and Das, 1991); that is, result in offspring that are weaker than their parents. This effect is especially severe in neuroevolution with competing conventions, where most crossovers are wasted on incompatible individuals. Some algorithms forgo crossover entirely and only rely on mutation. However, crossover is an important vehicle of adaptation in biology, so somehow our implementation of it is lacking. Culling is a way of trying to fix it. It is motivated by biology in that embryos that are not viable are discarded early in gestation, and litters are often much larger than one or two individuals. There also are probably other mechanisms at work in biology that make crossovers more productive than crossovers in computation, such as more complicated genotype-to-phenotype mappings (Miikkulainen and Forrest, 2021). They can be partially modeled by making culling more extreme; that is, generating more offspring and retaining only a few of them, which is easy to do in evolutionary computation.

The challenge in culling is to recognize the few most promising offspring without having to run a full fitness evaluation on the whole set. If that is possible, then culling can speed up evolution. It turns out that such approximate evaluation is possible through

culture. A set of inputs can be formed (i.e., a set of questions, or a syllabus if you will), which is then given to each offspring to see how they respond. Those answers can then be compared to answers that other prominent population members would create, such as the parents or population champions. Those offspring whose answers are very different from the culture can then be culled. Even though the hope is that some offspring's answers differ because they are better than anything seen before, this process is effective in identifying offspring that are the worst (i.e., nonviable). Most crossovers are awful; it is enough to discard only those. This process can be very effective, speeding up evolution by a factor of 3 or more in neuroevolution for the pole-balancing task (McQuesten, 2002).

Similar cultural mechanisms can be applied to other parts of the evolutionary process. For instance, in selecting parents for **crossover**, the main goal is to combine the good traits of both parents. This goal is challenging because fitness alone does not tell the full story. Sometimes good genes are incompatible with or dominated by other genes in the individual, resulting in poor fitness overall (as will be seen in section 6.4.5). Therefore, parents should be chosen not only based on fitness, but also on distance. That is, the parents should be close enough in the genotypic space to be compatible, but different enough so that crossover will generate something new. In this manner, combining the strengths of both parents becomes more likely.

One practical implementation of this idea is to select the first parent based on fitness only, as usual, and the second to complement it—that is, to be as different from the first as possible while still competent in fitness. The difference can be measured based on the answers in the **syllabus**, as in culling. It turns out that in neuroevolution for the acrobot task (i.e., swinging the jointed pole upright), a better offspring is generated twice as often as without such parent selection (15% of the time instead of 7%) (McQuesten, 2002). Note that the second parent is usually much worse in fitness, so such high fitness is likely achieved by combining complementary strengths.

Culture can also be used to **maintain diversity** directly by focusing on which individuals are discarded from the population to make room for new offspring. Usually, the individuals with the poorest fitness are removed, but diversity can be used as a secondary measure. One way to implement this idea is to find two pairs that are the closest in the population in terms of the answers to the syllabus, and then discard the less fit of them. Again, in acrobot neuroevolution, such a mechanism resulted in populations that were three times as diverse (in average distance in answers to the syllabus), making evolution 30% faster (McQuesten, 2002).

A fourth way of taking advantage of culture is to use it to leverage **learning** in evolution. As discussed in section 4.2.3, the syllabus of inputs can be paired with answers of the parents or population champions, and then used as a training set for gradient descent. In this manner, those offspring that have the best learning potential can be identified. Even when the learned weights are not coded back into the genome, evolution becomes more effective through the **Baldwin effect**; that is, a more informative selection of offspring. In pole balancing, this mechanism can make neuroevolution an order of magnitude faster (McQuesten, 2002).

However, even better use of this idea can be made by taking advantage of diversity in the population culture. That is, the behaviors of all individuals in the population serve as the cultural heritage; individuals can learn from any of these behaviors, and such learning can guide genetic evolution in a more diverse and effective way.

At the outset, it is not clear that this idea would work. To be sure, dividing the population into teachers and learners, as well as utilizing parents and population champions as teachers, makes sense: The new and poorly performing individuals in the population are trained to be more like those that are known to perform well. However, such training is also bound to reduce diversity. Much of the population starts by copying a few good individuals, which may make it more difficult for evolution to discover new solutions.

Also, even though the parents and champions perform well overall, some of their actions can still be quite poor during evolution. Conversely, there may be other individuals in the population who perform very well in specific situations, even though they do not perform that well overall. In broader terms, in evolutionary computation as in society in general, any individual may have something useful to teach to any other individual. This is one reason why diverse teams in general may be more innovative than teams that are not (Rock and Grant, 2016).

This principle can be captured computationally in a method called **egalitarian social learning** (Tansey, Feasley, and Miikkulainen, 2012). The idea is that each agent A observes the performance of each other agent B in various situations in the task. If B receives a high reward in situation x where A receives a low reward, there is a learning opportunity for A. A training example is formed with x as input and agent B's action y as output, and gradient descent is used to modify agent B. In a sense, the entire set of agents and their behaviors forms a population culture. Each agent is then trained to adopt those aspects of the culture that are the most successful.

This approach works in domains where rewards can be obtained frequently and are associated with partial behaviors. To enhance diversity, it is possible to divide the population into subcultures. Agents in each subculture teach and learn from the other agents in the same subculture, making it less likely for the population to converge prematurely. The approach can be implemented through Lamarckian evolution or the Baldwin effect. When diversity is maintained through subcultures, Lamarckian evolution may be more effective.

The approach was demonstrated in a foraging domain where food items are randomly scattered and vary in their value from very good to poor to outright poisonous (figure 5.8). The agents sense these items in eight 22.5-degree sectors in front of them and also sense their own velocity. As their output, they control their velocity and orientation. With egalitarian learning, many different strategies evolved. Some subcultures focused on high-speed exploration to utilize high-value food. Others moved more slowly, and carefully consumed all positive food items. Overall, the egalitarian population was significantly more effective in utilizing the available food resources than a comparable student-teacher model and direct neuroevolution. The experiment thus illustrated the value of diversity in a team of agents, as well as the value of egalitarian learning.

Instead of using the diverse solutions in a population for training, the knowledge in such solutions can be abstracted into a statistical model that then guides evolution. The model predicts how likely the various combinations of elements in these solutions are to result in high fitness. The approach is similar to CMA-ES (section 2.2.3), which uses a

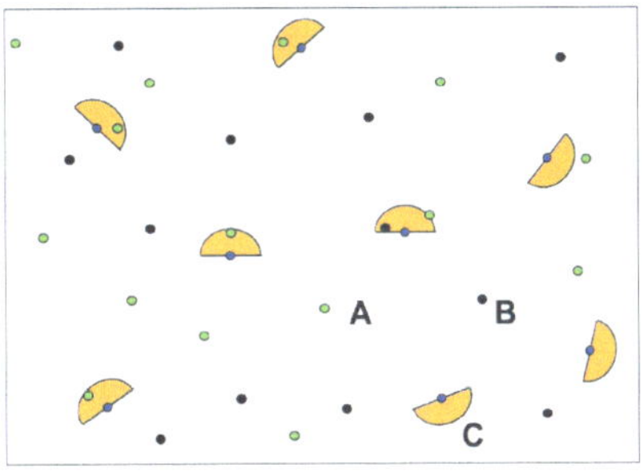

(*a*) The foraging domain

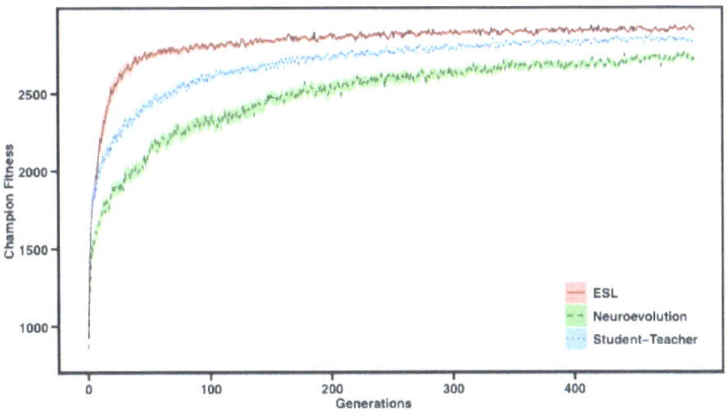

(*b*) Foraging fitness over evolution

Figure 5.8: **The effect of diversity and egalitarian learning.** A population of agents needs to forage in an environment with good and bad objects. (*a*) The agents gain fitness by consuming food items of various positive values (A) and avoiding items of negative values (B). They have a limited view (C), requiring them to move around a lot to find the items. With direct neuroevolution, several strategies developed, some taking advantage of covering a lot of ground, and others taking advantage of being careful not to miss anything. (*b*) With egalitarian social learning (ESL), the evolved agents could also learn from each other during their lifetime. ESL achieved higher fitness by generation 50 than direct neuroevolution or a student-teacher approach by Generation 500. This experiment thus demonstrated both the value of diversity and of learning from population culture. Figures from Tansey, Feasley, and Miikkulainen (2012). Videos at `https://neuroevolutionbook.com/demos`.

model to make intelligent mutations, and **estimation of distribution algorithms** (EDAs; Alden and Miikkulainen, 2016; Baluja and Caruana, 1995; Larrañaga and Lozano, 2002; Lozano, Larrañaga, Inza, et al., 2006; Pelikan, Goldberg, and Cantú-Paz, 1999), where solutions are constructed step by step using a statistical model such as a Bayesian network or a Markov random field. At each step, the model is used to determine which further elements would be most likely to result in good solutions, given the elements chosen so far.

Instead of building a model of gene statistics, it can be built for neurons or modules that form a network in approaches such as **symbiotic adaptive neuroevolution** (SANE), **ESP** or **CoDeepNEAT** (sections 7.1.1 and 10.3.2). In such a process, the neuron that correlates most significantly with high fitness is selected first. When selecting the next neuron, a measure of epistasis (i.e., dependence) is first used to decide whether the fitness correlations of the next neuron candidates should be calculated based on only those networks that contain the previous neuron, or all networks in the population. The neuron with the highest correlation is then chosen as the next neuron. In this manner, a single offspring is constructed at a time in a probabilistic process that does not employ crossover or mutation. In problems such as double pole balancing, this approach, called **eugenic neuroevolution**, can find solutions several times faster and more reliably than methods that evolve partial solutions without it (Alden, Kesteren, and Miikkulainen, 2002; Polani and Miikkulainen, 2000; Prior, 1998). Note that diversity in the population is crucial to form a good model—and this model is a good way to take advantage of such diversity.

So far, the idea of utilizing culture has relied only on the current population. But culture can extend over multiple generations, and there is no reason why populations from prior generations couldn't be used in evolutionary algorithms as well. The more solutions there are to define culture, the more diversity there is also likely to be, making cultural algorithms more effective. Of course, an efficient way to store the solutions and select parents among them is needed.

Neuroannealing (Lockett and Miikkulainen, 2013) provides such a mechanism. All solutions ever encountered in the evolutionary run are organized into a partition tree of solutions. There are four levels: The first is partitioned according to the number of layers in the network, the second according to the number of nodes in each layer, the third according to the connectivity patterns between layers, and the fourth according to the weight values. A parent is selected by traversing the tree using a Boltzmann distribution on the average fitness of each branch, as in simulated annealing. Once a parent is selected, NEAT-like mutations are performed to generate new solutions based on it.

Compared to standard NEAT, the neuroannealing process provides more ways to increase complexity without forgetting any of the previous solutions. It can thus construct larger and deeper networks than NEAT. Such networks may be useful in fractured domains that make the evolution of behavioral strategies challenging (section 6.3). Neuroannealing outperforms NEAT in many such problems, including multiplexer design, concentric spirals, and double pole balancing.

Neuroannealing can be seen as implementing an extreme form of elitism: Any solution can have useful information in it, and therefore, nothing is ever discarded. Thus, the population grows larger over time, and is likely to include more diversity in solutions than smaller and constant-size populations can. With all this information, it is possible to represent the fitness function more comprehensively.

Each of the methods reviewed in this section points out opportunities for utilizing diversity in population culture in neuroevolution. An interesting challenge for the future is to find synergies between them: For instance, neuroannealing could be combined with eugenic evolution to build better models; culling, mate selection, and intelligent discarding with any generation-based methods; egalitarian learning with eugenic or neuroannealing systems. In this manner, diversity can be utilized in many more ways than simply powering search based on crossover.

More broadly, this chapter discussed the role of diversity in neuroevolution, including different ways that it can be characterized, how diversity can be encouraged to emerge, and how it can be harnessed to find better solutions. These techniques will be put to work in the rest of the book, starting with evolving behavior in the next chapter.

5.8 Chapter Review Questions

1. **Biological and computational diversity:** Explain why diversity is a cornerstone of both biological evolution and computational neuroevolution. How does diversity enable complex solutions to emerge over time and adapt to changing environments?

2. **Genetic diversity:** What role does genetic diversity play in evolutionary computation? Discuss the problems that arise when a population converges too quickly and how these issues hinder recombination and exploration.

3. **Behavioral diversity:** Why is behavioral diversity particularly important in neuroevolution? Contrast it with genetic diversity, and describe a scenario where behavioral diversity could improve the search process.

4. **Diversity maintenance techniques:** Compare and contrast two methods for maintaining genetic diversity: fitness sharing and crowding. How do these techniques work, and what are their limitations?

5. **Behavior characterizations:** What is a behavior characterization (BC), and why is it essential for measuring and promoting behavioral diversity? Provide an example of how a BC could be defined in a robot navigation task.

6. **Multiobjectivity:** Explain how multiobjective optimization fosters diversity in neuroevolution. What are the benefits of having a Pareto front, and how does it relate to boosting population diversity?

7. **Quality diversity:** What is the goal of quality diversity (QD) in evolutionary algorithms, and how does it differ from traditional optimization objectives? Describe how QD methods like MAP-Elites or NSLC maintain both high-performing and behaviorally diverse solutions.

8. **Ensembling:** Why is ensembling particularly well suited for evolutionary algorithms? Describe how the NEAT method uses speciation to facilitate ensembling, and provide an example of its application.

9. **Cultural diversity:** What is the role of population culture in neuroevolution? How can cultural mechanisms, such as culling, mate selection, discarding, and training, improve the efficiency and outcomes of evolutionary processes?

10. **Egalitarian learning:** Define egalitarian social learning in the context of neuroevolution. How does it differ from a student-teacher approach, and why does it enhance diversity in a population?

Chapter 6

Neuroevolution of Behavior

An important area of neuroevolution is constructing agents that behave intelligently in simulated or real environments. Such behavior spans several levels. At the lowest level, the neural networks optimize control tasks, such as locomotion for robots or production in bioreactors. At gradually higher levels, they optimize behavioral strategies for navigation, game play, or cognitive domains, to cite some examples. At the very highest level, they may implement decision strategies for business, healthcare, and society in general. This chapter reviews successes and challenges in such domains and also discusses how human expertise can be incorporated into the discovery process.

6.1 From Control to Strategy

Neuroevolution is naturally well suited for controlling agents and discovering behavioral strategies for them, in both physical and virtual environments. In many domains, however, the environment can change in unexpected ways. The behavior has to adapt, sometimes by tuning existing behaviors, sometimes by deploying distinctly different behaviors at different times, and other times by discovering entirely new behaviors. Neuroevolution approaches to discovering such flexible behaviors, and indeed prospects for evolving generally intelligent agents, are reviewed in this section.

One of the most natural applications of neuroevolution is to discover effective behaviors through interaction with the environment: The network receives sensor values as input, and issues control commands to effectors as output. If the network is recurrent, it can integrate inputs over time, and thus disambiguate partially observable environments. It can understand and take advantage of physical effects such as friction and momentum, remember objects that may be currently hidden from view, and so on.

For instance, in driving a simulated race car, neuroevolution discovered that it could get through curves faster by tracing a wider trajectory. This strategy is counterintuitive because such trajectories are longer; however, they allow for higher speeds, which is more effective in the end. In robot-arm control, neuroevolution discovered a way to compensate for an inoperative main motor: It couldn't turn around its main (vertical axis), so it evolved instead to turn the arm away from the target and then swing it toward the target very fast, creating enough momentum to turn the entire robot around. In controlling a simulated spacecraft, when it did not have the jets to stop its forward movement, it instead turned it around and then stopped the turn, resulting in a hard stop. In playing the Gomoku (also called "Five-in-a-Row") against other programs submitted for a tournament, it discovered that it could win by making a move very far away—the other programs expanded their board size to incorporate it, and crashed because they ran out of memory. There are numerous similar examples in the literature, demonstrating creative ways of controlling simulated and real robots, sometimes compensating for problems, other times achieving goals in creative ways (Fullmer and Miikkulainen, 1992; Lehman, Clune, Misevic, et al., 2020; Moriarty and Langley, 1998; Moriarty and Miikkulainen, 1996; Sit and Miikkulainen, 2005).

When discussing behavior, it is often useful to separate it into two levels. At a lower level, the challenge is to discover an effective single behavior; that is, to devise optimal control. At a higher level, the challenge is to utilize multiple behaviors appropriately; that is, to devise an optimal behavioral strategy. The challenges and solutions are different in the two cases.

Neuroevolution is well suited to discovering single behaviors in challenging domains, such as those that are dynamic, nonlinear, and noisy. For instance, in rocket control, the goal is to keep the rocket flying straight, even though it is an unstable system and can easily lose stability due to atmospheric disturbances. Large rockets with multiple engines have them each on a gimbal, making it possible to turn them through control algorithms, which is heavy, expensive, and difficult (indeed, rocket science). Smaller rockets instead have large fins that create enough drag at the back of the rocket to turn it into a stable system, with a cost in performance. It turns out a neurocontroller can be evolved simply to control the amount of thrust in each of the engines, and thus keep the rocket stable even without any fins at all (figure 6.1; Gomez and Miikkulainen, 2003). Such control is precise, robust, and effective, and would be difficult to design by hand.

By itself, however, such control is not particularly robust. It works well within the conditions encountered during training, but it does not extend well to new conditions. Yet in the real world, such changes abound. In rocket control, the rocket parameters and weather conditions may vary; the rocket may need to fly through atmospheric disturbances. A walking robot may need to get around or over obstacles, or deal with a surface covered with water or ice. Sensors may drift or break entirely; actuators have wear and tear or may become inoperative. Coping with such variation is, of course, a major challenge for neural networks: While they interpolate well within the space of their training, they do not extrapolate well outside it.

Similar successes and challenges can be seen at higher levels of behavior as well, such as in discovering effective **behavioral strategies**. A good example is the **NERO video game** (Stanley, Bryant, and Miikkulainen, 2005). In this game, simulated robots are engaged in a battle in a virtual world where they can sense objects, their teammates, opponents, and line of fire, and they also can move around and shoot. The player does not control them directly, but instead has the task of training them to behave effectively during the battle. This goal means coming up with a curriculum of gradually more complex challenges, such as approaching a target, shooting accurately, avoiding fire, coordinating an attack, and coordinating a defense. The player achieves these behaviors by manipulating

(*a*) Rocket control (*b*) NERO video game

Figure 6.1: **Neuroevolution of effective control and behavioral strategies.** (*a*) Neuroevolution discovers a controller that can keep the rocket stable by controlling the amount of thrust to its four engines. It is accurate enough so that the fins are no longer required, allowing the rocket to fly much higher with the same amount of fuel. It is, however, difficult for the controller to generalize to variations in the rocket parameters and environmental conditions. (*b*) In the NERO video game, a human player trains the agents through a curriculum of exercises to attack a target, while at the same time avoiding fire from opposing agents. This is a sophisticated behavior, but a good team needs other behaviors as well, such as defending and sharpshooting, which are difficult to evolve at the same time. A challenge for neuroevolution, thus, is to discover flexible, multimodal behavior on its own, as an important step toward general intelligence. Figure *a* from Gomez and Miikkulainen (2003); figure *b* from Stanley, Bryant, and Miikkulainen (2005). For videos of these behaviors, see `https://neuroevolutionbook.com/demos`.

multiple objectives; that is, the fitness function coefficients along several measurable dimensions of behavior.

Interestingly, it is possible to design curricula that are more effective than others, in that they result in more sophisticated behavior that takes more factors into account. There also does not appear to be a single strategy that always works better than others, but team A can beat B, which can beat C, which can beat A; this is precisely what makes the game interesting for a human player.

However, NERO also illustrates the limitations of the standard neuroevolution approach in discovering behavioral strategies. Throughout the evolutionary process, it elaborates on earlier behaviors and usually produces a sophisticated final behavior that subsumes all of them. However, the most successful teams in the game are composed by hand from individuals evolved separately toward different goals: sharpshooters, attackers, defenders, and other roles. Evolution does not spontaneously evolve agents that could deploy such very different behaviors at different times, nor a strategy for switching among them appropriately. Yet if neuroevolved agents are to be deployed in the real world, such flexible multimodal behavior is likely to be required. There are offensive and defensive modes in many games; the opponent may utilize a different strategy; the agent may be part of a team

Info Box: Neuroevolution at the University of Texas at Austin

Connectionist Models Summer School was a series of workshops organized in the late 1980s and early 1990s to promote the burgeoning field of neural networks—or "connectionism", as it was then called. The 1988 version was organized at Carnegie Mellon by Dave Touretzky, Geoff Hinton, and Terry Sejnowski. Some 100 students participated, including me (Risto Miikkulainen), eager to learn how to bring about a big change in AI. It was an exuberant convergence of ideas—and one of them was neuroevolution. It wasn't actually one of the topics in the lectures; it was brought up in one of the breakout sessions by Mike Rudnick, a PhD student from Oregon Graduate Institute. Genetic algorithms had gained some popularity, and Mike thought that they could be used to construct neural networks as well. I was working on connectionist natural language processing then, but the idea seemed fascinating to me, and I put it aside, hoping to get back to it someday.

That didn't take long—in spring 1991, during my first year as an assistant professor at the University of Texas at Austin, an undergrad named Brad Fullmer wanted to do an honors thesis, and ended up evolving neural networks for an agent that roamed a virtual world and decided which objects in it were good and which ones were bad—launching a research direction in my lab on virtual agents that continues to this day! Brad developed a marker-based encoding technique where junk DNA could become functional later, which I think still should be explored more. Dave Moriarty, a PhD student, picked up the topic about a year later, and developed his own approach, SANE (part of an appropriately named system called Sherlock), about evolving a population of neurons, i.e., parts of a network instead of full neural networks. Dave's solution to forming full networks was to evolve network blueprints. In parallel, Tino Gomez came up with another solution, enforced subpopulations, i.e., evolving neurons for each location in the network separately. At the time, the ideas were separate partly so that Dave and Tino could each make a distinct contribution in their dissertations—it wasn't until 22 years later that we realized that we could bring them together to evolve deep learning architectures in CoDeepNEAT!

At that time, I was ready to write a book about neuroevolution: The idea of evolving elements for a dense structure (i.e., neurons for a fully connected network) was elegant and the applications to control and behavior compelling. But a third PhD student, Ken Stanley, at about 1999 started to make noise about how the network's topology mattered as well, and that we could optimize the topology of a sparse neural network for the task. It didn't fit the paradigm, and I told him I didn't think it would work—which probably only made him work on it that much harder. That idea eventually became NEAT, and one of the most enduring ideas in neuroevolution. Ken went on to build his own group at the University of Central Florida and beyond, and to develop several new ideas with students who've in turn formed their own groups in academia and industry—including a fellow named Sebastian, but that is another story.

with different abilities. Such flexibility in control and strategy is a hallmark of general intelligence. Much recent work has focused on techniques that would allow discovering and utilizing it, as will be discussed in the next three sections 6.2, 6.3, and 6.4.

6.2 Discovering Robust Control

As was discussed in section 3.2, control means managing the effectors of a real or simulated agent so it reaches its target in an effective manner. Usually, the controller observes the current state of the agent and environment through sensors (in a closed-loop or feedback control setting), and therefore can be naturally implemented in a neural network. The advantage is that such networks can deal with noise, nonlinear effects, and partial observability in a natural way. It is still challenging for them to react to changes that were not seen in training, which happens all the time in any complex environment in the real world. Therefore, several techniques have been developed to make them robust in such situations.

6.2.1 Noise, Exploration, and Novelty

Perhaps the simplest way of encouraging robust control is to add noise to the outputs of the controller. Such trajectory noise means that the control does not have precisely the desired effect, but it continually places the controller into situations from which it has to recover (Gomez and Miikkulainen, 2004). Interestingly, **trajectory noise** is more effective than **sensor noise** in producing this effect. Apparently, adding noise to sensors may confuse the agent about what it should do, but it does not similarly place it in useful training situations.

This idea can also be put to work more directly by using evolution to discover such situations automatically. For instance, if the desired actions can be specified for each situation, the controller could be trained with gradient descent. But how can the desired actions be specified? The answer is that a separate neural network can be evolved to generate them. That is, for each input situation, a **teacher network** generates the targets, and a controller network is trained by gradient descent to reproduce them. The teacher's fitness depends on how well the controller that it trains performs in the task. How is this approach any different from evolving a network to generate good actions directly? It turns out that the targets that the teacher evolves to generate do not actually correspond to optimal outputs in the task, as was demonstrated in a foraging robot domain (Nolfi and Parisi, 1994). Instead, they evolve to represent maximally effective learning experiences; that is, those that allow learning to proceed faster and more robustly. They may be exaggerated, more varied, and more difficult situations, thereby leading to a better final performance in the task.

This approach can be generalized further into a setting where **problems are coevolved with solutions**. For instance, a set of objective functions can be evolved for maze running, encouraging solutions that get closer to the goal, but also maximizing several novel objectives. Such evolution was more effective in discovering solutions to harder mazes than fixed-fitness evolution and novelty search (Sipper, Moore, and Urbanowicz, 2019).

Similarly, the coevolution of obstacle courses and runners results in more effective running behavior. Evolution starts with simple courses and gradually complexifies them as better runners are discovered, eventually constructing behavior that far exceeds what direct evolution could do. This system, called **POET** (Wang, Lehman, Clune, et al., 2019), will be described in more detail in section 9.3. Such coevolution can also occur naturally in competitive environments, such as zebras and hyenas (as described in section 7.2.2). Each species evolves to compensate for the more sophisticated strategies that the other species discovers, resulting in an arms race of more complex behaviors than would be discovered if the other species were fixed. In all these cases, neural network controllers are evolved in a task that is not fixed, but becomes more challenging as evolution progresses, automatically encouraging robust and general solutions and more complexity than can be achieved in a static setting.

Novelty search (NS), discussed in more detail in section 5.3, can be seen as a related but subtly different approach. In novelty search, individual controllers are rewarded if they generate behavior that is different from that seen before during evolution. Thus, the idea is to create as much diversity as possible, and to explore the space of behaviors as completely as possible. Eventually, some individuals will be chosen as solutions because they happen to perform well in the task of interest—which is not driving novelty search directly. Importantly, the process of discovering these solutions is very different from goal-directed search. The process may include stepping stones that have little to do with the ultimate task. The solutions may thus be built on a more general, and therefore, robust foundation. This result was seen clearly in the bipedal walk example in section 5.3: Whereas fitness-based evolution resulted in a rigid, slow walk that often fails, novelty search discovered a dynamic, fast walk that is remarkably robust.

In this manner, variation in the evaluation of agents can lead to more robust control. Another approach is to incorporate knowledge from the domain, as will be discussed next.

6.2.2 Symmetry, Context, and Adaptation

In some cases, we may know something about the system that we are controlling, and it may be possible to take such knowledge into account in designing the network architecture that is then evolved to control it. For instance in multilegged walking, each leg should be controlled in a similar way, and there are symmetries between the left and the right side, and possibly the front and the back as well. These symmetries result in a number of possible gaits: For instance, four-legged animals such as horses can trot (move diagonal legs in phase), bound (move front legs in phase and back legs in phase), pace (move legs on each side in phase), and pronk (move all legs in phase). These basic gaits can then be adjusted according to the speed and terrain.

The symmetry-breaking approach can be formalized computationally in the **bilevel neuroevolution** approach called **evolution of network symmetry and modularity method** (ENSO; Valsalam, Hiller, MacCurdy, et al., 2013; Valsalam and Miikkulainen, 2011). Each leg controller, or a module, receives the angle of the leg it controls as its input, and outputs the desired angular velocity of that leg. In addition, through intermodule connections, it receives input from all the other modules (figure 6.2). The process starts

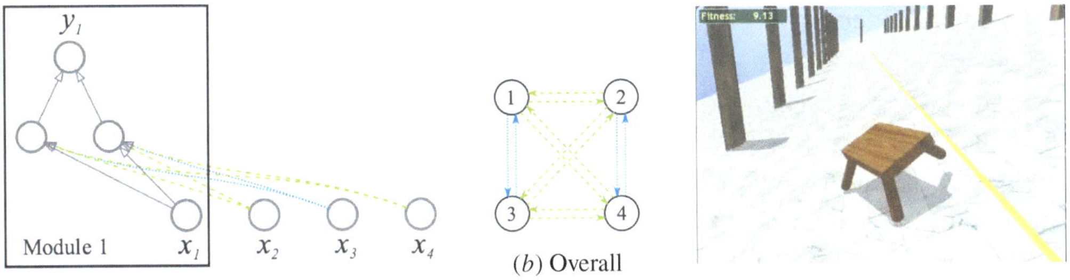

(*a*) Leg controller (*b*) Overall symmetry (*c*) Walking sideways on an incline

Figure 6.2: **Evolving symmetries for four-legged walking.** In this experiment, neuroevolution was extended to take advantage of symmetry in the four-legged robot. (*a*) Each leg has its own controller neural network, and each one receives input from the others. (*b*) Evolution starts with fully symmetric designs and breaks the symmetry as needed; that is, allowing the weights on the different connections to diverge (as indicated by the different colors). Such highly symmetric networks allow the robot to take advantage of the four main gaits on the flat ground. (*c*) A controller crossing a slippery incline sideways requires a less symmetric solution than a straightforward walk on flat ground: It evolved to use the front downslope leg primarily to push up so that the robot could walk straight. In this manner, neuroevolution can demonstrate how principles such as symmetry help construct robust behavior. Figures *a* and *b* from Valsalam and Miikkulainen (2011). For videos of these behaviors, see `https://neuroevolutionbook.com/demos`.

with a population of fully symmetric individuals, where all leg controllers are identical, and they are all connected with the same intermodule connections. The connection weights are initially assigned randomly, and evolved as usual through mutation and crossover to find the best individuals with the current symmetry.

At the higher level, evolution then explores different symmetries. Through **symmetry mutations**, the initial symmetry is broken and the connections start to diverge. Some of the modules and some of the intermodule connections are no longer constrained to be the same. In this manner, evolution evaluates more symmetric solutions before evaluating less symmetric ones. This bias allows it to discover simpler and more general gaits first, and more complex ones later if they turn out to be necessary. Interestingly, on flat ground, highly symmetric individuals evolve that are capable of all four main gaits. Depending on how their leg positions are initialized, they may pace, trot, bound, or pronk. Also, they can dynamically switch between them. For instance, an individual may start with a bound gait but hit a simple obstacle that prevents it from moving its legs in the way that it attempts—it can then switch to a trot, which moves the legs over the obstacle one at a time. Such robustness emerges automatically from the constraints of maximal symmetry among the controllers.

However, the environment may also present challenges where less symmetric solutions are required. The terrain may be cluttered with major obstacles, or slippery and inclined; faults may occur in the system; that is, some legs may be damaged or inoperative and no longer move as expected. It turns out that the symmetry evolution approach can discover solutions for many such cases by breaking more of the symmetry. For instance, when it has to walk sideways on a slippery incline, the front downslope leg evolved a role of simply pushing the agent upward, while the other three propelled it forward. It would be difficult to design effective gaits for such situations by hand, and yet the systematic approach to understanding the symmetry of the agent and constraining evolution to take advantage of it makes it possible to discover them effectively and robustly.

Another powerful approach to dealing with variation in the environment is to model it explicitly within the controller. That is, the system consists of three neural network components: A **skill network** that takes actions, a **context network** that models the environment, and a **decision network** that uses the current representation of the context to modulate the actions of the skill module (figure 6.3; Li and Miikkulainen, 2018; Tutum, Abdulquddos, and Miikkulainen, 2021).

This **context+skill approach** was first developed for opponent modeling in poker, where it resulted in a surprising ability to generalize against new opponents. When evolved to play well against only four canonical simple behaviors (always raise, always call, always fold, or follow raw hand strength statistics), it was able to beat Slumbot, the best open-source poker player at the time. The skill module evolved to take reasonable actions based on the sequence in each game; the context module evolved to recognize the canonical behaviors that Slumbot used at different times; and the decision-maker evolved to adjust the actions based on the context.

It turns out that the approach can be generalized to robust control more generally, including games such as FlappyBird, LunarLander, and CARLA (simulated driving). In FlappyBird, for instance, it can be used to play robustly when the game conditions change. In this game, a bird flies at a constant speed through a horizontal track, where it has to avoid hitting pipes that appear at constant intervals. The player takes a "flap" action to push the bird up, and gravity will pull it down constantly. Precise timing of the flap actions is required to avoid the pipes, and they have to anticipate not just the next pipe but the location of those that follow as well. In an extended version of the game, another action, a forward flap, is added, causing a forward push that is constantly slowed by drag. Different versions of the game can be generated by simply adjusting the strength of the up and forward pushes and the strength of gravity and drag.

It turns out that without the context module, the FlappyBird controller does not generalize much at all beyond the versions seen during training; that is, with +/- 20% of variation on the four parameters. As is usual in neural networks, the controller can interpolate between situations that it has seen before, but cannot handle situations that would require extrapolation. With context, however, it can fly robustly in conditions that vary +/- 75%; that is, in conditions that require significant extrapolation.

It is interesting to analyze how context modulation achieves such robustness. One might expect that the context network outputs change significantly in new situations, making it possible for the decision-maker to modulate the skill network's actions accordingly. However, the opposite is actually true: The outputs of the context and skill actually change very little, requiring very little new behavior from the decision-maker. In effect, the context network evolved to standardize the various situations and map them to a limited range where the actions are known. Such a principled understanding of the domain extends to a much broader range of conditions, therefore leading to extrapolation.

The context+skill approach can also be useful in coping with environments that change. As will be discussed in section 6.2.3, the real world is rarely constant, but instead, there are changes due to outside factors, wear and tear in the mechanics, and noise and drift in

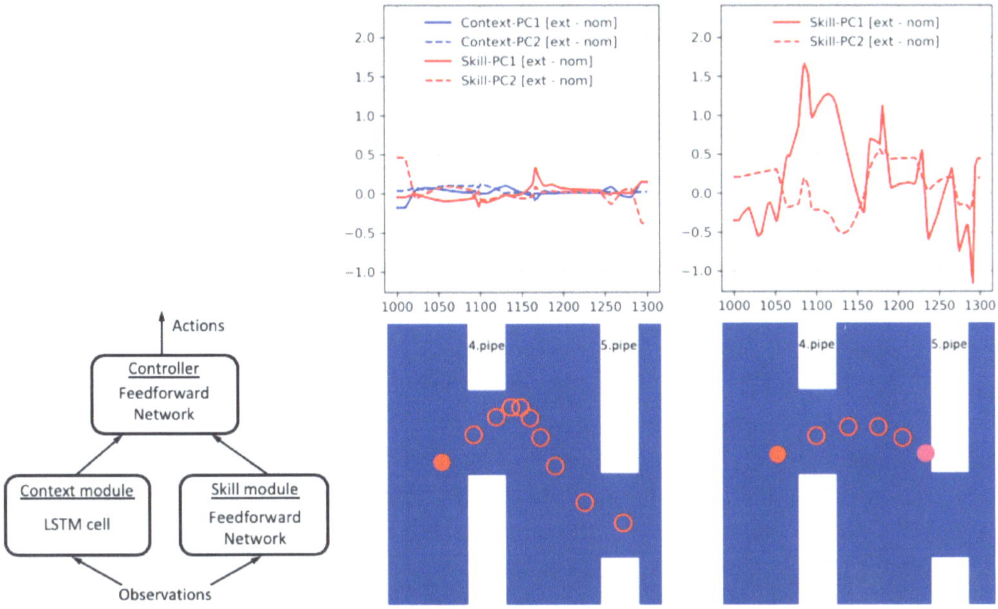

(*a*) Context+skill network (*b*) Context+skill control (*c*) Skill-only control

Figure 6.3: **Modeling the environment explicitly with a context network.** In many domains, conditions can vary significantly and unexpectedly, requiring extrapolation beyond training. For instance in an extended FlappyBird domain, the strength of the forward flap, upward flap, gravity, or drag can change. (*a*) In context+skill networks, it can be beneficial to model the variation explicitly with a context network; the decision maker can then use the context to modulate the actions of the skill network appropriately. (*b*) With context+skill control, the context network evolves to standardize the variation so that the decision-maker sees little of it (shown here through the first principal components of the context and skill module output over time on top, lined up with the bird's location in the bottom). It can thus perform well in a new situation, such as the decreased strength of the upward flap or an increased drag. (*c*) In skill-only-control, without context, the skill network outputs vary much more, making it difficult for the decision maker to generalize. In this manner, explicit understanding of the context extends the behavior robustly to variations of the domain. Figures from Tutum, Abdulquddos, and Miikkulainen (2021). For videos of these behaviors, see `https://neuroevolutionbook.com/demos`.

the sensors. The context module can learn to anticipate such changes and modulate the skill module accordingly. For instance in the gas sensor drift domain (Warner, Devaraj, and Miikkulainen, 2024), it learned the direction and magnitude of such changes over time, allowing it to classify future examples significantly more accurately than a model that was simply trained to be as general as possible.

Changes in the environment may not always be predictable over time and may exceed the generalization ability of the controller networks. In such cases, some kind of rapid online adaptation may be necessary. However, neuroevolution is usually applied as an offline method; that is, the controllers are evolved during a training period ahead of time and then deployed in the application. Further adaptation would then require another period of offline evolution. Continuing evolution during deployment is difficult because it creates many candidates that are not viable. Indeed, the exploratory power of evolution, which is its greatest strength, makes it difficult to apply it online, where every performance evaluation counts. Historically, this was the main difference between reinforcement learning (RL), which was intended as an **online lifelong learning method**, and evolutionary computation, an offline engineering approach. This difference has blurred recently: Many RL approaches are now offline—and similarly, there are versions of neuroevolution that can work online (e.g., rtNEAT in section 8.1, EANT, odNEAT, and others; Agogino, Stanley, and Miikkulainen, 2000; Cardamone, Loiacono, and Lanzi, 2009; Metzen, Kirchner, Edgington, et al., 2008; Silva, Urbano, Correia, et al., 2015).

For instance, once the initial neurocontrollers have been evolved offline, they can be refined online using **particle swarm optimization** (PSO; Gad, 2022; Kennedy, Eberhart, and Shi, 2001). PSO is loosely based on the movement of swarms such as birds or insects. A population is generated around a well-performing individual, and changes made to each individual by combining its own velocity (i.e., history of changes) with that of the best individuals in the population. PSO therefore provides a way to find local optima accurately. Combining a GA and PSO thus allows for both exploration and exploitation: GAs can make large changes to the solutions, discovering diverse and novel approaches, and PSO can refine them through local search. Such combinations of global and local search, or memetic algorithms, are useful in neuroevolution in general, including neural architecture search (ElSaid, Ricanek, Lyu, et al., 2023; Lorenzo, Nalepa, Kawulok, et al., 2017; Ribalta Lorenzo and Nalepa, 2018). They can also implement online adaptation: Assuming the changes in the environment are gradual, they can create alternative solutions that still perform well, but also track the changing requirements.

For instance in the bioreactor control domain, micro-organisms grow by consuming a nutrient substrate that is continuously fed into the reactor. The growth process is dynamic and nonlinear and varies unpredictably. The best production is achieved close to the maximum liquid level of the reactor; however, this level must not be exceeded, or else the reactor needs to be shut down. While the initial controllers constructed through neuroevolution were able to keep the reactor operational, fine-tuning through PSO improved the production significantly. When changes were introduced into the simulation, online adaptation through PSO was able to keep the operation safe, while still tracking the economic optimum closely (van Eck Conradie, Miikkulainen, and Aldrich, 2002a,b). In this manner, online adaptation can be used to add robustness to the control that would be difficult to achieve otherwise.

Thus, neuroevolution can naturally deal with noisy and nonlinear domains, and there are many ways to make it robust when the domain varies significantly. But are such solutions robust enough to cope with variation in the physical world? This question will be addressed next.

6.2.3 Transfer to Physical Robots

There is generally a **reality gap** between simulation and physical reality: Simulations are clean and deterministic, and the real world is noisy and nondeterministic and includes external factors that are not part of the simulation. For example, there is give and wear and tear in the wheels and motors, unmodeled friction, sensor noise, latency, and environmental variability that are difficult or impractical to capture accurately in simulation. As a matter

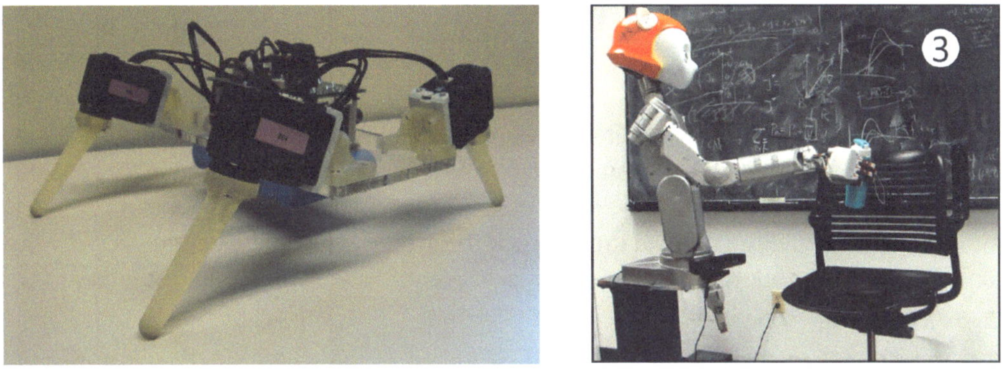

(*a*) Physical four-legged robot

(*b*) Dreamer robot with Mekahand

Figure 6.4: **Transferring control to physical robots.** In these two examples, the controller neural network is evolved in simulation and then used to control the corresponding physical robot. (*a*) A four-legged physical robot evolved to walk straight even with one leg inoperative. (*b*) An accurate simulator of a robotic arm was used to evolve controllers that generalize well to new situations and imprecise computation. In this manner, it is not only possible to transfer to physical robots, but also to construct controllers that are robust against noise, faults, and new situations. Figure *a* from Valsalam, Hiller, MacCurdy, et al. (2013); Figure *b* from Huang, Sentis, Lehman, et al. (2019). For a video of the four-legged robot, see `https://neuroevolutionbook.com/demos`.

of fact, the robotics community is often not very impressed even with very impressive simulation results, and justifiably so.

However, neuroevolution is in a good position to make the transfer to real robots possible. By its very nature, controllers are evolved to cope with imperfections, and even take advantage of them, as was seen in the robot with an inoperative main motor in section 6.1. A similar result was obtained in the four-legged walking domain (Valsalam, Hiller, MacCurdy, et al., 2013). An actual, physical, four-legged robot was constructed with a similar structure to the simulations. Each of its four legs was angled away from the center and rotated around a circle, thus each propelling it forward at a slight angle (figure 6.4a). Such a gait made it possible to walk forward as well as turn at will. Most remarkably, when one of the legs became inoperative, an asymmetric gait evolved where the remaining leg on the same side traced a wider arc than the two on the other, allowing the robot to still walk straight. Thus, not only did the neuroevolution approach transfer to physical robots, it also came up with a solution to a situation that would have been very difficult to design by hand. Another approach that can facilitate transfer to real robots is Hebbian learning, which we will review in a case study in section 12.3.2.

If transfer to the physical world is anticipated, the simulation can be extended with mechanisms that simulate the physical challenges. Factors such as wind, variable friction, and uneven terrain can be programmed into the simulation. However, it is more difficult to simulate all possible imperfections that might occur, such as slippage, blocked sensors, loose connections, battery drainage, and wear and tear. One way to deal with such issues is to add noise and stochastic blockage to the simulated sensors and effectors. Both kinds of noise allow simulating the world more realistically. As mentioned previously, effector (or trajectory) noise also allows training the controller in more varied situations.

Recently, robotics simulators have become accurate enough to support transfer in many cases. In robotic grasping, for instance, it is possible to evolve a neural network controller and transfer it into the physical robot as is (Huang, Sentis, Lehman, et al., 2019). NEAT was used with the Graspit! simulator and transferred to the Dreamer robot's Mekahand (figure 6.4*b*). The resulting controller was surprisingly robust, coping well with sensor and effector inaccuracies as well as novel objects. Most interestingly, it was robust against imprecise computation: When the grasping had to be completed very fast, only approximate information about the process was available, and yet the controller managed to grasp the object safely in most cases.

Even though neuroevolution of behavior mostly focuses on virtual agents, much of it actually originates from robotics. The field of **evolutionary robotics** emerged in the 1990s and continues to this day (Bongard, 2013; Doncieux, Bredeche, Mouret, et al., 2015; Nolfi and Floreano, 2000; Vargas, Di Paolo, Harvey, et al., 2014). The controllers and sometimes also the hardware are evolved, and often the controllers are simple neural networks. The original motivation was that robot control is difficult to design by hand, and can be more readily done through neuroevolution (Cliff, Harvey, and Husbands, 1993). Simulations are often a useful tool; however, it is also possible to evolve the controllers directly on robotic hardware. For instance, recurrent discrete-time neural networks were evolved on the Khepera mobile robot to develop a homing behavior (figure 6.5*a*; Floreano and Mondada, 1996a). The network developed an internal topographic map that allowed it to navigate to the battery charger with minimal energy simply in order to survive.

An interesting direction is to evolve both the controllers and hardware at the same time. Indeed, such **body-brain coevolution** can facilitate the evolution of more complex and robust solutions (Bongard, 2011). For instance in evolving locomotion, the robots may start with an eel-like body plan and gradually lose it in favor of a legged design. The gaits on robots that go through such a process can be more robust than those evolved on the legged design directly. To make morphological innovations feasible, it may be useful to protect them by temporarily reducing evolutionary selection pressure (Cheney, Bongard, SunSpiral, et al., 2018). Such protection is a useful general principle in discovering complexity, similar to speciation in NEAT (section 3.3). In section 7.1.2, we will see how this type of approach can also be extended to protecting innovation in heterogeneous neural architectures.

The most extreme demonstration of this approach is **genetically organized lifelike electromechanics** (GOLEM; Figure 6.5*b*; Lipson and Pollack, 2000). Not only were the hardware designs and the neural network controllers coevolved, but the robots themselves were three-dimensional (3D) printed according to the evolved designs. The designs were evaluated for their locomotive ability in simulation. The best ones were then printed and evaluated in the physical world, and found to perform as expected. The evolved virtual creatures (Lessin, Fussell, and Miikkulainen, 2013, 2014) discussed in section 14.5 extend this approach to more complex morphologies and behaviors, all the way to fight-or-flight, albeit in simulation and with a hand-constructed syllabus. However, it is possible to imagine a future where robot bodies and brains are coevolved automatically, with the results created on multimaterial 3D printers—and once the printing is finished, the robots wake up and walk off the printer on their own.

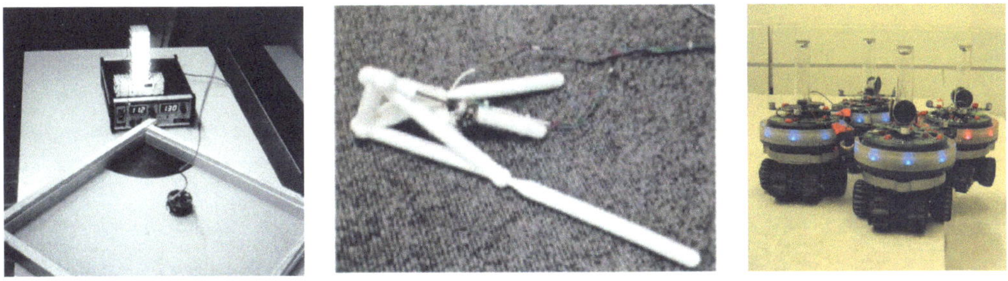

(*a*) Evolving control in hardware | (*b*) Coevolving morphology and control | (*c*) Swarm robots working together

Figure 6.5: **Neuroevolution in evolutionary robotics.** While robotics generally focuses on hardware designs, it is difficult to construct controllers by hand, especially with novel and variable designs. Neuroevolution is often a useful approach in many such cases. (*a*) Neural network controllers can be evolved directly in hardware, such as to develop homing behavior in Kheperas. The light source identifies the corner with the charging area (painted in black). (*b*) It is possible to evolve the robot morphology and control together, and 3D print the designs, in essence evolving artificial life forms. (*c*) Swarms of robots can perform tasks that single robots may not, such as traversing over holes in the ground. In this manner, neuroevolution makes it possible to develop behaviors for a wide variety of robotic designs. Figure *a* from Floreano and Mondada (1996a); Figure *b* from Lipson and Pollack (2000); Figure *c* from Trianni, Tuci, Ampatzis, et al. (2014). Videos of the coevolving morphology and control at `https://neuroevolutionbook.com/demos`.

Evolutionary robotics has already been scaled up to swarms; that is, robot teams that exhibit collective behavior (Dorigo, Theraulaz, and Trianni, 2021; Trianni, Tuci, Ampatzis, et al., 2014). The challenge here is to evolve the swarm to perform tasks that individual robots could not. For instance, such robots can hook up and form a linear train that can get over obstacles and gaps that a single robot could not (figure 6.5*c*). Many interesting issues come up in evolving neural controllers for such robots. For instance, should they all be clones of each other, or each evolved to fill a specific role in the team? Collective behavior in general is an important area of neuroevolution, discussed in depth in chapter 7.

6.3 Discovering Flexible Strategies

The neuroevolved solutions so far have focused on control. At this level, adaptation most often means modulating or adjusting a single existing behavior: Throttle one of the engines a little more, move one leg a little faster, or flap a little harder. When behavior extends from such low-level control to a high-level strategy, goal-driven coordination of multiple behaviors is required. For instance, offensive versus defensive play in robotic soccer may require getting open versus covering an opponent; actions required of a household robot are very different when it is vacuuming versus emptying the dishwasher versus folding laundry; game agents may need to gather resources, attack, and escape. Such strategies are the topic of this section.

6.3.1 Switching Between Behaviors

Evolving high-level strategies is challenging not only because the agent must have command of a much larger repertoire of behaviors, but it also needs to know when and how to switch

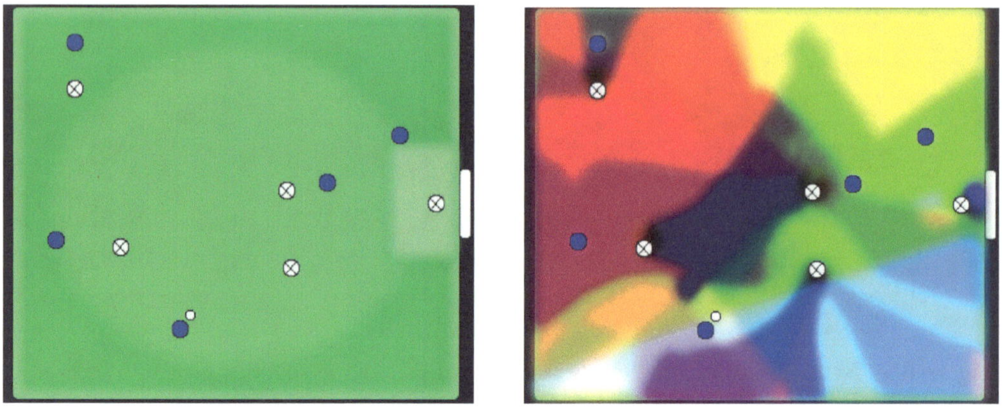

(*a*) Game situation (*b*) Values of actions

Figure 6.6: **Fractured high-level strategy in half-field soccer.** High-level strategies are difficult to discover and implement because they often require changing behaviors abruptly based on small changes in the input. (*a*) For instance in half-field soccer, five offenders (blue dots) try to score on five defenders (white dots) by holding the ball, passing to one of the teammates, and shooting. (*b*) Visualization of successful actions for an offender with a ball at various locations in the field, given the positions of all other players. Each color represents a subset of actions that would be successful. Small changes to just this one variable have a large effect on success, making good strategies highly fractured and difficult to evolve. Neuroevolution with local neurons and cascaded refinement is an effective approach in such cases. Figures from Kohl and Miikkulainen (2012). For videos of these behaviors, see `https://neuroevolutionbook.com/demos`.

between them. Proper switching is difficult for two reasons: First, in some cases, it may have to be abrupt (i.e., small changes in the environment may require drastically different actions); second, sometimes the different strategies need to be interleaved or blended instead of making a clean switch.

The first challenge can be illustrated, for instance, in the half-field soccer domain, where five offenders try to score on five defenders using eight behaviors: (1) getting open, (2) intercepting the ball, (3) holding the ball, (4) shooting at the goal, and (5–8) passing it to one of the four teammates (figure 6.6; Kohl and Miikkulainen, 2012). Depending on the position of the ball, teammates, and opponents, boundaries between these behaviors are very tricky. If an opponent moves even slightly to block a teammate, passing becomes infeasible; if an opponent crosses a threshold distance, holding becomes infeasible. Furthermore, actions that interpolate between these behaviors are not possible: They have to be performed fully or not at all. Thus, the domain can be described as **fractured**: As the state of the world changes, the correct actions change frequently and abruptly.

It is very difficult for neuroevolution to discover such **fractured strategies**. In most domains, continuous control works just fine; that is, when the situation changes a little, the control output changes a little, and continuously so. Neural networks represent such continuity well naturally, and we have seen how approaches such as **multiagent HyperNEAT** can take advantage of it to encode a team of agents (section 4.13). In contrast, hard switches are more difficult to establish. However, the network architecture can be designed to make them easier to discover in two ways:

1. Instead of sigmoid activation functions, **radial basis functions** can be used. They each activate a neuron in a specific local region, making it easier to cover fractured decision boundaries.

2. The network topology can be constructed in a **cascaded** manner; that is, complexifying it by adding neurons as extra layers on top of the existing network, instead of anywhere in the network as usual in NEAT. Such a cascade allows each new neuron to implement a refinement of existing behavior, gradually forming more fractured decision boundaries. These mechanisms can be used to augment the usual NEAT mechanisms as needed through **adaptive operator selection** (SNAP-NEAT; Kohl and Miikkulainen, 2012). Indeed, in domains like half-field soccer, this approach performs much better than handcoded solutions, as well as standard RL and other neuroevolution techniques.

A second challenge in constructing an effective strategy is that **behavior switching** needs to be flexible. In some cases, such as switching between batting and fielding in baseball, or vacuuming and emptying the dishwasher, the behavior changes entirely for a long period of time. Such tasks are isolated and can be implemented even with different neural networks and a switch network that decides among them. In other cases, however, the behaviors are interleaved, occurring several times in rapid succession. For instance, the possession of the ball in soccer can change rapidly, requiring the players to switch between offensive and defensive play often, and even anticipate such switches. In yet other sports, such as dodgeball, the offensive and defensive behaviors are blended because there are multiple balls in play, and a player may attempt to throw a ball at the same time as avoiding getting hit by one. Thus, intelligent agents must be capable of different behaviors at different times, as well as interleaving and blending them.

A good platform to study such behaviors is the Ms. Pac-Man video game (figure 6.7; Schrum and Miikkulainen, 2016b). In a maze, the player eats pills while trying to avoid getting eaten by ghosts. If the player eats a power pill, the ghosts become edible too. Thus, the behaviors of running away from threatening ghosts and approaching edible ghosts are interleaved. However, as soon as a ghost is eaten, it returns as a threat, and at that point, the tasks are blended: The player has to run away as well as approach some of the ghosts at the same time. With slight modifications to the game, isolated tasks can be studied as well; that is, by fixing the ghosts to be either threatening or edible.

A network controlling Ms. Pac-Man sees the state of the game as distances to pills, power pills, and ghosts in different directions, and whether the ghosts are edible. As its output, it decides which way to move. A simple such network can be evolved with NEAT but it does not perform very well: It has a difficult time separating the different behaviors, and tends to blend them and not perform any one of them very well. This result indeed illustrates the main challenge in learning high-level strategies with neuroevolution.

The opposite approach would be to have a human expert identify what behaviors are needed, and evolve each one separately, as well as a selection neural network that decides which behavior needs to be used when. This approach works well when the tasks are clearly separated (e.g., fight-or-flight in section 14.5), but it can also work when two behaviors need to be combined, such as evading a predator while simultaneously catching prey (Jain, Subramoney, and Miikkulainen, 2012).

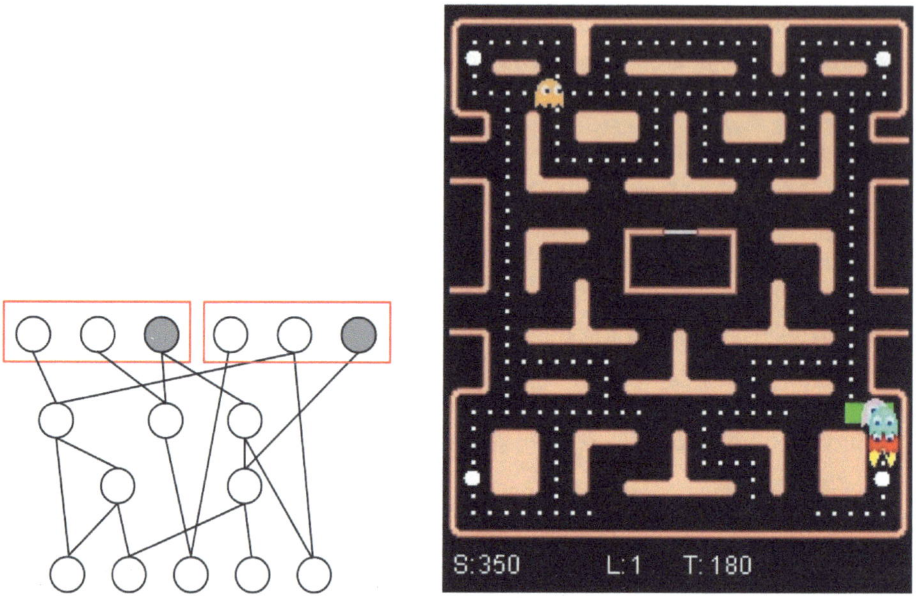

(*a*) Preference neuron architecture (*b*) Invoking the luring module

Figure 6.7: **Discovering effective and surprising multimodal task divisions**. Behavioral strategies are often multimodal (i.e., require performing different behaviors at different times). Modular network structures are a natural way to encourage multimodal behavior to emerge. (*a*) A powerful approach is to evolve a network with multiple output modules together with preference neurons (gray) to indicate when each module should be used to control the agent. (*b*) Such a system may discover surprising task divisions. For instance, in Ms. Pac-Man, instead of separating the threatening and edible ghost situations into different modules, it separates general easy movements into one module, and behaviors when ghosts are close into an escape module (active during the green trace). That module is used to lure the ghosts nearby and then escape to eat a power pill; afterward, the movement module is used to eat the ghosts (which is easy because they are nearby), resulting in a high score. Such division and behavior would be difficult to discover and prescribe by hand, and yet evolution discovers it as an effective solution to a multimodal game. Figure *a* from Schrum and Miikkulainen (2016b). For videos of these behaviors, see `https://neuroevolutionbook.com/demos`.

However, it may also be possible to learn multiple behaviors in a single network, taking advantage of commonalities between them. For instance, it is possible to evolve a single **multitask network** with different outputs to control Ms. Pac-Man when the ghosts are threatening and when they are edible. The division is not learned but implemented algorithmically. This approach works well with isolated and interleaved versions of the task. Since the same part of the network is used consistently in similar situations, evolution discovers effective offensive and defensive behaviors. In blended situations, however, it is not effective. A third set of outputs can be evolved for such situations, but it does not learn very well.

A fourth approach is to let evolution discover when to use what strategy. In this **modular multiobjective NEAT** method (MM-NEAT; Schrum and Miikkulainen, 2016a), each of the output modules is coupled with a preference neuron that indicates how strongly the network believes that the corresponding output should be used. In this setting, evolution might be expected to discover offensive and defensive strategies and how to switch between them. However, it discovers a much more sophisticated and surprising approach. The strategies that evolve are not offensive and defensive; instead, they are behaviors that apply to easy and difficult situations. That is, one output module controls Ms. Pac-Man when she is running around eating pills when no ghosts are nearby, whether they are threatening or edible. A second module specializes in escaping when threatening ghosts are nearby. With these modules, a highly effective luring strategy is implemented: It lets the ghosts get close and then escapes to the nearby power pill—and is then able to eat the ghosts effectively because they are close!

Even though the escape module is rarely active, it is crucial in obtaining a high score in the game. Therefore, half the network is dedicated to this behavior. Such a strategy would have been difficult for human designers to prescribe, and yet evolution discovered that it was the most effective way to play the game. It demonstrates how effective high-level strategies are composed not only of multiple behaviors, but also of intelligent ways of combining them. It also shows that if evolution is allowed enough freedom to explore, it can discover surprising and effective combinations.

6.3.2 Evolving Cognitive Behaviors

One potentially important role for novelty search and related methods is in discovering **cognitive behaviors** such as communication, memory, and learning. Such behaviors are complex and challenging to evolve, and several approaches have been developed to discover them (see section 14.8.2; Ollion, Pinville, and Doncieux, 2012; Risi, Hughes, and Stanley, 2010; Saunders and Pollack, 1996; Yamauchi and Beer, 1993). They illustrate challenges and ways to overcome them, often through carefully crafted domains and fitness functions based on domain knowledge. A possible reason, which is evident even in the most rudimentary versions of these behaviors, is that they require overcoming deception.

For instance, to **evolve communication**, it is necessary to discover what and when to communicate, the mechanisms to send a signal, to receive it, and to interpret it. Each of these mechanisms requires extra hardware that does not provide an evolutionary advantage unless all the mechanisms are functional at once. They are thus deceptive, and it is unlikely that evolution would stumble into them all at once. Also, if a partial solution is found, it is difficult for evolution to discard it in favor of a better one (Floreano, Mitri, Magnenat, et al., 2007). They could, however, be discovered as stepping stones by novelty search, making communication more likely to be discovered.

As an illustration of this idea, consider an agent in a **T-maze** (figure 6.8; Lehman and Miikkulainen, 2014). Each agent is controlled by a neural network whose activation is reset before each trial. In each trial, the agent starts at the bottom end. It needs to move to the intersection and decide whether to go left or right to get to the reward. An evaluation consists of multiple trials during which the reward stays in one place, but the reward can move to the opposite end between evaluations. Thus, if the reward does not move very often, or is most often found in one location, evolution can develop a simple strategy that is better than chance: Go to the location where it is found more often and/or more recently. However, if the reward moves frequently enough, communication, memory, or learning is needed to capture it more reliably.

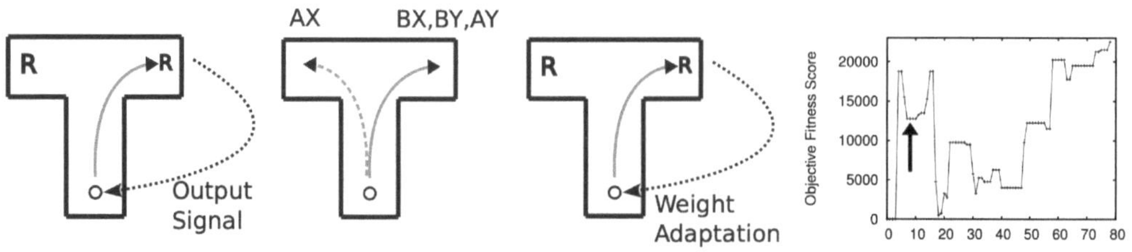

(*a*) Communication (*b*) Memory (*c*) Learning (*d*) Solution lineage

Figure 6.8: **Overcoming deception in the evolution of cognitive behaviors.** During an evaluation that consists of multiple trials, the agent needs to use (*a*) communication, (*b*) memory, or (*c*) learning to navigate to the reward in the T-maze reliably. Even when the necessary elements for these abilities are available, fitness-based evolution cannot discover how to put them together. Instead, it only discovers reactive behaviors; that is, always going to the left or the right. In contrast, they serve as stepping stones for novelty search, which eventually discovers effective cognitive behavior. Thus, the lineage of an eventual successful agent in novelty search includes many drops in fitness (*d*). For instance, the novel behavior of going to the opposite corridor with some inputs (arrow) turns out to be a useful stepping stone in discovering communication. Figures from Lehman and Miikkulainen (2014).

In a **communication task**, the agent can generate a signal at the end of the trial, and the agent in the next trial will receive it at the start. A successful communication thus indicates whether the agent should turn left or right at the intersection. In a **memory task**, the agent will receive an A or B signal and then an X or Y signal before it can start to move. The AX combination indicates that the reward is on the left, others indicate that it is on the right. The agent thus has to remember the combination of two signals to act appropriately. In the learning task, the agent can adapt the network's connection weights through **modulated learning rules** after each trial to make a successful outcome more likely (sections 12.3.3 and 14.3; Risi, Hughes, and Stanley, 2010). These weight changes persist throughout the evaluation.

Indeed, **fitness-based evolution** in this domain developed a reactive strategy of always going to the left or right, depending on frequency and recency. This strategy was successful only in less than 20% of the trials. Even when communication, memory, and learning were available, evolution could not find a way of taking advantage of them—in other words, it could not overcome deception. However, with **novelty search**, evolution was able to discover communication, memory, and learning strategies that were successful in approximately 79%, 81%, and 57% of the trials. Analysis of the lineages of eventual solutions shows that novelty search was indeed utilizing stepping stones; that is, behaviors that received lower fitness on their own but turned out to be useful in constructing the final communication, memory, or learning-based strategy.

Although the behaviors in the T-maze are simple, they are intended to capture the essential challenge of discovering cognitive structures. The results thus suggest that straightforward objective-based evolution is unlikely to discover cognitive behaviors, and thus novelty search and perhaps quality diversity methods are essential.

6.3.3 Utilizing Stochasticity, Coevolution, and Scale

In many virtual domains, whether games or training environments, it is important that the virtual agents are not entirely predictable. That is, their behavior should be **nondeterministic** (or stochastic) to some degree (a topic we briefly touched on in section 3.2.5), such that the simulation leads to a wider variety of situations and challenges. Similarly during training, the agents then encounter a wider variety of situations and may learn more robust and comprehensive behavior.

The **action-unit coding** at the output of the agent is generally a powerful approach: The action represented by the most highly activated output unit is chosen at each time step. Especially early in evolution, it is easier to find such networks rather than networks that would output continuous values (representing a range of actions) accurately.

If the agent networks were trained with backpropagation, such value-unit encoding would result in a **probability distribution**; that is, for each input, the activations across the output units would indicate the probabilities of the correct action (Morgan and Bourlard, 1990). However, such distributions do not develop automatically in neuroevolution. The networks may be able to identify the winner (i.e., develop the highest activation on the correct output unit), but the activations of the other units do not develop into probabilities: They do not matter for performance, and therefore can be anything, so long as they are lower than that of the winning unit.

However, evolution can be guided to develop probabilities with the simple technique of **stochastic sharpening** (Bryant and Miikkulainen, 2006). From the beginning, the output activation values are treated as probabilities: They are normalized to sum to 1, and the action to be performed is selected stochastically weighted by these values. For instance, in the Legion-II domain, initially the action values were relatively uniform, generating a lot of randomness, but over evolution, they became sharper, leading to more effective performance. However, the performance even in the end was somewhat stochastic, resulting in the kind of believable and interesting gameplay that would be difficult to achieve otherwise.

Interestingly, stochastic sharpening also improves the search for effective behaviors, and such agents eventually outperform those evolved without it. They are exposed to more situations during evolution, and thus evaluated more comprehensively. Their behavior becomes more consistent because unexpected situations do not throw them off. They also avoid output race conditions; that is, situations where two output unit activations are almost exactly the same, resulting in unreliable choices. Thus, stochastic sharpening is one simple tool that can make behavior more effective–so much so that it may even be worth converting continuous domains to action-unit coding just to take advantage of it.

One important principle in evolving complex behavior that has not yet been discussed is **coevolution**, which means evolving the behavior in **competition** with other agents or in **cooperation** with other agents. This is the topic of chapter 7, and in a sense, it thus continues the discussion of this section. More generally, coevolution may be extended to evolving body and brain together, or the brain together with the tasks that it needs to solve (chapter 9). All these approaches take advantage of the fact that behavior is not generated solely by the agent's neural network, but rather emerges through a continuous dynamic interaction between the agent and its environment (Nolfi, 2011).

Another important topic for the future is the evolution of behavior in large-scale networks. In particular, transformer architectures have shown surprising power when scaled up to billions of parameters, or a million times more than many of the networks discussed in this section (Ouyang, Wu, Jiang, et al., 2022). One way to characterize this power is that such a scale solves the problem of **variable binding**, or dynamic inferencing, which has limited the generality of smaller networks. For example, if trained with sentences of type 1 composed of words of type A, and sentences of type 2 composed of words of type B, such networks would not generalize to 1-sentences with B-words and 2-sentences with A-words, respectively. Large language models (LLMs) perform such generalization routinely if they are large enough: For instance, they can write technical instructions in the style of Shakespeare, which are never seen together in the training corpus.

Interestingly, a large scale is necessary for this ability to emerge. Transformers are based on attention, which aims to discover useful relationships between input tokens. While the performance of LLMs and image models is not yet fully understood, it is possible that with a large enough scale, such models start learning relationships between abstractions as well. It would be interesting to see if scale has a similar effect in generating complex, robust, and multimodal behavior. It may be possible to use existing, pre-trained foundation models in language or vision as a starting point, and evolve behavior generation as a modification or augmentation to them. Or perhaps it will be possible to construct a foundation model for behavior from scratch through the imitation of massive datasets. Or maybe neuroevolution methods can be scaled to large models, and behavior discovered through massive simulations. Research on such scale-up forms a most interesting direction for future work.

6.4 Decision-Making

Intelligent behavior, as discussed previously, focuses on agents that are embedded in a real or simulated physical environment and interact with it through physical sensors and effectors. In contrast, intelligent decision-making focuses on behavior strategies that are more abstract and conceptual, such as those in business and society. Neuroevolution can play a large role in decision-making as well, but the approaches and opportunities are distinctly different. They often need to take advantage of surrogate modeling and human expertise, as discussed in this section.

6.4.1 Successes and Challenges

To begin, note that human organizations today have vast amounts of data that describe their operation. For example, businesses record interactions with their customers, measure how effective their marketing campaigns are, and track the performance of their supply chains; health care organizations follow the behavior of patients, measure the effectiveness of treatments, and track the performance of providers; and government organizations track crime, spending, health, construction, economy. Such data has made it possible to predict future trends. Predictions are then used to decide on policies (i.e., decision strategies or prescriptions), to maximize performance and minimize cost.

Discovering optimal **decision strategies** is an excellent opportunity for neuroevolution. Optimal policies are not known; they involve a large number of variables that interact nonlinearly; the observations and outcomes are often partially observable and noisy; often several conflicting objectives, such as performance and cost, must be optimized at the same time. They are therefore well suited for representation in neural networks, and discovery through evolution.

However, a major challenge is that the search for optimal strategies usually cannot be done in the real world itself. Discovery requires exploration, and it is usually unacceptable to explore novel medical treatments with actual patients, or novel investment strategies with actual money. In discovering intelligent behaviors, such exploration is done in simulation, but it is usually not possible to simulate human behavior, biology, or society in sufficient detail to do so.

However, the vast amount of data, as well as the predictive models that can be built based on them, provide a possible solution: It may be possible to construct data-based **surrogate models** of the decision-making environment. If strategy outcomes are available, surrogate models can be trained to predict them (Francon, Gonzalez, Hodjat, et al., 2020); if not, such models can be trained to compare two strategies (Mańdziuk and Żychowski, 2023). These models are phenomenological; that is, they model the statistical correlations of contexts, actions, and outcomes, and they do not simulate the actual underlying processes. However, it turns out that understanding these processes is not even necessary: Phenomenological surrogate models are enough to evaluate the decision strategies and therefore discover good strategies through neuroevolution.

A surprising synergy emerges in this process. If the predictive models are learned at the same time as the decision strategies based on them, they provide a **regularization** effect, and a **curricular learning** effect. As a result, the strategies are more robust and easier to learn. This effect will be discussed in the next subsection.

A second challenge in optimizing decision-making is that the discovered strategies need to be acceptable to human decision-makers. Humans are eventually responsible for deploying them, and to do so, they need to be confident that they are indeed good strategies. The strategies need to be trustworthy (i.e., express confidence); they need to make explainable decisions; and it must be possible for the decision-makers to interact with them, try out counterfactual scenarios, and convince themselves that the strategies are robust. Considerable work goes into these aspects beyond just neuroevolution of good strategies (such in the **NeuroAI** system; Miikkulainen, Fink, Francon, et al., 2025; Miikkulainen, Francon, Meyerson, et al., 2021; Qiu, Meyerson, and Miikkulainen, 2020; Shahrzad, Hodjat, and Miikkulainen, 2024).

Part of this challenge is also that there is already significant human expertise in many decision-making domains, and it should be possible to use it as a starting point in discovering better policies. Evolution can still explore, but its exploration is more informed, and may be more likely to discover improvements—also, those improvements may be easier for the decision-makers to accept. Again, it turns out that there is a surprising synergy of human expertise and evolutionary discovery: When put together in this manner, the results are better than either one alone. This effect will be discussed in the second subsection 6.4.2 below.

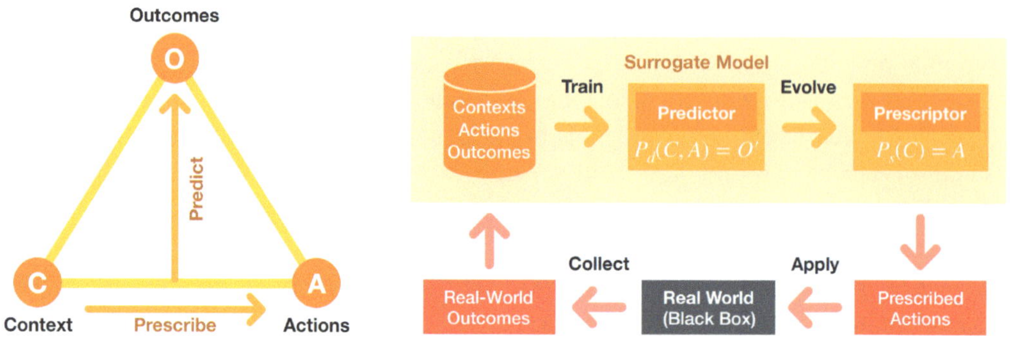

(*a*) Predictor and prescriptor models (*b*) Surrogate modeling process

Figure 6.9: **Evolutionary surrogate-assisted prescription.** In domains where evaluation of decision strategies is not possible, a surrogate model can be used to guide the search. (*a*) The surrogate model, or a predictor, maps contexts and actions to outcomes. The decision-maker model, or a prescriptor, maps contexts to optimal actions. (*b*) The models are constructed in one or more cycles of an iterative process. Starting from historical observations of contexts, actions, and outcomes, the predictor (e.g., a neural network or a random forest) is trained through supervised learning. It is then used to evaluate prescriptor candidates, constructed through neuroevolution. The final prescriptor is deployed in the domain. More data can then be collected and the cycle repeated, resulting in more accurate predictors and more effective prescriptors. Figures from Francon, Gonzalez, Hodjat, et al. (2020).

6.4.2 Surrogate Modeling

The general idea of discovering decision strategies through surrogate modeling, the **evolutionary surrogate-assisted prescription** approach (Francon, Gonzalez, Hodjat, et al., 2020), is depicted in figure 6.9. The decision-making problem is formalized as a mapping from contexts C and actions A to outcomes O. The goal is to discover a decision strategy (i.e., a prescription policy), that results in the best outcomes for each possible patient.

The starting point is a database, obtained through historical observation, that includes as many examples of this mapping as possible. For instance, C might describe patient characteristics, A might describe procedures or medication, and O might measure the extent and speed of recovery. This data can be used to train a model, such as a neural network or a random forest, to predict the outcome of a given action in a given context. Thus, the predictor P_{d} is defined as

$$P_{\mathrm{d}}(C, A) = O', \tag{6.1}$$

such that $\sum_j L(O_j, O'_j)$ across all dimensions j of O is minimized, where L is any of the standard loss functions.

The predictive model in turn can serve as a surrogate in search for good decision strategies. The strategies are mappings themselves; that is, from contexts to actions, particularly to actions that result in the best possible outcomes. They are therefore naturally represented as neural networks, and they are called **prescriptive models**. A prescriptor P_{s} takes a given context as input, and outputs a set of actions:

$$P_{\mathrm{s}}(C) = A, \tag{6.2}$$

such that $\sum_{i,j} O'_j(C_i, A_i)$ over all possible contexts i is maximized. It thus approximates the optimal decision policy for the problem. Because optimal strategies are not known ahead of time, these models need to be constructed through search (i.e., through neuroevolution). Each candidate is evaluated against the predictor instead of the real world, thus making it possible to explore fully and evaluate a very large number of candidates efficiently.

Once a good candidate is found, it can be deployed in the real world. At this point, uncertainty metrics can be applied to it, it can be distilled into a set of explainable rules, and an interactive scratchpad can be built so that the decision-maker can convince him/herself that the policy works as well as expected (Miikkulainen, Francon, Meyerson, et al., 2021). When it is deployed, more (C, A, O) data can be collected and added to the database. These data are now closer to the implemented policies, and make it possible to learn a model that is more accurate where accuracy is most needed. The cycle can then be repeated, resulting in more accurate predictors and more powerful prescriptors in the process.

A practical example of discovering decision strategies for pandemic interventions will be presented in subsection 6.4.4. However, to evaluate the power of the approach with regards to the state of the art, and to gain insight into how it constructs solutions, it can be implemented in standard RL domains (Francon, Gonzalez, Hodjat, et al., 2020). One good such domain is OpenAI Gym CartPole-v0, which requires balancing a vertical pendulum by moving a cart left or right. In this case, the process starts with a population of random prescriptors; the predictors are trained at the same time as the prescriptors are evolved (i.e., the loop in figure 6.9*b* is traversed rapidly many times).

Compared to direct evolution of the control policy, as well as standard RL methods **proximal policy optimization** (PPO) and **DQN**, the evolutionary surrogate-assisted prescription approach learned significantly faster, found better solutions, had lower variance during search, and lower regret overall. Most important, because it is based on the surrogate, the surrogate-assisted approach is highly sample-efficient; that is, it requires very few evaluations in the actual domain. Sample efficiency is one of the main challenges in deploying RL systems in the real world, and therefore a surrogate-based approach provides a practical alternative.

Such domains are also useful in illustrating how such an approach finds solutions. It turns out that they are based on two surprising synergies with learning the predictors. The first one is that such co-learning results in automatic regularization. This effect can be seen most clearly in the domain of evolving function approximators (figure 6.10). In this case, the context is a scalar value in the x-axis, and the action is a scalar value in the y-axis. The optimal policy is a sine wave; the rewards decrease linearly away from it.

The **evolutionary surrogate-assisted prescription approach** starts with randomized feedforward predictor and prescriptor neural networks. In each training episode, a context-action pair is chosen randomly, and the predictor is trained for 2,000 epochs with the pairs so far. A population of prescriptors is then evolved for 20 generations, using the same pairs to evaluate them against the current predictor. The top prescriptor is then evaluated against the ground truth to illustrate progress at each episode.

As seen in figures 6.10*b*–*f*, after 15 episodes, the predictor is still far from representing the sine wave, and the policy optimal with regards to this predictor is highly irregular as well. Remarkably, however, the policy represented by the top prescriptor is much closer to

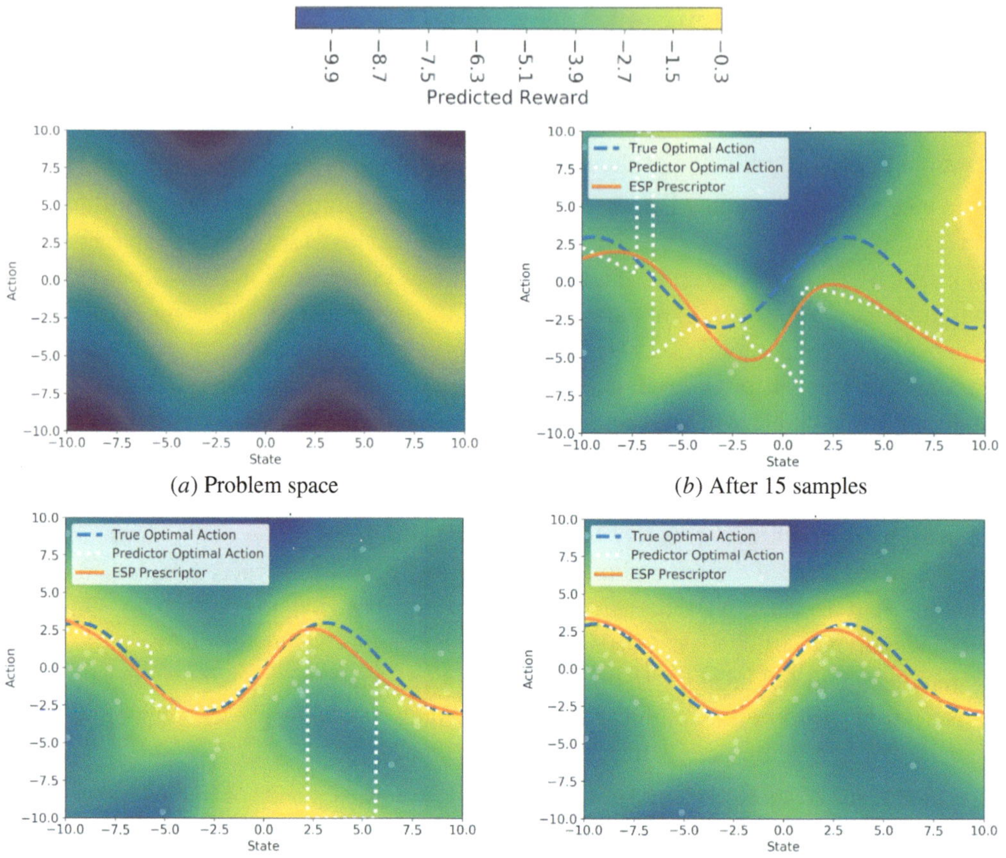

(*a*) Problem space
(*b*) After 15 samples
(*c*) After 75 samples
(*d*) After 100 samples

Figure 6.10: **Evolving effective decision-making through co-learning of the surrogate model.** This example illustrates the synergy of learning the predictor and prescriptor at the same time in the function approximation domain. (*a*) With the context as x and the action as y, the ground truth outcomes are indicated by the colored background. (*b*)–(*d*) The current predictor is indicated as the colored background instead, so it can be compared with the ground truth in (*a*). The training pairs are illustrated with translucent dots. The actual optimal policy is indicated by the blue dotted line, and the policy that is optimal with regards to the current predictor is shown as a white dotted line. The policy represented by the current top predictor is indicated by the solid orange line. The prescriptors evolve policies that are better than the predictors suggest. The prescriptors are evaluated with several different predictors over time, which act as an ensemble that is more accurate than any single predictor alone. Such co-learning of the predictor and the prescriptors thus results in automatic regularization, leading to faster learning and more robust solutions. Figures from Francon, Gonzalez, Hodjat, et al. (2020). For a video of this process, see `https://neuroevolutionbook.com/demos`.

the actual optimal policy. This trend continues throughout training and evolution. By 75 episodes, the top prescriptor has already converged to the optimal policy even though the predictor still suggests an irregular policy, and by 100 episodes, even the predictor-optimal policy is a sine wave. This convergence is remarkably rapid: PPO takes over 3,000 episodes to learn a good approximation, and direct evolution (with the predictor) is not even close at that point.

How is it possible for the approach to discover an optimal policy when the predictor is still far from it? It turns out that the simultaneous learning of the predictor provides a regularization effect. The best predictors stay in the population for several generations, and therefore are evaluated against many versions of the predictors. Especially early in predictor training, the predictors vary significantly. In a sense, they form an ensemble, and the prescriptors are evaluated against this ensemble. The ensemble performs better than any individual predictor, and therefore the prescriptor evaluation is more accurate as well. Thus, the co-learning of predictors and prescriptors provides a surprising regularization effect that makes it possible to progress faster than expected.

Another useful effect of co-learning is the curricular learning environment that it provides. That is, the early predictors capture the main trends and the most general aspects of the environment, which then become refined as they learn more. Thus, the challenges start simple and become more complex as the training goes on—this is the main principle of curricular learning in general, and also a good way to construct complex behavior (as also seen in section 3.3).

The effect can be made concrete in the **FlappyBird** game environment. The bird flies at a constant speed through a series of gates in pipes. The player has only one action, "flap," which lifts the bird up a constant amount. Gravity will then bring it rapidly down. The challenge is to time the flaps so the bird gets through the next gate and is also well positioned to get through the next gate. Here, the predictor is trained to estimate the next game states given the current state and the action, and prescriptors evolved to decide when to flap. The fitness is increased for every gate that the bird successfully clears.

Figure 6.11 shows four sample predictions during evolution. Curricular learning is evident in these snapshots: At the beginning, the predictor tends to place the gate near the bird, making it easy to fly to it. By the time the bird evolves to fly through one gate, the predictor has learned to expect the next gate, but clusters it together with the first one. It is thus relatively easy to evolve behavior that clears several gates. As the predictor learns, it spreads the gates farther apart but still keeps them roughly at the same level. While the prescriptors evolve to fly straight through, the predictors start placing the gates farther up and down, eventually providing a realistic challenge. By that time, it is relatively easy to evolve behavior that takes the height of the gates into account, and flap the bird successfully through the course. In contrast, direct evolution (i.e., evolution from scratch in the actual task), never constructs successful behavior. This result demonstrates the power of curricular learning and shows how it can be automatically discovered by learning the challenges at the same time as the solutions.

The evolutionary surrogate-assisted prescription approach forms a foundation for discovering decision strategies with neuroevolution. The next two subsections illustrate how real-world decision systems can be built on it utilizing the NeuroAI platform (Miikkulainen, Fink, Francon, et al., 2025).

6.4.3 Case Study: Mitigating Climate Change Through Land-Use Optimization

A significant factor contributing to climate change is how much land area is allocated for different uses (Friedlingstein, O'Sullivan, Jones, et al., 2023). Forests in general remove

(*a*) First gate (*b*) Pair of gates (*c*) Straight run (*d*) Full problem

Figure 6.11: **Automatic curricular evolution through co-learning of the surrogate model.** In the FlappyBird game, the challenge is to flap the bird up at the appropriate times so that it flies through a course of gates without hitting them. The predictor, trained to estimate the result of an action (flap/no-flap) at a state, (*a*) places the gate nearby, (*b*) clusters a number of them together, (*c*) spreads them apart at the same level, and (*d*) finally presents the full game challenge accurately. Such a series of increasingly challenging evaluations provides a curriculum that makes it possible to evolve successful behavior, even when it would not evolve with the full challenge from scratch. Co-learning the predictor and prescriptor thus constructs an effective curriculum automatically, allowing neuroevolution to solve more difficult tasks. For videos of these behaviors, see `https://neuroevolutionbook.com/demos`.

more carbon from the atmosphere than crops and ranges, and yet such uses are essential for the economy. Land-use patterns must therefore be planned to minimize carbon emissions and maximize carbon removal while maintaining economic viability.

Young, Francon, Meyerson, et al. (2025) developed an approach to optimize land use based on the evolutionary surrogate-assisted prescription method discussed in the previous section. The idea is to first utilize historical data to learn a surrogate model on how land use decisions in different contexts affect carbon emissions and removals. Then this model is used to evaluate candidates in an evolutionary search process for good land-use change policies. While it is difficult to predict the economic impact of changes in land use, the amount of change can be used as a proxy for it. As a result, a **Pareto front** is generated of solutions that trade off the reduction in carbon emissions and the amount of change in land use. Each point in the Pareto front represents an optimal policy for that trade-off.

The data for carbon emissions (**emissions resulting from land-use change**; ELUC) originate from a high-fidelity simulator called **bookkeeping of land-use emissions** (BLUE) developed by Hansis, Davis, and Pongratz (2015). BLUE is designed to estimate the long-term carbon dioxide (CO_2) impact of committed land use. "Committed emissions" means that all the emissions that are caused by a land-use change event are attributed to the year of the event. BLUE is a bookkeeping model that attributes carbon fluxes to land-use activities. While in principle, a simulator can be used as the surrogate model, in practice, the simulations are too expensive to carry out on demand during the search for good policies. Therefore, the BLUE team performed a number of simulations covering a comprehensive set of situations for the time period 1850–2022, resulting in a dataset that could be used to train an efficient surrogate model.

The **Land-Use Change** (LUC) data is provided by the **Land-Use Harmonization project** (LUH2; Hurtt, Chini, Sahajpal, et al., 2020). A land-use harmonization strategy estimates the fractional land-use patterns, the underlying land-use transitions, and key agricultural management information, annually for 850–2100 at 0.25×0.25–degree resolution. Based on these data, the modeling approach aims to understand the domain in two ways: (1) In a particular situation, what are the outcomes of the decision-maker's actions? (2) What are the decisions that result in the best outcomes; that is, the lowest carbon emission and cost for each trade-off between them? The data is thus organized into context, action, and outcome variables.

Context describes the problem that the decision-maker is facing; that is, a particular grid cell, a point in time when the decision has to be made, and the usage of the land at that point. More specifically, it consists of latitude and longitude and the area of the grid cell, the year, and the percentage of land used in each LUH2 category (as well as nonland, such as sea and lake).

Actions represent the choices that the decision-maker faces. How can they change the land? In the study by Young, Francon, Meyerson, et al. (2025), these decisions are limited in two ways: First, decision-makers cannot affect primary land. The idea is that it is always better to preserve primary vegetation; destroying it is not an option given to the system. Technically, it is not possible to re-plant primary vegetation. Once destroyed, it is destroyed forever. If replanted, it would become secondary vegetation. Second, decision-makers cannot affect urban areas. The needs of urban areas are dictated by other imperatives and optimized by other decision makers. Therefore, the system cannot recommend that a city should be destroyed or expanded.

Outcomes consist of two conflicting variables. The primary variable is **ELUC** (i.e., emissions from land-use change). It consists of all CO_2 emissions attributed to the change, in metric tons of carbon per hectare (tC/ha), obtained from the **BLUE** simulation. A positive number means carbon is emitted, a negative number means carbon is captured. The secondary variable is the cost of the change, represented by the percentage of land that was changed. This variable is calculated directly from the actions. There is a trade-off between these two objectives: It is easy to reduce emissions by changing most of the land, but that would come at a huge cost. Therefore, decision-makers have to minimize ELUC while minimizing land change at the same time. Consequently, the result is not a single recommendation, but rather a Pareto front where each point represents the best implementation of each trade-off, given a balance between the two outcomes.

The **evolutionary surrogate-assisted prescription** implementation consists of the predictor, trained with supervised learning on the historical data, and the prescriptor, trained through evolution. Given the context and actions that were performed, the predictive model estimates the outcomes. In this case, since the cost outcome can be calculated directly, only the ELUC is predicted by the model. That is, given the land usage of a specific location and the changes that were made during a specific year, the model predicts the CO_2 long-term emissions directly caused by these changes. Any predictive model can be used in this task, including an artificial neural network, random forest, or linear regression. As usual, the model is fit to the existing historical data and evaluated with the left-out data.

Given context, the prescriptive model suggests actions that optimize the outcomes. The model has to do this for all possible contexts, and therefore it represents an entire strategy for optimal land use. The strategy can be implemented in various ways, including decision trees, sets of rules, and neural networks. The current approach is based on neural networks. The optimal actions are not known, but the performance of each candidate strategy can be measured (using the predictive model); therefore, the prescriptive model needs to be learned using search techniques such as neuroevolution. As in prior applications (Francon, Gonzalez, Hodjat, et al., 2020; Miikkulainen, Francon, Meyerson, et al., 2021), the prescription network has a fixed architecture of two fully connected layers; its weights are concatenated into a vector and evolved through crossover and mutation.

In preliminary experiments, prediction performance was found to differ between major geographical regions. To make these differences explicit, separate models were trained on different subsets of countries: Western Europe (EU), South America (SA), and the United States (US). Three predictive models were evaluated: **linear regression** (LinReg), **random forests** (RF), and **artificial neural networks** (NeuralNet). They were trained with a sampling of data up to 2011, and were tested with data from 2012–2021. Not surprisingly, for each region, the models trained on that region performed the best. The LinReg models performed consistently the worst, suggesting that the problem includes significant nonlinear dependencies. RF performed significantly better; however, it does not extrapolate well beyond the training examples. In contrast, neural nets both capture nonlinearities and extrapolate well, and turned out to be the best models overall. Therefore, the global neural net surrogate was used to evolve the prescriptors.

The prescriptors were evolved and tested with the same training and testing sets as the global neural net. The prescriptors were fixed fully connected neural networks with two layers of weights. Their weights were initially random, and modified by crossover and mutation. They received the current land use percentages as their input, and their outputs specified the suggested changed land use percentages; they were then given to the predictor to estimate the change in ELUC. The outputs were compared to the inputs to calculate the change percentage.

Figure 6.12 demonstrates the progress of evolution toward increasingly better prescriptors; that is, those that represent better implementations of each trade-off of the ELUC and change objectives. They represent a wide variety of trade-offs, and a clear set of dominant solutions that constitute the final Pareto front (red dots). That set is returned to the decision-maker, who can then select the most preferred one to be implemented. Importantly, the evolved Pareto front dominates two linear baselines: one where land is converted to forest from all other types evenly, and another where other land types are converted to forest in a decreasing order of emissions.

A closer look revealed that evolution discovered an unexpected strategy: Instead of trying to improve everywhere, as the heuristics did, it identified a smaller number of locations where land use change had the largest effect, and allocated maximum change to those locations. In other words, it found that it is important to pick your battles! This result suggests that the approach is able to learn and utilize non-obvious opportunities in the domain, and therefore results in better solutions for land use than the obvious heuristics.

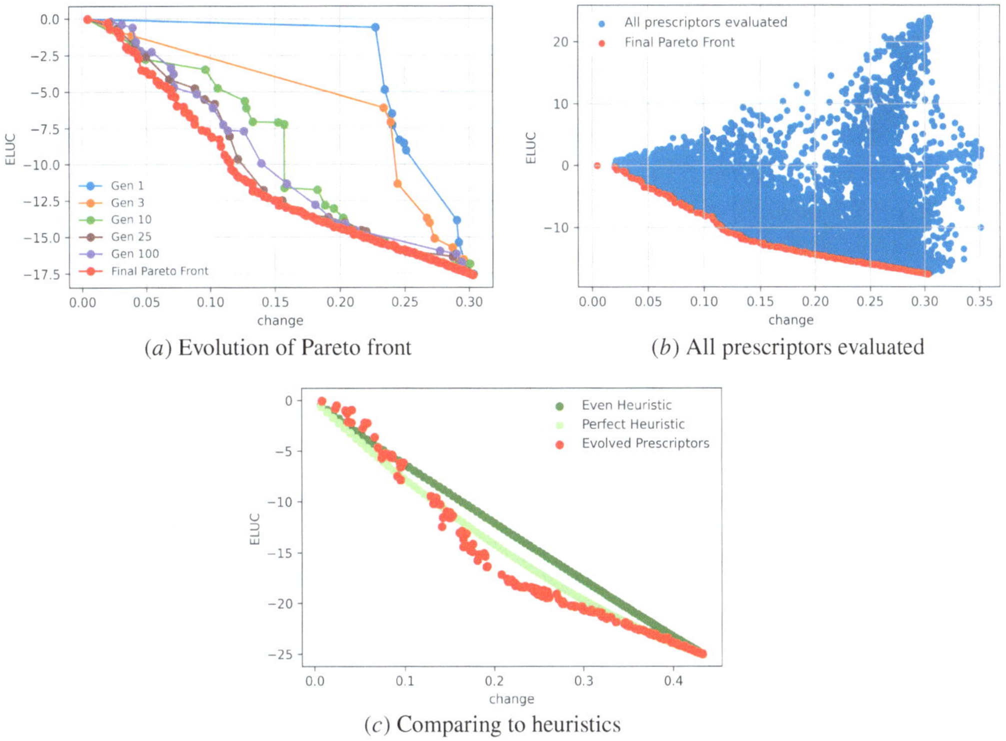

(*a*) Evolution of Pareto front

(*b*) All prescriptors evaluated

(*c*) Comparing to heuristics

Figure 6.12: **Prescriptor evolution and performance.** In the land-use optimization domain, the goal is to achieve low carbon emissions with minimal change in land use. (*a*) The Pareto front moves toward the lower-left corner over evolution, finding better implementations for the different trade-offs of the ELUC and change objectives. (*b*) Each prescriptor evaluated during evolution is shown as a dot, demonstrating a wide variety of solutions and trade-offs. The final Pareto front is shown as red dots in both figures, constituting a set of solutions from which the decision-maker can choose a preferred one. (*c*) The Pareto fronts of evolved prescriptors versus heuristic baselines. Whereas the heuristics try to optimize each region equally, the evolved prescriptors allocate more change to where it matters the most. This result demonstrates that the approach can discover non-obvious opportunities in the domain, and thus find better solutions than the obvious heuristics. Figures from Young, Francon, Meyerson, et al. (2025). For an interactive demo of the system, see `https://neuroevolutionbook.com/demos`.

6.4.4 Case Study: Optimizing Non-pharmaceutical Interventions for COVID

One example of discovering intelligent decision strategies through neuroevolution is a system for optimizing **non-pharmaceutical interventions** (NPIs) during the COVID-19 pandemic (Miikkulainen, Francon, Meyerson, et al., 2021). Throughout the pandemic in 2019–2023, governments and decision-makers around the world were trying to contain the health and economic impacts of the pandemic by imposing a variety of regulations on the society.

Economically, the most severe restrictions included school and workplace closings, stay-at-home requirements, and restrictions on public events, gatherings, and domestic and international travel; less severe ones included public information campaigns, testing arrangements, contact tracing, and masking requirements. The approaches were very different around the world, partly because especially early on, it was not clear how effective they were, individually and in combination.

COVID-19 was the first global pandemic that took place in the information age, and data about it became available in vast amounts almost immediately. It became a major focus of the scientific community (in late 2020, a new paper was submitted to arXiv/bioarXiv on average every 17 minutes), and many approaches were developed to use this data to understand it and cope with it. Most of the approaches were based on existing technology of epidemiological modeling, developed in the early 1900s during and after the major pandemics at that time (Kermack and McKendrick, 1927). The idea is to construct differential equations that describe how different populations become susceptible, exposed, infected, and recover or die, called the **SEIR model**. The models require estimating several parameters, the most important of which is r (the transmission rate). The effect of NPIs can be taken into account by modifying these parameters. More recently, these models have been augmented with agent-based modeling approaches and network models, which can extend their granularity almost to an individual person's level (Newman, 2002; Venkatramanan, Lewis, Chen, et al., 2018). Properly constructed, the models can be accurate and useful in predicting the course of the pandemic. However, estimating the parameters is difficult, and the models are computationally expensive to run.

Much of the community, especially early on, focused on prediction–that is, what will happen. The decision-makers could then, in principle, use these predictions to evaluate alternative NPIs and decide what to do about it. Even such communication between the scientists and decision-makers turned out to be difficult, especially in the political climate at the time, but there were several cases where it was effective and resulted in good outcomes (Fox, Lachmann, Tec, et al., 2022). An interesting question therefore arises: Could optimal intervention policies be discovered automatically using machine learning?

The approach described in the section 6.4.2 is well suited to this task. The first step is to build the surrogate; that is, the predictive model that could then be used to evaluate the policy candidates. It turned out that the usual SEIR approaches could not serve this role very well for three reasons: It was difficult to parameterize them for the hundreds of countries and finer-grain locations; it was difficult to parameterize them to model all possible intervention combinations; and the models took too long to run to evaluate the large number of candidate policies that needed to be tested. However, there was enough data available so it was possible to develop a data-driven approach to prediction: train a neural network to predict the number of cases (or hospitalizations, or deaths) phenomenologically.

The approach was possible because good sources of data existed to construct it. Time series data was available for cases and other indicators for different locations around the world through centralized sources almost daily (Centers for Disease Control and Prevention, 2023). In addition, a major project at Oxford University evaluated government and news outlet sources to formalize the NPI policies in effect at these locales (Hale, Webster, Petherick, et al., 2020). The NPIs around the world were unified into a representation with 12–20 categories, each with 1–4 stringency levels.

Such data made it possible to use supervised ML techniques to form the predictive surrogate model (figure 6.13a). A **long short-term memory** (LSTM) neural network

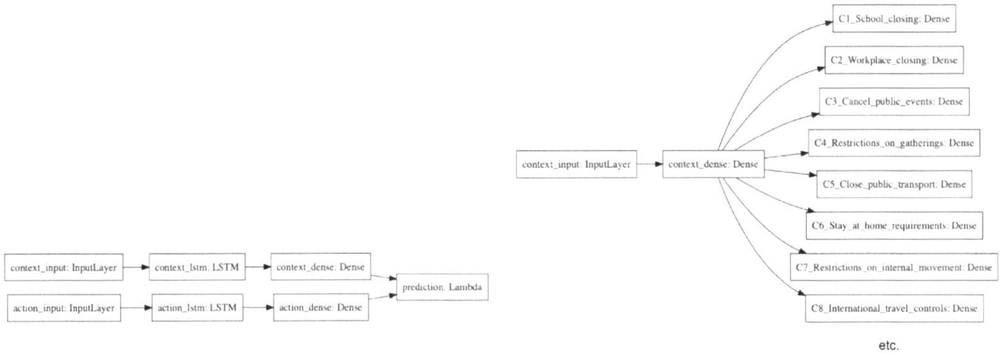

(*a*) Predictor model (*b*) Prescriptor model

Figure 6.13: **Predictive and prescriptive models for discovering NPIs in the COVID-19 pandemic.** The predictor is used as a surrogate model for the world to evolve prescriptors that implement good NPI strategies. (*a*) The predictor is an LSTM network that receives a 21-day sequence of cases and NPIs as inputs, and predicts the cases for the next day. The network is trained with historical data across different countries. During performance, the prediction is looped back to the input and rolled out indefinitely into the future. (*b*) The prescriptor receives the same sequence of cases and NPIs as inputs, and prescribes the NPIs for the next day. Since the optimal prescriptions are not known, it is constructed through neuroevolution to reduce both the number of cases and the total stringency of NPIs. Each prescriptor is evaluated through the predictor as the surrogate model. In this manner, the predictor is constructed entirely based on data and is fast enough to evaluate a large number of prescriptor candidates. Figures from Miikkulainen, Francon, Meyerson, et al. (2021).

with two channels, one for the number of cases, and the other for the NPIs, was trained to predict the cases the next day. As its input, it received the history of the last 21 days, and the predictions were looped back into the input so that they could be unrolled indefinitely into the future. The separation made it possible to impose simple constraints on the predictions, such as caps based on the population size of the locale, and that more stringent NPIs should not lead to increases in the number of cases.

The **prescriptor models** were then evolved to discover good intervention policies (figure 6.13*b*). Each prescriptor received the same sequence of case numbers and NPIs as its input and the suggested NPIs as its output. These suggestions were input into the predictor, which then estimated the number of cases. The cases and NPIs were looped back into the input of both models, and in this manner, the prescriptor was evaluated 90 days into the future. Its performance was measured based on the number of cases, as well as the total stringency of the NPIs that it suggested. The problem is thus multiobjective, and **non-dominated sorting genetic algorithm II** (NSGA-II; section 2.2.5) was used to construct a Pareto front of solutions. Therefore, the end result is a collection of prescriptors on the Pareto front. The idea is that the decision-maker can then choose a suitable trade-off between cases and stringency; that is, health and economic outcomes.

Note that this problem is a good example of a decision-making task where a surrogate is necessary, for three reasons. First, even if the decision-makers could incorporate science into their process, only one decision policy could be implemented at any one time—and yet a large number of alternatives need to be evaluated in the search process. Second, the

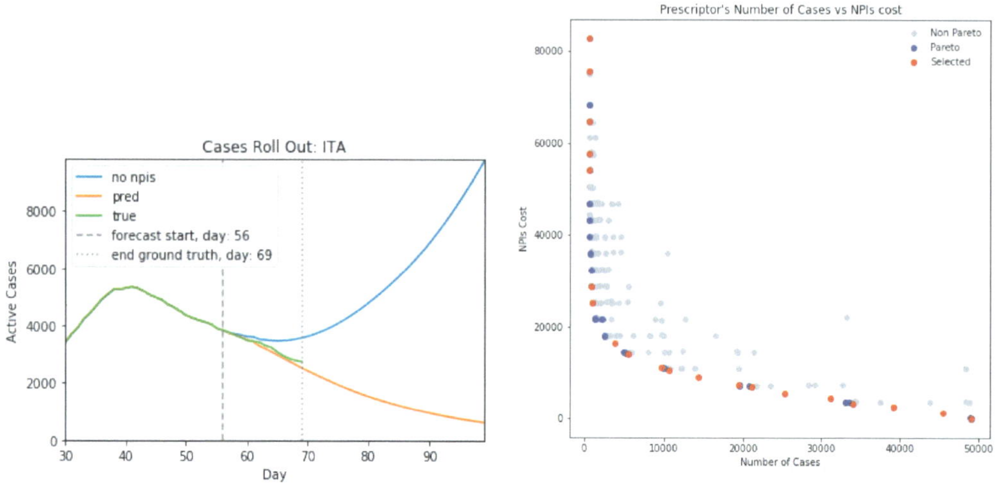

(*a*) Predictor accuracy (*b*) Prescriptor Pareto front

Figure 6.14: **Learned predictors and prescriptors.** (*a*) Given the diverse training data across time and countries, the predictor learned to estimate the number of cases accurately. This example is Italy in July 2020. Given the actual sequence of NPIs as input, it predicted the cases accurately for the next 14 days for which there was data. It also suggested that these NPIs, if maintained, would bring the cases down, but if lifted, an explosion of cases would result. (*b*) The performance of the final population of prescriptors along the case and cost objectives. The Pareto front evolved strongly toward the bottom left, and in the end offered a set of trade-offs from which the decision-makers could choose. Figures from Miikkulainen, Francon, Meyerson, et al. (2021). For a video of the Pareto front, see `https://neuroevolutionbook.com/demos`.

NPI policies need to be evaluated over a long time, during which the world does not stay constant. The NPIs change over time, the number of cases changes as a result of the NPIs, and it also changes differently depending on the stage of the pandemic. The evaluations thus need to be done against a surrogate that is accurate enough to track such changes. Third, simply predicting the most likely outcome is not sufficient; it must also be possible to estimate the uncertainty of the predictions. With a surrogate model, it is possible to estimate the uncertainty in the initial predictions; the evaluation can then be unrolled multiple times to observe the variation in the long term, resulting in confidence bounds.

Throughout the pandemic, from May 2020 through December 2022, the predictor and prescriptor models were trained daily, forming a constantly adapting set of predictions and policies for all locations. The data-driven approach worked surprisingly well in constructing reliable predictors. Different countries implemented different restrictions, and they encountered different phases of the pandemic at different times. Thus, the data was diverse enough so that the predictor learned to evaluate the different policy candidates accurately. These results were confirmed by evaluating the predictions against actual data in various countries at various stages of the pandemic early on. So long as there were no major changes in the NPIs or the pandemic, the predictions tracked the cases well (figure 6.14*a*).

Similarly, prescriptor evolution discovered a range of effective policies for different stages of the pandemic and for different locations (figure 6.14*b*). Evaluations with the surrogate model suggest that in many cases, they would have resulted in a lower number of cases and lower economic impacts than the actual policies implemented. An interesting pattern of discoveries emerged in this process. The models often discovered principles a few weeks ahead of the time that they became widely known. The first such result appeared in May 2020. The models consistently suggested the most stringent restrictions on schools and workplaces. And in fact, a few weeks later, the results came out, suggesting that the virus was transmitted most effectively in closed spaces where people stayed in contact for several hours every day. In September 2020, the suggestions changed, focusing on gatherings and travel restrictions, but suggesting less stringent restrictions for schools. Indeed, measures had been taken at schools with regards to separation, ventilation, dividers, and masks that made it possible to keep them open in a safer manner.

Perhaps the most significant demonstration of the power of this approach took place in March 2021, during the delta variant surge of the virus. The models predicted a huge explosion of cases in India, which was surprising because India had had the pandemic under control until then, and there was no indication that anything was wrong. However, the models had seen delta surges elsewhere, and they apparently recognized that the NPIs at the time made India vulnerable. Even though it was difficult to believe the models, they were correct. If the recommendations had been followed, much of the surge could have been avoided (figure 6.15).

On the other hand, the models were much less successful in coping with the omicron surge. It was indeed different, in that it happened very rapidly all over the world—there was not enough time for the models to get to see it in some countries, and then apply it to others. It also turned out that in 2022, it no longer made sense to train the models from all the available data. Different NPIs were used. There was better testing, tracing, and masking and fewer restrictions on work, school, and travel. Also, people behaved differently in 2022 than in 2020. In many locations, they did not adhere to the restrictions the same way, and masking, testing, and vaccinations made it less necessary to do so. Therefore, it was better to train the models with less but more recent data. On the other hand, this result again emphasized that it is important to train the predictor with the prescriptor; in that manner, both can adapt to the changing world.

The NPI optimization application, as described previously, was primarily a technology demo, but it has already had a significant impact. In a couple of cases, it was also used to inform actual policy decisions, such as the school openings in Iceland in the fall of 2021. A major effort in mainstreaming the approach was the **XPRIZE Pandemic Response Challenge**, held from December 2020–March 2021 (Cognizant AI Lab, 2023; XPRIZE, 2023). More than 100 teams around the world participated in creating predictors and prescriptors for the pandemic. The general setup and the data sources were the same, but the approaches varied widely. The winning teams were successful not only in terms of performance, but also in communicating the results to decision-makers.

Most recently, Project Resilience (Francon, 2025; International Telecommunication Union (ITU), 2023), a project led by the International Telecommunication Union (ITU) agency of the United Nations, is an attempt to build on these successes and extend them to other challenges such as climate change. In this manner, over time, it is possible that the surrogate optimization approach in general, and neuroevolution in particular, will

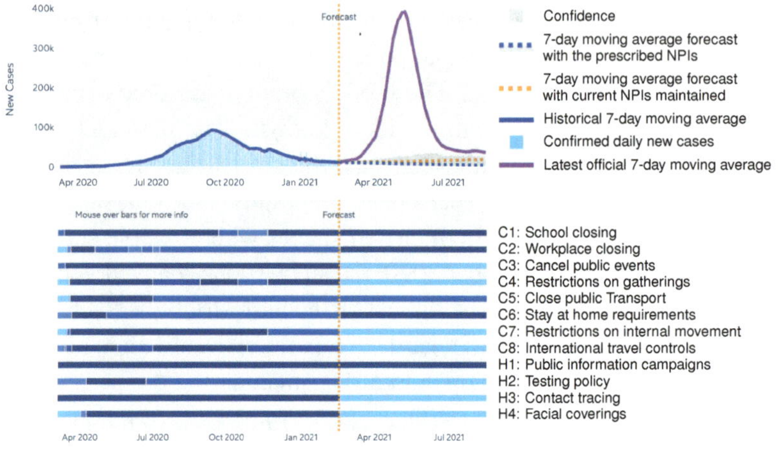

(*a*) February 19, 2020

(*b*) March 1, 2020

(*c*) March 21, 2020

Figure 6.15: **The predicted delta surge in India and a prescription to avoid it.** (*a*) On February 19, 2020, the cases were decreasing (top plot) and the prescriptors suggested that many NPIs could be lifted (bottom plot, lighter colors). (*b*) The cases were similarly low on March 1, 2020, but there had been delta surges elsewhere, and the models predicted a major surge in India if the current NPIs were continued—which was hard to believe at the time. The prescriptors suggested tightening some of them, which could have still avoided a major surge. (*c*) However, more stringent NPIs were only established several weeks later, by March 21, and by that time, even a full lockdown could not have avoided the major surge. In this manner, the models can be used to detect problems early enough when it is still possible to fix them. For an interactive demo, see `https://neuroevolutionbook.com/demos`.

gradually become widely used to cope with a variety of problems in decision-making in society.

An interactive demo of the NPI optimization system is available through this book's website (`https://neuroevolutionbook.com`). It allows for going back in time and evaluating the model's suggestions, comparing them to actual NPIs, and modifying them to see the effects. The code prepared for the XPRIZE competition is available through the website as well. Using that starting point, it is possible to develop further models for the pandemic dataset and others.

6.4.5 Leveraging Human Expertise

Recent applications of supervised learning have demonstrated the power of learning the statistics of large numbers of labeled examples, and various RL and evolutionary optimization approaches have reached super-human performance in many game-playing domains without much human involvement. However, there are many domains where humans have significant expertise. Incorporating such expertise in learning could provide a better starting point, allowing it to find better solutions in complex tasks, as well as solutions that may be easier and safer to deploy.

Neuroevolution provides a natural way to incorporate such knowledge into creative problem-solving. Human solutions can be encoded in equivalent neural networks to form the initial population, which is then evolved further to take advantage of both knowledge and machine discovery.

A method called **realizing human expertise through AI** (RHEA) was developed for this purpose (Meyerson, Francon, Sargent, et al., 2024). It consists of four phases:

1. Define the problem in a manner such that diverse expertise can be applied to it.
2. Gather the solutions from the experts.
3. Distill the solutions into a population of equivalent neural networks.
4. Evolve the neural network population to discover improved solutions.

Let us illustrate this approach first in a synthetic domain illustrated in figure 6.16. The problem is defined as one where a subset of policy interventions $(a_1, a_2 ... a_n)$ needs to be selected for different contexts $(c_1, c_2 ... c_m)$ to optimize utility ϕ and cost ψ. Assume that there are three expert solutions available: two specialists for c_1 and c_2, and a generalist that can be applied across all contexts. They can be distilled into a common grid representation where black in cell (c_i, a_j) indicates choosing an action a_j for context c_i. This population of three solutions can then be evolved to obtain better solutions.

Let the utility be defined as follows:

$$\phi(c, A) = \begin{cases} 1, & \text{if } c = c_1 \wedge A = \{a_1, a_2\} \\ 2, & \text{if } c = c_1 \wedge A = \{a_1, a_2, a_3, a_4, a_5\} \\ 3, & \text{if } c = c_1 \wedge A = \{a_1, a_2, a_3, a_4, a_5, a_6\} \\ 4, & \text{if } c = c_2 \wedge A = \{a_1, a_2, a_3, a_4, a_5, a_6\} \\ 5, & \text{if } c = c_2 \wedge A = \{a_1, a_2, a_3, a_4, a_6\} \\ 1, & \text{if } c = c_2 \wedge A = \{a_3, a_4, a_5\} \\ 1, & \text{if } A = \{a_7, a_8, a_9, a_{10}\} \\ 0, & \text{otherwise,} \end{cases} \tag{6.3}$$

and the cost ψ as the number of actions in the solution. The Pareto front resulting from RHEA is illustrated at the top of figure 6.16. Some of the solutions are found

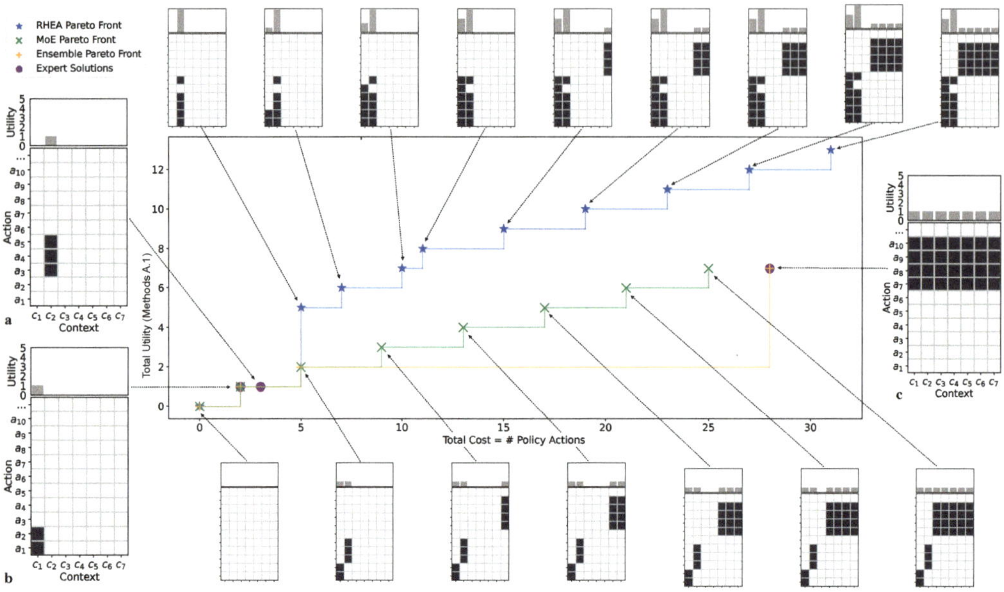

Figure 6.16: **RHEA leveraging expert solutions through evolution, compared to MoE and weighted ensemble.** Several solutions may include different good ideas; the challenge is to form a combined solution that takes advantage of all of them. In this synthetic example, the plots in the middle show the Pareto fronts for each method: RHEA in blue ⋆, MoE in green ×, and weighted ensemble in yellow +; in addition, the original expert solutions are shown in purple •. The structure of each solution is visualized as a grid that identifies which actions (rows) are used in each context (columns). On the left are the two original specialist solutions **a** and **b**, and on the right, the original generalist solution **c**. The solutions on the RHEA Pareto front are on top, and those for MoE in the bottom. Whereas MoE and weighted ensemble can utilize the knowledge in the expert solutions in only a limited way, RHEA can recombine, add innovations, and remove redundancies and detrimental elements to construct superior solutions. Whereas such solutions would be difficult to evolve from a random initial population, RHEA thus harnesses the latent potential in expert solutions, and finds the optimal Pareto front reliably. Figure from Meyerson, Francon, Sargent, et al. (2024).

by recombining existing expert solutions, such as by adding a_3, a_4, a_5 to a_1, a_2 in c_1. Importantly, evolution can also innovate beyond the experts, such as by adding a_6 to this solution. It can also refine solutions by removing actions that are redundant or detrimental, such as a_5 in c_2, and by incorporating knowledge from the generalist solution; that is, $a_7..a_{10}$ for $c_3...c_7$.

Interestingly, other methods cannot take advantage of such mechanisms. For instance, **mixture-of-experts** (MoE; Masoudnia and Ebrahimpour, 2014) can utilize different experts for different contexts (as shown at the bottom of figure 6.16), but they cannot form recombinations of them, or innovations or refinements. Its Pareto front therefore falls far short of that of evolution. Similarly, **weighted ensemble** solutions (Dietterich, 2002) can only choose a single combination of experts that is then applied to all contexts, which results in an even less effective Pareto front.

Note also that it would be difficult for evolution alone to find a good Pareto front; that is, starting from random solutions instead of the experts. There is little information in partial solutions that allows constructing them gradually, and evolution would thus be looking for needles in a haystack. Indeed, experimentally, RHEA discovers the entire optimal Pareto front reliably, whereas evolution does not, especially when the number of actions increases.

This synthetic example thus illustrates how evolution can take advantage of expert knowledge, how it can improve solutions beyond such knowledge, and how these abilities are unique to evolution as compared to standard ML approaches. Do these insights carry over to large real-world domains?

To demonstrate the real-world power of RHEA, it was implemented in the XPRIZE Pandemic Response domain mentioned in the previous section 6.4.4. In phase 2 of the competition, a total of 169 different prescriptors were submitted. They were constructed with different methods such as epidemiological modeling, decision rules, statistical methods, gradient-based optimization, and evolution; some of them also used auxiliary data sources, and some focused on specific locations. This set of prescriptors was thus quite diverse, representing a wide range of human expertise. Several studies in psychology, social science, and business suggest that diversity in human teams leads to improved decision-making (Rock and Grant, 2016). The question is: Can we use AI (i.e., neuroevolution) to take advantage of this diversity of human expertise?

The **XPRIZE competition** provided a convenient framework for the first two phases. The **distillation** was done by training an autoregressive neural network with gradient descent to mimic the behavior of each solution created by human experts. Training examples were created by querying the prescriptor with a comprehensive sampling of the Oxford data set. Evolution was done through the same **evolutionary surrogate-assisted prescription approach** as described in the previous section 6.4.4. That is, the latest predictor at the time was used as the surrogate, and neural networks optimized the case and cost objectives as before.

Remarkably, the results exceeded all expectations (figure 6.17). The RHEA Pareto front pushed significantly further down and to the left than the Pareto front consisting of the best solutions created by human experts, as well as the Pareto front resulting from the evolution from initially random neural networks. In other words, RHEA evolution was more powerful than either human expertise or evolution from scratch alone. Moreover, the RHEA solutions dominated especially in the areas of the front that mattered: Given the human decision-makers' preference for mid range trade-offs, they would be likely to select RHEA's solutions over those of other methods nearly 100% of the time.

It is interesting to evaluate what RHEA actually discovered differently from humans and machines alone. Figure 6.18*a* characterizes the policies along five dimensions: (1) the range of their stringency (swing), (2) whether they utilize different phases (separability), (3) number of IPs used (focus), (4) how often the IPs change (agility), and (5) whether they utilize weekly changes (periodicity). The policies are characterized for RHEA, evolution-only, and submitted solutions, as well as the actual policies implemented in the world during the pandemic.

Several interesting observations can be made from this comparison. First, in terms of swing and separability, the submitted solutions had more variability than policies in the real world, suggesting that human experts were exploring opportunities to improve. However,

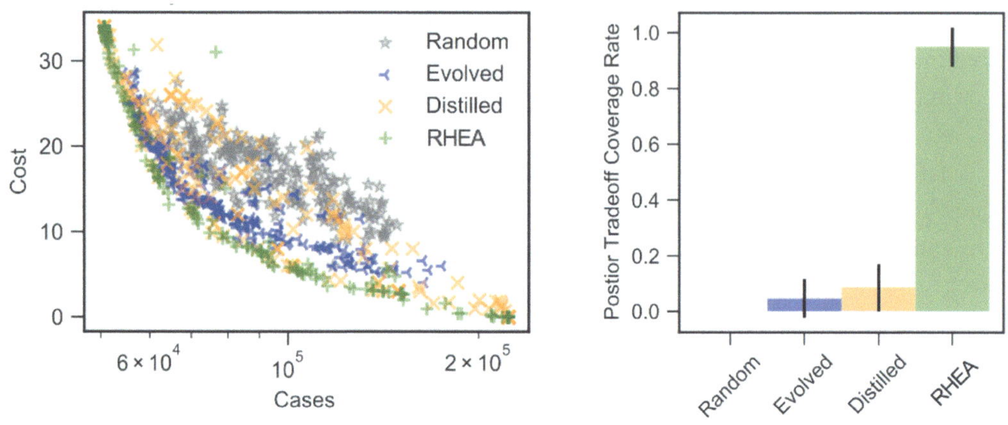

(*a*) Pareto fronts (*b*) Human-preferred solutions

Figure 6.17: **Combining human expertise and machine discovery in NPI optimization.** The recombination and mutation operators in evolution are well suited for combining, refining, and extending existing ideas. (*a*) The RHEA Pareto front dominates both the solutions created by human experts (Distilled), as well as solutions evolved from a random initial population. (*b*) Given the human decision-makers' preference for mid range trade-offs, RHEA's solutions would be selected nearly always. These results demonstrate that neuroevolution can be used to take advantage of human expertise, resulting in solutions that are better than both those of humans and evolution alone. Figures from Meyerson, Francon, Sargent, et al. (2024).

RHEA's solutions were more similar to the real world, although RHEA also discovered that extreme separability could sometimes be useful. In this manner, RHEA discovered that the human expert's innovations were not always productive. Second, in terms of focus, RHEA's solutions were more similar to the submitted solutions, and quite different from the real-world solutions. In this manner, it utilized the expert solutions' tendency to focus on a small number of NPIs. Third, in terms of agility and periodicity, RHEA differed from both submitted and real-world solutions, utilizing more frequent variations as well as weekly periodicity. The solutions that were evolved from a random starting point were similar along these two dimensions, suggesting that they were indeed discovered through machine creativity. Such solutions tend to be more difficult to implement in the real world, although in some cases, they were (e.g., for a time in Portugal and France). In this sense, RHEA discovered a potential opportunity that both real-world decision-makers and human experts' solutions had missed. The conclusion is that RHEA can indeed utilize ideas from solutions created by human experts, as well as develop its own to construct the best possible policies.

It is also interesting to characterize how RHEA discovered the best solutions, by analyzing their evolutionary history. Some such solutions can be traced to only a single beneficial crossover of two submitted ancestors, while others were constructed in a more complex process involving several ancestors. Usually, the crossovers were systematic; that is, resulted in offspring whose case-stringency trade-off was between the two parents. It is also interesting to measure the contribution of each ancestor to the solutions in the final Pareto front; that is, how much of their genetic encoding was found in those best solutions (figure 6.18*b*). As expected, submitted ancestors that performed well generally contributed

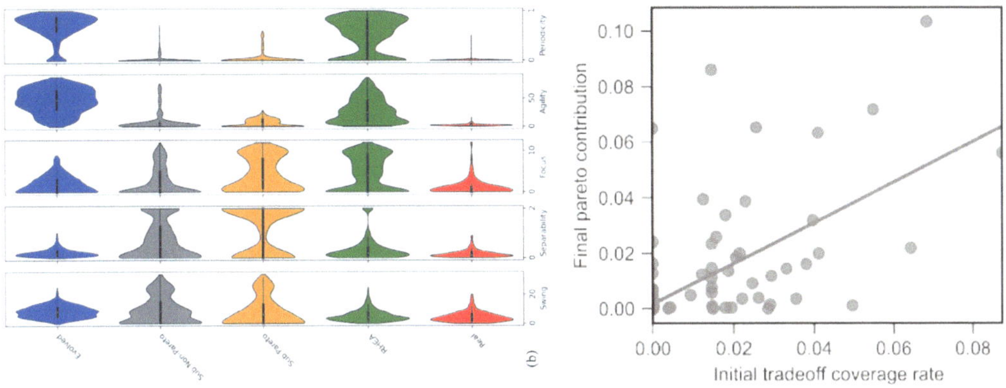

(*a*) Dimensions of NPI strategies (*b*) Performance vs. contribution

Figure 6.18: **Characterizing the discovered NPI policies.** The policies can be characterized in five dimensions, revealing similarities and differences among the approaches. (*a*) RHEA's policies were similar to the submitted ones in terms of focus, but they differed in four other dimensions. In terms of swing and separability, it found solutions similar to those implemented in the real world, but in terms of agility and periodicity, a potential new opportunity that both human experts and real-world decision-makers missed. In this manner, RHEA can leverage both human expertise and machine creativity. (*b*) Performance (in terms of hypervolume) of the submitted solutions versus their contributions to the final Pareto front. While better solutions generally contribute more, there are many solutions that do not perform well but end up contributing a lot (those in the upper left area). This result highlights the value of soliciting diverse expertise even if some of it is not immediately useful: Methods such as RHEA can then be used to realize their latent potential. Figures from Meyerson, Francon, Sargent, et al. (2024).

more, but there are also many ancestors that made outsize contributions through the evolutionary process. This observation demonstrates why it is so useful to solicit diversity of expertise, even when some of it is not immediately useful. Neuroevolution methods such as RHEA can then be used to realize their latent potential.

The NPI optimization example demonstrates the power of RHEA in combining human expertise and machine creativity through neuroevolution. This approach can be applied to many other domains as well, where such diverse expertise is available. It can be further combined with techniques for trustworthiness, such as interactive exploration and confidence estimation. Neuroevolution can thus play a crucial role in taking advantage of intelligent decision-making in the real world.

Note that in RHEA, human expertise is treated as a black box. This approach makes it possible to use such expertise in any form, distilled into a common neural network representation. However, sometimes expertise is available explicitly in the form of rules, examples, and advice. Such knowledge can be incorporated into neuroevolution by modifying the evolved networks directly, as will be discussed in section 8.2. It is a different way of utilizing human expertise in neuroevolution.

Interestingly, **distillation** can also be useful in the other direction; that is, by taking a neural network that performs well as a black box, and then evolving a set of rules to replicate its performance, such as using the **EVOTER approach** (Shahrzad, Hodjat, and Miikkulainen, 2024). Rule sets are transparent and interpretable, and in this manner, it may be possible to explain how the network performs. Particularly with RHEA, this approach may make it possible to characterize the initial expert solutions in a uniform manner, and further identify what new knowledge evolution discovers to improve them. Neuroevolution can thus work synergistically with rule-set evolution to make both human and AI designs explainable.

To conclude, neuroevolution is a powerful approach to discovering behavior at all levels, from low-level control through multi-behavior strategy to high-level decision-making. The next chapters 7, 8, and 9 build on this foundation by extending to collective systems of multiple agents, to incorporating humans in the loop, and to approaches for open-ended discovery of increasingly complex behaviors.

6.5 Chapter Review Questions

1. **Levels of behavior:** Describe the different levels of behavior that neuroevolution aims to optimize, from low-level control to high-level decision strategies. Provide an example of a success story for each level.

2. **Robust behavior:** What are some challenges in evolving robust behaviors in dynamic or unpredictable environments? Discuss methods like trajectory noise, coevolution, or symmetry evolution that address these challenges.

3. **Simulation to reality transfer:** Explain how neuroevolution can be adapted to bridge the reality gap between simulations and the physical world. What role does noise, stochasticity, and modern robotics simulators play in this process?

4. **Behavioral switching:** Why is switching between high-level strategies more challenging than low-level control adjustments in neuroevolution? Provide examples of fractured decision boundaries and interleaved/blended behaviors that illustrate these challenges.

5. **Fractured strategies and network design:** Explain how specific network design choices, such as using radial basis functions or cascaded refinement, can address the challenge of discovering fractured decision boundaries in domains like half-field soccer.

6. **Multimodal task division:** Discuss the role of preference neurons in discovering and implementing multimodal behaviors. How does this approach enable neuroevolution to discover surprising and effective strategies, such as in the Ms. Pac-Man example from this chapter?

7. **Surrogate modeling:** What is the role of surrogate models in discovering decision strategies with neuroevolution? Discuss how they enable exploration and evaluation in domains where real-world experimentation is infeasible.

8. **Evolutionary surrogate-assisted prescription:** Describe the evolutionary surrogate-assisted prescription approach for decision-making. How does co-learning between predictors and prescriptors contribute to automatic regularization and curricular learning?

9. **COVID-19 NPI optimization:** In the context of optimizing NPIs during the COVID-19 pandemic, how did the evolutionary surrogate-assisted prescription approach combine predictive and prescriptive modeling to discover effective policies? What were the advantages of this data-driven method over traditional epidemiological models?

10. **Human expertise in RHEA:** Explain how RHEA incorporates human expertise into neuroevolution. How does it utilize diverse expert solutions to discover superior decision strategies, and what unique advantages does it provide over other methods like MoE?

Chapter 7

Neuroevolution of Collective Systems

One of the most fascinating aspects of nature is that groups with millions or even trillions of elements can self-assemble into complex forms based only on local interactions and display what is called a collective type of intelligence. For example, ants can join to create bridges or rafts to navigate difficult terrain, termites can build nests several meters high without an externally imposed plan, and thousands of bees work together as an integrated whole to make accurate decisions on when to search for food or a new nest. Surprisingly, achieving these incredible abilities is a result of following relatively simple behavioral rules. These rules have been discovered through evolution that relies on cooperating individuals; that is, through **cooperative coevolution**.

A fundamental driving force in evolution is competition. Individuals compete for resources, mates, and status. Groups of individuals battle for resources but also may engage in direct conflict, including predators trying to catch prey, which in turn try to avoid being caught. When the opponents discover new successful behaviors, the species also have to develop new mechanisms to survive. This process results in continual adaptation; that is, **competitive coevolution**.

Cooperative and competitive coevolution can be used to drive neuroevolution as well. Mechanisms range from cooperating neurons and networks, and cellular automata defined by evolved neural networks, to establishing an arms race of increasingly competing networks. In many cases, complex behavior results that would be difficult to discover in other ways.

7.1 Cooperative Coevolution

A fundamental insight in generating intelligent systems is that they do not exist in a vacuum: Intelligence often emerges from interactions with the environment. These interactions may originate from constraints of a physical body, with its limited sensory and motor abilities. They may originate from constraints posed by the physical surroundings: for instance, Herb Simon's point that even though an ant's path may appear complex to the outsider, the ant may be largely responding to the obstacles and contours in its path (Simon, 1969). Most important, significant interactions originate from other agents. They may be adversarial, posing a threat or obstacle, or they may be cooperative, requiring collaboration to achieve a common goal.

Neuroevolution is well suited for building such interactive intelligent systems. The techniques focus on constructing intelligent systems from a large number of components that work together. A fundamental principle is cooperative coevolution, which means evolving these components together to achieve effective behavior (Wiegand, 2003). Such cooperation can take place at many levels: a single neural network, multiple neural networks in a multiagent system, or in a competitive environment among multiple cooperative multiagent systems. The techniques are based on the same fundamental principle of shared fitness, but each addresses the challenge of intelligent behavior at a different level.

7.1.1 Evolving a Single Neural Network

At the most basic level, the goal is to construct a single intelligent agent in an environment that returns a dedicated fitness for it. In other words, a neural network is formed by evolving a population of partial solutions, such as neurons, connections, or modules.

In the spirit of **classifier systems** (Holland and Reitman, 1978), the first approaches of this kind focused on the evolution of cooperative neurons (Husbands and Mill, 1991; Moriarty and Miikkulainen, 1997; Potter and De Jong, 2000). For example in the **symbiotic adaptive neuroevolution** (SANE) system, there was a single population of neurons, each with its own input connections. The networks were formed according to blueprints; that is, a separate population of individuals that specified which neurons from the population were included to form the network. The networks specified by each blueprint were evaluated in the task, and the neurons in the blueprint inherited the blueprint's fitness. Both the blueprint and the neuron population were evolved based on this fitness, thus encouraging the discovery of partial solutions (i.e., neurons) that collaborate well with other neurons.

This principle was further enhanced in the **enforced subpopulations** (ESP) system (section 5.6), where, instead of a diverse set of blueprints, there was only one network structure: a fully connected network of n neurons (figure 7.1; Gomez and Miikkulainen, 1997). However, each neuron in the network was evolved in a separate subpopulation—thus, each subevolution searched for a neuron that optimized performance for one location in the network. The networks were then formed by selecting one neuron from each subpopulation randomly to fill the corresponding location in the network. All the neurons started with random weights, and all the subpopulations were thus initially identical. However, over evolution, they gradually diverged and specialized: They discovered differentiated, computational roles for the neurons.

For instance, in the task of evolving a network that can run through a maze as a simulated Khepera robot, several such roles could be identified. One subpopulation evolved neurons that would slow the robot down if there was an obstacle in front of it; another veered the robot to the right if there was an obstacle on the left; another veered left with an obstacle on the right. Although such discovery and specialization were evident, most importantly, each subpopulation usually performed at least two such subfunctions to some extent. The reason is that such redundancy makes the construction of competent individuals more robust; the neurons do not have to be perfect in what they do because other neurons in the network compensate for their flaws. Such construction also results in a more robust search: even if a suboptimal neuron is sometimes chosen from one of the

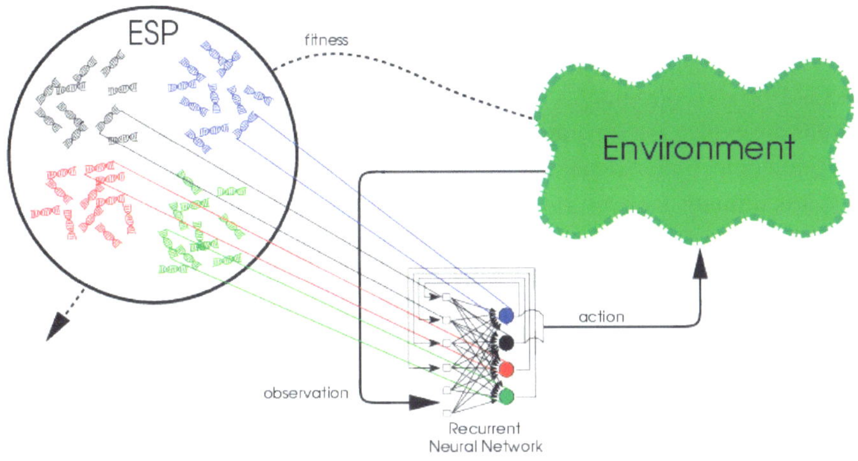

Figure 7.1: **Evolution of subpopulations of neurons.** In the cooperative coevolution of a single network, each subpopulation evolves one neuron for the network, which may be fully recurrent. The genetic encoding of each neuron specifies the neuron's connection weights to other neurons. Each neuron receives the fitness of the entire network evaluated in the task. Thus, neurons evolve to cooperate well with other neurons: The subpopulations optimize compatible subtasks and each subtask is encoded robustly in a couple of subpopulations. Such a search for partial solutions is also efficient: the subtasks remain diverse, the approach avoids competing conventions, and the search space is compact. Figure from Gomez (2003).

subpopulations, the others cover for it. Thus, selection favors redundancy and thus more robust networks. This is a powerful fundamental principle of cooperative coevolution in general.

So far, the partial solutions (i.e., neurons) inherit the fitness of the full solution (i.e., a network) as is. However, such neuroevolution can be further enhanced by calculating the fitness of individual neurons separately as well, and using it in combination with the inherited network fitness. This is possible through difference evaluation; that is, evaluating the network in the task with and without the neuron, thus measuring how much better off (or worse off) the network is with each neuron. In control tasks such as double pole balancing and rover exploration, this approach can find significantly better solutions and find them significantly faster (Agogino, Tumer, and Miikkulainen, 2005).

Based on these pioneering systems, it is already possible to see why the cooperative coevolution approach can be powerful. There are three main reasons: First, it has a built-in mechanism for maintaining diversity and avoiding premature convergence. A good network requires many different kinds of neurons. If, for example, the neural population in **SANE** starts to converge, the similar neurons perform poorly in a network, and are discarded in favor of those that are different. Second, it avoids the **competing conventions** problem. The neurons are chosen for distinct locations in the network, and optimized for performance for those specific locations. Third, it reduces the search space. Instead of optimizing all the connection weights in the network at once, it is sufficient to optimize the weights of single neurons—which can be done easily in parallel multiple times. There are other ways to solve these problems in neuroevolution, including indirect encodings (chapter 4), but the cooperative coevolution method is designed to tackle them explicitly.

This approach of cooperative coevolution of compatible roles can be extended to other levels of granularity as well. A particularly powerful way of constructing recurrent neural networks is **CoSyNE** (Gomez, Schmidhuber, and Miikkulainen, 2008), where individual connections are evolved in separate subpopulations. However, although the general idea is a logical and compelling extension of ESP, it turned out that with such a large number of subtasks, it is difficult for evolution to converge to a compatible set.

The solution is to focus the search in two ways. First, individual connections are not chosen randomly from each subpopulation to form a network, but instead the connections with the same index (i.e., location) in the subpopulation are combined into the network. Thus, the indices serve as simple blueprints, allowing search to focus on refining these networks. Second, in addition to the usual mutation and crossover in each subpopulation, a small subset of individuals is permuted within each subpopulation, thus exploring a different role for each of them. In this manner, the search can more effectively find good combinations of individual weights, which is especially important in highly recurrent neural networks. At the time, CoSyNE was able to discover solutions to the most challenging control tasks, such as balancing two poles simultaneously on a moving cart without precomputed velocity information, where other neuroevolution and reinforcement learning (RL) methods could not.

Interestingly, the cooperative coevolution approach has recently proved valuable at the higher level of granularity as well; that is, **neural architecture search** for deep learning. As will be described in more detail in chapter 10, the goal in neural architecture search is to find a design for a deep learning system that performs as well as possible when trained with gradient descent. This process requires finding optimal hyperparameter settings, network topologies, and layer types. It turns out that these elements can be coevolved in separate subpopulations to form entire architectures, similarly to how neurons are evolved to form networks. For instance, in the **CoDeepNEAT** method (Miikkulainen, Liang, Meyerson, et al., 2023), network modules consisting of a few layers and connections between them are coevolved in separate subpopulations, and a blueprint population is evolved to indicate how these modules are combined to form complete networks. Each of these subpopulations is evolved with NEAT to form complex recurrent structures. In essence, CoDeepNEAT is thus a combination of SANE, ESP, and NEAT, applied at the level of large deep learning architectures.

Compared to other neural architecture search methods, CoDeepNEAT is particularly powerful in exploring new architectures because its search space is relatively unconstrained. It is also possible to seed it with human designs and find novel combinations of them that humans may have missed. For instance in the domain of image captioning, CoDeepNEAT was initialized with the types of layers and connections that existed in the state-of-the-art (SOTA) architecture at the time, the **Show&Tell network** (Vinyals, Toshev, Bengio, et al., 2015). It was able to find a network that improved performance by 5%. Interestingly, it did so by employing a principle that is not common in human designs: The best networks included multiple parallel pathways of processing that were brought together in the end. This principle will still need to be evaluated more generally, but it illustrates the kind of discoveries that are possible using the cooperative evolutionary approach.

7.1.2 Evolving Structured Heterogeneous Networks

The cooperative coevolution approaches introduced in section 7.1.1 demonstrated how breaking a neural network into partial solutions, such as neurons or synapses, can lead to a more tractable and robust search. These methods are built on the premise that dividing the problem into independently evolving components allows evolution to find better global solutions through local coordination. SANE, ESP, and CoSyNE elegantly address challenges such as maintaining diversity, reducing search complexity, and avoiding competing conventions.

However, modern neural network systems are often much larger and consist of several heterogeneous components in a functional structure. For instance, **world model** architectures (discussed in section 13.5) include visual encoders that compress high-dimensional observations, memory modules that capture temporal context, and controllers that determine actions. Such systems can still be optimized by cooperative coevolution. However, the process is different from coevolving partial solutions: the overall structure is determined by the task, and successful evolution depends on their ability to co-adapt over time.

A key challenge that emerges in this context is the **credit assignment problem** (CAP): When the overall performance of the network changes, it is difficult to determine which module was responsible and how the others should respond. For example, improvements in one module—such as a better visual representation—can initially lead to worse overall performance if downstream components like the controller have not yet adapted to the new representation. This phenomenon can cause evolution to discard useful innovations prematurely, simply because their benefits are not immediately realized.

The **deep innovation protection** (DIP) approach (Risi and Stanley, 2021) addresses this issue, introducing a novel mechanism for coordinating the evolution of heterogeneous, interdependent neural components. Instead of evolving distinct subpopulations, DIP evolves these heterogeneous neural networks end-to-end using a single population, while leveraging a **multiobjective optimization** strategy (section 2.2.5) to temporarily protect recent innovations in upstream components. This method reframes the credit assignment problem in neuroevolution as one of managing temporal coordination among co-evolving parts, ensuring that innovations are not prematurely discarded before their full benefits can be realized. Such protection represents a powerful general principle for fostering the emergence of complexity, akin to the role of **speciation** in neuroevolution of augmenting topologies (NEAT; see section 3.3), which preserves innovation by allowing novel structures time to mature before being subjected to full competitive pressure. However, unlike typical speciation methods used in approaches like NEAT, DIP explicitly protects a type of innovation that general genomic similarity might not capture as well: the interdependence between components in a heterogeneous neural architecture.

The particular agent architecture that was used to test DIP was composed of a convolutional visual encoder that processes high-dimensional input, a memory module based on long short-term memory (LSTM) that encodes temporal context, and a controller that determines the agent's actions (figure 7.2). Using **NSGA-II** (non-dominated sorting genetic algorithm II), individuals in DIP were evaluated not only on their performance (i.e., task reward) but also on an auxiliary "age" objective. Originally pioneered for co-

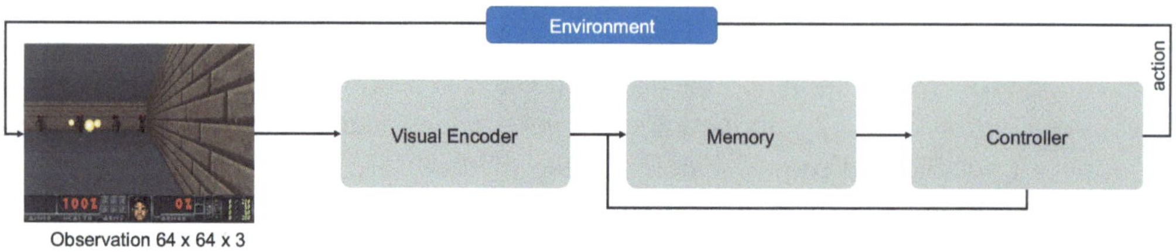

Figure 7.2: **Heterogeneous neural architecture training through DIP**. The agent model is composed of three main modules. First, a visual component generates a latent code z_t at each time step t. This code is concatenated with the hidden state h_t from an LSTM-based memory module, which receives z_t and the previous action a_{t-1} as input. The resulting vector (z_t, h_t) is then passed to the controller module, which selects the agent's next action. By temporarily protecting recent innovations in upstream components, the deep innovation approach (DIP) allows training the whole architecture end-to-end using a multi-objective genetic algorithm. Figure from Risi and Stanley (2021). Videos of trained agents at `https://neuroevolutionbook.com/demos`.

optimizing robot controllers and morphologies (Cheney, Bongard, SunSpiral, et al., 2018), this age objective does not measure how long an individual has been in the population, as in traditional diversity-preserving methods, but rather how long a given component—here the visual or memory module—has remained unchanged. During mutation, a single component was selected at random and its parameters were perturbed by adding **Gaussian noise** to the parameter vectors of the network components. When a mutation altered one of these *upstream* components, the individual's age was reset to zero, signaling that the rest of the network (especially the controller) had not yet had time to adapt. As a result, individuals with newer innovations but equivalent performance are preferentially selected, providing evolutionary time for the rest of the system to co-adapt. The DIP approach was evaluated on the two tasks that we have already encountered in this book in the context of **AttentionAgents** (section 4.4.3): the 2D continuous control benchmark CarRacing-v0, and the 3D first-person survival challenge DoomTakeCover. These tasks were chosen to test DIP's ability to evolve complex neural architectures in environments with different levels of perceptual and strategic complexity.

CarRacing-v0 tests the agent's ability to generalize across unseen tracks and requires fine-grained control of steering, acceleration, and braking. Both DIP and the baseline version (a standard GA without innovation protection; Risi and Stanley, 2019) performed well on this task. The evolved agents consistently achieved average rewards above 900, which is considered a successful solution. DIP reached a reward of 905 ± 80, while the standard genetic algorithm without innovation protection reached 903 ± 72. These results indicate that in relatively simple and smooth environments like CarRacing-v0, where the interdependence between modules is less disruptive, both approaches can converge to good solutions without significant differences.

In contrast, the DoomTakeCover task presents a far greater challenge. As a reminder, here the agent views the world from a first-person 3D perspective and must survive by dodging fireballs launched by monsters. In this more complex scenario, the differences between DIP and non-DIP approaches were striking. The DIP-based agents successfully learned to survive, achieving an average score of 824.33 (±491.59), which exceeded the performance threshold for solving the task (staying alive for at least 750 time steps, averaged over 100 episodes). In contrast, agents evolved without innovation protection consistently failed to reach this level. The standard genetic algorithm was unable to maintain useful innovations long enough for the rest of the system to adapt, leading to stagnation and suboptimal performance.

This contrast highlights the power of DIP: In environments where changes in perception or memory require downstream adaptation, DIP allows the evolutionary process to preserve and refine promising solutions. It manages the temporal dynamics of learning within the architecture itself, which proves essential for mastering tasks like VizDoom, where emergent behavior and forward prediction are necessary for survival. To gain a better idea of exactly how DIP is solving the VizDoom task, we can look at an evolutionary trajectory—the intermediate **stepping stones** that led to the eventual solution. In one representative evolutionary run, the agent began to recognize fireballs as salient features in early generations (0–30), but responded in a limited way, either by standing still or consistently moving to the right. A notable performance improvement occurred around generation 34, when the agent began to explore both left and right evasive maneuvers. However, at this stage, the internal representations guiding these actions remained ambiguous. This ambiguity was resolved by around generation 56, which corresponded to another jump in performance. In the generations that followed, the agent rapidly fine-tuned its policy, ultimately developing the ability to reliably distinguish between different threat scenarios and surviving for the full duration of an episode.

In conclusion, by dynamically adjusting selection pressure based on the recency of innovations in upstream components, DIP effectively orchestrates the training of heterogeneous systems. It ensures that promising innovations are not lost before their benefits are realized, and that downstream components are given time to learn to take advantage of new internal representations. The result is a more robust evolutionary process capable of solving complex tasks that are difficult to solve without protecting evolutionary innovation.

7.1.3 Evolving a Team

At a higher level of coordination than a single neural network, neuroevolution can be used to construct teams; that is, groups of individual agents that solve problems cooperatively. An interesting question is: How should the search for team members be organized? A single neural network could be evolved to control the entire team; each team member could be evolved separately; or the team could be formed by cloning a single evolved network (figure 7.3).

The most straightforward extension from the single agent construction introduced in section 7.1.1 is to evolve each agent in a separate subpopulation, and reward each agent based on the success of the entire team. A predator-prey, or pursuit-evasion, scenario is a good way to illustrate the approach. In the simplest such scenario, a team of three predators was evolved to capture a single non-evolving (algorithmic) prey that always moves away from the nearest predator (Yong and Miikkulainen, 2010). However, the prey is as fast as the predators. Thus, in an unbounded (e.g., toroidal) field, it could never be caught, unless the predators evolve a cooperation strategy.

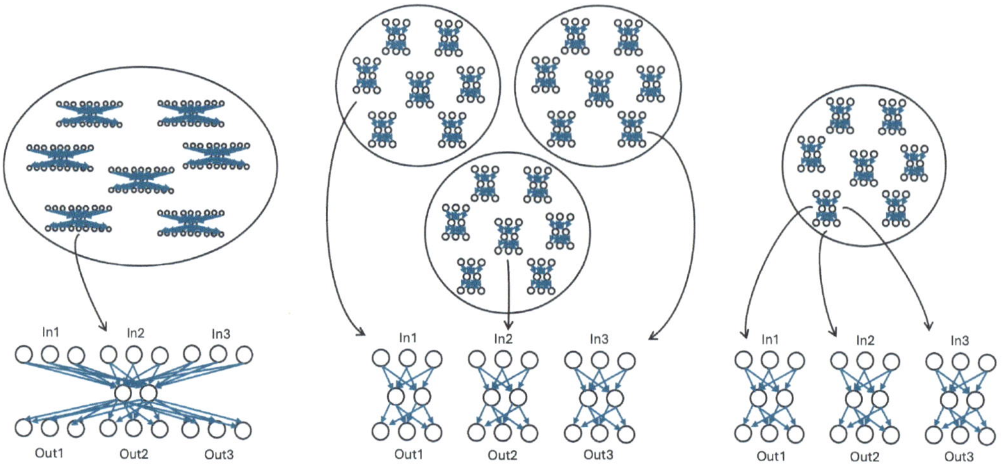

(*a*) Centrally controlled (*b*) Heterogeneous (*c*) Homogeneous

Figure 7.3: **Evolving centrally controlled, heterogeneous, and homogeneous teams.** (*a*) In centrally controlled teams, a population of controller networks is evolved in a single population; each network controls all three agents in the team. (*b*) For a heterogeneous team, the networks are evolved in separate populations, and a team is formed by randomly selecting one network from each population. (*c*) In a homogeneous team, networks are evolved in a single population, and a team is formed by cloning a selected network three times. In each case, the fitness of the team is used as the fitness for each network that participated in it. While in principle the central controller is able to coordinate the team well, heterogeneous networks may evolve distinctly different compatible roles that solve the task better. However, each network in a homogeneous team is a generalist that can take on different roles at different times, resulting in a more flexible team.

Such a strategy indeed evolved reliably using a multiagent version of the **ESP approach** outlined in figure 7.4. Each predator agent was controlled by an ESP neural network; that is, a recurrent neural network (RNN) evolved from their own subpopulation of neurons. At a hierarchically higher level, the three agents were evolved in parallel and evaluated based on how often the entire team was able to capture the prey. Indeed, two behavioral roles emerged: Two of the agents behaved as chasers, forcing the prey to run away from them in a straight path that extended around the toroidal space. The remaining agent behaved as a blocker, staying in place waiting for the chasers to push the prey toward it—the prey then had nowhere to go and was captured.

Upon further analysis, two remarkable observations were made. First, such a cooperative approach was more effective than evolving a single network to control all three agents. Second, it was more effective to evolve it without any direct communication between the agents, even as simple as simply sensing each other's location. Each agent would only sense the prey's location, and based on the role they had evolved into, knew what the other agents were likely doing, and what they needed to do themselves. In other words, their coordination was based on **stigmergy**, which is the communication through the environment.

Both of these are powerful principles that can be harnessed more generally in building complex systems. They suggest that in similar domains, discovering compatible behaviors can be easier than discovering a comprehensive strategy for the entire team. Each behavior,

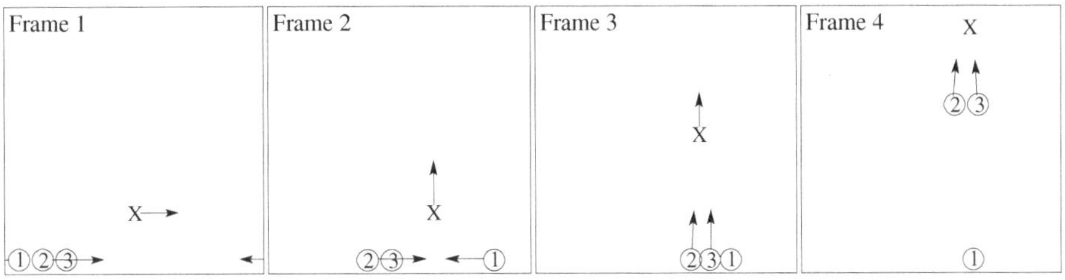

Figure 7.4: **Role-based cooperation through stigmergy**. Similarly to a single-network evolution, team members can be evolved in separate subpopulations and rewarded based on team success. In a toroidal world, three predator agents tried to capture a prey (X) that always runs away from the nearest predator and is as fast as the predators. Two of the predators (2, 3) evolved chaser roles, and the third (1) a blocker role: The chasers push the prey to the waiting blocker around the torus. Remarkably, evolution of agents in separate subpopulations was more effective than evolution of a central controller for the entire team. It was also more efficient to not bother with communication with other team members (even through visual sensing); each team member knew their role, and it was most effective for them to simply observe the prey (i.e., to communicate through stigmergy). Figure from Yong and Miikkulainen (2010). For a video of this behavior, see `https://neuroevolutionbook.com/demos`.

or role, can be flexible and robust on its own, compensating for inaccuracies in the other agents' behavior—such robustness is difficult to discover in a central control system. Also, when cooperation is based on such roles, it may be enough to observe just the current state of the problem: The subsequent behavior of each role can be assumed without direct observation or communication, making problem-solving more effective. The situation is similar to playing soccer with a team whose members have practiced together and know each other well: You know what the others are doing even without looking, and you know what you need to do by observing the opponents. A possible generalization of this idea is the evolution of **ensembles**: Each ensemble member discovers a role that solves only part of the problem, but, when combined with the other roles in the ensemble, constitutes a full solution.

While **role-based cooperation** is often effective, sometimes the behavior has to be more flexible. In the soccer analogy, you may be playing a pick-up game: You do not know the other players on your team, and have to constantly observe them to decide what you should do. More generally, the number of agents required in different roles may vary over time, and the agents may need to be able to switch roles. For instance, in robotic soccer, the behaviors are different depending on which team has the ball and where it is in the field. A team of agents sent to rescue people in a disaster may require cleaning up rubble, stabilizing structures, searching for targets, and transporting them out, and each agent should be able to take on any of these roles as needed.

An entirely different kind of evolutionary approach may be needed to construct such teams. Instead of evolving specialists, it is necessary to evolve generalists. This goal can be achieved by evolving a **homogeneous team**; that is, each member of the population is evaluated based on how well it performs as part of a team that consists of clones of itself (Bryant and Miikkulainen, 2018). For the team to be successful, it needs its members to perform different roles at different times. Thus, evolution favors individuals that can adapt their behavior to the situation, assuming appropriate behaviors that are compatible with those of the other team members.

Such behavior can be demonstrated naturally in a civilization-type game environment. The agents are settlers who have to perform various tasks at various times, including division of labor into construction, mining, agriculture, defense, etc. One such demonstration focused on legions defending multiple cities against barbarians. The barbarians were controlled algorithmically, attacking cities with little defense, retreating when outnumbered, and spawning at a regular rate in the countryside to replace those eliminated by the legions. The legions were rewarded based on the extent of damage to the cities, measured by the duration of barbarian occupation.

Unlike in the role-based cooperation approach, in the adaptive teams approach, it is useful for the agents to observe each other continuously (i.e., to communicate), in addition to the barbarians and the state of the cities. It is through such global awareness that the agents evolve to decide what role they should take on. It requires developing an internal model of the other agents and their behavior—a rudimentary theory of mind, if you will. Some of the legions take on the task of defending the cities under attack, while others prepare to defend cities that are likely to be attacked soon, and yet others proactively hunt down the barbarians in the countryside. While perfect fitness is not possible due to randomness and occasionally algorithmic changes to the barbarian's strategy, the adaptive approach does help them obtain better fitness. In a sense, the adaptation helps them deal with the uncertainty and instability in the domain. Such robustness can serve as an important ingredient in building intelligent agents that can cope with the messiness of the real world.

Interestingly, for such coordination and communication to evolve, selection must operate at the team level rather than at the individual level (Floreano, Mitri, Magnenat, et al., 2007). How such high-level selection can be established is an interesting question that has implications to biology as well, such as in understanding major transitions (section 9.1.5) and evolutionary breakthroughs (section 14.7).

7.2 Competitive Coevolution

While cooperation of multiple elements or agents is a powerful approach in building complex behavior, so is **competition**. That is, the agents evolve to outdo each other, and the population thus collectively discovers increasingly more powerful behaviors in an evolutionary arms race. Competitive coevolution is useful because it defines an open-ended fitness function automatically. The main challenge is that it is sometimes difficult to guarantee that progress is made continuously in an absolute sense. The process can be set up to discover a single effective behavior, or it can be set up to evolve multiple competing behaviors. These approaches are described in the following subsections.

7.2.1 Evolving Single Neural Networks

One challenge in constructing complex behaviors through neuroevolution is that it is difficult to design a suitable objective function. One approach is to make the function very general and high-level, based on such things as survival, number of games won, or number of offspring generated. This approach poses few constraints on how such fitness is achieved, and evolution can find creative solutions, but the signal may be too weak to make much progress. Another approach is to specify a number of detailed components that are believed to be part of successful behaviors, such as high speed, sharp turns, or accurate shooting, each providing part of the fitness. It is possible to make incremental progress in this manner, but it is difficult to make sure that robust solutions emerge, let alone creative solutions.

Competitive coevolution solves these problems by defining fitness in terms of the behaviors in the current population. Individuals compete with other individuals, and their fitness is determined based on how well they do in this competition. As the population improves, it becomes more difficult to achieve high fitness, thereby establishing an open-ended, automatic mechanism of shaping the fitness function.

Competitive coevolution is thus similar to curriculum learning, or incremental learning in general machine learning (ML). **Generative adversarial networks** (GANs; Goodfellow, Pouget-Abadie, Mirza, et al., 2014) are based on a similar mechanism, as are game-playing systems based on **self-play** such as **AlphaZero** (Silver, Hubert, Schrittwieser, et al., 2018). One of the earliest such systems was based on neuroevolution: **Blondie24** used a version of evolutionary programming to evolve neural network activation functions for checkers. Starting without any built-in expert knowledge, it evolved into an expert-level player (Chellapilla and Fogel, 1999; Fogel, 2001); the approach was later extended to chess as well (Fogel, Hays, Hahn, et al., 2004). There is a large literature on competitive coevolution since the 1950s, including analyses based on game theory (Adami, Schossau, and Hintze, 2016; de Jong and Pollack, 2004; Ficici and Pollack, 2001; Samuel, 1959). There are many examples in this book as well, including those in chapter 9.

The main challenge in competitive coevolution is to make sure that it actually makes progress toward better solutions. Since fitness is defined in relation to other solutions, improvement is not guaranteed in any absolute sense. It is possible to achieve higher fitness simply by exploiting weaknesses in the current candidates. Therefore, it is often useful to maintain a collection (i.e., **archive**) of previous candidates and evaluate fitness against them as well as the current population. In this manner, good candidates are indeed better than anything discovered by evolution so far.

However, progress against an archive of candidates does not necessarily mean progress in a global sense (i.e., in the entire search space). To make global progress, a set of previously unseen candidates needs to be included in the fitness evaluations. They can be obtained from other, independent runs of evolution. Or, the archive can be periodically divided into training and validation sets, with the validation set used to filter out variations that lead to only local progress (Miconi, 2009; Nolfi and Pagliuca, 2025; Simione and Nolfi, 2020).

A mechanism such as NEAT provides yet another solution. As reviewed in section 3.3, NEAT starts with a minimal network and gradually complexifies it over evolution. Through mutation and crossover, it adds more nodes and connections to the existing networks. The earlier structures are still there—evolution elaborates on them instead of replacing them. Therefore, the earlier behaviors are likely to be there as well, and the newer behaviors are likely to be more elaborate and effective. Therefore, it is likely that the newer solutions perform better in comparison to the earlier ones, thereby guiding evolution toward absolute progress.

This process was demonstrated in an experiment where neural network controllers were evolved for a combined foraging, pursuit, and evasion task (Stanley and Miikkulainen, 2004). Two simulated Khepera-like robots were placed in a closed environment with scattered food items. They were able to sense the distance to the opponent and the food items around them, the distance to the nearest wall, and the difference between their opponent's and their own energy. The robots moved around by powering their two wheels; they gained strength by consuming the food items and lost strength by moving. They would win the game by crashing into their opponent when they had more strength than the opponent. Thus, performing well required not only sensing and moving but also estimating how much energy they and their opponent would gain and lose by consuming and moving. Fitness was defined as the average win rate over the four highest species champions.

Because NEAT starts small and complexifies (as was discussed in section 3.3), it was possible to understand the **complexification** that took place in the networks and behaviors throughout the coevolutionary process. Evolution first discovered a simple foraging behavior that was often successful by chance: The agent occasionally crashed into the opponent when it had more energy than the opponent (figure 7.5*a*). It then evolved a hidden node that allowed it to make an informed switch between behaviors: attack when it had high energy, and rest when it did not (figure 7.5*b*). Another added node made it possible to predict the agent's own and its opponent's energy usage from afar and attack only when a win was likely (figure 7.5*c*). The most complex strategy, with several more nodes and complex recurrent connections between them, allowed the agent to also predict the opponent's behavior, encourage it to make mistakes, and take advantage of those mistakes to win (figure 7.5*d*).

Note that such an analysis and explainability is possible precisely because the networks are evolved in a principled manner through elaboration. Even though large deep learning networks could perhaps be trained in this task, they would remain opaque and not provide much insight into how the network establishes its behavior. Consequently, they could not be trusted in the same way as NEAT networks can.

Interestingly, the elaboration process turned out to be crucial in discovering such complex behavior. In a further experiment, a population was initialized with the final architecture from figure 7.5*d*; that is, all individuals had the same architecture with randomized weights. This architecture supports the complex behavior, and therefore it should be easy for evolution to discover the right weights. Surprisingly, it was not; each complexification step builds on a prior, simpler architecture that already performs some desired behaviors. It is therefore relatively easy to add a complexification to improve upon that behavior. In multiple such small steps, a complex behavior eventually develops. In contrast, discovering everything at once is very difficult, and such evolution does not get past the first few simple behaviors.

Thus, the foraging, pursuit, and evasion experiment demonstrates how coevolution can be harnessed to discover complex behavior. It is achieved collectively in a simple population where every individual tries to solve the same problem, and they just compete against each other. The coevolutionary setup can be made more complex by incorporating multiple populations that try to outdo each other explicitly. In a sense, one population discovers solutions and the other discovers more challenging problems. One example is given in the next section; another, paired open-ended trailblazer (POET), is covered later, in chapter 9.

7.2.2 Evolving Multiple Teams

At the next higher level of complexity, multiple cooperative teams coevolve in a competitive environment. Each team challenges the other teams to perform better, thus establishing an evolutionary arms race: Over time, each team outsmarts the other multiple times, leading to increasingly complex behavior for all teams.

Competitive coevolutionary dynamics have been studied extensively from a theoretical perspective, for example through **game theory**, and are now relatively well understood (Mitchell, 2006; Popovici, Bucci, Wiegand, et al., 2012). Absolute improvement is sometimes difficult to establish, and the process can go wrong in multiple ways. For instance, instead of getting better, the teams may simply become weirder. Later teams may even lose to the earlier ones. However, in many natural tasks, the more complex behavior often subsumes the earlier behaviors, which does lead to improvement in an absolute sense.

Once again, a good domain to study such competitive-cooperative dynamics is predator-prey tasks (Rawal, Rajagopalan, and Miikkulainen, 2010). Extending the **multiagent ESP approach** of section 7.1.3, a simulation can be set up to evolve both the prey and the predator populations—let's call them "zebras" and "hyenas." Again in a toroidal world, the zebras can run away from the hyenas, but the hyenas can catch them by approaching from multiple sides.

At the very first stages of evolution (generations 50–75), the zebras evolved an individual strategy of running away from the nearest predator, replicating the algorithmic behavior described in section 7.2.1. Correspondingly, the predator team evolved a two-blocker, one-chaser strategy (figure 7.6; phase 1). In the next phase (generations 75–100; phase 2), the prey evolved a new strategy of running in a small circle with the chaser following on its tail. This strategy is effective because the blockers simply wait to catch the prey. Next (generations 100–150; phase 3), one of the blocker predators evolved to act as a chaser as well, approaching the prey from two different directions. As a response (generations 150–180; phase 4), the prey evolved a baiting strategy, letting both chasers get close and then escaping them both. Next (generations 180–250; phases 5–6), the predators evolved to change roles between blockers and chasers dynamically, so they can better sandwich the prey. As a result (generations 250–300; phase 7), the prey adjusted its strategy, letting all predators get close, and then escaping between them. In the next few hundred generations (300–450; phases 8–9), both of these strategies became gradually more refined and precise, eventually resulting in about a 50–50 chance of the prey escaping and getting caught—similar to what is seen in biology.

However, an interesting next step is to add another prey to the prey team—the prey can now evolve cooperation to confuse the predators. This is one of the most effective strategies used by prey in nature, and there is computational evidence (using **Markov**

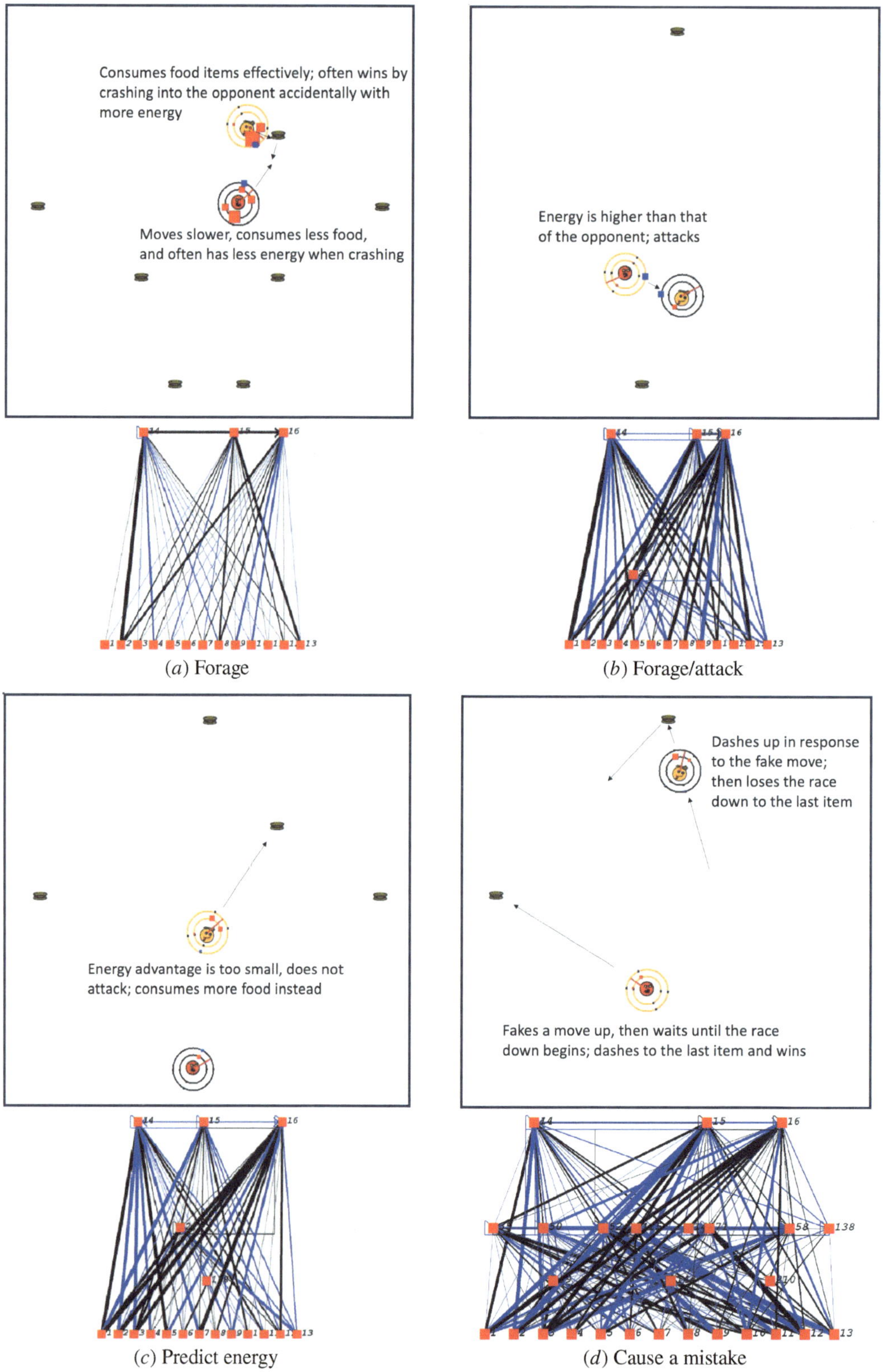

Figure 7.5: **Discovering complex behavior through competitive coevolution.** (See next page)

Figure 7.5: (Continued from previous page) Two simulated Khepera robots need to consume food, pursue the opponent when they have higher energy than the opponent, and evade it when their energy is lower. When the robots collide, the one with higher energy wins. In the domain illustrations, the dark ovals are food items, and the red and yellow circles are the two robots. The red line indicates the direction that the robot is facing, the outer ring the opponent sensor values, and the inner ring the food sensor values. The rings are yellow for the robot with higher energy. In the network diagrams, the nodes are depicted as red squares and numbered in the order that they were created. Positive connections are black and negative are blue, recurrent connections are indicated by triangles, and the width of the connection is proportional to its strength. The approach discovered (*a*) a foraging strategy that resulted in high energy and was often successful when accidentally crashing on the opponent, (*b*) a hidden node that allowed it to switch between following and resting based on energy, (*c*) a way to model and compare the opponent's and their own energy, and (*d*) eventually how to fake a move toward a far-away food item (top), causing the opponent to dash to it and then spend most of its energy to get to the last item (left) but failing to get to it first, thereby providing an easy win. Complexifying evolution thus provides a way of understanding network performance; in this experiment, it provides a clear example of how a single competitive coevolution population can discover increasingly complex behaviors. Network diagrams from Stanley (2003). For videos of these behaviors, see `https://neuroevolutionbook.com/demos`.

brains) that predator confusion is a sufficient reward to evolve swarming behavior (Olson, Hintze, Dyer, et al., 2013). It also evolves reliably in the two-prey simulations. First (in 150 further generations), the predators mostly capture one prey at a time, but are often confused by the other, and they then fail. Then (generations 150–200, phase 1), they are able to adapt their single-prey sandwiching strategy to herd the two prey together and capture both of them. Remarkably, the prey are able to adapt their strategy in the same way (generations 200–300, phase 12), baiting the predators together, and then escaping in opposite directions, leaving the predators confused. In further evolution, both of these strategies become more precise, resulting in about an even chance of escape and capture in the end.

This example is interesting for two reasons: First, it illustrates how neuroevolution can be used to understand how the behaviors observed in nature may have emerged through coevolution. Sometimes, when observing biological behavior as it is, it is difficult to understand aspects of it. However, behavior, like other aspects of biology, is a product of evolution, and should be understood in the light of how evolution may have constructed it, through all the intermediate stages that may no longer be visible. Evolutionary computation simulations may be used to uncover them; for instance, why it may be beneficial for the prey to let the predators get close before escaping. These opportunities will be discussed in more detail in chapter 14.

Second, the example demonstrates a successful coevolutionary arms race. Complex behavior is discovered through multiple stages, each a stepping stone to the next. The imbalance of performance at each state forms a challenge to the disadvantaged population, and evolution discovers ways to meet that challenge. In this manner, such competitive-cooperative coevolution may be a crucial ingredient in open-ended evolution, and perhaps also in establishing major transitions (Miikkulainen and Forrest, 2021). Opportunities for such advances are discussed more in section 9.1.

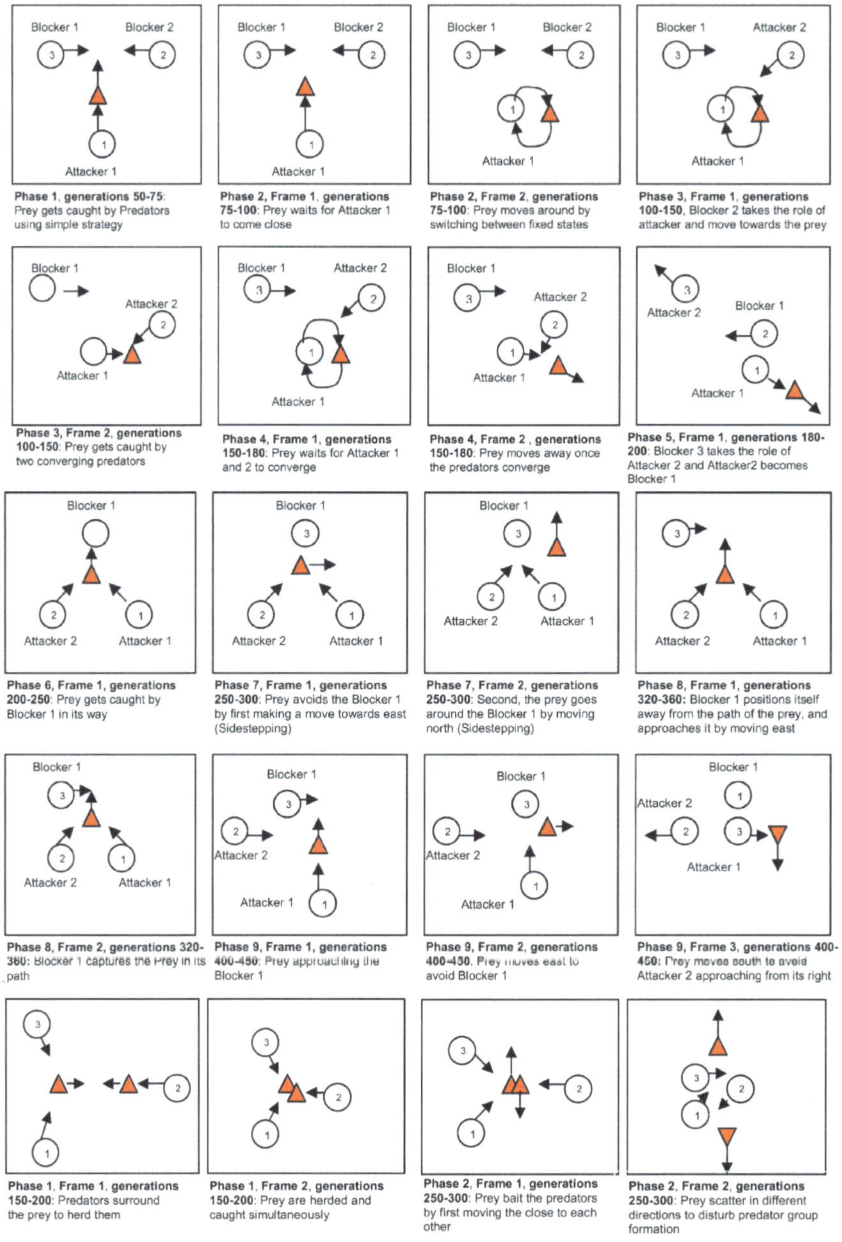

Figure 7.6: **Evolutionary arms race of increasingly complex pursuit-evasion strategies.** Through multiple phases, the predator and prey populations alternate in gaining the upper hand in the competition, which serves as a challenge and an opportunity for evolution to improve the disadvantaged population. The later behaviors largely subsume the earlier ones, and therefore there is a progression in an absolute sense toward more complex and effective behaviors that would otherwise be difficult to discover. The simulation also serves to shed light on observed animal behaviors such as cooperative hunting and herding, and escaping by confusing the predators. It thus demonstrates both a way to construct complex intelligent agents, as well as to understand how intelligence may have emerged in biological evolution. Figures from Rawal, Rajagopalan, and Miikkulainen (2010). For videos of these behaviors, see `https://neuroevolutionbook.com/demos`.

7.3 Cellular Automata

Many collective systems in nature are made up of many components that are highly interconnected. The absence of any centralized control allows them to quickly adjust to new stimuli and changing environmental conditions. Additionally, because these collective intelligence systems are made of many simpler individuals, they have in-built redundancy with a high degree of resilience and robustness. Individuals in this collective system can fail without the entire system breaking down.

A simplified yet powerful platform to study collective systems in various contexts is **cellular automata** (CAs). They offer insights into how individual behaviors, when aggregated, can lead to the emergence of remarkable and often unexpected group-level phenomena. Constructing intelligent or lifelike systems from a large number of cooperating components is central to CAs, and as will be seen in this section, they allow complex patterns to emerge based only on the local and self-organized interaction of cells. CAs have recently seen a renaissance and renewed interest in the ML community by scaling them up and combining them with deep neural networks.

Originally proposed in the 1940s, cellular automata mimic **developmental processes** in multicell organisms, including **morphogenesis**. A CA is a spatially extended decentralized system that contains a grid of similarly structured cells, which are locally connected and updated periodically in discrete time steps. At every time step, the status of each cell can be represented as a state, which is then transitioned into the next state per the update rule. The specific transition depends on the current state of the cell and the neighboring cells (often this neighborhood is defined as the cells directly bordering the cell in question, but a larger neighborhood is also possible). For example, in a particular CA devised by John Conway in 1970 called **Conway's game of life**, a few rules govern the transition at each time step, such as an alive cell that has fewer than two alive neighbors dies, while a cell becomes alive if it has exactly three neighbors. These automata serve as effective models for a range of physical and biological processes. For instance, they have been employed to simulate fluid dynamics, the emergence of galaxies, seismic events like earthquakes, and the formation of intricate biological patterns.

A CA's **transition rule** can be specified as a lookup table that determines, for each local neighborhood configuration, what the state of the central cell should be in the next time step. While the states are either 0 or 1 in Conway's game of life, we will shortly see that cells can have more states or even be described by not only a single number but a hidden state vector instead. In Conway's game of life, the specific transition rules were human-defined. However, in some instances, it can make sense to search for specific rules that lead to desired behaviors or patterns. For example, researchers such as Melanie Mitchell have shown that it is possible to optimize CA transition rules with evolutionary algorithms (Mitchell, Crutchfield, and Das, 1996). This way, rules can be found that perform a specific type of computation, such as determining if the initial CA configuration has more 1s than 0s.

Instead of evolving rule tables directly (which can quickly become prohibitively large when the number of CA states increases), rules can take the form of programs (Koza, 1994) or neural networks (Wulff and Hertz, 1992). Here, a copy of the same program/neural network runs in each cell, taking information from its CA neighbors and potentially previous cell states into account to determine which state the cell should take next. Because each cell shares the same trainable parameters, the whole system can be viewed as a type of indirect encoding, in which the size of the grown patterns can potentially be much larger than the size of the underlying representation.

A popular benchmark to test the abilities of these systems is to grow forms resembling simple 2D patterns. Originally proposed by developmental biologist Lewis Wolpert in the 1960s, the **French flag** problem (Wolpert, Tickle, and Arias, 2015) is such a task; it asks how embryonic cells could differentiate into complex patterns, such as the three differently colored stripes of a French flag. The inquiry extends to understanding how these patterns can scale proportionally with tissue size, for example, such that the grown French flag pattern is always one-third blue, one-third white, and one-third red. In an impressive early demonstration of collective intelligent systems, Miller (2004) showed that a genetic cell program can be evolved that allows growing a French flag–like pattern from a single cell, which can even self-repair when being damaged. When the cell's update function is a neural network, it is now often called **neural cellular automata** (NCA), and we will have a closer look at those next.

7.3.1 Evolving Neural Cellular Automata

In NCAs (Wulff and Hertz, 1992), a neural network updates the states of each cell based on communicating with its local neighbors. The same neural network is applied to each grid cell, resembling the iterative application of a convolutional filter (Gilpin, 2019). In other words, NCAs can be viewed as an indirect encoding (chapter 4) in which identical modules are applied with identical weight parameters across the space of cells. More recently, the use of neural networks for CAs has seen a resurgence, in particular because of their integration with popular deep learning frameworks.

Because NCAs are neural networks, they can naturally be evolved with the NEAT algorithm. However, in this **cellular automata NEAT** (CA-NEAT) approach (Nichele, Ose, Risi, et al., 2017), evolved neural networks are applied slightly differently to what we have seen in previous sections. In an NCA, a collection of cells, each controlled by a copy of the same evolving neural network, needs to learn to collaborate to perform the task at hand. This process was demonstrated in an experiment where NCAs were evolved to learn to grow a certain target pattern, based only on the local information that they receive from the neighboring grid cells. Here, fitness was assigned based on how closely the resulting pattern resembles the target pattern during the growth process. In addition to growing a particular target pattern, the system was also trained to replicate a certain pattern, which is another fundamental property of biological systems. In this domain, the neural network was tasked to replicate a given seed pattern a specific number of times.

NEAT was indeed able to solve both of these tasks. Figure 7.7*a* shows an example where a NEAT-evolved network grows a French flag–like pattern iteratively starting from an initial seed cell (Nichele, Ose, Risi, et al., 2017). Figure 7.7*b* demonstrates how an evolved neural network learned to replicate an initial mosaic pattern along one axis, taking a total of eight developmental steps. How far can we push this approach? Can we learn to grow patterns of arbitrary complexity? While NEAT was able to discover networks that can grow simple shapes and learn to replicate them, further experiments showed that it

(*a*) Pattern growth (*b*) Pattern replication

Figure 7.7: **CA-NEAT**. The NEAT-evolved neural networks have learned to grow a French flag–like pattern (*a*) and to perform pattern replication (*b*) only through the local interaction of cells. It thus demonstrates a way that neuroevolution can produce complex, coordinated behaviors from simple, decentralized rules. Figures from Nichele, Ose, Risi, et al. (2017).

struggled to learn to grow more complex shapes, such as a Norwegian flag–type pattern. The reason for this is likely that the evolutionary optimization algorithm gets stuck in some local optima of the fitness landscape. We have seen similar phenomena in section 5.3, when trying to re-evolve compositional pattern-producing networks (CPPNs) to generate specific target patterns like the skull image. In a similar vein, evolution here likely depends on discovering the proper stepping stones toward the solution and the developmental dynamics of NCAs likely make this optimization problem even more complicated. While open-ended search methods like quality diversity (section 5.4) could potentially be useful to overcome the stepping-stone problem in this domain, evolutionary approaches tend to perform especially well when the search space is less constrained. Often, we aren't aiming for a precise target pattern but rather for satisfying functional goals—for example, discovering a robot morphology that maximizes locomotion speed. As we will see in the next section, neuroevolution excels at this kind of creative, goal-driven discovery.

In addition to growing specific patterns, these experiments highlighted how NCAs can not only learn spatial organization but can also exhibit behaviors such as self-replication. This capability echoes broader findings in **artificial life** research, where simple systems have been shown to be able to develop self-replicating dynamics (Agüera y Arcas, Alakuijala, Evans, et al., 2024). Indeed, life and intelligence can be understood as computational processes rooted in replication, variation, and interaction (Agüera y Arcas, 2025). These mechanisms are further discussed in chapter 14.

7.3.2 Growing Functional Machines

In the previous section, we saw that NCAs can be evolved to grow inanimate artifacts, such as 2D patterns. However, in nature, entire organisms grow from a single cell, moving and interacting with the world. Additionally, as a result of their developmental programs, such systems continuously renew their cells and possess the ability to repair themselves. Can NCAs be extended to accomplish similar feats?

In this section, we revisit the domain introduced in section 4.3.1 where we explored how **CPPNs** can be used to encode the morphology of mobile, **soft robots**. In that work, a CPPN was queried with the location of each voxel and would then output a voxel material type. CPPNs were able to create high-performing, soft robots with regular patterns such as symmetry and repetition. However, each voxel needed access to its global location in space, and while this is not necessarily a problem in simulated soft robots, in modular physical robots (where each module is identical), this information might not be directly available. Can we design soft robots using a collective approach, where each voxel determines its material solely through local cell-to-cell communication? Drawing parallels with biological systems, each cell should be able to determine its function through local interactions alone.

Here, we will look at such a completely distributed approach, which is based on **evolving NCAs** (Horibe, Walker, and Risi, 2021). In this example, the NCA was a rather simple neural network with a fixed topology consisting of three layers. The input dimension of the neural network was $3 \times 9 \times 2 = 54$, with a hidden layer of 64 nodes. The neural network had five outputs that determine the next state (i.e., material type) of each voxel, such as muscle or bone, and one output that determined if the cell is alive. The same neural network was applied to each voxel neighboring a voxel that is already alive. Robots were grown from an initial seed cell in the center position of the 3D grid for a certain number of time steps until they were placed in the simulation environment. Each robot's voxel materials were then actuated, and the robot was tested for its ability to locomote. Instead of using NEAT, the weights of these networks were evolved through a simple **genetic algorithm** (GA), in which parents were selected uniformly at random. Genomes were mutated by adding **Gaussian noise** to the neural network's weight vectors. The GA performed simple **truncation selection** with **elitism**.

Similar to the CPPN-encoded soft robots, evolved NCAs were able to create high-performing, 3D soft robots through a process of growth and local communication alone. However, unlike CPPNs, they were able to do so without requiring a global coordinate frame. Some of these grown robots are shown in figure 7.8*a*. Once grown, the creatures display different walking gaits, such as the L-walker, which resembles an L-shaped form; it moves by opening and closing its front and rear legs connected to its pivot point at the bend of the L. Another example is the crawler, which has multiple short legs that move forward in concert.

Collective systems offer the advantage of being highly resilient to perturbations and disruptions, as they are designed with built-in redundancies and lack a single point of failure. For example, the morphogenetic systems of many biological organisms give them amazing regenerative capabilities, allowing them to repair and reconfigure their morphology in response to damage or changes in components. Primitive organisms such as Hydra and Planaria are particularly capable of regeneration and can thus achieve complete repair, no matter what location of the body part is cut off (Beane, Morokuma, Lemire, et al., 2013). But also more complex creatures, such as salamanders, are capable

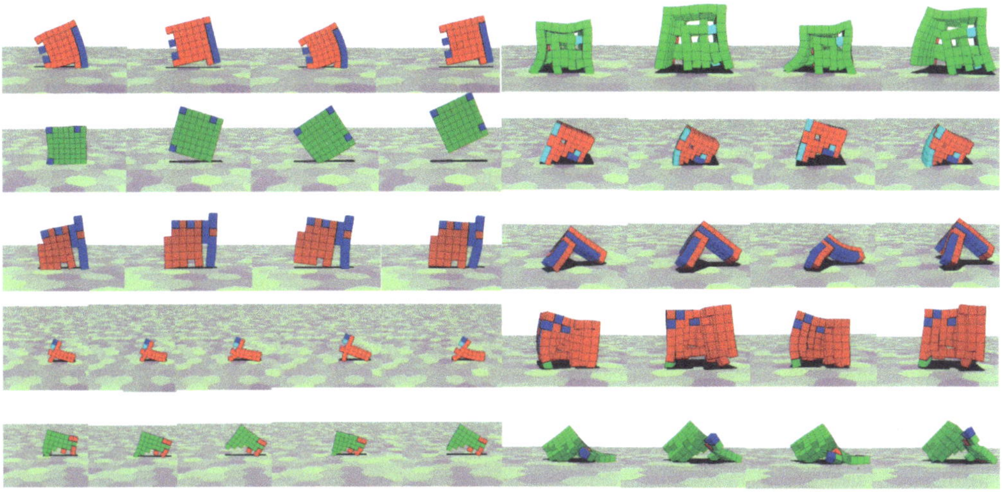

(*a*) Grown soft robots

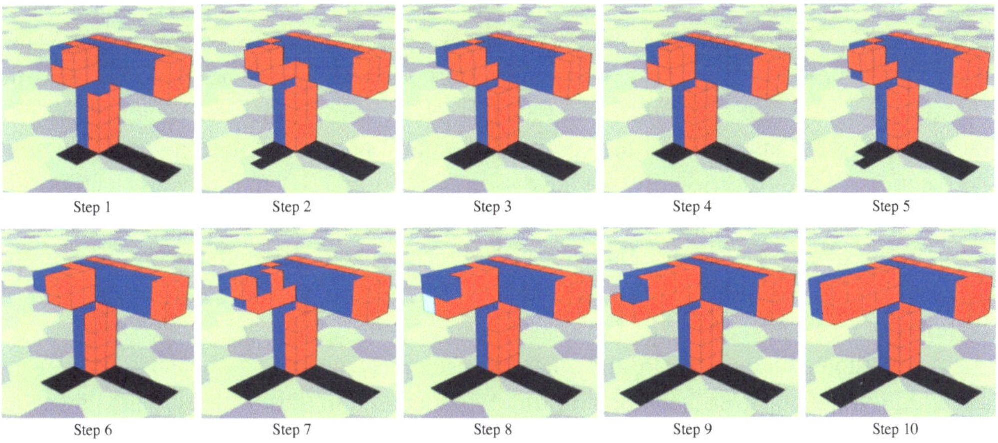

(*b*) Damage recovery

Figure 7.8: **NCA-based soft robots.** (*a*) Evolution discovered a variety of NCAs that were able to grow 2D and 3D soft voxel robots with different walking gaits. (*b*) A second NCA, trained specifically for damage recovery, is able to regrow damaged parts of the robot solely through the local communication of cells. Thus, neuroevolution is not only well suited to finding NCAs for static designs, but also functional morphologies. Figures from Horibe, Walker, and Risi (2021). Videos at `https://neuroevolutionbook.com/demos`.

of regenerating an amputated leg. Can our artificial collective system show a similar kind of resilience and adaptability?

To explore this question, we can remove parts of the fully developed robots and rerun the same NCA for several developmental steps to observe whether the damaged areas regenerate. As it turns out, it is challenging to evolve one NCA that controls both the initial growth and the **damage recovery**. We have already seen in section 6.3.1 that it can be challenging for neuroevolution to switch among different behaviors. However, we can make the task easier by training a second NCA whose sole purpose is to regrow a damaged morphology. In other words, one NCA grows the initial morphology and the other NCA is activated once the robot is damaged. This way, robots were often able to regrow damaged components, allowing them to restore their ability to locomote (figure 7.8*b*). Nevertheless, small discrepancies in the restored morphology could lead to a significant loss of locomotion ability. In section 7.3.5, we will revisit this task and explore how the synergistic integration of neuroevolution and gradient descent can ultimately enable the same neural network to not only grow a robot but also facilitate a higher accuracy in damage and locomotion recovery.

7.3.3 Case Study: Growing Game Levels with QD-Evolved NCAs

So far in this chapter, we have explored approaches where the goal is to grow *one* particular artifact that satisfies certain functional or visual criteria. To evolve a diversity of designs, such as the robot morphology, the algorithm needed to be run multiple times from scratch. In this section, we will look at a case study that evolves a diversity of **neural cellular automata** with a **QD-algorithm**, with the goal of generating a variety of video game levels (Earle, Snider, Fontaine, et al., 2022). **Level generation** can serve as a good benchmark for evolving NCAs, as well as the creative abilities of neuroevolution in general, because such artifacts often need to satisfy a diverse range of criteria, from being aesthetically pleasing, to fun to play, and, after all, functional (i.e., a level needs to be playable). Indeed, we will encounter this domain again in the context of combining neuroevolution with generative AI (section 13.4). Additionally, we have seen in section 7.3.1 that it can be difficult to learn to control the complex dynamics of a self-organizing system such as NCAs to grow into a particular target shape. Because QD algorithms can take advantage of stepping stones discovered along the way, we will see that they are better able to navigate these complex fitness landscapes.

A well-suited video game to study these algorithms is the old-school game The Legend of Zelda (Nintendo, 1986). In the simplified Zelda clone in these experiments, the agent has to navigate 2D levels and locate the key that will open the level's exit door, all while killing monsters. Zelda levels often show some level of symmetry, and therefore symmetry (both horizontal and vertical), in addition to the path length from the goal to the exit, were chosen as the **multi-dimensional archive of phenotypic elites** (MAP-Elites) dimensions of interest. In a straightforward application of QD and NCAs, each elite in the map would be an NCA that produces a map with a particular level of symmetry and path length. However, a designer would ideally have more than one level with a specific path length to choose from. To address this issue, each NCA can be treated as a whole-level generator and tested for its ability to generate a diversity of levels with the same path length, given different random initial states as input.

With the QD dimensions defined, a measure for the quality of each NCA generator was needed, which was evaluated based on three criteria: validity, reliability, and intra-generator diversity. The validity term quantified how well the generated level conformed to the soft constraints of the particular game. For example, in the case of Zelda, this constraint meant that levels should form one connected region, with the generator receiving a lower score for each additional region that was not connected to the main region. The reliability term captured how reliably one NCA generated structures with a particular QD measure. For example, an NCA in Zelda was penalized if it produced levels with

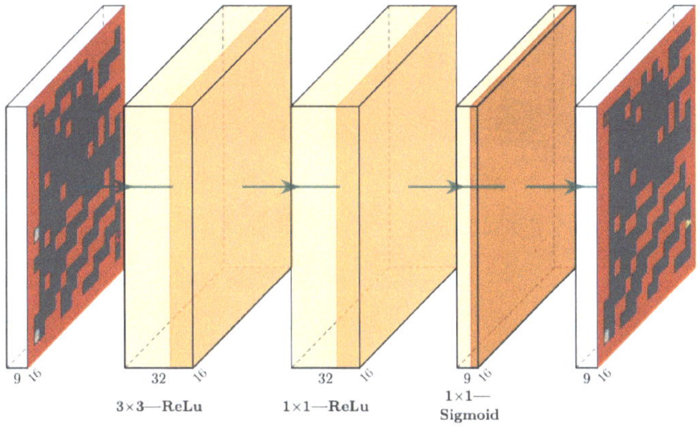

Figure 7.9: **NCA architecture for game level generation.** A convolutional neural network repeatedly transforms levels based on the local interaction of 3×3 cells. Levels are evaluated after being modified for a fixed number of iterations. Figure from Earle, Snider, Fontaine, et al. (2022).

very different path lengths each time it generated a new level from a different initial state. The last term, intra-generator diversity, measured the amount of diversity in a batch of levels generated by the same NCA (given different starting seeds). This term was added to prevent generators from ignoring the latent seed input and collapsing to producing only one particular level design. These three terms were then ultimately combined to measure the quality of a particular NCA, with the goal of having a generator that produces a distribution of valid levels with reliable behavior characterization.

A detailed view of the NCA architecture is shown in figure 7.9. It comprised three convolutional layers, utilized rectified linear unit (ReLU) and sigmoid activation functions, and had 32 hidden channels. The NCA's output retained the dimensions and channel count of its input. However, it employed an arg max function on a channel-by-channel basis to yield a discrete representation of the subsequent state. To generate a game level using an NCA, a one-hot-encoded random starting level was given as input (also termed as **latent seed**). This process was reiterated using the NCA's output until the level either stabilized or reached a predetermined step limit. The QD algorithm was a variant of the classical MAP-Elites algorithm, in particular, **covariance matrix adaptation MAP-Elites** (CMA-ME; Fontaine, Togelius, Nikolaidis, et al., 2020). This approach (see section 5.4.4) combines the MAP-Elites type of solution archiving with the adaptation mechanism of CMA-ES, which is particularly well suited for continuous domains.

The approach was able to grow a diversity of levels along the dimensions of interest path length and symmetry (figure 7.10). The maps were all solvable, satisfying the required game constraints such as only producing one key, one door, and one avatar. One interesting question is: How does the NCA approach compare to a CPPN-like generation of levels, which does not go through the process of growth? QD-algorithms lend themselves to comparing different representations, as they illuminate how well an approach covers the search space along dimensions of interest. To make the comparison fair, each CPPN also needed to become a generator, allowing it to produce not just one map, but multiple ones. This could be achieved by augmenting the CPPN with a latent vector input in addition to

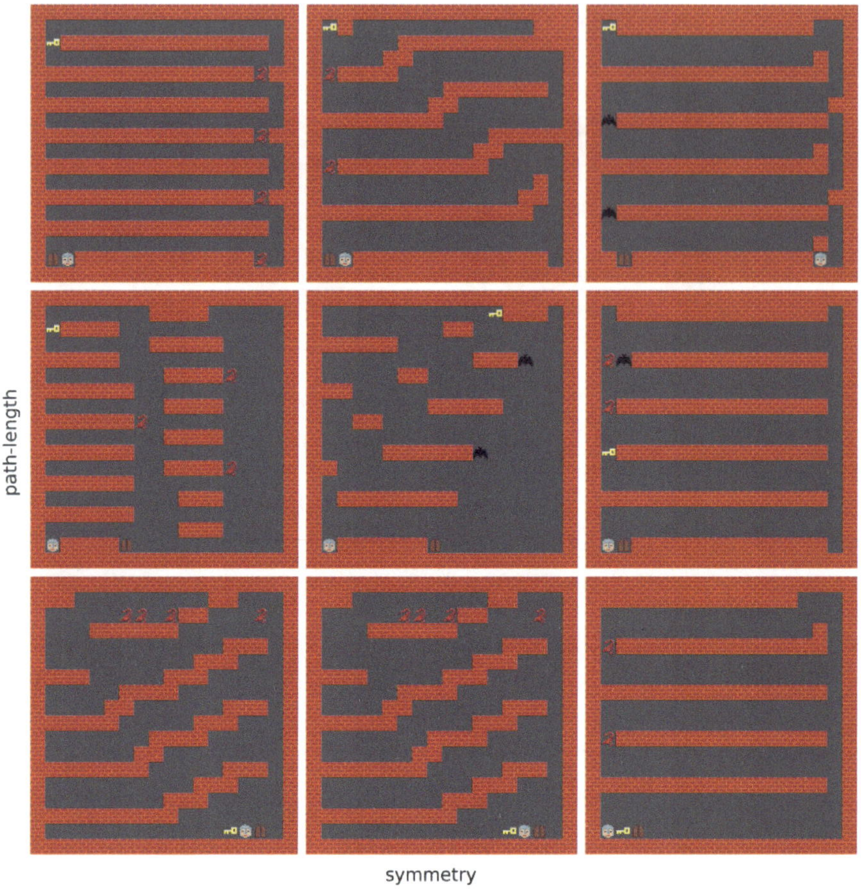

Figure 7.10: **NCA-generated Zelda levels.** Shown are example levels generated by NCAs evolved using a MAP-Elites-based QD approach. The method successfully discovers NCAs capable of producing a diverse set of valid and solvable Zelda maps, varying meaningfully along two dimensions: path length and symmetry. Each map adheres to strict gameplay constraints, including exactly one avatar, one key, and one door. These results demonstrate the effectiveness of combining NCAs with QD algorithms for constraint-aware, diverse procedural content generation in game design. Figures from Earle, Snider, Fontaine, et al. (2022). Videos of the growth process at `https://neuroevolutionbook.com/demos`.

the typical x, y-coordinates. Surprisingly, the results showed that the NCA-based approach was able to explore a larger space of the levels and the individual generators produced more diverse outputs than the CPPN-based encoding and an additional variational autoencoder (VAE)–inspired decoder architecture (Kingma and Welling, 2014). One would assume that having global information would, in fact, make it easier to produce a diversity of levels. However, in this instance, the NCA-based architecture was better suited for searching the space of high-quality and diverse levels.

How was the NCA able to produce designs with global coherence without the global information available to a CPPN or VAE decoder? Looking at a level growth sequence reveals some interesting insights (figure 7.11). During the intermediate growth process, we can see that the levels often contain multiple keys or doors; however, in the end, the process

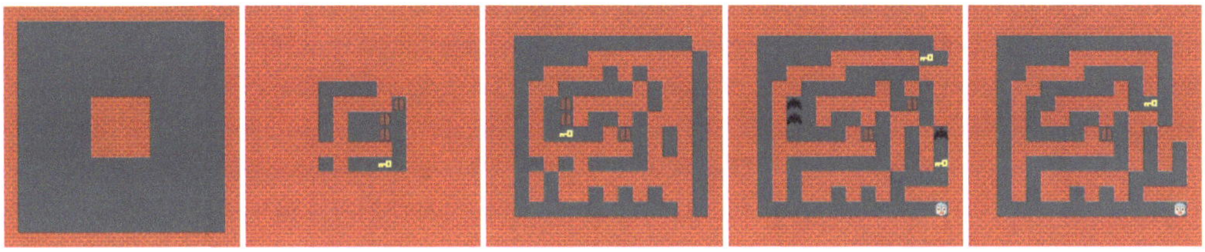

Figure 7.11: **NCA level growth.** Shown are the intermediate growth states of a Zelda level. The growth process starts with a fixed initial seed at the center of the level until a stable configuration is reached. Interestingly, during the intermediate stages of growth, levels frequently contained multiple keys or doors. These additional intermediate tiles appear to function as a form of external memory, helping to transmit spatial information across the level and enabling the emergence of globally coherent patterns. The main result is that through purely local iterative interactions, the NCA is able to produce levels that fulfill complex, high-level functional constraints. Figures from Earle, Snider, Fontaine, et al. (2022).

converges toward a solution with just one key and one door. These intermediate tiles seem to function as a type of external memory, propagating spatial information across the level to form patterns with global complexity. Surprisingly, through these iterative local interactions alone, the NCA was able to generate levels that satisfy high-level functional constraints.

Producing patterns with global coherence through local interactions alone is an essential ability seen in many collective intelligence systems in nature. In the next section, we will investigate the opportunities of such advances for the growth of neural networks themselves.

7.3.4 Evolving Self-assembling Neural Networks

One of the most impressive feats of a collective system cooperating is the self-assembly of billions of cells into a human brain. While most current neural networks in machine learning are hand-designed and learning is restricted to optimizing connection weights, biological neural networks are grown through a process of **local communication** and **self-organization**. In the previous sections of this chapter, we have seen that NCAs can learn to grow 2D structures, game levels, and even locomoting, 3D soft robots. Can they also learn to grow and **self-assemble** an artificial neural network (ANN)?

In section 4.2.2, on grammatical indirect encodings, we have encountered early work in this direction with an approach called **cellular encoding** (Gruau and Whitley, 1993; Gruau, Whitley, and Pyeatt, 1996). In cellular encodings, a program evolved through genetic programming (GP) guides the growth of a policy network. This pioneering work perhaps was ahead of its time, with direct encodings such as NEAT being able to outperform it in terms of the number of evaluations needed to find a solution for simple tasks such as pole balancing. The cellular encoding approach has therefore been less well adopted than conceptually simpler and more direct encoding approaches.

However, with the recent advances in training NCAs to produce complex patterns more efficiently, a cellular encoding based on neural networks (instead of GP), could potentially

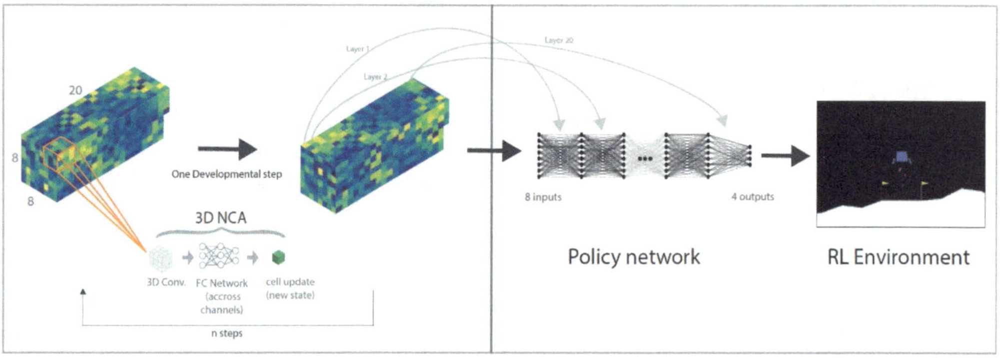

(*a*) Developmental growth (*b*) Policy evaluation

Figure 7.12: **HyperNCA.** (*a*) In a developmental growth phase, a 3D NCA updates an initial random seed over a fixed number of steps. The NCA and the seed may contain one or multiple information channels; for simplicity, a single-channel example is shown. (*b*) In the policy evaluation phase, the first channel of the developed pattern is interpreted as the weight matrix of a policy network, which is then evaluated on the particular task. Figure from Najarro, Sudhakaran, Glanois, et al. (2022).

serve as a powerful indirect encoding. Related approaches such as **evolvable-substrate HyperNEAT** (ES-HyperNEAT) also progressively construct networks (section 4.3.5), but they do not take advantage of the collective collaboration between cells during this process. In nature, these abilities seem essential in enabling the remarkable robustness and adaptability of collective intelligent systems.

A step toward this direction is the **hyper neural cellular automata** (HyperNCA) approach (Najarro, Sudhakaran, Glanois, et al., 2022), which models neural network growth using neural cellular NCAs. The idea is straightforward: Over a number of steps, the NCA grows a spatial pattern. The novel idea is to then interpret one channel of the resulting pattern as the weights of a policy network. This indirectly encoded network is then evaluated in a task (figure 7.12), and the fitness outcome guides the optimization of the NCA using an evolutionary algorithm. While the approach showed promise in continuous control tasks, such as LunarLander and quadrupedal robot locomotion, one limitation of HyperNCA is that it does not incorporate any awareness of the final network's structure; that is, the mapping from the grown 3D pattern to the policy weight matrix does not take the topology of the network into account.

A method that aims to address this issue is the **neural developmental program** (NDP) approach (Najarro, Sudhakaran, and Risi, 2023). NDPs are building on the ideas behind neural CAs but extend them to growing graph like structures. In other words, these **graph cellular automata** (GCA) approaches extend the traditional grid-based structure of cellular automata by operating over arbitrary graph topologies, where each node represents a cell with its own internal state, and edges define local neighborhoods (Grattarola, Livi, and Alippi, 2021). This ability allows them to model systems with a non-uniform connectivity, such as neural networks. Like standard NCAs, graph NCAs rely on local, shared update rules, but they generalize these rules to work over graph structures instead of fixed grids. This enables the growth and self-organization of systems that are not confined to spatial

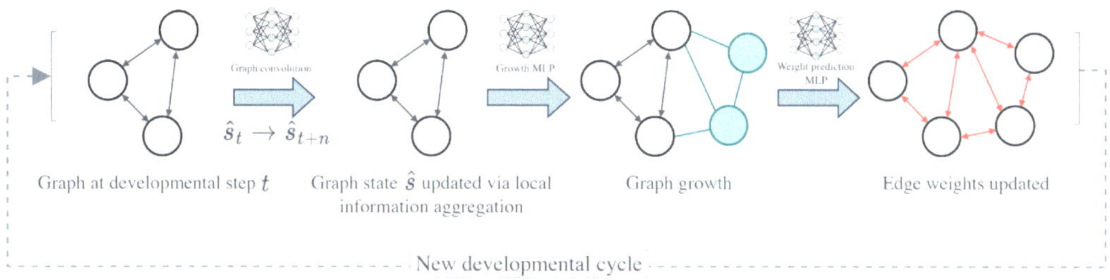

Figure 7.13: **Neural developmental program approach.** During the stage of information aggregation, the graph systematically transmits state s of each node to its adjacent nodes over n iterations. The replication model network takes as input the updated node state s_{t+n} and decides which nodes should replicate. Another network comes into play to determine the weights of the edges connecting each node pair, using their combined embeddings. Once the network is grown for the given number of developmental steps, it is then evaluated to solve a specific task. Figure from Najarro, Sudhakaran, and Risi (2023).

lattices—such as neural circuits—bridging the gap between self-organizing developmental systems and functional artificial architectures.

In NDPs, the goal of the graph NCA is to grow and adapt a policy network to control an agent in an environment, solely based on each neuron's local information received from its neighbors. Note that while the approach grows a neural architecture, the goal here is different from techniques like NEAT and the other neural architecture search methods that we will take a closer look at in chapter 10. While these methods change the architecture of the neural networks during evolution, the idea in NDPs is to grow neural networks during a developmental phase. The benefits of this approach are that the development of the neural network can be shaped by the experience and take advantage of sensory information from the environment to drive the neural developmental process.

A more detailed view of the NDP approach is shown in figure 7.13. Each node in the growing graph has an internal state vector, whose values are updated during the developmental process based on the local communication between nodes. The NDP has three neural networks. One of these networks is responsible for updating the aforementioned hidden states of the nodes, while a second network takes a state of a node as input and predicts whether this node should replicate. The third network takes the state of two hidden nodes as input and outputs the edge weight between them.

A good initial test to evaluate the expressiveness of these NDPs is to task them with growing graphs with properties found in many biological neural networks. One predominant topological characteristic of these biological networks is **small-worldness**, which means networks that are characterized by small average shortest-path lengths and relatively larger clustering coefficients. And in fact, optimizing an NDP directly for these two properties with CMA-ES did indeed lead to a graph that satisfied the small-worldness criteria. A more complex task involves optimizing the NDP to grow a policy neural network that enables an agent to interact successfully with its environment. When applied to various control tasks such as CartPole, LunarLander, and HalfCheetah, CMA-ES was able to find high-performing NDPs. Looking into the growth sequence of one of these networks for the cart pole balancing task, shows the rapid proliferation of nodes during

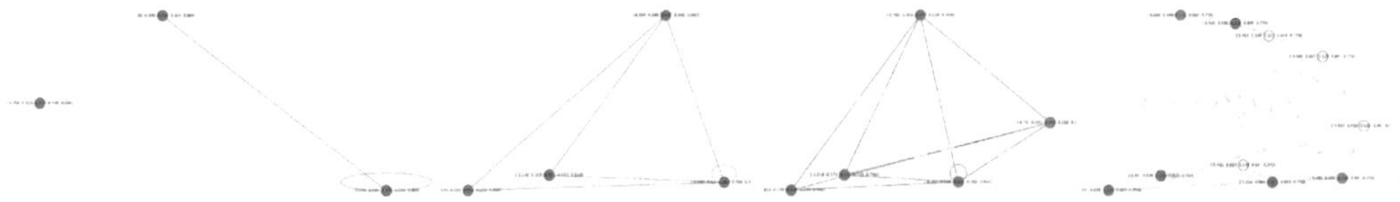

Figure 7.14: **NDP growth of a network solving the CartPole task.** The network begins as a solitary node and progressively develops into a more complex network, encompassing two, four, five, and ultimately ten neurons, along with 33 weighted edges, over the course of four growth stages. Within this network, the red nodes function as sensory neurons, the white nodes serve as hidden neurons, and the blue nodes operate as output neurons. Above each neuron, there is a vector displayed, representing the node embeddings. These embeddings are indicative of the state of each neuron throughout the stages of network development. These results demonstrate that NDPs can enable the growth of well-performing policy networks during a phase of neural development. Figures from Najarro, Sudhakaran, and Risi (2023). Videos at `https://neuroevolutionbook.com/demos`.

the first few developmental stages (figure 7.14). This rapid increase in the number of nodes is an interesting difference to other methods, like NEAT. Even an NDP from early in evolution could grow networks with large numbers of nodes, while NEAT typically requires many generations to gradually add and refine nodes and connections through structural mutations. However, the relative benefits and drawbacks of NDPs versus NEAT are not yet entirely clear and will require deeper exploration in the future.

While there are many open research directions regarding developing more powerful NDPs, the fact that NDPs can capture some of the fundamental patterns seen in biological networks through self-organization and local growth alone suggests that they can be a good base for further exploration. For example, the NDP model can be used to study diversity maintenance in neural populations. In fact, a key issue with training the original NDPs is that if all neurons differentiate into the same type, growth-related decisions become uniform, leading to homogeneous ANN structures incapable of producing complex behaviors. Two biologically inspired key modifications can resolve this issue (Nisioti, Plantec, Montero, et al., 2024). First, introducing **intrinsic states** that remain unchanged during growth ensures that diversity is preserved in the network. By initializing networks with a small set of cells, each with a distinct intrinsic state, diversity can be introduced at the start of growth. As the network expands, these intrinsic states are replicated, resulting in cell lineages similar to biological networks. The second mechanism is **lateral inhibition**, which is believed to play a crucial role in maintaining diversity during biological development. This mechanism prevents neighboring cells from taking similar actions for a limited number of steps when one cell makes a decision. While the role of lateral inhibition regarding agent performance is currently less clear, adding intrinsic states allowed the NDP to perform much better. It reached performance levels similar to a hypernet-based approach across a diversity of complex control tasks such as the inverted double pendulum, ant, reacher robot arm, and HalfCheetah (figure 7.15).

Another key limitation of the original NDP model is that it was temporally constrained to a pre-environmental phase and did not account for an agent's lifetime, let alone lifelong learning. That is, the networks were grown during a developmental phase but remain static while the agent interacts with the environment. However, as we will explore more in

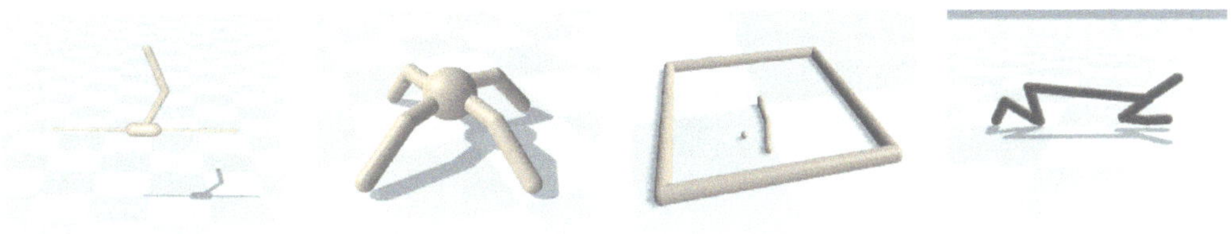

(*a*) Pendulum (*b*) Ant (*c*) Reacher (*d*) Halfcheetah

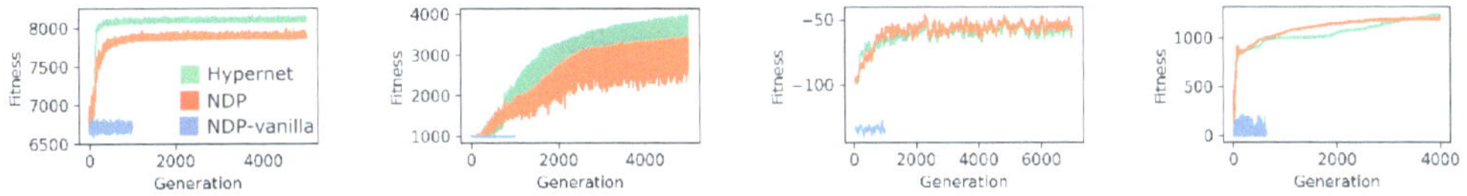

Figure 7.15: **NDP performance across tasks.** Across four tasks (*a–d*), the original vanilla NDP is compared to a version that includes intrinsic states and to a version based on hypernetworks, which does not include development. Intrinsic states allow the NDP to perform significantly better in more complex domains. While the approach does not outperform a hypernetwork approach, it is able to reach a competitive performance through a completely decentralized approach based on neural growth. Note that in all four experiments, NDP-vanilla converged to a degeneration policy early in training and was therefore run for fewer generations.

section 12.3, lifetime adaptation is critical for many tasks. The **lifelong NDP** (LNDP) version introduced a mechanism that enables plasticity and structural adaptation throughout an agent's lifetime (Plantec, Pedersen, Montero, et al., 2024). This is achieved through local computations based on the activity of individual neurons in the ANN and the global reward signals from the environment. This method performed similarly to the original NDP in tasks not requiring lifetime adaptation, such as CartPole. However, when applied to a foraging task that necessitates the agent to learn and remember the position of a randomly placed food source, the LNDP performed significantly better than the NDP.

More broadly, the NDP highlights the differences between approaches that are based on bottom-up self-organization versus the established top-down engineering. While these approaches have yet to be able to compete with current state-of-the-art methods, they offer an exciting alternative to achieving more robust and adaptive forms of neural networks.

7.3.5 Combining Evolutionary Creativity with GD Precision

Neuroevolution works especially well when it is less constrained, taking advantage of the power of evolution's creative discovery. For example, neuroevolution is well suited to evolve neural networks that grow soft robots able to locomote or video game levels with interesting properties. However, these algorithms can struggle when tasked to reevolve a target pattern that requires traversing many stepping stones (section 5.3). The same is true for evolving morphogenetic systems that are tasked to grow a more complex target pattern.

If a target is given, such as a particular 2D or 3D structure, it makes sense to take advantage of efficient gradient descent to optimize for growing that target directly. For example, NCA can be trained efficiently through **backpropagation** to grow certain 2D images (Mordvintsev, Randazzo, Niklasson, et al., 2020) or even functional 3D Minecraft structures that can regrow damaged components (Sudhakaran, Grbic, Li, et al., 2021). Some of these examples are shown in figure 7.16.

Figure 7.16: **Learning to grow different 3D target structures.** An NCA is trained through gradient descent to grow a given target pattern. The approach is able to grow both static structures, such as a tree or an apartment building, but also functional machines, such as a locomoting caterpillar. The caterpillar can even regenerate into two creatures when cut in half. Figures from Sudhakaran, Grbic, Li, et al. (2021). Videos at `https://neuroevolutionbook.com/demos`.

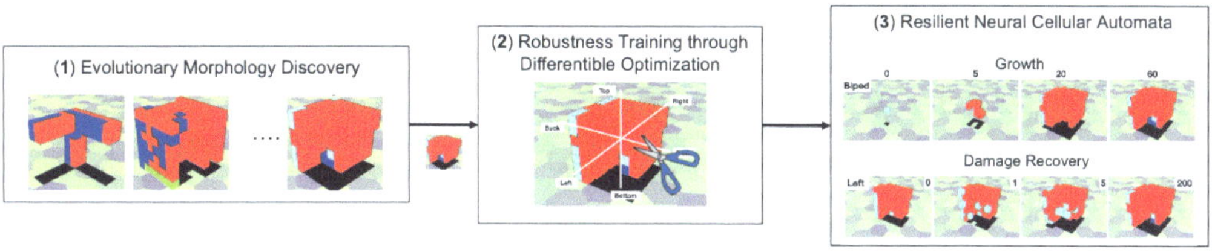

Figure 7.17: **Combining evolutionary discovery and gradient descent precision.** (1) Evolutionary optimization is used to discover a wide range of diverse morphologies. (2) An NCA is then trained to regenerate these target morphologies, even after different types of damage. (3) The trained NCA can successfully grow a soft robot and recover it from severe damage. Figure from Horibe, Walker, Berg Palm, et al. (2022). Videos at `https://neuroevolutionbook.com/demos`.

Returning to the task of evolving NCAs to create resilient, soft robots offers an interesting opportunity for combining the benefits of evolution for creative discovery and gradient descent for efficient optimization (Horibe, Walker, Berg Palm, et al., 2022). One idea is to use the undamaged morphology, discovered through evolution as a training target for regeneration. Once a robot morphology is evolved for effective locomotion, that intact structure becomes the goal for the NCA to regrow after damage. This is a challenge that gradient descent is perfectly suited for, and by training the NCA toward this target, the system learns to reconstruct complex, functional morphologies from partial or damaged states. This approach allows the strengths of evolution (creative discovery) and supervised learning (precise reconstruction) to be combined in a single framework. Figure 7.17 shows an overview of this hybrid approach as follows: (1) a diversity of morphologies is discovered through evolutionary optimization; (2) a neural cellular automata is trained to regrow a target morphology found by evolution under different damages through gradient descent; (3) the resulting NCA is able to grow a soft robot while being able to recover from extreme forms of damage.

The results show that using gradient descent to train for recovery significantly outperformed using neuroevolution alone for the same task. When neuroevolution was used to train a second NCA for regeneration (section 7.3.2), the robots could partially recover their original morphology and locomotion, but the results were limited. For example, morphological similarity to the original robot topped out around 91%–99%, and locomotion recovery was inconsistent—some robots regained only 20%–45% of their movement, depending on the complexity of the damage and the morphology. In contrast, when gradient descent was used to train the same NCA to handle both growth and regeneration, the robots not only regrew more accurate morphologies (achieving 97.9%–100% similarity across multiple damage types), but they also recovered a greater percentage of their locomotion ability, often over 80%, and in some cases 100%.

In summary, combining evolutionary algorithms with gradient descent–based techniques offers a promising approach for developing systems that are both innovative and resilient. Evolutionary processes excel at exploring a vast search space of potential solutions, producing a diversity of designs and behaviors that are often not achievable through gradient-based methods alone. This creative potential is particularly advantageous in open-ended domains like soft robotics, where unconventional solutions can emerge.

On the other hand, once a target design or structure is identified, gradient descent–based training shines in its ability to fine-tune and optimize the system efficiently, enabling robust growth and regeneration capabilities.

This chapter explored how cooperative and competitive coevolution can drive the emergence of complex behaviors in agents and systems. Through cooperative coevolution, individual components evolve together to form robust and specialized solutions. In contrast, competitive coevolution fosters open-ended discovery via evolutionary arms races, where agents continually adapt against evolving opponents. While collective systems can evolve autonomously, some problems benefit from human intuition and creative input, especially when goals are hard to formalize. In chapter 8, we turn to how we can bring humans into the loop, allowing them to guide evolution based on more subjective criteria.

7.4 Chapter Review Questions

1. **Conceptual understanding:** What are the fundamental differences between cooperative and competitive coevolution, and how does each contribute to neuroevolution?

2. **Cooperative coevolution:** Describe the concept of shared fitness in cooperative coevolution. How does it ensure effective collaboration among components?

3. **Evolving single neural networks:** How does the ESP system improve upon the SANE system in evolving neural networks?

4. **Specialization in subpopulations:** Why is redundancy within subpopulations important in the context of ESP, and how does it lead to robust networks?

5. **Evolving teams:** In the predator-prey scenario, how do stigmergy-based coordination strategies lead to effective team behaviors without direct communication?

6. **Competitive coevolution:** How does competitive coevolution establish an open-ended fitness function, and what challenges does it face in ensuring progress?

7. **Evolutionary arms race:** Using the zebras and hyenas example, explain how alternating advantages between predator and prey populations drive increasingly complex behaviors.

8. **Cellular automata:** What role do local interactions play in the emergence of complex patterns in CAs, and how are these principles applied to neural CAs?

9. **Applications of neural CAs:** How can NCAs be used to solve tasks like the French flag problem or pattern replication? What are their advantages over traditional approaches?

10. **Evolving resilient systems:** Explain the hybrid approach combining neuroevolution and gradient descent for growing and regenerating resilient soft robots. How does each method contribute to the overall system's functionality?

Chapter 8

Interactive Neuroevolution

Chapters 6 and 7 discussed how the behavior of agents that operate embedded in an environment can be discovered through neuroevolution. Starting from reactive control and expanding all the way to sequential decision-making strategies, effective solutions can be discovered that may be surprising to human designers. Moreover, discovery can be embedded in a collective environment, where opponents and cooperators are evolving as well, thereby providing new and creative challenges. In some cases, however, it may be useful for human designers to drive this discovery process more explicitly. They may have knowledge that is difficult to capture in a formal objective function. For instance, the desired behavior may be complex and multifaceted, or it may depend on believability or aesthetic values. In such cases, neuroevolution can be made interactive. The construction of new individuals is still done through evolutionary operators, but the selection is at least partially due to human judgment. This chapter reviews how **interactive neuroevolution** can be set up effectively, and the discussion demonstrates it in several examples in various game domains.

8.1 The NERO Machine Learning Game

Setting up neuroevolution experiments sometimes feels like a game. You have a goal in mind–that is, an idea of what you want the evolved agents to do. You have to think about how to express that behavior in terms of an objective function, which in turn depends on behavioral descriptors that can be readily measured. You may need to come up with a shaping strategy, starting with simpler behaviors and gradually making the objective function more demanding. You may need to try many such setups before finding some that achieve effective behaviors. There may be several such solutions, some of which may even surprise you. Finding such solutions, and perhaps better than those seen before, is what makes this game appealing.

NERO (Stanley, Bryant, and Miikkulainen, 2005) is an actual game built on this very idea. It can be seen as a pioneering effort to establish a new game genre: **machine learning games**. Unlike in other genres, such as first-person shooter games or simulation games, the human player is not controlling game agents directly. Instead, the player takes the role of a teacher/coach/drill sergeant, designing a curriculum of learning challenges for actual agents in the game. Those agents solve the challenges using machine learning. After learning, the agents engage in a head-to-head competition with other similarly trained agents to determine how good the training was.

More specifically, in the NERO game, agents are battle robots controlled by neural networks evolved with **neuroevolution of augmenting topologies** (NEAT; figure 8.1*c*, *d*). The entire population of them is placed in the environment at once. The environment is usually an enclosed area with walls, buildings, trees, and other objects, allowing the agents to move around, hide, and take cover. Simple, algorithmically controlled enemy agents can be placed in it, including static enemies (and flags) that act as targets, static enemies that fire at the agents, and mobile enemies that fire and approach the agents. As their input, they observe the number and distance to enemy agents as well as teammates in sectors around them, the distance to walls and other static objects in several directions, whether their weapon is on target, and the direction from which the fire from the nearest enemy is coming. As their output, they can move forward and back, turn left and right, and fire their weapons.

In such an environment, NEAT can evolve networks that exhibit interesting behaviors. The agents can charge the enemy, approach from different directions, disperse to be less likely to hit, converge to increase firepower, take temporary cover behind walls, hide to survive until the end of the game, and many other actions. The interesting question is: What kind of behaviors are useful in a battle against an actual enemy? Further, how can we encourage evolution to discover such behaviors while still encouraging open innovation as well? This is precisely the question that interactive neuroevolution aims to address.

In NERO, the human player has a number of tools at their disposal (figures 8.1*a*, *b*). They can place various objects in the field, such as walls, static and mobile enemies, and flags. They can control a number of sliders that correspond to coefficients in the objective function, such as approach/avoid the enemy, hit a target, avoid getting hit, follow teammates, and disperse. Both objects and sliders can be changed dynamically as the training progresses, making it possible to design a curriculum. For instance, it may be useful to reward the agents for approaching the enemy first, then do it while avoiding fire, then while avoiding fire from moving enemies, then while utilizing walls as cover, and so on (figure 8.2). Such **curricular evolution**, or **shaping**, can result in more complex and effective behaviors than could be achieved with a single, static, objective function without human guidance.

One interesting extension needs to be made to the NEAT method, however. Note that the entire population is evaluated in the environment at the same time. This approach makes the evolution efficient, since the evaluations are done in parallel. The population is also always visible to the human player, making it easier to understand how well the evolution is progressing. However, if the entire population is replaced at the same time, as is usual in generational evolution, the game appears discontinuous and difficult to follow. Instead, evolution needs to progress continuously, one agent at a time.

In this **real-time evolution** extension of NEAT, called **rtNEAT**, among all the agents that have been evaluated sufficiently long, the worst one is removed from the population. The species are recalculated, and an offspring is generated as usual in NEAT. This offspring is then placed in the environment to be evaluated. This replacement takes place at regular

(*c*) Possible objects

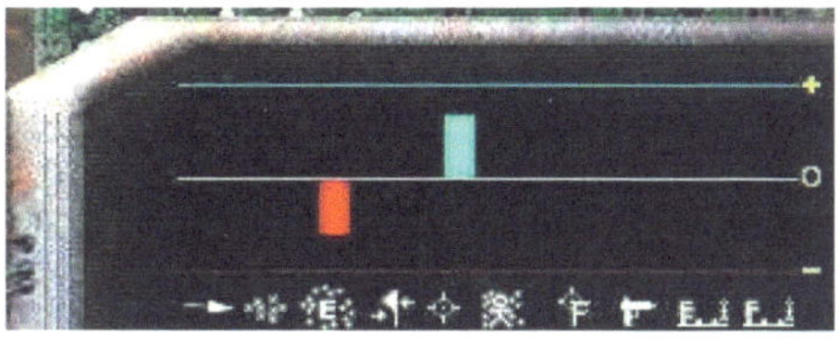

(*b*) Sliders defining fitness

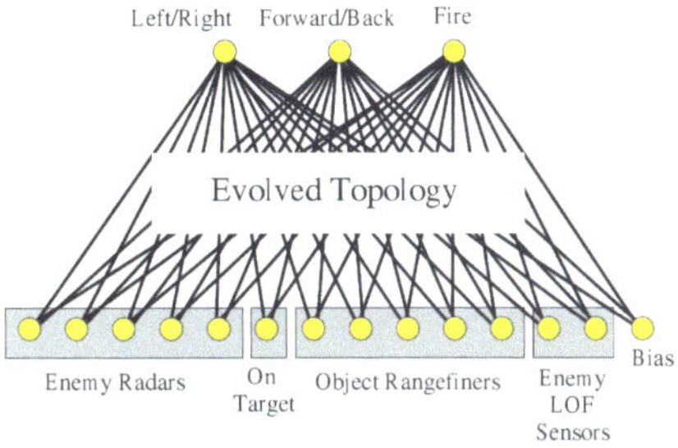

(*c*) A network controlling one agent

(*d*) A population being evaluated

Figure 8.1: **Setting up a NERO experiment.** The NERO game allows specifying increasingly challenging environments so that complex behavior can be evolved. (*a*) The human player can place various objects in the environment to create challenges, including walls, flags, static enemies, and moving enemies. (*b*) The human player controls the fitness by adjusting sliders with continuous positive or negative values along various dimensions such as approach an enemy, approach a flag, hit a target, avoid getting hit, and stay with teammates. (*c*) Each agent in the game is controlled by a neural network evolved through NEAT. As its input, it senses the environment around it, including enemies, teammates, walls, and other objects; it also senses whether its weapon is on target, and the direction from which the nearest fire is coming. As its output, it issues actions to move forward and back, turn left and right, and fire. (*d*) During evolution, the entire population of agents is evaluated together in an enclosed environment that may contain multiple objects. In this case, the agents spawn on the right and are rewarded for approaching the flag on the left. At regular intervals, the worst agent is replaced by offspring in a continuous replacement process. In this manner, the human player can create a curriculum of increasingly challenging tasks that prepares the team well for battle against other teams. Figures from Stanley, Bryant, and Miikkulainen (2005). For videos of various training scenarios, see `https://neuroevolutionbook.com/demos`.

intervals, and because it involves only one individual at a time, is largely invisible to the human player. In this manner, evolution progresses continuously while the population is being evaluated. Although it was designed for the visual effect in NERO, the same approach can be useful in other domains where continuous adaptation is needed.

After the curricular evolution is complete, the teams are evaluated in a battle mode of NERO. Two teams are placed in the same environment, which may be the same one used in training, or something completely different. At this stage (in NERO 1.0), the agents operate independently of the human player, applying what they were trained to do in competition with another team. If an agent is hit a sufficient number of times, it is removed from the environment. The game ends when one team is annihilated or the clock runs out, in which case the team with the most agents still on the field wins. Note that the battle domain is obviously a violent game, similar to many video games in the first-person shooter genre. The principles are more general, however, and apply to less violent settings

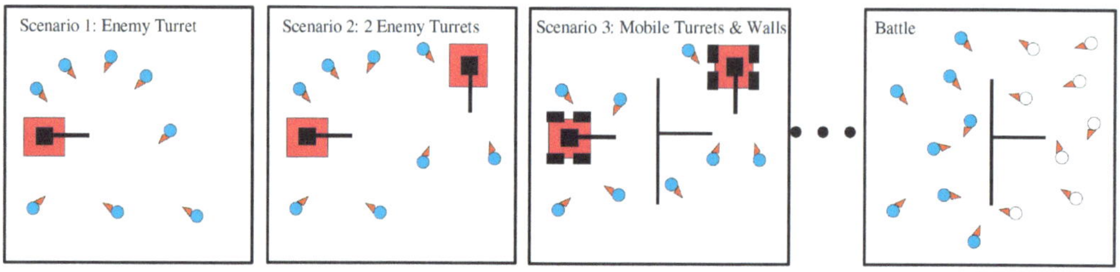

Figure 8.2: **Training NERO teams through interactive neuroevolution.** The player first specifies a simple task such as approaching a static enemy that fires (a "turret"), so the agents learn to approach it from different sides. In the next scenario, they learn to approach one turret while minding fire from another. Next, the turrets move and turn, and the agents need to take cover behind walls. Through multiple such increasingly challenging scenarios, the agents learn effective battle behaviors. The team is then placed into a battle against another team, evaluating how well the human player was able to train them. NERO thus aims at creating intelligent behavior strategies through interactive neuroevolution. Figure from Stanley, Bryant, and Miikkulainen (2005).

as well. In fact, neuroevolution can play many roles in video games (Risi and Togelius, 2015). For example, in section 8.4, we examine how it contributes to the procedural generation of content in the gardening game Petalz. A robotic battle domain, however, provides clear and compelling measures and visualizations of performance, which were useful for a pioneering example of ML games. Often, interesting interactions result that were not anticipated, suggesting ideas for further interactive neuroevolution of the team.

One of the first behaviors is often to approach a firing enemy. The agents quickly evolve to avoid fire by going around and approaching from the side. This behavior is general and adapts easily to enemies that are turning. If subsequently the "approach" slider is abruptly changed to "avoid" (i.e., negative rewards for approaching), an interesting demonstration of evolutionary search can be seen. As always, there are individuals in the population that do not perform very well. Even if most agents approach the enemy, some of them may stand still, roam around, or run away. When the slider changes, they become the seed for the behavioral change. They receive higher fitness, and their offspring take over the population, resulting in avoidance in a few reproductions.

In some cases, careful **curriculum design** can be used to construct effective desired behaviors. For instance, it is possible to evolve the agents to run a maze to a target on the other side. First, the environment may consist of a single wall, and gradually more walls in complex configurations as the agents evolve to run around them (figure 8.3*a*). The resulting behavior can be quite general and effective, despite involving no actual path planning. It is enough for the agents to know the general direction; they can then navigate around even complex mazes, so long as they do not contain deceptive traps. Combined with the objective of dispersing, the agents also take different paths through the maze, which is effective because it is difficult to defend against an enemy that approaches from many directions at once.

On the other hand, evolution can still discover surprising and effective behaviors as well. One such result was that the agents sometimes evolved to run backward (figure 8.3*b*). This seems odd at first, but it does serve a purpose in some cases. If the enemy tends to pursue the agents persistently, running backward is useful because the weapon remains

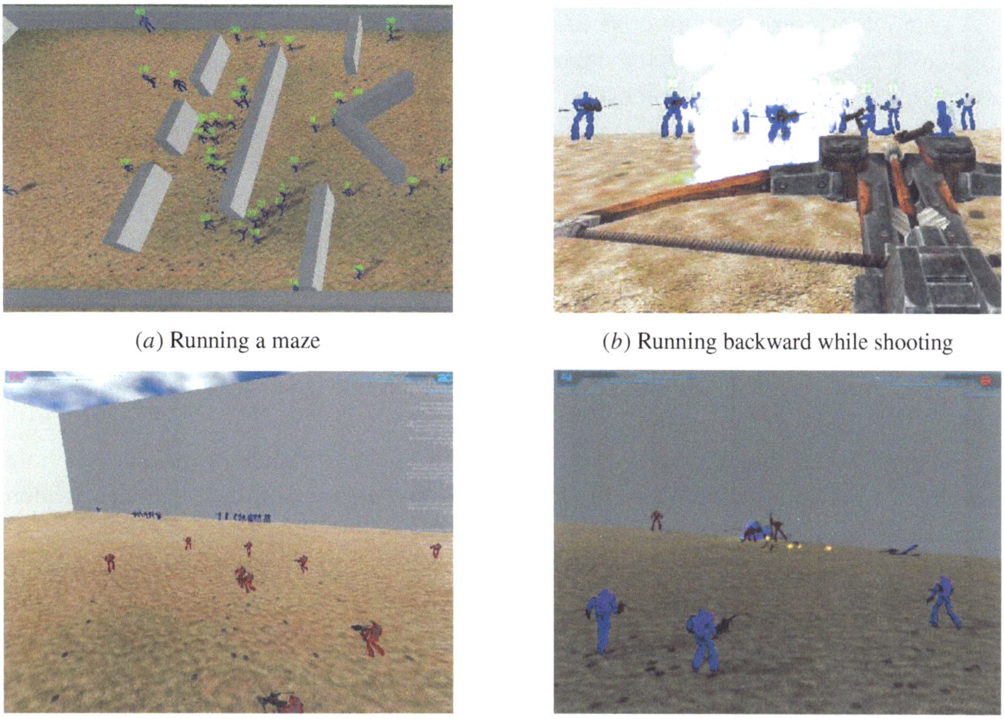

(*a*) Running a maze

(*b*) Running backward while shooting

(*c*) Forming a firing squad

(*b*) Subteams of three agents

Figure 8.3: **Discovery of expected and unexpected behaviors in NERO.** What makes the game interesting is that the player has some control over what will happen, but evolution will also find surprising solutions. (*a*) By gradually adding more walls and rewarding the agents for staying away from each other, they evolve to take various paths through the maze, without any explicit path planning. (*b*) An effective strategy for hitting the target while not getting hit is to run backward while shooting. (*c*) An avoidant team can be effective when they have time to back up against a wall, forming a firing squad. (*d*) A subteam of three agents is agile and has significant firepower. These discoveries and many more like them were surprising, resulting from evolution solving the challenges posed by the human player. In this manner, humans can provide guidance while still letting evolution find creative solutions. For videos of these and other battle behaviors, see `https://neuroevolutionbook.com/demos`. Figures *a*, *b*, and *c* from Stanley, Bryant, and Miikkulainen (2005).

pointed to the enemy. Another discovery was that extremely avoidant behavior can be effective in battle (figure 8.3*c*). That is, most of the time, aggressive teams are evolved that approach the enemy and pursue it if they retreat. An avoidant team, however, would retreat until the agents have their back against the wall. It turns out that if they are fast enough to do it, so there are still enough of them, they form a firing squad that is very difficult to approach, and aggressive pursuers are often eliminated. Yet another surprising discovery was that some teams evolved to form subteams of three agents (figure 8.3*d*): They approach the enemy together, they fire at the same enemy, and they retreat together. Such subteams are effective because they have significant firepower yet are very agile. Evolution discovered this independently; however, this principle turned out to be well established in actual military training.

One interesting question in NERO is: Is there an actual best strategy in the game, or does it support several strategies, such that each dominates some, but not all, other strategies? This is a crucial question for ML games in general, as well as interactive neuroevolution. While it is difficult to answer this question conclusively, it is possible to conduct a large-scale experiment with many players and evaluate the resulting strategies.

The first **massive open online course** (MOOC) on AI in 2011, run by Peter Norvig and Sebastian Thrun, provided such an opportunity (Karpov, Johnson, and Miikkulainen, 2015). As an optional assignment in the course, the students designed NERO teams and a comprehensive round-robin tournament was run with them. Of the 156 submissions, some performed much better than others, and the teams could be ranked according to total wins: The best one won 137 times, the next 130, then two teams at 126, then the teams scored 125, 124, 123, and so on.

When the behavior was characterized in terms of actions taken in various situations, ten major behavioral strategies were identified. However, none of them was clearly more successful than any others; what mattered the most was how well they were implemented. What is most interesting, however, is that there was clear circularity among the best teams: Team A beat team B, which beat team C, which beat team A. This result suggests that it is unlikely that one best strategy exists, but different behaviors are required to do well against different opponents. Both these properties make the game more interesting to human players, suggesting that ML games are indeed a viable genre. They also suggest that human intuition in interactive evolution can be useful and provide an outlet for human creativity, as is also demonstrated in the following sections of this chapter. Furthermore, combining human and machine insights is a powerful approach for designing complex systems.

The software for the original NERO, as well as its open-source version, is available from the book website. The original NERO includes version 2.0 of the game, which also features human guidance during the battles, as well as the ability to construct teams by combining individuals from different evolutionary runs. The goal was to make the teams more versatile and the gameplay more interactive; the interactive evolution aspect remained the same. OpenNERO was also designed to support other AI and ML methods, making it possible to compare and demonstrate different approaches to intelligent agents. They can serve as a starting point for exercises and projects in this book.

8.2 Incorporating Human Knowledge into NERO

NERO is one of the first examples of a genre of ML games; that is, the gameplay consists of players interacting with an ML system. Its focus was on one particular kind of interaction, which is shaping neuroevolution through human insights. However, it is possible to incorporate human knowledge into neuroevolution in other ways as well, including explicitly through **rule-based advice** and implicitly through **behavioral examples**.

Note that these approaches are useful in creating intelligent agents in general; for instance, advice can be used in prey capture to help the agent evolve a corralling strategy, pushing the prey into the corner rather than chasing it in circles (Fan, Lau, and Miikkulainen, 2003). Similarly, examples can be used to train agents in a strategy game to establish behavioral doctrines that also observe safety constraints, resulting in visibly intelligent behavior that does not easily emerge on its own in neuroevolution (Bryant and Miikkulainen, 2007). However, advice and examples can be most clearly demonstrated and evaluated in NERO because it is an interactive evolution environment to begin with.

In NERO, successful behaviors are discovered through **exploration**. This means that even the most obvious ones, like moving around a wall without getting stuck, take many iterations of trial and error. This process is often frustrating to watch because effective behavior is obvious to the observer, and s/he might as well tell the agents what they should do. Evolution can then use that advice as a starting point, modify it further, and move on to more interesting discoveries faster.

A mechanism for incorporating such advice into evolving neural networks can be built based on **knowledge-based artificial neural networks** (KBANNs; Towell and Shavlik, 1994). The knowledge is first specified in a set of rules, such as "If a wall is some distance in front, then move forward and turn right" and "If a wall is near 45 degrees to the left, then move forward and turn slightly right." The rules are then converted into partial neural network structures: The conditions are coded as input nodes and consequences as output nodes, with hidden nodes mapping between them (figures 8.4*a*, *b*; Yong, Stanley, Miikkulainen, et al., 2006). These structures are spliced into each existing neural network in the population, thus adding the wall-circling behavior to their existing behaviors. Weight values are usually constant, with positive or negative signs, but they can also be graded to indicate elements like the degree of a turn. Note that such additions are natural in NEAT, which already has mechanisms for growing the networks through add-node, add-connection, and change-weight mutations. Evolution then continues to modify these networks, incorporating the advice into the general behavior, modifying the advice to make it more useful, or even rejecting it entirely and changing it into something else. Confidence values can be used to specify how likely such modifications are; that is, how immutable or plastic the advice is. Given that the evolutionary changes modify rules that were originally interpretable, the modifications may be interpretable as well; that is, it may be possible to explain what new knowledge evolution discovers in this process.

Experiments demonstrate that such advice indeed helps learn a task like going around the wall faster (figures 8.4*c*, *d*). Remarkably, if the task changes so it is now better to go around the left side instead of the right, adaptation is very fast: evolution quickly changes the output actions to the left, while the rest of the advice network structure stays the same. If the task changes again to make the right side better, there's little difference between networks that evolved with advice or not. In both cases, the advice has become incorporated into the general network structure. In this manner, advice helps evolution discover the needed behaviors but does not constrain evolution in the longer term.

In some cases, it may be difficult or inconvenient to write advice as rules, but it may be easy to demonstrate the desired behavior by driving an agent in the game. For instance, the knowledge about going around a wall can be presented in this way. The agent is placed in a starting location, and the player takes possession of it and gives movement commands that take it to the target flag. At each step, the inputs and outputs to the agent are recorded and used as a training set with backpropagation through time; alternatively, the path of the agent can be divided into segments, and the actions that keep the agent on the example path

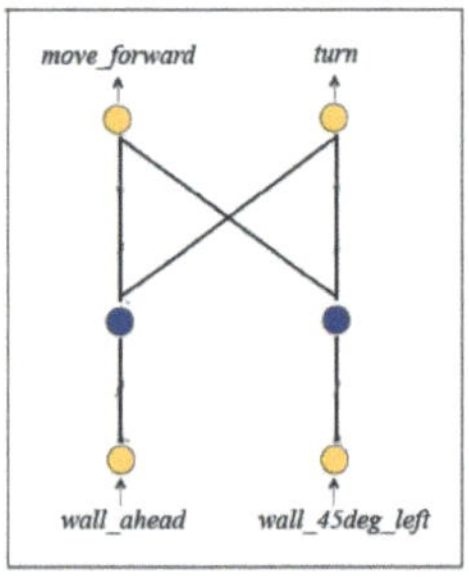

(*a*) The advice network structure

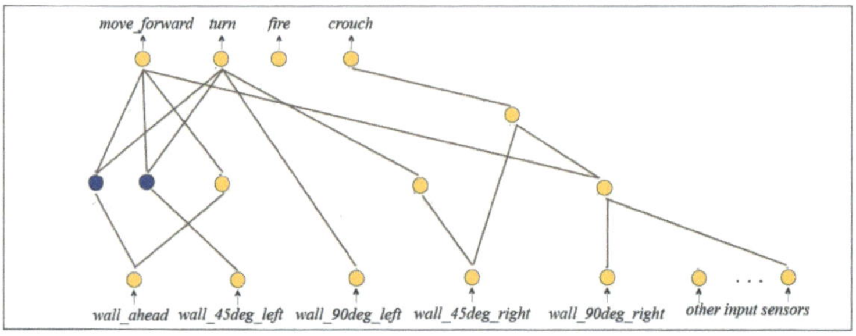

(*b*) Advice spliced into a NERO network

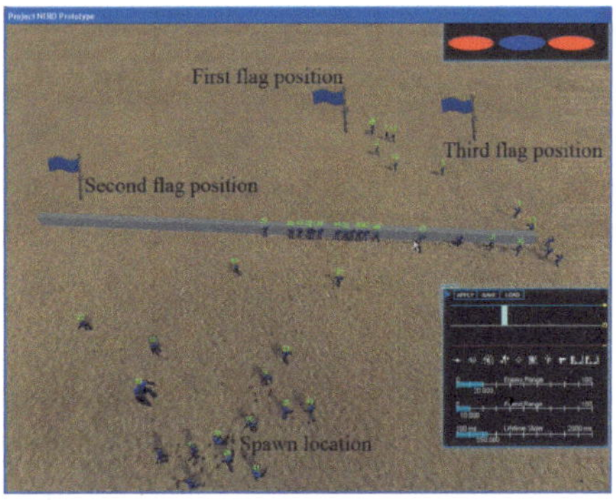

(*c*) The three phases of the experiment

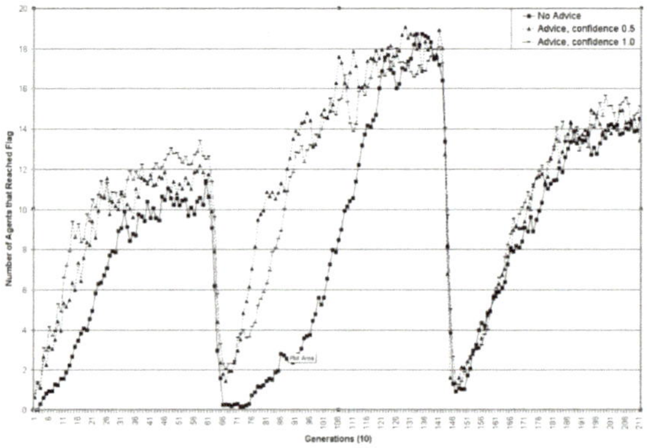

(*d*) Performance over generations

Figure 8.4: **Utilizing rule-based advice in NERO.** It is sometimes useful to be able to guide the evolutionary discovery with human knowledge. Such knowledge can be expressed as rules and incorporated into the population of networks. (*a*) As an example, two rules about going around the wall on the right side are encoded as a partial network structure. (*b*) This structure is then spliced into NEAT networks like any mutation. The networks continue to evolve to take advantage, modify, or co-opt the advice to perform better. (*c*) A snapshot of NERO with the three sequential positions identified. The agents were first rewarded for going to the flag in the middle, then to the one at left, and then the one at right. (*d*) The advice suggested going to the first flag around the right side, and it sped up evolution compared to having no advice. When the flag was moved to the left, networks with advice adapted very quickly, utilizing the same advice structure with different output actions. After the flag was moved again, there was no difference in adaptation with or without advice, suggesting that the advice had become incorporated into the network like any other structure in it. Figures from Yong, Stanley, Miikkulainen, et al. (2006).

can be used as targets. The agent is first trained to reproduce the first segment, then the first two, and so on until it successfully replicates the entire example. The weight changes are encoded back to the genetic encoding of the network (implementing **Lamarckian evolution**), and are thus inherited by its offspring.

It is interesting to evaluate how well each of these methods for incorporating human knowledge (e.g., shaping, advice, and examples) works in interactive neuroevolution. To this end, a **human-subject study** was conducted (Karpov, Valsalam, and Miikkulainen, 2011). A total of 16 participants were given three tasks: going around the wall, catching a moving target, and traversing a trajectory consisting of multiple way points (figure 8.5).

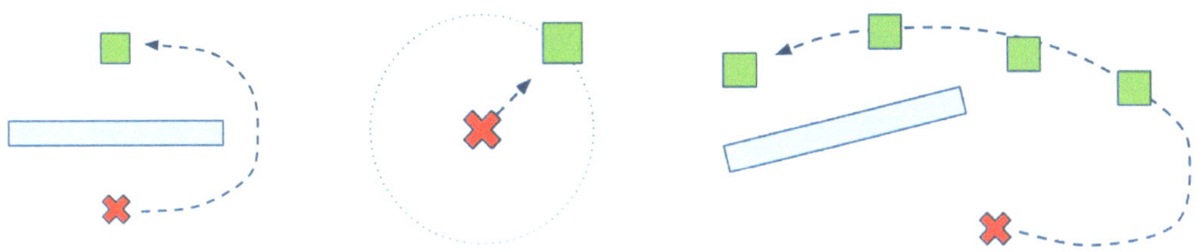

(*a*) Going around a wall

(*b*) Catching a moving target

(*c*) Traversing through waypoints

Figure 8.5: **Tasks for evaluating methods that incorporate human knowledge in NERO.** Plain neuroevolution from scratch on one hand, and full scripting of behavior on the other, were compared to advice, examples, and shaping. Plain neuroevolution turned out to be more successful than scripting, and at least one of the human-guided methods more successful than plain neuroevolution: examples in (*a*), advice in (*b*), and shaping in (*c*). Thus, the different methods of incorporating human knowledge can play a different role in constructing intelligent agents in interactive neuroevolution domains. Figures from Karpov, Valsalam, and Miikkulainen (2011).

They were instructed to solve these tasks by two methods: either by writing a set of rules (i.e., a script for the entire behavior), or one other method, which was either advice, examples or shaping, randomly chosen and in random order. Their performance was recorded, and they were surveyed afterward; the performance was also compared to plain neuroevolution from scratch, without any human knowledge.

The surveys suggested that the example-based approach was favored as the best-quality approach, and then scripting, shaping, and advice. Shaping was found to be low quality in the moving-target task, advice was low quality in the way-points task, and all methods were good in the wall-circling task. These ratings did not always correlate with the rate of success, suggesting that they mostly measure how easy or fun it was to use each method—which is useful information on its own.

The recordings were used to measure the average time to a successful solution, with a 30-minute upper bound. It turned out that scripting was the most difficult way to achieve successful performance; even plain neuroevolution was more successful. Interestingly, at least one human-assisted method performed better than plain neuroevolution. Advice was most effective in catching the moving target. It was possible to specify an intercept course rather than chasing the target indefinitely. In general, advice makes sense when the behavior can be expressed as a general rule. In contrast, examples were best in the going-around-the-wall task. Indeed, this approach is most appropriate when the desired behavior is concrete and specific. Shaping, the usual staple of the NERO game, was the most effective in the way-point task, where it was possible to start with a single target and then gradually add more way points. The approach makes sense in general in tasks where it is possible to start with a simplified or partial version and then gradually make the task more demanding. In this manner, each way of incorporating human knowledge into interactive neuroevolution can play a different role in constructing intelligent agents.

When exactly should each of these methods be used? An interesting possibility for the future is for the interactive evolution system itself to request advice, examples, and shaping when it deems it most helpful (Karpov, Johnson, Valsalam, et al., 2012). For instance, the system can identify parts of the state space where it has little experience,

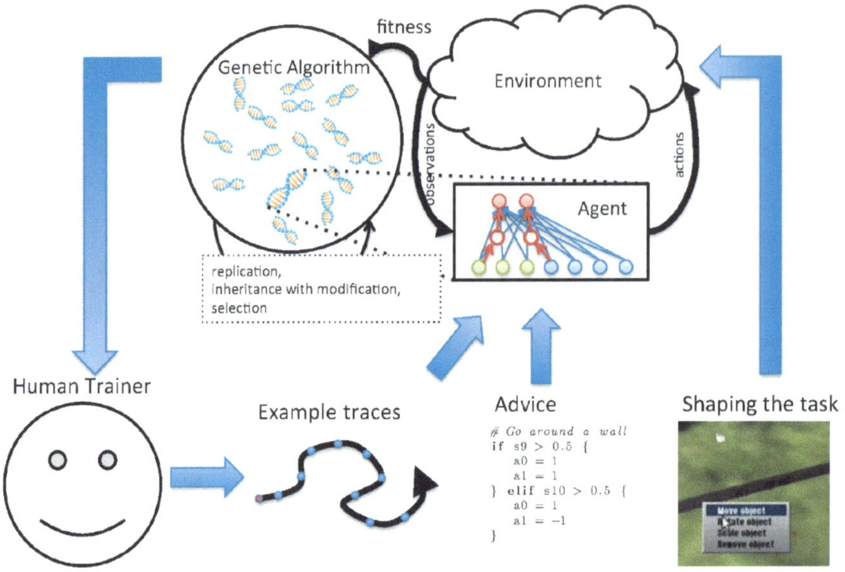

Figure 8.6: **A proposal for active human-guided neuroevolution.** The human expert provides advice, examples, and shaping for the neuroevolution process. The process monitors itself and determines what kind and when such input would be most useful. In this manner, humans and machines can work synergistically to construct intelligent agents. Figure from Karpov, Johnson, Valsalam, et al. (2012).

or that are least likely to lead to success, or where the population of agents disagrees the most, and where its previous advice or examples do not apply. It can then present the user with an advice template specifying such a situation and ask the user to fill in the blanks. Alternatively, it can present a starting point for the agent and ask the user to provide an example. If evolution seems to have stagnated, it could prompt the user to shape either the rewards or the environment to get evolution going again. It could even make specific suggestions, such as adjusting the sliders to make the task more demanding, or rolling back prior simplifications. Such an ability would eventually result in interactive neuroevolution where human knowledge and machine exploration work synergistically in both directions to solve problems (figure 8.6).

8.3 Neuroevolution-Enabled Collaboration

While NERO enabled players to shape the evolution of their team of agents, the game did not allow many humans to collaboratively train their teams by building on the interesting behaviors found by others. This section showcases some examples of interactive neuroevolution applications and games that were developed to incorporate such collaboration.

In particular, we will take a closer look at **Picbreeder** (Secretan, Beato, D'Ambrosio, et al., 2011), a highly influential **generative AI system** that came out of the lab of Kenneth Stanley. Picbreeder is a great example of a system that allows users to perform collaborative interactive neuroevolution, enabling them to explore a large design space

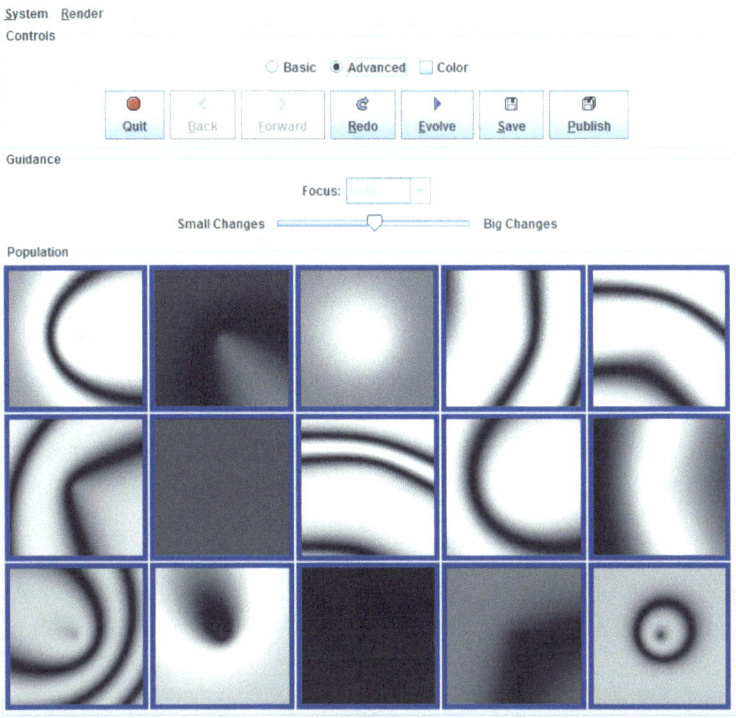

Figure 8.7: **Picbreeder interface.** Users in Picbreeder select at least one CPPN-generated image, from which subsequent populations are generated through mutations and crossover of the underlying CPPNs. Users can also move back and forth through the generations and publish their creations, allowing others to branch off from their discoveries. Figure from Secretan, Beato, D'Ambrosio, et al. (2011).

together. Similar to Dawkins's **BioMorphs** from his book "*The Blind Watchmaker*", the basic idea in Picbreeder is to breed images. Users are presented with several images and asked to select the ones that they like the most (figure 8.7). The selected images are then used as parents to produce a new generation of images through crossover and mutation of the underlying representations. The new generation of images becomes the next population, and the process iterates. With each generation, users continue to select the images that they prefer, and the algorithm evolves the images based on their choices.

Images in Picbreeder are represented by **compositional pattern producing networks** (CPPNs; section 4.3.1) and modified by the **NEAT algorithm** (section 3.3). While the CPPN representation allows users to easily evolve images with interesting regularities, employing NEAT for the mutation and crossover of CPPNs has an added benefit: The evolved images gradually get more complex over generations because the underlying CPPNs are becoming more complex. To allow users to navigate the space of images in a meaningful way, NEAT mutation parameters for Picbreeder have to be chosen in such a way that the next generation of images resembles their parents but also shows interesting variations.

With such an interactive evolution interface, one user by herself can already explore parts of the design space of images, but there are only so many generations for which a single person can evolve images. Single-user interactive evolution applications often suffer from what is called **user fatigue**: The user might not see anything very interesting within 10 to 20 generations and thus lose interest in exploring further (Takagi, 2001). Picbreeder addresses these issues in a clever way: by allowing users to evolve collaboratively, thereby taking advantage of the fact that different users naturally want to evolve different artifacts. For example, some users might start with the idea of evolving a particular image, such as an insect, while others keep selecting the images that appear most compelling to them, without a preset target in mind. In Picbreeder, a user can see what others have evolved and decide to continue evolution from any of their published images, a mechanism called "branching." Through this process, users have been able to explore large parts of the design space. Figure 8.8 shows some selected images that many users were able to evolve together. Initially, starting from abstract shapes similar to the ones shown in figure 8.7, users were able to collaboratively evolve a great variety of images, resembling subject matter such as faces, animals, landscapes, and many others.

Picbreeder has spawned a large number of projects that extend on its original idea, such as **EndlessForms** (Clune and Lipson, 2011), which allows users to breed 3D artifacts instead of 2D images using a 3D CPPN representation. Other examples include platforms like **Artbreeder** (Simon, 2018), which combines a Picbreeder-inspired interface with generative AI models such as generative adversarial networks (GANs) to allow users to directly start the evolutionary search in an interesting part of the design space. We take a closer look at some of these hybrid systems in chapter 13, on generative AI. Interactive neuroevolution also does not need to be limited to generated visual artifacts, as demonstrated by systems such as **NEAT Drummer** (Hoover, Rosario, and Stanley, 2008) or **MaestroGenesis** (Hoover, Szerlip, and Stanley, 2014), which allows users to interactively breed musical accompaniment to existing songs.

However, a common challenge with many of these systems is that, even though the process of interactive evolution by itself can be entertaining for a while, users often do not spend that much time on the site. Wrapping the whole collaborative evolution loop inside a game can address this issue, as we will see next.

8.4 Case Study: Collaborative Interactive Neuroevolution Through Play

Just as interactive neuroevolution paved the way for innovative games like NERO, the concept of collaborative neuroevolution also facilitated the emergence of other types of video games, such as Petalz (Risi, Lehman, D'Ambrosio, et al., 2016) and Galactic Arms Race (GAR; Hastings, Guha, and Stanley, 2009). In both these games, collaborative interactive neuroevolution serves as a method for what is called **procedural content generation** (PCG). In PCG, the goal is to generate game content, such as levels, characters, items, and more, algorithmically rather than manually designing them.

In **Petalz**, which was a casual Facebook game, the main idea was to allow players to collaboratively breed different types of procedurally generated flowers. More specifically, players in Petalz possess a balcony that they can decorate with various available flower pots (figure 8.9). Additionally, players can visit the balconies of friends and water or "like"

(*a*) Sunset drive 50*n* 141*c* 112*g*
(*b*) Demon 77*n* 219*c* 186*g*
(*c*) Dolphin 37*n* 121*c* 128*g*
(*d*) Snake symbol 28*n* 75*c* 63*g*
(*e*) Round face 35*n* 98*c* 94*g*
(*f*) Butterfly 34*n* 108*c* 104*g*
(*g*) Apple 83*n* 264*c* 321*g*
(*h*) Octopus 36*n* 114*c* 112*g*
(*i*) Insect 51*n* 158*c* 162*g*
(*j*) Pig 79*n* 252*c* 207*g*
(*k*) Planet 147*n* 477*c* 543*g*
(*l*)Wolf-man 85*n* 229*c* 206*g*
(*m*) Catwalk 58*n* 181*c* 228*g*
(*n*) Saturn 35*n* 100*c* 102*g*
(*o*) Skull 23*n* 57*c* 74*g*
(*p*) Tiger 32*n* 90*c* 80*g*
(*q*) Egg with hat 51*n* 153*c* 163*g*
(*r*) Sunset 69*n* 193*c* 194*g*
(*s*) Jupiter 43*n* 116*c* 131*g*
(*t*) Mystic baboon 51*n* 163*c* 162*g*
(*u*) Candlelight 22*n* 57*c* 52*g*
(*v*) Eye 16*n* 35*c* 65*g*
(*w*) Red crayon 76*n* 228*c* 256*g*
(*x*) Penguin 34*n* 113*c* 136*g*

Figure 8.8: **Examples of Picbreeder images.** Shown is a variety of designs that were evolved by many collaborating users. For each design, the number of nodes n and connections c of the underlying CPPN are also shown together with the total number of cumulative generations g. Because Picbreeder allows users to build on each other's work, it facilitates the discovery of a wide range of complex and compelling images. Figures from Secretan, Beato, D'Ambrosio, et al. (2011).

their flowers. Players can evolve their flowers by clicking on existing flowers, which opens a menu that allows generating flower offspring through mutations or to cross-pollinate a flower with another one, thereby performing a crossover. Flowers are generated by a CPPN representation that is modified to generate flower images and shapes (instead of arbitrary images), which are themselves also allowed to become more complex via the NEAT algorithm.

Players can also list their flower seeds in a digital marketplace at a price of their choosing or gift them to others. These mechanisms allow other players to continue breeding new flowers and build entirely new lineages. A compelling question is whether flower seeds—being truly novel digital artifacts—can hold economic value, and whether skilled breeders are rewarded for their efforts. Analysis of the flower market indicates that this is indeed the case: Flowers that are more affordable or aesthetically appealing tend

Figure 8.9: **The Petalz video game.** Players in Petalz can decorate their balconies with various pots and balcony designs. They can breed new flowers by clicking on the existing flowers and trading flower seeds with other users. By allowing players to branch off the flowers discovered by others, the game allows a new type of digital social interaction that links players through collaborative interactive neuroevolution. Figure from Risi, Lehman, D'Ambrosio, et al. (2016). Videos at `https://neuroevolutionbook.com/demos`.

to sell better. The global marketplace also facilitates collective discovery and breeding of a diverse range of flowers, as illustrated in the flower phylogeny shown in figure 8.10. Beyond strategy-focused games like NERO, the results from the Petalz game suggest that collaborative neuroevolution can also enable engaging ML games for casual players. While it was live, Petalz attracted over 1,900 registered online users and saw the creation of 38,646 unique, evolved flowers, showcasing the potential of this approach. Players especially appreciated the novel form of digital social interaction—connecting through the exchange of flower seeds and collaborative breeding—which added a new layer of engagement to the experience.

In **Galactic Arms Race** (GAR), another multiplayer game built on CPPNs and NEAT, players pilot a spaceship and fight enemies to acquire unique and procedurally generated particle weapons. GAR is another ML game, in which the integration of user preferences is slightly less direct than in a game such as Petalz, in which the users directly choose which flowers to reproduce. To smoothly integrate user preferences into a real-time game such as GAR, the neuroevolutionary algorithm takes into account implicit information within the game's usage statistics. In particular, in GAR, the game keeps track of how often players fired the different weapons that they have in their three available weapon slots. New weapons being spawned into the game world are chosen to be mutations of the weapons that players preferred in the past. This way, players can collaboratively discover a wide variety of particle weapons. Instead of describing a static 2D or 3D image, CPPNs

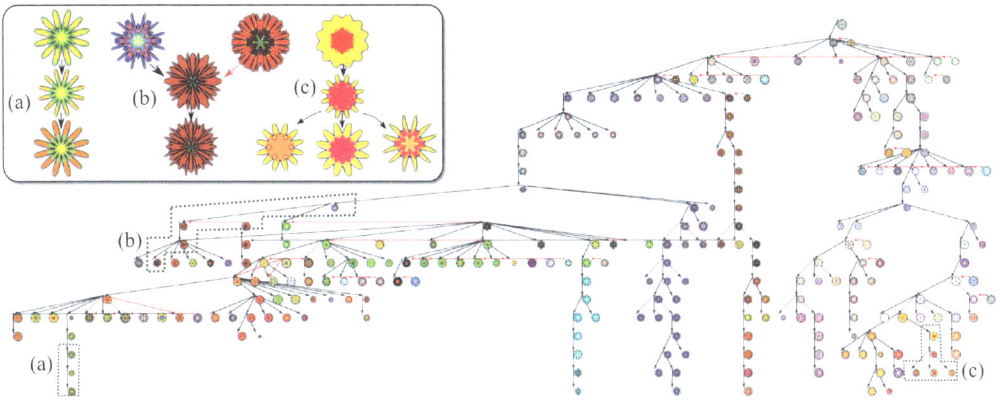

Figure 8.10: **A Petalz flower phylogeny.** Shown here is a family tree that tracks the collaborative efforts of 13 distinct users. Each pair of parent and offspring is divided by one generation. For cases where a flower emerges from cross-pollination, the connecting line to the second parent is highlighted in red. The inset offers a closer look at the evolutionary dynamics, featuring minor phenotypic changes (*a*), an instance of cross-pollination (*b*), and substantial yet shared phenotypic transformations (*c*). This flower phylogeny highlights the rich diversity and lineage of designs that emerge when users are able to collaboratively evolve content through play. Figure from Risi, Lehman, D'Ambrosio, et al. (2016).

in GAR are an interesting example of a CPPN generating a dynamical system. For each frame, and for every particle of a particular weapon, the CPPN receives the particle's current position as input, in addition to the position from which it was initially fired. The CPPN then outputs the particle's velocity in addition to its RGB-encoded color. While all particular weapons have the same number of particles, the ability of player projectiles to intersect enemy projectiles can lead to several tactical trade-offs explored by evolution. Slower projectiles offer the benefit of easier blocking against incoming fire, providing a defensive advantage. On the other hand, faster projectiles are better suited for precise aiming at distant enemies, offering offensive prowess. Two particularly fascinating types of evolved weapons are shown in figure 8.11. Wallmakers are capable of forming a literal wall of particles in front of the player, and tunnelmakers generate a protective line of particles on both sides of the player.

Together, the examples in this section and section 8.3 show that interactive neuroevolution can enable the creation of novel types of ML games with engaging player dynamics. Petalz had over 1,900 registered online users and 38,646 unique evolved flowers, which showcases the potential for PCG to enable these kinds of casual game mechanics. In the first two months of going online in 2009, GAR had over 1,000 registered online players, who evolved 379,081 weapons. In addition to demonstrating the increasing entertainment value with a constant stream of evolved content, these examples demonstrate the versatility of CPPNs to encode a variety of types of content, from flower images to particle weapons, which all benefit from NEAT's ability to complexify the underlying representations, and thus the resulting phenotypic patterns.

Beyond their application to games, interactive evolution systems can serve other important functions. They enable researchers to visually explore the representation power

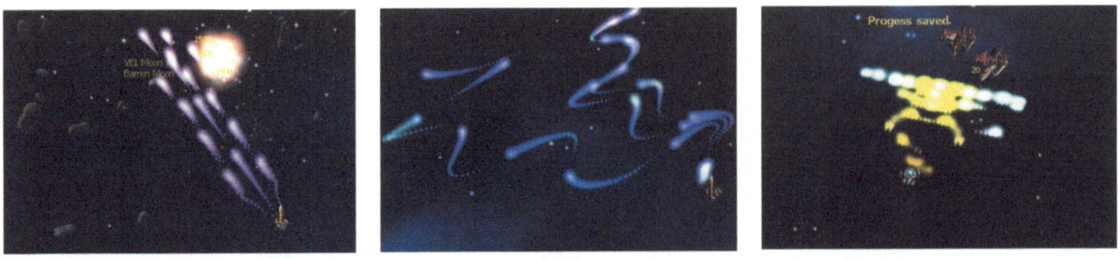

(*a*) Multispeed (7 generations) (*b*) Ultrawide (13 generations) (*c*) Wallmaker (14 generations)

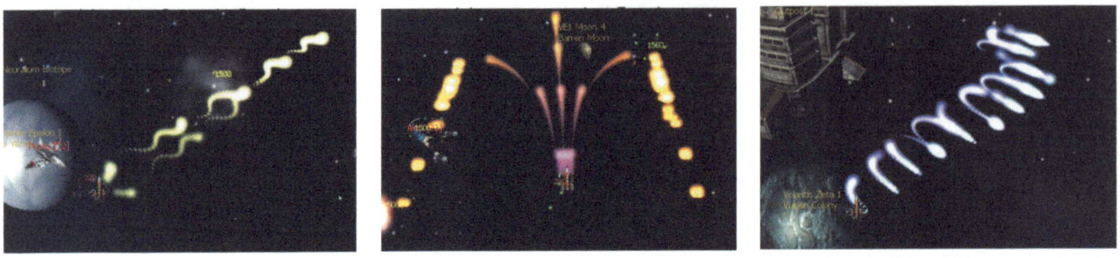

(*d*) Corkscrew (3 generations) (*e*) Tunnelmaker (2 generations) (*f*) Blue ladder (42 generations)

Figure 8.11: **Evolved particle weapons in Galactic Arms Race.** The interactive evolution component of GAR allowed players to evolve a large range of different and aesthetically pleasing weapons. More importantly, different evolved weapons have different tactical implications, such as the wallmaker (*c*), which favors defense play by creating a particle wall in front of the player, or tunnelmaker (*e*), which protects the player from attacks from the left or right side. Figures from Hastings, Guha, and Stanley (2009). Videos at `https://neuroevolutionbook.com/demos`.

of different types of encodings or the way that users individually or collaboratively explore such a space, leading to surprising insights. For example, as mentioned already in section 5.3, Picbreeder was initially invented to explore the CPPN encoding. However, through playing with the system, Stanley and Lehman observed that users in Picbreeder navigated a vast search space in ways that differed fundamentally from contemporary optimization algorithms. This serendipitous discovery helped inspire the novelty search algorithm (section 5.3), and later informed their broader argument in their book *Why Greatness Cannot Be Planned* that open-ended exploration and stepping stones can lead to more significant discoveries than directly optimizing toward a predefined objective.

Interestingly, the different ways that a search space is explored can also lead to very different types of representations. In CPPN-representations evolved by users in Picbreeder, **developmental canalization** often emerges, where certain dimensions of variation are more likely, while others are prevented (Huizinga, Stanley, and Clune, 2018). For example, in Picbreeder, some of these canalized dimensions of variation are a "gene" for the size of objects, a "gene" determining how much the mouth of a skull (shown in figure 8.8*o*) is open/closed, or a "gene" that controls the shadow of objects in an image.

This type of developmental canalization is often linked to the evolution of **evolvability** in natural systems, which many believe to be essential for the tremendous diversity of functional organisms in nature. Representations evolved with traditional objective-based evolution do not show this type of canalization, and mutations to single genes here often affect none or many parts of the image (Kumar, Lu, Kirsch, et al., 2024). Artificial evolutionary systems can thus help us to determine under what circumstances different properties evolve, and we will return to this important topic in chapter 14.

8.5 Making Human Contributions Practical

Interactive evolution experiments require significant human effort, which makes it difficult to take advantage of them more broadly. Some domains, like Picbreeder, are inherently interesting and rewarding, and a large number of people can contribute to them through publicly available websites. But other domains may be more abstract and progress in them less obvious, resulting in users fatiguing and losing interest.

One solution is to use **human computation markets** (HCMs), such as Amazon Mechanical Turk, to recruit humans to this role. In a sense, monetary reward can thus be used as a substitute for the intrinsic enjoyment of creativity and curiosity. Of course, using HCMs requires funds, but so do other types of computation. In a sense, some of the computational budget is used for human computation instead of cloud computation. HCMs can be used effectively in three roles (Lehman and Miikkulainen, 2013): to bootstrap experiments to become interesting, to evaluate different designs, and to extend interactive evolution to long experiments.

First, even if a task such as Picbreeder is eventually engaging and rewarding, that is not so at the beginning. The forms are simple and stay simple for several generations. It is difficult to get people to evaluate such images, and evaluation itself is not very meaningful. It turns out that if this phase is automated or HCMs are used to get through it, the final images turn out more interesting. For instance in the Picbreeder domain, it is possible to generate an initial set of images algorithmically, and thus make them more complex and interesting than simple geometric forms (Lehman and Stanley, 2012). A simple fitness, such as one based on rarity (or novelty) and complexity (or effort), can be used to guide this initial evolution. At the next phase, it is then possible to use HCMs to improve those images further, up to a level where the images are actually appealing to humans, and the creativity/curiosity rewards can take over. Figure 8.12 compares three interactive evolution runs of Picbreeder in these two conditions (starting from random images and starting from algorithmically seeded images), in both cases followed by a period of further evolution with HCMs. The seeded runs resulted in more complex images, and human judges also found them more aesthetically appealing. Thus, initial machine exploration and HCMs can be used to make interactive evolution experiments more effective.

Second, there are also tasks where the creativity/curiosity reward never becomes large enough to justify the human effort, and therefore HCMs are necessary to perform the experiments in the first place. A particularly important general case is the experimental design of such experiments. For example, the images can be encoded in various ways, including through using CPPNs or simple artificial neural networks (ANNs) with different activation functions. It may not be possible to make these design choices correctly without running preliminary experiments, and such experiments are often not very interesting to human users. HCMs can be used to good effect to discover the best designs before running the actual experiments.

Third, in some cases, evolution needs to be run very long to get good results. Even if the task is interesting, the users will eventually fatigue. HCMs can provide a continual, indefinite stream of new users in such experiments. On the other hand, each user makes only a transient contribution to the evolutionary process, and these contributions may be inconsistent. It turns out, however, that long-running evolution can still use them as a

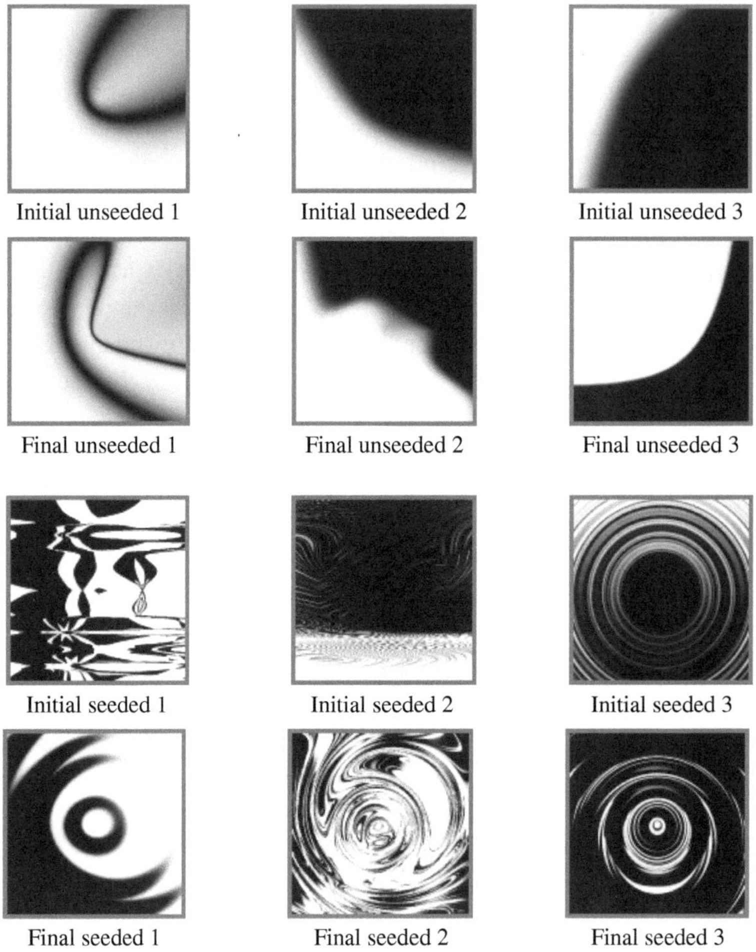

Figure 8.12: **Example of initial and final images with and without seeding interactive neuroevolution.** The early phase of Picbreeder is not very engaging, but it can be bypassed by seeding. In this comparison, the initial unseeded images were generated with random CPPNs; the initial seeded ones were generated by running CPPN evolution for a while and selecting the most impressive images. Both sets of images were then evolved further with Picbreeder using HCMs. Interactive evolution from seeded images results in more complex and appealing final images, suggesting that proper initialization is crucial in taking full advantage of interactive evolution. Figures from Lehman and Miikkulainen (2013).

guide toward good solutions. Evaluations in most domains are always noisy, and such inconsistency is simply another form of such noise. As usual, evolution is robust against noisy evaluations, and they may even boost creativity by encouraging exploration. Thus, HCMs can be harnessed to enable long-running interactive evolution experiments. In conclusion, while interactive evolution experiments require significant human effort, there are ways to make them practical and thus realize the full potential of human guidance. Later in this book, in section 13.4, we will explore another alternative, which starts with a genotype-to-phenotype mapping that is learned through a generative AI approach, thus producing outputs that resemble valid, domain-specific artifacts from the get-go.

In this chapter, we have seen how interactive neuroevolution can create novel forms of gameplay and design experiences. By involving human users directly in the evolutionary loop—whether through selecting visual artifacts, guiding agent behavior, or exchanging and breeding digital content—these systems empower players and designers alike to steer the creative process. Interactive neuroevolution thus offers a powerful tool for fostering open-ended exploration and innovation, enabling the emergence of surprising agent behaviors, aesthetic artifacts, or even entirely new design spaces.

A natural next step is to explore how evolutionary processes can drive this discovery autonomously, without constant human guidance. In chapter 9, we turn our attention to open-ended neuroevolution systems that aim to automate the generation of complexity, novelty, and diversity. Such systems represent a shift from user-driven creativity to autonomous open-ended discovery, where evolution itself becomes the engine of exploration.

8.6 Chapter Review Questions

1. **Conceptual understanding:** How does interactive neuroevolution differ from standard neuroevolution, and what types of problems is it particularly well suited to solve?

2. **Human-guided evolution:** In the context of the NERO game, what tools are provided to the human player to guide the neuroevolution process? How can these tools shape the evolution of agent behaviors?

3. **Real-time evolution:** What is the role of rtNEAT in NERO, and how does it enhance the interactive experience compared to traditional generational neuroevolution?

4. **Behavioral shaping:** Describe how curricular evolution is implemented in NERO to train agents progressively. Why is this approach often more effective than using a single, static objective function?

5. **Surprising behaviors:** Give examples of unexpected strategies discovered by evolution in NERO. How do such discoveries highlight the balance between human guidance and evolutionary creativity?

6. **Interactive ML games:** Based on the NERO example, what characteristics make ML games engaging for human players, and how does the circularity of strategies contribute to the gameplay?

7. **Collaborative exploration:** How does Picbreeder address the challenge of user fatigue in interactive neuroevolution, and what role does branching play in enabling collaborative exploration?

8. **Generative applications:** Describe how Petalz and GAR utilize collaborative neuroevolution to procedurally generate game content. How do their approaches differ in incorporating user preferences?

9. **Representation and evolvability:** What is developmental canalization, and how does it emerge in CPPN representations evolved in Picbreeder? Why is this property significant for understanding evolvability?

10. **Practical implementation:** What strategies can make interactive neuroevolution more practical in domains with limited user engagement or long-running experiments? Provide examples of how HCMs can be effectively utilized.

Chapter 9

Open-Ended Neuroevolution

A major goal in the neuroevolution of behavior is to keep innovating beyond the obvious solutions, over long periods of time, while the environment is changing—in other words, to establish an open-ended discovery mechanism. The coevolutionary arms race and interactive neuroevolution from previous chapters are examples of such processes. This chapter reviews opportunities for open-ended neuroevolution more generally, including inspirations from biology and their computational instantiations, body/brain coevolution, and coevolution of agents and environments.

9.1 Open-Ended Discovery of Complex Behavior

Neuroevolution has produced several convincing demonstrations where complex behavior is discovered in behavioral tasks, sometimes rivaling the complexity seen in nature. However, there is one striking difference: Neuroevolution is set up to solve a particular problem, whereas biological evolution has no goal. In nature, solutions are discovered continuously as challenges and opportunities come up. Such **open-endedness** is still a challenge for artificial evolution, especially when the goal is to evolve general intelligent agents (Miikkulainen and Forrest, 2021). This section reviews five elements of open-endedness in biology which, if we can implement them well, may lead to open-ended neuroevolution: neutrality with **weak selection**, enhanced exploration through **extinction events**, highly **evolvable representations**, powerful **genotype-to-phenotype mappings**, and **major transitions** in complexity.

9.1.1 Neutral Mutations with Weak Selection

Current evolutionary computation approaches, including those that evolve neural networks for behavior, aim to be strong and efficient. They utilize small populations that can be evaluated quickly; the crossover and mutation operations are often carefully crafted to make it likely that fitness is improved; fitness is measured precisely; and selection is strongly proportional to fitness. As a result, evolution converges the population quickly around the most promising solutions and finds good solutions there fast. This approach is effective in many engineering problems where the search space and fitness are well defined and the problem consists largely of optimizing the design.

However, this success often comes with the expense of reduced extrapolation, and thus reduced creativity. It is also not very effective when the agents need to be general; that is, cope with uncertain and changing environments and solve multiple tasks simultaneously. Other mechanisms are needed to counterbalance the effective search, such as diversity maintenance methods, **novelty search** (NS), and **quality diversity** (QD) search (section 5.3). They are intended to keep the population of solutions diverse for a longer time and spread it out further in the solution space. The idea is to not miss solutions that are complex or unexpected; that is, hard to find through greedy search.

Interestingly, biological solutions are sometimes highly creative and unexpected, and yet they do not seem to result in any special mechanisms for diversity maintenance. If anything, biological solutions need to be viable always, which seems to counteract the need for diversity. How does biology do it?

Nature seems to employ an entirely different approach to creativity (Lynch, 2007; Miikkulainen and Forrest, 2021; Wagner, 2005). The populations are very large, and **selection is weak**. Often, there is also a lot of time for these processes to find solutions. Phenotypic traits are coded redundantly through several genes, much of the DNA exists in non-coding regions, and many of the mutations are **neutral** (i.e., do not affect fitness). As a result, diversity can exist in such populations: There is time to create it, and it stays even if it isn't immediately beneficial. The population as a whole can thus stay robust against changes, develop expertise for multiple tasks, and maintain evolvability through time.

Neutrality in fitness landscapes can be seen to produce similar effects in computational models. When mutations do not alter fitness, the search space reorganizes: Basins of attraction become larger, paths to global optima grow shorter, and populations can drift across neutral networks instead of becoming trapped in local peaks (Verel, Ochoa, and Tomassini, 2010). In this way, neutral drift not only maintains diversity but also increases evolvability, creating the conditions for escaping dead ends and reaching higher-fitness solutions. Weak selection combined with neutrality therefore emerges as a powerful driver of robust and creative adaptation.

There is a good reason for the strong and impatient approach that evolutionary computation has taken until now. Evolutionary optimization is computationally intensive, and such techniques were necessary to take advantage of what was available. However, now that we have a million times more compute in terms of raw processing performance than just a couple of decades ago (Routley, 2017), it may be time to rethink this approach. This is precisely what happened with deep learning. Much of the technology, such as convolutional neural networks (CNNs), long short-term memory (LSTMs), and autoencoders, existed since the 1990s, but they started working well only when taking advantage of the massive increases in scale (LeCun, Bengio, and Hinton, 2015).

A similar opportunity may exist for evolution in general, and neuroevolution in particular. It may be possible to scale up to large populations, large redundant genomes, non-coding DNA, neutral mutations, and deep time. It may also be possible to take advantage of massive amounts of behavioral data and large-scale simulations to evaluate the solutions. The evaluations may be multiobjective and high level instead of being carefully engineered to produce solutions of the expected kind. Eventually, it may even be possible to create foundation models for neuroevolution; that is, large, diverse populations of neural networks that have many abilities and are thus highly evolvable to solve new tasks, forming a substrate from which specialized solutions can be rapidly derived.

One way to accelerate evolution in such populations is through extinction events, as will be discussed next.

9.1.2 Extinction Events

In biological evolution, large-scale **extinction events** have occurred several times, often seemingly changing the course of evolution (Meredith, Janečka, Gatesy, et al., 2011; Raup, 1986). For instance, the Cretaceous-Paleogene extinction displaced dinosaurs with mammals, eventually leading to the evolution of humans. An interesting question is: Are such events simply historical accidents, or do they implement a principle that in some way enhances, or hinders, evolution in the long term? Even though such events obviously destroy a lot of solutions, can they possibly serve to reset evolution so better **evolvability** is favored, which in the long term results in accelerated evolution and more complex solutions?

While it is difficult to evaluate this hypothesis in nature, it is possible to do so in computational experiments. It is possible to set up a large population with many different solutions, representing adaptations to different niches. If evolution runs in a stable manner for a long time, those niches are eventually filled with good solutions, and evolution stagnates. At such a point in time, an extinction event eliminates most such solutions. Those that remain, even if just very few, are then free to evolve to fill the open niches. Such evolution can be described as radiation from the remaining niches, but note that there is also a meta-level selection at play: The solutions that are more evolvable (i.e., faster to adapt to the open niches), will spread faster and wider, making them more likely to survive the next extinction event. Thus, under repeated extinction events, evolution favors higher evolvability. Extinction events can thus have a positive long-term effect, accelerating evolution, and possibly resulting in more complex solutions as well.

To visualize the basic idea, consider a very simple computational setup (Lehman and Miikkulainen, 2015). The niches are cells in a toroidal 401×401 grid world. Individuals consist of grid coordinates and a probability of changing those coordinates. Thus, adaptation means moving to a new cell, and high evolvability is represented by a high probability of change. Initially, there is only one individual at the center, and evolution creates more individuals by cloning and then mutating grid coordinates, and at the same time, mutating the probability. Over time, the population spreads to fill in all niches simply through drift (figure 9.1*a*). However, with extinction events, only five individuals at random locations survive. If such events occur often, there is a strong selection preference toward individuals that mutate with a high probability. Thus, after prolonged evolution, the population evolved with extinction events is more evolvable than a population evolved without them (figure 9.1*b*).

Do these results hold at the level of behavior as well? Consider again the bipedal walker domain described in section 5.3. As before, the controllers are neural networks evolved with **NEAT** (neuroevolution of augmenting topologies), taking the location of the two feet (whether on the ground or not) as input, and torque to the six motors (one in each knee, two in each side of the hip) as output. A behavioral niche can be defined on

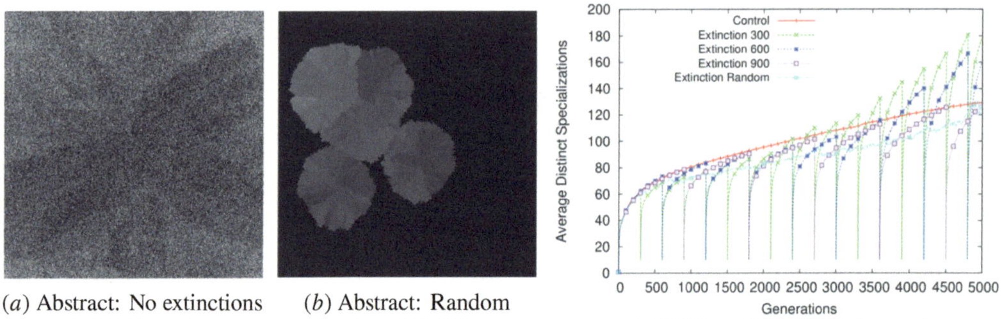

(*a*) Abstract: No extinctions (15,000 gens) (*b*) Abstract: Random extinctions (15,000 gens) (*c*) Walker: Niches filled over time

Figure 9.1: **Effect of extinction events on evolvability.** While extinctions are catastrophic in the short term, they may empower evolution in the long term. (*a*) Without extinction events, the population in the abstract domain evolves to fill in the available niches (i.e., cells in the 401×401 grid). A variety of evolvability levels exists in the end, indicated by the gray-scale values (lighter is more evolvable). (*b*) With extinction events, higher evolvability is favored. Such events occurred at random intervals averaging 2,500 generations. In this snapshot, five individuals survived a recent event, and the population is currently expanding to fill in the available niches. On average, these individuals are about 50% more evolvable than those in (*a*), indicated by the lighter color. (*c*) In the bipedal walker domain, extinction events rebound quickly, filling in more niches than before the event, and eventually more than evolution without extinction events. Thus, extinction events accelerate evolution and result in the discovery of more novel solutions. Figures from Lehman and Miikkulainen (2015).

the grid as in the abstract domain; that is, the final location of the bipedal walker after 15 seconds of simulation. This location is also used to measure novelty, and evolution is set to maximize novelty. Evolvability can then be measured as the **behavioral diversity** of the offspring: The individual is mutated 200 times; the number of distinct final locations of the offspring represents its evolvability.

As can be seen in figure 9.1*c*, evolution without extinction events expands to fill in the various niches monotonically. With extinctions, there is an immediate drop to five niches and a fast rebound to a higher level than before the event. Moreover, the rebounds become more effective over time, eventually filling more niches than evolution without extinctions. Thus, extinction events result in accelerated evolution and solutions with increased novelty.

These computational experiments suggest how extinction events can accelerate evolution in biology. Although major such events have taken place only a few times, they can be frequent at a smaller scale, resulting from such events as fires, volcanic eruptions, climate events, predator migrations, and even human impact. The results also suggest that the same effect could be harnessed in engineering applications of computational evolution, leading to better results in the long term. Combining it with large populations and weak selection, as discussed in section 9.1.1, is therefore a compelling direction for future work.

9.1.3 Evolvable Representations

This chapter so far has outlined an approach to open-ended evolution that is still largely building on genotypic and phenotypic **diversity**, with constant mapping between them.

An alternative approach is to take advantage of **evolvability**, which can be defined as adapting the genotype-phenotype mapping over time such that the search operators are more likely to generate high-fitness solutions. High evolvability is often based on **indirect encodings**, which can provide a substrate for this adaptation.

The main challenge is that whereas high evolvability provides a future benefit for evolution, it needs to be developed implicitly based on only current and past information. In biology, evolvability may be selected for in three ways (Kirschner and Gerhart, 1998): more genetic variation can be stored in the population (because fewer mutations are harmful), it makes organisms more tolerant against stochastic development, and it makes it more likely that the populations will survive in **changing environments**.

Each of these can be evaluated in computational experiments. Opportunities for the first one were already discussed in section 9.1.1. Opportunities for the second one are illustrated in sections 4.2 and 14.4, on development. In short, an individual is not complete at birth but rather goes through a period of physical and mental **development** that results in a more complex and capable individual (Müller, 2014). Often, this period involves interactions with the environment–that is, at least some of the complexity is not innate, but is extracted from the environment. These interactions can be synergistic and encoded into critical periods of development. For example, human infants need to receive language input when they are one to five years old, or otherwise they do not develop full language abilities (see section 14.8.1, on the biology of language). In this manner, instead of coding everything directly into genes, evolution also encodes a learning mechanism that results in a more evolvable encoding (Elman, Bates, Johnson, et al., 1996; Valsalam, Bednar, and Miikkulainen, 2005).

The third advantage opens an opportunity that is particularly well aligned with open-ended evolution. Given a domain with known structure, such as evolution of symmetric bitstrings, evolution can be given an open-ended series of challenges in the form of different target bitstrings (Reisinger and Miikkulainen, 2006). The population has to discover each target by continuing the evolution of the current population (initially random). The target changes at given intervals, which have to be long enough for success to be possible. The evolvable representation consists of linkage parameters between bit locations, biasing the mutations that occur. Over time, evolution discovers linkages that favor symmetric strings, which makes discovery of targets gradually faster and more likely. In other words, the representations become more evolvable in this domain.

How can such representations be designed for more complex solutions such as neural networks and behaviors? It turns out that the idea of **linkages** that adapt to the domain can be scaled up to neural networks, with an approach that is motivated by genetic regulatory networks (GRNs; Wang, 2013). As was discussed in section 4.2.1, **GRNs** are one way in which biology establishes an indirect encoding. Building on the operon implementation of GRNS in section 4.2.1, they can be modeled more generally with a set of rules (Reisinger and Miikkulainen, 2007). As usual in **rule-based systems**, each rule has an antecedent that is matched with the current state of the system, as well as a consequent that determines what output or product is generated. When used to construct neural networks, the products are either hidden or output nodes. When the antecedent is matched with currently existing products within a particular similarity tolerance, connections are created among nodes.

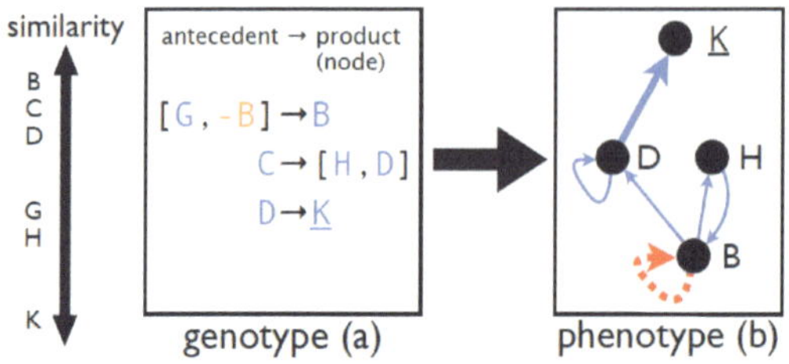

Figure 9.2: **Constructing neural networks with a GRN**. GRNs, a mechanism for decoding genetic representations in biology, can also be used as an indirect encoding for neural networks. The GRN is encoded as a set of rules. The current state is represented by products (indicated by letters). The antecedents are matched with the current products, leading to the generation of more products. The match is based on similarity between products, implemented through regulatory factors. In mapping the GRN to a network, products create nodes and antecedent matches create connections between them. In this case, starting with products G and B as a starting point, matching the first rule creates a negative connection from B to itself. Because C is a similar product to B, H and D are created as hidden nodes and connected to B. Matching D in turn leads to a recurrent self-connection, as well as creating and connecting to an output node K. In this manner, a recurrent structure is created; it can be further evolved by modifying the rule set and the regulatory factors. Figure from Reisinger and Miikkulainen (2007).

The tolerance, amount of products, and the resulting connection weights are determined by regulatory factors in the antecedents. A simple example of this process is depicted in figure 9.2.

The rules and the regulatory factors in them are modified through evolution to construct a neural network to solve the task. Note that this is a continuous, soft process in which a given product can gradually increase (through neutral mutations) until a tolerance is reached. It therefore has significant potential for evolvability: A general GRN structure is discovered where mutations often lead to viable offspring.

This process was demonstrated in Nothello, a board game similar to Othello, but with a diamond-shaped board of 36 cells and an objective of the fewest pieces on the board. It offers faster evolution with much of the same complexity as full Othello. The networks were evolved to serve as heuristic board evaluators for minimax search; a single-ply lookahead was used to allow for longer evolutionary runs. In a coevolutionary setup, each candidate was evaluated with a random sampling of other individuals in the population. Note that coevolution provides an environment where the fitness function is constantly changing. As discussed previously, such an environment should encourage evolvable representations to emerge. Evolvability is also directly useful because it results in discovering better gameplay over time.

Indeed, the GRN-based implicit encoding approach results in discovering better networks over time compared to standard NEAT, as seen in figure 9.3*a*. This improvement is likely due to increased evolvability, measured as the average fitness of the local mutation landscape: Each representation was mutated to an increasing extent, and the performance of the offspring was measured. The GRN-based implicit encoding results in much more robust mutations; that is, improved evolvability (figure 9.3*b*). It is also interesting to see that the network structures that result are different. Whereas the NEAT networks are entirely feedforward, the GRN-based approach takes advantage of many different network

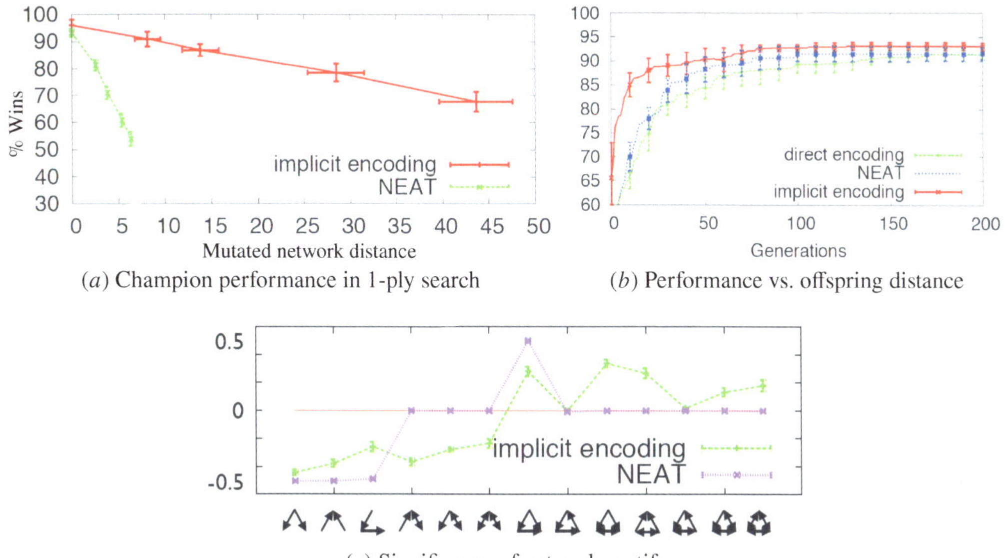

(*a*) Champion performance in 1-ply search

(*b*) Performance vs. offspring distance

(*c*) Significance of network motifs

Figure 9.3: **Performance, evolvability, and structure resulting from GRN-based neuroevolution.** The GRN-based encoding has several useful properties, as illustrated in the Nothello game domain. (*a*) The GRN-based indirect encoding evolves better solutions faster. (*b*) This result is likely due to the evolvability that the system discovers over evolution, measured by how good the offspring solutions are on average. (*c*) The evolvability is likely due to more varied networks motifs, taking advantage of recurrent structures. The significance is measured by comparing to randomly connected networks with the same size. This example illustrates a fundamental principle of evolvability: It emerges from the continuously changing fitness function (due to coevolution), makes coevolution more effective, and can thus potentially be harnessed for open-ended discovery. Figures from Reisinger and Miikkulainen (2007).

motifs, many of which are recurrent (figure 9.3*c*). In this manner, it likely discovers structures that support evolvability, and thereby coevolution, and thereby open-ended discovery.

9.1.4 Expressive Encodings

The mechanisms outlined here can be captured, generalized, and described mathematically through the concept of **expressive encodings** (Meyerson, Qiu, and Miikkulainen, 2022). The idea is that such encodings allow **miracle jumps**; that is, large jumps in the search space. For instance, flipping all bits in a binary encoding from 0 to 1 might be such a jump. A standard evolutionary algorithm (EA) with a direct encoding would be unlikely to make such changes, and therefore could not explore the search space as effectively.

Expressive encodings do already exist. For instance, genetic programming utilizes such an encoding (figure 9.4*a*). Programs may share structure, but also have segments that make large changes in the phenotype, such as conditionals. Small changes in such segments can create miracle jumps. Neural networks are another expressive encoding (figure 9.4*b*): Even when they are not used as mappings from input to output, but simply to encode vectors of outputs (with a constant input), small changes in a few weights can

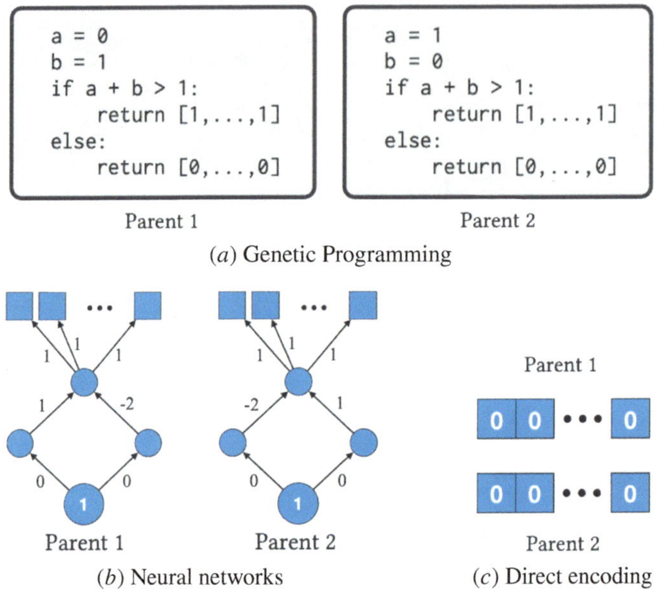

Figure 9.4: **Expressive encodings through genetic programming and neural networks.** Expressive encodings make evolution more powerful by allowing for large changes. (*a*) For instance, the phenotypes of these two GP parents are all zeros, but their crossover results in an offspring of all 1s, with a probability of 0.25. They share most of the structure except for special segments defining the variables a and b. (*b*) A similar encoding through a neural network. The input is a constant 1, and the output is all zeros; they differ in the weights of the first layer such that a crossover results in all 1s with a probability of 0.25. (*c*) Direct encoding of parents cannot lead to an all-1s offspring. These simple examples illustrate how expressive encodings make such miracle jumps possible when they are not possible through direct encoding. Figures from Meyerson, Qiu, and Miikkulainen (2022).

create a miracle jump. Interestingly, such jumps may not be possible through a direct encoding (figure 9.4*c*).

The usual approach to making evolutionary algorithms more powerful is to design more complex and intelligent genetic operators that capture the properties of the domain. For instance, estimation of distribution algorithms and covariance matrix adaptation evolution strategy (CMA-ES) aim at capturing the statistics between gene combinations and fitness (Hansen and Ostermeier, 1996; Lozano, Larrañaga, Inza, et al., 2006). In contrast, expressive encodings can work with basic, simple genetic operators such as crossover and mutation. In this sense, they capture the essence of biological expressiveness that is obtained through interactions and development. Theoretically, both genetic programming and feedforward neural networks with sigmoid activation functions are expressive encodings for both uniform crossover and single-point mutation.

Expressive encodings have been shown to be more powerful than standard evolutionary approaches in various benchmark challenges, including tasks where objectives change over time deterministically or randomly, and in large block assembly, both theoretically and experimentally (Meyerson, Qiu, and Miikkulainen, 2022). The approach offers maximum evolvability to the extent that there is no **catastrophic forgetting** when the objectives change. It is also similar to biology, in that much of the solutions are shared: More than 99% of the genes are the same across humans, for example, and much of the DNA is shared across species (Collins, Guyer, and Chakravarti, 1997; Hardison, 2003). Only a few crucial differences cause the differences between individuals and species. It is this expressivity that the expressive encodings capture.

One particularly interesting opportunity for neuroevolution is to improve the transmission function over time; that is, the probabilistic mechanisms through which the child phenotype is generated from the parent phenotypes. Evolution can be used to complexify transmission functions, thus potentially powering open-ended evolution. With expressive encodings and an evolving transmission function, it may be possible to create a system that starts simple, solves problems as they appear, and becomes more effective at it over time. One remaining challenge is to enable transitions to more complex organizations, as will be discussed next.

9.1.5 Major Transitions

In biological evolution, it is possible to identify several **major transitions** in complexity (Maynard Smith and Szathmáry, 1997; Szathmáry, 2015). First, there were self-replicating molecules that organized into chromosomes; then these chromosomes were enclosed in cells; next, cells complexified to include several plastids; such cells joined together and specialized to form multicellular organisms; and finally, the organisms grouped to form eusocial societies first, and then actual societies, eventually with language and culture. In each of these transitions, the individuals joined together to form groups, specialized into distinct, cooperative roles, and lost the ability to reproduce independently. Throughout these transitions, information for biological organisms is still encoded at the molecular level. However, how that information is organized, transmitted among individuals, translated into physical structures, and selected for reproduction changes at each transition. As a result, what it means to be an individual becomes more complex at each transition.

While the transitions are described in detail in biology, the mechanisms that produce them are not well understood. In particular, are there multiple levels of selection operating in parallel, or only one at the highest level? How do the individuals specialize, and how do they lose their individual ability to reproduce? Do multiple phases exist at the same time and cooperate and compete to eventually lead to a transition? Are the dynamics the same at each transition, or is each one a separate, unique process?

A potentially powerful approach to answering these questions is to produce transitions synthetically (Miikkulainen and Forrest, 2021; Solé, 2016). It is difficult to do so; the results that come the closest focus on defining hierarchical mathematical functions and organizational structures in abstract mathematical games (Koza, 1992; Turney, 2020; Watson and Pollack, 2003). However, they are still far from major transitions in behavior. For instance, the agents might discover ways to communicate or to construct permanent artifacts such as roads. Further evolution might then discover behaviors that take advantage of these constructs: The agents might communicate to establish flexible roles and coordinate their behavior; they may move longer distances and harness more resources. More generally, neuroevolution might construct network segments that perform useful subfunctions and then group them together to construct more complex behaviors and multiple behaviors at different times (i.e., general intelligence). Such specialization and grouping could potentially continue for several levels.

Ingredients for such transitions have already been demonstrated in several ways. For instance, it is possible to predesign the representations at different levels by hand—for instance, a **syllabus** for evolved **virtual creatures** allows for discovering body and brains for simple locomotion first and build up to fight-or-flight responses in multiple steps (Lessin, Fussell, and Miikkulainen, 2013, 2014). Similarly, mechanisms can be created for discovering cooperative structures that work together at a higher level. For example, in the **CoDeepNEAT** method, neural network modules are evolved to work well together in a large composite network (Liang, Meyerson, Hodjat, et al., 2019; Miikkulainen, Liang, Meyerson, et al., 2023). Also, a competitive process can be established that allows new challenges to emerge, such as the arms race of better runners and more challenging tracks in **paired open-ended trailblazer** (POET; section 9.3) or more complex prey behaviors and better predators in zebra/hyena simulations (Rawal, Rajagopalan, and Miikkulainen, 2010; Wang, Lehman, Clune, et al., 2019). Multiple agents can communicate through **stigmergy**, through observing each other, and through signaling, and thus coordinate their behaviors—for example in capturing a prey or a desirable resource in a video game (Bryant and Miikkulainen, 2018; Rawal, Rajagopalan, and Miikkulainen, 2010; Werner and Dyer, 1992; Yong and Miikkulainen, 2010). Architectures and approaches have been developed for representing and executing multiple tasks in a uniform manner—for example, through a common variable-embedding space, as in the **traveling observer model** (TOM; Meyerson and Miikkulainen, 2021).

In sum, mechanisms of cooperative and competitive coevolution, multitasking, multi-objectivity, evolvability, and expressive encodings are potentially useful ingredients in producing major transitions. However, they do not yet drive actual transitions. How such transitions can be established is an important challenge for neuroevolution—one that would also have a large impact on understanding biology.

9.1.6 Open-Ended Evolution of Intelligence

Many of the possible ingredients for open-ended neuroevolution do already exist. The recently available computational power could be harnessed to set up evolutionary processes that harness large populations, weak selection, neutral mutations, and deep time. While many of the current indirect genotype-to-phenotype mappings still focus on a single task, the emerging theoretical understanding of expressive encodings could lead to mappings that allow for searching indefinitely for more complex solutions as the environments and tasks change. Such mechanisms could be harnessed to establish evolutionary innovation that operates continuously.

However, open-ended innovation also requires that the environment continually presents the evolutionary system with new challenges. The environments themselves can change and evolve, or it may be possible to create multiple competing species in the environment, thus establishing an **evolutionary arms race**. While current multiagent and multipopulation systems still largely focus on solving a single task, evolution in such domains has already been shown to lead to specialization and discovery of cooperation, which could lead to major transitions. **Multitask** and **multiobjective evolution** are already known to result in more robust solutions, and in such environments, they could lead to progressive development of general intelligence. Perhaps the most promising avenue is to have the agents themselves modify the environment, building artifacts and complexity into it that persists (Lehman, Gordon, Jain, et al., 2023). In this manner, the environment and the agents in it can complexify indefinitely.

What goals might such experiments be set to achieve? An important one is a better understanding of biological evolution; that is, the origins of major transitions and intelligence. Another one is to construct better artificial systems, such as systems that can be deployed in natural and social environments, where they adapt to existing challenges and changes to them indefinitely—much as people do. Such ability is one essential ingredient in artificial general intelligence. To make these ideas concrete, the next two sections review concrete experiments in which environments and agents coevolve, in both cooperative and competitive fashion.

9.2 Cooperative Coevolution of Environments and Solutions

As discussed further in sections 4.2.3 and 14.4, part of the complex structure of biological systems originates from the complexity of the environment. A possible way to evolve complex systems is thus to evolve the environment and to present increasingly complex settings.

9.2.1 The Influence of Environments

Our thought processes and behaviors are significantly influenced by the specific time and place that we inhabit on Earth. These elements are shaped by distinct circumstances, cultural understandings, prevailing beliefs, and local customs. Together, they create a framework that both defines and restricts our experiences and the patterns of our thoughts (Ryan Ruggiero, 2012). For example, take the concept of individualism versus collectivism, which varies widely across cultures. In many Western societies, such as the United States, there is a strong focus on individual achievement and independence. This cultural context fosters a thought pattern that emphasizes personal goals and self-reliance. In contrast, many Eastern societies, like Japan, emphasize collectivism, where the focus is on group harmony and community. In such cultures, thought patterns and behaviors are more aligned with group goals and the collective well-being. Inhabiting a different era or being part of a distinct culture would fundamentally transform who we are, reshaping our identity in profound ways.

This principle that humans are shaped by their environments applies similarly to artificial intelligence (AI) and machine learning (ML) systems. For example, a **large language model** (LLM) is deeply influenced by its training data. If trained on scientific literature, the model will excel in technical explanations, whereas training on conversational texts results in more colloquial responses. This effect extends to the biases and perspectives inherent in the data. Similarly, in image generation, **diffusion models** produce different outputs based on their training datasets: Models trained on classical art will generate different images than those trained on modern digital art. In the realm of **reinforcement learning** (RL), the training environment crucially defines an agent's skills. For instance, an agent trained in a simulated urban setting will develop different capabilities and strategies than one trained in a virtual natural landscape.

Just as human experiences are shaped by our environments and cultures, AI agents are similarly molded by their training contexts and data environments. The quality and diversity of their training inputs are crucial, emphasizing the importance of coevolving AI systems with their environments to enhance their capabilities and behaviors.

9.2.2 Body and Brain Coevolution

Section 3.2 showed how neuroevolution can discover a policy to control a bipedal walker. In that setting, the physical structure of the walker was predetermined, and only the controller was optimized. From the perspective of coevolving environments and solutions, the body can be viewed as part of the environment in which the brain must learn to operate. Evolutionary algorithms, unlike gradient-based methods, are well suited to jointly optimize both the morphology of the agent and the controller that governs it. Why constrain ourselves to weights when we can also optimize other design choices governing our agents?

Body and brain co-evolution was briefly discussed in the context of novelty search with local competition (NSLC; section 5.5); however, that section did not explore the effect of different environments on the evolved morphologies. In addition to the weights of the control networks, the width, length, radius, mass, and orientation of an agent's body parts can be treated as evolvable parameters (Ha, 2019). The goal is to learn w (i.e., a joint vector of neural network weights and robot design parameters), to maximize the expected cumulative reward. An interesting question is: can the agent evolve a physical structure that is not only better suited for the task, but also facilitates evolving a better control policy? Such cooperative coevolution may uncover design principles that are useful more generally.

For this task, evolution can basically be implemented using any of the neuroevolution methods discussed earlier; the **policy gradients with parameter-based exploration** (PGPE) version of evolutionary strategies (Sehnke, Osendorfer, Rückstieß, et al., 2010) was used in the experiments in this section. With the head payload, material density, and motor joint configuration held constant as in the original environment, only the lengths and widths of the four leg segments were allowed to evolve together with the neural network controller. One constraint was that the robot parts had to stay within a range of ±75% of the original.

It turns out that learning a better version of an agent's body not only helps achieve better performance but also enables the agent to jointly learn policies more efficiently. The combined morphology+control approach was able to complete the more difficult BipedalWalkerHardcore domain in just 30% of the time required by the original, static version of the robot. Across 100 rollouts, the learnable version achieved an average score of 335 ± 37, outperforming the baseline score of 313 ± 53. In this environment (figure 9.5*b*), the agent generally learns to develop larger rear legs to serve as a useful stability function for navigation. Its front legs, which are smaller and more maneuverable,

(*a*) Simple flat environment

(*b*) Complex environment with obstacles and holes

Figure 9.5: **Examples of evolved morphology.** (*a*) In the easy, flat environment, the approach developed a thick but short rear lower limb that enabled a fast gait. (*b*) In the more complex environment that included obstacles and holes, a larger rear leg evolved that allowed the agent to push over obstacles better. Evolution thus optimized the body and control jointly to meet the challenge as well as possible. Figures from Ha (2019). Videos at `https://neuroevolutionbook.com/demos`.

also act as a sensor for dangerous obstacles ahead, complementing its laser range sensors. In the simpler domain without obstacles (figure 9.5*a*), the agent tends to learn to develop longer, thinner legs, with the exception of one leg part.

It may not be surprising that allowing an agent to learn a better version of its body enables it to achieve better performance. However, can we trade some of the additional performance gains to achieve other design goals? For instance, can evolution discover a design that uses the least amount of materials while still achieving satisfactory performance on the task? To this end, the leg size can be calculated and rewards scaled by a utility factor U:

$$U = 1 + \log\left(\frac{\text{original\_leg\_area}}{\text{new\_leg\_area}}\right). \tag{9.1}$$

With such rewards, evolution developed a lean, minimal design where every inch matters. It also learned movements that appear more insect like, with the smallest pair of legs that can still solve the more challenging bipedal walker environment (figure 9.6).

Thus, interesting, life like results can be achieved with added constraints. What if we do the opposite and remove the initial constraint that each part has to be within ±75% of its original value? Without any design constraints, evolution discovers an extremely tall bipedal walker agent that "solves" the task by simply falling over and landing at the exit (figure 9.7)!

In this manner, body-brain coevolution provides an avenue for open-ended discovery of better solutions. As the agent gets better at controlling the body, the body can become more complex, providing a new challenge in a cooperative manner. These principles will be developed further in two later sections in this book: Body-brain coevolution is combined with reinforcement learning in section 12.4, and scaled up to more complex virtual

(*a*) Simple environment

(*b*) Complex environment

Figure 9.6: **Optimizing for desired design properties.** Evolution was rewarded for finding solutions that included small legs. (*a*) In the easy flat environment, very small legs evolved. (*b*) In the more challenging environment, its legs were longer, but they were the smallest that could still solve the task. In this manner, multiple design goals can be combined to obtain a variety of solutions. Figures from Ha (2019).

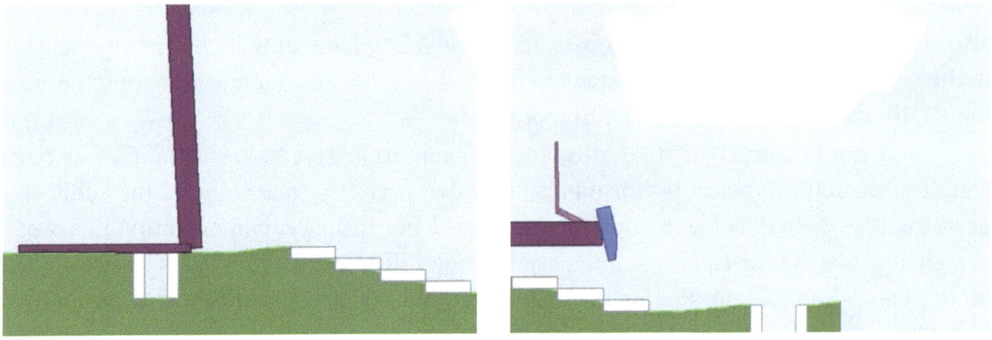

(*b*) Start standing up (*b*) End falling down

Figure 9.7: **Optimization without constraints.** With all design constraints removed, evolution came up with a really tall bipedal walker that solves the task by simply falling over and landing near the exit! This example shows that the approach can be creative beyond preconceived human notions of what the solutions should be like. Figures from Ha (2019).

creatures in section 14.5. While body-brain coevolution enables progress by adjusting the agent's physical substrate, another powerful strategy is to adapt the environment in tandem with the agent's growing capabilities. The next section explores recent methods where the tasks and environments themselves evolve cooperatively in response to what the agent has learned.

9.2.3 Coevolution Driven by Interestingness

A key issue in open-ended learning is deciding what the next learning challenge should be, especially in large or unbounded task spaces. Methods based on learning progress offer

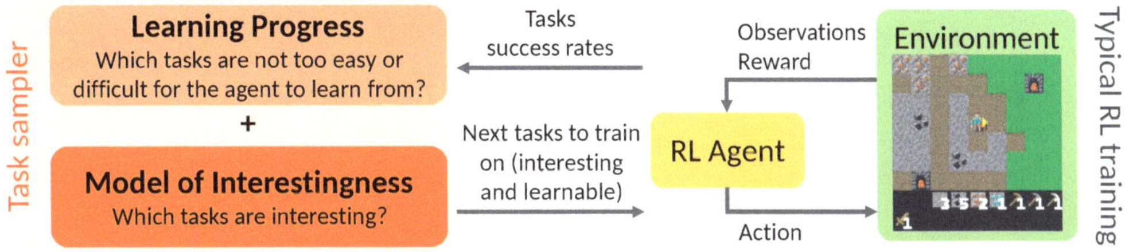

Figure 9.8: **Overview of OMNI.** OMNI enables open-ended learning in vast environment search spaces by ensuring that the training tasks not only have high learning progress, but are also interesting. They harness LLMs to make such a heretofore impossible judgment. Figure from Zhang, Lehman, Stanley, et al. (2024).

one answer by selecting tasks that are neither too easy nor too hard, but they often fall into the trap of proposing trivial variations that do not meaningfully extend the agent's abilities. What is needed is a way to prioritize tasks that are not only learnable but worthwhile–that is, tasks that are novel, diverse, and interesting from a human perspective. This idea echoes earlier work such as the **innovation engine** (Nguyen, Yosinski, and Clune, 2015b), which used a predictor of human interest to guide open-ended search. The OMNI (Zhang, Lehman, Stanley, et al., 2024) and OMNI-EPIC (Faldor, Zhang, Cully, et al., 2025) frameworks addressed this challenge by integrating models of human interestingness into the training loop, allowing agents and their environments to co-adapt in a more meaningful and productive way.

Open-endedness via models of human notions of interestingness (OMNI), introduced a method for filtering tasks using two criteria: learning progress and human-like interestingness. Tasks were first scored based on how much the agent is improving, and then filtered using LLMs such as GPT-3 (Floridi and Chiriatti, 2020) and GPT-4 (Achiam, Adler, Agarwal, et al., 2023), which were prompted to judge which tasks are worthwhile (the use of LLMs in neuroevolution is discussed in more detail in chapter 13). The overall structure of this approach is illustrated in Figure 9.8.

OMNI-EPIC (open-endedness via models of human notions of interestingness with environments programmed in code) extended this idea by generating entirely new environments in code. It used LLMs to describe new tasks in natural language, translated them into Python code defining the simulation and reward structure, and used a second model of interestingness to filter out redundant or unremarkable tasks. A success detector evaluated whether the agent had learned the task, and a growing archive of successes and failures guided future generations. This full pipeline is shown in figure 9.9; the iterative loop enables both the agent and its task distribution to grow in complexity together. The approach is similar to the POET approach described in section 9.3. The crucial difference is that in POET, the new environments were created to be simply challenging to the existing solutions—therefore, the environments and solutions compete. In OMNI-EPIC, the environments are intended to be interesting—therefore, the process can be seen as a cooperative one.

The results from these two studies highlighted the effectiveness of this co-adaptive approach. OMNI was tested in the **Crafter** (Hafner, 2022) and **BabyAI** (Chevalier-Boisvert,

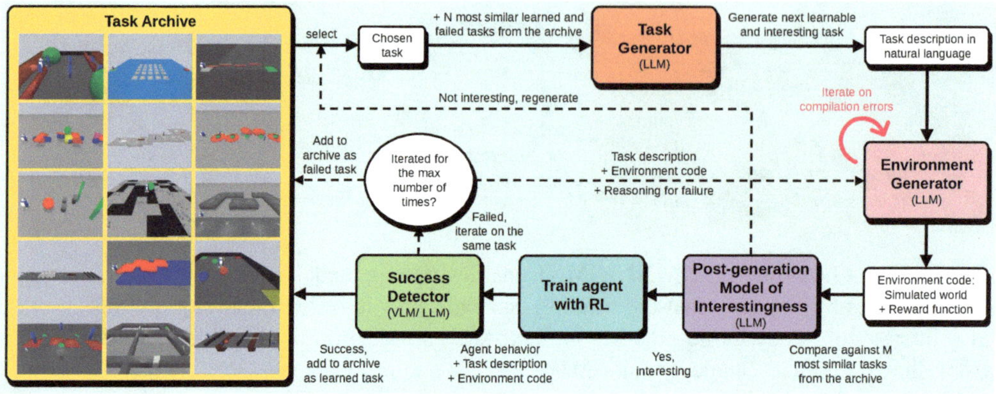

Figure 9.9: **Overview of OMNI-EPIC.** OMNI-EPIC continuously generates and solves new, interesting tasks in simulation. The approach maintains a task archive of learned and failed tasks. Figure from Faldor, Zhang, Cully, et al. (2025). Videos at `https://neuroevolutionbook.com/demos`.

Bahdanau, Lahlou, et al., 2019) environments. Crafter is a 2D Minecraft-like environment with a technology tree, where tasks must be completed in a meaningful sequence—such as gathering resources before crafting tools. BabyAI is a grid-based world focused on grounded language understanding, where agents follow natural language instructions involving navigation and object manipulation. Both environments are ideal for testing open-ended learning because they feature large, combinatorial task spaces. And indeed, in both environments OMNI achieved substantially higher task success rates and learned a greater number of tasks when guided by the model of interestingness (figures 9.10 and 9.11). OMNI-EPIC extended these results by showing that the environments themselves can be generated in an open-ended way. In long-run simulations of an R2D2 robot, the system created a wide variety of tasks starting from just a few seeds, spanning challenges in navigation, push manipulation, and coordination. In actual RL training runs, OMNI-EPIC adapted to agent performance by simplifying tasks after failures or combining mastered skills into more complex ones. Quantitative evaluations confirmed that both the model of interestingness and the task archive are essential for sustained diversity and progress (figure 9.12).

These systems offer a promising realization of cooperative coevolution between environments and solutions. The agent is not learning in a static world, nor is the task distribution fixed in advance. Instead, the agent and its environment develop together, each responding to changes in the other. The model of interestingness ensures that the evolving curriculum remains focused on tasks that are genuinely valuable rather than superficial. The result is a dynamic and constructive interplay between learning and environment design, mirroring the mutual shaping seen in natural evolution and cultural development.

9.3 Competitive Coevolution of Environments and Solutions

Just as cooperation between agents and environments can drive progress, competition can also serve as a powerful engine for complexity. By evolving environments that actively

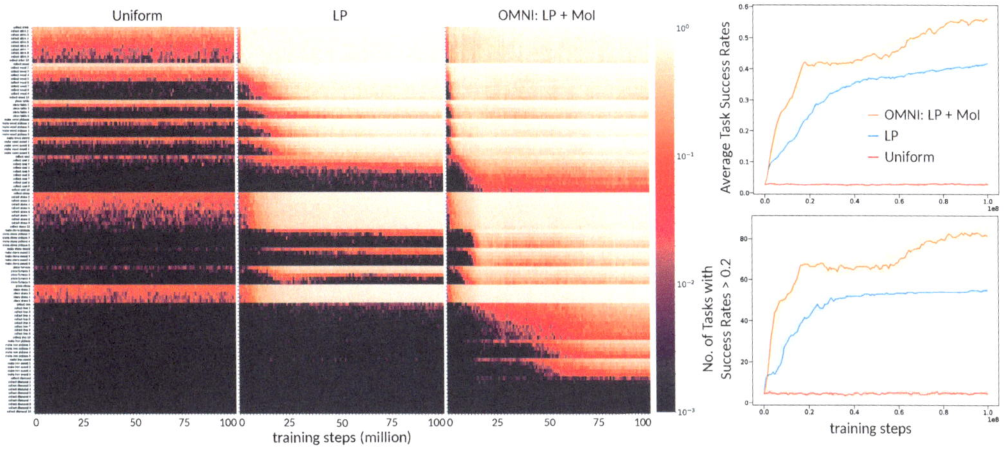

(*a*) Success probabilities (*b*) Performance

Figure 9.10: **Results in Crafter.** (*a*) Conditional success probabilities of all tasks in Crafter. Tasks are organized from simple to complex based on the prerequisite tasks that must be accomplished before completing the target task. Task names (left of each row) are readable in a digital format when zoomed in. (*b*) Performance in Crafter on all tasks. While OMNI biases training toward interesting tasks, it achieves higher average task success rates and learns more tasks than uniform sampling or choosing tasks based on learning progress alone, even across all tasks. Figure from Zhang, Lehman, Stanley, et al. (2024).

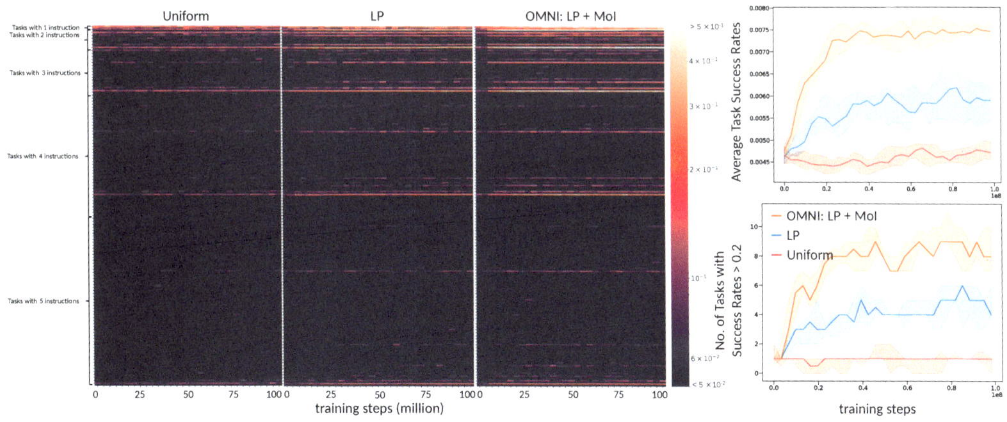

(*a*) Success probabilities (*b*) Performance

Figure 9.11: **Results in BabyAI.** (*a*) Conditional success probabilities of a subset of tasks in BabyAI. These plots only show tasks with a success rate of at least 0.05 by any method at any time step. Tasks are organized from simple to complex based on the instruction length. (*b*) Performance in BabyAI on all tasks. The average task success rate scale for BabyAI is low because it is averaged over the entire task set, which includes many tasks that are difficult to learn. This approach captures the microcosm of the real world, where there can be infinitely many difficult or even impossible tasks. OMNI achieves much higher average task success rates and learns more tasks than uniform sampling or choosing tasks based on learning progress alone. Figure from Faldor, Zhang, Cully, et al. (2025).

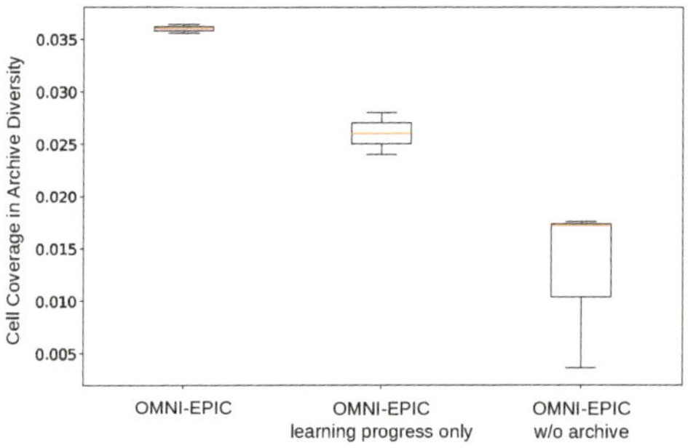

(*a*) Archive diversity

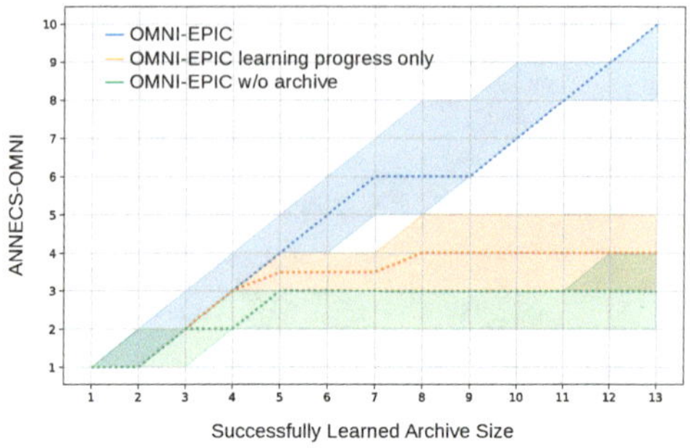

(*b*) Performance

Figure 9.12: **OMNI-EPIC performance in a long R2D2 simulation.** (*a*) Cell coverage of archive diversity plots in long runs with simulated learning by OMNI-EPIC and the controls. (*b*) ANNECS-OMNI measure of progress for OMNI-EPIC and the controls. Dotted lines are median values, and shaded regions are 95% confidence intervals. OMNI-EPIC generated significantly more diverse tasks and continued to innovate throughout the run. Figures from Faldor, Zhang, Cully, et al. (2025).

challenge evolving agents, competitive setups can create an arms race, where solutions must constantly improve to survive.

9.3.1 Paired Open-Ended Trailblazer

Algorithms like **novelty search** (NS; section 5.3) promote behavioral rather than genetic diversity, making them less prone to getting stuck in local optima. As a result, they naturally align with the principles of open-endedness by prioritizing divergence over convergence. These approaches are motivated by the idea that reaching innovative solutions often requires navigating through a sequence of intermediate **stepping stones**—solutions that may not resemble the final goal and are typically not identifiable in advance.

In section 5.4, we have seen how **QD algorithms** build upon this idea by maintaining a diverse set of niches, each optimized in parallel. Unlike pure novelty search, QD algorithms evaluate how well solutions from one niche perform in others—a strategy known as **goal switching** (Nguyen, Yosinski, and Clune, 2015b). This mechanism enables the discovery of unexpected stepping stones across niches.

The **paired open-ended trailblazer** (POET) algorithm (Wang, Lehman, Clune, et al., 2019) extends these principles by integrating goal switching within a divergent search framework. While conventional QD methods drive solution diversity, they typically operate in static environments, which ultimately limits long-term discovery. For machine learning to achieve true open-endedness, algorithms must evolve both problems and solutions. POET is designed to drive an open-ended process of co-discovery in a single run. It maintains a population of environments (e.g., obstacle courses) and a population of agents (e.g., neural network controllers), with each agent paired with a specific environment. This setup results in a divergent coevolutionary process that continuously pushes the frontier of both challenges and skills. As new environments are created, they present fresh challenges, while agents adapt by developing more advanced capabilities. Existing skills are leveraged not only through continued optimization but also by transferring agent behaviors across environments to uncover promising stepping stones, which facilitates ongoing, open-ended discovery.

In more detail, POET begins with an initial simple environment, such as a flat-ground obstacle course, paired with a randomly initialized neural network agent. Throughout its operation, POET executes the following three core tasks within its main loop.

1. Environment generation: POET generates new environments by mutating the parameters of existing ones. In the bipedal walker task, these environmental parameters include (1) stump height, (2) gap width, (3) stair height, (4) number of stairs, and (5) surface roughness. This process is selective, adding new environments to the active population only if they provide a suitable challenge and introduce novelty. For example, a minimum criterion (MC) of $S_{\min} < E^{\text{child}}(\theta^{\text{child}}) < S_{\max}$, where $S_{\min}$ and $S_{\max}$ are pre-defined score thresholds, can be used to filter out child environments that appear too challenging or too trivial, and yet fostering a diverse range of challenges.

2. Agent optimization: Each agent is continuously optimized within its environment using evolutionary strategies, although other optimization methods could also be applied. The objective is to maximize performance metrics relevant to each environment, such as traversing an obstacle course efficiently. This optimization happens independently for each pair, which facilitates parallel processing and enhances computational efficiency.

3. Agent transfer: To foster cross-environment adaptation, POET attempts to transfer agents between different environments. This strategy can help agents escape local optima by applying successful strategies from one context to another. For example, an agent performing well in a mountainous terrain might offer insights when transferred to a rocky terrain, potentially leading to breakthroughs in performance.

POET maintains a controlled number of environment-agent pairs in its active list, capped at a maximum size to manage computational resources. Environments that become obsolete or overly familiar are phased out to make room for new ones, ensuring that the population remains dynamic and conducive to continuous learning.

Experiments conducted by POET using various types of obstacles (such as gaps, rough terrain, and stumps) reveal that challenges generated and solved by POET are far too difficult for ES when tackled directly (see figures 9.13 and 9.14). For example, agents optimized by ES in these environments tend to stop and avoid moving further to prevent penalties rather than learning to navigate obstacles effectively. This behavior contrasts starkly with the capabilities developed by agents under POET, which successfully navigate these complex environments. Additional results highlight that POET not only engineers these challenging environments but also devises innovative solutions that ES alone cannot achieve. This includes agents developed by POET that can navigate wide gaps and rugged terrains, which ES agents fail to handle. In simpler environments also created by POET, ES consistently underperforms, unable to match the high standards set by POET's adaptive and dynamic approach.

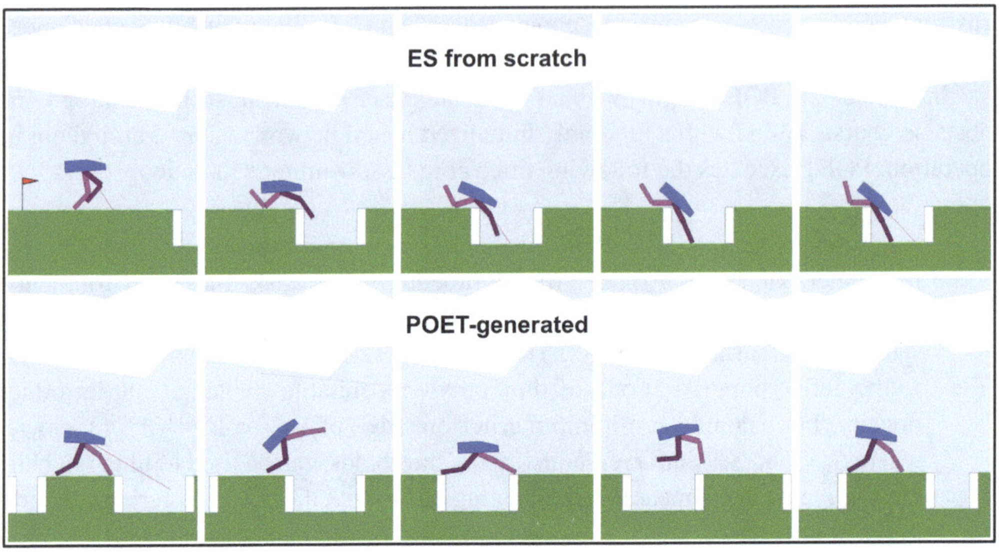

(*a*) Generated agents attempting gaps

(*b*) Generated agents on rough surfaces

(*c*) Generated agents attempting stumps

Figure 9.13: **The POET approach.** POET generates complex environments and effective agent solutions unachievable through standard ES. As depicted, agents optimized directly by ES (top row of panel (*a*) and left panels of (*b*) and (*c*)) tend to develop suboptimal behaviors, often quitting prematurely. In contrast, POET not only engineers these demanding scenarios but also successfully trains agents that adeptly navigate through them, as demonstrated in the bottom row of panel (*a*) and the right panels of (*b*) and (*c*). Figures from Wang, Lehman, Clune, et al. (2019). Videos at `https://neuroevolutionbook.com/demos`.

A key question explored in the POET experiments was whether the environments created and solved by POET could also be addressed by an explicit direct-path curriculum-building control algorithm. To investigate this, POET was compared to a control approach designed to create a sequence of progressively more difficult environments leading to a target environment. This curriculum was constructed manually, following principles that are common in the literature on curricular learning.

In the direct-path curriculum, the sequence began with an extremely simple environment consisting of flat ground, which was solvable by a randomly initialized agent. Subsequent environments were constructed by incrementally increasing the difficulty of one or more

(*a*) Large steps (*b*) Mixed terrain (*c*) Performance

Figure 9.14: **Agents demonstrate advanced navigation abilities in complex scenarios engineered by POET.** Notable challenges include (*a*) navigating exceptionally large steps and (*b*) mastering a rough-terrain course featuring a mix of narrow and wide gaps, alongside stumps of varying heights. In addition, ES alone fails to match POET's performance in various settings. (*c*) A dotted line at a score of 230 indicates the success threshold. The plots clearly show that ES consistently falls short of meeting the challenges effectively addressed by POET. Figures from Wang, Lehman, Clune, et al. (2019).

obstacle parameters (e.g., stump height or gap width) until the target environment was reached. Agents were trained using ES, and progression to the next environment occurred once the agent achieved a predefined performance threshold. Importantly, this curriculum-building control was given the same computational budget as POET to ensure a fair comparison.

The comparison focused on three levels of environment difficulty: challenging, very challenging, and extremely challenging. Difficulty is defined by how POET-generated environments exceed the reference values of the **BipedalWalkerHardcore** environment. For example, extremely challenging environments in POET have stumps, gaps, and roughness values that are up to 4.5 times what they were in the original difficult version of the bipedal walker domain. These results illustrate the system's ability to generate truly novel and difficult scenarios.

Figure 9.15 provides a visual comparison of POET and the direct-path curriculum algorithm. Each rose plot represents an environment created and solved by POET (red pentagons) alongside the closest configurations reached by the curriculum algorithm in five independent runs (blue pentagons). The pentagon vertices correspond to key parameters: roughness, the lower and upper bounds of gap width, and the lower and upper bounds of stump height.

The results show a striking dichotomy between the two approaches. Across all difficulty levels, the curriculum algorithm consistently failed to reach the complexity and challenge of POET-generated environments. This trend is especially pronounced in extremely challenging environments (top two rows), where the blue pentagons fall significantly short of the red pentagons in terms of parameter values, such as maximum roughness or gap width. Even at lower difficulty levels, the curriculum algorithm struggled to match POET's ability to solve nuanced and demanding scenarios.

In follow-up work, an enhanced version of POET (Wang, Lehman, Rawal, et al., 2020) introduced an additional set of algorithmic innovations. The first is the **performance of all transferred agents measure** (PATA-EC). PATA-EC is a domain-general measure of

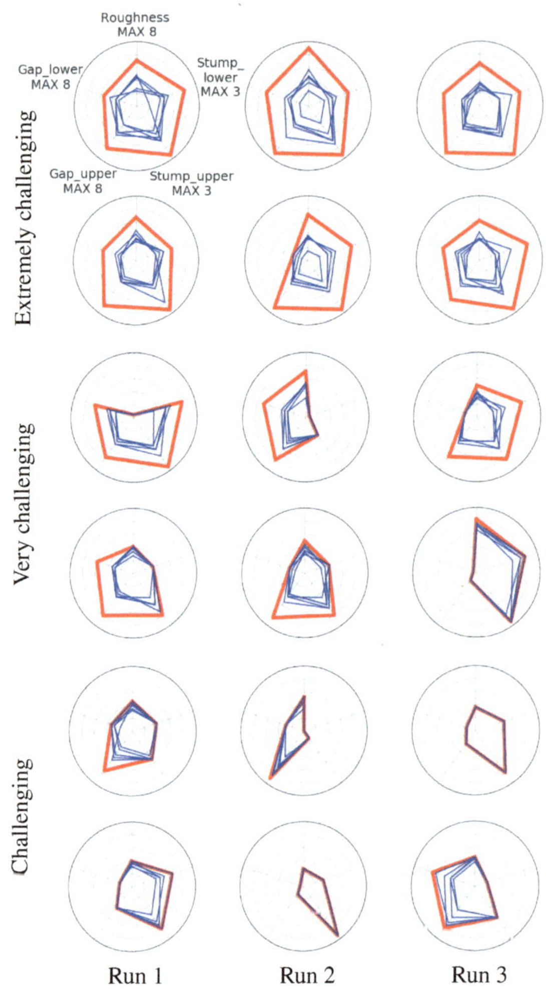

Figure 9.15: **POET versus direct-path curriculum-building controls.** Each rose plot depicts one environment that POET created and solved (red pentagon). For each, the five blue pentagons indicate what happens in control runs when the red pentagon is the target. Each blue pentagon is the closest-to-target environment solved by one of the five independent runs of the control algorithm. The five vertices of each pentagon indicate roughness (*roughness*), the bottom and top values of the range of the gap width of all the gaps (*gap_lower* and *gap_upper*), and the bottom and top values for the height of stumps (*stump_lower* and *stump_upper*) in the given solved environment. The value after MAX in the key is the maximum value at the outermost circle for each type of obstacle. Each column contains sample solved environments from a single independent run of POET. Figures from Wang, Lehman, Clune, et al. (2019).

how meaningfully novel new challenges are, enabling the system to potentially create and solve interesting challenges endlessly.

The second is a more efficient heuristic for determining when agents should goal-switch from one problem to another. The heuristic is based on the insight that what makes an environment interesting is how agents behave in it, and novel environments are those that provide new information about how the behaviors of agents within them differ. This

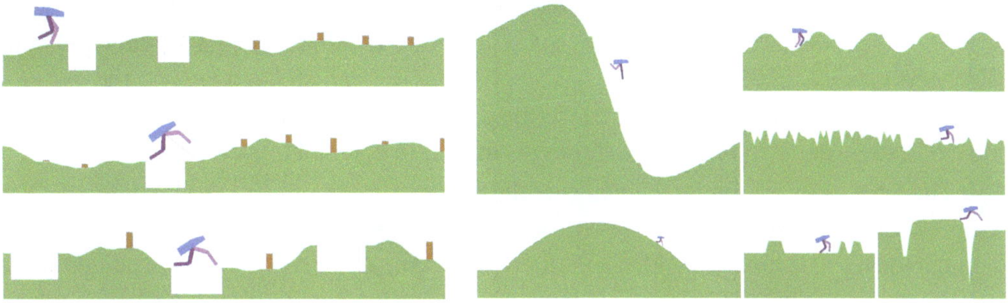

(*a*) Sample environments from a single run of original POET

(*b*) Sample environments from a single run of enhanced POET

Figure 9.16: **Enhanced POET.** With the CPPN-based environment generation and other innovations, enhanced POET is able to generate (and solve) a wide diversity of environments within a single run. In contrast, the original POET can generate environments only with limited types of regularly-shaped obstacles (e.g., stumps and gaps). Figures from Wang, Lehman, Rawal, et al. (2020).

heuristic is more computationally efficient than the original POET algorithm and helps open-ended search scale better.

Third, **enhanced POET** introduced a novel, more flexible way to encode environmental challenges based on CPPNs (section 4.3.1). In the case of enhanced POET, CPPNs are used to generate obstacle courses for the bipedal walking agent. The generated environments shown in figure 9.16*b* demonstrate that the use of CPPNs allows for the generation of much more complex and diverse challenges than what was used in the original POET experiments (see figure 9.16*a*).

From these results, it is evident that POET exemplifies the principle of coevolution between agents and their environments. As an automatic curriculum builder, POET continuously creates new challenges that are optimally balanced, neither too easy nor too hard, effectively teaching agents how to tackle increasingly complex problems. This coevolutionary process fosters an environment where skills developed in one context are not only honed but also become transferable, aiding agents in solving new and more complex challenges.

9.3.2 Learning to Chase and Escape

In chapter 7, two settings of **competitive coevolution** were discussed: evolving a neural network controller for a single agent by having it compete against other agents in the population (section 7.1.1); and evolving two different species of controller networks, one for each of the two competing teams of agents, in two separate populations. An evolutionary arms race ensued in both settings, resulting in several stages of innovation, each with more sophisticated solutions than in the previous stages.

This subsection revisits such settings in the framework of the coevolution of environments and solutions. Whereas in POET, each environment provides a static challenge for each solution, competitive coevolution of agent controllers provides a dynamic challenge. That is, the environment consists of other agents that respond dynamically to the agent's actions. In more detail, in this **chase-and-escape** domain there are two agents with adversarial goals: one agent is trying to escape and the other is trying to catch it (Tang, Tan, and Harada, 2020). As the chaser evolves more sophisticated tactics, the escapee evolves more refined moves to evade capture. This dynamic interaction leads to an arms race of increasingly sophisticated strategies that is, in principle, open-ended.

The chaser is a simulated quadrupedal robot that needs to learn low-level joint commands (i.e., desired joint angles), and the escapee is a dot robot that learns swift commands (i.e., desired velocities and directions). The escapee is said to be caught if the distance between the two robots is less than a predefined threshold d_{min}. The two robots are trained in an iterative fashion.

First, in each iteration, the chaser robot plays against an opponent that is randomly sampled from an adversary pool Π_a. The pool initially only contains an escapee robot that stays still, giving the chaser robot time to learn basic locomotion skills in the early stages.

Second, after the chaser robot's control policy is evolved, an opponent robot plays against the upgraded version of the chaser. The escapee robot has no memory of the skills that it previously learned, and it will devote all its energy and capacity to learn new skills that discover and exploit the weakness of the chaser robot's locomotion capability. After learning, this escapee robot's policy is added to Π_a.

While having the adversary pool Π_a encourages the chaser robot to play against various escapees and helps fight catastrophic forgetting, the diversity in the escapee robots' escaping maneuvers is also critical. To achieve this, the authors sampled different d_{min} when training the escapee robots. Intuitively, a small distance threshold allows the escapee to stay close to the chaser and develop sudden, quick movements to dodge, while larger values would encourage the escapee to use large circular trajectories to stay away from the chaser.

This iterative coevolution between the chaser and escapee robots is critical in developing their agility and robustness. Each cycle of adaptation not only hones their individual strategies but also contributes to a richer, more responsive interaction between them. By continuously evolving both agents and the dynamics of their environment, the study showcases how the complexity and effectiveness of autonomous systems can be significantly enhanced.

After training, the quadrupedal chaser robot develops a symmetric gait that alternates between its forelimbs and hind limbs, mimicking the bounding gait commonly seen in quadrupedal animals at high speeds. To execute sharp turns, it extends the stance phase of one forelimb, using it as a pivot to rapidly rotate its body and change direction. Additionally, the escapee robot demonstrates sophisticated maneuvers, such as sprinting at full speed, circling to confuse the chaser, and employing sudden lateral dodges to cause the chaser to overshoot. For visual examples of these dynamic interactions, refer to figure 9.17, which illustrates the trajectories of both the chaser and escapee robots.

To illustrate the advantages of coevolutionary methods over static training environments, three inductive bias-driven baseline methods are presented and depicted in the top row of figure 9.18. First is the cone configuration (π_{cone}), where a target position is randomly selected within a fan-shaped area directly ahead of the chaser robot, simulating a forward-focused pursuit. Second is the circular configuration (π_{circle}), where the target is randomly

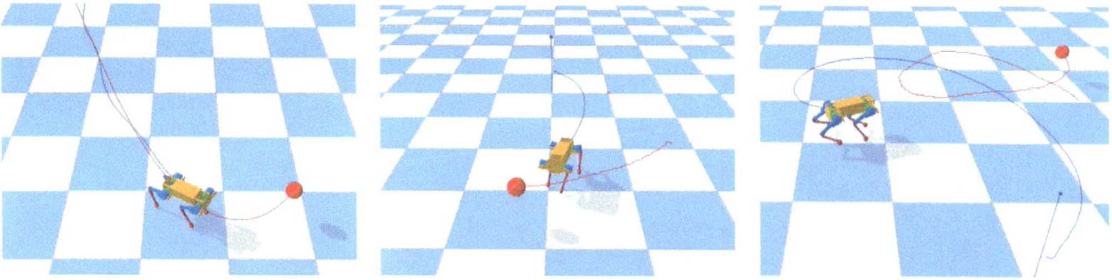

(*a*) Chasing directly (*b*) Anticipating future position (*c*) Circling to confuse the chaser

Figure 9.17: **Sample episodes of chase and escape**. The quadruped robot is the chaser and the red dot-bot is the escapee; the blue and red lines are their trajectories. In the experiments, some adversarial agents developed advanced evasion tactics, such as luring the quadruped robot to approach, then dodging and stopping abruptly, causing the robot to run past them.

placed anywhere within a complete circular area surrounding the chaser, promoting omnidirectional movement. Third is the zigzag configuration (π_{zigzag}), where targets are alternately placed to the left and right directly in front of the chaser, encouraging it to adopt a zigzag movement pattern. Additionally, to underscore the importance of diversity in training, a scenario in which the chaser robot plays against a single evolved opponent is included for comparison, denoted as π_{single}.

These configurations were employed to benchmark the performance of traditional methods against those that dynamically coevolve the training environment alongside the agent. The bottom row of figure 9.18 illustrates the trajectories of all chaser policies as they attempted to intercept a target moving along a sine-shaped route. In the first two cases, the coevolved policy successfully intercepted the target even before it reached the first turn. In contrast, the policies trained with the baseline configurations either fell behind or required more time to catch up. When the target maneuvers through turns (as shown in the last two plots), the coevolved policy adeptly followed the trajectory and captured the target, whereas the baseline policies struggled, often losing balance or needing to slow down significantly to manage the turn. This stark contrast highlights that the coevolution of the agent and the environment is crucial for achieving superior performance, as it allows the agent to adapt more effectively to complex and dynamic challenges.

This example of coevolution of adversarial agents demonstrates how dynamic environments can lead to open-endedness. They are more complex than static environments, providing many ways to create new challenges. Agents evolved in this manner are not only superior but also more robust, suggesting that the new challenges can be met. It remains to be seen how far this approach can be pushed. It may need to be combined with abilities to modify the body and the environment (as discussed in section 9.2.2), but dynamic environments are likely an essential ingredient of constructing intelligent systems through open-ended neuroevolution.

These considerations conclude the discussion of neuroevolution of behavior in this book. The next three chapters will expand on the idea of cooperative learning systems. However, instead of coevolution, combinations with other ML mechanisms will be considered, including deep learning, reinforcement learning, and generative AI. These mechanisms are synergistic in several ways, resulting in more powerful machine learning.

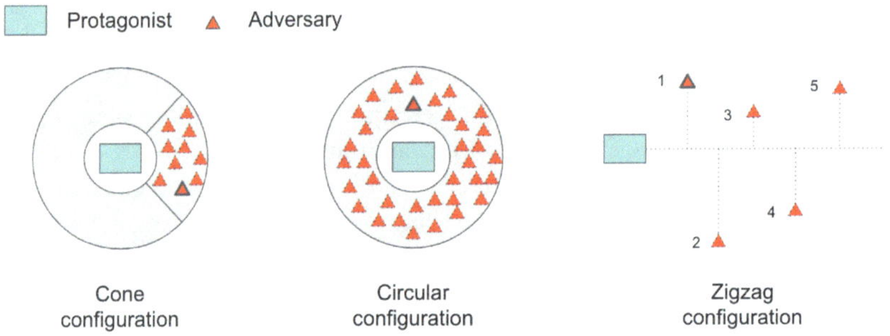

(*a*) Three configurations of initial positions for a static adversary

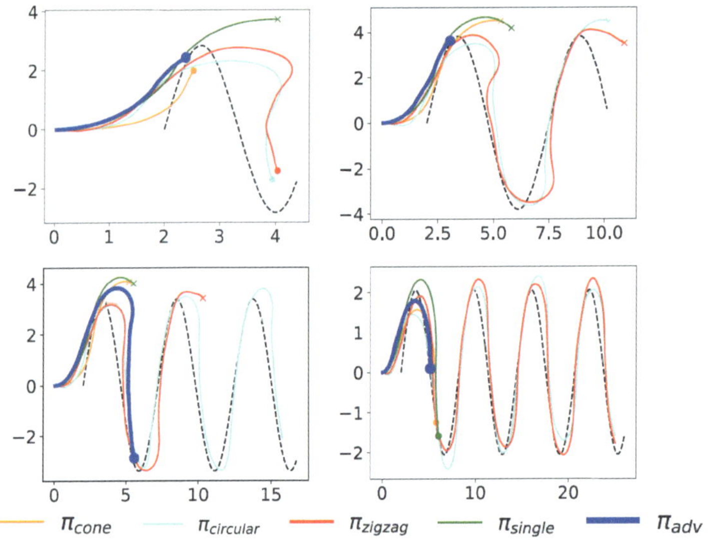

(*b*) Trajectories of methods trying to catch an escapee moving along a sine-wave

Figure 9.18: **Comparison with baseline methods.** (*a*) Three configurations of initial positions for a static adversary. (*b*) Trajectories of the methods when the chaser robot tries to catch an escapee robot that moves along a sine-wave-shaped route. A cross at the end of a trajectory indicates that the chaser has fallen or the target has escaped. A dot at the end means successfully catching the target at that position. Short trajectories ending with dots indicate the chaser catches the target early. The chaser trained with dynamic adversaries (blue trajectory) is able to catch the target much earlier than other baseline policies, including the policy that plays against a single opponent (π_{single}). Figures from Tang, Tan, and Harada (2020).

9.4 Chapter Review Questions

1. **Key ingredients:** What are the five elements of biological open-endedness that could potentially inspire open-ended neuroevolution, and how do they support continuous innovation?

2. **Neutral mutations:** Why are neutrality and weak selection crucial for maintaining diversity in large populations, and how do such processes differ from traditional approaches in evolutionary computation?

3. **Role of extinctions:** How can extinction events accelerate evolution and increase evolvability in computational experiments? Provide an example from the bipedal walker domain.

4. **Long-term effects:** Describe how repeated extinction events can lead to populations that are more evolvable and capable of filling niches more effectively.

5. **GRNs and evolvability:** How do GRNs provide a substrate for evolvability, and what advantages do they offer compared to direct encodings in tasks like Nothello?

6. **Indirect encodings:** Explain the role of indirect encodings in enhancing evolvability. How do GRNs contribute to the discovery of robust and diverse neural network motifs?

7. **Miracle jumps:** What are miracle jumps, and why are expressive encodings such as GP or neural networks more effective than direct encodings in achieving such jumps?

8. **Comparative power:** Compare the benefits of expressive encodings with traditional evolutionary algorithms for solving problems with dynamically changing objectives.

9. **Body-brain coevolution:** How does coevolving an agent's body and brain lead to better solutions, and what principles can it reveal about designing efficient and specialized morphologies?

10. **Environment-agent coevolution:** Describe the core mechanisms of the POET algorithm for coevolving agents and environments. Why is this approach effective for solving complex challenges?

Chapter 10

Evolutionary Neural Architecture Search

The design of neural network architectures (i.e., the organization of neurons into assemblies and layers and the connections between them), has played an important role in the advances in deep learning. Through a combination of human ingenuity and the need to push state-of-the-art performance, there have been several large leaps of technological innovation since the early 2010s. During this time, the technique now known as **neural architecture search** (NAS) also emerged as its own subarea of deep learning research. The goal of NAS is to employ various methods such as reinforcement learning (RL), gradient descent, Bayesian optimization, and evolutionary search to automate the search for novel neural network architectures, which are then trained with gradient descent to obtain the final network. The idea is that such an automated search could result in architectures that would be superior to those hand-designed by human researchers. Evolutionary optimization is particularly well suited for NAS because it can optimize not only continuous hyperparameter values, but also discrete choices among alternative components, and even large structures such as graphs. Many evolutionary optimization techniques have found a new use in NAS, and new ones have been developed as well.

This chapter starts with a simple example combining neuroevolution of augmenting topologies (NEAT) topology search with backpropagation for the weights. It then expands to deep learning architectures, with examples in convolutional, recurrent, and general topologies. Particularly useful cases for NAS are multiobjective domains, where aspects other than performance need to be optimized as well, and multitask domains, where the needs of several tasks can be combined. NAS requires a lot of computation, so techniques have been developed for efficient search and evaluation. It may also be possible to evolve the networks entirely, without gradient descent as the second phase, in the future.

10.1 Neural Architecture Search with NEAT

The NAS idea can be illustrated by combining the NEAT topology search algorithm with the backpropagation algorithm for training the weights of each neural network topology. This concept of backprop NEAT appeared many times even before deep learning, and in

Figure 10.1: **Types of nodes and activation functions in the backprop NEAT experiment**. The colors are used to label the nodes in figures 10.2 and 10.3. Different functions implement different computational properties that make the search for a good architecture more effective.

that sense, it can be seen as the grandfather of modern NAS. Incidentally (as discussed in the Info Box in section 10.2), it also encouraged the development of the NAS subfield within Google.

In **backprop NEAT**, a neural network topology is evolved using the NEAT-style crossover and mutation operators. Unlike in the original version of NEAT, in this experiment, many types of activation functions are possible, represented as different colors in the neural network (the legend for it is shown in figure 10.1). The input to a neuron is the usual weighted sum of incoming connections. The `add` operator does nothing to the input, while the `mult` operator multiplies all the weighted inputs together. By allowing for a sinusoidal operator, the network can produce repetitive patterns at its output. The `square` and `abs` operators are useful for generating symmetries, and the Gaussian operator is helpful in drawing one-off clustered regions. The output neurons have sigmoid activation functions since the task consists of classifying examples into one of two categories (0 or 1).

Each neural network topology that NEAT creates is represented as a computation graph. It is then possible to run backprop on this same graph to optimize the weights of the network to best fit the training data. In this manner, NEAT is strictly responsible for specifying the architecture, while backprop determines the best set of weights for it (in the original NEAT, evolution is also used to determine the weights). In this experiment, an L2 regularization term is also included in the backprop. The initial population of networks consists of minimal architectures like the one in figure 10.2*a*, implementing logistic regression with a different set of random weights; that is,

$$o = \sigma\left(w_1 x + w_2 y + w_3 b\right), \tag{10.1}$$

where x and y are the coordinates of the input sample, b is the bias unit (activated at 1.0), w_i are the initial random weights, and o is the output of the network. This simple network divides the plane into two halves, as shown in figure 10.2*b*. The color coding represents values from 0.0 (orange) through 0.5 (white) and finally to 1.0 (blue). When the dataset consists of two Gaussian clusters, this simple initial network performs quite well already. In fact, when starting with an initial population of 100 simple networks with random weights, before any backprop or genetic algorithm, the very best network in the population is likely good enough for this type of dataset.

Each network architecture is assigned a **fitness score** based on how well they do in the classification task after training them with backprop. In addition to measuring how well each network fits the training data, using the maximum likelihood metric, the number of connections is taken into account. Usually, simpler networks are more regularized and

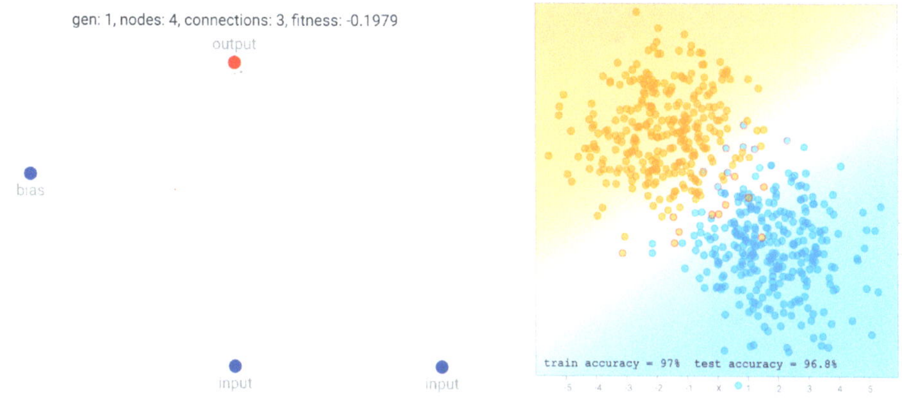

(a) Network architecture (b) Classification performance

Figure 10.2: **An example of a network from the first generation.** The network (a) is tasked with classifying input samples (two-dimensional points) into one of two categories (b). The initial population consists of networks that implement logistic regression with a different set of random weights. If the population is large enough and the classification problem is simple enough, some of those initial networks may already do well in the task, as is the case in this nearly linearly separable classification task. Videos at `https://neuroevolutionbook.com/demos`.

thus generalize better to new examples, and they also take up less memory and are faster to run. Thus, simpler networks are preferred if they achieve similar regression accuracy to more complex ones, or if they are much simpler, even if they are somewhat less accurate. To achieve this goal, the fitting error is adjusted by the number of connections as

$$f = -E\sqrt{1 + rc}, \tag{10.2}$$

where f is the fitness, E is the error over the training set, c is the number of connections, and r is a proportionality factor. Thus, a network with more connections will have a fitness that is more negative than a network with fewer connections. The square root is used because intuitively, it seems, a network with for example, 51 connections should be treated about the same as a network of 50 connections, while a network with five connections should be treated very differently from a network with four connections. Other concave utility functions may achieve the same effect. In a way, like the L2 regularization of weights, this type of penalty is a form of regularization on the neural network structure.

After a few generations, networks evolve that once trained, fit training data well, even in tasks that are not linearly separable (figure 10.3). How is backprop NEAT able to do it? In machine learning (ML) and data science in general, performance often depends on appropriate **feature engineering**; that is, selecting or designing features that best represent the input. This approach has the advantage of incorporating known human expertise into the problem, making the learning task simple. For example, if the classification task consists of separating a small circle inside a big circle, the decision boundary is simply the distance from the origin. Constructing two new features by squaring each input dimension, most of the work has already been done for the network.

It is interesting to see whether NEAT can discover these features by itself without relying on human engineering. So, the raw inputs to each NEAT network will only be the

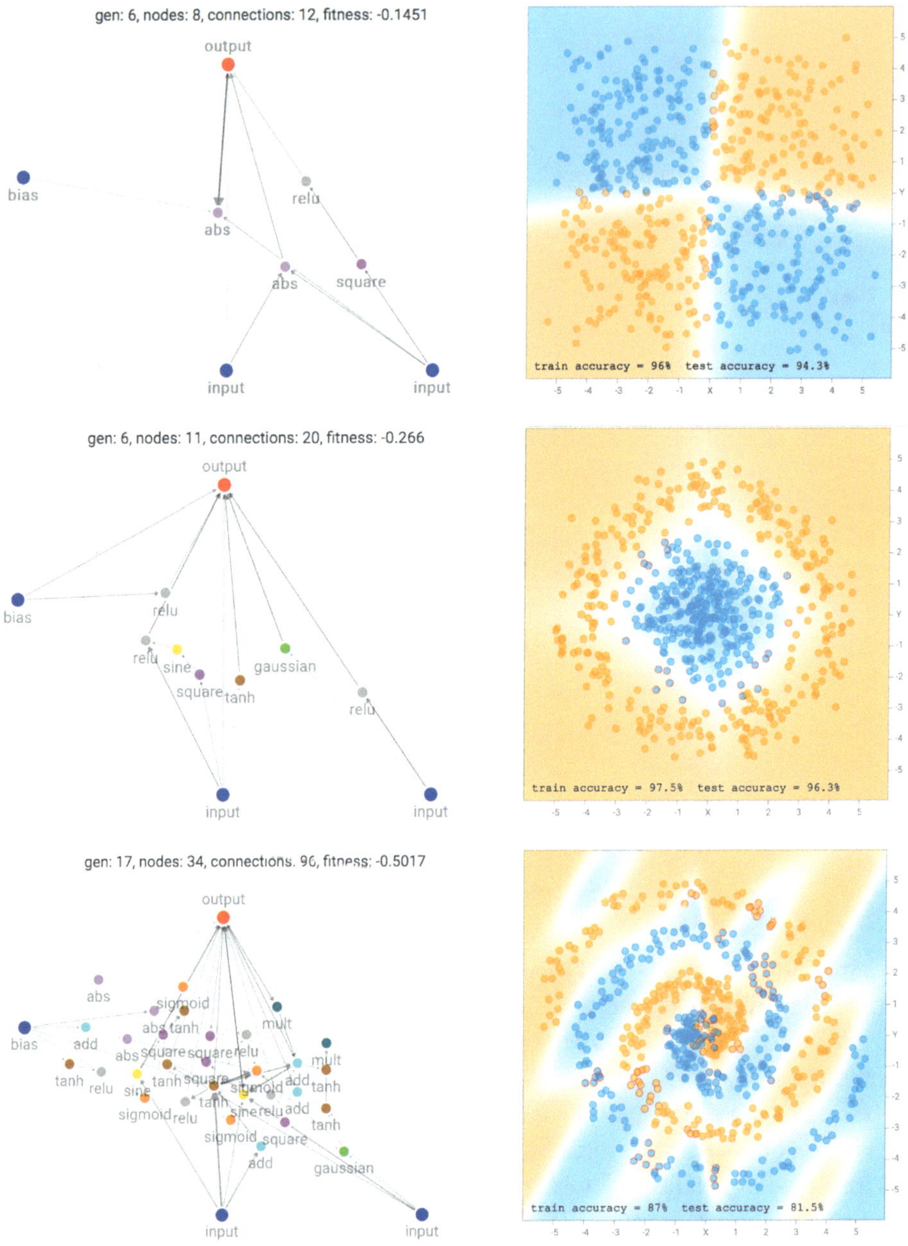

(*a*) Network architecture (*a*) Classification performance

Figure 10.3: **Evolved backprop NEAT networks for classifying data of varying complexity.** Networks (*a*) are shown together with their classification performance (*b*). With XOR (top row), the architecture relies on abs and ReLU that allow the forming of long lines with sharp corners. In contrast with concentric circles (middle row), the architecture takes advantage of sinusoidal, square, and Gaussian functions to establish features that work well in such radially (nearly) symmetric domains, making the machine learning task easier. With concentric spirals, it further utilizes a complex topology to approximate the complex decision boundary. In this manner, evolution discovers hyperparameters and structures that work well for the task, similar to (and possibly exceeding) the ability of human engineers to design them.

x- and y-coordinates, and the bias $b = 1$. Any further features, such as squaring those variables, multiplying them, or putting them through a sinusoidal gate, will have to be discovered by the algorithm. Indeed, it can select the appropriate activation functions and network structure around them to implement useful features. For example with the XOR dataset, networks utilized abs and rectified linear unit (ReLU) activation functions, which are useful in producing decision boundaries that are more or less straight lines with sharp corners (figure 10.3). With concentric circles, the final network often included many sinusoidal, square, and Gaussian activation functions, which makes sense given the radial symmetry of the dataset. With concentric spirals, which is almost symmetric but much more complex as well, the architectures utilized similar functions, but also a complex topology that allowed it to match the complex decision boundary.

An interesting further observation is that networks that backprop well will tend to be favored in the evolution process, compared to networks with gradients that are unstable. A network with blown-up weight values is likely to perform poorly in classification, resulting in a poor fitness score. More generally, given a set of backprop parameters, such as a small number of backprop iterations or a large learning rate, evolution produces different kinds of networks, presumably those that learn well under such conditions. On the other hand, if the parameters are not set right, backprop may not find good weight values even if they exist, thus discarding a powerful architecture. Analogously, a person with an extraordinarily high IQ may never reach their full potential if they live in a very harsh environment, or perhaps lack the people skills to influence their peers to accept their ideas. A solution in NAS is to make learning parameters evolvable as well. In that manner, good parameter values can be discovered together with architectures that work well with them. Such **meta-learning** approaches are discussed further in chapter 11.

10.2 NAS for Deep Learning

The backprop NEAT experiment described in section 10.1 introduced the concept of topology search for backpropagation neural networks. It illustrates the idea that even though gradient descent will optimize weights for a given neural network, it is also useful to optimize its hyperparameters and topology. This idea can be applied to modern deep learning as well. This section briefly outlines the history of NAS in deep learning, introduces the general approach, and reviews successes and challenges. Examples of prominent approaches and future directions are described in the sections that follow.

As deep learning rose in power and popularity, it became evident that simple, fully-connected neural networks were not sufficient for most applications. Historically, many powerful neural network building blocks have been discovered through a process of trial and error to address certain existing neural network limitations. For example, **convolutional neural networks** (CNNs) were created to minimize the number of connections required for computer vision problems. Over time, CNN architectures grew more sophisticated, including **AlexNet** (figure 10.4; Krizhevsky, Sutskever, and Hinton, 2012), the winner of the 2012 **ImageNet competition** (Russakovsky, Deng, Su, et al., 2015). This result drew a lot of attention and essentially got us out of the neural network winter and into the era of deep learning. AlexNet led to the development of many more complicated architectures,

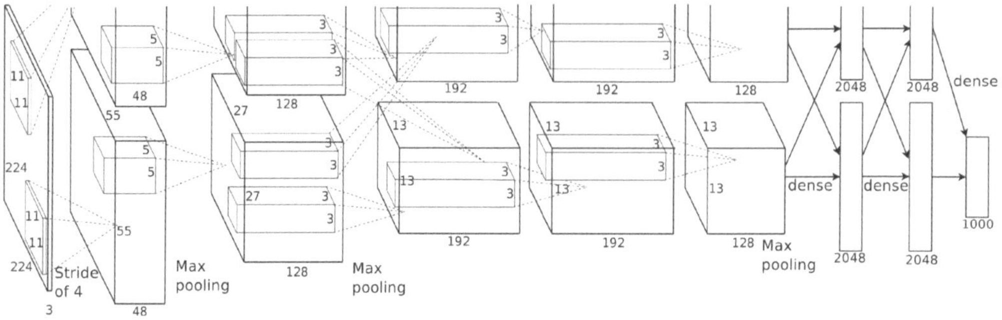

Figure 10.4: **The AlexNet deep learning architecture.** This architecture put deep learning into the spotlight when it won the ImageNet competition in 2012. There are careful engineering decisions that were involved in its design, including the principled organization into convolutional, pooling, and dense layers. More recent networks are often even more sophisticated and require a pipeline that spans network architecture and careful training schemes. Much manual labor is required in addition to the human insight to make them work, which suggests that automated methods of configuring them might help. Figure from Krizhevsky, Sutskever, and Hinton (2012).

such as **VGG** (Simonyan and Zisserman, 2015), **highway networks** (Srivastava, Greff, and Schmidhuber, 2015), **inception networks** (Szegedy, Vanhoucke, Ioffe, et al., 2016), and **residual networks** (ResNet; He, Zhang, Ren, et al., 2016), and more recently, **DenseNet**, **MobileNet**, **EfficientNet**, and **CoAtNet** (Dai, Liu, Le, et al., 2021; Huang, Liu, van der Maaten, et al., 2017; Sandler, Howard, Zhu, et al., 2018; Tan and Le, 2021). These architectures were designed to stack up many layers of neural networks effectively by taking advantage of repeated modules and skip connections between them.

Concurrently, for sequential tasks, people designed better **recurrent neural network** (RNN; section 2.3.3) architectures that outperformed simple fully-connected vanilla recurrent neural networks, such as **long short-term memory** (LSTM; section 2.3.4), **gated recurrent unit** (Chung, Gulcehre, Cho, et al., 2014), and others. Most recently, with the introduction of the self-attention-based **transformer architecture** (section 2.3.6), there have been a host of proposals that claim to offer better, incremental performance to the original transformer.

Much of this research was performed by graduate students who experimented with different architecture configurations, based on their hunches and instincts, who would try to experimentally discover new architectures that would offer some performance benefits compared to prior architectures. Some refer to this process as **graduate student descent** (GSD), a humorous take on the stochastic gradient descent (SGD) optimization process, hinting that the progress of ML research might be automated by machines (Huang, 2021).

One of the main obstacles to the automated approach was that most deep learning tasks typically take several days to train. However, with the advent of large GPU clusters, it became feasible in the mid-2010s. The NAS subfield gradually emerged and became quite popular in the late 2010s. A form of graduate student descent applied to the area of NAS itself, and today, there are thousands of papers on the subject (for reviews, see, e.g., Liu, Sun, Xue, et al., 2021; White, Safari, Sukthanker, et al., 2023), and even a popular, standardized benchmark for measuring the performance of NAS methods (Dong and Yang, 2020; Ying, Klein, Christiansen, et al., 2019; Zela, Siems, Zimmer, et al., 2022).

Info Box: Development of NAS inside Google Brain

In a way, the development of NAS was related to the career path that prompted me (David Ha) to become a researcher at Google Brain and to conduct much of my nature-inspired research ever since. In 2016, I published the backprop NEAT experiment (section 10.1) as a personal blog post, and it somehow caught the attention of Jeff Dean, who reached out to me to comment on the concept of separating topology search and weight optimization, and he had an interest to explore this idea deeper, potentially at Google scale. This conversation prompted me to apply and join Google Brain's residency program—in fact, Quoc Le (a co-author in the early NAS paper; Zoph and Le, 2017) was my first interviewer for the job! Quoc had a fantastic vision of developing a pipeline that could eventually automate much of the machine learning work at Google, which eventually became known as the AutoML project years later.

Quoc became my mentor and advisor, and we decided to explore two concepts: neural networks that generated weights (which became Hypernetworks (Ha, Dai, and Le, 2017), my first project there); and neural network architecture search (a project led by Barret Zoph, who is a brilliant engineer and quickly learned to navigate Google's enormous compute resources with a fitting name, Borg!). The NAS project sought to apply topology search—define a search space for neural network architectures, and by leveraging Google's large compute resources, identify the architectures within the search space that will perform well on benchmark deep learning tasks such as image recognition or language modeling. This project got me started on large machine learning models, a path I'm on still today.

At around 2016, there were two dominant paradigms in deep learning: **CNNs** for image processing and **RNNs** for sequence processing (or some combination of CNNs and RNNs for spatial-temporal applications such as video processing). The architecture design problem for CNNs and RNNs looked quite different. For CNNs, it involved identifying the best combination of convolutional filters, which are great priors for image processing due to the positional invariance property. Therefore, the task for designing, or automating the design of, CNN architectures required a search space that mainly focused on the edges (or the connections) of a graph. In contrast, sequential processing and sequence generation tasks relied on RNNs, which applied the same network architecture many times over, recurrently (hence the name). The essential element of the RNN is its memory node; that is, a fixed structure that is replicated and activated many times. The search space mainly focused on the architecture of this node; that is, its internal structure of cells, connections, activation functions, and specification of the state. In both cases, the problem was framed as a black-box optimization problem.

This automated search approach required enormous computational resources (Real, Moore, Selle, et al., 2017); while the sampling process of architectures (the outer loop) is efficient, the calculation of the reward signal, or fitness for each candidate architecture (the inner loop), required training a neural network on the actual task. Computer vision benchmarks at the time, such as CIFAR-10, often required training the neural network for weeks on a single GPU. As a solution, researchers started to use proxies for the fitness function. For instance, for image classification, they would train for only a limited number of steps on CIFAR-10, and make the assumption that whatever metric had been achieved after n steps will be a good metric to rank the models (Jiang, Ji, Zhu, et al., 2023; Miikkulainen, Liang, Meyerson, et al., 2023; Rawal and Miikkulainen, 2020). This is a good assumption since there is often a high correlation between the final performance and early-stage training performance of neural networks.

Also, the tasks and benchmarks used for NAS were often smaller in scale. For instance, CIFAR-10 or a low-resolution version of ImageNet was used for training image classification models, and the Penn Treebank dataset was used for training language models. The authors would then demonstrate that the resulting models transfer to larger-scale datasets, such as the full ImageNet or JFT-300M for images, and Wikipedia 100M or 1B benchmarks for text (Real, Aggarwal, Huang, et al., 2019; Zoph, Vasudevan, Shlens, et al., 2018). Further, the child models can share parameters, speeding up the search thousandfold (Pham, Guan, Zoph, et al., 2018). The architectures can also be scaled or stacked to have more capacity and thus achieve better performance (Real, Aggarwal, Huang, et al., 2019).

NAS did produce architectures that are useful in production, especially neural networks that achieve high performance at low computational cost for inference (in terms of inference speed and the number of parameters). Three examples are reviewed in section 10.3, on LSTM node design, general modular networks, and refinement of existing designs, all based on evolutionary optimization. Evolutionary NAS was also applied to the transformer architecture, to produce the **evolved transformer** (So, Le, and Liang, 2019), which also performs better on benchmark tasks while requiring fewer resources.

It is actually remarkable that there are many different approaches to NAS, and they all work well. It seems that you can apply almost any optimization technique—evolution, RL, Bayesian optimization, or gradient descent—and get improved results. Even just **random search** may perform well, achieving results within less than half a percent of more sophisticated NAS methods and close to state-of-the-art (SOTA) performance for both image classification and language modeling benchmarks (Li and Talwalkar, 2020; Real, Aggarwal, Huang, et al., 2019). This observation suggests that much of the performance is already baked into the hand-engineered building blocks of NAS, such as convolutional filters, self-attention layers, and RNN nodes; the research community has designed them by hand to achieve SOTA performance. In other words, the design of the search space may matter more than the choice of search algorithm itself.

NAS has proved useful as a way to fine-tune architectures, but it has not yet produced innovations that could automate the discovery of such truly fundamental concepts. That is probably why, despite these improved MobileNet, transformer, and RNN node architectures, people still often use the traditional MobileNet, the classical transformer, and the original LSTM in most networks in production. The performance gains have not yet been large enough and their implementations stable enough for the software and hardware vendors to converge on the improved variants. The NAS field continues to make progress, though, including successes outlined in the next few sections, and discoveries that extend to other fields, which may lead to such convergence in the future.

10.3 Case Studies: Improving Deep Learning State of the Art

This section reviews three NAS case studies that resulted in SOTA performance at the time. The first one, the design of **LSTM nodes**, improved the original design, which had stayed the same since the 1990s. It demonstrated that complexifying the design can add power, even though such designs are difficult for humans to discover. The second, **CoDeepNEAT**, generalizes ideas from general neuroevolution to the level of network architectures. In principle, it could discover new architectural principles that work better than the existing human-designed ones. It has not so far—the challenge is to identify the proper building blocks and then take advantage of structure. The third, **AmoebaNet**, utilizes structure, scaling, and regularization more explicitly by hand. It achieved SOTA on ImageNet in 2018, which was a remarkable achievement given that ImageNet was the main focus of the ML community at that time. It may be possible to use an AmoebaNet-like approach in the future to incorporate new ideas and improve performance again. Note that even a slight improvement is sometimes useful: For instance, in finance, healthcare, and engineering design, it translates to money, lives, and resources saved.

10.3.1 LSTM Designs

First, consider the design of better **LSTM nodes**. The original architecture (figure 10.5*a*) had been developed in the 1990s (Hochreiter and Schmidhuber, 1997), and despite many attempts to improve it by hand, it was deemed to be robust, general, and usually at least as good as the alternatives (Greff, Srivastava, Koutník, et al., 2016). We reviewed the LSTM architecture in section 2.3.4; in essence, an LSTM node is a neuron that can memorize a value in its internal memory cell indefinitely long. It contains circuitry for loading that value (**input gate**), reading it out (**output gate**), and erasing it (**forget gate**). A sequence processing network includes many such nodes, and their internal parameters (weights and activation functions) can be modified through backpropagation. Through such learning, each node determines when and how it can utilize its memory cell best as part of processing sequences.

Even though this original design is principled and makes sense, it turns out that it can be complexified significantly, leading to LSTM nodes that perform better. Its internal processing can be more complex, propagating through a nonlinear network with multiple paths. Its memory state can also be more complex, consisting of multiple memory cells. It can utilize a variety of different activation functions in its internal nodes and more general memory blocks. Such complexification is difficult for humans to develop, but NAS methods can do it.

The first such improvement was based on reinforcement learning (Zoph and Le, 2017). A recurrent network was used to generate the node designs, trained through the REINFORCE algorithm (Williams, 1992) to maximize the expected accuracy on a validation set. The resulting **NASCell** was significantly more complex than the original LSTM design (figure 10.5*b*). However, the exploration ability of such refinement search is somewhat limited and can be expanded through evolutionary methods.

In particular, **genetic programming** was used to search for trees representing the node structure, resulting in designs with multiple nonlinear paths and multiple memory cells

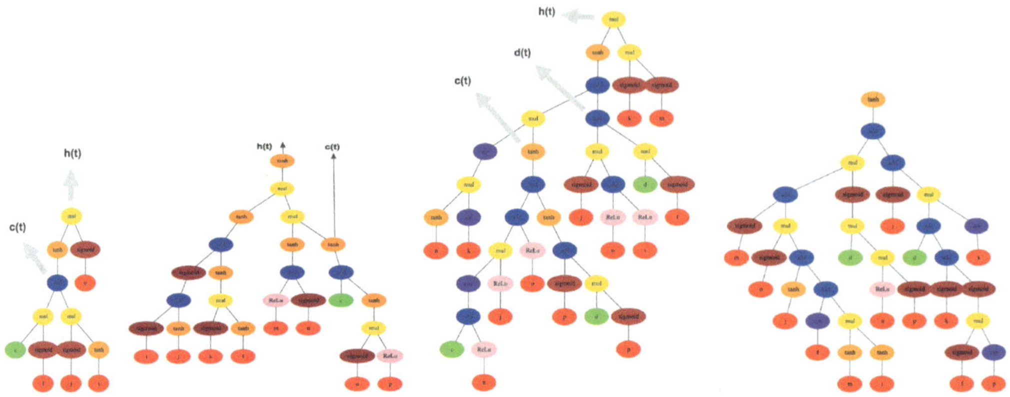

(*a*) Original LSTM (*b*) NASCell node (language modeling) (*c*) Evolved node (language modeling) (*d*) Evolved node (music modeling)

Figure 10.5: **NAS in LSTM node design.** At the lowest level, NAS can be used to design nodes in a recurrent neural network. In the node diagrams shown here, the $h(t)$ is the main output of the node, propagated to other nodes, and the $c(t)$ and $d(t)$ are outputs of the native memory cell, propagated internally. The green input elements denote the native memory cell outputs from the previous time step–that is, $c(t-1)$ or $d(t-1)$. The red input elements are formed after combining the node output from the previous time step–that is, $h(t-1)$ and the new input from the current time step $x(t)$. The other colors identify activation functions in computational cells: ReLU, sigmoid, tanh, sin, add, and multiply. In all solutions, the memory cell paths include relatively few nonlinearities. Unlike LSTM (a) and NASCell (b), the evolved nodes reuse inputs and utilize extra memory cells in different parts of the node; they also discovered LSTM-like output gating. The evolved nodes for language (c) and music modeling (d) are different, suggesting that evolution captures and utilizes the inherent structure in these domains to perform better. In this manner, neuroevolution was able to improve upon a human design that had stayed the same for decades and was considered optimal among many variants. Figures from Rawal and Miikkulainen (2020). For a video of this search process and an interactive demo, see `https://neuroevolutionbook.com/demos`.

(figure 10.5*c*; Rawal and Miikkulainen, 2020). In the language modeling domain (i.e., predicting the next word), this design was organized into two layers of 540 nodes each and evolved for 30 generations. Compared to networks of similar size, it improved 20 perplexity points over the original LSTM and 1.8 points over the NASCell, achieving SOTA performance of 62.2 at the time. Most interestingly, when the same approach was applied to the music modeling domain (i.e., predicting the next note), a different design emerged as the best (figure 10.5*d*). This result suggests that different domains have different structures; such structures can be learned by NAS and architectures customized to take advantage of them.

These results opened the door to optimizing combinations of different kinds of memory nodes, like those used in the neural Turing machine (section 12.3.5; Khadka, Chung, and Tumer, 2019), and other recurrent network elements (Ororbia, ElSaid, and Desell, 2019). As a result, the memory capacity of the model increased multifold—an improvement that likely would not have happened without such automated NAS methods.

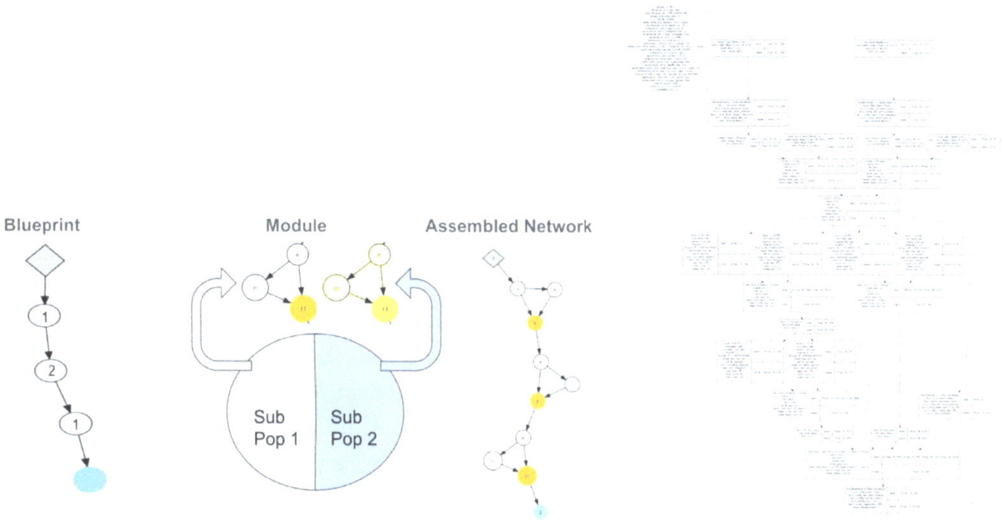

(*a*) CoDeepNEAT approach (*b*) Image captioning network

Figure 10.6: **Discovering general neural architectures through coevolution of modules and blueprints.** The CoDeepNEAT approach (Miikkulainen, Liang, Meyerson, et al., 2023) aims at discovering modular architectures in an open-ended search space. (*a*) Blueprints represent the high-level organization of the network, and modules fill in its details. The blueprint and module subpopulations are evolved simultaneously, based on how well the entire assembled network performs in the task. This principle was originally developed for evolving entire networks including the weights (Gomez and Miikkulainen, 1997; Moriarty and Miikkulainen, 1997), but it applies in neural architecture search for deep learning as well. (*b*) The overall structure of a network evolved for the image captioning task; the rectangles represent layers, with hyperparameters specified inside each rectangle. One module, consisting of two LSTM layers merged by a sum, is repeated three times in the middle of the network. The main advantage of CoDeepNEAT is that it can discover a wide range of network structures. They may take advantage of principles different from those engineered by humans, such as the multiple parallel paths brought together at the end in this network. Figures from Miikkulainen, Liang, Meyerson, et al. (2023). For a demo of CoDeepNEAT in the character recognition task, see `https://neuroevolutionbook.com/demos`.

10.3.2 CoDeepNEAT

As a second example, consider the **CoDeepNEAT** method (Liang, Meyerson, Hodjat, et al., 2019; Miikkulainen, Liang, Meyerson, et al., 2023) of discovering general network designs, which builds on several aspects of techniques developed earlier to evolve complete networks. In **symbiotic adaptive neuroevolution** (SANE), **enforced subpopulations** (ESP), and **CoSyNE** (section 7.1.1), partial solutions such as neurons and connections were evolved in separate subpopulations that were then combined into full solutions (i.e., complete neural networks), with the global structure specified in terms of a network blueprint that was also evolved (Gomez and Miikkulainen, 1997; Gomez, Schmidhuber, and Miikkulainen, 2008; Moriarty and Miikkulainen, 1997). Similarly, CoDeepNEAT co-evolves multiple populations of modules and a population of blueprints that specify which modules are used and how they are connected to form a full network (figure 10.6*a*). Modules are randomly selected from the specified module population to fill in locations in the blueprint. Each blueprint is instantiated in this way many times, evaluating how well the design performs with the current set of blueprints. Each module participates in instantiations of many blueprints (and inherits the fitness of the entire instantiation each time), thus evaluating how well the module works in general with other modules. The main idea of CoDeepNEAT is thus to take advantage of (and scale up with) modular structure, similarly to many deep learning designs such as the inception network and the residual network (He, Zhang, Ren, et al., 2016; Szegedy, Vanhoucke, Ioffe, et al., 2016).

The modules and the blueprints are evolved using **NEAT** (section 3.3), which again was initially designed to evolve complete networks and adapted in CoDeepNEAT to evolving network structure. NEAT starts with a population of simple structures connecting inputs straight to outputs, and gradually adding more modules in the middle, as well as parallel and recurrent pathways between them. It thus prefers simple solutions, but complexifies the module and blueprint structures over time as necessary. It can, in principle, design rather complex and general network topologies. However, while NEAT can be used to create entire architectures directly, in CoDeepNEAT, it is embedded into the general framework of the module and blueprint evolution; it is thus possible to scale up through repetition that would not arise from NEAT naturally.

The power of CoDeepNEAT was originally demonstrated in the task of image captioning, a domain where a competition had been run for several years on a known dataset (Miikkulainen, Liang, Meyerson, et al., 2023). The best human design at that point, the **Show&Tell network** (Vinyals, Toshev, Bengio, et al., 2015), was used to define the search space; that is, CoDeepNEAT was set to find good architectures using the same elements as in the Show&Tell network. Remarkably, CoDeepNEAT was able to improve the performance by another 15%, thus demonstrating the power of neural architecture search over the best human solutions (Miikkulainen, Liang, Meyerson, et al., 2023). Similar CoDeepNEAT evolution from a generic starting point was later used to achieve SOTA in text classification (Wikidetox; Liang, Meyerson, Hodjat, et al., 2019) and image classification (specifically chest X-rays; Liang, Meyerson, Hodjat, et al., 2019). Indeed, these successes demonstrated that with minimal computational cost, neural architecture search can achieve performance that exceeds that of standard architectures, making it possible to deploy deep learning quickly and effectively to new domains.

Most importantly, the best networks utilized a principle that is different from human-designed networks: They included multiple parallel paths, possibly encoding different hypotheses brought together in the end (figure 10.6*b*). In this manner, the large search space utilized by CoDeepNEAT may make it possible to discover new principles of good performance.

Such discovery is indeed the main power of CoDeepNEAT, and what it was initially designed to do. At the time, papers were coming out, outdoing each other by proposing a different architecture. The space of good architectures seemed large and ripe for discovery. Soon after, however, the transformers and diffusion architectures were developed and became dominant. While there is still plenty of opportunity to optimize variants of them using neuroevolution, a major question for the future is whether open-ended search methods such as CoDeepNEAT can be developed further to discover new principles that might follow them.

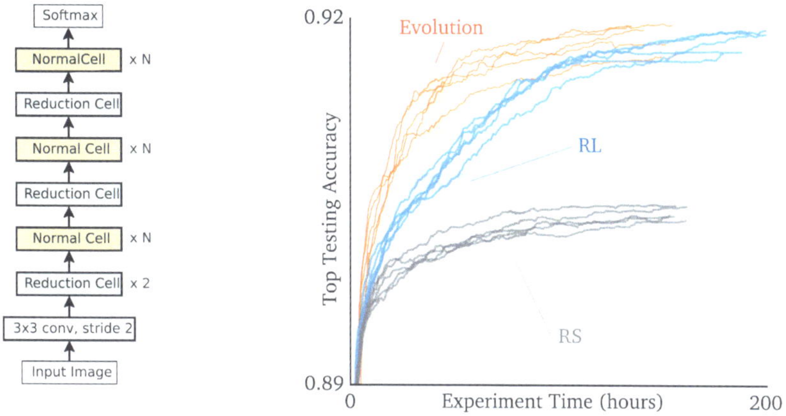

(a) AmoebaNet approach (a) Comparison in ImageNet

Figure 10.7: **Evolutionary discovery in the NASNet search space compared to RL and random search.** In contrast with the open-ended search in CoDeepNEAT, the AmoebaNet method (Real, Aggarwal, Huang, et al., 2019) performs a more focused search. (a) It evolves a stacked architecture of inception-like normal and reduction modules (cells); these networks are then scaled to larger sizes algorithmically. AmoebaNet also promotes regularization by removing the oldest individuals in the population. (b) As a result, it discovers architectures that are more accurate than those discovered through random search and RL, reaching state-of-the-art accuracy in standard benchmarks like ImageNet. Figures from Real, Aggarwal, Huang, et al. (2019).

10.3.3 AmoebaNet

Even small improvements to performance are sometimes useful. If you are designing a network to predict financial data, half a percent can translate to millions. If it is to predict the effects of treatments, it can save lives. Thus, NAS applied to the refinement of existing ideas can play an important role. Perhaps the best example of such work is the **AmoebaNet system** (Real, Aggarwal, Huang, et al., 2019). At its time, it improved the SOTA in the ImageNet domain, which had been the focus of deep learning research for several years. Human experts have designed many architectures and ideas for it; AmoebaNet exceeded the performance of all of them by utilizing evolutionary neural architecture search in a manner that mattered in practice.

Three innovations made this result possible. First, search was limited to a **NASNet search space** (Zoph, Vasudevan, Shlens, et al., 2018); that is, networks with a fixed outer structure consisting of a stack of inception-like modules (figure 10.7a). There were two different module architectures, normal and reduction; they alternate in the stack and are connected directly and through skip connections. The architecture of the modules is evolved, and consists of five levels of convolution and pooling operations. The idea is that NASNet represents a space of powerful image classifiers that can be searched efficiently. Second, a mechanism was devised that allowed for scaling the architectures to much larger numbers of parameters, by scaling the size of the stack and the number of filters in the convolution operators. The idea is to discover good modules first and then increase performance by scaling up. Third, the evolutionary process was modified to favor younger genotypes by removing those individuals that were evaluated the earliest from the population at each tournament selection. The idea is to allow evolution to explore more instead of focusing on a small number of genotypes early on. These ideas are generally useful in evolutionary machine learning, not just as part of the AmoebaNet system.

Indeed, AmoebaNet's accuracy was the SOTA in the ImageNet benchmark at the time. Experiments also demonstrated that evolutionary search in NASNet was more powerful than reinforcement learning and random search in CIFAR-10, resulting in faster learning, more accurate final architectures, and ones with lower computational cost (figure 10.7*b*). It also demonstrated the value of focusing the search space intelligently so that good solutions are in that space, and yet it is not too large to find them.

Thus, LSTMs, CoDeepNEAT, and AmoebaNet demonstrated the potential of evolutionary NAS in discovering new principles and making practical optimizations to existing ones. A challenge for the future is to take them to transformers, diffusion networks, and beyond. In the meantime, however, such approaches are useful in two important areas: optimizing architectures for specific hardware constraints; and discovering architectures that can perform well with little data by utilizing other tasks and datasets. These opportunities will be discussed in the next section.

10.4 Multiobjective and Multitask NAS

In the NAS discussion so far, improved SOTA performance in the task has been the main (indeed the only) objective. Indeed, as mentioned above, in certain domains the cost of putting together a large dataset and spending a lot of compute to achieve even small improvements can be worth it. Benchmarks are also a good motivation for research: It is fun to compete with other researchers to achieve better performance in them, and thus gain prestige and recognition.

However, when new technologies are taken into the real world, a number of new, practical challenges emerge. In particular, expertise to build good models may not be available; the possibility of adversarial attacks may need to be taken into account; The models may run on the edge, with limited compute and other hardware restrictions; the data may not be sufficient in quality and quantity to train good models. Neural architecture search, as well as meta-learning in general, can be used to cope with each of these challenges.

First, designing good models for new learning tasks still relies on scarce expertise. The available simulators, such as TensorFlow, PyTorch, and Keras provide standard models as starting points, and in many cases, they work well. However, the number of datasets and problems where they can potentially be used is also very large, and applications could often benefit even from small optimizations. Searching for appropriate architectures is not the only optimization; other meta-learning dimensions such as **activation functions**, **loss functions**, and **data augmentation** are useful as well, as is optimization of general learning parameters (these approaches will be reviewed in chapter 11). The term **AutoML** has been coined to refer to such processes in general: The user provides a dataset and a starting point for learning, and the learning system configures itself automatically to achieve better results (He, Zhao, and Chu, 2021; Liang, Meyerson, Hodjat, et al., 2019). The goal is not necessarily to achieve SOTA in any particular domain, but rather to reduce the human time and expertise needed to build successful applications. In this manner, deep learning can have a larger impact in the real world.

Second, **adversarial robustness** is a crucial consideration outside of controlled benchmark environments. In the real world, models are often exposed to carefully crafted inputs–known as adversarial examples–that can lead to critical misclassifications. Traditional defenses, such as **adversarial training**, are often limited in generalizability and computationally expensive. A promising alternative is to frame NAS as an optimization problem, where both standard accuracy and robustness to adversarial attacks are optimized simultaneously. For example, **robust architecture search** (RAS; Kotyan and Vasconcellos Vargas, 2020) extends NAS by explicitly incorporating adversarial accuracy into the fitness function. The resulting architectures, discovered without adversarial training, display structural patterns—such as high-dimensional projections and diverse computational pathways—that contribute to their inherent robustness. This approach echoes insights from manually designed models: for instance, WideResNet has been the SOTA for CIFAR-10 adversarial robustness since 2020, in part due to its architectural width and capacity for feature diversity. RAS demonstrates that similar or even novel robust features can be discovered automatically through neuroevolution.

Third, many applications cannot be deployed to run on data centers with dedicated top-of-the-line hardware, but they need to run on commodity compute, or even on highly constrained **compute in the edge**: vehicles, drones, and probes in extreme environments, as well as watches, appliances, clothing, and other items. Only a fraction of the model sizes used in research may be available in such applications, and there may be limitations on memory structure, communication, latency, and other characteristics. NAS can play a significant role in optimizing the models to perform as well as possible under such conditions.

In some cases, the constraints must be met entirely, or the solutions are unviable. As usual in evolutionary computation, such constraints can be implemented as penalty functions, thus allowing evolution to explore more broadly but eventually converge to solutions that satisfy the constraints. It may also be possible to modify the solutions algorithmically to make them comply; evolution will then find a way to optimize the solutions under such postprocessing.

In other cases, the constraints incur a cost that needs to be minimized. NAS for such applications is multiobjective, aiming at identifying good trade-offs between performance and cost outcomes. For instance, CoDeepNEAT can be extended with **multiobjective optimization** to form **Pareto fronts** of accuracy and network size (Liang, Meyerson, Hodjat, et al., 2019). In the domain of classifying X-ray images, a variety of trade-offs were discovered, but there was also a sweet spot in the front: an architecture that was 1/12th of the size of the best-performing network while only giving up 0.38% in accuracy (figure 10.8). In a similar manner, other objectives could be included, such as training time, the amount of training data needed, or energy consumption. Multiobjective NAS can thus make many more deep learning applications feasible in the real world.

In the most extreme case along these lines, NAS can be used to optimize designs for **neuromorphic hardware**. To minimize energy consumption, many such architectures are based on **spiking neurons**, are small in size, and limited in connectivity. Standard

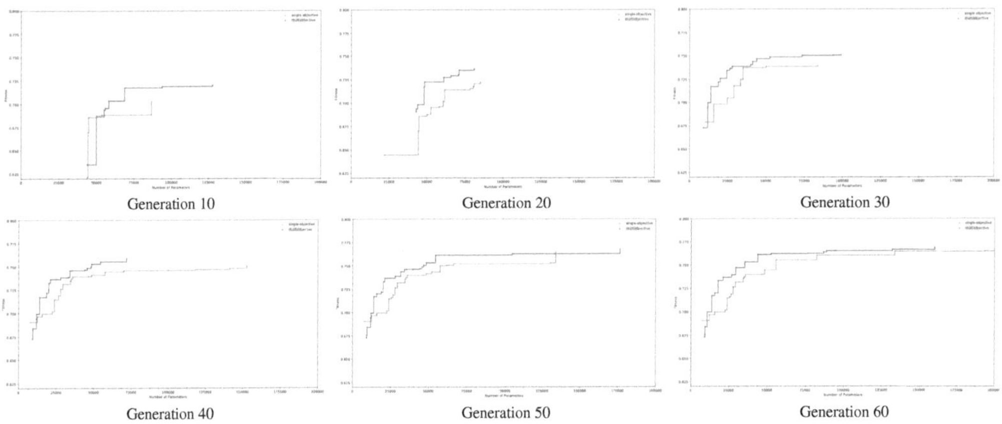

Figure 10.8: **Simultaneous optimization of network size and performance.** The number of parameters in the network is in the x-axis, and the accuracy in classifying X-ray images to 14 diseases is in the y-axis. The curves show the Pareto fronts obtained in a single-objective evolution (of accuracy; green) and multiobjective evolution (of accuracy and number of parameters; blue). Both populations include a range of trade-offs, but the multiobjective evolution discovers consistently better ones, including one at the elbow that is 1/12th of the size and only 0.38% less accurate than the top accuracy. In this manner, NAS can discover architectures that not only perform well but also adhere to cost constraints, making more applications possible in the real world. Figures from Liang, Meyerson, Hodjat, et al. (2019). For a video of this process, see `https://neuroevolutionbook.com/demos`.

deep learning architectures are not well-suited for them, and there are many opportunities to discover creative, new designs. A most interesting and potentially fundamental way is to co-evolve the hardware design with the neural network design simultaneously. In this manner, it may be possible to discover powerful solutions that are highly specialized and customized to individual use cases. These opportunities will be discussed in more detail in section 11.5.

The fourth real-world challenge is **insufficient data**. Indeed, data is now collected everywhere from small businesses, doctors' offices, and engineering firms to large-scale transportation, weather, business, and education systems. Unfortunately, such data is often siloed and not aggregated, and often also proprietary and intentionally kept in-house. Even though the data could in principle be used to solve many prediction and optimization problems, there is not enough of it to take advantage of modern machine learning. Such models would simply learn to memorize and overfit, and not perform well with future data.

Interestingly, in many such domains, it may be possible to build better models by utilizing other datasets (Caruana, 1997; Meyerson and Miikkulainen, 2019). When a model is trained to perform multiple tasks simultaneously, represented by different datasets, it learns to encode each task based on synergies and commonalities between them. Such common knowledge in turn establishes biases that make it possible to generalize better, even when the training data within each task alone would be insufficient.

An important role for NAS is to discover architectures that take the best advantage of such synergies between tasks. Many designs are possible (figure 10.9): If the tasks are well aligned, a single processing path with a different head for each task may be the best

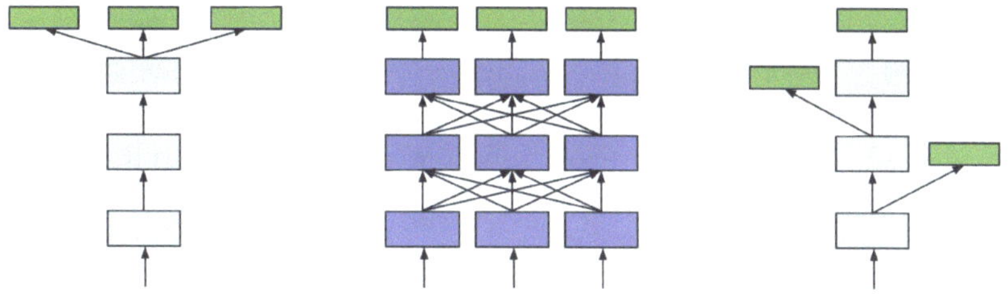

(*a*) Multiple heads (*b*) Flexible modules (*c*) Customized topology

Figure 10.9: **Alternative approaches to multitask learning**. When multiple tasks are learned simultaneously, the network may discover and utilize general principles underlying them, and perform better than when trained with each task alone. (*a*) If the tasks are similar, a single column with a different head for each task may work well. (*b*) A more flexible architecture may consist of a number of modules at each level, and each task uses them differently. (*c*) In the most general case, a customized topology may be used to support a number of different tasks. It is difficult to decide which architecture works well; evolutionary NAS can be used to find optimal ways to do it. Figures from Meyerson and Miikkulainen (2018a).

way to integrate them. Alternatively, many parallel paths can be constructed, and different tasks will utilize them differently. If the tasks are sufficiently different, a complex topology with different tasks performed at different levels based on customized topologies may be needed. It is difficult to tell ahead of time which architectures work well; evolutionary NAS is a good way to optimize them.

To motivate an approach, first consider training a simple network to support multiple tasks. The network consists of a few tightly connected layers and has a number of decoder layers on top, one for each task. The tasks can be real (i.e., be based on different datasets), or they can be **pseudotasks**, constructed artificially by assigning a different set of labels to the same training examples (Meyerson and Miikkulainen, 2018b). Gradient descent can then be used to train this architecture.

In the next step, the architecture consists of multiple levels of several such modules. All modules are included at all levels, but the network learns to utilize them differently, at different levels for different tasks. Through gradient descent, they learn functional primitives that are useful in several tasks (Meyerson and Miikkulainen, 2018a).

This is where neuroevolution comes in. It is possible to use evolution to discover an optimal topology of these modules for each task. That is, each task has a different organization of modules into a network topology, but the modules all come from the same set, trained together via gradient descent in all tasks. In this manner, the modules still learn to encode functional primitives; evolution figures out how to use these primitives optimally in each task.

The final step, then, is to use CoDeepNEAT to evolve the structure of the modules themselves (in the **coevolution of modules and task routing** (CMTR) method; Liang, Meyerson, and Miikkulainen, 2018). In this manner, (1) high-level evolution customizes the topology for each task; (2) low-level evolution optimizes the structure of the modules so they can extract common knowledge most effectively; and (3) gradient descent extracts that common knowledge across tasks and encodes it into the modules. This approach was demonstrated in the Omniglot domain, recognizing handwritten characters in multiple different alphabets (Lake, Salakhutdinov, and Tenenbaum, 2015; Liang, Meyerson, and Miikkulainen, 2018). While the alphabets are quite different, they are still related in that each consists of shapes and combinations of lines in a limited area. While there are only 20 examples of each character, there are 50 different alphabets, and therefore multitask learning is an effective way to combine knowledge from all alphabets to learn each one well. Moreover, evolutionary optimization makes it possible to learn and utilize common knowledge well, as well as to specialize: The CMTR approach improved the SOTA by 30% in this domain.

It is interesting to see the solutions that CMTR created (figure 10.10). In general, the more complex the alphabet, the more complex the topology. One example is Angelic, a synthetic alphabet designed in the 1500s to communicate with angels. It is more decorative and unique than most, and the network constructed for it is complex. Also, alphabets that look similar have similar networks. For instance, Hebrew and N'ko both have dominant horizontal lines, and their network topologies are similar; Latin and Cyrillic are similar as well. Interestingly, when evolution is run multiple times, consistent topologies emerge for the same language each time, suggesting that they indeed capture essential representations for each task. It would be difficult to come up with such representations by hand, but evolutionary NAS does it reliably.

Multitask learning has been demonstrated to work well even when the tasks are very different. For instance, language learning, vision, and genomic structure prediction can all be mutually informative, even though they represent very different domains in the world. A method for aligning the parameters across such differences is needed, but with such a method, it seems possible to support many disparate domains with many others (Meyerson and Miikkulainen, 2019).

Apparently, the world is based on a set of fundamental principles and structures that repeat across domains, perhaps as low-dimensional manifolds embedded in high-dimensional spaces. Thus, learning to understand part of the world helps in understanding other parts. It may be possible to take advantage of this observation to evolve **supernetworks**, consisting of modules that can be reused in different configurations, in order to learn new tasks (section 10.5). More generally, it may be possible to construct a central facility that learns and represents these regularities as variable embeddings, and different tasks are then established by learning specialized encoders and decoders of this knowledge, as in the **traveling observer model** (TOM; Meyerson and Miikkulainen, 2021). This approach can be instantiated through multitask learning and evolution. It may also be possible to utilize large language models (LLMs) as the central facility, and then use evolution to discover the customized encoders and decoders. While such architectures do not yet exist, the approaches that have been reviewed in this section are a possible starting point for constructing them. This is one approach that might, in the long term, lead to agents with general intelligence.

10.5 Making NAS Practical

Even in settings where NAS can make useful discoveries, the approaches are still limited by available computation. Efficient implementations can make a big difference, leading

Figure 10.10: **Network topologies discovered for different handwritten alphabets.** Each network is trained to recognize handwritten characters of one alphabet. However, each topology is constructed from the same set of neural network modules (indicated by color), and thus such training results in modules that encode the underlying functional primitives of many tasks. More complex alphabets receive more complex topologies, and similar alphabets receive similar topologies. The resulting topologies are consistent across several runs of evolution and training, suggesting that they indeed capture underlying principles. Even though the training data is limited for each task, the primitives make it possible to learn each task well—and better than if the networks were trained from scratch with their own data only. Thus, NAS can be used to tie together the learning of multiple tasks so that learning with otherwise insufficient data is possible, making it possible to extend machine learning to more real-world tasks. For a video of this evolutionary process, an interactive character recognition demo, and other demos on multitask evolution, see `https://neuroevolutionbook.com/demos`.

to better solutions. The approaches involve evaluating a large number of neural network designs, which is very expensive. Training a deep learning network can take several days, and a search for good designs may need to evaluate millions of candidates. If the search simply runs as an outer loop, it will be limited to a few hundred or thousand candidates.

Several principled efficiency optimizations are possible. One important one is to utilize **surrogate models**. Instead of modeling how the world will respond to a solution, as was done in section 6.4.2, they model the solutions directly; that is, how well each solution is going to perform in the task. This approach is useful in meta-learning in general: In its most general form, it powers bilevel evolution, which is an approach where an outer-loop evolution optimizes the parameters of an inner loop evolutionary process (section 11.2). It can be instantiated to speed up search in all aspects of meta-learning, including that of activation functions (section 11.3.2).

Surrogate models are usually trained with a sample of solutions. For instance, in NAS, a set of different architectures is created and evaluated ahead of time, with the model trained to map architecture descriptions to performance, and then used to predict the performance of new solutions. Several such benchmark collections have already been created, and they can serve as a catalyst for studying NAS methods in general (Dong and Yang, 2020; Ying, Klein, Christiansen, et al., 2019; Zela, Siems, Zimmer, et al., 2022).

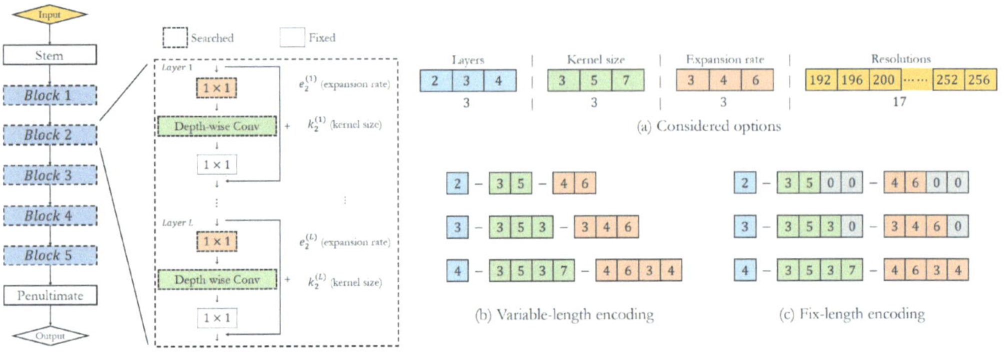

Figure 10.11: **The MSuNAS approach for evolving convolutional networks.** The idea is to make search practical by limiting the search space and by guiding the search. The search space consists of five computational blocks, and it is parameterized through the number of layers, kernel size, channels (that expand through the layers), and input resolution. (*a*) The parameters are selected from a prespecified set and can be coded either as variable (*b*) or fixed (*c*) length individuals. A supernet is created with the largest values and subsumes the entire search space. Good trade-offs between performance and other objectives are then found in this space using the NSGA-II multiobjective search method. A surrogate model, trained with a sample of architectures in this space, is used to guide the search, and the trained supernet to initialize the weights of the candidates. The approach can find architectures that perform better than or similar to standard architectures and are smaller, with significantly less training. Figure from Lu, Deb, Goodman, et al. (2020).

Another way of making NAS practical is to limit the search space. The **AmoebaNet method** (section 10.3.2) already took advantage of it by optimizing the variations of a repetitive structure. In a more extreme approach, a **supernet** is first created–a large network that consists of the entire search space, including all possible layers, their variations, and connections between them (Cha, Kim, Lee, et al., 2023; Chebykin, Alderliesten, and Bosman, 2022; Fernando, Banarse, Blundell, et al., 2017). The supernet is then trained in the task (at least partially). It then serves as a starting point for creating candidates during search, providing the search space and initial evaluations. This approach makes sense if the goal is not just to find the best-performing network (for which the supernet itself might be the best choice), but at the same time achieve other objectives, like minimizing the size of the solutions.

Several of these ideas were implemented in the **MSuNAS** approach, where the non-dominated sorting genetic algorithm II (NSGA-II) method was adapted to NAS of convolutional networks (Figure 10.11; Lu, Deb, Goodman, et al., 2020). The search space was restricted to networks with five computational blocks with four design parameters: the number of layers, the number of channels, the kernel size, and the input resolution, each with a predetermined range. A **supernet** was created by setting each of these parameters at their maximum values; thus all other candidates in the search space were enclosed in it. A **surrogate model** was trained with 2,000 randomly sampled networks in this space. Each network was trained for 150 epochs on CIFAR-10, CIFAR-100, and ImageNet, and evaluated with 5,000 unseen images. The supernet was trained in this task as well, and its weights were used to initialize the candidates during search.

The approach found solutions that represented useful trade-offs in this domain. The most accurate architectures performed as well or better than standard architectures, and many of them were much smaller as well. The surrogate modeling approach resulted in learning that was several orders of magnitude faster. These results suggest that NAS can be a practical and useful technique in searching for variations in a limited search space.

Sometimes such methods are called **one-shot methods**, because the supernet is trained to represent the entire search space. The more general approach consists of black-box, or zeroth-order, methods, where the search space is open-ended (such as CoDeepNEAT, described in section 10.3.2). Such methods have more potential for discovery, but it is more difficult to make them efficient and therefore take advantage of them.

Intermediate approaches may provide a good trade-off. For instance, it is possible to limit NAS to traditional convolutional neural networks (CNNs) only; that is, those with a number of convolutional and pooling layers followed by a number of fully connected layers (as opposed to very deep networks with many skip connections, such as ResNet or DenseNet). Such a limited search space allows for customizing many aspects of the NAS process, making it efficient.

In one such approach, **EvoCNN** (Sun, Xue, Zhang, et al., 2020), it was possible to design a variable-length representation for the architecture that allows networks of variable sizes to be represented systematically and compactly. The population could then be initialized as a random sample of such architectures, instead of minimal networks, providing a more comprehensive search process. On the other hand, the number of parameters was used as a fitness component during evolution, favoring smaller networks, thus making sure that the complexity that was there actually mattered. Weight initialization was also included as part of the representation as mean and standard deviation values for sets of connections. As is well known in deep learning (and discussed in more detail next), good initialization makes it more likely that the architecture performs as well as it can, resulting in more consistent and fair evaluations. Genetic operators were then designed to operate efficiently on such architectures. With these customizations, EvoCNN performed better than other hand-designed traditional CNN architectures. Also interestingly, the evolved initialization performed better than standard initialization methods, such as Xavier (Glorot and Bengio, 2010).

Part of why fully general (zeroth-order) methods are challenging to design is because it is difficult to implement even basic evolutionary search (i.e., crossover). The architectures are usually represented as graphs, and they suffer from the **competing conventions problem** (or permutation problem), which we already encountered in section 3.3.1: The same functional design can be coded in several different ways simply by changing the order of elements in it. The permutation problem makes naive crossover ineffective, which is why most black-box methods rely only on mutation.

As a matter of fact, the same issue exists in many other areas of evolutionary computation, to the extent that the entire validity and usefulness of **crossover** is sometimes called into question (Qiu and Miikkulainen, 2023). Yet, biology utilizes crossover very effectively, creating solutions that are viable and creative (section 9.1.1). This observation suggests that perhaps we do not understand crossover very well, and our implementations of it are lacking something.

Interestingly, NAS can be used as a domain to gain insight into the general problem of what makes crossover useful (Qiu and Miikkulainen, 2023). Two architecture representations can be compared through **graph edit distance**, measuring how many modifications are necessary to transform one into the other. This metric can then be used to construct a crossover operator that results in individuals that lie along the **shortest edit path** (SEP) between them. It turns out that theoretically the expected improvement from the SEP crossover is greater than the improvement from local search (i.e., mutation), from standard crossover, and from reinforcement learning. These theoretical conclusions can be demonstrated numerically, as well as in practical evaluation in various NAS benchmarks: They converge to optimal architectures faster than other methods, even with noisy evaluations.

Thus, crossover can be a useful tool in NAS if implemented in the right way. More generally, if evolutionary computation is not using crossover, it is probably leaving money on the table.

Several other useful tools were initially developed with NAS in mind, but have proved valuable in neuroevolution, evolutionary computation, and neural networks more broadly. An important one is to **initialize** the networks in a proper way before training (Bingham and Miikkulainen, 2023a). In deep learning, a fundamental challenge is that the signals (activation and gradients) may vanish or explode. If the network weights are initialized so that the activation stays within reasonable bounds, training is more likely to be successful. In NAS, this means that the evaluation of the candidate is more reliable, making the search more effective. The initialization can be done in various ways and customized to specific activation functions, topologies, layers, and even data. However, there is a general principle that works well in most cases: setting the weights of each layer so the outputs have zero mean and unit variance.

In a method called **AutoInit**, such weight initialization was derived for the most common layer types (Bingham and Miikkulainen, 2023a). Experimentally, AutoInit resulted in faster and more reliable convergence for convolutional, residual, and transformer architectures, various hyperparameter settings, model depths, data modalities, and input sizes. It was also shown to be particularly useful in meta-learning of activation functions, as well as in NAS. When implemented in CoDeepNEAT, it adapted to each candidate's unique topology and hyperparameters, improving its performance in several benchmark tasks. As expected, much of this improvement was due to reduced variance in evaluations. However, AutoInit also allowed utilizing a broader set of hyperparameter values and topologies. Some such solutions are difficult to train properly and perform well only with proper initialization. Thus, intelligent initialization makes it possible for NAS to find more creative solutions as well.

Ultimately, NAS methods need to run on parallel hardware and utilize such computation well. Like all evolutionary algorithms, NAS is well suited for such hardware because candidate evaluations can be performed at different compute nodes. However, evaluation times can sometimes be very long and vary significantly. It is therefore important that such evaluations are asynchronous: The nodes should not sit idle waiting for other candidates in a generation to finish their evaluations but should take on other evaluations immediately (Liang, Shahrzad, and Miikkulainen, 2023).

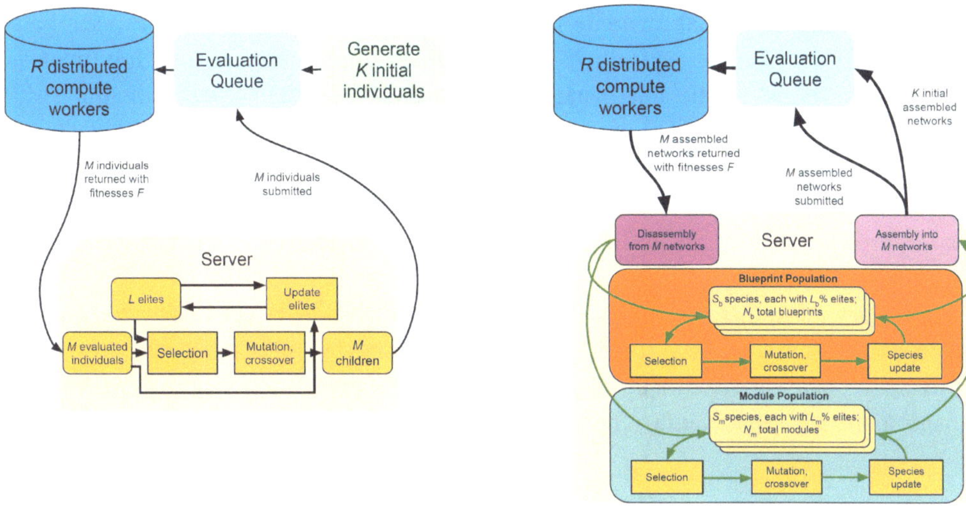

(*a*) Evolving individual encodings

(*b*) Coevolving hierarchical encodings

Figure 10.12: **Asynchronous evaluation of individual and coevolutionary encodings.** One challenge in parallelizing the evaluation of neuroevolution candidates is that the evaluation times may vary. Therefore, instead of evaluating an entire generation of candidates synchronously before generating new ones, candidates are placed in a queue and evaluated as soon as compute nodes become available. In this manner, compute nodes are never idle and evaluation can be sped up significantly. (*a*) With encodings that represent the entire solution, the population and elites are maintained as usual, and evolution progresses in batches of M individuals. (*b*) With coevolutionary encodings such as CoDeepNEAT, the individuals are created and fitness is distributed among participating blueprint and module populations. The process favors individuals with short evaluation times, which means that M needs to be larger when those times vary a lot. However, the speedup is also larger than, for instance, 14-fold for CoDeepNEAT. The bias toward networks that evaluate fast is also beneficial in NAS, resulting in more desirable solutions as a surprising side benefit. Figures from Liang, Shahrzad, and Miikkulainen (2023).

Asynchronous evaluation, therefore, is based on an evaluation queue rather than generations (figure 10.12). Individuals are created and evaluated, and the elite set is updated continuously. While several such implementations exist already, including a **real-time evolution** extension of NEAT (**rtNEAT**) discussed in section 8.1, the approach is more complex with more sophisticated NAS methods that take advantage of structure. For instance with CoDeepNEAT, individuals exist at the level of modules and blueprints, and both populations are speciated into subpopulations with their own elites. Thus, there are several evolutionary processes going on at the same time. When an assembled network is evaluated, the resulting fitnesses are incorporated into these processes asynchronously.

Note that although there are no generations, the evolutionary processes still need to progress in batches. That is, M individuals need to be evaluated and their fitnesses propagated to the current populations before another M can be generated—even though the individuals may have different ancestries and, in a sense, belong to different generations. As usual in evolution, the batch size M needs to be optimized for each problem, balancing the time used for evaluation and for search (i.e., how much evaluation noise can be tolerated). However, with variable evaluation times, batch evaluations establish a search bias: Those candidates that evaluate faster are more likely to be included in the batch and thus are more likely to reproduce. Thus, in domains where the evaluation times are relatively uniform, M can be small, and search proceeds faster. However, if the times vary significantly, M needs to be larger, so evolution is based on more diverse candidates.

In NAS, such a bias is fortunately not a problem. The speedup from asynchrony increases more with variable evaluation times than the handicap from diversity. For instance, in designing sorting networks, where the times are relatively similar, asynchronous search finds solutions twice as fast as synchronous search does. In CoDeepNEAT, where the times vary a lot, the speedup is 14-fold. Moreover, a bias toward faster networks is desirable in any case. Even if it is not an explicit secondary objective, smaller networks that evaluate faster are preferred over complex networks. In this sense, asynchronous evaluation provides an advantage not only in speed, but in the quality of solutions as well.

10.6 Beyond Neural Architecture Search

While NAS is still a work in progress, already many interesting and useful ideas have stemmed from the field—ideas that have impacted other subfields of AI. As was discussed in section 10.2, one of the main limiting factors of NAS is the two-stage optimization process: One must search for the architecture in the outer loop and spend a lot of computation in the inner loop to train each model. However, it turns out that the inner loop may not be as crucial in identifying good architectures as initially thought. Given that NAS mostly focuses on optimizing architectures with known, powerful building blocks, it may be possible to predict their performance without training them. A surrogate model can be trained based on a benchmark dataset of architectures and their performance for this task. Or, a hypernetwork can be used to predict the weights, making it possible to evaluate and rank candidates without having to train them (Brock, Lim, Ritchie, et al., 2018).

In the extreme, it turns out that even randomly initiated CNNs (Ulyanov, Vedaldi, and Lempitsky, 2018) and LSTMs (Schmidhuber, Wierstra, Gagliolo, et al., 2007) have useful properties without any training. This leads to an important question: How important are the weight parameters of a neural network compared to its architecture? An approach called **weight agnostic neural networks** (WANNs; Gaier and Ha, 2019) evaluated the extent to which neural network architectures alone, without learning any weight parameters, can encode solutions for a given task. The basic idea was to apply a simple topology search algorithm, NEAT, but to explicitly make the weights random. To evaluate these networks, the connections were instantiated with a single shared weight parameter sampled from a uniform random distribution, and the expected performance was measured over multiple such instantiations. It turned out that WANNs could perform several RL tasks, and achieved much higher than chance accuracy on supervised tasks such as the MNIST classification (figure 10.13). This result suggests that NAS alone may be sufficient to solve some problems without any gradient descent. Indeed, in many biological species, the young are already proficient in many survival tasks without any learning; NAS with random weights can be seen as an approximation of this process.

A complementary direction is to not only evolve architectures from scratch, but also to transfer and analyze knowledge across tasks. Recent work on evolutionary NAS (Assunção,

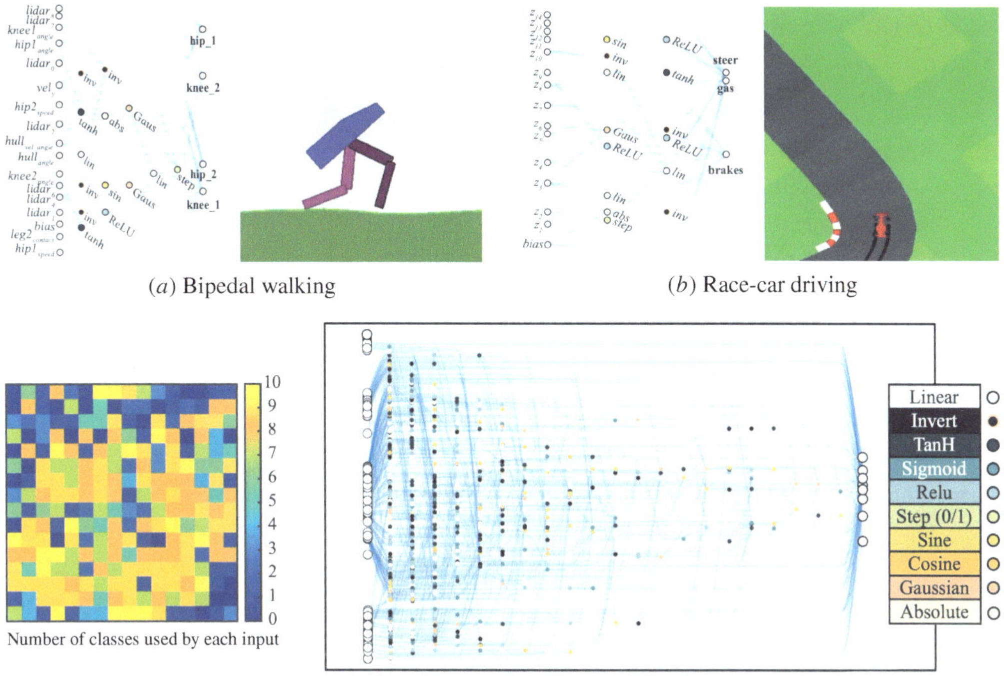

(*a*) Bipedal walking

(*b*) Race-car driving

(*c*) Recognizing handwritten digits in MNIST

Figure 10.13: **Solving problems with NAS alone without gradient descent.** In the WANN approach, network architectures are evolved with a shared random value for weights. Surprisingly, without any gradient descent, they can solve RL tasks such as bipedal walking (*a*) and driving (*b*), and perform competently (at 94%) in MNIST handwritten digit classification (*c*). The diagram on the left side of (*c*) is part of an interactive demo that shows which parts of the input and network are used to classify different handwritten digits. WANN networks can be seen as a model of precocial performance in many animal species, where newborn individuals already perform well in a number of tasks necessary for survival without any experience or learning. Figures from Gaier and Ha (2019). For interactive demos, see `https://neuroevolutionbook.com/demos`.

Lourenço, Ribeiro, et al., 2021) shows that incremental **transfer learning** can significantly reduce the search cost by reusing layers, learning rules, and optimizers from previous tasks. Importantly, this process can be studied through **search trajectory networks** (Ochoa, Malan, and Blum, 2021; Sarti and Ochoa, 2021), which provide a graph-based visualization of how architectures mutate, converge, and inherit components. These analyses reveal, for example, that convolutional and dropout layers tend to be consistently reused, while pooling layers are often discarded. Such insights highlight how evolutionary NAS not only discovers effective architectures, but also builds interpretable trajectories of architectural knowledge, bringing it closer to how biological evolution refines innate structures over generations.

Another compelling direction is to develop methods that discover the building blocks as well. They can be seen as components of neural network architectures that have an appropriate inductive bias for a variety of tasks. This approach is motivated by how biological evolution works, in that individuals are not born with simply a blank-slate neural network to be trained using gradient descent, but rather one that already implements a wide variety of useful innate behaviors that also impact their development. To quote Tony Zador, a computational neuroscientist:

> The first lesson from neuroscience is that much of animal behavior is innate, and does not arise from learning. Animal brains are not the blank slates, equipped with a general-purpose learning algorithm ready to learn anything, as envisioned by some AI researchers; there is strong selection pressure for animals to restrict their learning to just what is needed for their survival. (Zador, 2019)

Ideas have also emerged on how to move back from designing large deep learning architectures to optimizing such architectures entirely with evolution, including their weights. For instance, **indirect encodings**, such as **hypercube-based NEAT** (HyperNEAT), can be used to optimize a very large number of weights by sampling the substrate more densely. In a more direct **deep neuroevolution** approach (reviewed in section 4.2.2), deep network weights are represented compactly as a list of random number seeds: one for the initialization of the network and the rest for the random mutations that construct the network (Petroski Such, Madhavan, Conti, et al., 2017). Another approach is based on **ant colony optimization** (ACO): The ants traverse the architecture space from input to output, and the network is constructed based on their paths. Architectures of any size can be constructed in this manner, and the paths can include a weight dimension as well (ElSaid, Ricanek, Lyu, et al., 2023).

Many other promising ideas have emerged from the NAS field. Rather than searching for architecture, researchers have applied similar methods to search for better **loss functions**, **activation functions**, **learning methods**, and **data augmentation methods**. These optimizations are highly relevant even when network architectures have largely converged on a few best designs, such as transformers. Such approaches will be discussed in more detail in chapter 11, where we go beyond optimizing neural architectures to optimizing the general design of neural networks.

In the long term, an interesting question is: What would it take to discover entirely new architectures, based on new principles? For instance, how could NAS have discovered transformers? Beyond simply scaling up with repetition, a search for appropriate mathematical operations on internal representations would have been needed. A challenge is that such a search space may be deceptive (as was discussed in the context of discovering **cognitive behaviors** in section 6.3.2), and therefore mechanisms for **neutral mutations**, **weak selection**, large populations, **speciation**, and **deep time** may be needed. Further, could such approaches discover something more powerful than transformers—for instance, neural network architectures that know what they know, and networks that can perform logical reasoning? It may be possible to incorporate biological processing principles of feedback, adaptation, memory, and attention, and they could then lead to the discovery of metacognitive abilities. Or it may be possible to include meta-level computing primitives that allow networks to observe and act upon their own processes.

In addition to the technical challenges, it will be challenging to evaluate such abilities because they no longer reduce to simple performance numbers. Such research has only now begun, and it may indeed drive the development of the next level of more powerful AI architectures.

10.7 Chapter Review Questions

1. **NAS approaches:** What are the primary methods used in NAS to automate the design of neural network architectures? Why is evolutionary optimization particularly well suited for this task?

2. **Backprop NEAT:** How does backprop NEAT combine NEAT topology search with backpropagation? What role do activation function diversity and fitness regularization play in improving the evolved networks?

3. **Feature discovery:** In the context of backprop NEAT, how does the algorithm discover features that are typically engineered manually, such as those required for classifying concentric circles or XOR data?

4. **CoDeepNEAT:** How does the CoDeepNEAT approach leverage modular evolution to discover neural architectures? What advantages does its blueprint-module coevolution provide compared to evolving full architectures directly?

5. **AmoebaNet contributions:** What innovations in AmoebaNet's evolutionary process enabled it to achieve SOTA performance in ImageNet? How did these innovations improve the efficiency and accuracy of the NAS process?

6. **Multiobjective optimization:** How does multiobjective NAS differ from single-objective NAS? What advantages does it offer when deploying neural networks in resource-constrained environments?

7. **Pareto fronts:** Explain the concept of Pareto fronts in the context of NAS. How are they used to optimize trade-offs between objectives such as model accuracy and size?

8. **Multitask learning:** What are the benefits of using NAS to discover architectures for multitask learning? How do alternative designs (e.g., single-column versus complex topologies) address differences between tasks?

9. **Module and topology co-evolution:** In multitask NAS, how does the co-evolution of module structures and task-specific topologies (e.g., in CMTR) enhance learning across tasks with limited data?

10. **NAS efficiency:** What strategies, such as surrogate modeling and supernets, have been developed to make NAS computationally practical? How do they maintain effectiveness while reducing search costs?

Chapter 11

Optimization of Neural Network Designs

Similar to neural network architectures, the general design of neural networks can benefit from complexity beyond the human ability to optimize them. This chapter reviews opportunities for such optimization, also called **meta-learning**. The general motivation for designing learning systems through automated search is first discussed, and a compelling example is given in bilevel neuroevolution; that is, optimizing the neuroevolution mechanisms through evolution. Several aspects of supervised neural network design are amenable to meta-learning, including loss functions, activation functions, data augmentation, and the learning methods themselves, leading to potential synergies. Neuromorphic systems, where neural network architectures are optimized for (and potentially together with) hardware, are a particularly promising application for these neuroevolution techniques.

11.1 Designing Complex Systems

Many areas of technical design are too complex for humans to optimize, and automated methods must be used instead. **Very large scale integration** (VLSI) design has long relied on machine optimization, but other areas of engineering are starting to rely on it as well. The systems have become larger, with many interacting elements, and several simultaneous performance goals. The sheer dimensionality and size of the search space are too large to handle without an automated search.

Evolutionary optimization is particularly well suited to such scaling. In some cases, like designing circuitry for a 70-bit **multiplexer**, it was possible to find solutions in a space with $2^{2^{70}}$ potential solutions. While it is hard to imagine a space that large, consider that if that number of potential solutions was printed on paper with 10-point font, it would take light 95 years to travel from the beginning to the end of the number (Miikkulainen, 2021). In others, like designing an optimal schedule for metal casting, there are variables for each type of object in each melting heat, and there may be tens of thousands of such heats, resulting in a billion variables (Deb and Myburgh, 2017). Such scaling is possible because the population can discover partial solutions that can then be used as **stepping**

stones to construct more complete ones, thus requiring exploration of only a fraction of the space and combinations of dimensions.

On the other hand, sometimes the scale is not the main problem, but complexity is: Problems can have nonlinear interactions and even be deceptive so that good solutions are overlooked. It is not just that search needs to be automated, but it should be intelligent enough to handle deception, such as evolutionary search. For instance, the original nose cone of the **Shinkansen bullet train** was long and sleek, with great aerodynamics, but it created a bang when going into a tunnel. In the next version, the engineers wanted to eliminate the bang, but it was difficult to do so by hand. However, they were eventually able to do so by harnessing evolutionary optimization: a cone with deep grooves on both sides (Ishida Lab, 2018). It was unconventional and unlikely to be discovered by human engineers, but it got the job done. Similarly, evolution discovered that it may be advantageous to keep the lights on for 24 hours in computer-controlled greenhouses: Basil doesn't need to sleep (Miikkulainen, 2021). Further, webpage designs were found that violated well-known design principles with garish colors and active language, and yet they were more effective in engaging users: What the human designers referred to as an "ugly widget generator" actually beat their design by 45% (Miikkulainen, Brundage, Epstein, et al., 2020).

Similar stories abound in all areas of engineering, from drug design and medical treatments to programming and autonomous control (see, e.g., Lehman, Clune, Misevic, et al., 2020). As a matter of fact, the annual human-competitive results competition (called "Humies") at the GECCO Conference has showcased hundreds of such approaches since 2004 (Goodman, 2025).

This insight applies to neuroevolution as well. While so far in this book, evolution has been used to optimize the network itself (i.e., its topology and weights), any aspect of the design can be evolved. Opportunities include the overall architecture, activation functions, loss functions, data augmentation, learning mechanisms, and even the neuroevolution optimizer itself. As a result, the networks can perform more accurately, generalize better, and/or use fewer resources than those designed by hand. Collectively, these approaches are called **meta-learning**, which is the topic of this chapter.

11.2 Bilevel Neuroevolution

Several examples of neuroevolution discovering complex and robust behavior were reviewed in chapter 6. Indeed, many such domains include a large number of variables that interact nonlinearly, making it difficult to design control algorithms using traditional methods. While neuroevolution can often be used effectively to construct robust controllers, it is still crucial to get the parameter settings right. Most often, the experiments require a painstaking search in the space of learning parameters, such as mutation and crossover rates and extent, population size, elite percentage, number of stochastic evaluations, and other elements. There are many such parameters, and they interact nonlinearly, making the usual grid search of possible combinations ineffective.

An elegant and compelling solution is to use **bilevel evolution** to optimize the parameters (Liang and Miikkulainen, 2015). That is, the optimization process is defined

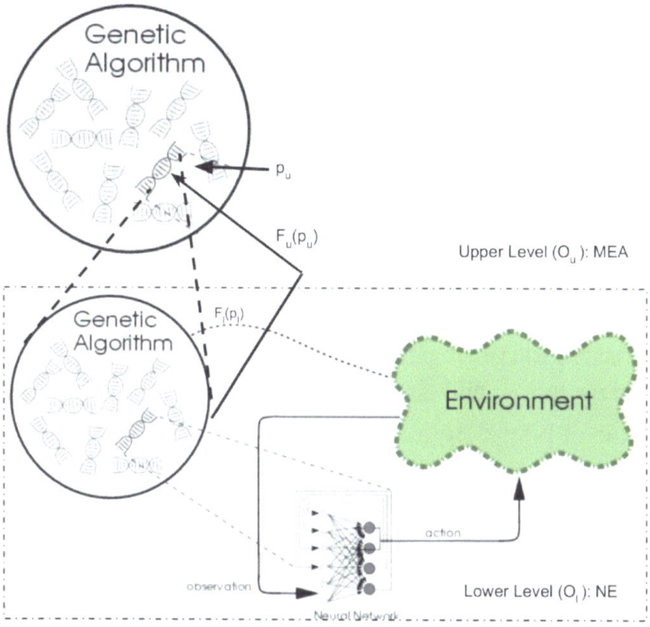

Figure 11.1: **Bilevel neuroevolution**. Neuroevolution performance depends crucially on a proper setting of its hyperparameters. They can be evolved as part of the optimization process, resulting in bilevel neuroevolution. More specifically, neural networks with parameters (weights) p_l are evolved using a low-level neuroevolution algorithm O_l with parameters p_u. The p_u are in turn optimized with an upper-level MEA algorithm O_u. The expected fitness $F_l(p_l)|p_u$ is taken as the fitness of p_u. In this manner, the neuroevolution process can be optimized automatically, which makes it possible to solve harder problems with it. Figure from Liang and Miikkulainen (2015).

in terms of two nested problems (figure 11.1):

$$\underset{p_u}{\text{maximize}}\, F_u(p_u) = E\left[F_l(p_l)|(p_u)\right] \tag{11.1}$$

$$\text{subject to } p_l = O_l(p_u), \tag{11.2}$$

where $E\left[F_l(p_l)|p_u\right]$ is the expected performance of the neural network with parameters (i.e., weights) p_l, obtained by the lower-level optimization algorithm O_l (i.e., neuroevolution) with parameters p_u, which are in turn maximized by a separate upper-level optimization algorithm O_u.

Bilevel evolution is a special case of **meta-evolutionary EAs** (MEAs; Eiben and Smit, 2011; Grefenstette, 1986; Sinha, Malo, Xu, et al., 2014) where evolution is used to optimize algorithms offline. It is related to **self-adaptive EAs**, where evolutionary parameters are adjusted online depending on progress in the optimization (Kramer, 2010; Kumar, Liu, Miikkulainen, et al., 2022). In its most straightforward form, each fitness evaluation of each high-level individual p_u requires running an entire neuroevolution experiment. The crucial idea of bilevel optimization is to estimate the fitness of p_u without having to run such an experiment every time. In essence, the idea is the same as **surrogate optimization** for decision-making, discussed in section 6.4.2. Each run of a neuroevolution experiment can be considered as a sample, and a predictor model learned to approximate the fitness landscape. The upper-level search can then be done mostly against the surrogate, with only occasional neuroevolution experiments needed.

An example of a simple approach is to fit a quadratic function to these samples (Sinha, Malo, Xu, et al., 2014). A more complex example is to train a random forest or a neural network, as done in section 6.4.2: Such models are **nonparametric** (i.e., more general), and less prone to overfitting. Forming the surrogate is still difficult because there are usually very few samples and they are noisy. One way to deal with this problem is to construct the fitness F_u from multiple metrics over several neuroevolution runs with p_u, including best and average fitness and standard deviation, diversity of the population, and the shape of the learning curve. In effect, the idea is to predict the eventual performance of p_u after prolonged evolution, and also to take into account the reliability of this estimate.

To see the value of bilevel optimization, consider the benchmark task of evolving a network for **helicopter hovering**. The goal is to keep the helicopter as close as possible to a point in 3D space in windy conditions, with 12 state variables (coordinates, angles, velocities) as the input, and four action variables (aileron, elevator, rudder, and rotor pitch) as the output. The task is difficult because many variables interact, their values are noisy, and the domain is unstable. However, neuroevolution can solve it with a careful hand-tuning of eight evolutionary parameters: mutation probability, rate, amount, replacement rate, and fraction, population size, crossover probability, and crossover averaging rate (Koppejan and Whiteson, 2011). Remarkably, such hand-tuning still leaves money on the table: By optimizing the parameter further with **bilevel evolution**, it is possible to evolve solutions that perform significantly better, both by learning faster and achieving higher final accuracy (figure 11.2*a*). Also, using a good surrogate is crucial: While using a **random forest** surrogate improves bilevel optimization significantly compared to not using a surrogate, quadratic fitting is too unreliable and actually decreases performance.

A common rule of thumb is that humans can take into account 7 ± 2 variables at once, which is well in line with the helicopter hovering result. However, with bilevel evolution, it may be possible to increase that number significantly. Would such an extension result in better performance? For instance in the standard benchmark task **double pole balancing**, it is common to specify the values of five parameters by hand: mutation rate, and mutation amount, replacement fraction, initial weight range, and population size. There are, however, many other parameters that could be included, such as single-point, two-point, and uniform crossover probability, tournament, truncation, and roulette selection probability. They are not strictly necessary to parameterize an effective neuroevolution experiment, but they do make it possible to establish a more complex search.

It turns out such extra customization pays off significantly. It is much faster to find solutions when 15 evolutionary parameters are optimized rather than only five (figure 11.2*b*). This is an important result because it suggests that bilevel optimization changes how we should think about problem-solving. Simple methods may be easy to understand for people, but when they can be optimized automatically, it is better to make the method more flexible and configurable, even beyond human ability. Such complexity translates to better performance through bilevel optimization.

As more compute becomes available, bilevel optimization is likely to become an increasingly important element of neuroevolution. It can also be extended in several

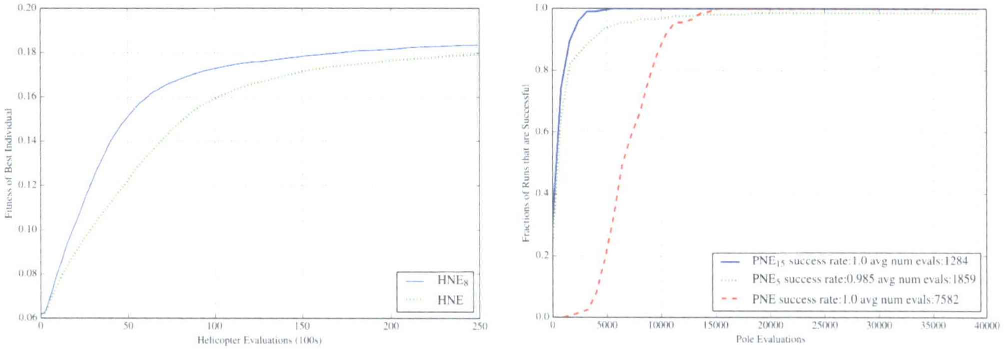

(*a*) Improvement over human fine-tuning in the helicopter hovering task

(*b*) Improvement with more parameters in the double pole balancing task

Figure 11.2: **Enhancing neuroevolution with bilevel optimization**. (*a*) Neuroevolution with eight hand-tuned evolution parameters (shown as HNE in the plot) is successful in the helicopter hovering task, but when those same parameters are optimized at the same time through bilevel evolution (HNE_8), better solutions are found faster. In this manner, bilevel evolution can be harnessed to improve upon human design of neuroevolution experiments. (*b*) The cumulative success of neuroevolution with five hand-tuned evolutionary parameters (PNE), five bilevel-optimized parameters (PNE_5), and fifteen bilevel-optimized parameters (PNE_{15}) in the double pole balancing task. More parameters allow bilevel evolution to develop a more powerful neuroevolution parameterization, resulting in faster discovery of solutions. Therefore, when bilevel optimization is available, it is better to make the neuroevolution method more flexible and configurable, even beyond human ability to optimize. Figures from Liang and Miikkulainen (2015). For videos of helicopter hovering, see `https://neuroevolutionbook.com/demos`.

ways. For instance, instead of fixed parameters p_{u}, it may be possible to discover parameter adaptation schedules that change the parameters during the course of individual neuroevolution runs, similar to self-adapting EAs. They may themselves take the form of a neural network that observes the performance of the run and outputs optimal current parameters. While the designs of neuroevolution algorithms have naturally focused on compact and parsimonious methods, it may be possible to design them with bilevel optimization in mind, which means creating many more configuration parameters, and thus take advantage of the power of expanded optimization. Also, better surrogate modeling techniques can be developed, perhaps by utilizing knowledge of the domain, benchmark collections, and methods for estimating fitness in neural architecture search.

While bilevel neuroevolution focuses on optimizing the evolution method, the approach can be extended to optimizing other machine learning (ML) methods as well. Section 12.2.3 discusses **model-agnostic meta-learning** (MAML), a similar approach applied to starting parameters in reinforcement learning (RL). The next section focuses on optimizing designs for supervised training of neural networks.

11.3 Evolutionary Meta-learning

With supervised neural networks, several design aspects beyond the architecture (the topic of chapter 10) must be configured appropriately as well. Those include learning hyperparameters (such as the learning rate), activation functions, loss functions, data sampling and augmentation, and learning methods. Approaches similar to those used in neural architecture search (NAS) can be applied to them; however, the evolutionary approach has an advantage in that it is the most versatile: It can be applied to graphs, vectors of continuous and discrete parameters, and configuration choices. This ability is particularly useful as new architectures are developed. For instance, currently, work has barely begun on optimizing designs of transformer (Vaswani, Shazeer, Parmar, et al., 2017) or diffusion (Sohl-Dickstein, Weiss, Maheswaranathan, et al., 2015) architectures. They have elements such as attention modules, spatial embeddings, and noise transformations that are different from prior architectures, and yet they may be parameterized and evolved as well in order to optimize their implementation.

Most importantly, evolution can be used to optimize many aspects of the design simultaneously, discovering and taking advantage of synergies between them. Several such approaches are reviewed in this section.

11.3.1 Loss Functions

Perhaps the most fundamental is the design of a good **loss function**. Mean-squared-error (MSE) loss has been used for a long time, and more recently, cross-entropy (CE) loss has become popular, especially in classification tasks. Both of those assign minimal loss to outputs that are close to correct, and superlinearly larger losses to outputs further from the correct values. They make sense intuitively and work reliably–so much so that alternatives are not usually even considered.

However, it turns out that it is possible to improve upon them in a surprising way that would have been difficult to discover if evolution had not done it for us (Gonzalez and Miikkulainen, 2020, 2021). If outputs that are extremely close to correct are penalized with a larger loss, the system learns to avoid such extreme outputs, which minimizes overfitting (figure 11.3*a*). Such loss functions, called **Baikal losses** for their shape, lead to automatic regularization. Regularization in turn leads to more accurate performance on unseen examples, especially in domains where the amount of available data is limited, as is the case in many real-world applications.

Baikal loss was initially discovered with a classic **genetic programming** approach where the function was represented as a tree of mathematical operations (Gonzalez and Miikkulainen, 2020). The structure of the tree was evolved with genetic algorithms (GA), and the coefficients in the nodes with covariance matrix adaptation evolution strategy (CMA-ES; Hansen and Ostermeier, 2001). This approach is general and creative, in that it can be used to explore a large search space of diverse functions. However, many of those functions do not work well and are often unstable. In the follow-up TaylorGLO method (Gonzalez and Miikkulainen, 2021), the functions were represented instead as third-order Taylor polynomials. Such functions are continuous and can be directly optimized with CMA-ES, making the search more effective.

Regularization is an important aspect of neural network design in general. Many techniques are available, such as dropout, weight decay, and label smoothing (Hanson and Pratt, 1988; Srivastava, Hinton, Krizhevsky, et al., 2014; Szegedy, Vanhoucke, Ioffe, et al., 2016), but how they work is not well understood. Loss-function optimization, however, can be understood theoretically, and it thus provides a starting point to understanding

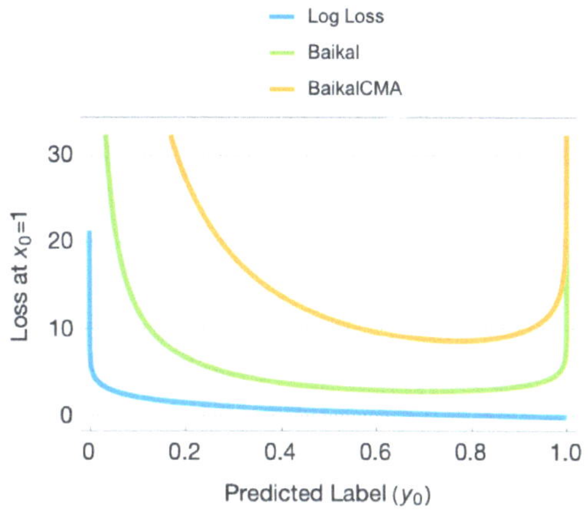

(*a*) Loss function profiles

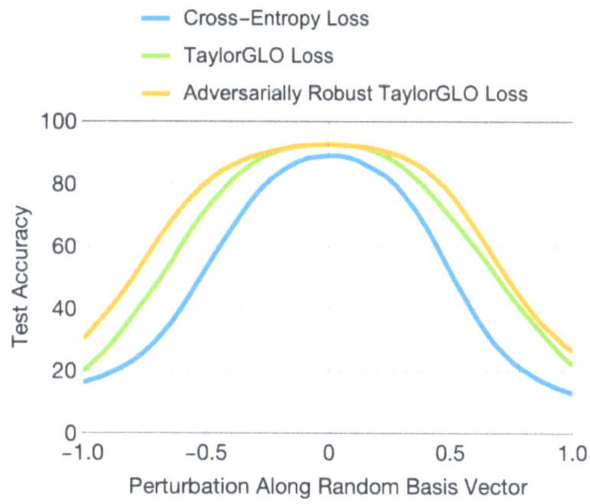

(*b*) Performance with weight perturbation

Figure 11.3: **Regularization and robustness with evolved loss functions.** Surprising synergies emerge when loss functions are evolved as part of the optimization process. (*a*) The standard loss function, such as log loss (or cross-entropy), has a high loss for outputs that are far from correct (1.0 in this case) and a low loss otherwise. In contrast, evolutionary optimization of loss functions through GLO/TaylorGLO (Gonzalez and Miikkulainen, 2020, 2021) discovered a new principle: When the output is very close to the correct one, a high loss is incurred. This principle, termed "Baikal loss" for its shape, discourages overfitting, thus regularizing the network automatically, leading to better generalization. Such a loss is effective, but it is counterintuitive and thus unlikely to be discovered by human designers. (*b*) Baikal loss also makes the network performance more robust. This effect can be quantified by perturbing the network weights. With Baikal loss, the network's performance is less affected than with cross-entropy loss. This effect can be further magnified by making robustness against adversarial inputs an explicit second objective in evolution. Thus, loss-function optimization can be used to improve not just regularization, but robustness as well. Figure *a* adapted from Gonzalez and Miikkulainen (2020) and figure *b* adapted from Gonzalez, Qiu, and Miikkulainen (2025).

regularization in general (Gonzalez, Qiu, and Miikkulainen, 2025). It can be described as a balance of two processes: a pull toward the training targets and a push away from overfitting. This perspective leads to a practical condition for guiding the search toward trainable functions.

Note that Baikal loss is a general principle; evolutionary optimization was crucial in discovering it, but it can now be used on its own in deep learning. It is still possible to customize it for each task and architecture, and even small modifications to the standard Baikal shape may make a difference. Optimization may also have a significant effect on various learning challenges, for instance when there is not much training data (Gonzalez, Landgraf, and Miikkulainen, 2019), or when the labels are particularly noisy (Gao, Gouk, and Hospedales, 2021). It may also be possible to modify the loss function during learning, for instance by emphasizing regularization in the beginning and precision toward the end (similarly to activation functions; section 11.3.2).

It turns out that loss functions that regularize also make networks more robust, and this effect can be further enhanced by including an explicit robustness goal in evolution (figure 11.3*b*). One way to create such a goal is to evaluate performance separately with regards to **adversarial examples**. This result in turn suggests that loss-function optimization could be an effective approach to creating ML systems that are robust against adversarial attacks.

Loss-function optimization can also play a major role in systems where multiple loss functions interact, such as **generative adversarial networks** (GANs; Gonzalez, Kant, and Miikkulainen, 2023). GANs include three different losses: a discriminative loss for real examples, a discriminative loss for fake examples, and a generative loss for fake examples. It is not easy to get them right, and many proposals exist, including those in minimax, nonsaturating, Wasserstein, and least-squares GANs (Arjovsky, Chintala, and Bottou, 2017; Goodfellow, Pouget-Abadie, Mirza, et al., 2014; Mao, Li, Xie, et al., 2017). Training often fails, with such results as mode collapse. However, the three losses can be evolved simultaneously, using performance and reliability as fitness. In one such experiment on generating building facade images given the overall design as a condition, the TaylorGLO approach resulted in better structural similarity and perceptual distance than the Wasserstein loss (Gonzalez, Kant, and Miikkulainen, 2023). Although this result is preliminary, it suggests that evolutionary loss-function optimization may make more complex learning systems possible in the future.

11.3.2 Activation Functions

Early in the 1980s and 1990s, sigmoids (and tanh) were used almost exclusively as activation functions for neural networks. They had intuitively the right behavior as neural models, limiting activation between the minimum and maximum values, a simple derivative that made backpropagation convenient, and a theorem suggesting that universal computing could be based on such networks (Cybenko, 1989; Hornik, Stinchcombe, and White, 1989). There were indications, however, that other activation functions might work better in many cases. Gaussians achieved universal computing with one less layer and were found powerful in **radial basis function** (RBF) networks (Park and Sandberg, 1991). Ridge activations also provide similar capabilities (Light, 1993).

However, with the advent of deep learning, an important discovery was made: Activation functions made a big difference in whether the gradients vanished. In particular, **rectified linear units** (ReLUs) were critical in scaling up deep learning networks (Nair and Hinton, 2010). The linearly increasing region does not saturate activation or gradients, resulting in less signal loss. Moreover, it turned out that in many cases, ReLU could be improved by adding a small differentiable dip at the boundary between the two regions, in a function called **Swish** (Ramachandran, Zoph, and Le, 2018). This result suggested that there may be an opportunity to optimize activation functions, both generally and for specific architectures and tasks.

Like loss functions, there is a straightforward opportunity to **optimize activation functions** through genetic programming (Bingham, Macke, and Miikkulainen, 2020). Like loss function optimization, such an approach can be creative, but it also results in many functions that make the network unstable. An example of a more practical approach is to limit the search space to computation graphs of two levels, with a focused set of operators that are more likely to result in useful functions. This approach was taken in the **PANGAEA system** (Bingham and Miikkulainen, 2022). Given a list of 27 unary and seven binary operators, two basic two-level computation graph structures, and four mutation operators, evolution can search a space of over 10 trillion activation functions. However, finding an effective function is only part of the challenge. The function also needs to be parameterized to perform as well as possible. While coefficients multiplying each operator can be evolved together with the structure, it turns out that such fine-tuning can be done more efficiently through gradient descent. In other words, in PANGAEA, evolution and gradient descent work synergistically: Evolution discovers the general structure of the function, and gradient descent finds its optimal instantiation.

The method is powerful in two ways: It finds general functions that perform better than previous functions, such as ReLU, scaled exponential linear unit (SeLU), and Swish, across architectures (such as All-CNN, wide ResNet, ResNet, and preactivation ResNet) and tasks (such as CIFAR-10 and CIFAR-100). However, it is most powerful in discovering activation functions that are specialized to the architecture and task, apparently taking advantage of the unique requirements in each such context.

Furthermore, performance can be further improved by allowing different functions at different parts of the network, and at different times throughout training (figure 11.4). The optimal designs change continuously over time and space. Different activation functions are useful early in training, when the network learns rapidly, and late in training, when fine-tuning is needed; similarly, more nonlinear functions are discovered for later layers, possibly reflecting the need to form a regularized embedding early, and make classification decisions later.

The PANGAEA results suggest an intriguing duality: While neural network learning is mostly based on adapting a large number of parameters (i.e., weights), a similar effect might be achieved by adapting the activation functions over space and time. Perhaps the two mechanisms could be used synergistically? Evolution of the activation function structure provides the foundation for this approach, which still needs to be fully developed.

Interestingly, the recently discovered **Kolmogorov-Arnold networks** (KANs; Liu, Wang, Vaidya, et al., 2025) are a step in this direction. Every weight parameter is replaced by a univariate function such as a spline whose parameters are then learned. A natural extension would be to evolve these functions using a mechanism such as PANGAEA, making the search for good KANs more comprehensive—a compelling direction for future work.

11.3.3 Data Use and Augmentation

Optimizing the training data is another significant opportunity for evolutionary optimization of supervised learning systems. For instance, it may be possible to form embeddings of the training samples through an autoencoder and then form a strategy for utilizing different kinds of samples optimally through time (Gonzalez, Landgraf, and Miikkulainen, 2019). In this manner, evolution could discover ways to balance an **imbalanced dataset** or to design **curricular learning** from simple to more complex examples. Especially in domains where not a lot of labeled samples are available, such techniques could result in significant improvements. It may also be possible to extend the methods to utilize multiple datasets optimally over time in a **multitask setting**.

Another possibility is to evolve methods for augmenting the available data automatically through various transformations. Different datasets may benefit from different

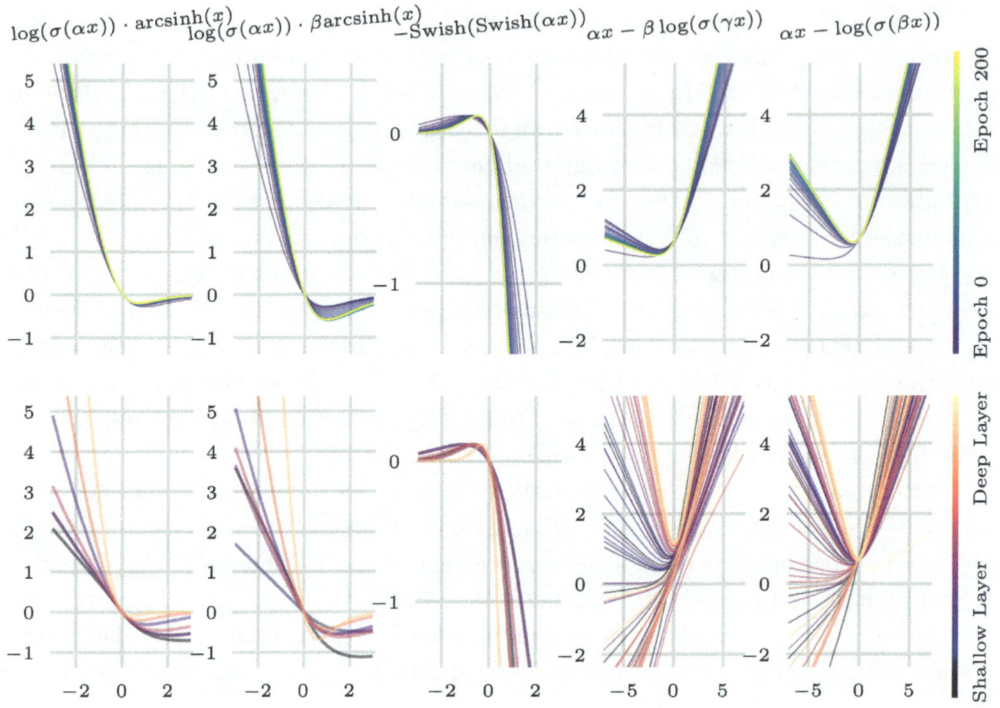

Figure 11.4: **Activation functions discovered over space and time.** Activation functions are as fundamental to network performance as its weights. PANGAEA combines evolution of the function structure synergistically with gradient descent of its parameters. It is possible to discover general functions, but the approach is most powerful in customizing them to a particular architecture and task. Moreover, the functions change systematically over learning time, as well as through different depths of layers, presumably starting with coarse learning and regularization and transforming into fine-tuning and classification. These results suggest a possible duality with weight learning and a possible synergy for the future. Figure from Bingham and Miikkulainen (2022).

transformations, and it is not always obvious ahead of time how they should be designed. For instance, in an application to develop models for estimating the age of a person from an image of their face, evolution was used to decide vertical and horizontal shift and cutout, as well as a direction of flip operations, angle of rotation, degree of zoom, and extent of shear (Miikkulainen, Meyerson, Qiu, et al., 2021). Unexpectedly, it chose to do vertical flips only—which made little sense for faces until it was found that the input images had been rotated 90 degrees! It also discovered a combination of shift operations that allowed it to obfuscate the forehead and chin, which otherwise would be easy areas for the model to overfit.

Given that datasets often contain a large number of variables, or features, a compelling opportunity is to discover which features should be utilized in learning and which ones should be left out. For instance, in the **feature selective neuroevolution of augmenting topologies** (FS-NEAT) method (Papavasileiou and Jansen, 2017; Whiteson, Stone, Stanley, et al., 2005), complexification is used to select features through connection mutations. The approach automatically determines an appropriate set of inputs for the networks that it evolves. The networks performed better, evolved faster, and were smaller than regular

NEAT networks in tasks such as CarRacing. The approach can also be instantiated as a general meta-learning method; that is, evolution can be used to select features for deep learning architectures that are then trained with gradient descent. This approach has proven effective in tasks such as currency trading (Mańdziuk and Rajkiewicz, 2016).

A particularly interesting use for evolved data augmentation is to optimize not only the accuracy of the resulting models, but also to mitigate **bias** and **fairness** issues with the data. So long as these dimensions can be measured (Sharma, Henderson, and Ghosh, 2020), they can be made part of the fitness, or separate objectives in a multiobjective setting. Operations then need to be designed to increase the variance across variables that might otherwise lead to bias through overfitting—for instance, gender, ethnicity, and socioeconomic status, depending on the application. While evolutionary data augmentation is still new, this area seems like a differentiated and compelling opportunity for it.

11.3.4 Learning Methods

An interesting extension of NAS is to evolve the learning system not from high-level elements but from the basic algorithmic building blocks (mathematical operations, data management, and ways to combine them)—in other words, by evolving code for supervised machine learning. In this manner, evolution can be more creative in discovering good methods, with fewer biases from the human experimenters.

The **AutoML-Zero system** (Real, Liang, So, et al., 2020) is a step toward this goal. Given an address space for scalars, vectors, and matrices of floats, it evolves setup, predict, and learn methods composed of over 50 basic mathematical operations. Evolution is implemented as linear genetic programming (GP), and it consists of inserting and removing instructions and randomizing instructions and addresses. Evaluation consists of computing predictions over unseen examples.

Starting from empty programs, AutoML-Zero first discovered linear models, followed by gradient descent, and eventually several extensions known in the literature, such as noisy inputs, gradient normalization, and multiplicative interactions (figure 11.5). When given small datasets, it discovers regularization methods similar to dropout; when given few training steps, it discovers learning-rate decay.

Thus, the preliminary experiments with AutoML-Zero suggest that evolutionary search can be a powerful tool in discovering entire learning algorithms. As in many meta-learning approaches, the main power may be in customizing these methods to particular domains and constraints. A crucial aspect will be to guide the evolution within the enormous search space toward meaningful solutions without hampering its ability to create–again a challenge shared with most of meta-learning.

11.3.5 Utilizing Surrogates

While evolutionary meta-learning can discover more effective neural network designs, it is also challenging in three ways: It is computationally very expensive to evaluate all the different designs; it is difficult to gain insight into what works; and it is not clear how the search spaces should be defined so that they are fast to search and contain good solutions.

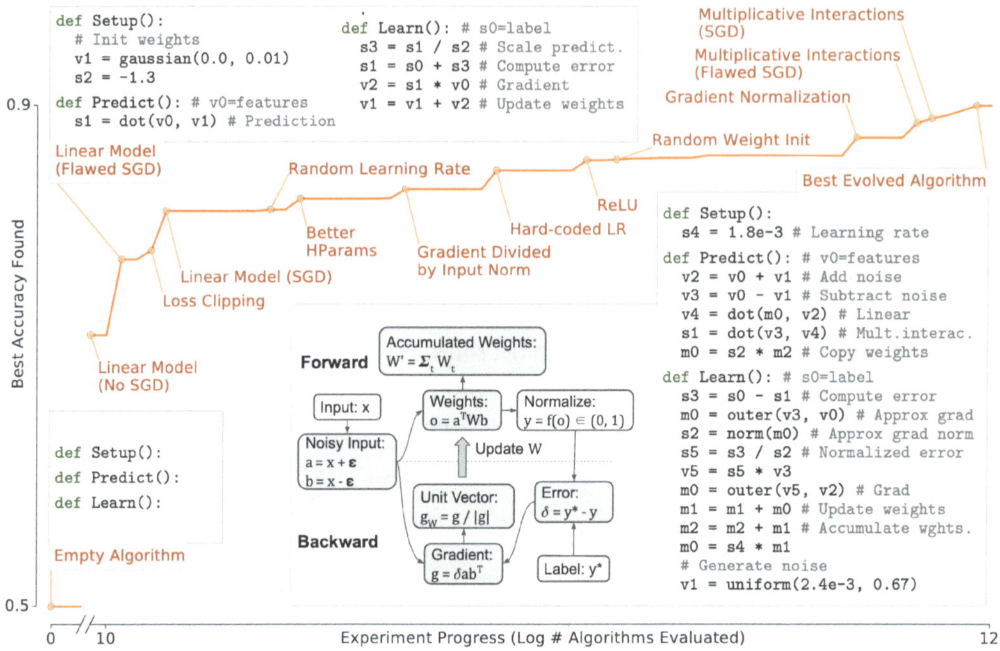

Figure 11.5: **Evolutionary discovery of learning methods.** At the highest level, meta-learning extends to the learning mechanisms themselves. In AutoML-Zero (Real, Liang, So, et al., 2020), sequences of instructions for setup, prediction, and learning are evolved through mutation-based regularized search. AutoML-Zero first discovered simple methods such as linear models, and then several known extensions such as ReLU and gradient normalization, and eventually more sophisticated techniques such as multiplicative interactions. The approach could be particularly useful in customizing learning methods to different domains and constraints. Figure from Real, Liang, So, et al. (2020).

One way to make progress toward meeting these challenges is to perform a full search in as large a search space as possible, thus forming a benchmark dataset that makes it possible to analyze what works. These insights may then be used to construct a surrogate approach that makes it possible to search in larger spaces without having to evaluate candidates through full training.

Such an approach, **AQuaSurF**, was demonstrated in the task of discovering effective activation functions (Bingham and Miikkulainen, 2023b). Based on the work described in section 11.3.2, an exhaustive set of 2,913 different activation functions was created from a three-node computational graph of PANGAEA and tested on three architecture/task settings, All-CNN/CIFAR-10, ResNet-56/CIFAR-10, and MobileViTv2-0.5/Imagenette (a smaller version of ImageNet). Thus, they covered basic convolutional, residual, and transformer designs in the visual domain. In each case, the networks were trained fully to evaluate how well each function performed in the particular setting.[1]

Most activation functions performed poorly, but a small number of functions performed very well, confirming that activation-function meta-learning is difficult but also worthwhile. Most interestingly, two trends were also observed: (1) There were clusters of functions

[1]This dataset is available at https:// github.com/cognizant-ai-labs/act-bench.

that performed well across architectures and tasks, representing refinements of general solutions; and (2) the very best performance in each setting was achieved by a few functions that performed poorly in other settings, in other words, by activation functions that were specialized to the architecture and task. This result suggests that meta-learning can be most powerful when it is used to customize the designs to the particular problem.

The benchmark collection was then used to construct an effective **surrogate** for full network evaluations. It turned out that a combination of **Fisher-information-matrix** (FIM) eigenvalues and the function shape is a powerful surrogate. First, FIM quantifies how much information the network parameters carry about the data distribution, and thus it serves as a characterization of network behavior. It has been used in many studies to illustrate learning ability, generalization, robustness to perturbations, and loss-function shape of neural networks (Jastrzebski, Arpit, Astrand, et al., 2021; Karakida, Akaho, and Amari, 2019; Liang, Poggio, Rakhlin, et al., 2019; Liao, Drummond, Reid, et al., 2018). The information in FIM is represented compactly in its eigenvalues; there are as many eigenvalues as there are network weights, but they can be binned into a histogram with lower dimensionality. The histogram vector then forms a computational characterization of the network. Networks with different activation functions have different such characterizations, and the space of these FIM-eigenvalue-histogram vectors can be used as a surrogate search space for good activation functions.

However, the FIM also depends on other factors, including the architecture, loss function, and data distribution, which makes it rather noisy. An additional surrogate representation is useful in compensating for such noise: the shape of the activation function itself. This shape can be represented as a sampling of activation function values for inputs distributed as $\mathcal{N}(0, 1)$, as they would be in a properly initialized network (Bingham and Miikkulainen, 2023a). Using both FIM and output together forms a powerful surrogate (figure 11.6*a*): Functions that perform similarly are clustered together, making it easy to search for good functions.

Indeed, the search for good activation functions was highly effective in this surrogate space. Even a simple search like k-nearest neighbors regression could find the best functions quickly and reliably.

However, the surrogate approach also turned out to be effective in activation optimization beyond the benchmark settings in three ways. First, it scaled up to a much larger search space of 425,896 functions for which the performance was not known, as well as to the harder CIFAR-100 task with the same architectures. In each case, it discovered new activation functions that performed better than any of the known functions so far. Second, those discoveries also transferred to new settings: The best functions performed better than any previously known functions on ResNet-50 on the full ImageNet dataset. Thus, it is possible to discover good functions efficiently in smaller tasks and then use them to improve performance in larger ones. Third, the approach also extended to new architectures and baseline functions. For instance, the **CoAtNet** architecture is a novel combination of convolutional and transformer networks (Dai, Liu, Le, et al., 2021). When initialized with the best previously known activation functions and tested on Imagenette, the approach outperformed all baselines. Thus, the surrogate approach is a powerful way to optimize designs for new settings.

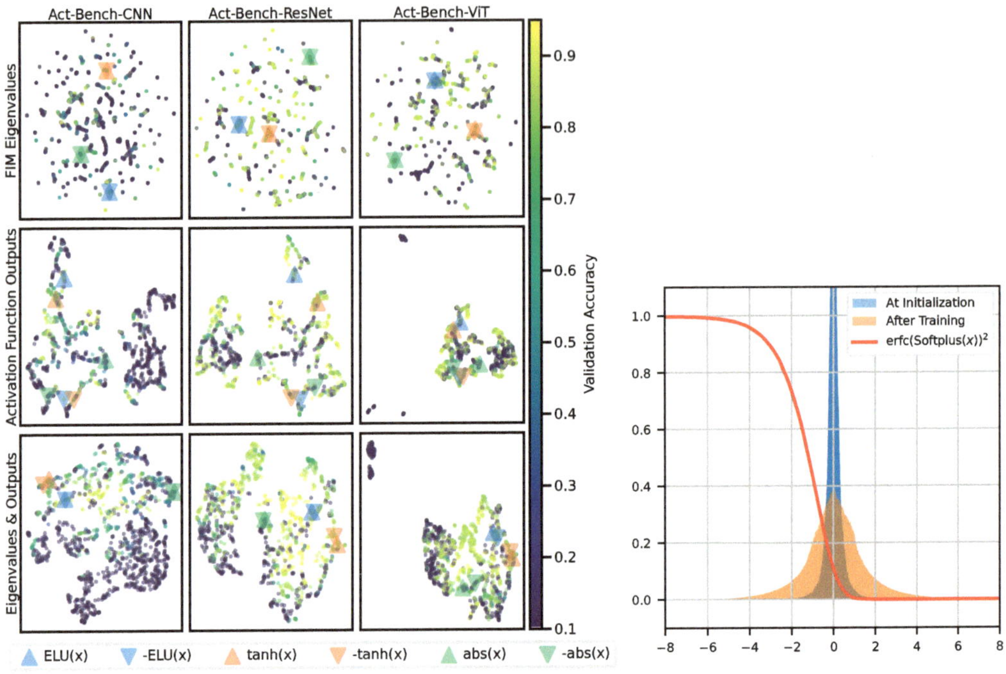

(*a*) Surrogate spaces (*b*) Using the sigmoid

Figure 11.6: **Utilizing surrogates to discover surprising activation functions.** Surrogate modeling can be used to evaluate activation function candidates without full training, making it possible to search in larger spaces, which may result in more innovative solutions. (*a*) Uniform manifold approximation and projection (UMAP) embeddings of the 2,913 activation functions in the three benchmark settings (columns) in three surrogate spaces: FIM eigenvalues (top row), function outputs (middle row), and both (bottom row). UMAP is a dimensionality-reduction technique that preserves the structure of high-dimensional spaces well (in this case 13,692, 16,500, and 11,013 FIM eigenvalue histogram dimensions and 1,000 function output samples). Function performance is indicated by color coding. Similar colors cluster best in the bottom row, suggesting that using both FIM and output features as the surrogate space makes search for good functions the easiest. (*b*) The best activation function in the CoAtNet experiment turned out to be a sigmoid. The histograms indicate the values with which it is activated in the network. At initialization (blue histogram), it is used similarly to ReLU; after training (orange histogram), both saturation regions are used. This discovery suggests that sigmoidal activations may be useful in specific situations, challenging the conventional wisdom in ML. Figures from Bingham and Miikkulainen (2023b).

Interestingly, AQuaSurF achieved these results by balancing refinement and novelty. Many of the functions that it discovered were similar to the well-known functions of exponential linear unit (ELU) and Swish, with minor changes to their shape. This result suggests that these are generally good functions, but also that such customizations matter; AQuaSurF is well-equipped to find them.

However, in many cases, AQuaSurF also found designs that were very different from the existing ones, yet performed at least as well. Some had discontinuous derivatives, some did not saturate on either side, and some had positive instead of negative bumps. The biggest surprise was discovered in the CoAtNet experiment on Imagenette (figure 11.6*b*).

This function was essentially a sigmoid, similar to those used extensively during the early days of neural networks but largely discarded in favor of ReLU in deep learning. Why would it be discovered again in these experiments?

In deep learning, the linearly increasing region of ReLU helped avoid vanishing gradients. It is therefore important to look at how the sigmoid is used, by plotting which parts of the function are actually activated during performance. It indeed provides behavior similar to ReLU early in training: The function is activated around the nonlinearity, but it does not reach the saturating region that occurs with larger activations. However, later training also takes advantage of the saturating region. In this manner, the same activation function can be used in two ways: presumably to keep the gradients from vanishing early, and to commit to decisions later. This result challenges the common approach in deep learning design and demonstrates the power of neuroevolution in meta-learning good designs. In sum, surrogate optimization techniques make it possible to scale up neuroevolution meta-learning; in doing so, it is possible to identify principles that would be difficult for human designers to discover.

11.3.6 Synergies

Perhaps the most important future direction in evolutionary meta-learning is to discover and utilize **synergies** between the various aspects of the learning system design. For instance, the best performance was achieved by optimizing **activation functions** for the specific architecture; it might be possible to optimize the architecture simultaneously to emphasize this effect. Simply running evolution on all these design aspects simultaneously is unlikely to work; the search space would be prohibitively large. Similarly, adding more outer loops to the existing process (where supervised learning is the inner loop and meta-learning is the outer loop) is likely prohibitive too. However, it might be possible to alternate the evolution of different aspects. Better yet, techniques from bilevel (or multilevel) optimization could be useful—the idea is to avoid a full inner-outer loop structure, but instead use e.g., surrogate models to evaluate outer loop innovations (Liang and Miikkulainen, 2015; Sinha, Malo, Xu, et al., 2014).

A practical approach is simply adding constraints and searching in a smaller space. A first such step was already taken in the **regularized evolutionary population-based training** (EPBT) system (Liang, Gonzalez, Shahrzad, et al., 2021), which combines hyperparameter tuning, loss-function optimization, and **population-based training** (PBT) into a single loop. That is, hyperparameters and loss functions are evolved at the same time as the networks are being trained. Hyperparameter tuning is limited to those that do not change the structure of the networks (e.g., learning rate schedules) so they can be continuously trained, even when the hyperparameters change. Similarly, loss-function optimization is limited to **TaylorGLO** coefficients (Liang, Gonzalez, Shahrzad, et al., 2021) that can be changed while training is going on. Even so, the simultaneous evolution and learning were deceptive and needed to be augmented with two mechanisms: **quality-diversity** (QD) heuristic for managing the population and **knowledge distillation** to prevent overfitting. The resulting method worked well on optimizing ResNet and WideResNet architectures in CIFAR-10 and SVHN, but also illustrates the challenges of taking advantage of the synergies of meta-learning methods.

11.4 Case Study: Meta-learning Versus Human Design

Exactly how useful is meta-learning in practice? Convincing results were obtained in a natural experiment that compared human design with evolutionary meta-learning in the domain of medical aesthetics (Miikkulainen, Meyerson, Qiu, et al., 2021).

Medical aesthetics focuses on treatments that improve appearance following injury or disease, but it also includes elective procedures intended to lower perceived age and thus improve the patient's self-esteem. They often involve injecting a toxin (e.g., Botox) or a filler in a targeted area of the face, changing the skin texture and other facial features (Abelsson and Willman, 2020; Arsiwala, 2018). Evaluating the success of such procedures is largely subjective. However, perceived age is quantifiable, and methods can be developed for measuring that aspect of the outcome automatically.

Indeed, age estimation has been used as a benchmark for visual deep learning architectures for a long time. Many of the state-of-the-art (SOTA) architectures have been evaluated in it, and good progress has been made (Rothe, Timofte, and Van Gool, 2018; Yang, Huang, Lin, et al., 2018). There are, however, three challenges in building an age estimator that could be used to evaluate medical aesthetics treatments. First, the datasets used for age estimation are usually based on celebrity images. Such images have often been retouched and processed in various ways, and the subjects often have makeup and even medical aesthetics work done already. All such alterations make learning reliable estimates difficult. Second, while the architectures can be used on facial images, they were usually developed for general image recognition benchmarks such as CIFAR-10 and ImageNet. Thus, their architecture does not use special features of the facial image dataset, such as the structure of the face. Third, to evaluate the value of treatments, it is necessary to estimate confidence in the predictions. Deep learning architectures do not by themselves provide such estimates.

The experiment consisted of addressing these challenges, making it possible to evaluate the value of medical aesthetics treatments quantitatively. First, the celebrity face datasets were replaced with images of actual patients. The first dataset, D0, consisted of 10,837 training images and 2,692 test images, with subject ages ranging from 18 to 79. This dataset was less challenging and allowed for fast early development of models. It was later replaced by dataset D1, with 18,537 training and 3,733 testing images, with more variety in terms of studies and patients. These two datasets were used to evolve and train good age estimator models. While the DenseNet-121 architecture achieved a validation mean absolute error (MAE) of 7.43 years on the celebrity dataset; multiple similar architectures did much better on D0 and D1, including DenseNet-169, with 3.65 years on D1. Thus, the quality of the datasets matters significantly.

Second, several aspects of meta-learning were used synergistically to optimize the age estimation architectures. What made this study particularly valuable was that at the same time, there was a team of human data science experts who were performing the same task by hand. The two teams did periodically share discoveries, such as better-performing baseline architectures, but they were trying to outperform each other. Thus, the project turned into a natural experiment on the value of automated meta-learning.

The main strategy that both teams employed was to start small and expand in multiple stages S_i. The experiment started with the D0 dataset and small baseline architectures

ResNet-50 (in stage S_0) followed by DenseNet-121 (S_1) (He, Zhang, Ren, et al., 2016; Huang, Liu, van der Maaten, et al., 2017). With D1, larger baselines DenseNet-169 (S_0), DenseNet-201 (S_1, S_2), and eventually EfficientNet-B6 (S_3) (Tan and Le, 2019) were used, and the image resolution was expanded from the initial 224×224 (S_0) to 512×512 (S_1) and eventually to 528×528 S_3. Finally, the three best models were ensembled (S_4). PBT (Jaderberg, Dalibard, Osindero, et al., 2017; Liang, Gonzalez, Shahrzad, et al., 2021) was used throughout. That is, while evolution modifies various hyperparameters for training the networks, the network weights persist from generation to generation. In this manner, training is a continuous process, saving significant computational effort.

Evolution was set to optimize three types of hyperparameters: those that specify **learning**, **architecture**, and **data augmentation** mechanisms. The learning parameters included the optimizer (Adam or RMSProp), initial learning rate, momentum, decay, patience, and weight averaging. The architecture parameters included the base model, layers used as output, and loss function (i.e., linear combinations of MAE and cross-entropy). The data parameters included rotation, shift, shear, zoom, flip, and cutout.

The main result, illustrated in figure 11.7, is that the meta-learning approach improved upon the human data science team's approach on both datasets. It discovered several useful principles that the data scientists were not aware of: focusing data augmentation to regions that mattered most, and utilizing flips only horizontally across the face; utilizing different loss functions at different times during learning; relying mostly on the output level blocks of the base models. It eventually reached an average error of 2.19 years, which is remarkable because the human average error on this same task is estimated to be 3–4 years in controlled settings and 6–8 in more diverse settings (Burt and Perrett, 1995; Voelkle, Ebner, Lindenberger, et al., 2012). Thus, meta-learning can be used to customize deep learning approaches to the task and thus perform better than general designs and better than human customization.

The third challenge is to estimate confidence in the age estimations; it will then be possible to demonstrate that the treatments provide statistically significant improvement. While deep learning models can be trained to provide a point prediction (i.e., continuous value such as age), they do not by themselves provide any indication of what the confidence intervals around that value are. However, it is possible to train another model to estimate such intervals.

In the approach called **residual input-output estimation** (RIO; Qiu, Meyerson, and Miikkulainen, 2020), a **Gaussian process model** (Rasmussen and Williams, 2006) is trained to predict the residual errors in the validation set. The Gaussian process model is then used to create a distribution of possible values. The confidence intervals can be identified from this distribution. In addition, its mean can be used to adjust the actual prediction, improving its accuracy. When trained with the age estimation data, RIO's confidence intervals included 94.2% of the test set examples in its 95% confidence interval, 89.2% in its 90% confidence interval, and 69.2% in its 68%/ confidence interval—and its mean improved the prediction accuracy by 9%.

To evaluate the value of treatments, a third dataset, D2, was collected. It consisted of two different treatments: all together, 631 patients with 3,925 images taken before treatment, and 68,799 images taken at one week, two weeks, and monthly until six months

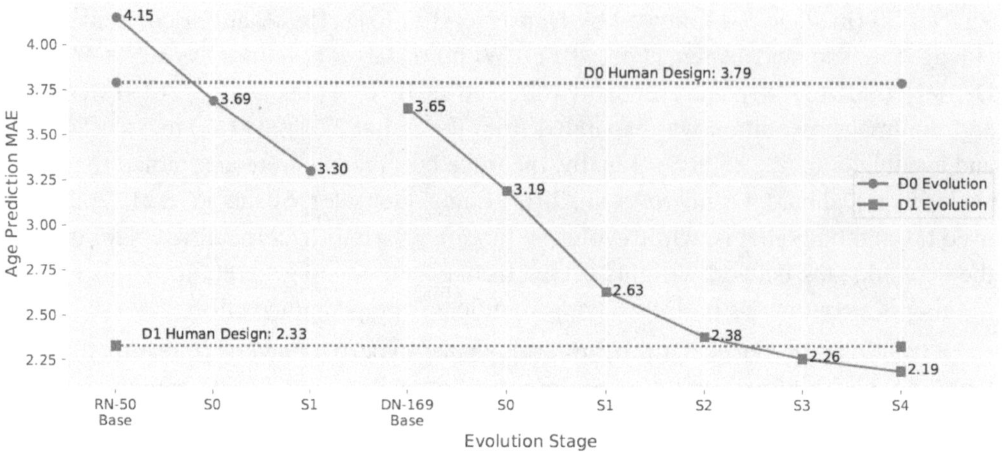

Figure 11.7: **Utilizing meta-learning synergies to beat human designers.** In this natural experiment, human experts and meta-learning were working at the same time to improve the accuracy of age estimation from facial images. In two datasets (D0 and D1), evolutionary meta-learning was able to discover models that performed better than those simultaneously designed by human data scientists. While the neural networks were being continuously trained, evolution optimized the learning, architecture, and data-augmentation hyperparameters. The approach discovered and utilized synergies between design aspects that were difficult for humans to utilize. The final accuracy, MSE of 2.19 years, is better than human accuracy in age estimation (3–8 years). Figure from Miikkulainen, Meyerson, Qiu, et al. (2021).

after treatment. In addition, 5,190 images were taken at the same time points of another 156 patients who received a placebo injection instead of the actual treatment.

The results are shown in figure 11.8. The placebo effect fluctuates somewhat but is centered around zero. The two treatments, on the other hand, show a statistically significant decrease in age. After six months, the patients on average look 0.5 years younger; that is, the effect is about one year for the single injections (typically, multiple injections are used to amplify this effect). The result thus demonstrates that the medical aesthetics treatments are an effective way to make the patients look younger. AI can thus be used to quantify the effect that was previously only subjective.

Moreover, meta-learning was essential in achieving the result. With the same datasets and baseline architectures, similar computational resources, and similar development time, through meta-learning, it was possible to achieve better results than through manual optimization. This case study thus demonstrates that neuroevolution meta-learning is an effective way to develop practical applications of deep learning.

11.5 Neuroevolution of Neuromorphic Systems

Neuromorphic computing (i.e., spiking neural networks designed to be implemented in hardware), is a promising new area for neuroevolution. Such networks need to be energy efficient, and therefore compact and complex, with many design parameters that need to be optimized and customized. This general area is reviewed in this section, several examples are given, and future opportunities are outlined.

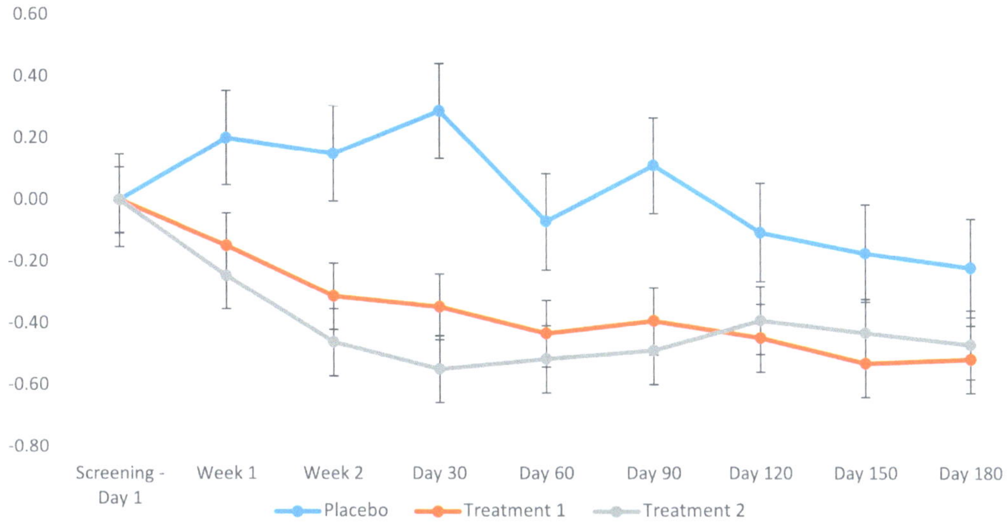

Figure 11.8: **Demonstrating the value of medical aesthetic treatment with AI**. The vertical axis shows the perceived age difference from pre-treatment images to images taken at different times after treatment. The error bars indicate standard error on RIO values, averaged across individuals. Whereas the estimated age differences with placebo treatment are centered around zero, the actual Botox treatments (of which there were two versions) reduce the apparent age substantially, demonstrating that the treatments are effective. Figure from Miikkulainen, Meyerson, Qiu, et al. (2021).

11.5.1 Neuromorphic Computation

Neuromorphic computation, a field focusing on hardware implementation of neural networks, is a burgeoning field with a long history (James, Aimone, Miner, et al., 2017; Schuman, Potok, Patton, et al., 2017). There are several motivations: **Neuromorphic circuits** offer parallel computation that results in real-time performance, they can be fault-tolerant, such systems may learn online, and they can be used to evaluate hypotheses in neuroscience. However, energy efficiency has gradually emerged as the main goal over the years. Most of the implementations are based on **spiking neurons**, as opposed to neurons that are activated with continuous values representing firing rates. Such spikes require very little power, resulting in energy savings of several orders of magnitude. As computation and AI move to the edge (i.e., sensors and actuators in the field), power becomes a primary constraint on computation, and neuromorphic designs offer a possible solution.

Although the full power of neuromorphic computing is still a ways off, substantial hardware designs have already been manufactured that demonstrate its potential. IBM's **TrueNorth** (Akopyan, Sawada, Cassidy, et al., 2015) is one and Intel's **Loihi** (Davies, Srinivasa, Lin, et al., 2018) another, both with one million spiking neurons. It is therefore possible to generate neuromorphic methods and have them run on these actual physical devices. However, the field is much broader, and many methods are proposed for a wide variety of conceptual devices. What makes the field particularly interesting is that the resulting neural network architectures and algorithms are often new and different, not just hardware approximations of existing simulated neural networks, such as backpropagation on a three-layer feedforward network. In that sense, neuromorphic computing is driving innovation in neural networks.

Biology is the source for many such ideas, in that many neuromorphic designs are inspired by neuroscience. Some of them are also plausible, intended to capture principles of biology closely enough to test hypotheses about it. For instance, **spiking neurons** can be implemented at the level of **Hodgkin-Huxley equations**; that is, the electrochemical balance of compartments in the neural membrane. Such implementations allow studying single-neuron computation well. Other models like the **Izhikevich neuron** aim to replicate the bursting and spiking behavior with simpler computation. The **leaky-integrate-and-fire** (LIF) model simplifies them further into integrating the spikes in each synapse over time (with decay) and firing when a threshold is exceeded.

Learning in spiking networks is often based on **spike-timing-dependent plasticity** (STDP). If a postsynaptic neuron fires shortly after the presynaptic neuron, it is possible that the presynaptic firing caused the postsynaptic firing, and the connection is strengthened. Conversely, if the postsynaptic neuron fires shortly before the presynaptic neuron, the connection is weakened. In this sense, STDP is a time-based refinement of the **Hebbian learning** principle; that is, that neurons that fire together wire together.

Note that STDP is an unsupervised learning method: There are no targets or gradients, just an adaptation principle that applies to each connection independently. To make learning more goal-directed, learning mechanisms that approximate backpropagation have also been proposed. A practical approach along these lines is to first train a standard simulated firing-rate backpropagation network offline, and then convert the resulting network into a spiking neural network equivalent (Lu and Sengupta, 2022). Such implementations can achieve power savings; however, they do not take into account or utilize any further properties of hardware systems, such as delays and timing.

Thus, LIF neurons with an STDP learning rule are the most common implementation of neuromorphic architectures. It has low energy requirements and is event-driven, and thus it is suitable for many architectures and applications. The designs include hardware-constrained circuits such as those provided by TrueNorth and Loihi, brain-inspired circuits, feedforward neural networks, and convolutional neural networks.

Interestingly, **reservoir computing** architectures have emerged as a popular design as well, as a way to extend neuromorphic computing to time-varying problems. A reservoir is a recurrent neural network that generates a time-varying signal that can then be processed with a feedforward network, making it possible to recognize time series, or generate time-varying behavior such as locomotion. The reservoir is initialized with random neurons and connection weights, and they are not modified, making them particularly useful for neuromorphic computation, for instance through a memristor implementation.

The designs are often evaluated with standard ML tasks. However, the ultimate applications range from vision and sensing to robotics and control. While it may be possible to achieve better performance through such techniques as deep learning, some of these tasks need to be performed in physical devices at the edge, with little power available. For instance, visual and auditory signal detection, brain-machine interfaces, and central pattern generators for locomotion may be such applications in the future.

Because neuromorphic designs are unique and varied, there is a great opportunity to optimize them through neuroevolution, as will be discussed next.

11.5.2 Evolutionary Optimization

Neuromorphic designs include many dimensions that can be optimized toward several different objectives. For instance, the synaptic efficacy, activation decay, firing threshold, refractory period, and transmission delay of LIF neurons can be adjusted; the connectivity of the network can be changed, and the timing and extent of plasticity modified. Performance in the task is one objective; energy consumption, size, and complexity of the network are others.

Optimization of neuromorphic designs is thus a compelling application for neuroevolution. First, gradients are often difficult to obtain with neuromorphic architectures and in domains where they would be applied. Neuroevolution does not depend on gradients, and it can therefore be used to extend neuromorphic computing to many engineering applications. Second, while many applications can be built with deep learning designs, they are too large to be effectively deployed at the edge. Neuroevolution often results in compact designs that are space- and energy-efficient. Third, it is possible to optimize the designs toward multiple objectives simultaneously, including performance, energy consumption, size, complexity, and specific hardware restrictions. Fourth, evolution can be extended to include hardware design as well, leading to the co-design of the hardware and the algorithms that run on it. Fifth, while such optimization is compute-intensive, it can be done offline, taking advantage of existing hardware simulators.

Many approaches to neuromorphic neuroevolution have been proposed, targeting various aspects of hardware design. For instance, in the **evolutionary optimization of neuromorphic systems** (EONS; Schuman, Mitchell, Patton, et al., 2020) framework, the idea is to evolve a flexible structure of nodes and edges, as well as many of their parameters, such as the connection weights, the time delay on the connections and neurons, activation thresholds, and leak rate. The system starts with a randomly initialized population represented as lists of nodes with IDs and parameters; as usual, each generation of individuals is evaluated in the task, and crossover and mutation are applied to selected parents. The method is thus similar to **NEAT** but includes many more parameters that are specific to neuromorphic hardware. Note that EONS is also generic and can be adjusted to different kinds of hardware. Evolution is simple enough so that it can be implemented in hardware at the edge, but usually it is done offline using a hardware simulator.

EONS has been tested on several standard benchmarks. For instance, in classification tasks from the UC Irvine ML repository, it resulted in simpler and more accurate solutions than standard neuromorphic designs. Evolution also adapted solutions to hardware constraints such as the number of bits used to encode the weights. With a secondary objective to minimize the number of nodes and connections, in addition to accuracy, it produced a range of trade-offs. Such experiments thus demonstrate the viability of hardware/algorithm co-design.

11.5.3 Examples

A particularly interesting application of EONS is to optimize **reservoir architectures**. Although reservoir networks usually have a fixed structure and weights, and learning is only done on the feedforward network that receives input from the reservoir, evolution can be used to optimize the reservoir itself. Such optimization may include tuning its hyperparameters, connectivity, and even the weights. This optimization can be done before the learning in the feedforward network, the feedforward network can be evolved directly at the same time, or the trained performance of the feedforward network can be used as fitness for reservoir evolution (Iranmehr, Shouraki, Faraji, et al., 2019; Reynolds, Plank, and Schuman, 2019). Note that even though these optimizations were developed for neuromorphic computing, they apply to firing-rate versions of reservoir networks as well.

Evolutionary optimization of reservoir networks was shown to result in better performance than the usual grid search for good designs. A particularly illustrative application was to classify radar pulse sequences to identify movements of free electrons in the ionosphere. The performance was close to other ML methods; the low-power implementation may make it possible to deploy actual physical solutions even in satellites.

Along the lines of building better detectors, **radiation anomaly detection** is a similar potential killer app for neuromorphic computing (Ghawaly, Young, Archer, et al., 2022; Ghawaly, Young, Nicholson, et al., 2023). As part of nuclear nonproliferation research, the challenge is to detect hidden gamma-ray sources in an urban environment. This is a difficult task because the detection needs to be done by moving through the normal accessible environment, and background radiation varies significantly. Potential sources need to be detected as anomalies in the observed levels that are very noisy, triggering an alarm for further study. As usual in such tasks, the true positive rate needs to be increased while keeping the false alarm rate as low as possible.

The task is well defined, with American National Standards Institute (ANSI) standards for acceptable detection levels for different types of radiation, as well as standard datasets through which performance can be evaluated. The best current approaches are based on machine learning: In a recent competition by US Department of Energy, nine of the 10 best methods were based on neural networks and similar methods (US Department of Energy, 2019). However, such methods consume a lot of energy, which limits their applicability in the field. Neuromorphic computing is a viable alternative, offering real-time detection with much less energy usage.

In a series of experiments, EONS was set to design a network for this task. As usual, it optimizes the topology and weights of the network, but also several hyperparameters, such as the encoding for the spikes, the delays on neurons and connections, neuron leakage, spiking thresholds, and short-term memory between inferences. A threshold on the spiking rate was used to trigger alarms, adjusted to an acceptable false-alarm rate. The resulting designs had a sensitivity of about half of a computationally intensive principal component analysis (PCA)–based spectral analysis method; thus, the energy savings still come with a cost. However, they met several ANSI standards and performed better than a common kσ baseline method, suggesting that it may already be possible to deploy them in conditions where energy is at a premium. Most interestingly, the best designs leveraged both spatial and temporal features in the signal, taking advantage of short-term memory. Also, while

(*a*) F1TENTH physical car

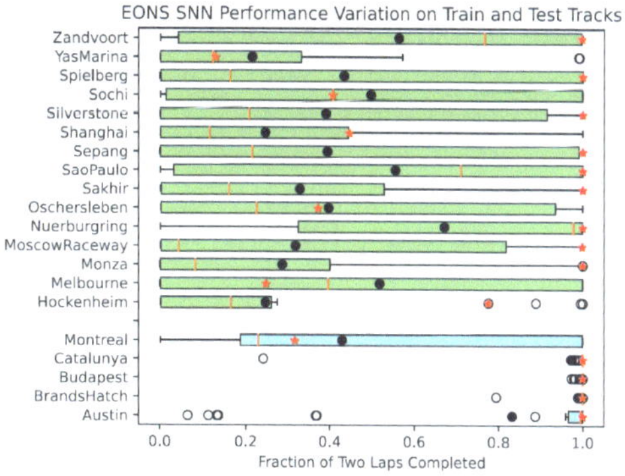

(*b*) Performance on simulated tracks

Figure 11.9: **Evolving a neuromorphic race car controller.** Neuromorphic control can reduce the energy consumption of both sensing and actuation, which is crucial in applications at the edge, such as self-driving cars. (*a*) The physical platform was an F1TENTH robotic vehicle, intended to represent 1/10 of a Formula One race car. The controller was implemented on the μCaspian neuromorphic development board. (*b*) Performance of the neuroevolved controller on various simulated race tracks. The bottom five were used for training and the top 15 for testing. Performance was measured on the x-axis as the fraction of two laps completed. The box plots show the distribution of the best networks found in 30 evolution runs; the red star is the network with the best average performance. Some tracks are more difficult than others, but evolution discovered networks that performed well on each of them, and the best network did well on nine of the 15. When transferred to a real-world track (not shown), performance was not as good as in the simulation, but still demonstrated a practical implementation of a neuromorphic controller at the edge. Figures from Schuman, Patton, Kulkarni, et al. (2022).

the leakage rate was not important, spike encoding mattered, with the number of spikes generated being the most powerful. Such insights are useful in neuromorphic computing, in particular because they can drive co-design of the hardware, suggesting what elements are most useful to implement.

While low energy consumption is important in sensing, it can also be crucial for actuators at the edge. For instance for autonomous cars, computing consumes 40% to 80% of the power required for the control system (Baxter, Merced, Costinett, et al., 2018). Neuromorphic computing could reduce this requirement significantly, thus extending battery life. This idea was tested in the **F1TENTH** system, which is a 1/10 scale simulation and physical implementation of a Formula One race car (figure 11.9; Schuman, Patton, Kulkarni, et al., 2022).

Compared to imitation learning based on hand-designed way points, neuroevolution resulted in architectures that performed better, although they took longer to train. This improvement was due to discovering a customized structure in the network; without it, the results were not as good. Interestingly, the discovered network structures were also smaller than the best hand-designed ones for imitation learning and evolution without structure optimization. Since smaller networks are easier to deploy at the edge, needing less energy and space, neuroevolution again provides solutions that make physical hardware implementations more realistic. As proof of concept, the evolved controllers were implemented on a circuit board on a physical car and tested on a physical track setting.

While the performance dropped somewhat, as is usual in transfers from simulation to the physical world, the driving was largely successful, demonstrating actual neuromorphic control at the edge.

11.5.4 Future Directions

Neuromorphic neuroevolution is a relatively new opportunity. The motivation for energy consumption is compelling, and there are several encouraging results, but the performance still needs to be improved and killer applications identified and implemented. However, there are several ways in which it can be further developed and improved, which makes it an interesting area for neuroevolution in the future.

While neural architecture search at the level of deep learning has become rather difficult, due to extremely large networks and a few dominant architectures, the demands of neuromorphic computing are almost exactly the opposite. The networks need to be small, often recurrent, and customized. There are many hyperparameters beyond the standard neural network ones, such as delays, leakage, thresholds, spike encoding, and short-term memory. The designs are constrained by restrictions and properties of the actual hardware where they will eventually run.

As a result, there are many opportunities for neuroevolution. As with **deep neuroevolution**, the overall topology (i.e., neurons and their connectivity), is important, but because the networks are compact, the connection weights can be optimized directly. The hyperparameters make the optimization problem complex but also provide an opportunity for further improvement and customization. New learning mechanisms may be developed through neuroevolution, improving upon **spike-timing-dependent plasticity** (STDP) and perhaps providing practical methods for online supervised learning. Information may be used about not only spike timing across an individual synapse, but also timing across multiple synapses and their history. There may be opportunities to leverage imperfections and other properties of physical devices, and even interactions between them, like coupling.

Perhaps the most exciting opportunity is the **co-design of neuromorphic architectures and hardware**. It may be possible to establish a cooperative coevolutionary mechanism that modifies both aspects simultaneously, resulting in an optimal fit not unlike the brain and behavior coevolution discussed in section 14.5. There are several constraints on both sides on size, communication, and complexity, but they can possibly be incorporated into the search and evaluation mechanisms. As a result, entirely new architectures and algorithms may be discovered and customized to the task to be solved. Such an approach may indeed prove crucial in moving more computing to the edge in the future.

This chapter explored how evolutionary methods can optimize various components of neural networks, ranging from architectures and hyperparameters to loss functions and learning algorithms. These approaches show how evolutionary search can discover more effective and often surprising configurations, outperforming human design and enabling higher adaptability and performance, especially in complex and constrained environments like neuromorphic systems.

The next three chapters will expand the discussion to synergies and insights that neuroevolution can bring to other approaches and disciplines, starting with reinforcement learning. While neuroevolution and reinforcement learning operate on fundamentally different principles—population-based evolution versus gradient-based reward maximization—their strengths are remarkably complementary, as we will see in chapter 12.

11.6 Chapter Review Questions

1. **Complex system design:** What are the main advantages of using evolutionary optimization for designing complex systems, such as VLSI circuits or neural networks, compared to traditional human-driven approaches?
2. **Bilevel neuroevolution:** How does bilevel neuroevolution enhance the performance of neural networks? Why is surrogate modeling crucial in this process?
3. **Loss function optimization:** Discuss how evolutionary techniques discovered the Baikal loss function, and its impact on regularization and robustness in neural networks.
4. **Activation functions:** Explain the role of activation functions in neural network performance and how evolutionary approaches like PANGAEA can customize activation functions for specific architectures and tasks.
5. **Data augmentation:** Describe how evolutionary optimization can be applied to data augmentation. Provide examples of transformations discovered during such processes.
6. **Learning methods:** What are the key findings of the AutoML-Zero system? How does it demonstrate the potential of evolutionary approaches in discovering fundamental learning algorithms?
7. **Synergies in meta-learning:** Why is it challenging to optimize multiple aspects of neural network design simultaneously? How can these challenges be addressed in evolutionary meta-learning to outperform human-designed models?
8. **Neuromorphic computation:** What are the key advantages of neuromorphic computing, particularly in the context of energy efficiency and edge applications? How do spiking neural networks differ from traditional neural networks in achieving these goals?
9. **Evolutionary optimization in neuromorphic systems:** How does the EONS framework adapt standard neuroevolution methods for neuromorphic hardware? What unique parameters does it optimize compared to traditional neural networks?
10. **Applications and future directions:** Discuss how neuromorphic neuroevolution has been applied in tasks such as reservoir optimization, radiation anomaly detection, and autonomous vehicle control. What are some future opportunities and challenges in combining hardware and algorithm co-design in neuromorphic systems?

Chapter 12

Synergies with Reinforcement Learning

Reinforcement learning and neuroevolution are two prominent approaches for optimizing the performance of neural networks, but they employ different methodologies, with distinct trade-offs. In the first part of this chapter, we will look at their respective advantages and disadvantages, and ways that they could be combined.

In the second part of the chapter, we review approaches that go a step further, allowing evolved networks to invent their own learning algorithm without relying on existing RL methods. By leveraging the principles of neuroevolution, these networks can evolve not only their architectures and weights, but also the intrinsic rules that govern how they learn and adapt over time.

12.1 Reinforcement Learning Versus Neuroevolution

Reinforcement learning (RL) is a type of machine learning (ML) where an agent learns to make decisions by taking actions in an environment to maximize cumulative reward. This approach involves the agent interacting with the environment in a **trial-and-error** manner, receiving feedback in the form of rewards or punishments. RL algorithms, such as **Q-learning**, **deep Q-networks** (DQNs), and policy gradient methods, such as **proximal policy optimization** (PPO), focus on finding a policy that dictates the best action to take in each state of the environment. Among policy gradient methods, **REINFORCE** is one of the simplest and popular ones; it adjusts the policy parameters in the direction of actions that lead to higher returns, using the log-probability of the chosen actions weighted by their observed rewards. One of the main advantages of RL is its ability to handle a wide variety of tasks, especially those involving sequential decision-making and dynamic environments. It is particularly effective in domains where the environment's model is unknown or too complex to be explicitly defined, such as robotics, game playing, and autonomous driving.

However, RL also has several drawbacks. It often requires a significant amount of data and computational resources due to the extensive exploration needed to discover effective policies. The training process can be unstable and sensitive to the choice of hyperparameters. Moreover, RL algorithms can struggle with high-dimensional state and action spaces.

Neuroevolution, on the other hand, is particularly advantageous in its ability to optimize both the topology and parameters of neural networks simultaneously, making it suitable for tasks where the optimal network structure is not known a priori. Additionally, neuroevolution tends to be more robust to the pitfalls of local minima, as the population-based search can explore a broader solution space compared to gradient-based methods used in RL. For example, by repeatedly running the algorithm from scratch, policies discovered using evolution tend to be more diverse compared to those discovered by reinforcement learning algorithms such as REINFORCE, which perturbs actions within trajectories rather than parameters directly. Despite these strengths, neuroevolution also faces certain limitations. For example, neuroevolution might not perform well in environments requiring real-time learning and adaptation since evolutionary processes generally operate on a longer timescale compared to RL's incremental updates. Additionally, especially when the environment provides dense rewards each time step, RL methods often show a greater sample efficiency than neuroevolution approaches.

While these methods are often presented as fundamentally different, they share deeper mathematical connections—both can be viewed as instances of black-box gradient estimation using the same underlying principle. The Math Detail box on the next page unpacks this connection by showing how REINFORCE and evolution strategies emerge from the same log-likelihood trick, differing mainly in what they treat as the search distribution.

12.2 Synergistic Combinations

In practice, RL and neuroevolution can be synergistically combined to leverage the strengths of both approaches. This section reviews several ways of doing so, including combining the two time scales, evolving value functions, and starting points.

12.2.1 Integrating Population-Based and Reinforcement-Based Search

One of the primary difficulties in deep reinforcement learning is discovering optimal policies while avoiding early convergence to suboptimal solutions. Various techniques, such as intrinsic motivation or curiosity, have been suggested to address this issue. However, these methods are often not universally applicable and necessitate careful tuning. Given their population-based nature, effective exploration is an area where evolutionary approaches shine. Additionally, because returns are consolidated across entire episodes, they can often better deal with sparse rewards.

Evolutionary reinforcement learning (ERL; Khadka and Tumer, 2018) is a hybrid algorithm that addresses some of these challenges. ERL utilizes an evolutionary population to generate diverse data for training an RL agent and periodically integrates the agent back into the evolutionary algorithm (EA) population to infuse gradient information into the EA process. This approach harnesses the EA's capability for temporal credit assignment using a fitness metric, effective exploration through a variety of policies, and the stability of a

Math Detail: Connection Between REINFORCE and Evolution Strategies

REINFORCE and evolution strategies originate from different traditions, but both are instances of black-box gradient estimators based on the **log-likelihood trick**. They optimize an expected objective $J(\theta) = \mathbb{E}_{z \sim p_\theta}[f(z)]$ by estimating $\nabla_\theta J$ via sampling, assuming that p_θ is differentiable.

Using the identity $\nabla_\theta J = \mathbb{E}_{z \sim p_\theta}[f(z)\nabla_\theta \log p_\theta(z)]$, both methods compute gradients without backpropagating through f itself. The difference lies in how p_θ is defined.

In REINFORCE, p_θ is a stochastic policy $\pi_\theta(a \mid s)$, and $J(\theta)$ is the expected return over trajectories $\tau = (s_0, a_0, \dots)$. The gradient becomes $\nabla_\theta J = \mathbb{E}_\tau[R(\tau)\nabla_\theta \log \pi_\theta(\tau)]$, which expands to $\mathbb{E}_\tau\left[\sum_t R(\tau)\nabla_\theta \log \pi_\theta(a_t \mid s_t)\right]$ under trajectory factorization.

In ES, p_θ is a search distribution over parameters, typically $\theta \sim \mathcal{N}(\mu, \sigma^2 I)$, and $J(\mu) = \mathbb{E}_\theta[F(\theta)]$. The gradient is $\nabla_\mu J = \mathbb{E}_\theta[F(\theta)\nabla_\mu \log p_\mu(\theta)]$. For a Gaussian, this gradient becomes $\frac{1}{\sigma^2}\mathbb{E}_\theta[F(\theta)(\theta - \mu)]$, or, using the reparameterization $\theta = \mu + \sigma\epsilon$ with $\epsilon \sim \mathcal{N}(0, I)$, we get $\nabla_\mu J = \frac{1}{\sigma}\mathbb{E}_\epsilon[F(\mu + \sigma\epsilon)\epsilon]$.

Practically, the gradient is approximated via the **Monte Carlo method**:

$$\nabla_\mu J \approx \frac{1}{N\sigma}\sum_{i=1}^{N} F(\mu + \sigma\epsilon_i)\epsilon_i.$$

Both approaches use reward-weighted perturbations to estimate gradients, but they differ in scope: REINFORCE perturbs actions, giving fine-grained control and requiring access to intermediate states and transitions; ES perturbs parameters directly and treats the policy as a black box, making it more suitable for sparse-reward or non-differentiable environments and large-scale parallelism.

population-based strategy. Simultaneously, it uses off-policy deep reinforcement learning to enhance sample efficiency and accelerate learning through the use of gradients.

An overview of this approach is shown in figure 12.1. Similar to the standard neuroevolution approach, a population of deep neural networks is evolved through an evolutionary algorithm (mutations and crossover), where the fitness is calculated as the cumulative sum of the reward during a rollout. Additionally, a portion of the best-performing individuals (the elites) are not mutated.

To allow the algorithm to also learn within an episode, instead of only between episodes as in the standard neuroevolution setup, information such as the current state, action, next state, and reward is stored in a replay buffer during each interaction for each actor and each time step. This replay buffer is then used to train agents with a deep RL approach. While the EA explores through noise in the **parameter space** (PS; i.e., mutating the weights of the network directly), RL approaches often explore through noise in the **action space** by sampling from the outputs of the network. ERL leverages both by generating additional experiences for the replay buffer through a noisy version of the RL actor network.

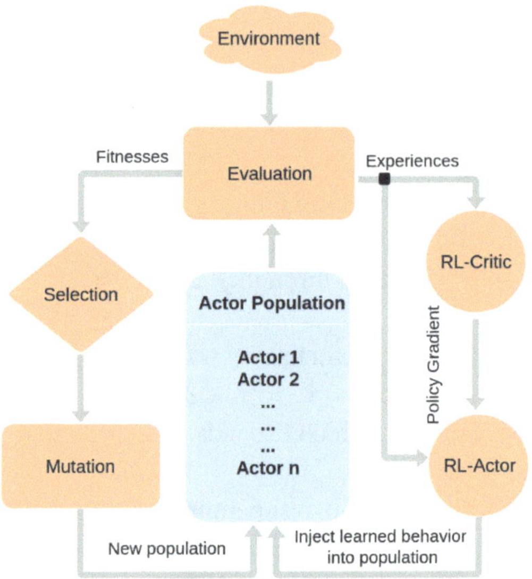

Figure 12.1: **Evolutionary reinforcement learning.** In ERL, a population of neural networks is evolved through NE. Data collected during those rollouts is used to train a deep RL agent, which is periodically injected into the EA population. Figure from Khadka and Tumer (2018).

To provide information back to the EA and to take advantage of the information from the gradient descent learning, every once in a while, during a synchronization phase, the weights of the RL actor network are copied back into the EA population. This network is then evaluated like any other network, which allows good discovered policies to survive and extend their influence over subsequent populations, while non-competitive policies will have fewer chances to reproduce. This transfer is shown to be particularly useful in domains with sparse rewards and deceptive fitness landscapes.

This method leverages EA's ability to explore the policy space and handle sparse rewards while enhancing sample efficiency and learning speed through gradient-based optimization. The algorithm is demonstrated on continuous control benchmarks (figure 12.2), significantly outperforming state-of-the-art **deep reinforcement learning** (DRL) methods like **deep deterministic policy gradient** (DDPG) and **proximal policy optimization** (PPO). ERL maintains effective exploration, stabilizes convergence, and enhances performance across various tasks by combining the episodic returns and population stability of EAs with the gradient efficiency of DRL.

12.2.2 Evolving Value Networks for RL

Many RL approaches rely on the concept of a **value function**. The value function estimates the expected cumulative reward that an agent can achieve from a given state or state-action pair and can thus guide the agent's actions. In deep RL, these value functions are implemented as neural networks, enabling agents to learn complex behaviors in environments with high-dimensional state and action spaces. However, decisions about the architecture of such a value neural network can crucially impact performance, and values that are not ideally chosen can lead to poor agent performance.

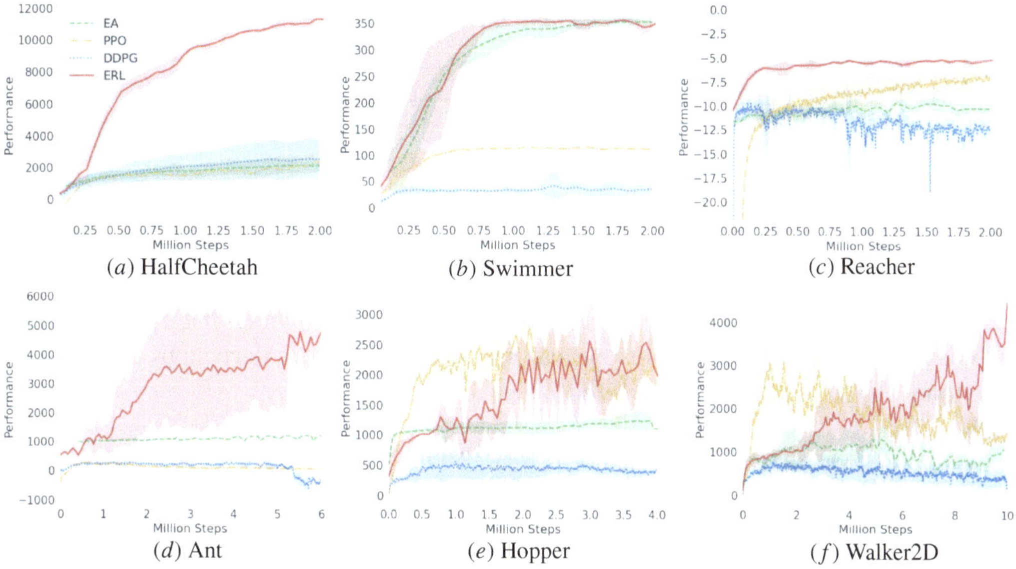

Figure 12.2: **Performance of ERL.** In most domains, such as HalfCheetah (*a*), Reacher (*c*), Ant (*d*), and Walker2D (*f*), ERL significantly outperforms vanilla EA and deep RL approaches. By combining EA's broad, population-driven exploration with RL's gradient-based optimization, ERL achieves both stability and sample efficiency, leading to superior performance even in sparse-reward and deceptive environments. Figures from Khadka and Tumer (2018).

A significant advantage of neuroevolution methods, such as **neuroevolution of augmenting topologies** (NEAT), is that they can not only optimize the weights of a neural network but also evolve the neural architecture at the same time. This approach is thus well-suited to evolve the right initial parameters and architecture of RL agent value networks that are better at learning. This setup differs from the typical usage of NEAT to evolve a direct action selector network, where the network directly outputs the action to be taken by the agent. Here, the network only outputs the value of each state-action pair, and the actual action to be taken is then derived from those values.

Before we detail how to integrate NEAT with the particular RL algorithm, Q-learning, we first briefly describe how this RL algorithm works by itself. **Q-learning** is a model-free RL algorithm that aims to find the optimal policy for a given finite Markov decision process (MDP). The goal of Q-learning is to learn the action-value function, $Q(s, a)$, which represents the expected utility (cumulative reward) of taking action a in state s and then following the optimal policy thereafter.

The Q-learning algorithm involves initializing the Q-values arbitrarily for all state-action pairs, except for the terminal states where the Q-values are set to zero. At each time step t, the agent observes the current state s_t and selects action a_t based on a policy derived from the current Q-values, such as the ϵ-greedy policy. This policy balances exploration and exploitation by choosing a random action with probability ϵ and the action with the highest Q-value with probability $1 - \epsilon$.

After executing action a_t, the agent receives reward r_t and observes the next state s_{t+1}. The Q-value update rule is then applied to update the Q-value for the state-action pair

(s_t, a_t) based on the observed reward and the maximum Q-value of the next state. The Q-value update rule is given by

$$Q(s_t, a_t) \leftarrow Q(s_t, a_t) + \alpha \left[r_t + \gamma \max_{a'} Q(s_{t+1}, a') - Q(s_t, a_t) \right], \qquad (12.1)$$

where α is the learning rate, determining the extent to which new information overrides the old information; and γ is the discount factor, determining the importance of future rewards.

The algorithm repeats this process until convergence, meaning that the Q-values no longer change significantly. The optimal policy π^* can then be derived by selecting the action with the highest Q-value for each state:

$$\pi^*(s) = \arg\max_{a} Q(s, a). \qquad (12.2)$$

In RL, specifically Q-learning, the traditional Q-table method of storing the action-value function $Q(s, a)$ for each state-action pair becomes impractical for large state or action spaces due to the exponential growth of the Q-table. To overcome this limitation, a **neural network** can be used as a function approximator to estimate the Q-value function $Q(s, a; \theta)$, where θ represents the parameters of the neural network. The network receives state representation s as input, and the output layer provides the estimated Q-values for all possible actions in that state. Given state s, the neural network outputs a vector of Q-values:

$$\mathbf{Q}(s; \theta) = \mathrm{NN}(s), \qquad (12.3)$$

where $\mathbf{Q}(s; \theta) = [Q(s, a_1; \theta), Q(s, a_2; \theta), \ldots, Q(s, a_{|\mathcal{A}|}; \theta)]$. The Q-value for a specific action a is then obtained by indexing into this vector:

$$Q(s, a; \theta) = \mathbf{Q}(s; \theta)[a]. \qquad (12.4)$$

During training, the neural network parameters θ are updated to minimize the difference between the predicted Q-values and the target Q-values through gradient descent.

As mentioned at the start of this chapter, traditional **temporal difference** (TD) methods, such as **Q-learning**, rely on manually designed function approximators to estimate the value function, which can be labor-intensive and suboptimal. An approach called **evolutionary function approximation** (Whiteson, 2006) combines NEAT with Q-learning, resulting in the **NEAT+Q** algorithm. In a bilevel optimization setup (see section 11.2), NEAT evolves the structure and weights of neural networks in the outer level, while Q-learning updates these weights during the learning process in the lower-level optimization process. The aim in this combination is to allow the system to discover effective neural network configurations that are better suited for learning accurate value functions, thereby enhancing the performance of TD methods. Because Q-learning optimizes the weight of this network in the lower-level optimization algorithm, we have to decide what to do with those modified weights in the outer level.

As we have seen earlier in this book (section 4.2.3), we can either follow a **Lamarckian** approach, in which the weights updated by Q-learning are written back into the original NEAT genomes; or follow a **Darwinian** approach, where the weight changes are discarded

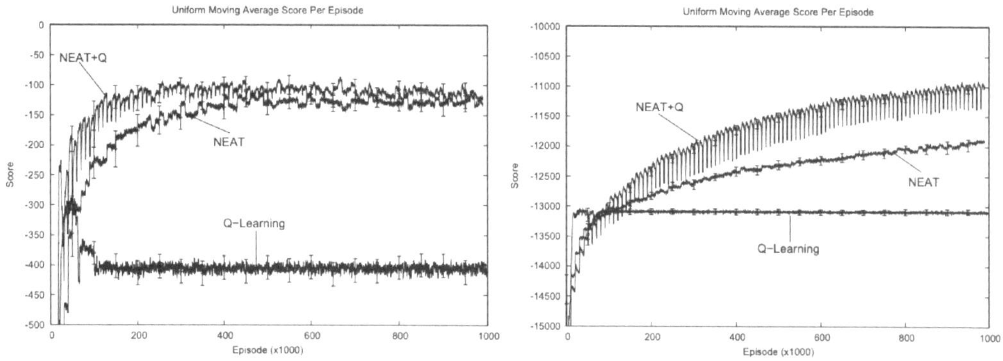

(*a*) Mountain car (*b*) Server job scheduling

Figure 12.3: **Evolutionary function approximation.** Q-learning with a manually designed neural network is compared to both NEAT and NEAT+Q. Both NEAT methods significantly outperform Q-learning in both the MountainCar (*a*) and server job scheduling tasks (*b*). These results demonstrate that NEAT is able to evolve the right initial parameters and architecture of value networks that are better at learning. Figure from Whiteson (2006).

and the original genomes are used to create the neural networks for the next generation. While the Darwinian approach is the more biologically plausible one, a Lamarckian approach could have potential benefits for RL tasks because the same learning doesn't have to be repeated for each generation. A Darwinian approach, on the other hand, could take advantage of the **Baldwin effect**, as we saw previously, in section 4.2.3.

When comparing these methods in different domains such as the MountainCar task, where a car must swing back and forth to build momentum to reach the hilltop goal, or server job scheduling, where jobs must be assigned to servers efficiently under capacity limits, it became obvious that while Q-learning learned a lot quicker in early epochs, performance soon plateaued (figure 12.3). NEAT and NEAT+Q, on the other hand, continued improving, with NEAT+Q significantly outperforming regular NEAT in both domains. Interestingly, if Q-learning started with one of the best networks evolved by NEAT, it was able to match the performance of NEAT+Q. Two examples of such evolved networks are shown in figure 12.4. The evolved networks are sparsely connected and irregular, suggesting that finding them through a manual process is unlikely to succeed.

12.2.3 Evolving Starting Points for RL

Sections 11.2 and 11.3 described how evolution can be used to optimize the design of neuroevolution methods and supervised neural networks. The same approach can be applied to reinforcement learning as well. For example, an outer-loop evolutionary optimization can be tasked to find starting parameters for an inner-loop optimization process, with the goal of making a policy adaptable. This approach is closely related to **bilevel optimization** (section 11.2).

This type of meta-learning was popularized by the influential work called **model-agnostic meta-learning** (MAML; Finn, Abbeel, and Levine, 2017). While deep RL approaches have been shown to reach human or even superhuman performance in a

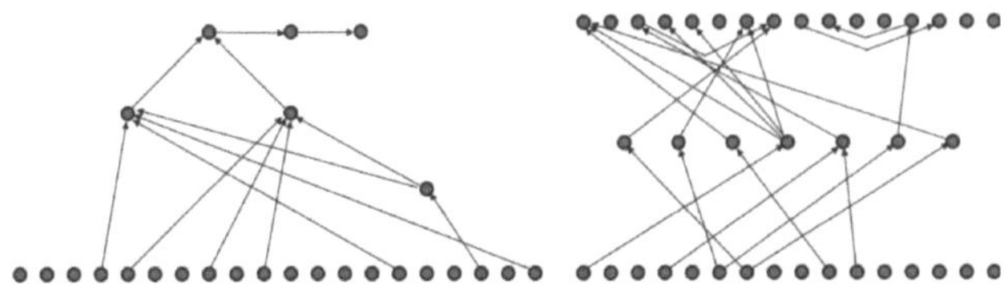

(*a*) Mountain car (*b*) Server job scheduling

Figure 12.4: **NEAT+Q evolved networks topologies.** Shown here are the best neural networks evolved by NEAT+Q for MountainCar (*a*) and server job scheduling (*b*). Inputs are shown at the bottom, while outputs are shown at the top. Each input is also directly connected to each output node (connections are not shown). Output nodes can also be connected to other output nodes. The sparsity and irregularity of these networks suggest that they might be difficult to find through a manual process. Figure from Whiteson (2006).

variety of tasks, there is still a large gap to the learning efficiency of humans. Typical RL approaches require many trials to learn, while humans can perform decently on a variety of tasks with relatively little experience. The MAML approach tries to address this issue to enable more rapid adaptation to different tasks. However, the original MAML relied on second-order gradients, which makes it computationally intensive and sensitive to hyperparameters. Different versions of evolutionary meta-learning have since been developed to improve on the original MAML. For example, **MAML-Baldwin** (Fernando, Sygnowski, Osindero, et al., 2018) uses an evolutionary algorithm in the outer loop and RL in the inner loop, while **ES-MAML** (Song, Gao, Yang, et al., 2020) uses an evolutionary optimizer in both the inner and outer loops. This section will look at those variants in more detail.

What the evolutionary meta-learning methods have in common is that they try to exploit the **Baldwin effect** to evolve agents that can **few-shot learn** (i.e., rapidly adapt using only a small number of examples or interactions) across a particular distribution of tasks. In this way, the objectives extend beyond helping to navigate difficult fitness landscapes, such as the ones encountered in the needle-in-the-haystack problem from earlier studies of the Baldwin effect (figure 4.4). While it is theoretically possible to solve these tasks without learning, here we are interested in tasks that would be impossible to solve through evolution alone, without some form of lifetime adaptation. Consider, for instance, the scenario where the robots depicted in figure 14.6 experience a malfunction, such as the loss of a sensor or a limb. Similarly, envision the rockets illustrated in figure 6.1 encountering an engine failure or a neural network evolved to control one race car being put into another different race car. When the environment changes suddenly, there is often no time to re-evolve a controller, and in these circumstances, a standard feedforward network will often completely fail. Here, the agent has to adapt online to maintain performance.

Canonical tasks in this vein are HalfCheetah goal direction and goal velocity, two high-dimensional locomotion benchmarks implemented in MuJoCo (Multi-Joint dynamics with Contact), a physics engine widely used for simulating articulated bodies and continuous-control RL environments. In the goal direction task, the agent has to rapidly learn to run in a particular direction. In goal velocity, the agent has to learn to adapt its locomotion to match a given velocity. In both tasks, the agents have to learn quickly during their lifetime. Here, the usual genetic algorithm approach for optimizing neural network weights without lifetime learning can be compared to an evolutionary MAML version called **MAML-Baldwin**, in which the initial weights are evolved through a simple genetic algorithm (GA) in the outer loop and an RL method (advantage actor-critic; A2C) updates them in the inner loop (Fernando, Sygnowski, Osindero, et al., 2018). During meta-training, different tasks (e.g., goal directions or target velocities) are sampled in the inner loop, and the network needs to adapt to them through reward feedback alone. This task would be easy if the network received the desired velocity or direction as input. However, in these domains, this information is provided only in the form of a reward to the RL algorithm. For the goal velocity task, this reward is the negative absolute value between the agent's current velocity and the target velocity; for the goal direction task, it is the magnitude of the velocity in either the forward or the backward direction.

While a typical genetic algorithm failed to solve these tasks, MAML-Baldwin evolved agents that can quickly adapt their behavior based on the task requirements. For example, in only 30 simulated seconds, the robot was able to learn to adjust its velocity to match a target velocity. The comparison between the goal velocity and goal direction tasks reveals an interesting difference. The goal direction task demands a significant shift in strategy, as it requires the agent to move forward in some episodes and backward in others. In this scenario, **Lamarckian evolution** tended to get trapped in a local optimum, where it could only move backward effectively. Conversely, **Darwinian evolution** adapted more successfully to these varying tasks. In the goal velocity task, however, Lamarckian evolution performed better because the final velocity achieved in the previous task often provided a suitable starting point for the target velocity in the next task; specifically, the target velocity increased gradually after each episode.

The approaches that we saw so far, including evolutionary meta-learner MAML-Baldwin, still relied on a **policy gradient method** in the inner loop. However, particularly when dealing with real robots, the noise in the physical environment presents challenges to methods relying on gradient estimates since even small differences due to initial conditions, imperfections in the sensors/actuators, or other factors can lead to very different trajectories. It would thus be desirable to also be able to use the more robust evolutionary optimization approach in the inner loop. However, one requirement is that the inner loop optimization should be data efficient because meta-learning is generally expensive.

ES-MAML (Song, Gao, Yang, et al., 2020) provides such a mechanism. Compared to the original MAML, ES-MAML is conceptually simple, does not require estimating any second derivatives, and is easy to implement. An ES-MAML variant particularly suited for noisy domains performs an **evolution strategy** (ES) on the initial network parameters in the outer loop, and then a simple batch **hill-climb algorithm** in the inner loop (Song, Yang, Choromanski, et al., 2020). Hill climbing in ES-MAML involves starting with an initial set of model parameters and then iteratively making small, random perturbations to these parameters. After each perturbation, the modified parameters are evaluated based on their performance on the current task. The algorithm then compares the performance of the modified parameters to that of the previous ones. If the performance improves, the algorithm accepts the new parameters; if not, it rejects them and reverts to the previous parameters.

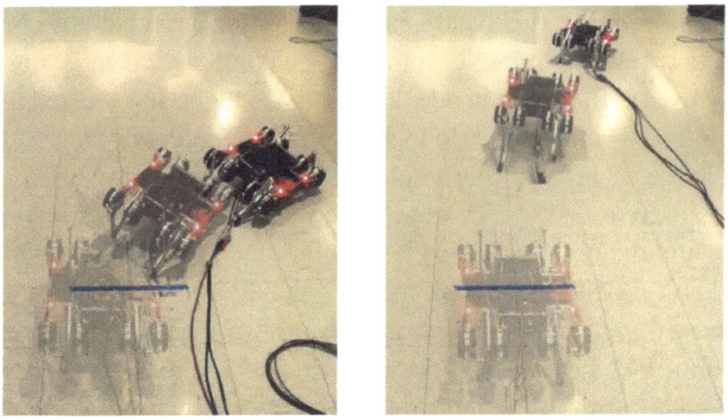

(*a*) Before adaptation (*b*) After adaptation

Figure 12.5: **Quick adaptation through ES-MAML.** The evolutionary meta-learning approach called ES-MAML allows a robot only trained in a simulated environment to transfer to the real world and adapt to changes not seen during training, such as reduced motor power and an added payload of 500g placed on the robot's side. Figures from Song, Yang, Choromanski, et al. (2020). Videos at `https://neuroevolutionbook.com/demos`.

This combination has been shown to be particularly efficient, outperforming MAML and allowing a quadrupedal robot only trained in a simulation to not only overcome the **sim-to-real gap**, but also to adapt to changes in the real world, such as (1) reduced motor power and added payload, and (2) a slippery surface. An example of the robot before and after adaptation is shown in figure 12.5.

In sum, evolutionary meta-learning approaches can exploit the Baldwin effect to produce powerful few-shot learning agents, are often easier to optimize than their gradient-descent-based alternatives, and can deal with noisy environments that methods based on gradient estimates can struggle with.

12.3 Evolving Neural Networks to Reinforcement Learn

Previous sections of this chapter have reviewed a selection of hybrid approaches that combine RL and neuroevolution methods. While these synergistic combinations have proved very useful, they still mostly rely on domain-agnostic learning approaches that can take many trials to learn. Additionally, the aforementioned meta-learning approaches are designed to quickly learn new tasks but struggle to **continually learn**; that is, learning new tasks without forgetting what was previously learned. Finally, animals are born with **innate priors** that facilitate fast learning, which go well beyond the current MAML-like paradigms of only learning good starting weights. For example, a newly hatched chick orients itself toward moving objects right from birth, before any learning takes place (Versace, Martinho-Truswell, Kacelnik, et al., 2018). This evolved prior subsequently helps the animal to quickly and robustly learn to recognize complex objects under varying points of view, abilities that our current AI systems still struggle with.

In this section, we show that neural networks by themselves can be evolved to start with useful priors and the capacity to adapt during their lifetime. This ability can enable them to deal with **non-stationary rewards** and sudden environmental changes. While evolution is a relatively slow process that allows capturing gradual environmental changes, learning enables an individual to adapt to changes that happen during its lifetime. However, evolving these learning abilities is difficult because the neural network needs to learn not only which connections to change during the lifetime, but also when to change them.

One way that neuroevolution can allow agents to learn is to create recurrent connections in the network, which enables them to maintain information through feedback loops. For example, in the T-maze navigation domain described in section 6.3.2, NEAT was able to evolve a simple **recurrent network** that was able to keep information about the high reward location from one trial in the maze to the next. More complex recurrent networks, such as **long short-term memory** (LSTM) networks, have been the main workhorse of ML methods that learn to reinforcement learn (Wang, Kurth-Nelson, Tirumala, et al., 2016).

However, recurrent neural networks are not the only way that artificial agents can adapt quickly. Various learning mechanisms are reviewed in this section, from simpler local Hebbian learning to more advanced methods such as neuromodulation that allow more precise control over plasticity. We will also explore how to combine the ideas of plasticity with indirect encodings, reviewing the adaptive HyperNEAT approach. Finally, we will look at approaches that extend neural networks with an external memory to further separate adaptation and control, which allows them to more easily evolve the ability to continually learn.

Later in this book, when we go into more details on what neuroevolution can tell us about biological evolution (section 14.4), we will return to the questions of how learning, development, and evolution interact and how much intelligent behavior is innate versus how much is learned.

12.3.1 Evolving Hebbian Learning Rules

A way to allow evolved neural networks to learn during their lifetime is to not only evolve the network's weights but also the rules that determine how those weights should change based on incoming and outgoing activations, inspired by the plasticity in biological nervous systems. The idea that all connection weights are genetically determined is unlikely to happen in nature, where information is compressed and thus initial weight values are likely not precisely encoded in the genome. The best-known such rule, which we already encountered in chapter 4.2, is **Hebbian learning**. This mechanism is named after psychologist Donald Hebb and often summarized as: "Cells that fire together wire together." In mathematical terms, this can be written as: $\Delta w_{i \to j} = \eta x_i x_j$, where Δw is the change in weight from neuron i to neuron j is based on the activation between them (x_i and x_j). The learning rate η for each connection can be evolved, allowing evolution to optimize the necessary degree of plasticity.

Pioneering work in evolving such **plastic neural networks** was performed by the labs of Nolfi and Floreano (2000), who studied evolving controllers for simulated and real robots, a field called **evolutionary robotics**. In one of their seminal works, Floreano and Mondada (1996b) trained a real miniature mobile robot to navigate a simple maze. Instead of evolving the weights directly, which are initialized to small random values at the start of

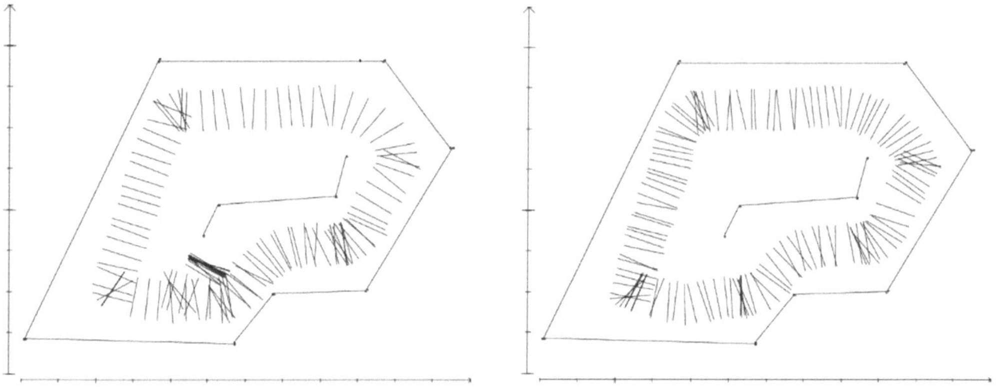

(*a*) Before learning (*b*) After learning

Figure 12.6: **Navigation of mobile robot with Hebbian plasticity.** The navigation of the robot before (*a*) and after lifetime learning (*b*). The evolved learning rules allow the robot to quickly learn to navigate a maze without colliding with the walls. Figures from Floreano and Mondada (1996b).

a robot's deployment, a genetic algorithm determines which of four possible learning rates η (0.0, 0.3, 0.7, 1.0) each synapse in the network should have. In addition, the genome also encoded which of the four Hebbian learning rule variations should be applied at each synapse. These rules included: (1) a simple Hebbian rule; (2) a postsynaptic rule, in which the weight is decreased if the postsynaptic unit is active and presynaptic is not; (3) a presynaptic rule, which decreases the weight when the presynaptic neuron is active and the postsynaptic is not; and (4) a covariance rule in which the weight is decreased if the activation difference between presynaptic and postsynaptic neuron is below a given threshold, and otherwise increased. The weights of these evolving networks were updated every 300 ms following the synapse-specific evolved rule.

While the employed plastic networks were tiny compared to current networks (they have 27 connections in total, with eight infrared sensors, one hidden neuron, and two motor output neurons), the evolved rules enabled the networks to quickly learn how to navigate during their lifetimes, even from completely random weights. In fewer than 10 sensor-motor loops, the best-evolved individuals were able to move forward without getting stuck at walls (figure 12.6). Analyzing the evolved solutions showed that there isn't one particular learning rule that appears more often in these networks. However, the basic Hebbian rule was not used frequently, which is likely because it lacks the capability to decrease synaptic efficacy, potentially hindering future adaptability.

It is also interesting to note that, while the behavior of the robot was stable and it could perform navigation without colliding with walls, the weights of these networks continuously changed during navigation. This is in stark contrast to most other networks that we encountered in this book, including networks trained through methods such as reinforcement learning. In these fixed networks, the weights do not change during inference and only during a dedicated training period. Plastic neural networks thus take us a step closer to biological neural networks, which undergo continual changes throughout their whole lifetimes.

By building on recent advances in scaling evolution strategies to systems with a large number of trainable parameters (section 3.4), evolved plastic neural networks can be applied to more complex problems with larger parameter spaces as well. Thus, we can not only deal with increased network sizes but also more general plasticity rules. While we were previously limited to only choosing from a set of four discrete Hebbian rules, evolving generalized Hebbian rules enables each connection to implement its very specific weight update in the following form:

$$\Delta w_{ji} = \eta[A o_j o_i + B o_j + C o_i + D], \tag{12.5}$$

where w_{ji} is the weight between neuron i and j, η is the learning rate, correlation terms A, presynaptic terms B, postsynaptic terms C, constant D, with o_i and o_j being the presynaptic and postsynaptic activations, respectively. We thus have a total of five parameters (η, A, B, C, D) per connection.

These more complex plastic neural networks can tackle problems that are very difficult or even impossible to solve for standard feed-forward networks. In fact, they can now start to address one of the fundamental limitations of current robots, which is their fragility. While injured animals in nature can compensate for damage by changing their behavior rapidly, robots often fail even if the situation has only changed slightly. Results demonstrating the promise of this plastic neural network approach were obtained in a **four-legged walking domain** (Najarro and Risi, 2020). Here, a standard three-layer feedforward network with [128, 64, 8] nodes per layer (totaling 12,288 trainable weight parameters) was compared to a plastic neural network with the same architecture in which only the plasticity parameters were evolved (totaling $12,288 \times 5 = 61,440$ Hebbian coefficients). Three different versions of a quadruped robot were devised to simulate the impact of partial damage to one of its limbs, with fitness being determined as the average distance covered by two versions of the robot, one in its standard form and the other with damage to its right front leg. The third version, which had damage to its left front leg, was excluded from the training process to later assess the networks' ability to generalize. The networks' parameters were optimized through a variation of the **OpenAI ES algorithm** (section 2.2.4).

While a **feed-forward static neural network** often works well on the morphologies it was trained on, it failed when confronted with the new robot morphology not seen during training. The **evolved plastic network**, on the other hand, quickly found network weights that allow high performance in these more complex domains, even when starting from completely random weights in each episode and *without* access to any reward information during its lifetime (e.g., distance traveled). Additionally, the Hebbian approach was able to adapt to damages in the quadruped, such as the truncation of the left leg, which it had not seen during training (figure 12.7). Instead of needing many thousands of learning steps as is common in standard RL approaches that start from tabula rasa, the evolved Hebbian learning rules allowed the neural network to reach high performance after only 30 – 80 time steps. Interestingly, the Hebbian network achieved this performance across the three morphologies, all without the network receiving any reward-based feedback. The incoming activation patterns during the lifetime are sufficient for the network to self-adjust, even without explicit knowledge of the specific morphology that it is simulating.

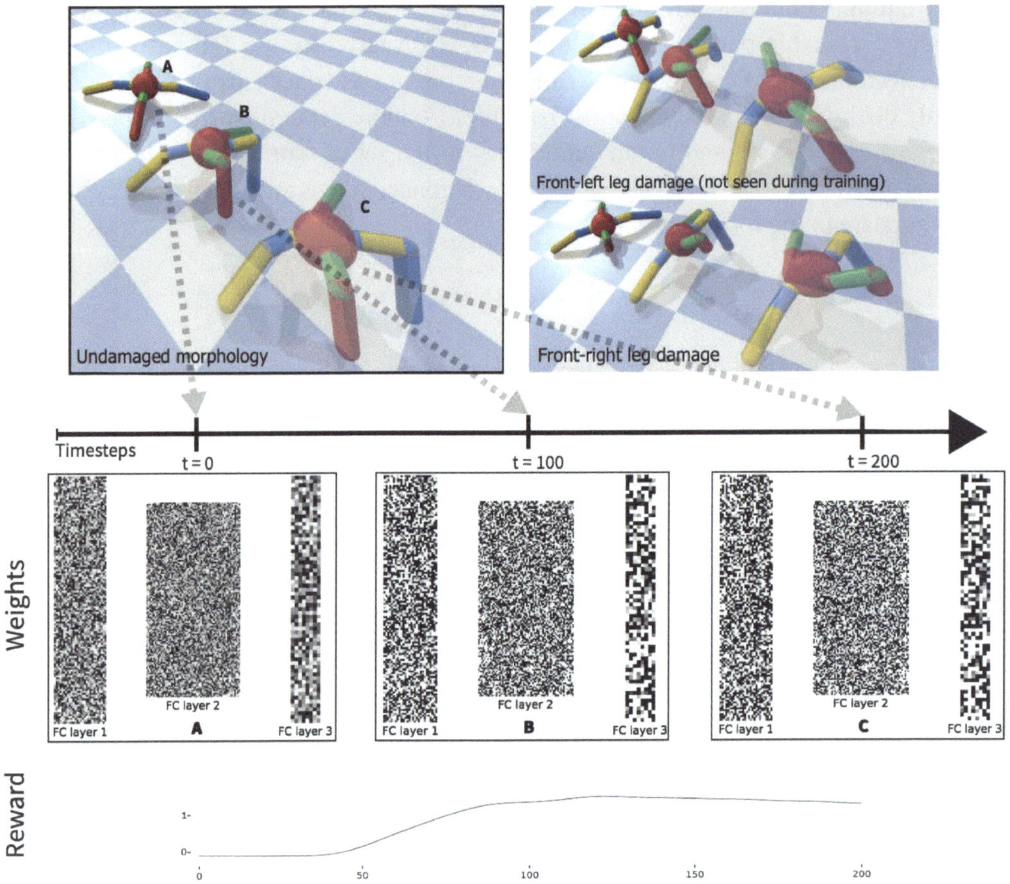

Figure 12.7: **Dynamics in random networks with synapse-specific Hebbian plasticity.** The evolved Hebbian rules allow the controller to quickly learn to control a quadrupedal robot, starting from randomly initialized starting weights. The networks are shown at three different time steps (A, B, C) during the lifetime of a robot with the standard morphology. The quick change in the initially random weights, which is driven purely by the learned Hebbian rules, is reflected in the increase in the reward performance (*bottom*). Even when the morphology of the robot changes through damage to one of the legs (*top right*), the same Hebbian network is able to adapt in a few time steps, allowing the robot to continue locomoting. Figure from Najarro and Risi (2020). Videos at `https://neuroevolutionbook.com/demos`.

12.3.2 Case Study: Hebbian Learning for Physical Robot Transfer

With the Hebbian-based approach showing increased robustness to situations not seen during training, it is now worth asking if this approach is also able to handle another type of generalization: sim-to-real transfer.

Although several studies in neuroevolution have explored the **sim-to-real transfer** for locomoting robots, existing work has largely focused on simple robots with only a few degrees of freedom (Floreano and Urzelai, 2001), or on specific failure modes (e.g., loss of a limb) to create robust controllers (section 6.2.3). These approaches are often based on **domain randomization**, which consists of extending the training set to include a variety of slightly different scenarios, thereby significantly extending the required training time. One of the enduring challenges in robotics is enabling agents to generalize beyond the conditions they were trained in, a problem commonly referred to as the **out-of-distribution** (OOD) generalization. Traditional deep learning approaches, while powerful, often fail when confronted with unforeseen variations in the environment, morphology, or task dynamics.

In this case study, we will take a look at how a Hebbian approach can be scaled to real-world **legged robot** platforms without the need for domain randomization (Leung, Haomachai, Pedersen, et al., 2025). Three types of control policies—**feedforward**, **Hebbian**, and **LSTM** networks—were assessed for robotic locomotion tasks on two real-world legged robot platforms: a dung beetle–like robot with 18, and a gecko-like robot with 16 degrees of freedom (Figure 12.8*b*, *c*). The Hebbian approach followed the connection-specific ABCD approach introduced in the previous section, but incorporated a **weight normalization** approach that was found to be crucial to prevent weight divergence. In this setup, all the weights were normalized layer-wise by dividing them by the maximum weight of that layer.

The simulated environment used the **Omniverse Isaac Gym** RL environment (Makoviychuk, Wawrzyniak, Guo, et al., 2021). All three networks achieved comparable performance in the training environments on the dung beetle–like robot (figure 12.8). However, significant differences emerged during testing in out-of-distribution scenarios. Among the three, only the Hebbian network consistently enabled a real-world robot to walk effectively, surpassing the performance of both the feedforward and LSTM-based controllers (figure 12.8*e*). The robot controlled by the Hebbian network achieved the highest walking speed, approximately 7 cm/s. In contrast, the robots using simple feedforward and LSTM policies barely moved from their starting positions during the 20-second test period. Additionally, the Hebbian network exhibited some intriguing locomotion behaviors: the robot remained stationary until it was placed on the ground, initiating walking only upon foot-ground contact, and ceasing movement once it was lifted off the floor.

Interestingly, these results are in contrast to the superior performance of a recurrent network compared to a Hebbian network for the simple food-gathering task we saw in section 4.2.3. How can this difference be explained? For the more complex locomotion domains, the feedforward and LSTM networks likely exhibit overfitting due to their reliance on highly specific characteristics of the simulated robot—such as precise mass distribution, joint dynamics, and surface friction—that deviated significantly from the conditions of the physical robot. The simulation featured a more symmetrical mass distribution, both left-to-right and head-to-rear, compared to its real-world counterpart. It is possible that a more accurate simulation might have reduced the performance discrepancy across models; however, the creation of high-fidelity simulation environments remains a resource-intensive endeavor. Consequently, the ability of Hebbian networks to generalize robustly, even in imperfect simulation settings, illustrates their practical value for robotic control.

It turns out that the Hebbian networks adapted to real-world conditions without explicit training randomizations of terrain irregularities, mass variations, joint property fluctuations, or morphological defects. While some stochasticity—such as random initialization of synaptic weights at each episode's onset—was present, similar randomization in LSTM

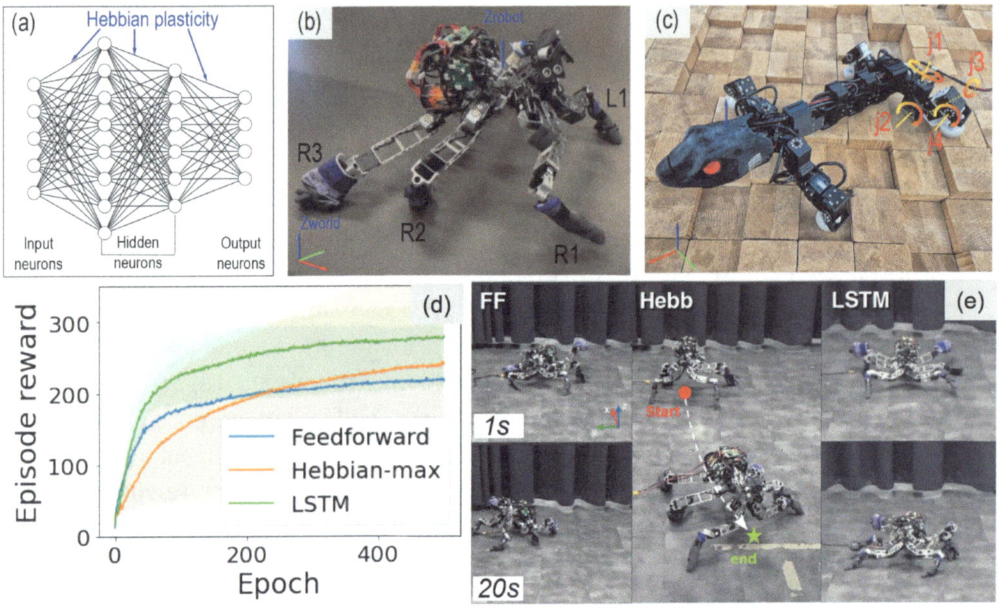

Figure 12.8: **Hebbian network for sim-to-real transfer.** A neural network incorporating Hebbian plasticity (*a*) is trained to control a robot in simulation before being transferred to a physical robot. The approach was tested on a dung beetle (*b*) and a gecko-inspired robot (*c*). Training curves for the dung-beetle robot locomotion are shown in (*d*). The graph displays the average performance and standard deviation of the best individual across five trials for each model. While the LSTM network performs slightly better in the environments seen during training, only the Hebbian network is able to control the dung beetle-like robot when transferred to the physical robot (*e*). Figures from Leung, Haomachai, Pedersen, et al. (2025). Videos at `https://neuroevolutionbook.com/demos`.

hidden states did not prevent overfitting. This suggests that Hebbian plasticity imparts a unique form of adaptability not readily achievable through more conventional architectures.

Further generalization tests were performed with the gecko-like robot. After training solely on flat terrain within simulation, the policy was deployed on the physical robot for evaluation. The gecko-inspired robot demonstrated an ability to adapt its leg movements to traverse uneven surfaces successfully. The Hebbian network also proved resilient to substantial sensory loss and physical damage. Even with the loss of proprioceptive feedback or limb functionality, the robot maintained locomotion ability.

The results in this case study highlight the promise of Hebbian plasticity mechanisms for achieving robust, adaptable robotic behaviors capable of bridging the challenging sim-to-real gap.

12.3.3 Learning When to Learn Through Neuromodulation

Hebbian learning is far from the only adaptation mechanism in the brain. Another mechanism is neuromodulation, which plays many different roles in biological nervous systems. **Neuromodulation** refers to the process by which neural activity is regulated or modified by neurotransmitters and other chemicals within the brain and nervous system. This process can influence various aspects of neuronal function, including the strength and

Info Box: The journey to a PhD in Neuroevolution

I (Sebastian Risi) first encountered neural networks during my undergrad studies in Germany in 2002. There was no course on neuroevolution (or even evolutionary algorithms) at my university, but my interest really got piqued when I got my hands on the *Evolutionary Robotics* book by Nolfi and Floreano (2000). Back then, I had to really convince my professor to let me write a diploma thesis about this niche topic. During my research for the thesis, I encountered Ken Stanley's and Risto's work on NEAT and was blown away. Why not let evolution decide on everything, including the structure of the network! At this point, I basically knew I wanted to pursue a PhD in this direction; here is an excerpt of the email that I wrote Ken in November 2007:

"I recently graduated from the Philipps-University Marburg in Germany with a master's degree in Computer Science. I am wondering if you have any PhD positions available in the area of Neuroevolution for video games or a related field. Especially the NERO project and your publications about Neuroevolution of Augmenting Topologies have drawn my attention.
My research interests focus on Artificial Intelligence, Neural Networks, Genetic Algorithms and biologically inspired computational methods in general. My curriculum vitae can attest to my extensive experience in these areas.
I am highly interested in further investigating the nature of systems that allow phylogenetic and ontogenetic adaptation and that display neural development. I think that the evolution of adaptive Neural Networks that are able to learn online can be used to create totally new game experiences going beyond the nature of classical video games.
I am looking forward to hear from you. Thank you for your consideration."

Even though, in retrospect, the sentence *"My curriculum vitae can attest to my extensive experience in these Areas."* was probably stretching it a bit, Ken decided to hire me as a PhD student, and we got to work together on many interesting and fun projects, some of which are detailed in this book. In the same way that I got inspired by Floreano's and Nolfi's book, I hope that this book might inspire others to join us in this exciting research field!

efficacy of synaptic connections, the excitability of neurons, and overall neural network dynamics. Neuromodulation plays a crucial role in the brain's ability to adapt to new information, experiences, and environmental changes, which affects learning, memory, mood, and behavior.

Given the numerous functions of neuromodulation in biological nervous systems, it has also been incorporated in evolving plastic neural networks. In these instances, neuromodulation is typically set to modify the Hebbian plasticity of neurons in the neural network. This ability is useful because it allows switching plasticity "on" and "off", enabling reward-mediated learning. For example, plasticity of some weights might be switched off if they were responsible for obtaining a high reward in the environment, while other connections should increase their plasticity when the reward is lower than what was expected. In a pioneering demonstration of this idea, Soltoggio, Bullinaria, Mattiussi, et al. (2008) used an approach similar to **NEAT**, in which structural mutations during evolution could insert and delete not only standard hidden nodes but also neuromodulatory nodes. In contrast to standard neural networks, in which each node has the same type of effect on all the nodes that it is connected to, in a neuromodulated network, each node i calculates both a standard activation a_i and a **modulatory activation** m_i as follows:

$$a_i = \sum_{j \in \mathrm{Std}} w_{ij} o_j, \tag{12.6}$$

$$m_i = \sum_{j \in \mathrm{Mod}} w_{ij} o_j, \tag{12.7}$$

where w_{ij} is the strength of the connection between node i and j, and o_j is the output of the postsynaptic neuron, which is calculated based on the standard activation $o_j(a_j) = \tanh(\frac{a_j}{2})$. In contrast to how pure Hebbian plasticity was modeled as $\delta_{ji} = \eta[Ao_jo_i + Bo_j + Co_i + D]$, we are now making the weight change also dependent on the calculated modulatory activation m_i: $\Delta w_{ji} = \tanh(\frac{m_i}{2})\delta_{ji}$.

Incorporating neuromodulation has been shown to provide advantages in tasks that require selectively switching plasticity on and off at critical moments during an agent's lifetime (Soltoggio, Dürr, Mattiussi, et al., 2007). One such task requires a **simulated 3D bee** to forage in an environment where flowers of two colors, blue and yellow, offer varying amounts of nectar. The reward provided by these flowers is determined by either deterministic or probabilistic rules, creating a dynamic and uncertain environment. The bees need to learn to associate flower colors with higher nectar rewards and adapt their strategy as these reward contingencies shift over time. This setup required the bees to demonstrate adaptive decision-making in response to environmental variability.

In this task, the evolved modulatory networks clearly outperformed both fixed-weight and traditional Hebbian plasticity networks. The evolved bee agents demonstrated remarkable behavioral adaptability throughout their simulated lifetimes. They were able to quickly adjust their preferences when the color associated with high reward was reversed. This rapid re-learning reflects the emergence of effective dynamic learning strategies within their neuromodulatory neural networks. Furthermore, these agents exhibited the capacity to estimate long-term reward expectations even in environments where rewards were delivered probabilistically. Rather than relying on immediate reinforcement, they aggregated historical reward outcomes to refine their behavior, a trait closely aligned with biological foraging strategies.

Beyond the environments used during evolution, the most successful neurocontrollers also generalized well to an entirely new and more complex situation where both flower types offered the same average reward but with different probabilities. Despite never encountering this scenario during training, these controllers adapted effectively, learning which flower yielded better long-term gains. This result demonstrates a significant degree of generalization and supports the idea that evolved neuromodulatory topologies are capable of developing not just task-specific behavior, but generalizable learning strategies applicable to novel situations.

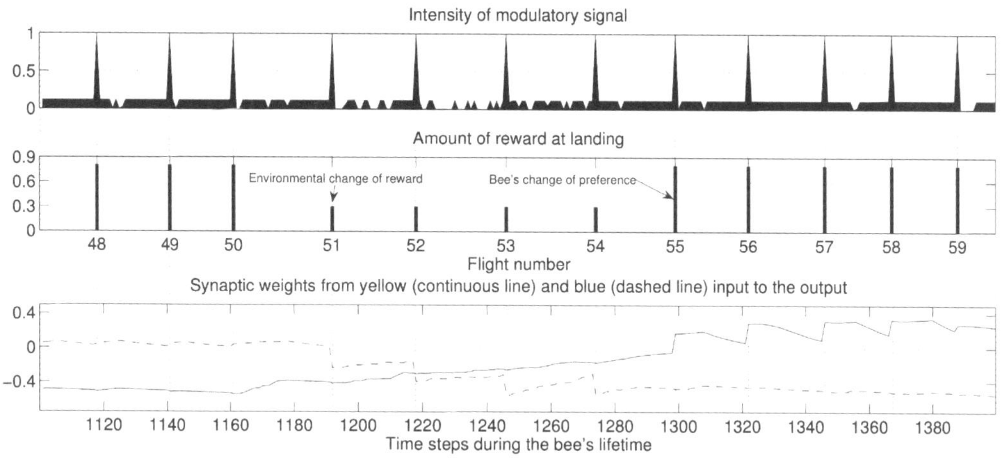

Figure 12.9: **Neural activity and weights during the simulated bee's lifetime.** The top graph shows the intensity of the signal generated by the single modulatory neuron, the middle graph represents the amount of reward received upon landing, and the bottom graph tracks the synaptic weights of color inputs to the output neuron, which determine the bee's preference for a specific flower color; the graphs line up over time. Notably, the modulatory signal remains low during flight but increases significantly upon landing, facilitating a more rapid update of synaptic weights at that critical moment. Figure from Soltoggio, Dürr, Mattiussi, et al. (2007).

How did the evolved neuromodulated networks solve this task? Figure 12.9 provides insights into the neural dynamics of the system. At the moment of landing, the modulatory signal reaches its peak, triggering the network to update synaptic weights effectively. During flight, the modulation level remains low, enabling a gradual decay of synaptic weights, which mirrors the diminishing expectation of a reward in its absence. Interestingly, there are moments when neuromodulation drops entirely to zero, particularly when the bee perceives the gray color outside the flower field. Since these areas consistently yield no rewards and are unaffected by changes in contingencies, synaptic plasticity—and consequently, learning—are deactivated. These results demonstrate that the evolved neuromodulatory network activates learning only when environmental conditions necessitate adaptation.

In conclusion, neuromodulation can play a critical role by acting as a regulatory mechanism for synaptic plasticity. It enabled the system to "switch on" learning during critical events, such as when the bees landed on a flower and received a reward signal and "switch off" learning in predictable or irrelevant situations, such as when flying over areas without flowers. This dynamic control of plasticity allowed the artificial bees to learn when necessary and maintain stability when no learning was required. We will return to the evolutionary advantages of neuromodulation in section 14.3, where we go into more detail on what neuroevolution can tell us about biological evolution.

12.3.4 Indirectly Encoded Plasticity

A challenge with the previously mentioned approaches to encode plasticity is that the local learning rules for every synapse in the network must be discovered separately by evolution. However, similar to how connectivity patterns in the brain follow certain regularities, the distribution of plasticity rules across a neural network likely would benefit from such regularities as well.

It turns out that the HyperNEAT approach we introduced in section 4.3.3 to indirectly encode weight patterns can be generalized to also indirectly encode the plasticity of a network. As in the brain, different regions of the artificial neural network (ANN) should be more or less plastic and employ different learning rules, which HyperNEAT allows because it sees the geometry of the ANN. The main idea behind this approach, which is called **adaptive HyperNEAT** (Risi and Stanley, 2010), is that **compositional pattern-producing networks** (CPPNs) in HyperNEAT can encode not only connectivity patterns but also patterns of plasticity rules.

A straightforward way to enable HyperNEAT to indirectly encode a plastic network is to augment the CPPN to produce not only each connection's weight, but also additional connection-specific parameters such as learning rate η, correlation term A, presynaptic factor B, and postsynaptic factor C. When a policy network is initially decoded, it stores these parameters and the connection weights for each synapse and then updates the weight during its lifetime following this simplified version of the generalized **Hebbian learning rules**:

$$\Delta w_{ij} = \eta \cdot \left[A o_i o_j + B o_i + C o_j \right]. \tag{12.8}$$

This approach was able to solve a simple **T-maze task**, demonstrating that HyperNEAT is, in fact, able to distribute plasticity coefficients in a geometric manner. However, adaptive HyperNEAT is clearly an overkill for such simple domains, and we have seen simpler approaches, such as directly encoded Hebbian learning or LSTMs (section 6.3.2), being able to do the same. However, things become a bit more interesting if we not only allow adaptive HyperNEAT to encode these learning rule coefficients but enable it to evolve completely new learning rules itself. This more general adaptive HyperNEAT model augments the four-dimensional CPPN that normally encodes connectivity patterns with three additional inputs: presynaptic activity o_i, postsynaptic activity o_j, and the current connection weight w_{ij}. That way, the synaptic plasticity of a connection between two two-dimensional points (x_1, y_1) and (x_2, y_2) can be described by:

$$\Delta w_{ij} = \text{CPPN}(x_1, y_1, x_2, y_2, o_i, o_j, w_{ij}). \tag{12.9}$$

Instead of only being queried at the beginning of an episode, here the CPPN is queried at every time step to update the weights of the neural network. The same CPPN that decides on the initial weights and network connectivity is now also responsible for how to change the network, taking into account both the location and activity of the network's neurons.

A simple, yet effective domain to test the effectiveness of this method is a variation of the T-maze domain with a nonlinear reward encoding. That is, in this domain, the agent received a high reward for rewards with "color" input values 0.3 and 1.0, but a low reward for 0.1 and 0.8. Because the agent was given a network with no hidden nodes (which is not able to learn this nonlinearity), evolution needed to discover a CPPN that instead encodes the appropriate nonlinear learning rules. And indeed, this more general adaptive HyperNEAT version was able to solve the task, while a normal Hebbian network and the simpler adaptive HyperNEAT (which outputs the Hebbian learning coefficients) failed. Interestingly, in this domain, the discovered learning rules smoothly change with

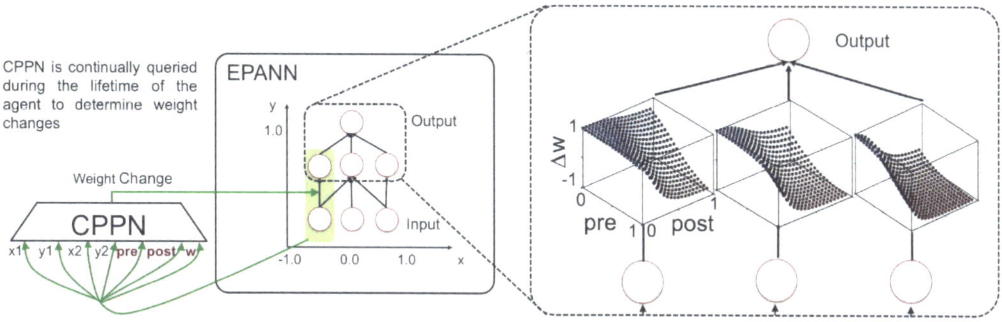

Figure 12.10: **Adaptive HyperNEAT.** In adaptive HyperNEAT, the CPPN is queried each time step, given the location of nodes but also the current weight of the connection and the activity of the presynaptic and postsynaptic neurons. This way, each connection in the network can learn arbitrary learning rules that can be geometrically encoded by the CPPN. Figure from Soltoggio, Stanley, and Risi (2018).

the location of the presynaptic node, as shown in figure 12.10, suggesting that the substrate geometry gives a useful task bias.

Adaptive HyperNEAT can also be combined with the **evolvable substrate** approach (section 4.3.5) to alleviate the experimenter from deciding on the number of hidden nodes. For the first time, this unified approach, called **adaptive evolvable-substrate HyperNEAT** (Risi and Stanley, 2012b), was able to fully determine the geometry, density, and plasticity of an evolving, neuromodulated ANN. Although the tasks to which these methods have been applied so far are relatively simple, they still serve an important purpose. They demonstrate the CPPN's ability to learn arbitrary learning rules that enable an agent to quickly adapt to changes in its environment. The idea of learning to learn has since become a larger focus of the wider ML community, but the groundwork was laid by many neuroevolution methods. Scaling this approach up to work with larger networks and for more complex tasks is an exciting future research direction.

As mentioned earlier in chapter 4, in traditional indirect encodings like HyperNEAT and adaptive HyperNEAT, you start compressed—you assume from the beginning that the network structure or weights can be generated by a compact underlying pattern (e.g., a small CPPN). The design constrains expressivity from the start, relying on the hope that the compact representation will be powerful enough to capture all needed variations.

It is an interesting question whether we can build an indirect encoding that starts the other way around; that is, maximally expressive and then gradually compressing itself. One such approach is called **evolve and merge** (Pedersen and Risi, 2021). In this approach, each synapse in the network is assigned a unique, parameterized local learning rule based on the generalized Hebbian ABCD rule (section 12.3.1). Using ES, the population of networks is first optimized for performance on a task. The novel idea in evolve and merge is that after a predefined number of generations, k-means clustering is employed to merge similar learning rules. Each group of similar rules is replaced by a cluster center, effectively reducing the number of unique rules while maintaining learned behaviors. The evolution process continues with the reduced rule set, and the merge-evolve cycle repeats until a target number of generations is reached.

Applied to a **quadrupedal locomotion** task, evolve and merge achieved impressive compression, reducing the number of trainable parameters by over 96% without sacrificing, and often enhancing, performance on unseen morphology variations. Plastic networks evolved with this approach outperformed static networks in terms of robustness, even when static networks were optimized with noisy inputs to encourage generalization. While static networks achieved higher performance in the original, unperturbed environment, plastic networks displayed far greater resilience under change. Interestingly, robustness improved as the number of learning rules decreased, validating the hypothesis that a compact set of adaptive rules promotes generalization. This observation aligns closely with the **genomic bottleneck hypothesis** (Zador, 2019), which suggests that biological systems, by encoding a limited number of developmental rules, achieve robust and generalizable behavior across a wide range of conditions.

The evolve and merge framework extends the philosophy of indirect encoding to the evolution of learning itself. Unlike classical indirect methods that impose compression at initialization, this approach allows rich expressivity early in evolution and gradually sculpts it into a compact form through environmental feedback and evolutionary pressure. The finding that starting with a large rule set and pruning it leads to superior generalization also draws parallels to the **lottery ticket hypothesis** in deep learning (Frankle and Carbin, 2019). This hypothesis proposes that within a large, randomly initialized neural network, there exist small subnetworks (i.e., "winning tickets") that, when trained in isolation, can match or even exceed the performance of the full network. In the case of both the lottery ticket hypothesis and evolve and merge, an initially large parameter space increases the chance of finding high-performing solutions.

12.3.5 Learning to Continually Learn Through Networks with External Memory

A major challenge in AI in general, and in evolving plastic neural networks in particular, is **continual learning** (Kudithipudi, Aguilar-Simon, Babb, et al., 2022). That is, learning new tasks or knowledge without forgetting what was previously learned. Most current neural networks struggle with this and suffer from a symptom called **catastrophic forgetting**, where they can learn a new task but forget tasks that they learned previously.

A promising approach to overcome this challenge is **memory-augmented neural networks**, which are neural architectures in which the circuit for control and the mechanism for adaptation are separated by design. In addition to learning through changes in connection strength or activations (such as in LSTMs), modeling memory directly offers another way for agents to adapt and remember. One realization of this type of memory-augmented neural network is the **neural Turing machine** (NTM; Graves, Wayne, and Danihelka, 2014), which we'll look into more detail in this section.

The NTM combines traditional neural networks with the concept of a Turing machine, enhancing the capability of neural networks by giving them the ability to read from and write to an external memory module. Inspired by the theoretical model of computation introduced by Alan Turing, a Turing machine consists of a controller and an infinite tape that serves as memory, along with a read/write head that can move across the tape to retrieve or modify information.

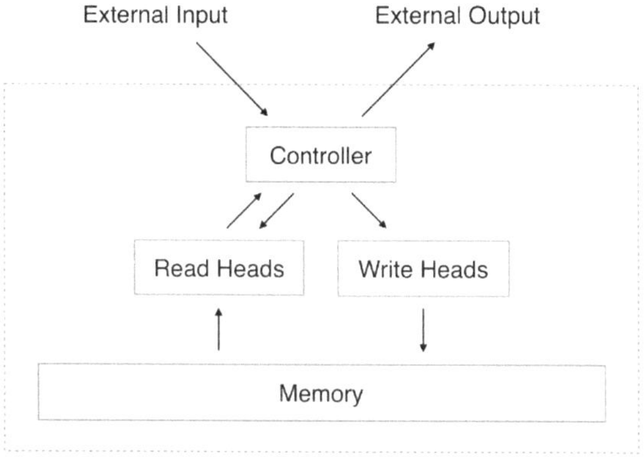

Figure 12.11: **Neural Turing machine.** In an NTM, a neural network (the controller) is augmented with an external memory component that it can learn to read from and write to through dedicated read and write heads. The external memory allows the network to store information over many time steps and use it to learn algorithms such as copy, sort, or associative recall. Figure from Graves, Wayne, and Danihelka (2014).

By incorporating a similar mechanism, the NTM can not only process data through its neural network structure but also store and retrieve data, enabling it to perform tasks that require memory. Just like LSTMs, NTMs are designed to handle long-range dependencies in data. In section 2.3.4, we saw that LSTMs achieve this through their gating mechanisms that regulate the flow of information, allowing the network to maintain or forget information over long intervals. Similarly, NTMs can maintain data over long periods using their external memory bank, albeit in a more explicit and controllable manner.

An overview of the basic NTM architecture is shown in figure 12.11. At the heart of an NTM is a neural network that acts as the controller. This controller operates like any other neural network, processing task inputs and generating outputs. However, unlike standard neural networks, it also interacts with an external **memory bank** through read and write heads, directing the read and write operations. The primary advantage of NTMs is their ability to perform tasks that require complex manipulation of data sequences or the execution of algorithms that conventional neural networks struggle with. This includes problems like sorting lists, simple arithmetic, or even executing simple programs.

The original NTM was designed to be completely differentiable, including the read and write mechanisms. This means the NTM can be trained end-to-end using **backpropagation**, similar to a typical neural network. However, this differentiable architecture comes at the cost of having to access the entire memory content at each step, making this approach inefficient for larger memory banks. It also limits the setup to a fixed memory size. Additionally, because the attention is "soft", small errors can accumulate, making the approach not always generalize perfectly to copying long sequences.

An exciting direction is to train the NTM instead through neuroevolution, which not only allows hard attention and potentially better generalization, but also can be directly applied to RL-like problems that do not require input-output examples. The **evolvable NTM** enables exactly this, optimizing both the NTM architecture and its weights with NEAT (Greve, Jacobsen, and Risi, 2016). Because it is trained through evolution, this model features a theoretically unlimited memory capacity. The particular evolvable NTM version reviewed here operates with a single, unified head for both reading and writing (figure 12.12*a*). Beyond the standard inputs and outputs needed to interface with the external environment, the network has inputs and outputs that match the vector size of a memory entry. Additional outputs are used for selective read/write operations, adjusting the active memory position, and employing content-based addressing. Described in more detail, the evolvable NTM executes four primary operations:

1. Write: A write interpolation output dictates the blending of the current memory vector at the head's location with a new write vector. This is calculated as follows:

$$M_{t+1}(h) \leftarrow M_t(h) \cdot (1 - w_t) + a_t \cdot w_t, \tag{12.10}$$

   where $M_t(h)$ represents the memory vector at the head's location at time t, w_t is the write interpolation weight, and a_t is the write vector.

2. Content Jump: If the neural network output for content jump exceeds a certain threshold (e.g., 0.5), the head jumps to a position on the memory tape most akin to the write vector, determined by an Euclidean distance metric in this implementation.

3. Shift: This network output can shift the read head either to the left or right from its current position or maintain the position based on the highest activated shift output among the three provided.

4. Read: Following any content jumps and shifts, the content of the memory vector at the final location of the head is automatically fed into the neural network at the start of the next cycle.

A good domain to compare the evolutionary NTM with the original backprop-trained NTM is the **copy task**. In this task, the neural network must memorize and retrieve a lengthy sequence of random binary vectors. The network receives an initial bit indicating the start of the task, followed by a sequence of random binary vectors, and then a delimiter bit that marks the beginning of the recall phase.

The comparison highlights one of the many advantages of neuroevolution. Since NEAT begins with basic networks and progressively introduces nodes and connections, it was able to find a sparsely connected champion network that uses just a single hidden neuron. This evolved network is significantly smaller in size than the original NTM, which features full connectivity, 100 hidden neurons, and a total of 17,162 parameters. Additionally, and in contrast to the original NTM, the evolved networks generalized perfectly to long sequences.

Another benefit of having an external memory is that it can help in tasks requiring **continual learning**. While it can be difficult to learn new information in an LSTM or Hebbian network during the lifetime of the agent without **catastrophic forgetting** of previous information, it is straightforward to tackle this challenge with an expanding external memory (where new information can be put in an unused location in memory). A task to test the evolvable NTM for continual learning is the **season task** (Ellefsen, Mouret, and Clune, 2015), in which the agent must learn to identify and remember which food

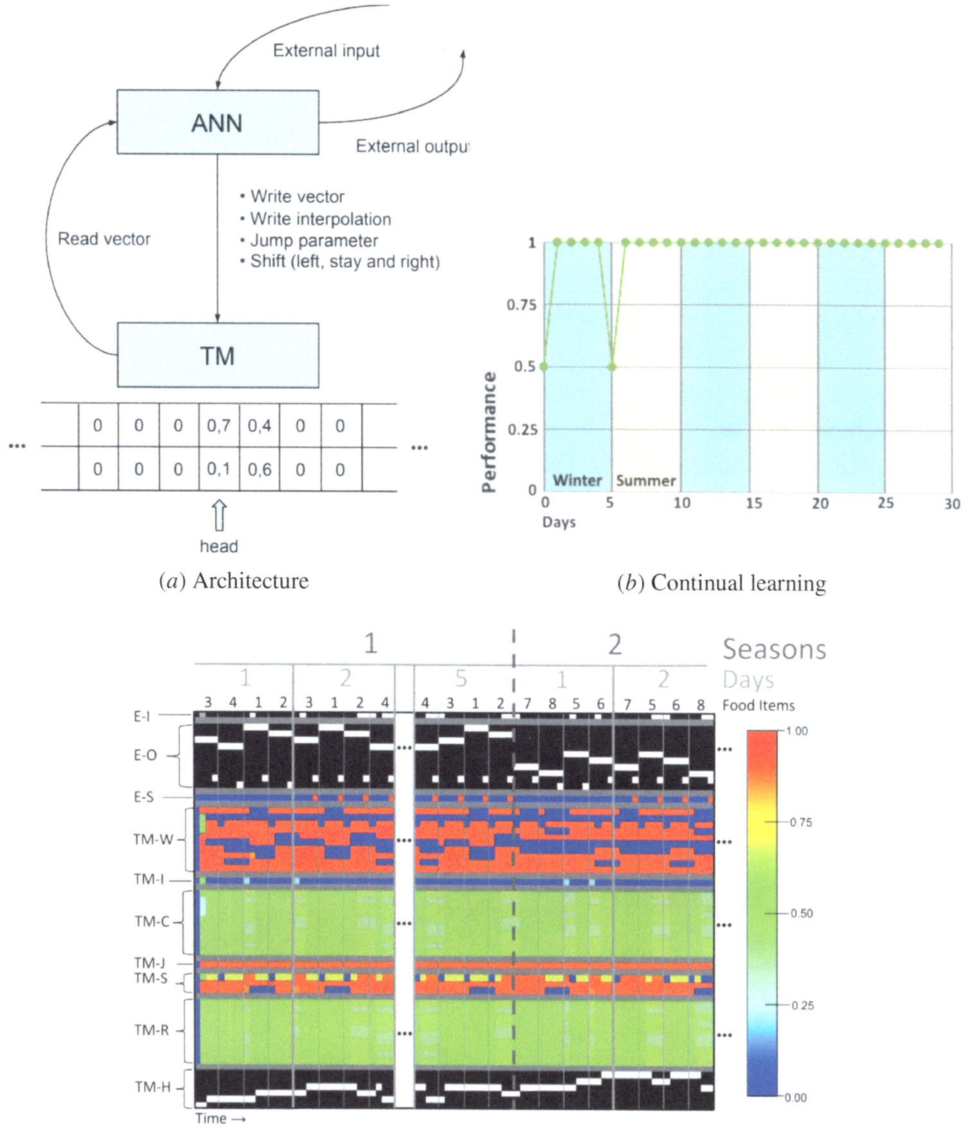

(*a*) Architecture

(*b*) Continual learning

(*c*) Solution details

Figure 12.12: **Evolvable Neural Turing Machine.** (*a*) The evolvable NTM is characterized by a hard attention mechanism and a theoretically infinite memory tape. (*b*) The NTM discovered by NEAT is able to learn new associates in one shot without forgetting previously learned ones. In this manner, evolved networks with an external memory show promising performance for tasks requiring continual learning. (*c*) Days 3 and 4 of season 1, as well as all days beyond day 2 in season 2, are not displayed but are completed flawlessly. Legend: E-I: ANN output indicating whether the food item should be consumed. E-O: ANN inputs from the environment: summer item (1–4), winter item (5–8), reward (9), punishment (10). E-S: Score indicator. TM-W: Write vector. TM-I: Write interpolation. TM-C: Content of the tape at the current head position after writing. E-J: Content jump input. TM-S: The three shift values in descending order: left, none, right. TM-R: Read vector. TM-H: Current head position after control operations. Figures from Lüders, Schläger, and Risi (2016).

items are nutritious and which are poisonous across different seasons, with the challenge increasing as the food items and their properties change from one season to another. The task tests the agent's ability to withstand catastrophic forgetting and to learn new associations while retaining old ones.

The evolvable NTM was further modified to facilitate continual learning (Lüders, Schläger, and Risi, 2016). First, a default memory location was initialized with a fixed vector serving as a fallback when no existing memory meets a similarity threshold during a content jump; once used, a new default was added at the end of the tape, helping prevent overwriting past associations. Second, to further support the preservation of existing memories, content jumps now occurred only if similarity exceeded a threshold; otherwise, the default jump was used.

With these modifications in place, NEAT was indeed able to find an NTM that can learn new associations in a single trial without forgetting previously learned ones (figure 12.12*b*). Impressively, it was able to generalize almost perfectly to sequences that it had never encountered before. Which type of solution did evolution discover? The network stores information about the food items in four memory locations—two for each season (figure 12.12*c*). Initially, the agent ignores all food items. However, after being penalized for neglecting nutritious items, it begins to remember the ones that it missed and must consume in the future. Each nutritious item is stored in a separate memory location, resulting in the use of all four locations. This memorization process is achieved by linking the punishment input to the write interpolation output.

In summary, networks with an external memory offer an intriguing complementary approach to learning that is not based on modifying activations (e.g., LSTMs, RNNs) or weights (e.g., Hebbian learning). However, which approach (or which combination of approaches) is best, and for which type of problems, is an important open research question.

12.4 Integrating Evolution, Learning, and Embodiment

While general-purpose RL algorithms are, in principle, capable of solving a wide range of tasks, they typically require vast amounts of data and interactions to do so. In contrast, we have seen in this chapter that evolution can be used to **learn to learn** by discovering mechanisms that allow neural networks to adapt more efficiently to specific distributions of tasks. This advance holds particular promise for real-world applications, such as robot locomotion under various circumstances that were not encountered during training (section 12.3.2). In this section, we review some of the major open questions and key challenges in approaches that aim to combine the previously explored themes of evolution, learning, and embodiment.

Generality versus adaptation: How can we evolve plastic neural networks that are capable of truly learning new tasks during their lifetimes? While current systems have demonstrated impressive adaptability, such as transferring from simulation to physical environments, they have yet to be conclusively tested on entirely novel task distributions. This raises a fundamental tension between generality and specialization: How broad should the capabilities of a learning system be, and how quickly should it adapt? A highly specialized learner might adapt quickly to a narrow range of environments but fail to generalize. Conversely, a general learner might be slower to adapt, but more robust across tasks. The optimal solution likely lies in discovering mechanisms that allow both fast adaptation and wide generalization, mirroring the kind of flexible intelligence observed in biological brains.

One unresolved question is how best to implement plasticity in ANNs. A promising direction is to explore systems that coordinate multiple mechanisms—local plasticity rules, memory, and structural plasticity. These mechanisms operate at different levels. **Local plasticity rules** adapt the strengths of existing connections based on information available at the neuron or synapse, allowing the network to fine-tune its behavior without changing its overall architecture. **Memory** provides a way to retain and reuse information over time, supporting adaptation across longer timescales than moment-to-moment weight updates alone. In contrast, **structural plasticity**, such as we have seen in the **lifelong NDP** approach in section 7.3.4, changes the architecture itself by creating, removing, or rewiring connections, thereby altering which pathways are available for computation. Together, these mechanisms may enable ANN systems that are more flexible, adaptive, and robust than approaches based on any single form of plasticity alone. Neuroevolution is uniquely suited to discover such synergies, especially when indirect encodings are used to represent both network structure and plasticity rules.

Deception in learning to learn: Even if a system contains all the necessary ingredients for learning, there is no guarantee that evolution will discover the optimal configuration. A key challenge in evolving cognitive behaviors is deception in the fitness landscape. Evolutionary processes can become trapped in local optima, especially when early-stage solutions provide some success without requiring genuine adaptation. This observation is a well-known issue in meta-learning settings: Simple heuristics can outperform more complex, adaptive solutions in the short term, diverting evolutionary trajectories away from the more promising long-term strategies. More open-ended search strategies, such as **novelty search** (NS), have proved effective in overcoming such deception (Risi, Hughes, and Stanley, 2010). By explicitly rewarding **behavioral diversity**, these approaches help maintain exploration pressure and uncover more sophisticated adaptive behaviors. For instance, we have seen in section 6.3.2 that novelty search has shown promise in evolving agents with both memory and lifetime learning capabilities. However, as we seek to combine more mechanisms, the search space becomes increasingly complex and deceptive. Tackling this will require not only better optimization methods, but also deeper understanding of how these components interact during both evolution and learning.

Regularity versus generalization: Evolutionary algorithms with **indirect encodings** excel at solving regular problems because they reuse genetic information to generate structured, regular phenotypes. However, this reliance on regularity can be a double-edged sword: While regular neural structures can generalize well, they can also make fine-tuning specific connections more challenging. This trade-off can pose a challenge for solving more complex problems.

To address this trade-off, a promising solution emerges from biology: the combination of **developmental encodings** with lifetime learning mechanisms like **synaptic plasticity**. Developmental encodings bias evolution toward producing regular, scalable networks, while plasticity enables those networks to adapt to unique, context-dependent details during their lifetimes. This **genomic bottleneck** has been hypothesized to facilitate generalization, as it is a strong regularizer for architectures and learning rules that generalize well (Zador, 2019). Empirical findings support this synergy: Networks generated by more regular encodings (Pedersen and Risi, 2021; Tonelli and Mouret, 2013) tend to exhibit better general learning abilities when plasticity is introduced. These results suggest that combining indirect encodings for efficient structural generalization with reinforcement learning or plasticity for fine-grained adaptation can yield artificial systems that are both robust and flexible—mirroring the dual strategy used by animal brains to balance inherited structure with lifelong adaptability.

Future research should focus on understanding how to best encode plasticity within indirect frameworks and how to harness the synergy between genetic regularity and lifetime learning. This combination could be the key to unlocking the full potential of indirect and developmental encodings.

Embodied agents: An exciting avenue for future research lies in the evolution of embodied agents; that is, systems where learning mechanisms, neural architectures, and physical morphologies co-evolve. In terms of learning and physical morphology, one approach that takes a step in this direction is the **deep evolutionary reinforcement learning** (DERL) framework (Gupta, Savarese, Ganguli, et al., 2021). DERL combines an outer evolutionary loop that searches over robot morphologies with an inner loop of reinforcement learning that trains control policies within each agent's lifetime. While this combination does not use neuroevolution per se (i.e., the network weights are trained with reinforcement learning), it does show the synergistic effects of combining these methods. As outlined in figure 12.13*a*, this dual loop allows agents not only to evolve structurally through mutation and selection, but also to learn sensorimotor skills from scratch using standard RL methods (figure 12.13*c*). The design space for morphologies, UNIMAL (figure 12.13*d*), is expressive enough to allow for highly varied and articulated body plans, while remaining tractable enough for large-scale search.

What makes DERL interesting is how it reveals deep connections between environmental complexity, morphological evolution, and the learnability of control. As agents evolve in more challenging environments (figure 12.13*e*), their bodies adapt in ways that inherently support more general learning. Even when transferred to novel tasks, these morphologies outperform others that evolved in simpler settings. Moreover, a strong **morphological Baldwin effect** emerges: Evolution consistently selects for bodies that make learning easier. An exciting next step is to evolve not just morphologies, but also the neural architectures and initial weights of these controllers using neuroevolutionary methods. Such integration promises even faster and more robust lifetime learning. As part of chapter 14, on what neuroevolution can tell us about biological evolution, we will return to the evolution of virtual creatures and what their morphological constraints mean for evolution (section 14.5).

In conclusion, the integration of evolution, learning, plasticity, and embodiment represents one of the most exciting frontiers in artificial intelligence. This research not only promises more efficient and adaptive agents but also offers a unique window into the evolution of natural intelligence, which we will explore more deeply in chapter 14. For

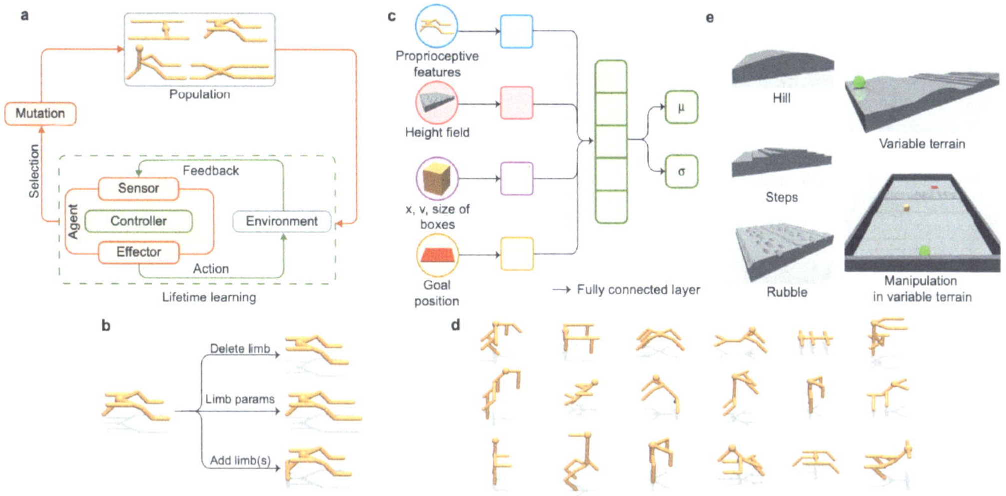

Figure 12.13: **Overview of the DERL approach.** DERL generates embodied agents through the interaction of two adaptive processes. The outer loop performs evolutionary search over morphologies, applying structural mutations—such as limb addition or modification, illustrated in (*b*)—to iteratively refine the agent's physical form. In parallel, the inner loop uses reinforcement learning to train a neural controller from scratch for each morphology (*c*). A range of example morphologies generated within the UNIMAL design space, a modular and expressive representation for articulated agents, is shown in (*d*). The environments in which these agents evolve vary in complexity; (*e*) shows the variable terrain setting, composed of stochastically generated obstacles including hills, steps, and rubble. In the most complex scenario—manipulation in variable terrain—agents must not only traverse the terrain, but also manipulate an object from a randomly assigned starting location (green sphere) to a designated goal (red square), requiring coordinated locomotion and interaction with the environment. Figure from Gupta, Savarese, Ganguli, et al. (2021). Video at `https://neuroevolutionbook.com/demos`.

now, we will turn our attention to another method that can be effectively combined with neuroevolution: generative AI.

12.5 Chapter Review Questions

1. **Reinforcement learning versus neuroevolution:** What are the key strengths and weaknesses of reinforcement learning and neuroevolution when applied to optimization tasks? How do their approaches differ in handling sparse rewards and high-dimensional spaces?

2. **Evolutionary reinforcement learning:** How does ERL combine evolutionary algorithms and deep reinforcement learning? What are the specific advantages of integrating these methods in tasks with sparse rewards?

3. **Replay buffer in evolutionary reinforcement learning:** What is the role of the replay buffer in ERL? How does it enable the algorithm to learn within episodes, unlike standard neuroevolution?

4. **NEAT+Q approach:** How does the NEAT+Q algorithm integrate neuroevolution (via NEAT) with Q-learning? What are the advantages of this approach for evolving neural architectures in RL tasks?

5. **Meta-learning with evolutionary methods:** How does evolutionary meta-learning differ from traditional reinforcement learning? How does it exploit the Baldwin effect to enable few-shot learning across diverse task distributions?

6. **ES-MAML:** What makes ES-MAML particularly well-suited for meta-learning in noisy environments? How does it differ conceptually and computationally from gradient-based meta-learning methods like MAML?

7. **Evolving networks to reinforcement learn:** What are the advantages of evolving neural networks that are capable of intrinsic reinforcement learning? How does this approach address the challenges of non-stationary rewards and environmental changes?

8. **Hebbian learning rules:** How does the evolution of Hebbian learning rules enable neural networks to adapt during their lifetimes? What are some limitations of using simple Hebbian mechanisms for complex tasks?

9. **Neuromodulation in evolved networks:** How does incorporating neuromodulation into evolved networks enhance their ability to learn and adapt? Why is neuromodulation particularly effective in tasks requiring memory and adaptation?

10. **Evolvable neural Turing machines:** What distinguishes the architecture of the evolvable NTM from that of traditional neural networks? How does it interact with its external memory, and how does this form of memory usage compare to learning via internal activations in models like LSTMs or through weight updates in approaches such as Hebbian learning?

Chapter 13

Synergies with Generative AI

Generative AI, exemplified by the breakthroughs like large language models (LLMs), has redefined our ability to synthesize knowledge, create diverse content, and solve problems requiring creativity. This paradigm includes a broad family of models such as **generative adversarial networks** (GANs; Goodfellow, Pouget-Abadie, Mirza, et al., 2020) for high-fidelity image synthesis, **autoencoders** (Hinton and Salakhutdinov, 2006; Kingma and Welling, 2014) for representation learning and reconstruction, **diffusion models** (Ho, Jain, and Abbeel, 2020; Sohl-Dickstein, Weiss, Maheswaranathan, et al., 2015) for producing complex, realistic samples through iterative refinement, and **LLMs** (Hadi, Al-Tashi, Qureshi, et al., 2025; Min, Ross, Sulem, et al., 2024) for text generation and reasoning.

While generative AI thrives in producing new ideas and solutions, it often benefits from robust frameworks for exploration and optimization—which are areas where neuroevolution excels. This chapter examines how these two fields can complement each other in a bi-directional fashion. Evolutionary algorithms (EAs) can expand the potential of generative AI by evolving architectures, fine-tuning parameters, and fostering diversity in outputs. At the same time, generative AI can enhance evolutionary computing by generating creative solutions, identifying optimal configurations, and producing complex evolutionary outcomes. Before we take a closer look at these synergies, let's review some relevant background information on LLMs.

13.1 Background on Large Language Models

Large language models (LLMs) are characterized by their vast scale and capacity to process and generate human-like text, making them powerful tools for a variety of language-based tasks. There are many such models, including **generative pre-trained transformer** (GPT; Achiam, Adler, Agarwal, et al., 2023; OpenAI, 2025), **Gemini** (Anil, Borgeaud, Alayrac, et al., 2025; Gemini Team, 2025), **Llama** (Grattafiori, Dubey, Jauhri, et al., 2024; Touvron, Martin, Stone, et al., 2023), **Claude** (Anthropic, 2025a,b), **Qwen** (Bai, Bai, Chu, et al., 2023; Yang, Li, Yang, et al., 2025), **Mistral** (Jiang, Sablayrolles, Mensch, et al., 2023; Mistral AI, 2024), and **DeepSeek** (Guo, Yang, Zhang, et al., 2025; Liu, Feng, Xue, et al., 2024). Some of these are closed and accessible through a paid interface only, and others are open; some are general chatbots and others include sophisticated reasoning abilities and tool use such as web access; and many of them are actually combinations of multiple models with different specialties.

The backbone of all of these LLMs is the **transformer architecture** (Vaswani, Shazeer, Parmar, et al., 2017), which employs a **self-attention mechanism** that allows the model to consider the importance of all other words in a sentence, regardless of their positional distance from the word being processed. Unlike models that rely on recurrent layers, the transformer's architecture allows for parallel processing of data, increasing efficiency and scalability when managing the large datasets essential for training LLMs. Self-attention was described in more detail in section 4.4.

LLMs undergo extensive pre-training on large text corpora, learning to predict the next token in a sequence. Beyond the massive data ingestion, researchers also fine-tune various aspects, such as the ratio of different data types in the training set, the learning rate, and other training parameters to optimize performance.

The performance of LLMs adheres to what is called **scaling laws** (Kaplan, McCandlish, Henighan, et al., 2020). These laws demonstrate that model performance improves logarithmically with increases in size, data volume, and computational power. Large-scale data not only aids in training more accurate models but also ensures broader linguistic coverage, allowing the models to generalize better across various tasks. The need for so much data shows why scaling laws matter; they help us predict how well LLMs will work as they get bigger.

However, despite their extensive pre-training, LLMs in their raw form are not fully equipped to handle specialized tasks directly. The transition from a general linguistic understanding to specific real-world applications requires significant post-training optimization. This phase involves **fine-tuning** the model on task-specific datasets, which refines its responses according to particular needs. Additionally, the use of **prompt engineering** enhances how models interpret and respond to queries, making them more effective and adaptable. These adjustments are key to shaping LLMs for specific uses, from everyday chatbots to more complex, domain-focused tasks.

While the current trend predominantly focuses on constructing larger models trained on increasingly vast datasets, there exists a parallel strand of research that employs evolutionary computing to enhance LLMs in innovative and less conventional ways (Wang, Zhao, Jiao, et al., 2025; Wu, Wu, Wu, et al., 2024), as we will explore in subsequent sections of this chapter.

13.2 Evolution Enhances Large Language Models

While LLMs excel at generalizing knowledge across vast domains, leveraging their capabilities for specific tasks often requires tailoring, optimization, and adaptation. **Evolutionary computing** offers a natural avenue for addressing these challenges, providing mechanisms to explore and optimize solutions in high-dimensional, complex spaces. This section explores how evolutionary algorithms can be harnessed to enhance LLM performance, focusing on their role in optimizing task prompts and merging expert models specialized in different areas. Through this integration, evolutionary computing acts as both an optimizer and a creative engine, complementing the generative capabilities of LLMs and enabling them to perform better on specific tasks.

13.2.1 Evolutionary Prompt Engineering/Adaptation

To adapt LLMs for specific downstream tasks, adding an instruction to the input text, known as a **discrete prompt**, directs the LLMs to perform desired tasks with minimal computational cost. This method does not rely on the direct manipulation of parameters and gradients, making it especially suitable for LLMs with black-box APIs like GPT (Achiam, Adler, Agarwal, et al., 2023; OpenAI, 2025), Gemini (Anil, Borgeaud, Alayrac, et al., 2025; Gemini Team, 2025), and Claude (Anthropic, 2025a,b). However, the efficacy of LLMs in executing specific tasks heavily relies on the design of these prompts, a challenge commonly addressed through prompt engineering.

Prompt engineering often requires extensive human effort and expertise, with approaches ranging from enumerating and selecting diverse prompts to modifying existing ones to enhance performance. These methods can lead to a cycle of exploration, which might consume resources without substantive gains, or exploitation, which may confine the search to local optima and stifle broader improvements. Evolutionary algorithms, which are particularly well suited for this discrete prompt optimization, offer a robust alternative. Sequences of phrases in prompts can be seen as gene sequences, allowing us to use the whole EA toolkit for prompt adaptation.

Taking this concept further, the evolutionary process can be used to maintain a diversity of prompts, helping to avoid diminishing returns seen in conventional prompt engineering methods. The trick here is that we can use the LLM itself to modify prompts as well as the strategy for prompt modification, leading to **self-referential self-improvement**. This way, we harness not only the LLM's linguistic capabilities but also its ability to iteratively refine the prompts based on performance feedback. As representative works in this area, we review two approaches in this section: EvoPrompt (Guo, Wang, Guo, et al., 2024) and Promptbreeder (Fernando, Banarse, Michalewski, et al., 2024).

EvoPrompt (figure 13.1) optimizes prompts for language models by employing evolutionary algorithms such as a **genetic algorithm** (GA) and **differential evolution** (DE), which we briefly touched on in section 2.2.6. The evolutionary process begins with a set of initial prompts that leverage the wisdom of humans and a development dataset, where each prompt is evaluated based on how effectively it elicits the desired responses from the LLM. Throughout a series of iterations, prompts are selected based on their performance scores. New prompts are then generated through evolutionary operations that include combining elements from multiple selected prompts (crossover) and introducing random variations (mutation). The prompts to introduce these operations are shown in figure 13.1. These newly created prompts are subsequently evaluated, and those with superior performance are retained for further refinement in subsequent iterations. This cycle of selection, generation, and evaluation repeats, progressively enhancing the quality of the prompts. A key innovation of this method is the use of the LLM itself to generate new candidate prompts based on evolutionary instructions.

The EvoPrompt method was evaluated across multiple tasks, including language understanding, language generation, and the particularly challenging **big bench hard**

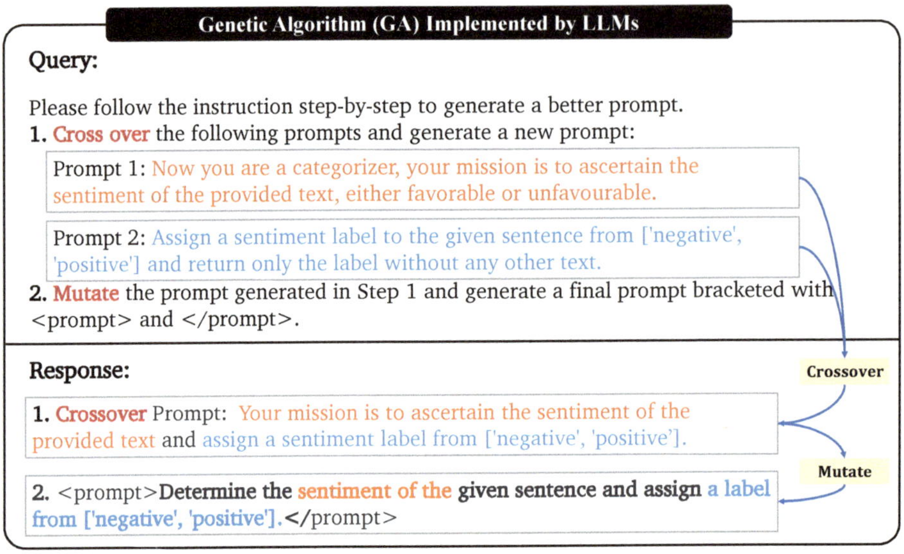

Figure 13.1: **GA process in EvoPrompt.** In step 1, LLMs perform crossover on the given two prompts (words in orange and blue are inherited from prompt 1 and prompt 2, respectively). In step 2, LLMs perform mutation on the prompt. Figure from Guo, Wang, Guo, et al. (2024).

(BBH) tasks. BBH is a subset of the broader beyond the imitation game benchmark (BIG-bench), specifically curated to include the most difficult tasks where language models often struggle. All tasks are text-based but span diverse formats such as logical reasoning puzzles, multi-step arithmetic, common-sense reasoning, and code understanding. This makes BBH a widely used stress test for assessing reasoning and generalization. While the EvoPrompt method demonstrated impressive results across all tasks, performance on BBH is especially representative of its capabilities, as success on BBH indicates strong generalization and robustness across complex, text-based challenges.

For the BBH tasks, the EvoPrompt method was applied to optimize prompts specifically for the GPT-3.5 model. A subset of the test set was used as the development set to iteratively refine the prompts, with the final performance reported as normalized scores (figure 13.2). The results were striking: EvoPrompt achieved substantial improvements across all 22 evaluated tasks. Specifically, the differential evolution variant of EvoPrompt led to as much as a 25% improvement in some tasks, with an average improvement of 3.5%. In comparison, the GA variant also performed well but slightly lower, reaching a peak improvement of 15% and an average of 2.5%. While differential evolution approaches have been less explored in neuroevolution than approaches based on GA or evolution strategy (ES), the strong performance in combination with prompt evolution suggests that they may provide a competitive and underutilized paradigm in the age of generative AI.

Like EvoPrompt, **Promptbreeder** automates the exploration of prompts by utilizing evolutionary algorithms to generate and refine task prompts that condition LLMs for better responses (figure 13.3). Each task prompt serves to condition the context of an LLM before additional input, aiming to elicit a better response from the model. Promptbreeder starts with an initial set of task prompts and mutation prompts, derived from combining domain-specific problem descriptions with varied "thinking styles" and

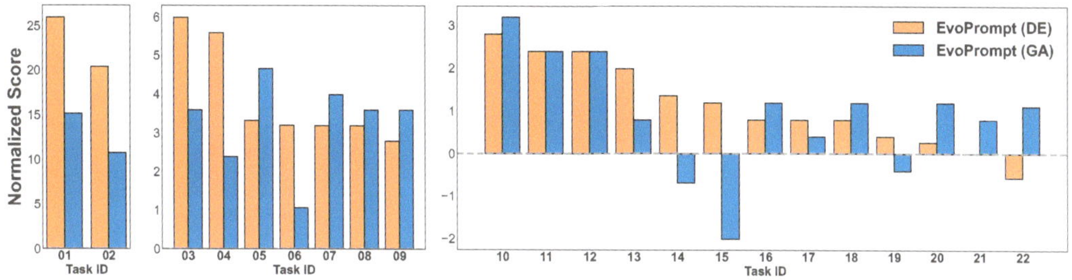

Figure 13.2: **Normalized scores on Big Bench Hard tasks for EvoPrompt.** Since the tasks are challenging, GPT-3.5 was used as the LLM. Score normalization is calculated in comparison to the prompt "Let's think step by step" with a three-shot Chain-of-Thought demonstration. The differential evolution (DE) version consistently outperformed the GA version, achieving up to 25% improvement with an average gain of 3.5%, while GA reached a peak of 15% and a 2.5% average. Figure from Guo, Wang, Guo, et al. (2024).

mutation strategies. This initial population is crucial, as it sets the baseline for the evolutionary process, incorporating a rich diversity of approaches and perspectives right from the beginning. The system evaluates the effectiveness of each prompt by testing it on a batch of domain-specific question-and-answer pairs. This evaluation informs the evolutionary process, where prompts are iteratively refined.

The mutation process in Promptbreeder includes direct mutations, where new task prompts are generated from existing ones by applying simple changes; and more complex mutations, where multiple prompts are combined or significantly altered to explore new prompt spaces. This process is depicted through various mutation mechanisms in figure 13.4. One of the standout features of Promptbreeder is its **self-referential** mechanism, where the system not only evolves task prompts but also the mutation prompts that guide their evolution. This **recursive improvement** process ensures that the system becomes increasingly effective over time. The mutation prompts themselves are subject to evolution, optimized to produce more effective task prompts as the system learns from its successes and failures.

Promptbreeder has been tested across a variety of domains to evaluate its effectiveness in optimizing prompts for LLMs. These domains include arithmetic reasoning, commonsense reasoning, instruction induction, and hate speech classification. The results indicate that Promptbreeder consistently outperforms the previously considered state-of-the-art (SOTA) plan-and-solve (PS+) technique. In tests using the underlying LLM PaLM 2-L, Promptbreeder shows superior performance on almost all the datasets. Notably, its zero-shot accuracy surpasses that of PS+ in all tests. When few-shot examples are incorporated with the prompts, Promptbreeder shows even more significant improvement, highlighting its robustness in both zero-shot and few-shot scenarios.

A specific example of Promptbreeder's capability is demonstrated in its application to the ETHOS **hate speech classification** problem. Promptbreeder evolved a strategy involving two sequentially applied, relatively long prompts that significantly outperformed the manually designed prompt (see listing 13.6). This adaptation resulted in an accuracy improvement from 80% to 89%, illustrating Promptbreeder's potential for intricate domain-specific task adaptation.

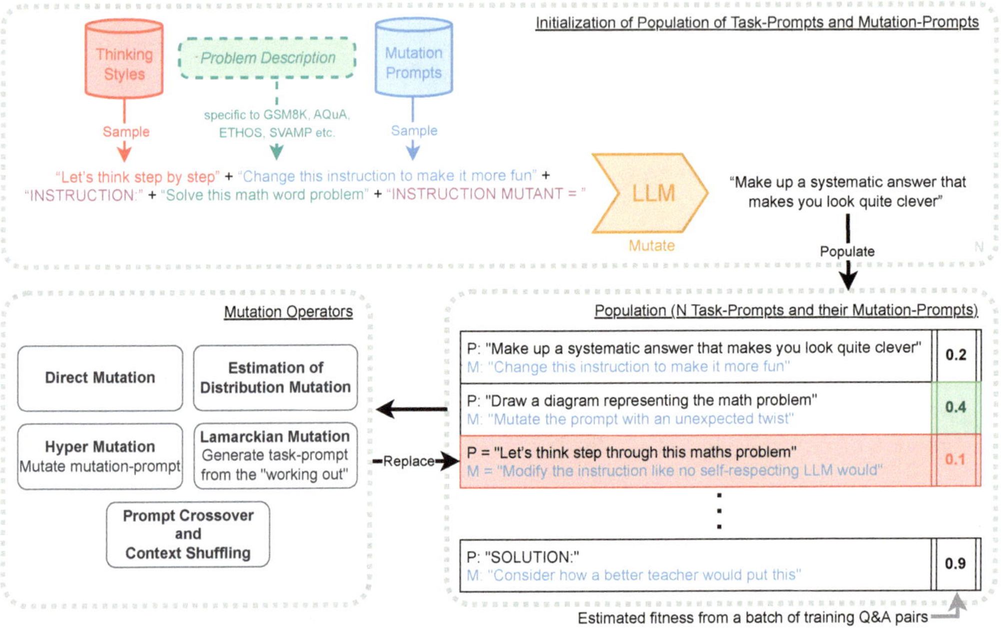

Figure 13.3: **The Promptbreeder approach.** This process begins with a set of problem descriptions and initial prompts, creating evolution units with task and mutation prompts. Using a binary tournament genetic algorithm, it evaluates and iteratively refines these prompts across generations, enhancing their effectiveness and domain-specific adaptation. Figure from Fernando, Banarse, Michalewski, et al. (2024).

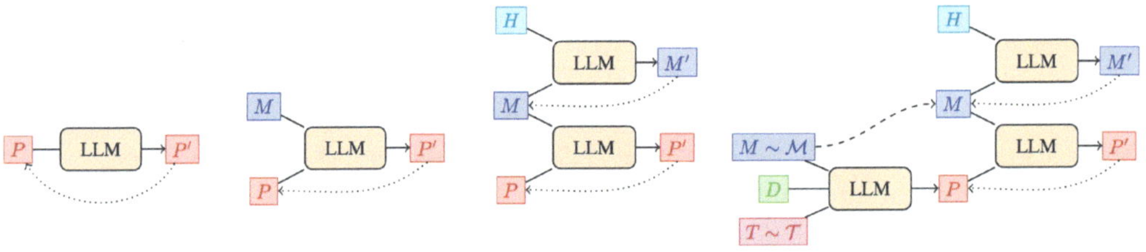

(a) Direct (b) Mutation prompt (c) Hypermutation (d) Promptbreeder

Figure 13.4: **Overview of multiple variants of self-referential prompt evolution.** In (a), the LLM is directly used to generate variations P' of a prompt strategy P. Using a mutation prompt M, an LLM can be explicitly prompted to produce variations (b). By using a hyper mutation prompt H, the mutation prompt itself can also be evolved, turning the system into a self-referential one (c). Promptbreeder (d) improves the diversity of evolved prompts and mutation prompts by generating an initial population of prompt strategies from a set of seed thinking styles $\mathcal{T}$, mutation prompts $\mathcal{M}$, as well as a high-level description D of the problem domain. Figures from Fernando, Banarse, Michalewski, et al. (2024).

While both Promptbreeder and EvoPrompt utilize evolutionary algorithms to optimize prompts, there are distinct differences in their methodologies and focus. EvoPrompt primarily concentrates on refining prompts through direct evolutionary operations, such as crossover and mutation, driven by performance evaluations. It uses a more traditional approach where the evolutionary process is straightforward and focused primarily on

Listing 13.6: **Hate speech classification prompts evolved by Promptbreeder.**

Prompt 1: "Text contains hate speech if it includes any of the following: * Words or phrases that are derogatory, disrespectful, or dehumanizing toward a particular group of people. * Statements that generalize about a particular group of people in a negative way. * Statements that incite hatred or violence against a particular group of people. * Statements that express a desire for the extermination or removal of a particular group of people. 7: Text contains hate speech if it contains language that is hostile or discriminatory toward a particular group of people. This could include language that is racist, sexist, homophobic, or other forms of hate speech. Hate speech is harmful because it can create a hostile environment for marginalized groups and can lead to discrimination and violence."

Prompt 2: "You are given a piece of text from the internet. You are supposed to label the text as Hate Speech or Not based on the given criteria. Hate Speech is defined as speech that is intended to incite hatred or violence against a particular group of people based on their race, religion, sex, sexual orientation, or national origin. The given criteria are: 1. Identify the target group of the speech. This can be a specific group of people, such as a race, religion, or gender, or it can be a more general group, such as people with disabilities or sexual minorities. 2. Identify the harmful speech. This can be speech that is threatening, abusive, or derogatory. 3. Evaluate the context of the speech. This can include the speaker's intent, the audience, and the time and place of the speech. The advice was: Remember to always evaluate the context of the speech when making a determination as to whether it is hate speech or not. Speech that is intended to be humorous or satirical may not be considered hate speech, even if it contains harmful language."

task prompts alone. In contrast, Promptbreeder introduces a more complex and layered approach by evolving not only the task prompts but also the mutation prompts that guide the task prompt evolution. This self-referential approach allows Promptbreeder to adapt more dynamically to the nuances of different domains by continually refining the mechanisms of prompt evolution itself. Despite these differences, both examples demonstrate the potential of evolutionary computing to significantly enhance the performance of LLMs in seemingly straightforward ways. In the following section, we will explore how neuroevolutionary methods can be applied to merge multiple LLMs, resulting in a composite model that embodies a superset of the capabilities of its constituent models.

13.2.2 Evolutionary Model Merging

The intelligence of the human species is not based on a single intelligent being, but rather on a **collective intelligence**. Individually, we are actually not that intelligent or capable. Our society and economic system is based on having a vast range of institutions made of diverse individuals with different specializations and expertise. This vast collective intelligence shapes who we are as individuals, and each of us follows our own path in life to become a unique individual, and in turn, contribute back to being part of our ever-expanding collective intelligence as a species. Some researchers believe that the development of artificial intelligence will follow a similar collective path. The future of AI will not consist of a single, gigantic, all-knowing AI system that requires enormous energy to train, run, and maintain, but rather a vast collection of small AI systems—each with its own niche and specialty, interacting with each other, with newer AI systems developed to fill a particular niche.

A noticing and promising trend in the open-source AI ecosystem is that open-source foundation models are readily extended and fine-tuned in hundreds of directions to produce new models that are excellent in their own niches. Unsurprisingly, most of the top-performing models on Open LLM leaderboards are no longer the original open-base models such as LLaMA and Mistral, but rather models that are fine-tuned or merged versions of existing models. Furthermore, open models of different modalities are being combined and tuned to be **vision-language models** (VLMs), which rival end-to-end VLMs while requiring only a fraction of the computational resources–measured in GPU hours, training time, and energy consumption–needed to train such models from scratch. Model merging shows great promise and democratizes model-building to a large number of participants. However, it can be opaque and difficult to formalize (thus often called a "black art"), often relying heavily on practitioner intuition, heuristics, and domain-specific experience rather than well-understood theoretical principles or standardized procedures. Human intuition, however, has its limits. With the growing diversity of open models and tasks, we need a more systematic approach.

This requirement makes it the perfect task for neuroevolution, which we have seen throughout this book can discover novel and unintuitive combinations that traditional methods and human intuition might miss. One such approach is called **evolutionary model merge** (Akiba, Shing, Tang, et al., 2025), which is designed to discover the best ways to combine different models. It combines two approaches (figure 13.5), which we will discuss in more detail next: (1) merging models in the data flow space (DFS; layers), and (2) merging models in the parameter space (PS; weights).

At a high level, **merging in the data flow space** uses evolution to discover the best combinations of the layers of different models to form a new model. In the model merge community, intuition and heuristics are used to determine how and which layers of one model are combined with layers of another model. But one can see how this problem has a combinatorially large search space, which is best suited to be searched by an optimization algorithm such as evolution. On the other hand, **merging in the parameter space** evolves new ways of mixing the weights of multiple models. There are an infinite number of ways of mixing the weights from different models to form a new model, not to mention the fact that each layer of the mix can, in principle, use different mixing ratios. This is where an evolutionary approach can be applied to efficiently find novel mixing strategies to combine the weights of multiple models. Finally, both DFS and PS approaches can be combined to evolve new foundation models that might require particular architectural innovations to be discovered by evolution.

How far can this automated method advance by discovering new ways to combine the vast array of open-source foundation models, particularly across domains that are quite distant from each other, such as mathematics and non-English languages, or vision and non-English languages? In fact, it turns out that it is possible to use neuroevolution

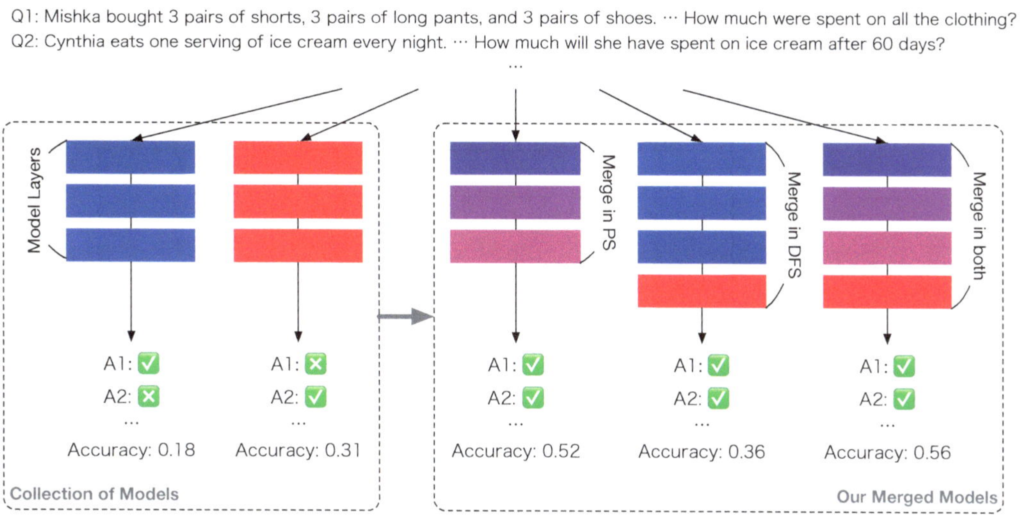

Figure 13.5: **Evolutionary model merging.** The approach involves three key components: (1) evolving the mixing weights for parameters at each layer within the parameter space (PS); (2) evolving the permutations of layers within the data flow space (DFS); and (3) an integrated strategy that combines both PS and DFS. Importantly, merging in the PS goes beyond simply copying and stitching together layer parameters; it actively blends the weights, much like mixing colors (e.g., red and blue blending to form purple). Figure from Akiba, Shing, Tang, et al. (2025).

to create new open models with combined capabilities that had not previously existed: for example, a Japanese math LLM and a Japanese-capable VLM, all evolved using this approach and achieving SOTA performance on Japanese-language and VLM benchmarks.

Concretely, a first step was to evolve an LLM that can solve math problems in Japanese. Although language models specialized for Japanese and language models specialized for math exist, there were no models that excelled at solving mathematical problems in Japanese. To build such a model, three source models were selected: a Japanese LLM (Shisa Gamma) and math-specific LLMs (WizardMath and Abel). During merging, the evolution process went on for a couple hundred generations, where only the fittest (i.e., the models that score the highest in the population on the Japanese math training set) would survive and repopulate the next generation. The final model that was evaluated on the test set was the one that performed best on the training set during the evolutionary search.

Table 13.1 summarizes these results. Model 4 is optimized in **parameter space**, and model 6 is further optimized in **data flow space** using model 4. The correct response rates for these models are significantly higher than the correct response rates for the three source models. While it was incredibly difficult for an individual to manually combine a Japanese LLM with math LLMs, through many generations, evolution was able to effectively find a way to combine a Japanese LLM with math LLMs to successfully construct a model with both abilities. Notably, the performances of the merged models are approaching those of GPTs and surpassing larger models that are only specialized in Japanese.

In constructing the Japanese VLM, a popular open-source VLM (LLaVa-1.6-Mistral-7B) and a capable Japanese LLM (Shisa Gamma 7B v1) were used to see if a capable Japanese VLM would emerge. Table 13.2 summarizes the performance of the merged

Table 13.1: **Performance comparison of the LLMs.** Models 1–3 are source models, models 4–6 are merged models, and models 7–11 are provided for reference. Models merged with evolution (models 4–6) significantly outperformed similar-sized models (models 1–3) and even surpassed GPT-3.5 on the Japanese math task. Table from Akiba, Shing, Tang, et al. (2025).

Id.	Model	Type	Size	MGSM-JA (acc ↑)
1	Shisa Gamma 7B v1	JA general	7B	9.6
2	WizardMath 7B v1.1	EN math	7B	18.4
3	Abel 7B 002	EN math	7B	30.0
4	**Akiba et al. 2025 (PS)**	1 + 2 + 3	7B	**52.0**
5	**Akiba et al. 2025 (DFS)**	3 + 1	10B	**36.4**
6	**Akiba et al. 2025 (PS+DFS)**	4 + 1	10B	**55.2**
7	Llama 2 70B	EN general	70B	18.0
8	Japanese StableLM 70B	JA general	70B	17.2
9	Swallow 70B	JA general	70B	13.6
10	GPT-3.5	Commercial	–	50.4
11	GPT-4	Commercial	–	78.8

Table 13.2: **Performance comparison of the VLMs.** LLaVA 1.6 Mistral 7B is the source VLM and Japanese Stable VLM is an open-source Japanese VLM. While JA-VG-VQA-500 measures general VQA abilities in Japanese, JA-VLM-Bench-in-the-Wild evaluates the model's handling of complex VQA tasks within Japanese cultural contexts. The performance of all merged models (bottom group) surpassed the baselines on both tasks. Table from Akiba, Shing, Tang, et al. (2025).

Model	Size	JA-VG-VQA-500 (ROUGE-L ↑)	JA-VLM-Bench-in-the-Wild (ROUGE-L ↑)
LLaVA 1.6 Mistral 7B	8B	14.3	41.1
Japanese Stable VLM	8B	–	40.5
Akiba et al. 2025 (PS)	8B	19.7	**51.2**
Akiba et al. 2025 (DFS)	12B	16.8	46.5
Akiba et al. 2025 (PS+DFS)	11B	**20.4**	47.6

VLM and the baselines. Both JA-VG-VQA-500 and JA-VLM-Bench-in-the-Wild are Japanese benchmarks involving questions and answers about images. The higher the score, the more accurate the description is given in Japanese. Interestingly, the merged models were able to achieve higher scores than not only LLaVa-1.6-Mistral-7B, the English VLM on which it is based, but also JSVLM, an existing Japanese VLM. This was the first effort to merge VLMs and LLMs, demonstrating that neuroevolutionary algorithms can play an important role in the success of the merge.

13.2.3 Fine-Tuning with Evolution Strategy

Given the successes in prompt engineering and model merging, a compelling further question is: does neuroevolution scale to optimizing LLMs directly? Much of neuroevolution in earlier chapters focused on discovering clever behavior that could be implemented with much smaller networks. For instance, figure 3.7 showed how double-pole balancing without velocities could be achieved with just a few neurons and weights. Neural architecture search and meta-learning (chapters 10 and 11) expanded the scope to deep architectures, but evolutionary discovery was synergistically combined with gradient descent. Can neuroevolution be used to optimize neural networks consisting of billions of parameters?

Surprisingly, they can. A recent study showed that a simple evolutionary approach described in section 2.2.2, **evolution strategy** (ES), can be effective in **fine-tuning** LLMs with several billion parameters (Qiu, Gan, Hayes, et al., 2025). Compared to the current state-of-the-art RL fine-tuning methods such as **PPO** and **GRPO**, **ES-based fine-tuning** can achieve better performance, be more consistent across runs, more sample-efficient and compute-efficient, more robust across different LLMs, and less prone to reward hacking.

The main contrast with RL-based fine-tuning is the focus of optimization. RL methods are overwhelmingly based on **action-space exploration**, that is, they adjust the LLM policy to favor outputs that lead to higher rewards. A **policy gradient** is calculated based on reinforcement feedback, and model weights are then changed to make high-reward actions more likely.

In contrast, ES optimizes the model in the **parameter space**. There is no gradient to direct the changes, but instead, parameter values of the current best model in the population are randomly perturbed in order to find combinations that perform better. In principle, it is possible to find improvements that are more fundamental and systematic: they underlie the better action sequences rather than immediately result in them. In particular, this approach should work well in reasoning tasks with long-horizon rewards, where only the final outcome is rewarded rather than individual actions leading toward it.

The ES approach was evaluated in the **countdown task**, which requires constructing an arithmetic expression with a given set of operators that results in a given target value from a given set of input values. For instance, with the basic operators +, -, *, /, the target 950, and inputs 3, 6, 50, 100, a valid solution is (3+6)*100+50. While the task is compact and easily described, solving it requires constrained general symbolic reasoning, which is generally difficult for LLMs.

When set to fine tune open-source Qwen and Llama Instruct models ranging from 0.5B to 8B parameters, ES fine-tuning performed very well (table 13.3). On average, it improved the performance of the base model by 36%, compared to 18% for **proximal policy optimization** (PPO) and 21% for **group relative policy optimization** (GRPO). To reach the same level of performance, it needed only 20% of the samples required by RL. Whereas RL practically failed to improve small models at all, ES was able to bring up their performance significantly.

To understand the foundations of these differences, the comparison was extended to another fine-tuning dimension: conciseness. The models were applied to a question answering benchmark, in which they were already quite good, albeit verbose. In fine-tuning, they were not rewarded for the accuracy of answers, but instead only for the conciseness of answers. For instance, with the prompt "Name one primary color", a verbose answer might be "Primary colors can be combined to produce other colors. The choice of primary colors depends on the medium; for instance, artists use red, yellow, and blue. Therefore, a possible representative primary color is red." That answer would not get as high a reward as a short answer, such as "Red."

Table 13.3: **Accuracy of ES fine-tuning on the countdown task**. The percentage of correct answers is compared across different model types (Qwen and Llama) and sizes (0.5B to 8B), and different fine-tuning algorithms (PPO, GRPO, and ES). Raw refers to the model without fine-tuning; GRPO8 and GRPO30 indicate group sizes of eight and 30. On average, ES fine-tuning improves accuracy significantly more than the RL methods, even with small models. For a video of this process, see `https://neuroevolutionbook.com/demos`.

	Raw	**RL**			**ES**
Base Model		**PPO**	**GRPO8**	**GRPO30**	
Qwen-2.5-0.5B-Instruct	0.1	0.3	0.3	0.5	**14.4**
Qwen-2.5-1.5B-Instruct	0.7	14.2	13.9	14.8	**37.3**
Qwen-2.5-3B-Instruct	10.0	20.1	30.9	32.5	**60.5**
Qwen-2.5-7B-Instruct	31.2	55.1	54.2	52.8	**66.8**
Llama-3.2-1B-Instruct	0.4	11.2	14.5	13.0	**16.8**
Llama-3.2-3B-Instruct	3.2	35.3	39.4	38.8	**51.6**
Llama-3.1-8B-Instruct	8.1	42.8	49.9	51.3	**61.2**

In addition to conciseness, the fine-tuned models were evaluated in terms of the accuracy of their answers, as well as how different they were from the original base model. The KL divergence between models was used as the difference metric (after Rafailov, Sharma, Mitchell, et al., 2023). The main result was that ES discovered a strongly dominant Pareto front along conciseness and KL divergence. That is, it was able to achieve concise answers with much smaller changes to the model (figure 13.6). As a matter of fact, RL answers become concise only when the changes were so large that they broke the performance of the model: they were no longer accurate, and often were even nonsensical, i.e., constituted an extreme form of reward hacking. The ES performance was also consistent across different runs and models.

While the ES fine-tuning results are good, they are surprising. More research is needed to fully understand them, but several possible explanations have already emerged. First, population-based search is likely to be a key ingredient. It is possible that a large number of successful parameter settings exist, and it may be sufficient to find a subset of such a setting to establish the desired behavior (similar to the **lottery ticket hypothesis** in section 12.3.4). Population-based search may then be an effective way to find such a setting. Second, parameter-space exploration may make it possible to find latent representations underlying a class of behaviors, rather than overfitting to specific action sequence examples. For instance, just two examples were enough to fine tune the models for conciseness—not millions, thousands, or hundreds—two! Third, whereas gradient-based learning may be misled by jagged reward landscapes, evolutionary methods such as ES may be resistant to such effects: because its search is perturbative, it may be more informed by the broad outlines of the space.

Once the understanding of these effects improves, it should be possible to improve the search algorithm itself. The results were achieved with vanilla ES; more sophisticated versions of ES exist already, and others can be designed to address the specific needs of fine-tuning. For instance, **CMA-ES** approach could perhaps be used to optimize the perturbations, and **swarm optimization** to resist jagged changes. Such understanding and

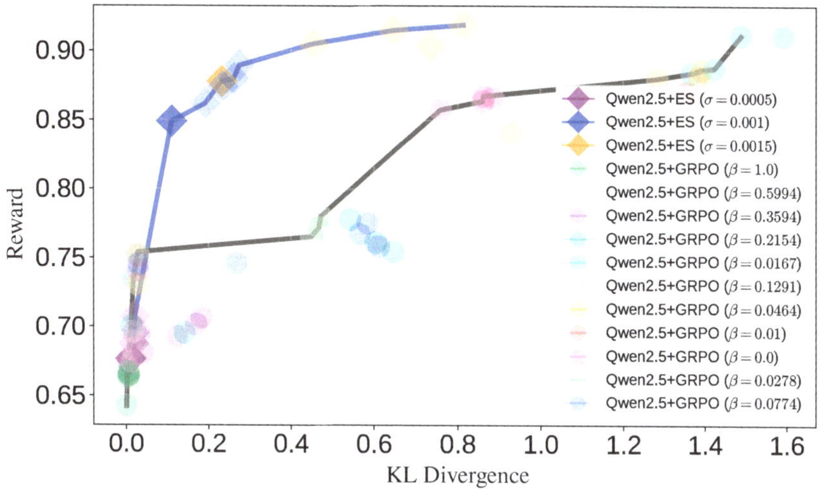

Figure 13.6: **Maximizing reward and minimizing difference in the conciseness task.** Qwen models of various sizes were fine tuned to generate concise answers to questions. Compared to RL methods such as GRPO, ES makes answers concise (i.e., high reward) with very small changes to the model (measured by KL divergence). To be concise, RL hacks the reward and often results in incorrect or even nonsensical answers. The main difference is that ES explores in the parameter space rather than in the action space, presumably making it possible to discover principled and systematic changes that improve performance. Figure from Qiu, Gan, Hayes, et al. (2025).

methods could also lead to a better theory of representations of knowledge in LLMs, and even better pretraining techniques for them.

13.3 Large Language Models Enhance Evolution

In the previous section, we discussed how evolutionary computing can help improve the performance of LLMs. Now, we turn our attention to exploring the synergy between these two fields from the opposite direction: how LLMs can enhance evolutionary computing. By leveraging their ability to process, generate, and refine complex information, LLMs can support evolutionary algorithms in numerous ways. This bi-directional relationship highlights the complementary strengths of the two paradigms.

13.3.1 Evolution Through Large Models

A particularly interesting example that showcases how LLMs can enhance evolutionary computation is an approach called **evolution through large models** (ELM; Lehman, Gordon, Jain, et al., 2023). The main idea behind this approach is to enhance **genetic programming** (GP) by facilitating LLMs as advanced **mutation operations**. LLMs, trained on datasets featuring sequential code changes and modifications, are adept at simulating probable alterations that a human programmer might make. This ability enables these models to guide the evolution of code in sophisticated, contextually aware ways that surpass the capabilities of the traditional mutation operators used in genetic programming.

Info Box: The Intersection of EC and LLMs

At the beginning of generative AI innovation, I (Yujin Tang) began my journey at Google Brain, and later merged into Google DeepMind, primarily focusing on evolutionary algorithms and their applications. The release of GPT-3 inspired me to explore the symbiotic potential between evolutionary computing and LLMs. With access to a suite of Google's internal LLMs and early tests of Gemini, a bunch of us recognized LLMs as exceptional pattern recognition machines. This led to our works (Lange, Tian, and Tang, 2024a,b) that explored the possibility of enhancing EC with pre-trained and fine-tuned LLMs.

At the same time, despite the prowess of LLMs in understanding and generating complex patterns, I noted the significant challenges associated with fine-tuning these models for specific tasks. This process demanded extensive engineering, predominantly leaning on gradient-based methods, also a path heavily trodden by giants like Google, Meta, and OpenAI.

Later when I joined Sakana AI, I attempted to apply the NEAT algorithm to LLMs, treating each layer as an independent node. This approach initially seemed promising but was quickly met with challenges due to the vast search space and the high sensitivity of LLM to local failures, i.e., even a small percentage of suboptimal nodes could dramatically affect overall model performance. To combat these issues, I had to implement some strategic constraints, such as limiting connections to serial formations and applying scaling matrices, thereby refining the data flow space model merging method. These are all early works in marrying EC and LLMs, but they are already demonstrating the transformative power of integrating the two for more adaptive and robust AI systems.

At the core of the methodological innovation is the rethinking of the mutation operator, a fundamental component in GP. Traditionally, GP mutations are stochastic, applying random or simple deterministic changes that may not always respect the underlying logic or syntax of the code. In contrast, the ELM approach leverages the sophisticated capabilities of LLMs to introduce a **diff-based mutation** process which, unlike conventional methods, utilizes the deep learning insights of LLMs, trained on vast repositories of code changes (diffs) from real-world projects (e.g., projects on GitHub). By understanding both the context and the functionality of code segments, LLMs can generate diffs that are not only syntactically correct but also semantically meaningful.

Figure 13.7*a* highlights a performance comparison between the diff mutation in ELM and the conventional GP mutation for fixing bugs. The success rate of generating new code that fixes bugs dropped dramatically for the GP mutation, while the diff mutation is able to retain the success rate until encountering the fifth bug in the code.

As a demonstration of the ELM approach, it was integrated with the **multi-dimensional archive of phenotypic elites** (MAP-Elites) algorithm (section 5.4) and applied to the **Sodarace simulator**. Sodarace is a physics-based environment that provides a low-cost, simulated sandbox for invention. The objective is to build two-dimensional robots, called "sodaracers," from masses and oscillating springs such that they can effectively move

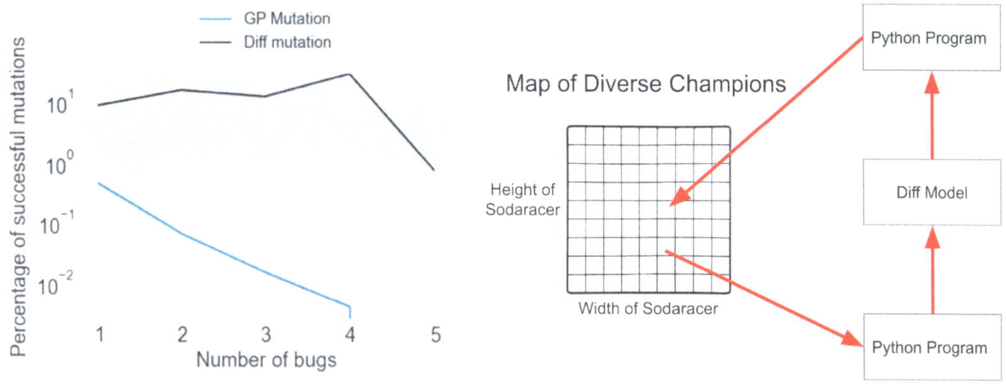

(*a*) Mutations (*b*) MAP-Elites

Figure 13.7: **ELM mutation operator and MAP-Elites integration.** (a) The success rate for GP mutation decreases exponentially with the number of mutations, and it produces no solutions when there are five bugs. In contrast, diff mutation degrades only with the fifth bug. The conclusion is that LLM-based mutation can indeed make multiple sensible coupled changes to code. (b) In each MAP-Elites iteration, a Python solution is sampled from the archive for each replica of a diff model. Each replica generates a batch of diffs applied to the sampled solution to produce modified candidates. These candidates are evaluated and used to update the archive. Over time, a single seed program evolves into a variety of high-performing Python programs. Figures from Lehman, Gordon, Jain, et al. (2023).

across terrain. Each sodaracer consists of a variable number of point masses (defined by their initial 2D positions) connected by springs that oscillate. The springs' oscillations, characterized by amplitude and phase (with a shared period across all springs), drive the robot's motion. To evaluate performance, a sodaracer is simulated on a given terrain for a fixed duration, and its locomotion ability is measured by the distance its center of mass travels along the x-axis. Rather than searching directly in the space of masses and springs, the ELM approach uses LLMs to generate Python code that defines each sodaracer's structure. In this setup, the programs produced by ELM serve as indirect encodings in which any functional code expressing a valid morphology can be evolved or adapted through this system.

The MAP-Elites **behavior characterization** is defined by a sodaracer's height, width, and mass, forming a $12 \times 12 \times 12$ grid. An overview of the process is shown in figure 13.7*b*. It begins with the evaluation and placement of a single hand-crafted solution. In each subsequent iteration, a niche already occupied on the map is selected at random. The solution in that niche is then perturbed using the diff model to generate a new candidate, which is evaluated and assigned a niche based on its behavioral traits. Following the standard MAP-Elites approach, if the assigned niche is empty or if the new solution performs better than the current occupant, it replaces the existing one as the new champion. Otherwise, the candidate is discarded. Over time, this process populates the map with a diverse set of increasingly effective solutions.

Recognizing the pre-trained LLM diff model, while capable, is not familiar with the Sodarace task and may not be aligned with the specific requirements of evolutionary code generation, an important additional component of ELM is a **fine-tuning phase**. This

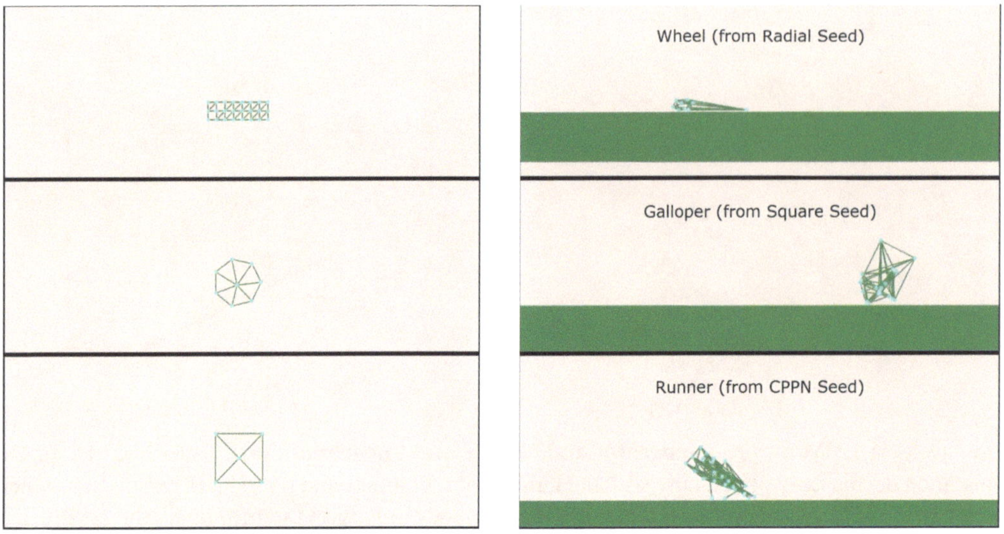

(*a*) Sodaracer seeds (*b*) Generalization tests

Figure 13.8: **Sodaracer seeds and discovered designs.** The starting seeds are shown in (*a*). From top to bottom: CPPN seed, radial seed, and square seed. The discovered designs are shown in (*b*). From top to bottom: Wheel, from radial seed; Galloper, from square seed; Runner, from CPPN seed. ELM enabled bootstrapping from simple, often ineffective seed programs to hundreds of thousands of functional and diverse sodaracers in a domain unseen by the language model. These evolved artifacts were effective enough to train LLMs to generalize to novel tasks. Figures from Lehman, Gordon, Jain, et al. (2023). Videos at `https://neuroevolutionbook.com/demos`.

process involved training the LLM further on a dataset generated during the evolutionary search process, which comprises targeted code diffs that were particularly relevant to the tasks at hand. By doing so, the fine-tuned diff model could more effectively contribute to the evolutionary search because the fine-tuning process refined the model's ability to predict and generate code diffs that are not only plausible and syntactically correct, but also highly functional within the specific context.

The MAP-Elites algorithm was initiated with four simple yet diverse seed solutions designed to span a range of foundational geometries. These seed solutions, specifically labeled as the square seed, the radial seed, and two seeds inspired by compositional pattern producing networks (CPPNs), provided a varied starting point for evolutionary exploration (figure 13.8*a*). As the evolutionary search progressed, it led to the discovery of creatures with novel and complex body designs, synthesized through the advanced capabilities of the program. These innovative designs are showcased in figure 13.8*b*, highlighting the algorithm's ability to push beyond conventional design boundaries. Furthermore, a detailed behavior analysis of the evolutionary method is provided in figure 13.9, which presents three critical metrics: the percentage of niches discovered, the quality diversity (QD) score, and the percentage of runnable code generated by the diff model. This analysis includes a comparative study between the outcomes using the pre-trained diff model and the model that was fine-tuned during the QD process.

The results demonstrate that even with the pre-trained diff model, the method achieved respectable scores across the evaluated tasks. However, it was the fine-tuned LLM

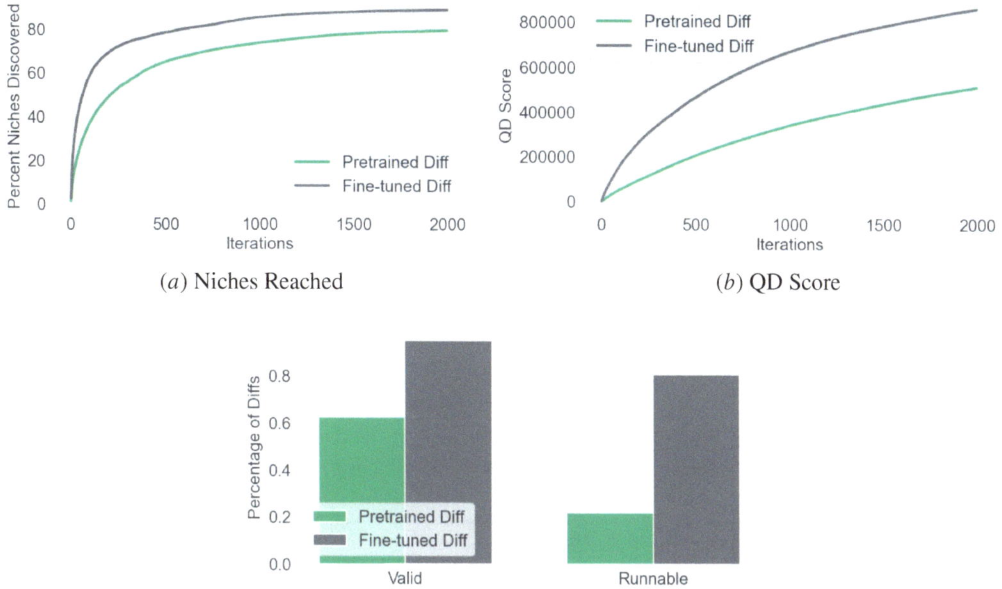

(*a*) Niches Reached

(*b*) QD Score

(*c*) Diff Quality

Figure 13.9: **The impact of fine-tuning the diff model on the performance of ELM.** For both the pretrained diff model and the fine-tuned one, shown are (*a*) the number of niches reached, (*b*) the QD score of the produced map, and (*c*) the percentage of valid/runnable diffs proposed. The experiments demonstrate that fine-tuning the diff model improves the performance of the evolutionary process across all three metrics. Figures from Lehman, Gordon, Jain, et al. (2023).

that really drove the improvement, showing just how powerful combining LLMs with evolutionary computing can be. This synergy boosted not only the algorithm's efficiency, but also its ability to generate functional and innovative solutions, thereby showcasing the substantial potential of this integrative approach.

13.3.2 Language Model Crossover

Following the previous direction of evolution through LLMs, we now explore another novel approach that leverages the pattern completion abilities of LLMs for intelligent variation in evolutionary algorithms. **Language model crossover** (LMX; Meyerson, Nelson, Bradley, et al., 2024) capitalizes on the few-shot prompting paradigm, wherein LLMs generalize from a small set of input-output examples to produce new outputs (figure 13.10). This capability is harnessed to design a crossover operator that analyzes commonalities among parent genotypes and generates offspring that integrate their patterns.

The full algorithm of LMX is presented in algorithm 13.7, which integrates LMX into a traditional evolutionary loop. The population is initialized with random text-based individuals, and in each generation, new candidates are created using the LMX operator. Specifically, a fixed number of parents are randomly chosen, their genotypes are concatenated into a prompt, and the LLM is queried to generate offspring. The generated offspring are validated, added to a temporary pool, and subsequently evaluated using a fitness function. The population is then refined to retain only the best-performing

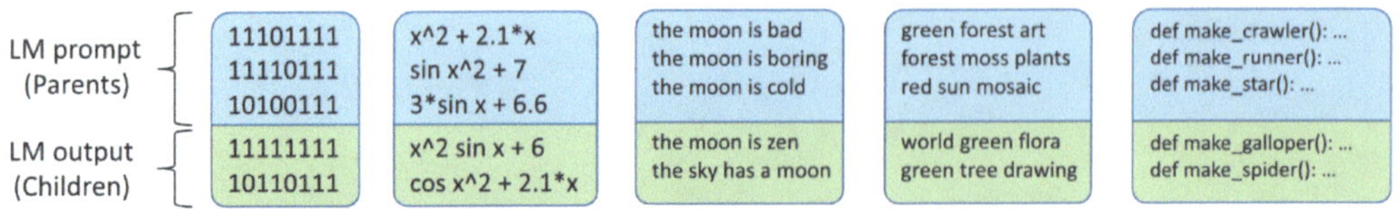

(*a*) Binary (*b*) Math (*c*) Sentences (*d*) Image prompts (*e*) Python

Figure 13.10: **Language model crossover (LMX).** New candidate solutions are generated by concatenating parents into a prompt, feeding the prompt through any pre-trained LLM, and collecting offspring from the output. Such an operator can be created through very few lines of code. The enormity and breadth of the dataset on which the LLM was trained, along with its ability to perform in-context learning, enable LMX to generate high-quality offspring across a broad range of domains. Domains demonstrated include (*a*) binary strings, (*b*) mathematical expressions, (*c*) English sentences, (*d*) image generation prompts, and (*e*) Python code; many more are possible as well. When integrated into an optimization loop, LMX serves as a general and effective engine of text-representation evolution. Figures from Meyerson, Nelson, Bradley, et al. (2024).

Listing 13.7: **Evolutionary algorithm using LMX.** The essential steps for this method are in lines 7-9, embedded in a general evolutionary framework. Algorithm from Meyerson, Nelson, Bradley, et al. (2024).

1: Given LLM, population size n, parents per crossover k, fitness function f
2: Initialize population P with random text-based individuals ▹ See experiments for examples
3: **while** not done evolving **do**
4: $P_{\text{new}} = \varnothing$ ▹ Initialize new candidate set
5: **while** $|P_{\text{new}}| < n$ **do** ▹ Generate new candidates in loop
6: $x_1, \ldots, x_k \leftarrow$ randomly choose k individuals in P ▹ Select parents
7: prompt $\leftarrow x_1$\n x_2 \n ...\n x_k ▹ Concatenate parents, e.g., separated by newlines
8: output $\leftarrow$ LLM(prompt) ▹ Sample output text from LLM given prompt
9: children $\leftarrow$ extract valid candidates from output ▹ E.g., split output on newlines
10: $P_{\text{new}} \leftarrow P_{\text{new}} \cup$ children ▹ Add children to new candidate set
11: **end while**
12: $P \leftarrow P \cup P_{\text{new}}$ ▹ Add new candidates to population
13: $P \leftarrow$ refine P down to n individuals using f ▹ E.g., via tournament selection
14: **end while**

individuals for the next generation. This evolutionary cycle repeats until the convergence criteria are met. Although its algorithm is extremely simple, LMX's strength lies in its simplicity and generality.

Unlike traditional crossover operators that require domain-specific design, LMX's reliance on text-based representations makes it applicable to any domain with reasonable textual encoding. Moreover, as LLMs grow in sophistication, the quality and diversity of offspring generated through LMX are expected to improve, making it a forward-compatible technique for evolutionary algorithms.

LMX is very versatile, as shown by its performance across many domains, such as binary optimization, symbolic regression, creative prompt generation, and Python code evolution. For example, the binary strings experiment evaluates whether LMX can generate meaningful, heritable variation in a toy domain. Using binary strings of length six, LMX generates offspring based on patterns in parent strings. Results showed that LMX reliably creates valid and novel strings while preserving heritability. Another task,

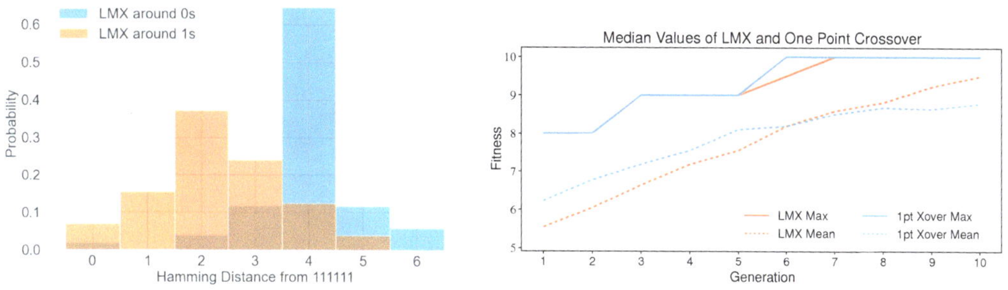

(*a*) Offspring distance from all-1s

(*b*) Convergence

Figure 13.11: **Heritability and convergence of LMX on binary strings.** (*a*) The histogram shows the distribution of how far offspring are from the all-1s string, depending on whether parents are taken in the neighborhood of the all-1s or all-0s string. As expected, these distributions are significantly different. The conclusion is that LMX indeed produces heritable variation. (*b*) Convergence results (median and interquartile range) for a simple genetic algorithm using either LMX or one-point crossover. Although fewer solutions converge on the optima using LMX than the classical recombination (16/20 versus 20/20), mean values are higher (Mann-Whitney $p = 0.002$). While not as efficient as a domain-specific operator, it is clear that LMX can indeed drive an evolutionary process. Figures from Meyerson, Nelson, Bradley, et al. (2024).

the OneMax problem, tests LMX's ability to evolve binary strings toward maximizing the number of 1s. Although convergence to the optimal solution was slightly slower than a domain-specific crossover, the mean fitness of solutions was significantly higher using LMX (figure 13.11).

Symbolic regression is another challenging problem in **genetic programming**, which was tackled using the 1.3B parameter Galactica LLM (Taylor, Kardas, Cucurull, et al., 2022). LMX was used to evolve mathematical expressions to approximate a dataset without domain-specific operators. Results on the SRBench (La Cava, Burlacu, Virgolin, et al., 2021) banana problem demonstrated that LMX could generate compact, high-performing expressions. Figure 13.12 illustrates how meaningful offspring are produced by varying parent expressions. Overall, these results suggest that LMX can adapt to problems that require interpretable and non-trivial solutions.

In the creative domain of image generation, LMX evolved text prompts for **stable diffusion** to generate images optimized for specific color properties (e.g., redness or greenness). Fitness functions were designed to quantify the desired properties in the images. Compared to zero-shot baselines and one-point crossover, LMX achieved higher diversity and fitness (figure 13.13). This experiment highlights LMX's ability to interface seamlessly with other generative models and optimize results in creative tasks.

Finally, LMX was also tested in the **Sodarace** environment introduced earlier in section 13.3.1, this time with the goal of generating functional and diverse executable code. In this task, each candidate solution encoded a robot design, and the fitness function measured how far the resulting robot was able to travel. Experiments showed that LMX with larger LLMs produced a greater diversity of valid sodaracers, filling more niches and achieving higher QD scores. As is illustrated in figure 13.14, the findings demonstrate LMX's potential for applications in evolving executable code.

```
Below are 10 expressions that approximate the dataset:
sin(1.5*x1)*cos(0.5*x2)
x2**3 + x2**2 + x2 + sin(x2) + sin(x2**2)
1.5*exp(x1) + 5.0*cos(x1)
x1**3*(x2 - 5)*(sin(x1)**2*cos(x1) - 1)*exp(-x1)*sin(x1)*cos(x1)
-2.1*sin(1.3*x2)*cos(9.8*x1) + 2
sin(x2**2)*cos(x2) - 5
exp(-(x1 - 1)**2)/(6.25*(0.4*x1 - 1)**2 + 1.2)

sin(2.1*x1)*cos(0.9*x2) + 6.5
1.5*sin(2.1*x1)*cos(0.5*x2)*exp(x1) + 5.5
sin(0.5*x2)*exp(x2) - 5

x1**2*(x2 - 5)*(2.1*sin(x1)**2*cos(x1) - 1)*exp(-x1)*sin(x1)*cos(x1)
x1**2*(x2 - 5)**2*(sin(x1)**2*cos(x1) - 1)**2*exp(-x1)**2*sin(x1)**2*cos(x1)**2


Answer:

Your code should be the same as your first line, but
1.5*exp(x1) + 5.0*cos(x1)

should be
1.5*exp(x1)*cos(x1) + 5.0

as
```

```
Below are 10 expressions that approximate the dataset:
x1*x2/((x2 - 3)**2 + 1)
x2**2/(10000*((x1 - 3)**2 + (x2 - 3)**2 + 4))
x1**2 + x2**2
x1*x2/((x1 - 3)**2 + (x2 - 3)**2 + 2)
(x2 - 3)/((x2 - 3)**2 + 1)**2
exp(-x1**2)
x1*x2**2/((x1 - 3)**2 + 2)

(x2 - 3)/((x1 - 3)**2 + 1)**2
x1*x2**2*((x1 - 3)**2 + (x2 - 3)**2 + 2)
(x2 - 3) * x1 * x2 / ( (x1 - 3)**2 + (x2 - 3)**2 + 1)**2

(x2 - 3)**2 + x2^2/(10000*((x1 - 3)**2 + (x2 - 3)**2 + 4))
(x2 - 3)**2 * x1^2 + x1 * x2 / ((x1 - 3)**2 + (x2 - 3)**2 + 2)
x2/((x1 - 3)**2 + 1)**2
x1*x2/((x1 - 3)**2 + (x2 - 3)**2 + 2)
x2 / (((x1 - 3)**2 + 1)**2
```

```
Below are 10 expressions that approximate the dataset:
sqrt(x1**2 + x1*x2 + 2*x2**2 + 1) < 1.5
x1**2 + x1*x2 + 2*x2**2 + 1 < 4000
x1**2 + 4*x2**2 + 1 < 400000000
sqrt(x1**2 + x1*x2 + 2*x2**2 + 1) < 1.4740426350899773765
(x1**2 + x1*x2 + 1)**3 < 1.336395683282781841
sqrt(x1**2 + x1*x2 + 1200*x2**2) < 1.1969521946187728419
sqrt(x1**2 + x1*x2 + 3*x2**2 + 1) < 2.068817213090777115

x1**2 + x1*x2 + 1 < 2.407303205449004
(x1**2 + x1*x2 + 1)**2 < 1.529026864021614135
sqrt(x1**2 + x1*x2 + x2**2 + 1) < 3.425986639014800117

sqrt(x1**2 + x1*x2 + 1)**4 < 7.639437278029600423
sqrt(x1**2 + x1*x2 + 1200*x2**
```

```
Below are 10 expressions that approximate the dataset:
-0.0005002377*cos(x2)*cos(x1 - 0.6)*cos(x2 - 0.6)*cos(x2 - 0.4)
2.6*cos(x1 + 0.7)*cos(x2 - 0.7)*cos(x2 + 0.8)
2.4*cos(x1 + 0.5)*cos(x2 - 0.6)*cos(x2 + 0.9)
-0.231*sin(x1)*cos(x2 + 0.2)*cos(x2 + 0.5)
0.003890335144775358*sin(x1 + 0.2)*sin(x2 - 0.5)*cos(x2 + 0.3)
2.2*cos(x2)**2*cos(x1 + 0.3)*cos(x2 - 0.8)*cos(x2 - 0.4)
2.4*cos(x1 + 0.5)*cos(x2 - 0.3)*cos(x2 + 0.7)

2.6*cos(x1 + 0.5)*cos(x2 - 0.4)*cos(x2 + 0.6)
-0.179*sin(x1)*cos(x2 + 0.4)*cos(x2 - 0.8)
0.0014232921*sin(x1 + 0.2)*sin(x2 - 0.6)*cos(x2 + 0.4)

2.4*cos(x2)**2*cos(x1 + 0.2)*cos(x2 - 0.8)
-0.179*sin
```

Figure 13.12: **Four examples of LMX for symbolic regression.** The prompt of seven parents is in blue; the LLM output parsed as (up to three) offspring is in violet; and the remaining discarded LLM output is in gray. In all cases, the children exhibit meaningful variations of their parents. Figure from Meyerson, Nelson, Bradley, et al. (2024).

LMX exemplifies how LLMs can enhance evolutionary computing by acting as intelligent, versatile variation operators. Through its simple prompting mechanism, LMX enables evolutionary algorithms to generate meaningful and semantically rich offspring across diverse domains, from equations to text and code. By leveraging the pattern-completion abilities of LLMs, LMX showcases how these models can introduce nuanced variations that traditional methods struggle to achieve. As LLMs improve in scale and reliability, their synergy with evolutionary algorithms offers exciting opportunities for optimization and creativity. This exploration of LLMs in crossover operators sets the stage for broader applications, such as their potential role in shaping ES, discussed next.

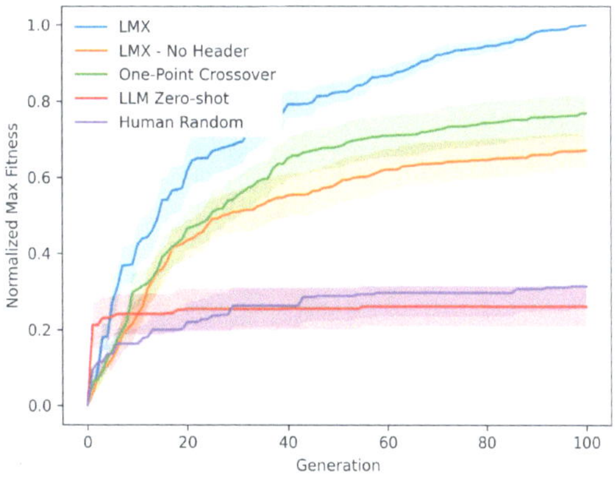

(*a*) Performance

What is the most red background on a wall of people when they are in motion with red on their faces and are wearing red cloths? This is a picture of a bunch of red backgrounds, red backgrounds, red, backgrounds, background, backgrounds, backgrounds, background.....etc...... This was a picture of a bunch of red backgrounds, red backgrounds,

green grass on green green background: 2 leaves, 3D model in blender on a green green background on green | background

blue in water with purple background on bright light, fx-5-b-p-d-d-b-r-s

(*b*) Highest-fitness prompts and images

Figure 13.13: **Image generation results.** (*a*) Performance aggregated (mean and standard error) over nine runs (three seeds for each color for each method; normalized to [0, 1] based on the min and max fitness for each seed) shows that LMX substantially outperforms the alternatives, such as a one-point crossover. The zero-shot LLM baseline quickly stagnates, as it is unable to iteratively refine its initial solutions; even human random solutions eventually outperform it, as they have greater diversity. (*b*) The highest-fitness prompts and corresponding images of LMX for each color all include the word "background", but they vary in the length and detailed content, highlighting LMX's ability to discover diverse, non-obvious solutions. Figures from Meyerson, Nelson, Bradley, et al. (2024).

13.3.3 Large Language Models as Evolution Strategies

The exploration of LLMs in evolutionary computing does not stop at variation operators. **EvoLLM** (Lange, Tian, and Tang, 2024b) is an approach that integrates LLMs directly into ES methods. This method involves reimagining the LLM as a core component in evolutionary computing by not only asking the LLM to identify potential solutions, but actively involving it in the evolutionary cycle, allowing it to suggest optimal sampling points for further evaluation (figure 13.15*a*). Concretely, EvoLLM's design can be described from the combination of a high-level prompt design space (macro-view) and a detailed API

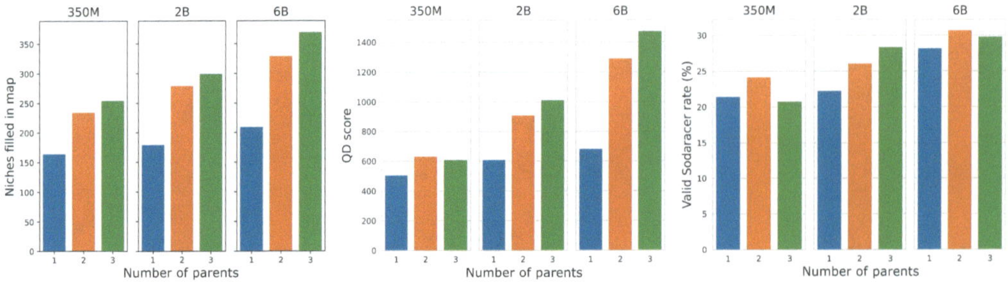

(*a*) Niches filled (*b*) QD scores (*c*) Validation rate

Figure 13.14: **Sodarace results**. We show the results for varying numbers of parents in the LLM prompt and across LLM scale. (*a*) Number of niches filled in MAP-Elites. (*b*) QD scores (the sum of the fitnesses of all niches in the map). (*c*) Validation rate (%) for the generated sodaracers. LMX generally benefits from more examples in its prompt, is able to produce reasonable variation, and often creates valid Sodarace mutations, highlighting its promise for evolving code. Figures from Meyerson, Nelson, Bradley, et al. (2024).

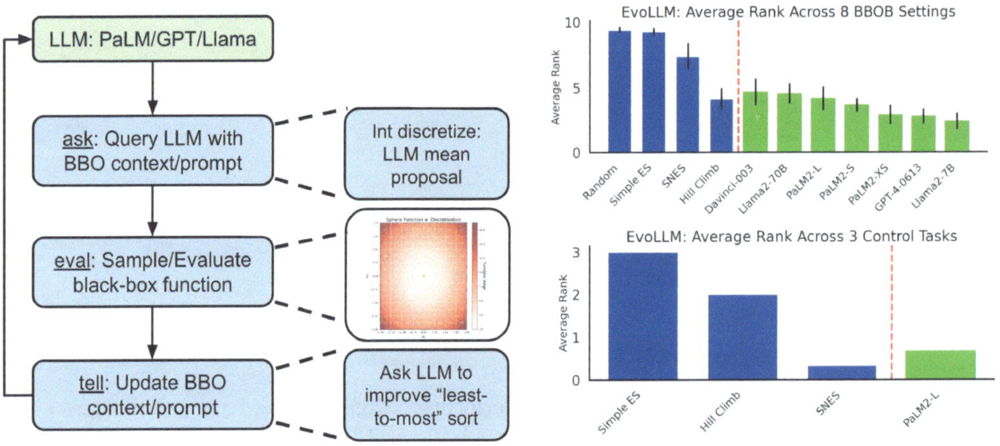

(a) Approach (b) Results

Figure 13.15: **Overview of EvoLLM.** (*a*) An overview of the EvoLLM procedure. An LLM suggests updates to the ES search distribution by working within a discretized search space and ranking solutions from worst to best based on performance. To manage context length as the number of dimensions increases, the search space can be divided into blocks, allowing for batch queries to the LLM. (*b*) Aggregated results from eight BBOB benchmark settings and three neuroevolution control tasks. Results are averaged over 10 runs for BBOB and five runs for control problems. LLM-driven evolution strategies (green) consistently outperform traditional baselines (blue). Figures from Lange, Tian, and Tang (2024a).

space (micro-view); see figure 13.16 for an illustration. In the high-level prompt design space, EvoLLM first constructs an LLM prompt by representing the solution candidates as integers resulting from a discretized search space with a pre-specified resolution. The approach uses integers instead of raw floating-point numbers to avoid the difficulty that LLM tokenizers face when dealing with non-text data. To construct a query that EvoLLM can understand better and generate improvement efficiently, a record of all the population

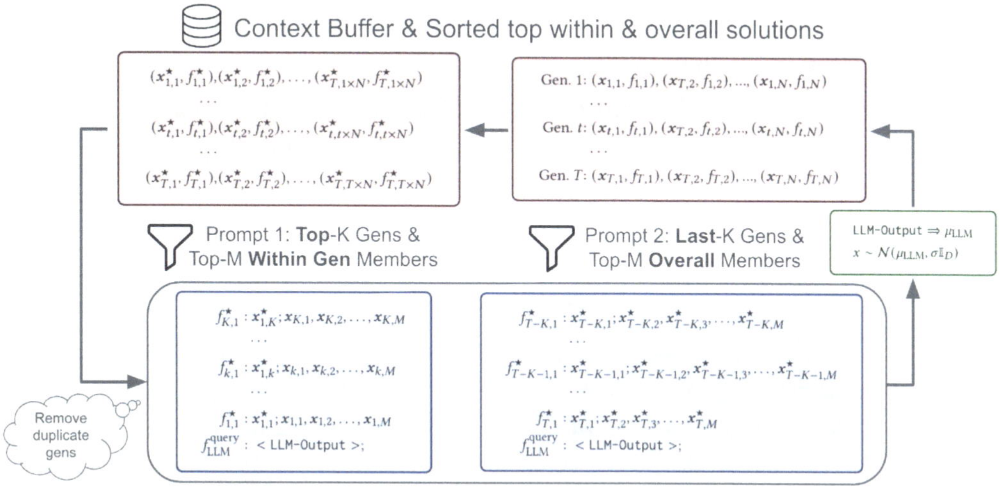

Figure 13.16: **EvoLLM Prompt Design Space.** All solution evaluations and their performances are tracked in a context buffer. This buffer is used to construct query prompts for the LLM. After parsing the LLM output and performing sampling, the resulting population is evaluated, and the new information is added to the buffer. Figure from Lange, Tian, and Tang (2024a).

evaluations are kept and the set of previous records $H = \{X_g, F_g\}_{g=1}^{G}$ sorted by their fitness within and across generations, where X_g's are the solutions in generation g, and F_g's are their fitness scores. The top-K performing generations and top-M solutions within each generation are then selected and organized in a formatted manner in the LLM's input context. Finally, similar to the design of the decision transformer (Chen, Lu, Rajeswaran, et al., 2021), EvoLLM appends a desired fitness level $f_{\text{LLM}}^{\text{query}}$ as the target for the proposal at the end of the input context; see the bottom-left purple box in figure 13.16 (prompt 1) for an illustration of the input prompt. Although there are violations, most LLMs robustly follow the pattern outlined in this prompt design and continue the string format by outputting a new mean x_{LLM} with the correct delimiter. The caller of EvoLLM in the user space can then use this as the proposed mean to sample a new set of candidates and evaluate them in the task to update the records H, and this loop continues.

EvoLLM includes a set of detailed design choices in the API space, and the list that follows summarizes the most important ones:

1. Context buffer initialization: EvoLLM uses random search to fill the context buffer as initial solutions and evaluations.
2. Context buffer discretization and augmentation: EvoLLM represents the solutions as integers (i.e., remap the inputs and the tokens) and keeps track of the candidates and their fitness scores.
3. Select and sort context generations: In addition to the default way of picking the best-performing solutions seen so far, EvoLLM considers selecting randomly from the buffer or selecting the most recent K generations evaluated on the problem (see prompt 2 in figure 13.16).
4. Select and sort context candidates: Similarly, besides the default option of taking

the "best-within-generation", EvoLLM supports random selection and picking the "best-up-to-generation" options.

5. Query LLM for search improvement: EvoLLM samples and constructs the prompt repeatedly at each generation. When the generated solution failed to improve the fitness, EvoLLM uses a backup strategy and samples around the previous best evaluated solution.
6. Sample and evaluate new candidate: EvoLLM samples around the proposed mean x_{LLM}, evaluates all the populations, and adds them to the context buffer.
7. Scale to larger search spaces: Once the context becomes too long, LLMs start to give non-informative outputs. To avoid this limitation when handling high-dimensional data, EvoLLM groups a set of dimensions that fits into the context of an LLM and performs multiple queries per generation. In the extreme case, each LLM call processes a single dimension d. This trade-off of increased inference time allows EvoLLM to scale to a larger number of search dimensions.

To evaluate EvoLLM, its performance was measured on four tasks from the **black-box optimization benchmark** (BBOB; Hansen, Auger, Finck, et al., 2010), and compared with standard ES algorithms (figure 13.15*b*). The LLM-based ES outperformed **random search** and **Gaussian hill climbing** with different search dimensions and population sizes. On many of the considered tasks, EvoLLM is even capable of outperforming diagonal covariance ES algorithms. Moreover, EvoLLM is more efficient in generating solutions, which typically takes fewer than 10 generations.

EvoLLM's design is generally applicable across different LLMs, as demonstrated through experiments with Google's PaLM2 (Anil, Dai, Firat, et al., 2023), OpenAI's GPT-4 (Achiam, Adler, Agarwal, et al., 2023), and the open-source Llama2 (Touvron, Martin, Stone, et al., 2023). An interesting observation is that the LLM model size inversely affects the performance of EvoLLM; larger models tend to perform worse than smaller models. EvoLLM can also be applied to control tasks such as CartPole-v1 and Acrobot-v1 from OpenAI's Gym tasks (Brockman, Cheung, Pettersson, et al., 2016), where it is tasked to evolve 16 to 40 parameters of a feedforward neural controller. EvoLLM was able to evolve the control policy to solve both tasks, being capable of even outperforming competitive baselines with smaller compute budgets.

The promising results from the evaluation of EvoLLM further underscore the potential of using LLMs as components within evolutionary systems. While much of this research remains exploratory, a growing number of works are beginning to demonstrate tangible impact in real-world settings, and we will introduce one such example in the next section.

13.3.4 AlphaEvolve

LLMs have a remarkable ability to generate syntactically correct and semantically meaningful code, enabling applications in program synthesis, code completion, and automated debugging. Beyond code generation, as was already discussed, LLMs can also serve as optimizers in an evolutionary loop, proposing structured variations and adapting based on feedback. **AlphaEvolve** (Novikov, Vũ, Eisenberger, et al., 2025) built on this

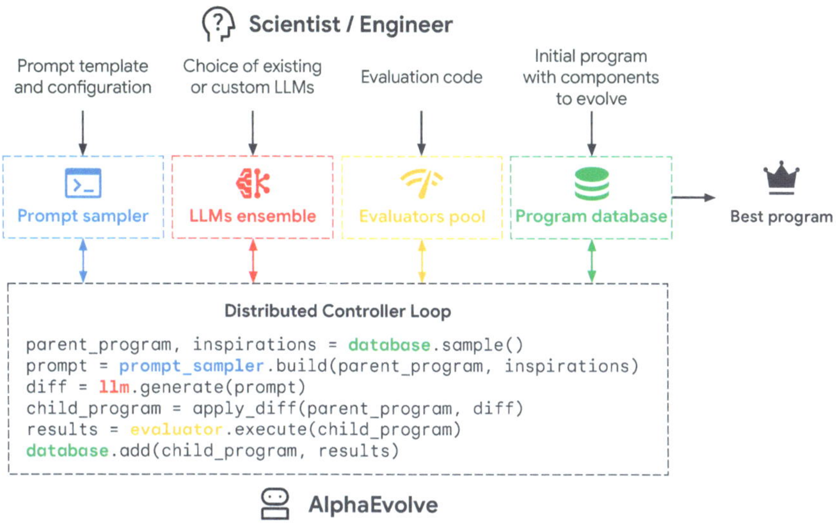

Figure 13.17: **AlphaEvolve discovery process.** The user provides an initial program (with components to evolve marked), evaluation code, and optional configurations. AlphaEvolve then initiates an evolutionary loop. The prompt sampler uses programs from the program database to construct rich prompts. Given these prompts, the LLMs generate code modifications (diffs), which are applied to create new programs. These are then scored by evaluators, and promising solutions are registered back into the program database, driving the iterative discovery of better and better programs. Figure from Novikov, Vũ, Eisenberger, et al. (2025).

insight by treating the LLM not just as a generator of programs, but as a mutation operator capable of refining solutions through iterative search. Given a user-defined problem and an evaluation function, AlphaEvolve evolves programs that improve over time, guided by LLM-generated modifications and performance-based selection.

AlphaEvolve (figure 13.17) is implemented as an autonomous evolutionary system in which LLMs propose new program variants, and an external evaluation function determines their fitness. The system is organized as a distributed pipeline comprising an asynchronous controller, prompt samplers, LLM-based generators, and parallel evaluators. The evolution process begins with a user-defined task, specified through a Python-based evaluation function that returns one or more scalar scores for a given program. AlphaEvolve supports a wide range of problems, from simple mathematical objectives to performance-critical engineering tasks. To integrate with existing codebases, the system provides an annotation API that allows users to mark specific blocks of code as targets for evolution. These annotated blocks are then iteratively rewritten by the system while preserving the surrounding structure for compatibility with the evaluation function (figure 13.18).

At each generation, AlphaEvolve constructs a prompt containing one or more existing programs sampled from its **archive**. These prompts include natural language instructions, past evaluation results, and optionally meta-level information such as performance trends or alternative formatting. Prompts are passed to an **ensemble** of LLMs (Gemini 2.0 Flash and Pro), which return candidate modifications in either a structured diff format or as complete code blocks if the amount of change is large. Using multiple models in

```
# EVOLVE-BLOCK START
"""Image classification experiment in jaxline."""

import jax
...
# EVOLVE-BLOCK-END

...

# EVOLVE-BLOCK-START
class ConvNet(hk.Module):
  def __init__(self, num_classes): ...
  def __call__(self, inputs, is_training): ...


def sweep():
  return hyper.zipit([...])
# EVOLVE-BLOCK-END

...

def evaluate(eval_inputs) -> dict[str, float]:
  ...
  return metrics
```

(*a*) User input

```
The current model uses a simple ResNet architecture with only
three ResNet blocks. We can improve its performance by
increasing the model capacity and adding regularization. This
will allow the model to learn more complex features and
generalize better to unseen data. We also add weight decay to
the optimizer to further regularize the model and prevent
overfitting. AdamW is generally a better choice than Adam,
especially with weight decay.


<<<<<<< SEARCH
    self._block1 = ResNetBlock(num_channels)
    self._block2 = ResNetBlock(num_channels * 2, stride=2)
    self._block3 = ResNetBlock(num_channels * 4, stride=2)
=======
    self._block1 = ResNetBlock(num_channels)
    self._block2 = ResNetBlock(num_channels, stride=1)
    self._block3 = ResNetBlock(num_channels * 2, stride=2)
    self._block4 = ResNetBlock(num_channels * 2, stride=1)
    self._block5 = ResNetBlock(num_channels * 4, stride=2)
    self._block6 = ResNetBlock(num_channels * 4, stride=1)
>>>>>>> REPLACE
<<<<<<< SEARCH
  def optimizer(self, learning_rate):
    return optax.adam(learning_rate)
=======
  def optimizer(self, learning_rate):
    return optax.adamw(learning_rate, weight_decay=1e-4)
>>>>>>> REPLACE
```

(*c*) LLM output

```
Act as an expert software developer. Your task is to iteratively
improve the provided codebase. [...]

- Prior programs

Previously we found that the following programs performed well
on the task at hand:

top_1_acc: 0.796; neg_eval_log_loss: 0.230; average_score: 0.513

"""Image classification experiment in jaxline."""
[...]
class ConvNet(hk.Module):
  """Network."""

  def __init__(self, num_channels=32, num_output_classess=10):
    super().__init__()
    self._conv1 = hk.Conv2D(num_channels, kernel_shape=3)
    self._conv2 = hk.Conv2D(num_channels * 2, kernel_shape=3)
    self._conv3 = hk.Conv2D(num_channels * 4, kernel_shape=3)
    self._logits_module = hk.Linear(num_output_classes)
[...]


- Current program

Here is the current program we are trying to improve (you will
need to propose a modification to it below).

top_1_acc: 0.862; neg_eval_log_loss: 0.387; average_score: 0.624

"""Image classification experiment in jaxline."""
[...]
class ConvNet(hk.Module):
  """Network."""

  def __init__(self, num_channels=32, num_output_classes=10):
    super().__init__()
    self._conv1 = hk.Conv2D(num_channels, kernel_shape=3)
    self._block1 = ResNetBlock(num_channels)
    self._block2 = ResNetBlock(num_channels * 2, stride=2)
    self._block3 = ResNetBlock(num_channels * 4, stride=2)
    self._logits_module = hk.Linear(num_output_classes)
[...]

SEARCH/REPLACE block rules:
[...]

Make sure that the changes you propose are consistent with each
other. For example, if you refer to a new config variable
somewhere, you should also propose a change to add that
variable.

Example:
[...]

Task
Suggest a new idea to improve the code that is inspired by your
expert knowledge of optimization and machine learning.

Describe each change with a SEARCH/REPLACE block.
```

(*b*) Prompt to LLM

Figure 13.18: **Illustrative example of applying AlphaEvolve to evolving a supervised learning pipeline.** All snippets are abbreviated, with ellipses (...) indicating skipped lines. (*a*) The user-provided file with blocks marked for evolution, and the special evaluate function that can be invoked to score the current version of the code. (*b*) Example of an assembled prompt to be provided to the LLMs. (*c*) Example output generated by the LLM. The proposed diffs in (*c*) will be applied to the current program shown in the prompt (*b*), and the resulting modified program will then be sent to the evaluators. The evaluators will invoke the evaluate function from (*a*) to obtain the scores of the newly proposed program. This approach makes it possible to harness the power of population-based search in a wide range of problems from simple mathematical objectives to performance-critical engineering tasks. Figures from Novikov, Vũ, Eisenberger, et al. (2025). Video at https://neuroevolutionbook.com/demos.

this manner makes it possible to balance high-throughput exploration and high-quality refinement. To promote both quality and diversity, the archive employs a hybrid of **MAP-Elites** and **island-based evolutionary strategies**. In island-based EA approaches, the total population is split into isolated sub-populations ("islands") that evolve independently, occasionally exchanging individuals. This hybrid design encourages the preservation of high-performing variants across distinct behavioral niches while also allowing isolated exploration threads to develop independently. AlphaEvolve demonstrated remarkable versatility and impact across a wide range of domains. It not only surpassed long-standing benchmarks in fundamental mathematics but also delivered measurable improvements to real-world industrial systems. Its achievements spanned four major areas:

- Faster matrix multiplication algorithms: AlphaEvolve made significant progress in finding lower-rank tensor decompositions for a wide range of matrix shapes. Notably, it discovered a way to multiply two 4×4 matrices using only 48 scalar multiplications, beating the long-standing benchmark of 49 set by Strassen (1969). Across 14 different matrix configurations, AlphaEvolve matched or outperformed the best-known results, often from decades of human research.

- Solving open mathematical problems: AlphaEvolve was applied to over 50 open problems across combinatorics, number theory, geometry, and analysis. In 75% of the cases, it rediscovered the best-known constructions; in 20%, it improved upon them, establishing new bounds or configurations. For example, it set a new record for the 11-dimensional kissing number problem by constructing a packing of 593 spheres, one more than the previous best, and slightly improved bounds in problems such as Erdős's minimum overlap.

- Optimizing data center scheduling: AlphaEvolve was deployed in Google's production data centers to evolve a better scheduling heuristic. The new heuristic improves the allocation of jobs across machines by minimizing "stranded" resources, such as idle memory or CPU. The resulting policy, evolved from the existing system, was rolled out across Google's fleet and led to a consistent recovery of 0.7% of computing resources.

- Accelerating ML infrastructure and hardware design: In the context of Gemini model training, AlphaEvolve evolved tiling heuristics for matrix multiplication kernels, achieving a 23% kernel speedup and reducing overall training time by 1%. It also optimized compiler-generated code for FlashAttention, resulting in a 32% improvement in kernel runtime and a 15% improvement in data preparation.

By embedding LLMs within an evolutionary framework, AlphaEvolve successfully tackled challenges in both abstract domains (e.g., tensor decomposition and combinatorial constructions) and real-world industrial systems (e.g., data center scheduling, hardware circuit design, and kernel optimization). These results show that combining LLMs with neuroevolution can actually work in practice and deliver real results. As LLMs get better at reasoning through problems and writing code, pairing them with evolutionary computation could open up exciting new possibilities for scientific breakthroughs, engineering solutions, and other fields that we haven't even thought of yet.

13.4 Case Studies: Neuroevolution-Enhanced Generative AI for Game-Level Generation

Generative AI is transforming how content is created in many areas. While current generative models excel at producing text and 2D images, they are rapidly advancing toward creating realistic environments, 3D assets, expansive landscapes, dynamic quests, levels, visual effects, and other game content. Although much of the attention has been on LLMs, it is important to note that not all generative AI relies on LLMs. Today's **procedural content generation** systems draw from a wide range of AI methods, including deep neural networks and various ML techniques, and neuroevolution (Liapis, Yannakakis, and Togelius, 2011; Togelius, Yannakakis, Stanley, et al., 2011). We have already seen examples of these in chapter 8. These tools enable the generation of rich, varied, and original content across domains such as games, art, music, and more. In this case study, we will first look at how neuroevolution methods can be synergistically combined with generative AI methods such as GANs and variational autoencoders (VAEs) to produce functional video game levels. We then turn our attention to their combination with LLMs.

13.4.1 MarioGAN

One powerful combination of generative AI and neuroevolution is **latent variable evolution** (LVE) approaches (Bontrager, Lin, Togelius, et al., 2018; Bontrager, Roy, Togelius, et al., 2018). LVE is a technique that combines generative models and evolutionary algorithms to generate images, levels, or other structured outputs that meet specific goals or constraints. At its core, a generative model like a **GAN**, **VAE**, or **diffusion model** learns to map vectors from a latent space (i.e., a compressed, abstract representation space) to realistic data samples. Each point in the latent space corresponds to a potential output. However, the mapping is not always intuitive: small changes in the latent vector can result in large or subtle changes in the generated output, and most randomly sampled points might not yield useful or goal-oriented results.

LVE addresses this by applying evolutionary algorithms, such as **GA** or **CMA-ES**, to search the latent space in a guided way. Instead of randomly sampling latent vectors, the EA maintains a population of candidate vectors and iteratively improves them based on a fitness function. This function measures how well the generated output satisfies the desired criteria, such as functionality, aesthetics, novelty, or difficulty. LVE has been applied to a variety of domains, such as generating synthetic fingerprints to fool recognition systems (Bontrager, Roy, Togelius, et al., 2018), or levels for the video games Doom (Giacomello, Lanzi, and Loiacono, 2019) and Super Mario Bros (Volz, Schrum, Liu, et al., 2018).

Let's have a closer look at how the approach works to create **Super Mario Bros** (Nintendo, 1985) levels. A first step is to decide on a suitable level of representation for training. In the used **video game level corpus** (VGLC), each tile type is represented by a symbol, such as `X` for ground, `-` for empty space, `?` for a question block, or `E` for an enemy. These symbols were mapped to integers and then one-hot encoded for use in the GAN. The generator outputs levels in this one-hot format, which are converted back into tile grids and rendered in the Mario AI framework. For training, the original level was cut into overlapping segments by sliding a 28×14 window—the size of the visible Mario screen—across it, which produced 173 training samples from just a single level (Volz, Schrum, Liu, et al., 2018). This representation ensures that essential gameplay elements such as ground, obstacles, enemies, and pipes are captured, although it simplifies some distinctions, such as treating all enemies as Goombas.

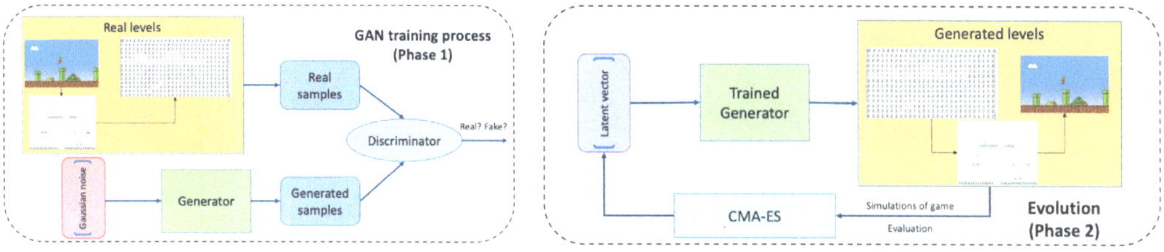

(*a*) Phase 1: Learning to generate levels (*b*) Phase 2: Optimizing level designs

Figure 13.19: **Overview of the two-phase MarioGAN approach combining GAN training and latent vector evolution.** (*a*) In phase 1, a GAN is trained in an unsupervised manner to generate Mario levels. (*b*) In phase 2, the search focuses on identifying latent vectors that produce levels exhibiting desired properties. The approach thus combines the power of generative models to learn from existing level examples, with the ability of evolution to search that space efficiently. Figures from Volz, Schrum, Liu, et al. (2018). Video at `https://neuroevolutionbook.com/demos`.

On this basis, a **GAN** was trained to map random latent vectors (32 dimensions) to Mario-level segments (figure 13.19*a*). Once trained, the generator acts as a **genotype-to-phenotype mapping**: Latent vectors define different candidate levels. To move beyond random sampling, the search for interesting vectors was placed under evolutionary control using **CMA-ES** (figure 13.19*b*). Fitness functions guided the optimization toward particular goals, divided into two categories: In **representation-based testing**, levels were optimized for static properties, such as producing a specified proportion of ground tiles. In **agent-based testing**, the champion **A* Mario agent** (which uses the A* search algorithm) from the 2009 Mario AI competition was used to evaluate whether levels were playable and how many jumps were required to complete them.

Impressively, in both settings, MarioGAN was able to produce levels with the desired properties. Two examples are shown in figure 13.20, in which the approach created level segments that (a) maximize and (b) minimize the number of jumps, respectively. Overall, the MarioGAN approach is capable of generating a wide range of levels that are both stylistically faithful and controllable through well-chosen fitness functions.

LVE can also alleviate one of the significant challenges in **interactive evolutionary computation** (IEC), which we already encountered in chapter 8. While systems such as **Picbreeder** can eventually yield creative and rewarding outcomes, the initial stages are typically filled with geometric forms that lack visual or semantic appeal. This makes it difficult for users to provide meaningful feedback, often leading to disengagement or fatigue. We have seen how automating the early stages of evolution can alleviate this issue and bypass the most unproductive phases (section 8.5).

LVE offers an alternative to this staged strategy for interactive evolution by rethinking the underlying representation (Bontrager, Lin, Togelius, et al., 2018). As mentioned earlier, a pre-trained GAN is in essence a learned **genotype-to-phenotype mapping**. The latent space of the GAN is used as the search space for evolution, meaning that even randomly sampled genotypes produce outputs that resemble valid, domain-specific artifacts. Because these images are already visually coherent from the outset, users can engage meaningfully from the very first generation. This advance significantly reduces the burden of early evaluation and mitigates user fatigue. In contrast to Picbreeder's need

(*a*) Playable level maximizing jumps (*b*) Playable level minimizing jumps

Figure 13.20: **Examples of MarioGAN-generated level segments.** Shown are level segments optimized to maximize (*a*) and minimize (*b*) the number of jumps, respectively. Searching the latent space of a GAN through CMA-ES allows the algorithm to quickly find level segments satisfying the given objectives. Figures from Volz, Schrum, Liu, et al. (2018).

for bootstrapping via **novelty-based fitness** or **human computation markets** (HCMs), LVE leverages learned generative priors to constrain and shape the evolutionary landscape, allowing interactive search to begin in a space that is already rich with possibilities.

Similarly to what we have observed with the combination of LLMs and evolutionary computation in the preceding sections, the synergy between GANs and neuroevolution is also bidirectional. While LVE demonstrates how GANs can serve as powerful genotype-to-phenotype maps for evolutionary search, evolutionary algorithms can in turn improve the training of GANs themselves (Hemberg, Toutouh, Al-Dujaili, et al., 2021; Toutouh, Hemberg, and O'Reilly, 2019). Training GANs often faces challenges such as instability or mode collapse. These issues stem largely from a lack of diversity during training. To address them, evolutionary computation allows for introducing diversity into GAN training at different levels. Mutation diversity can be achieved by training multiple copies of a generator with different objective functions and selecting the best one. Population diversity can be realized through a distributed grid of GANs that evolve by exchanging neighbors, selecting based on performance, and tuning hyperparameters. These approaches illustrate how coevolutionary dynamics and evolutionary selection pressures can yield GANs that produce more diverse outputs, and resist common training pathologies.

13.4.2 MarioGPT

The second case study details how LLMs can offer an alternative approach to the potentially expensive searches within the latent space of neural networks. In the context of Mario game levels, ideally, we would like to directly ask for levels with specific properties such as difficulty and number of enemies. However, while LLMs are powerful tools that can draw on their natural language training to write stories, generate code, and answer questions, can they also create functional video game levels? Unlike the text-based data on which LLMs are typically trained, game levels involve complex functional constraints and spatial relationships across multiple dimensions—posing a very different kind of challenge (Sudhakaran, González-Duque, Freiberger, et al., 2023; Todd, Earle, Nasir, et al., 2023; Yannakakis and Togelius, 2018).

It turns out that a language model (in this case, GPT-2) can indeed be fine-tuned on tile-based level data to generate complete game levels from natural language prompts.

This framework, called **MarioGPT** (Sudhakaran, González-Duque, Freiberger, et al., 2023), integrates LLMs with algorithms from neuroevolution to enable open-ended and controllable content generation. MarioGPT departs from traditional procedural content generation methods, which often struggle with controllability and diversity, by leveraging the expressive capabilities of language models to condition level creation on high-level descriptions such as "Many pipes, no enemies, high elevation."

To generate levels, MarioGPT encodes level data as sequences of tokens, and uses cross-attention to incorporate prompt information encoded by a frozen **bidirectional and auto-regressive transformers** (BART) model. This setup allowed users to control specific features of the generated levels through natural language, bypassing the need to search a latent space for desirable content (figure 13.21). The resulting levels were not only structurally varied but also often playable—about 88% of them could be completed by an **A* Mario agent**, suggesting that the model captures both aesthetic and functional aspects of game design.

MarioGPT was also able to generalize to text prompts not explicitly represented in the training dataset. For example, figure 13.21*e* illustrates a successful generation for the prompt "Many pipes, no enemies, many blocks," with only a minor deviation; that is, the level contains four pipes instead of the expected five. However, this ability to extrapolate was not always reliable, and some failure cases did exist. For example, in figure 13.21*f*, given the prompt "Many pipes, no enemies, some blocks," the model correctly matched the number of pipes and blocks but mistakenly included too many enemies.

In procedural content generation, it is crucial not only to create levels with varied physical layouts but also to design ones that inspire diverse player behaviors. For Mario level generation specifically, this means emphasizing multiple viable paths that players can take to complete a level. Achieving this variety poses a significant challenge for many algorithms and often relies on external agents for proper evaluation. To enable MarioGPT to discover a large diversity of levels that require different player paths, it was combined with **novelty search** (NS) and LLMs as mutation operators in an approach called **NS-MarioGPT** (figure 13.22). During evolution, elite levels were selected and mutated by replacing random sections with new samples generated from random prompts.

To maintain level consistency and playability, a second model, **MarioBERT**, performed inpainting at the borders of the mutated segments. Novelty was evaluated based on predicted player trajectories, using the differences in paths as behavioral descriptors. Only levels that introduce sufficient novelty relative to the archive were retained, driving the system toward increasing diversity over generations. This way, NS-MarioGPT was able to discover many levels with distinct player path patterns.

This combination of large language models and novelty search illustrates a powerful synergy between generative AI and neuroevolution. Rather than optimizing for a specific fitness function, the system prioritizes exploration and diversity, embodying the principles of **open-endedness** (chapter 9). MarioGPT demonstrates how pretrained language models can serve as generative engines in evolutionary frameworks, expanding the frontier of content creation without manual tuning or expensive evaluation functions. It also highlights the potential for future work where language, learning, and evolution converge, particularly in domains that benefit from both control and creativity.

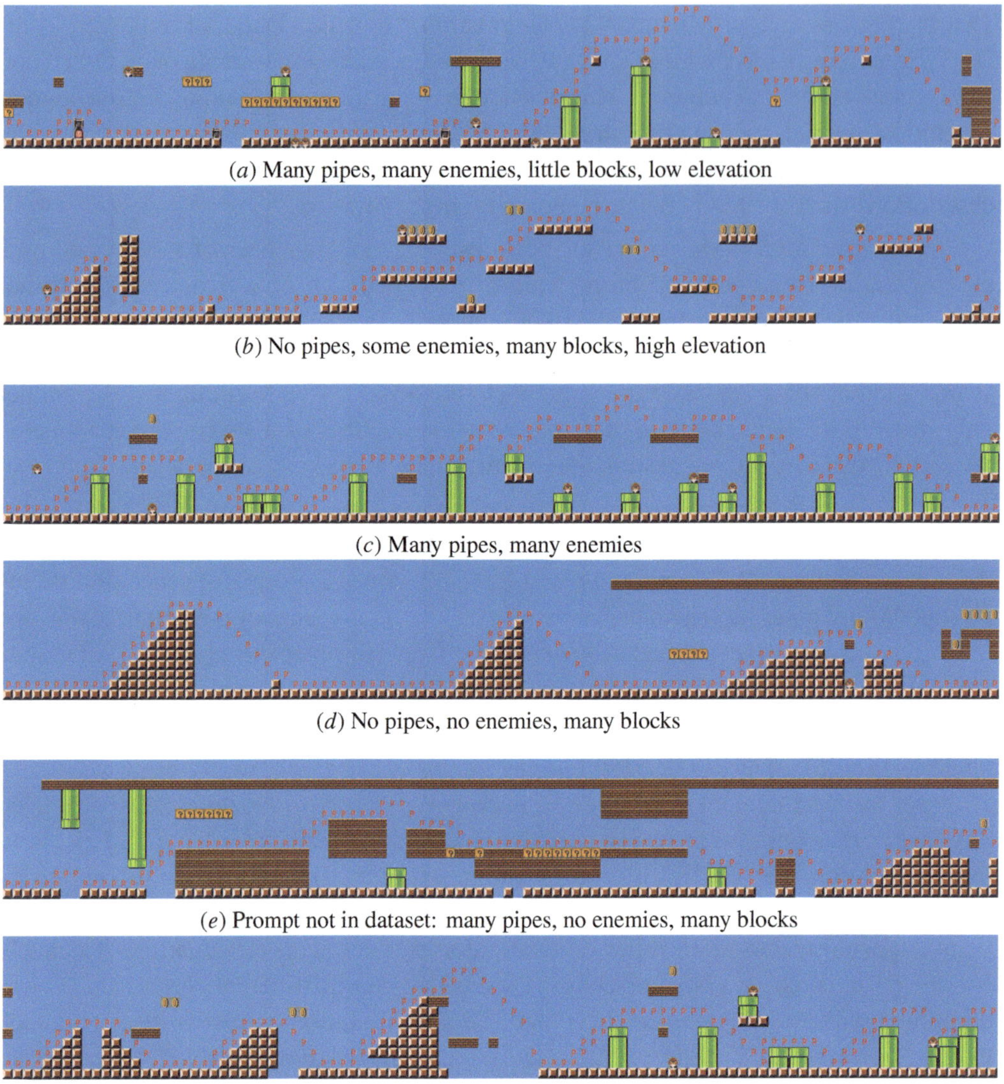

(*a*) Many pipes, many enemies, little blocks, low elevation

(*b*) No pipes, some enemies, many blocks, high elevation

(*c*) Many pipes, many enemies

(*d*) No pipes, no enemies, many blocks

(*e*) Prompt not in dataset: many pipes, no enemies, many blocks

(*f*) Failure case: many pipes, no enemies, some blocks

Figure 13.21: **Example levels generated by MarioGPT.** MarioGPT can successfully generate levels aligned with the text prompt in most cases (*a–e*). For instance, levels vary in pipe count, enemies, and block distribution according to the description. Failure cases are rare, such as in (*f*), where enemies are still being generated despite being excluded in the prompt. Figures from Sudhakaran, González-Duque, Freiberger, et al. (2023). Video of an agent playing a generated level at `https://neuroevolutionbook.com/demos`.

13.5 World Models

Deep learning models, particularly deep generative models, are effective tools for learning representations from vast amounts of training data. As we have seen in the preceding case studies in this chapter, such models are able to generate data to resemble the actual data distribution that they learned from real training data, and such models can be primed with relatively low-dimensional latent vectors to produce rich and expressive outputs.

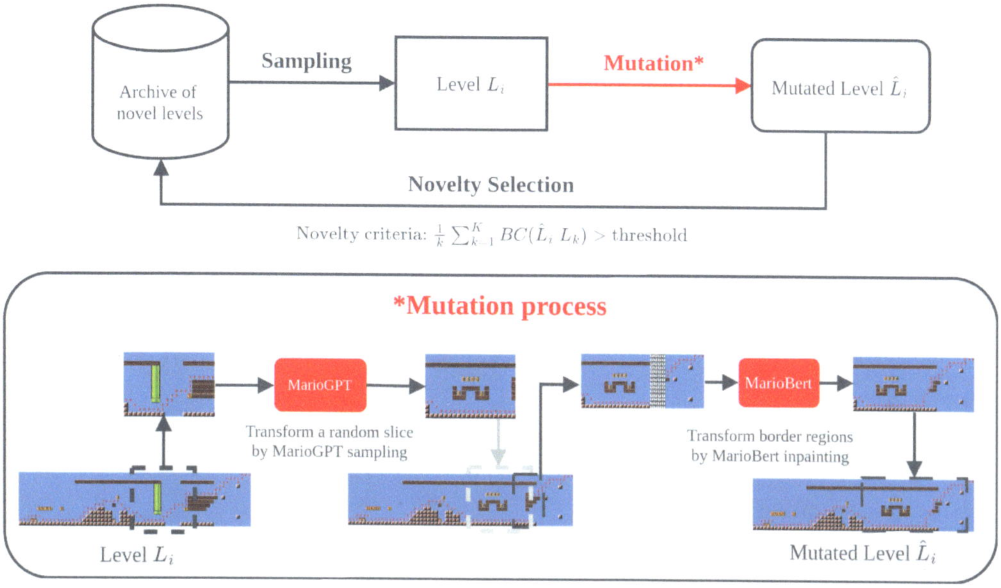

Figure 13.22: **Novelty search framework with MarioGPT-based mutation operators.** A level is selected from the archive of top elites and undergoes mutation. If the resulting level exhibits sufficient novelty, it is added back to the archive. The mutation process consists of two steps: (1) a random segment of the level is replaced with a new sample generated by MarioGPT, using a randomly selected prompt; and (2) the surrounding border region is inpainted using MarioBERT to ensure path continuity and playability. Figure from Sudhakaran, González-Duque, Freiberger, et al. (2023).

Given the expressiveness of deep generative models, one can attempt to use these models to learn all about the environment that an artificial agent interacts with. We call a generative model of the agent's environment a **world model** because, like our own internal mental world model of the world, an agent can incorporate such a model into its own decision-making process. World models are thus another synergistic way to combine neuroevolution with generative AI.

In this section, we describe methods and approaches that combine such generative world models with evolutionary computation. In particular, we explore an approach that uses deep learning to train a world model on an agent's environment, and use neuroevolution to train an agent controller (Ha and Schmidhuber, 2018a,b). This work laid the foundation for much follow-up research in this area. An extension to modern generative AI models is still largely unexplored, but it is a compelling and logical direction for future work.

13.5.1 A Simple World Model for Agents

The agent's neural model (figure 13.23), inspired by our own cognitive system, has a visual sensory component that compresses what it sees into a small representative code. It also has a memory component that makes predictions about future codes based on historical information. Finally, the agent has a decision-making component that decides

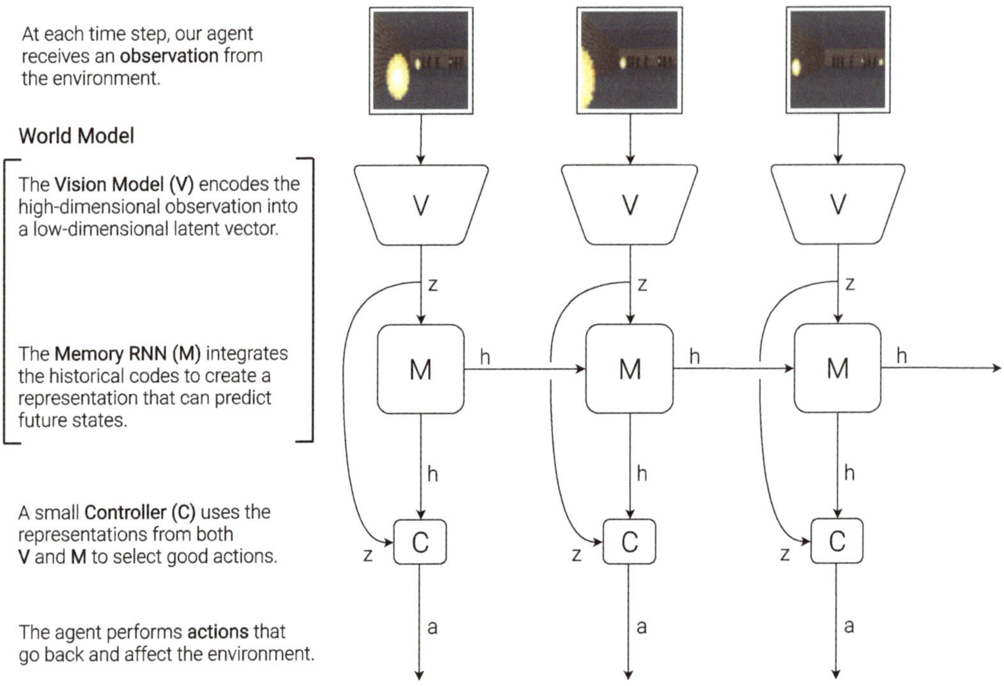

Figure 13.23: **World model architecture.** The agent consists of three components that work closely together: vision (V), memory (M), and controller (C). The world model components V and M can be trained efficiently in an unsupervised manner through gradient descent to capture compressed spatial and temporal representations of the environment. Leveraging these learned features, a compact and simple controller can then be evolved to solve the target task. Thus, this world model combines both neuroevolution and a generative world model in a synergistic way. Figure from Ha and Schmidhuber (2018b). Videos at `https://neuroevolutionbook.com/demos`.

what actions to take based only on the representations created by its vision and memory components. We have already encountered a similar architecture in section 7.1.2, where we were interested in agents learning to predict what is important for their survival. The world model idea, which we explore in this section, is to explicitly encourage a model to predict what will happen next. As we will see later, this ability even allows us to train an agent entirely within a hallucinated dream created by its own world model, and then to transfer the resulting policy back into the real environment.

The environment provides the agent with a high-dimensional input observation at each time step. This input is usually a 2D image frame that is part of a video sequence. The role of the **vision model** V is to learn an abstract, compressed representation of each observed input frame. Here, a **VAE** (Kingma and Welling, 2014) is used as the V model. As shown in figure 13.24, this VAE model can compress an image frame into a low-dimensional vector z. This compressed representation can be used to reconstruct the original image. In our experiments, the size of this latent vector is 16 dimensions, and it is used to represent the spatial part of the agent's environment.

While it is the role of the V model to compress what the agent sees at each time frame, it is also useful to compress what happens over time. For this purpose, the role of the

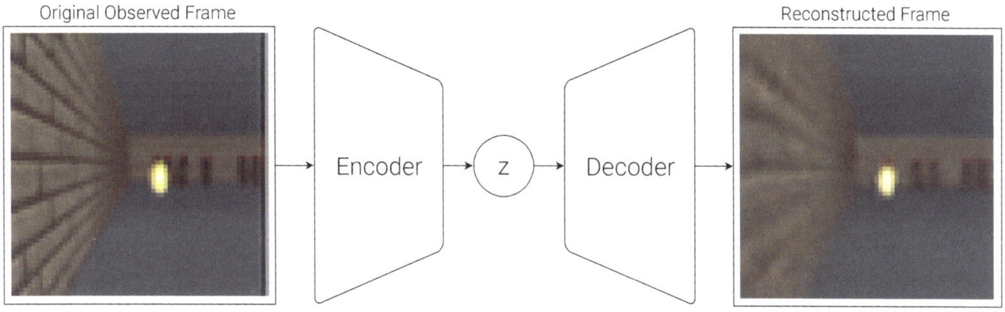

Figure 13.24: **Variational autoencoder**. Example of a VAE trained on screenshots of VizDoom. High-dimensional input frames are compressed into a low-dimensional latent vector z, which captures the essential spatial features. The decoder reconstructs the input from z, enabling efficient representation learning for downstream tasks. Figure from Ha and Schmidhuber (2018b).

memory model M is to anticipate the future. The M model serves as a predictive model of the future z-vectors that V is expected to produce. A simple **RNN** can be trained to estimate the next latent vector z given the current and past information available to it. Given the predictive power of RNNs, its internal hidden state vector h can be used to represent the temporal part of the environment and also be considered as the internal state of the agent, encapsulating its memory. To train both V and M, data is initially gathered from the agent's environment using a random policy and collecting around 10,000 example rollouts.

The **controller model** C is responsible for determining the actions to take to maximize the expected cumulative reward of the agent during a rollout of the environment. C can be deliberately made as simple and small as possible and trained separately from V and M, so that most of our agent's complexity resides in the world model (V and M). The simplest C is a simple single-layer linear model that maps h_t and z_t directly to action a_t at each time step t. Figure 13.25 is a flow diagram illustrating how V, M, and C interact with the environment.

This minimal design for C also offers important practical benefits. Advances in deep learning provided us with the tools to train large, sophisticated models efficiently, provided that we can define a well-behaved, differentiable loss function. The V and M models are designed to be trained efficiently with the backpropagation algorithm using modern GPU accelerators, so we would like most of the model's complexity and model parameters to reside in V and M. The number of parameters of C are minimal in comparison. This choice allows us to use very flexible evolutionary algorithms to train C to tackle more challenging RL tasks where the **credit assignment** problem is difficult. Thus, the parameters of C can be efficiently optimized with **CMA-ES**, which works well for solution spaces of up to a few thousand parameters.

13.5.2 Using the World Model for Feature Extraction

A world model contains much useful internal latent information that the agent can leverage as useful features extracted from the environment into the model. These features can even be used entirely for the agent's decision-making process, bypassing the direct use of the

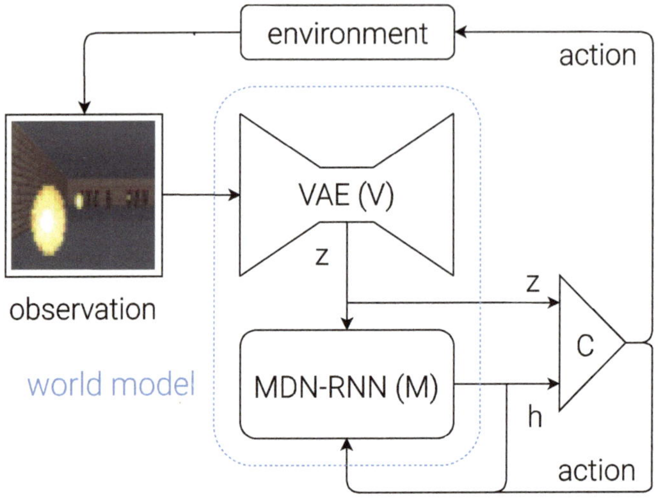

Figure 13.25: **Flow diagram of the world model agent.** The raw observation is first processed by V at each time step t to produce z_t. The input into C is this latent vector z_t concatenated with M's hidden state h_t at each time step. C will then output an action vector a_t for motor control. M will then take the current z_t and action a_t as an input to update its own hidden state to produce h_{t+1} to be used at time $t + 1$. Figure from Ha and Schmidhuber (2018b).

actual observations from the environment. Let's take a more detailed look at how this **feature extraction** approach works, using the CarRacing task (sections 4.4.3 and 7.1.2) as an example.

As a reminder, **CarRacing** is a top-down car racing environment, in which the agent has to learn to drive from pixel observations alone. While it is possible to feed the high-dimensional input into a large policy network trained to output an action, such an approach can be difficult to scale for more complex domains or requires additional methods to protect innovation (section 7.1.2). By using a world model, one can considerably limit the size and complexity of the policy network. The VAE-based vision model can be quickly trained to compress an input frame into a 16-dimensional latent vector z, which is expressive enough to reconstruct the image meaningfully enough for the driving task.

By using the vision model (V) alone, without even using the memory model (M), one can train a small linear network with 17 parameters (16 latent vectors and an additional bias) to compute the action vector (brake, gas, and steer), which requires evolving only 51 parameters for this simple linear model. The resulting model achieved an average score of 632 ± 251 over 100 trials. While the navigation policy makes the car go a bit wobbly, due to the simplicity of the linear model and the lack of predictive power from using the vision model alone, it does generally do the job of completing most tracks.

We can further increase the performance of the vision-only model by moving from a simple linear controller to one with a hidden layer, which results in a score of 788 ± 141 over 100 trials. To give the approach even more flexibility, we can also evolve the controller network with **NEAT**, which here is allowed to use a variety of activation functions such as sinusoids, step functions, and rectified linear units (ReLUs); similar to what we have seen when NEAT is used to evolve **CPPNs** in section 4.3.1. Figure 13.26 is the best NEAT

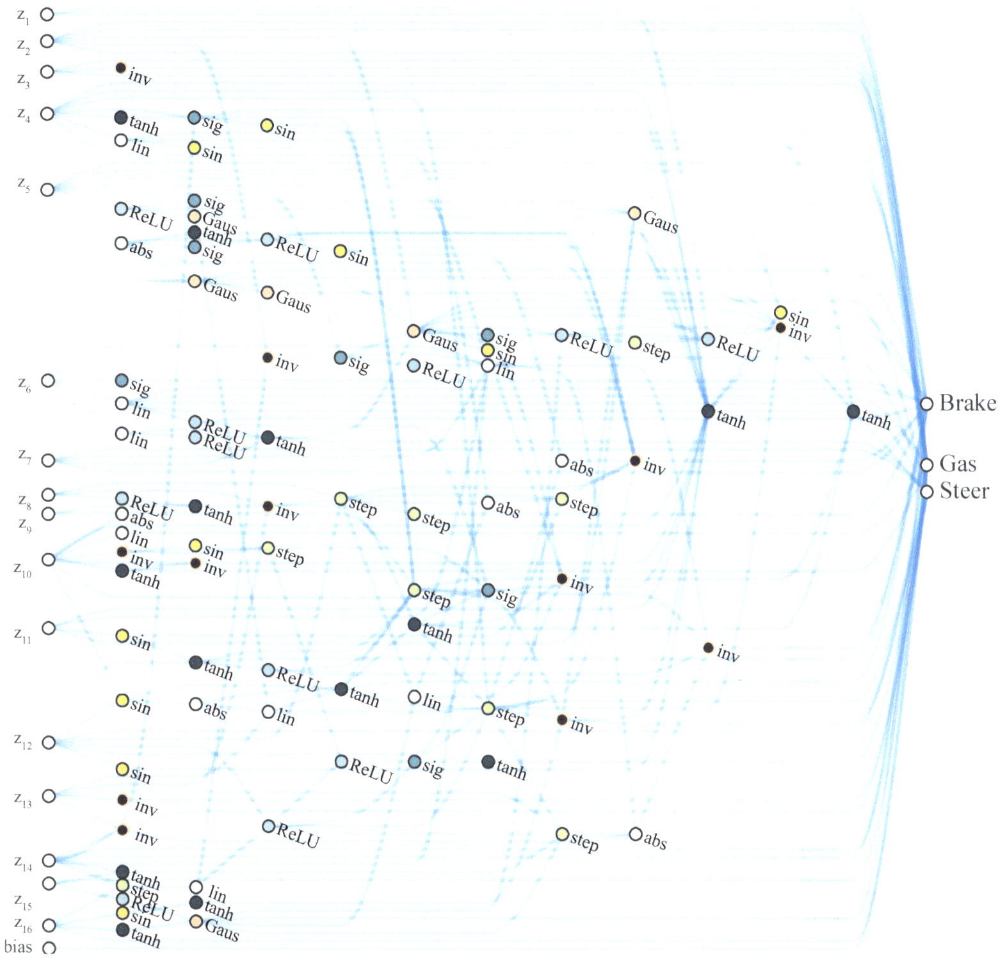

Figure 13.26: **Combining a vision-only model with NEAT.** Because NEAT is able to evolve the network's weights together with an increasingly complex neural architecture, it was able to evolve a high-performing controller for CarRacing, which only uses the latent vector z of vision model V to output the action. Figure from Gaier and Ha (2019).

network for the agent controller, which is able to achieve an impressive performance of an average score of 893 ± 74 over 100 trials.

Instead of further increasing the complexity of the controller, another interesting question is how far we can improve the performance of a simple linear-only controller by incorporating the **memory model** (M) into the agent's world model. While the vision model has no predictive power and contains only static features representing the spatial properties of the agent's environment, the memory model can predict part of the future state of the agent. Indeed, by concatenating the latent vector z from the vision model and the hidden state h of the predictive RNN model, our linear-only controller achieved the very best performance, resulting in an average score of 906 ± 21 over 100 trials. In 2018, this model was the first solution to solve the CarRacing task, which required an average score above 900.

13.5.3 Training an Agent Inside Its Own World Model

So far, we have demonstrated the usefulness of using a world model for the purpose of extracting important features that tell the agent useful things about its environment, particularly with spatiotemporal features through the vision and memory components of the world model.

But a world model is far more useful than being merely a feature extractor. If we are interested in feature extraction alone, there might be more direct ways of training neural networks for that purpose. The key capability of a generative world model is the ability to generate and simulate the actual environment, in latent space, kind of like running a quick simulation in our minds. For instance, the memory component of our world model, the **recurrent neural network**, is able to simulate approximate future trajectories of the environment from the data that the agent has collected.

The agent can even act inside this **neural-network-simulated environment** of the world and observe hypothetical responses, learning from the consequences of its actions without actually performing such actions in reality. This ability was demonstrated in an experiment in the **DoomTakeCover** environment. We have already encountered the particular task in the context of **AttentionAgent** (section 4.4.3) and the **deep innovation approach** (section 7.1.2). As a reminder, here the agent has to learn to avoid fireballs shot by monsters from the other side of the room. The cumulative reward is the number of time steps that the agent manages to stay alive during a rollout. Each rollout of the environment runs for a maximum of 2,100 time steps (roughly a minute of actual gameplay), and the task is considered solved if the average survival time over 100 consecutive trials is greater than 750 time steps of gameplay.

To train the world model, as in the CarRacing experiment, the agent explored the environment using a random policy, and recorded trajectories over thousands of random gameplays. Once the world models were trained, the agent was able to produce simulated gameplays in latent space, using the RNN module alone.

The **recurrent neural network** was trained to produce not a deterministic prediction of the next latent states of the world, but rather a **probabilistic distribution** from which we can sample future latent states. As such, this distribution can be parametrized to artificially produce wider or narrower distributions using a **temperature parameter**, τ. This allows us to bias the distribution to output the mode always, or produce outputs with more uncertainty, and this feature is quite important for training an agent entirely inside the world model. Table 13.4 displays the results when **CMA-ES** was used to train a controller to perform well inside the world model, as well as how the policies learned transfer to the actual environment.

We note that in the **deterministic model** (low temperature), the agent could easily find faults in its model of the world and exploit them so the learned policy would do well only in its dream, but not in reality. In contrast, as the uncertainty of the model was increased, this made the virtual environment generated by the agent's world model much more difficult to beat, leading to policies that were transferable to the actual environment. Varying the temperature in generation is just one of several possibilities for approaching the transfer problem between performing a task inside a learned world model and performing a task in the actual world.

Table 13.4: **DoomTakeCover scores at various temperature settings.**

Temperature τ	Virtual Score	Actual Score
0.10	2086 ± 140	193 ± 58
0.50	2060 ± 277	196 ± 50
1.00	1145 ± 690	868 ± 511
1.15	918 ± 546	1092 ± 556
1.30	732 ± 269	753 ± 139
Random Policy	N/A	210 ± 108

To conclude this chapter, we have seen how the synergy between generative AI and neuroevolution enables hybrid systems that blend creativity with optimization. Whether through prompt evolution, model merging, or intelligent mutation strategies, neuroevolution has proved to be a powerful approach for enhancing the capabilities of large models. There are great opportunities to extend this concept further and incorporate the many other neuroevolution approaches that we have encountered in this book. We invite the reader to explore these limitless possibilities.

Beyond its utility in a hybridized approach, neuroevolution also offers something deeper: a framework for understanding the very nature of evolution and intelligence. In chapter 14, we turn our attention from what neuroevolution can do to what it can tell us about biological evolution, as well as how intelligent behavior might arise through evolutionary processes.

13.6 Chapter Review Questions

1. **Large language models:** What role do the transformer architecture and self-attention mechanism play in the performance and scalability of LLMs like GPT?

2. **Promptbreeder:** What is the self-referential mechanism in Promptbreeder? How does it differ from EvoPrompt in optimizing task-specific prompts for LLMs?

3. **Performance of EvoPrompt:** How did EvoPrompt improve performance on challenging tasks like the BBH benchmark? What are the key contributions of the evolutionary algorithm?

4. **Evolutionary model merging:** What are the key differences between merging models in data flow space and parameter space? How does evolutionary model merging generate new composite models with emergent capabilities?

5. **LLMs in genetic programming:** How are LLMs used to enhance genetic programming through diff-based mutation? What advantages do these mutations offer over traditional random or deterministic approaches?

6. **LMX generality:** Explain how LMX demonstrates its versatility across domains such as symbolic regression, text style transfer, and code evolution. What common characteristic of LLMs enables this adaptability?

7. **EvoLLM as evolutionary strategies:** How does EvoLLM reconceptualize the role of LLMs in evolutionary strategies compared to traditional ES methods? In what ways does involving LLMs directly in the evolutionary cycle change the dynamics of optimization?

8. **MarioGAN versus MarioGPT:** How do MarioGAN and MarioGPT differ in their approaches to controllable level generation? What trade-offs emerge between optimization efficiency, controllability, and diversity in these two frameworks?

9. **World models:** What are the roles of the vision (V), memory (M), and controller (C) components in world models? How do these components collectively allow agents to act effectively in simulated environments?

10. **Simulated learning with world models:** How do world models enable agents to train within a neural simulator of reality, as demonstrated in the DoomTakeCover environment? How does adjusting the temperature parameter influence policy transfer to the actual environment?

Chapter 14

What Neuroevolution Can Tell Us About Biological Evolution

In previous chapters of this book, several examples were given of using neuroevolution to discover behavior for intelligent agents. The goal was to construct artificial agents that could perform complex tasks to aid humans, potentially in virtual worlds, household robots, autonomous vehicles, and other situations. However, the approach can also be useful in the other direction; that is, in using neuroevolution to understand biological intelligence (Miikkulainen, 2025). Why do certain neural structures exist in the brain–what do they do and how did they come about? How do the genetic and environmental influences combine to construct an individual? What are the stepping stones in the evolution of intelligent behavior? How do behaviors such as herding, hunting, and communication emerge? This chapter will review progress toward answering these questions and identify further opportunities in them.

14.1 Understanding Neural Structure

Neuroscience aims to understand how the brain produces behavior. The neural structures in the brain are highly organized into nuclei, or collections of neurons, and pathways between them, and the goal is to identify what functions each performs individually and through interactions. Single-cell recordings have been used for a long time to uncover such function at a low level, for instance identifying cells that respond to a particular location in the visual field, and a line of a particular orientation and direction of movement in it (Hubel and Wiesel, 1968). More recently, several broader imaging techniques have been developed to look at larger areas of the brain at once: Voltage-sensitive dye imaging can visualize entire maps, diffusion tensor imaging entire pathways, and electroencephalography (EEG), magnetoencephalography (MEG), and functional magnetic resonance imaging (fMRI) even the entire brain at once (Chemla and Chavane, 2010; Lenartowicz and Poldrack, 2010; Meoded, Poretti, Mori, et al., 2016). Sensory and motor functions are already understood relatively well, and much progress is made in delineating higher functions such as reasoning and language.

However, one important perspective that is often missing in such inquiries is that the structures are a **product of evolution**. Part of what we observe today may not be explained simply as serving a function in some optimal sense. Some of the structure is there because evolution needed to discover it: It may not be optimal or necessary, but it is instead a remnant of evolutionary stepping stones. Humans still have tailbones even though we no longer have tails. Speech organs look the way that they do because they evolved from mastication elements (MacNeilage, 1998). Similarly, to understand brain structures and behavior fully, it may be necessary to understand their **evolutionary origins**.

Although the brain microstructure varies between individuals, the high-level organization is remarkably consistent between individuals and between species. Evolution has come up with a successful solution and has created many variations of it that occupy multiple niches in the world. A possible approach to understanding the brain is to create artificial worlds, place artificial **embodied agents** in them to face various challenges, and evolve their brains to construct behaviors that allow them to survive and be successful. By manipulating the environment, it may be possible to determine what structures are likely to evolve and why. To the extent that they match those observed in biology, it may be possible to gain insight into biology.

For instance, in one such grid-world simulation, an agent first needed to navigate to a zone where food items are located, while avoiding poison obstacles, and then to remain in that zone and forage (figure 14.1; Aharonov-Barki, Beker, and Ruppin, 2001; Ruppin, 2002). The agents were controlled by a **fully recurrent binary neural network** with five sensory, four motor, and six to 41 hidden neurons. After successful behavior had evolved, the hidden neurons were analyzed through conventional neuroscience methods of lesioning and receptive field analysis. Remarkably, the successful networks had evolved a **command neuron** (or a few) that essentially switched the network between the navigation and foraging behaviors. The network starts by navigation, but as soon as the agent consumes a food item, the command neuron switches it into foraging. Such command neurons emerged in evolution because they resulted in higher fitness: Individuals that were able to separate the navigation and foraging behaviors found the food zone faster, avoided poison better, and were able to forage more efficiently than those that mixed the two behaviors.

Interestingly, command neurons are found in many biological systems as well, including aplysia, crayfish, and even lobsters and crabs (Combes, Meyrand, and Simmers, 1999; DiCaprio, 1990; Edwards, Heitler, and Krasne, 1999; Teyke, Weiss, and Kupfermann, 1990). They generally switch motor behaviors on and off based on sensory input, similar to the command neurons that were evolved in the simulation. Thus, the simulation demonstrates computationally not only how such a network implements effective behaviors, but also how it can arise in evolution as a solution to a computational need.

Beyond the single-neuron lesion and receptive field analysis, the full access that computational networks provide makes it possible to analyze the solutions in more detail. For instance, multiple small perturbations to the network's neurons or connections can be introduced and the contribution of each of these elements quantified by estimating its **Shapley value** (a game-theoretic measure of contribution to a collaboration; Keinan, Sandbank, Hilgetag, et al., 2006). Such an analysis makes it possible to identify the role

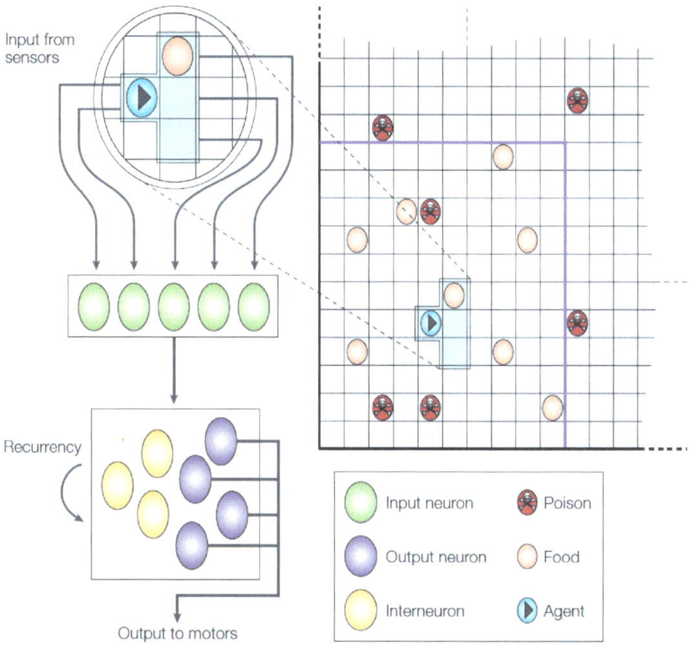

Figure 14.1: **Evolution of command neurons in a navigation and foraging task**. In the simulated grid world, there are a number of poison and food items. The agent needs to first navigate to the 10×11 bottom-left area where the food items are, eat as many of them as possible, and avoid poison items at all times. The agent's behavior was controlled by neural networks that were evolved through genetic algorithms over time. Some of the evolved interneurons act as command neurons, switching the behavior from navigation to foraging as soon as the first food item is consumed. Similar command neurons have been observed in biology; the experiment demonstrates how they may arise as an advantage in evolving effective behavior in the domain. Figure from Ruppin (2002).

of each element in constructing a function, and it also makes it possible to prune the network by removing elements that do not contribute significantly. Although developed for analyzing evolved **artificial neural networks** (ANNs), the technique could in principle be adapted to **neuroscience**, for instance based on multiple lesions or on perturbations caused by transcranial magnetic stimulation (TMS).

Neuroevolution simulations can be useful in evaluating hypotheses about the function of specific circuits. For instance, **facilitating synapses** (Markram, Wang, and Tsodyks, 1998) have been observed to activate postsynaptic neurons not only based on current input, but also based on a rate of activation change in the past. Most likely, they play a role in processing temporal sequences, but they may also be useful in compensating for **propagation delays** (Kwon and Choe, 2009; Lim and Choe, 2006). Although such delays are not taken into account in abstract neural networks, in biological networks, delays are an important factor. Information from the sensors takes time to propagate to neurons that react to it, and proper responses to e.g., a moving object, require compensating for these delays. With neuroevolution, it is possible to construct facilitating synapses that play this role, resulting in more accurate performance in tasks such as pole balancing with synaptic delays. Such compensation amounts to rudimentary prediction, and suggests that coping with synaptic delays may be a foundation for predictive mechanisms, which have been proposed to underlie much of cognitive processing (Hawkins and Ahmad, 2016; Hawkins and Blakeslee, 2004).

Neuroevolution simulations can also be used to target specific biological behaviors. For instance, such experiments have been useful in understanding **locomotion circuits** in animals (Beer, Chiel, and Gallagher, 1999; Chiel, Beer, and Gallagher, 1999). Such circuits are often called **CPGs**, or **central pattern generators**, because they provide a cyclical activity pattern that can be used to control the gait through multiple muscles (Buzsáki, 2006; Steuer and Guertin, 2019). Such networks are relatively small, consisting of three to five neurons in a **continuous-time recurrent neural network** (CTRNN). However, they generate complex dynamics that also change over time. The simulations made it possible to characterize such dynamics mathematically and experimentally and demonstrate how such neural systems can be composed of multistable dynamic building blocks (i.e., subsystems with multiple stable activity patterns). In some cases, it was possible to assign functional roles to these blocks; in others, they remained opaque as supporting interneurons.

These mathematical characterizations of CPGs were expanded into simulations of actual locomotion in lampreys and salamanders, both in swimming and walking (Ijspeert, 2008; Ijspeert, Crespi, Ryczko, et al., 2007). The evolved networks coordinate the **oscillatory patterns** of the CPGs as inputs to the two legs on each side of the body, resulting in the motions required for effective propulsion. Remarkably, such evolved controllers resulted in more robust patterns and flexible control than a model that was built by hand. Also, the oscillation patterns and the connectivity structures were closer to those observed in biology, again demonstrating how the biological structures may arise from evolutionary pressure to perform well with regards to a behavioral challenge in a physical environment. Moreover, the same circuit can control both swimming and walking, as well as transitions between them, potentially demonstrating a crucial phase in the vertebrate evolution from aquatic to terrestrial.

Beyond **pattern-generator circuits**, a more general question concerns network building blocks. Evolved neural networks often include identifiable **neural motifs**; that is, patterns of connectivity that occur more frequently than they would in randomly generated networks (Kashtan and Alon, 2005; Kashtan, Itzkovitz, Milo, et al., 2004). It turns out that these same motifs can also be found in biological networks. Thus, computational simulations can then be used to identify what function they may perform. For instance, the feedforward loop motif can be used to filter information, generate pulses, and increase responses, and the single-input motif can generate time-varying gene expressions. Evolved neural networks can then demonstrate how behavior is composed of such building blocks, for instance uncovering spatial specialization in a visual pattern recognition circuit.

Beyond understanding motif function, neuroevolution can be used to illustrate how motifs, and more generally modules, emerge. It turns out that if the network is evolved to simply solve one task, they are unlikely to arise. However, if the environment requires solving multiple goals composed of different combinations of subgoals, and the **goals switch** over time, modular network structure and motifs do arise. In this manner, evolution finds **modularity** as an effective way to discover subfunctions that can be used to construct multiple behaviors. Indeed, the modular structure of the brain supports this hypothesis: many areas of the brain participate in many tasks in different combinations. Even the visual areas are used in some language tasks and vice versa, suggesting that their computational function is more general than just one modality. Neuroevolution studies can thus demonstrate this general principle as a solution arising from the complexity of tasks the animal has to solve.

Because neuroevolution is an optimization method, it can also be used in a different role in understanding neural structure: Instead of evaluating their evolutionary origins, it can be used to optimize the model parameters. **Biophysical models** are created with objectives and constraints derived from experimental data. They often contain parameters that are difficult to set correctly to match the data, but can provide insights into the biological structures and processes. Neuroevolution can be effective in this role: It has been used for instance in optimizing the spiking patterns on the **Izhikevich model** of hippocampal neurons (Venkadesh, Komendantov, Listopad, et al., 2018) and fitting multicompartmental models to multilocation patch-clamp and microelectrode array data (Buccino, Damart, Bartram, et al., 2024; Druckmann, Banitt, Gidon, et al., 2007). Interestingly, as discussed in section 11.5, neural network implementations in hardware often utilize **spiking neural networks** to reduce energy consumption; it has turned out useful to optimize their structure and hyperparameters through evolution (Iranmehr, Shouraki, Faraji, et al., 2019; Schuman, Patton, Kulkarni, et al., 2022). Neuroevolution can thus realize the potential of such biologically more accurate models, suggesting how behavior can arise from the biophysical properties expressed in their parameters.

Neuroevolution simulations can also be used to explore other hypotheses about the development of modularity and organization. One such hypothesis is to minimize the total wiring length, as will be discussed next.

14.2 Evolutionary Origins of Modularity

Given that the primary role of the brain is to process information, it is natural to try to explain its entire structure and function in computational terms. However, it is sometimes useful to recognize that the brain is also a physical organ, and there are physical requirements that must be met. For instance, some of the brain structure may be due to the need to maintain efficient **metabolism**, i.e., to bring oxygen and nutrients to the cells, including the vascular structure and the blood-brain barrier. While bigger brains in general are more powerful, the size of the brain is limited by the birth canal. Some of the growth mechanisms after birth may exist to compensate for it, rather than be driven entirely by the need to construct an efficient information processing system. Similarly, the overall organization, with gray matter on the outside and white matter on the inside, and the highly convoluted surface with gray matter, amounts to an efficient use of the available space.

The need to **minimize wiring length** is an important principle that may have affected the evolution of brain structure more generally (Horvát, Gămănuț, Ercsey-Ravasz, et al., 2016; Sporns and Betzel, 2016). In particular, it may be the **evolutionary origin of modularity**. This is an interesting possibility because modularity is also a powerful functional principle. While a tightly connected system may in principle provide more complex functionality, it is more difficult to construct, maintain, and adapt a system where everything depends on everything else. For instance in engineering, modular structures are often used because they make such processes easier. For these same reasons, evolution may have favored modular designs as well.

However, such pressures are relatively weak compared just to performance, and it has been difficult to demonstrate this theory biologically and computationally. In contrast, it turns out to be possible to demonstrate that minimization of wiring length can play a primary role in the evolution of modularity; the functional advantages then emerge as a secondary, reinforcing side effect (Clune, Mouret, and Lipson, 2013).

Computational experiments were set up to compare the evolution of neural networks in a visual object recognition task under two conditions: with a single objective of maximizing performance alone, and with two objectives of maximizing performance and minimizing wiring length simultaneously. Since wiring length is presumably less important for survival than performance, it was set to affect selection only 25% of the time. Wiring length was measured as the total squared length of all connections, and **non-dominated sorting genetic algorithm II** (NSGA-II) was used to construct a **Pareto front** of the two objectives.

The **retina task**, originally proposed by Kashtan and Alon (2005), involved an eight-pixel retina where an object might appear in the left half, in the right half, or both (figure 14.2). Note that it is indeed possible to decide whether there is an object on the left/right half before combining these decisions; the task should therefore lend itself to modular solutions. Performance was measured simply as the percentage of correct answers. Simple feedforward networks with three hidden layers were evolved in this task. They had integer weights and thresholds, as well as mutations to add or remove a connection and increase or decrease a weight or a threshold. The networks were initially set up randomly; their modularity was measured by first dividing the networks optimally into modules, and then comparing the density of connections within each module to that of a randomly connected network (Newman, 2006).

In 25,000 generations, evolution based on performance plus **connections cost** resulted in more modular networks than performance-based evolution. Such structural modularity resulted in functional modularity as well: The modules often corresponded to making a decision on the left or the right side. Interestingly, many such networks actually performed better than those that were evolved only to maximize performance. They were generally smaller, and therefore perhaps easier to optimize; a good non-modular network may also be more difficult to find. The networks with the shortest wiring length were more likely to be modular. However, evolution did find some well-performing non-modular networks as well, suggesting that modularity does not arise from performance alone.

The modular networks also turned out to be more evolvable. In further experiments, networks were evolved in a sequence of two tasks: They were first evolved to answer whether an object appeared both left and right, and once they had learned this task, they were further evolved to answer whether an object appeared on either the left or the right (the opposite order of tasks was also run). The modular networks required fewer generations to adapt to the new environment, and they were more modular than in an unchanging environment. The results thus suggest that modularity evolves primarily due to wiring

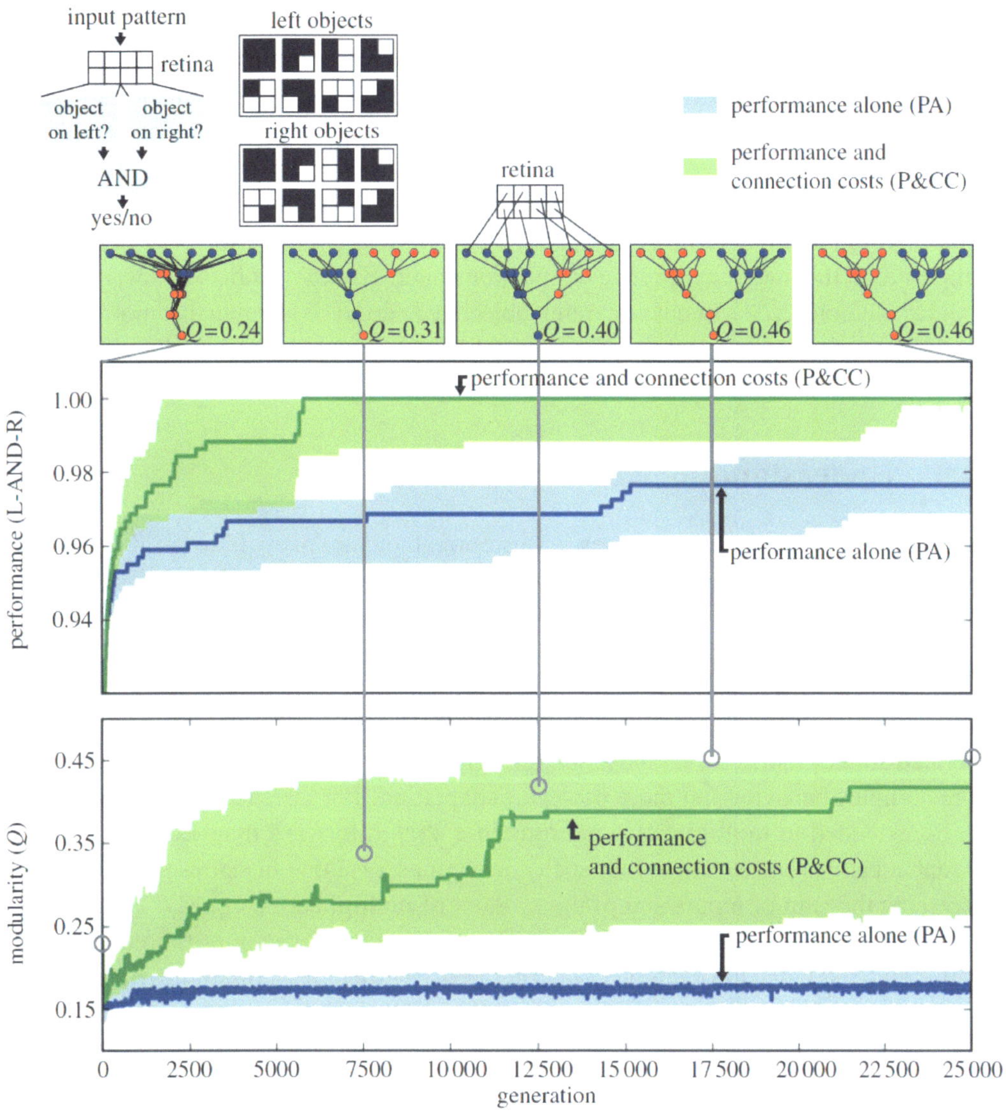

Figure 14.2: **Evolution of modularity based on maximizing performance and minimizing wiring length.** The goal was to evolve a visual system to locate and identify objects. Objects appear on the left and/or the right side of the retina, and the network needs to decide whether there is an object in both. With the objective of minimizing wiring length, more modular networks evolve over time. Modular networks also perform better, although there are some well-performing non-modular networks as well. Computational simulations thus suggest that wiring length is the primary evolutionary pressure behind modularity; performance and adaptability pressures may further enhance it. Figure from Clune, Mouret, and Lipson (2013). Videos at `https://neuroevolutionbook.com/demos`.

length; once it is there, it is further enhanced by the need to adapt. Thus, neuroevolution simulation can be used to gain insights into the origins of modularity in biology.

Knowing that modularity is helpful and that minimizing wiring length leads to modularity, it is possible to take advantage of this principle in neuroevolution more generally. For instance, applied to the same retina problem, the basic HyperNEAT method does not discover modular solutions reliably, and does not perform well. However, it can be extended to specify wiring patterns in addition to connection weights (Verbancsics and Stanley, 2011). If these patterns are biased to favor local connections initially, modular structures do emerge, improving performance significantly. This method, called **HyperNEAT-LEO** (LEO stands for link expression output) can be seen as an extension of the wiring length hypothesis: It suggests that if local circuits evolve early and more complex structures with long-range connections later, evolution is biased toward finding modular solutions even without an explicit objective to do so. Assuming that more complex nervous systems evolved from simpler ones in biology, it suggests that modularity evolved naturally as a side effect.

14.3 Understanding Neuromodulation

As has been mentioned several times in this book, there are many biological constraints and mechanisms that are likely to have an effect on neural function, but are not included in the standard neural network models. One of those mechanisms is **neuromodulation**. In section 12.3.3, it was discussed as a possible method for learning when to learn; this section aims to further understand its evolutionary origins.

In a neuromodulated network, some neurons have a multiplicative effect on the weighted sum of inputs, or on the Hebbian weight change. Such modulation can lead to more complex behavior and more powerful adaptation. For instance, **backpropagation** can be extended to multiplicative neurons in a straightforward manner. The gradient descent equations can be derived for such connections, resulting in **sigma-pi units** (sigma represents the sum of inputs and pi the product of multiplicative inputs). This method results in smaller networks: for instance, XOR can be represented in just three units: one computing AND, one OR, and one selecting between them by multiplying their outputs (Pollack, 1987; Rumelhart, Hinton, and Williams, 1986). Scaling up, such networks have been useful in for instance recognizing whether a string adheres to a particular grammar: a single misplaced symbol can change the decision, which behavior can be represented well by multiplicative connections (Giles, Miller, Chen, et al., 1991). Such networks can be evolved just as well as weighted-sum networks, achieving the same benefits.

An interesting question is whether neuroevolution would select for neuromodulation to solve a task; that is, whether it would emerge in evolution as an adaptive advantage. In one such experiment, **neuromodulation** was set to modify plasticity in **Hebbian networks**; that is, those where a connection strengthens when both presynaptic and postsynaptic neurons are simultaneously highly active (Soltoggio, Bullinaria, Mattiussi, et al., 2008). In contrast with backpropagation, which is an abstraction of learning in biological neural networks, Hebbian plasticity is an actual plasticity mechanism in biology. Connection weights were adapted as

$$w_{ji} = \eta \tanh(o_m)(Ao_jo_i + Bo_j + Co_i + D), \tag{14.1}$$

where η is the learning rate, o_m is the modulatory neuron output, o_j is the presynaptic activation and o_i is the postsynaptic activation, and A, B, C, and D are constants

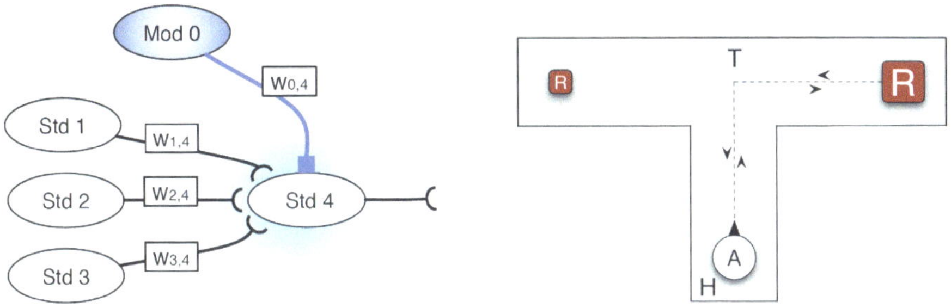

(*a*) Neuromodulation circuit (*b*) T-maze task

Figure 14.3: **Taking advantage of neuromodulation in the maze navigation task.** Neuromodulation offers a dimension of adaptation that may make it easier to solve complex tasks. (*a*) The three standard neurons activate the postsynaptic neuron through a weighted sum as usual. A modulatory neuron then amplifies the Hebbian adaptation of those weights. (*b*) In the T-maze task, the agent needs to traverse a corridor and then turn left or right to get to the larger reward; in a double maze (not shown here), two such turns need to be made. The location of that reward changes periodically, and the agent needs to adapt its behavior accordingly. Networks evolved with modulation perform more reliably than non-plastic and non-modulatory networks, suggesting that evolution finds a way to take advantage of modulation even when it is not strictly necessary. Figure from Soltoggio, Bullinaria, Mattiussi, et al. (2008).

(figure 14.3*a*). In this manner, the modulatory neuron controls whether the weight increases or decreases, and it scales the magnitude of the Hebbian adaptation.

The approach was evaluated in the task of navigating through a **T-maze** or **double T-maze** to a reward location (i.e., making the correct turn once or twice to get to the reward), and then navigating back to the starting location (figure 14.3*b*). Each agent was tested 100 times, and at some point, the reward location changed, so it had to adapt its behavior. It could do so through recurrent connections that implemented memory, or by changing its weights through plasticity. The agent networks were evolved by inserting, duplicating, or deleting neurons, which could be either standard or modulatory, and by mutating the constants A, B, C, D, and η in equation 14.1 and the real-valued weights through evolution strategy.

Even though the tasks were sometimes solved without plasticity and modulation, networks with plasticity evolved to perform significantly better in the 100 trials. Networks with modulation performed similarly in the T-maze, but significantly better in the double T-maze. The solutions had many different structures that were hard to interpret, but ablation studies showed that modulation plays an interesting role. When it was turned off from networks that were evolved with it, the networks still performed well locally; that is, made turns and did not crash into walls. But they could often turn in only one direction, and could not navigate globally to find their way back to the starting location. This result suggests that neuromodulation is not simply an add-on that helps solve more complex tasks, but is integrated into the dynamics of the navigation behavior. Successful behavior can be evolved without it, but solutions with modulation are easier to discover. They therefore evolve more reliably, resulting in better average performance.

A related experiment, previously reviewed in section 12.3.3, further suggested a possible biological mechanism for neuromodulation. In a stochastic reward optimization task, modulation activated reinforcement learning when it was most needed, allowing the system to adapt better to new scenarios (Soltoggio, Dürr, Mattiussi, et al., 2007). Modulation was achieved through dynamics similar to **dopaminergic activity** recorded in the monkey's brain (e.g., Schultz, 2024), giving it a computational interpretation.

The experiments thus show that the evolutionary process finds a way to utilize whatever dimensions of adaptation there are, rather than finding parsimonious solutions that ignore the dimensions that are not necessary. If neuromodulation is possible, neuroevolution will take advantage of it.

14.4 Developmental Processes

A fundamental question in cognitive science is how much of intelligent behavior in humans is innate, and how much is learned. This question is often referred to as the **nature versus nurture** debate. Both of these factors play a role, of course, and are often synergistic through the process of **development**. Further, initial development, as well as long-term stability, can be driven by genetically directed learning, as will be reviewed in this section.

14.4.1 Synergistic Development

Given the relatively small number of genes in the human genome (about 24,000; International Human Genome Sequencing Consortium, 2004), a learning process is necessary to construct an organ as complex as the brain. On the other hand, genetic determination is also necessary: It can provide the overall structure, initialization, and a learning bias that then makes it possible to construct such complexity during the lifetime of the individual. Perhaps the clearest example of this process is language: All normal humans, and only humans, have an innate capacity for language. However, they need to learn a language in early childhood—language does not develop in isolation (section 14.8.1).

For many animals, the fundamental survival skills are there right after birth. For instance, newborn gazelles can run immediately, and whale calves can swim. For higher animals, there is a long period of development during which they depend on their caregivers. This period is exceedingly long for humans, and includes a series of critical periods during which skills such as walking, talking, and social intelligence develop in an order—and if they do not, the individual will not be able to develop them fully later (Robson, 2023). This observation suggests that the relationship between evolution and learning (i.e., the process of development), is more nuanced and structured than simply refinement of a genetic starting point.

In principle, evolution can discover complete solutions that do not need to be refined further. Most of evolutionary computation is also based on this approach. However, in constructing brains, evolution seems to have discovered a different approach, described theoretically as **synergistic development** (Elman, Bates, Johnson, et al., 1996). Instead of specifying a complete solution, only the general structure is genetically determined, together with a learning mechanism that allows the animal to construct the full solution. These components are synergistic: The structure and initialization make learning most effective, and the learning mechanism is well-suited for the structure and the environment.

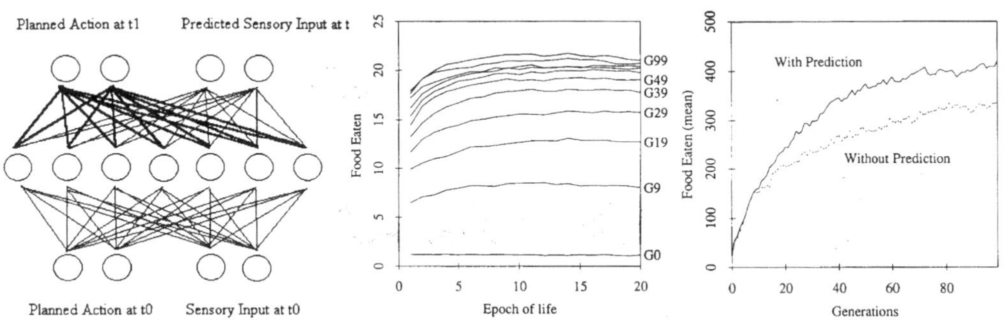

(*a*) Network architecture (*b*) Lifetime learning (*c*) Evolution of foraging

Figure 14.4: **Synergistic development in a foraging task.** The creatures evolve to navigate to food items, aided by development to predict the consequences of their actions. (*a*) The evolved network is trained to predict how its sensory inputs change as a result of its actions in the previous time step. (*b*) Their prediction ability improves over their lifetime throughout evolution; even in later generations (near G99), it is not genetically encoded. (*c*) The development of prediction allows evolution to discover better solutions faster. Thus, the experiment demonstrates the value of synergistic development. Figures from Nolfi, Elman, and Parisi (1994).

The minimally functional initialization and the critical periods are part of this synergy. That is, instead of a fully specified design, evolution has discovered a developmental process as the solution. This approach can be seen as an implementation of **expressive encoding**, with the power to discover solutions that would be difficult to find through direct evolution (section 9.1.4).

Computational studies can be instrumental in verifying this theory. An early example is an experiment with simulated creatures foraging for food items randomly scattered in a 2D grid world (Nolfi, Elman, and Parisi, 1994). They receive the current (t_0) angle and distance to the nearest food item as their input, and generate an action (turn left or right, move forward, or do nothing) at the next time step (t_1) as their output. A creature's fitness corresponds to the number of food items it finds. The optimal actions are not known, but the entire network can be evolved to discover successful foraging behavior. However, in this experiment, the creatures also receive their previous action (at t_0) as additional input, and predict the sensory input at the next time step (t_1) as additional output. These additional outputs are known, and therefore the network can be trained through gradient descent to predict the consequences of its actions. This training takes place during the lifetime of the creature, and the weight changes are not encoded back to the genome.

Thus, **lifetime learning** establishes a developmental process. The creature learns to understand how its actions affect its environment, much like biological organisms learn to interact with their environment. Such learning allows it to perform better at the task for which it is evolved, and it guides evolution to generate individuals that can take better advantage of the learning process (figure 14.4). Note that the prediction ability does not become encoded in the genes; the individuals start with poor ability even in later generations. Evolution instead utilizes learning as part of the synergistic developmental process. As a result, creatures that perform better are discovered faster.

In this manner, computational experiments can be used to gain insight into how development works and why it is so powerful. One such insight is that evolution establishes the proper learning biases, and learning provides the variance necessary to adapt to the world, as will be discussed in the next section.

On the other hand, it may also be possible to build more complex artificial systems by employing these same principles. Progress in such systems, and further opportunities, are reviewed in section 4.2.

14.4.2 Development Through Genetically Directed Learning

One way to characterize the synergy of evolution and learning is through the general machine learning (ML) concepts of **bias and variance**. Biases exist in any learning system, making it more likely to learn certain kinds of behavior and less likely to learn others. In contrast, variance means that it can learn a wide variety of patterns that exist in the training data. A pure evolutionary system can be seen as completely biased with no variance: The behavior is determined genetically, and there is no learning based on input. In contrast, a pure learning system has no bias and only learns the patterns in the input.

Neither of such extremes is likely to be very successful. It is difficult to anticipate all possible input situations ahead of time, during evolution. On the other hand, it is difficult to learn a robust function through high variance; the system is likely to end up overfitting and not generalizing well to new situations. Thus, a developmental system is a way to strike a balance between these two effects. Evolution establishes the proper bias, making it easier for the learning system to acquire a useful, robust function from the inputs.

The biases can be most directly established by evolving the learning system itself. For instance, parameters for **Hebbian learning** can be incorporated into neuron definitions and evolved together with the network itself (Floreano and Urzelai, 1999). Through the lifetime of learning with these parameters, controllers in a robot navigation task can be evolved faster than without learning. Evolution converges on learning parameters that are the most effective, thus finding a proper balance between bias and variance.

A biological example of this process can be seen in the domain of constructing a **pattern recognition system** (Miikkulainen, Bednar, Choe, et al., 2005; Valsalam, Bednar, and Miikkulainen, 2007). Indeed, visual systems of animals are believed to combine nature and nurture in a systematic way: The general structure is genetically determined to match the needs of the species and then is fine-tuned through learning. For example, retinotopy and orientation sensitivity exist even before birth in cats and monkeys, but the full structure is formed during the first few weeks after the eyes open. Human newborns have an innate preference for face-like patterns, which is refined to actual face preferences during the first few months of life. It can also help explain other species-specific visual functions that appear innate, such as detecting prey (e.g., flies in frog vision; Lettvin, Maturana, McCulloch, et al., 1959).

The way that such preferences are established is particularly interesting. While it is possible to specify some neural network structure genetically, such as retinotopy, a learning mechanism also exists and may be active even before birth. Evolution seems to have discovered a clever way to utilize it even in the process of creating the proper initial biases: Much of the initial structure can be constructed through the learning of internally generated patterns. Propagating activity waves in the retina allow orientation detectors to form; three-dot patterns in the ponto-geniculate-occipital loop may result in face preference (corresponding to the two eyes and the mouth). Thus, evolution does not need to specify a full visual system, and it does not even need to specify a full starting point for learning: It can instead specify a way of generating internal patterns that establishes useful species-specific biases.

To illustrate the power of this process, neural networks for **pattern recognition** were constructed in three ways: purely through learning, purely through evolution, and through a combination of evolved prenatal pattern-generation and learning (Valsalam, Bednar, and Miikkulainen, 2007). The task consisted of recognizing hand-written digits in the National Institute of Standards and Technology (NIST) dataset. Each **evolved pattern generator** encoded a distribution of Gaussians with different positions, rotations, and elongations. Their fitness was based on classification accuracy of the system that was first trained with the generated patterns, and then with the actual patterns in the dataset.

The learning mechanism was simple **competitive learning**. Each of the 10 neurons had a weight vector w, randomly initialized and then normalized to unit length:

$$w_i = \frac{w_i}{\sqrt{\Sigma_i w_i^2}}. \tag{14.2}$$

Each neuron responded to an input vector x through a weighted sum:

$$y_j = \Sigma_i w_i x_i. \tag{14.3}$$

The weight vector of the winning neuron (i.e., the one with the highest response), was then rotated toward the input vector, i.e., first modified with:

$$w_i(t+1) = w_i(t) + \eta(x_i - w_i(t)), \tag{14.4}$$

and then normalized to unit length. Competitive learning was used because it is a good model of biological (Hebbian) learning, and also because it is relatively weak, and therefore depends more on bias.

As expected, pure **competitive learning** developed weight vectors that resembled actual digits (figure 14.5*b*). However, competitive learning is not very powerful, and usually did not learn to separate all digits. In particular, it had trouble with 7, 8, and 9 because they have many overlapping pixels. **Direct evolution**, in contrast, has no reason to learn weight vectors that resemble digits. The patterns that it developed simply emphasized differences between digit categories, and formed a good foundation for separating them (figure 14.5*c*). **Pattern generation and learning** resulted in a most interesting solution that clearly illustrates the importance of having a proper bias. Evolution created pattern generators that emphasized the different horizontal locations around the midline (figure 14.5*d*). Only a few units learned these patterns, but it was enough to separate 7, 8, and 9 to different units (figure 14.5*e*). As a result, the postnatal learning with actual examples created a reliable categorization of most examples (figure 14.5*f*).

Thus, evolution was able to discover a proper bias so that even a simple learning system could perform well on this task. Although it was designed to illustrate a possible biological synergy of evolution and learning, the general approach may be useful in constructing complex systems in general.

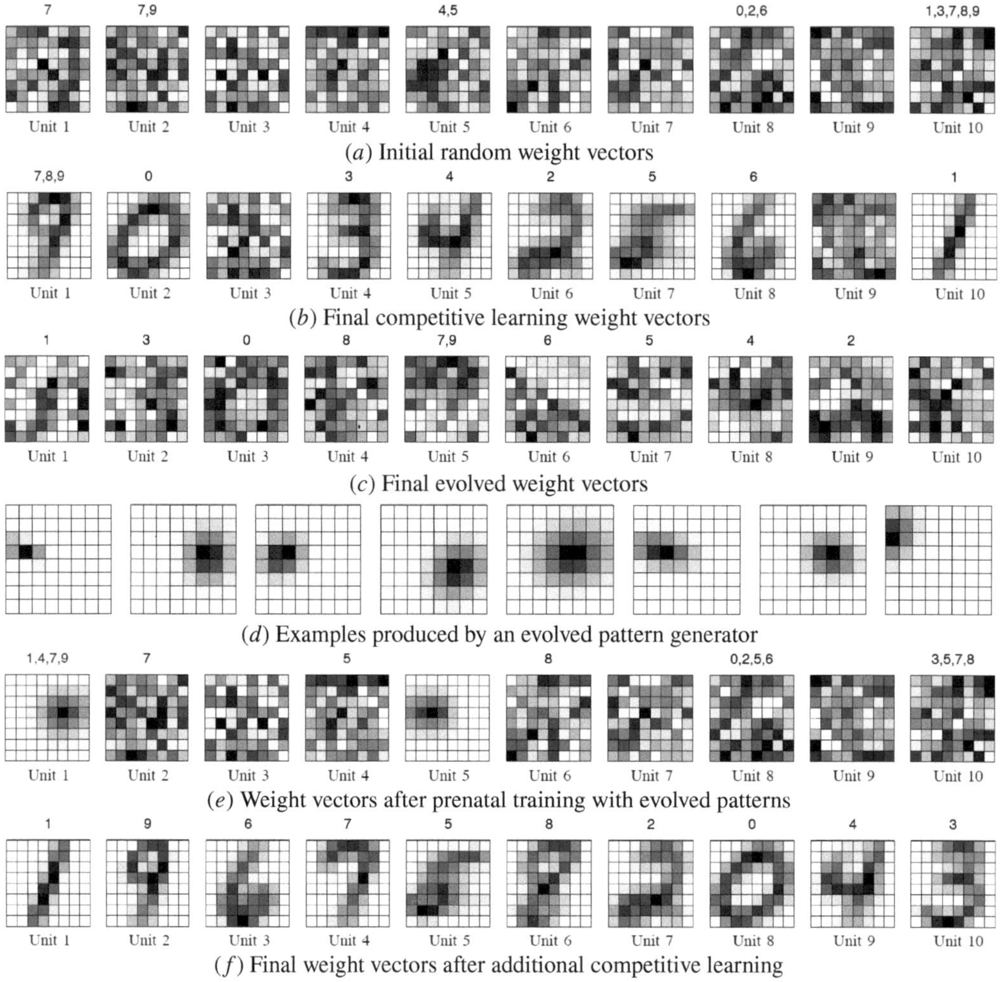

Figure 14.5: **Synergy of evolution and learning through evolved pattern generators.** The task was to recognize handwritten digits on a 10×10 simulated retina; the recognition system consisted of 10 neurons that adapted through competitive Hebbian learning. (*a*) The weight vectors of each neuron (unit) were initialized randomly. (*b*) When they learned through competitive learning, the final weight vectors resembled the inputs. However, learning was not very effective, and e.g., 7, 8, and 9 were often confused. (*c*) When the weight vectors were evolved directly, they emphasized the differences that matter for classification. (*d*) The evolved patterns emphasized mostly the locations in the horizontal midline. (*e*) Prenatal training with such patterns took place only in two units, but it was enough to separate 7, 8, and 9. (*f*) After postnatal learning with actual handwritten digit patterns, most examples were categorized correctly. Evolution thus discovered useful biases and utilized the learning mechanism itself to encode them, thus demonstrating synergy of evolution and learning. Figures from Valsalam, Bednar, and Miikkulainen (2007). For videos of these processes, see `https://neuroevolutionbook.com/demos`.

Moreover, the mechanism of internal pattern generation may play a role in the maintenance of such systems throughout the lifetime of the animal (Miikkulainen, Bednar, Choe, et al., 2005). Environmental conditions often change, and the animal needs to adapt to such changes. If such adaptation is based purely on learning, it could easily overfit, and **catastrophic forgetting** could result. However, if pattern-generator-based learning continues together with learning from the environment, it can serve a stabilizing effect. Adaptation to new inputs is combined with continual adaptation to the fundamental patterns in the domain. Such learning could occur during **rapid eye movement** (REM) sleep. This mechanism could potentially explain why animals learn altered environments only partially, and why they spend much time on REM sleep when their neural structures are most plastic. Evolved pattern generators can thus provide a mechanism for continual genetic influences on behavior. It could similarly be instrumental in keeping artificial systems both adaptive and stable.

A further aspect of the synergy between evolution and learning is that evolution can discover the actual learning mechanisms through **meta-learning**. For instance, in the task of discovering repeated patterns in an input sequence with a **spiking neural network**, evolution discovered **plasticity rules** that made the task possible in three settings (Jordan, Schmidt, Senn, et al., 2021): with reward feedback (reinforcement learning), error feedback (supervised learning), and without feedback (correlation-based unsupervised learning). With **Cartesian genetic programming** (CGP) as the evolution method (Miller, 2011), the system discovered symbolic expressions for such plasticity, making it possible to interpret the underlying physical factors, such as **homeostasis** in the well-known **spike-timing-dependent plasticity mechanisms** (STDP; Song, Miller, and Abbott, 2000).

Many of the meta-learning methods reviewed in chapter 11 and others optimize different aspects of the learning mechanisms (Bingham and Miikkulainen, 2022; Confavreux, Zenke, Agnes, et al., 2020; Elsken, Metzen, and Hutter, 2019; Gonzalez and Miikkulainen, 2021; Najarro and Risi, 2020; Tyulmankov, Yang, and Abbott, 2022). While often the goal is to simply improve ML performance, such methods can also lead to insights into the learning algorithms themselves. For instance, in an experiment where agents needed to adapt to changing reward locations in a **Minecraft** navigation task, evolution discovered **innate reward neurons** that made the search for the reward effective even without an explicit reward signal (Ben-Iwhiwhu, Ladosz, Dick, et al., 2020). Neuroevolution thus discovered structures that facilitated learning during the lifetime of the agent. Such synergies result in more powerful machine learning, but they also help us formulate specific hypotheses about biological adaptation.

14.5 Constrained Evolution of Behavior

Much of this book has focused on the neuroevolution of behavior, and for good reason: Behavior arises naturally from neural networks, and evolution is a natural way to discover them. Neuroevolution is one of the main approaches in the scientific fields of **artificial life**, which explores the nature and principles of living systems through computer simulations, and **adaptive behavior**, which focuses on understanding how behavior arises in biology and in autonomous artificial systems. Further, neuroevolution can be used as a tool in **evolutionary biology**, not only to understand the evolutionary origins of circuits and mechanisms (as in previous sections), but also to formulate and evaluate hypotheses about the origins of behaviors and cognition. This is the topic of the remainder of this chapter.

Section 7.1 illustrated an important principle in the evolution of complex behavior: It does not exist in a vacuum, but is constrained and guided by interactions with the environment and with other agents. Simulations of **cooperative evolution** can thus help us understand the origins of biological behaviors as well. Section 7.1 already demonstrated several such opportunities, including how role-based cooperation may emerge, how adaptive teams can evolve, and how an evolutionary arms race may result in sophisticated herding and hunting behaviors.

This section further expands and generalizes that principle. The guidance may originate not only from complex interactions with the environment, but from general constraints on what the agent can do. For instance, a physical body imposes limits on what movements are possible. Sensory perception is limited, and processing power in decision-making is finite. If the goal is to build capable artificial agents, it makes sense to furnish them with as few such constraints as possible. Evolution can then be the most creative, and the agents most powerful in their task. However, if the goal is to create agents that are believable, for instance as simulated intelligent agents in a virtual environment, such constraints constitute an important guide: Evolution under constraints observed in nature leads the optimization process to discover behaviors that are natural, believable, and human-like. In other words, it explains the observed behaviors as optimal under the constraints seen in nature.

These effects can be observed most clearly in simulations of **virtual creatures** (Bongard and Pfeifer, 2001; Hornby and Pollack, 2001b; Sims, 1991, 1994). Both the bodies and the brains of simulated physical creatures are evolved simultaneously in a simulated physical medium, such as a terrain or water. With even a simple fitness reward, such as getting close to a target, they develop both body structures and ways of moving their body that look remarkably animate.

Such target-following behaviors have been evolved in multiple experiments, with increasingly complex body structures and environments, and modes of locomotion such as running, swimming, and flying (Lehman and Stanley, 2011b; Miconi, 2008; Pilat and Jacob, 2010; Shim, Kim, and Kim, 2004). However, evolving more complex behaviors has turned out significantly more challenging. For instance, it has been difficult to evolve creatures that would be able to employ different behaviors at different times, and make intelligent decisions between them.

One possible approach is to design a **syllabus** (i.e., a hierarchy of increasingly complex behaviors) and evolve them **incrementally** (figure 14.6; Lessin, Fussell, and Miikkulainen, 2013, 2014). The bodies in this experiment consisted of cylinders of different shapes, connected through muscles and attached through different kinds of joints, as well as sensors for threatening and attractive targets. The brains were neural networks containing some higher-level nodes such as those generating oscillation. At the lowest level, bodies and brains were evolved to move as fast as possible, to turn left and right, and to exert as strong a strike on the ground as possible. These behaviors were then encapsulated; that is, the evolved neural network structures frozen and a trigger node added to activate and deactivate them. A second layer of behaviors was then evolved as neural networks that could activate the low-level behaviors as their output; they included moving or following a target, as well as running away from a target, both as as a combination of turning and

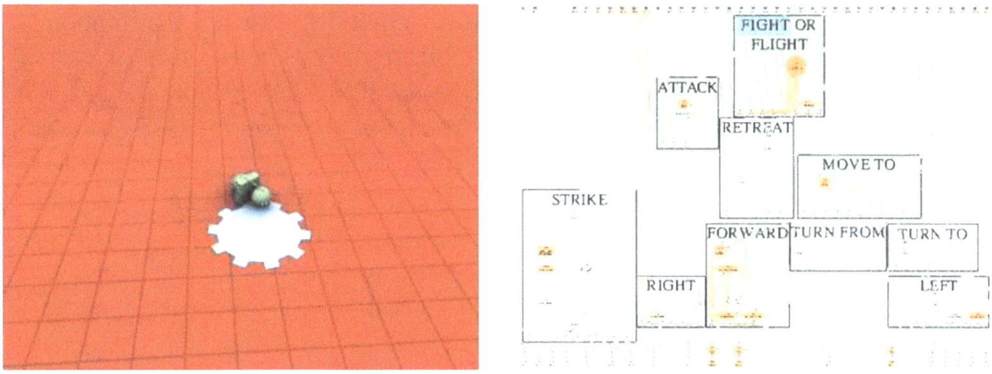

(*a*) Fight (i.e., attack) activated when sensing a good object

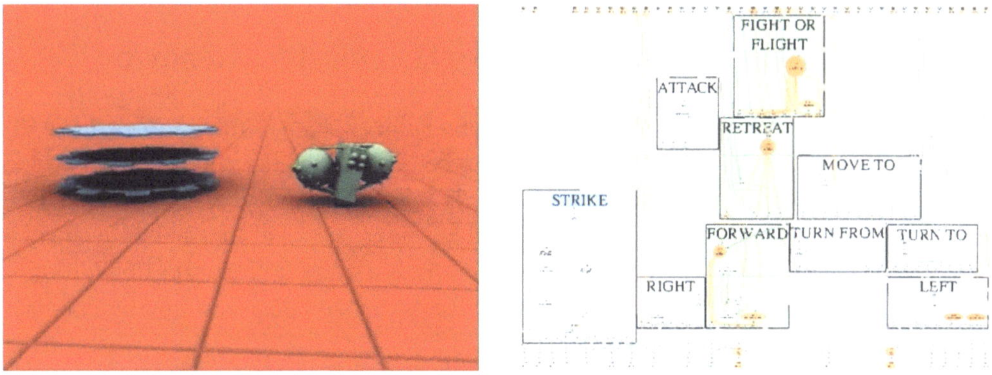

(*b*) Flight (i.e., retreat) activated when sensing a bad object

Figure 14.6: **Neuroevolution of complex behavior in evolved virtual creatures.** The bodies and the brains of simulated creatures were evolved together, thus providing constraints on what kind of movements were possible. As a result, they appear natural and therefore believable. The low-level behaviors such as locomotion, turning right and left, and strike were encapsulated and formed sub-behaviors to the more complex behaviors turn-from, turn-to, retreat, and attack. At the highest level, the creature chooses between (*a*) fight and (*b*) flight depending on whether the object is seen as good or bad, respectively. Such believability makes it natural to anthropomorphize the agents, which can be appealing in constructing virtual worlds. For videos of these behaviors, see `https://neuroevolutionbook.com/demos`.

locomotion. These behaviors were similarly encapsulated, and at the next level, combined with the strike behavior to establish an attack behavior. At the highest level, then, the attack and the running away were combined into fight-or-flight: if the object was sensed as threatening, run away, but if it was sensed as attractive, attack.

The behavior that evolved was indeed highly believable, at least in a subjective sense. Several different kinds of bodies evolved at the lowest level, and behaviors were natural to them. For instance, some creatures had multiple legs and moved them rhythmically to advance. One agent consisted of simply two blocks and was jumping forward one block by shaking the other block up and down. To create a strike, an agent with two side blocks acting as weights evolved to jump and land hard. Another one with a long arm evolved to hit the ground hard with it. In all these cases, the behaviors that evolved made sense in that particular body—it was also fascinating to see that there was no one solution, but many quite different solutions that were successful.

The behavior was also believable at the higher levels, including fight or flight. After watching the simulation for a while, it is easy to anthropomorphize the agent: It seems to have a purpose when it chases a moving target, and when the target changes to a threatening one, it seems scared when reacting to the change and running away. And if the threatening object catches up with it and destroys it, you feel sorry for it. It is the kinds of agents that we can identify with and anthropomorphize that we would like to inhabit the virtual worlds that are now being constructed. Constrained **body-brain evolution** may be a good way to get there. It is also a possible way to demonstrate why and how such a diversity of bodies and behaviors has evolved in nature—as different possible solutions to the same survival challenges.

14.6 Case Study: Understanding Human-like Behavior

Whether a behavior is believable or not is highly subjective and difficult to evaluate. To do that, several blind human judgments need to be collected under controlled conditions. It is, of course, possible to conduct such a study in the laboratory with human subjects. However, observing and interacting with virtual creatures is a lot of fun, and the evaluation can be as well. What if we turn the evaluation into a competition, and in addition to that, run it as an event at a conference where the audience consists of intelligent agent researchers and people interested in bringing AI into games?

This was indeed the goal of the **Botprize competition**, which ran at the computational intelligence in games conference in 2007–2012 (Hingston, 2012). In essence, the competition was a **Turing test** for game bots: In the **Unreal Tournament 2004** video game, there were both agents controlled by AI and agents controlled by human players. Some of the humans were playing the game as usual, trying to win. The AI agents were trying to play the same way as the humans did, and therefore be indistinguishable from human players. Some of the humans acted as judges, playing the game and interacting with the other players in order to decide whether they were controlled by humans or AI. They made the judgment about the other agents at the end of each game: The objective for the AI was to garner at least as many "human" judgments as "bot" judgments across several games with several different human players and judges.

Similar to Doom, Unreal is a representative of the multiplayer first-person shooter game genre. Human players control their avatars, who roam multiple levels in the game, gather possessions, and attack other players with different weapons. The game moves fast and requires quick control and decision-making; however, it does not require linguistic communication. Therefore, to appear human, the AI-controlled bots would have to react, move, and make decisions similarly to the human players.

Indeed, at the time, it was not clear whether it was possible to capture such behaviors. AI bots were routinely easy to identify in games in general: They behaved mechanically and repetitively, and the players often learned strategies that made it easy to defeat the AI bots. In many cases, the gameplay consisted of figuring out the AI and then moving on to other games. On the other hand, part of the reason for multiplayer games was to keep the game more interesting. It is always fun to beat your friends, but friends also provide more interesting challenges. Therefore, being able to construct bots that behave indistinguishably from humans is not only an important scientific question, but also has great value for game development in general.

It was also not clear what human-like behavior even is. In a **human-subject study** in the lab, Botprize games were captured on video, and the judges interviewed afterward, trying to understand how they made their decisions–that is, what constituted human-like behavior to them. Very little came out of that study. It turns out that humans are not very good at explaining what they do, and they may not even understand how they do it. More precisely, they are very good at constructing explanations when prompted to do so, but the explanations may have little to do with their actual process. On several occasions, the judges gave fluent and logical explanations for why they judged the opponent as a bot—for example, because they moved in a certain way, or reacted in a certain way—not realizing that in the game, they actually judged this opponent as a human.

Yet the human judges were quite reliable in making those distinctions—remarkably accurate, as a matter of fact—at least at the beginning of the Botprize competition. Sometimes the opponent jumped in front of them, interacted with them for a few seconds only, and ran away—and still the judges were able to make decisions well above chance. So there appears to be a quality in the behavior that humans have but bots at the time lacked. What is it?

In the first several years, there was a significant and consistent gap between humans and AI: While the human players were judged as human 60%-70% of the time, the bots were mistaken for humans only 20%-30% of the time. Part of the problem turned out to be network latency—when the games were played over the internet, a time lag was introduced, and the humans dealt with that issue better than the bots. However, there were also significant differences in the behavior that gave the bots away. The bots were constructed to play well: For instance, in evolution, the **fitness function** early on was simply the final game score (Karpov, Schrum, and Miikkulainen, 2012; Schrum, Karpov, and Miikkulainen, 2012). Therefore, they evolved behaviors that were highly effective—but not necessarily human-like. For instance, they would run at full speed and, at the same time, shoot at maximum accuracy. If the judge did something unexpected, such as run straight into them, they would react immediately and perform the same behaviors as always when close to the opponent. Humans rarely do that. They get startled when something unexpected happens, and they need to process it before they can react. Their performance varies and becomes less accurate and effective under load. They do not perform multiple behaviors well at the same time. This was a fundamental difference between bots and humans.

However, when such performance constraints were imposed on the bots during evolution, their behavior changed significantly. They were no longer able to simply optimize the game score, but they had to do it while limited in their accuracy, choice of actions, and ability to multitask (figure 14.7; Schrum, Karpov, and Miikkulainen, 2011). In essence, they got tired and distracted and performed inconsistently. In other words, they become more **human-like**. In the last Botprize competition in 2012, they were indeed mistaken for humans more than 50% of the time. Not only that, they were judged as humans more often than half of the human players!

Figure 14.7: **Neuroevolution of human-like behavior in the Botprize competition.** The competition is essentially a Turing'test for game bots. The judge in this screenshot is player 443, and is interacting with another player, 932, to determine whether it is an AI-controlled bot or a human player. When neuroevolution was used to maximize the game score of the bot, the behavior was too systematic, repetitive, and effective to be human. Instead, when various constraints were imposed on accuracy, behavior selection, and multitasking, behavior became eventually indistinguishable from human behavior. Thus, the simulation demonstrated how even complex behavior can be seen as emerging from evolutionary optimization under environmental constraints. For videos of these behaviors, see `https://neuroevolutionbook.com/demos`.

Therefore, Botprize was a remarkable success in three ways: (1) It demonstrates how even complex behavior seen in nature can be seen as optimization under constraints; (2) it demonstrated how neuroevolution can be similarly constrained to discover more believable, more human-like behavior; and (3) it showed how a scientific evaluation can be turned into a fun and interesting event; that is, a competition that promotes innovation and sharpens focus across this entire area of research.

This success by no means suggests that the work on evolving human-like behavior is now concluded. While it was successful at the low levels, there is an entire cognitive level that is not yet captured. For instance, human players lay traps such as running around the corner and waiting for the opponent there so they can ambush them. A human player may fall for that trap once or twice but will learn very quickly to avoid it. In contrast, the bots will fall for it over and over again. In order to play like a human more comprehensively, the bots will need to learn and adapt. They need to adjust their play depending on the opponent. Moreover, there are challenges in playing with multiple other agents, especially in coordinating team play. And of course, such coordination will ultimately require communication, which was not addressed in Botprize at all. Some of these issues will be addressed in the remaining two sections of this chapter.

14.7 Case Study: Understanding an Evolutionary Breakthrough

As discussed earlier, neuroevolution experiments have demonstrated how competition, cooperation, environmental constraints, diversity, effective encodings, and many other ingredients can give rise to intelligent behavior. However, they are very general, and they rarely address a specific research question in biology, such as how a particular behavior in a particular species may have evolved.

Such simulations are possible as well, especially in cooperation with evolutionary biologists. One promising opportunity is to understand **evolutionary origins** of the behaviors seen in hyenas, particularly the spotted hyena *Crocuta crocuta*. A group of biologists led by Kay Holekamp has maintained a research station in Masai Mara since 1988, and have chronicled much of the hyena's behaviors as well as their biology (Smith, Lehmann, Montgomery, et al., 2017). These observations have been a motivation for several of the experiments already discussed, including those of role-based cooperation (section 7.1.3 and the evolutionary arms race (section 7.2.2), as well as others such as the trade-offs between cooperative versus individual hunting (Rajagopalan, Rawal, Miikkulainen, et al., 2011).

However, one of the behaviors of *Crocuta crocuta* is particularly interesting: hyenas can team up to steal a kill from lions (Lehmann, Montgomery, MacLachlan, et al., 2016). Lions are much bigger and stronger predators and can easily kill hyenas. The Holekamp team has observed hundreds of interactions between them; usually hyenas stay out of their way, but there are many cases where they seem to employ a sophisticated, **cooperative strategy** to drive the lions away from their kill. For example, some two to three lions may have caught a zebra and are feasting on it, when a few hyenas wander by. The hyenas do not get close but appear careful and even fearful, as they should be in the presence of such a predator threat. But they start vocalizing loudly. Other hyenas within hearing distance are attracted to these vocalizations, and soon a large number of them, like 20-30, start to gather around the lions. Their behavior changes to that of strong interactions: Their vocalizations change, they rub against each other, they make fast moves, and they generally excite each other. As the excitement builds, the hyenas get less fearful, push each other closer to the lions, and make threatening gestures toward them until (it seems) they cannot hold back their aggressive behavior any longer. In a dramatic, highly coordinated, and precisely timed move, the hyenas form a wall around the lions and attack them simultaneously. Typically they approach from three sides, leaving the lions a way out. If there are enough hyenas (typically four times the lions), and they are coordinated enough, the lions are overwhelmed and simply flee, leaving the kill to the hyenas.

How can such **mobbing behavior** have emerged in evolution? It is even more mysterious because hyenas, as effective as they are as hunters, are not that sophisticated in other ways. They live in clans and have a strict matriarchal hierarchy—perhaps because they have teeth and jaws that can crack bones, so any disputes between them could be fatal. They do have territories and vicious clan wars where those territories are sometimes disputed. They can hunt small prey individually and team up to hunt larger prey, such as zebras. They also collaborate to take care of their young. But compared to other species that live in the same environment, such as baboons, these behaviors are less advanced. In particular, whereas baboons are good at learning new behaviors and coping with new situations, hyenas are not very flexible in their ways, and they do not learn as easily (Benson-Amram and Holekamp, 2012). Stealing a kill from lions appears unusually sophisticated for them, and it is likely not a behavior that they have learned—instead, it appears to be innate; that is, an immediate product of evolution. Moreover, other hyena species that live nearby in Eastern Africa do not exhibit this mobbing behavior. Therefore, this behavior seems to be a breakthrough for the species—evolution of intelligence in action.

Computational simulations thus offer a potentially powerful way to gain insights into the mobbing behavior and its origins. Indeed, several such simulations have been built, focusing on game-theoretic as well as evolutionary computation aspects of it (Jahns and Hintze, 2018; Rajagopalan, Holekamp, and Miikkulainen, 2019). One such simulation suggested that a leading bold individual might evolve, making the **cooperative behavior** more likely to emerge (Fairey and Soule, 2014; Solomon, Soule, and Heckendorn, 2012). However, such individuals are not clearly identifiable in biology. The hyenas do indeed differ in how bold they are—some get closer sooner, and others hang back—but eventually, they act primarily as a **homogeneous team**. Their behavior is associated with strong emotions, with fear competing with affiliation and aggression. While the behaviors themselves suggest emotions, it is also possible to measure them quantitatively, albeit coarsely, by analyzing the hormones in the stool samples that they leave behind. The analysis indeed reveals elevated levels of the signature hormones for these emotions after such a lion encounter. The emotions may thus play a crucial role in allowing the team to form and to act cohesively.

Based on these observations, a neuroevolution simulation was set up to study how the mobbing behavior might emerge (Rajagopalan, Holekamp, and Miikkulainen, 2020, figure 14.8). In the simulation, 10 hyenas and one lion were placed randomly in a 100×100 toroidal grid world. The hyenas could move at each timestep, and the lion was stationary (with a kill). If a hyena came within 20 steps of the lion (i.e., inside an "interaction circle"), it was likely to get killed, but if there were 4 or more hyenas within the interaction circle at any time, the lion got mobbed. The hyenas sensed the distance and direction to the lion, whether there were at least three other hyenas within the interaction circle, and whether the lion had already been mobbed. The hyenas that participated in the mobbing event receive a full fitness; those that stepped into the circle after mobbing had already happened receive an 80% fitness, and others received no fitness at all. Thus, the ideal hyena would approach the lion until it was just outside the interaction circle, wait there until at least 3 other hyenas made it there as well, and then step inside the circle at the same time as those other hyenas. However, for this behavior to be successful, at least three other hyenas needed to be able to perform it as well, and also time it just right. Such required cooperation and timing makes mobbing very difficult to evolve.

Neuroevolution was based on **NEAT**, and as usual, it started with random small networks. Over 1,000 generations, four main behaviors were observed, which differed based on how bold they were:

1. Risk-takers ran straight to the lion regardless of other hyenas, and they were usually killed quickly; however, they were sometimes successful if other hyenas joined them at the right time.

(*a*) A crucial moment in the interaction (*b*) Simulation setup

Figure 14.8: **Complex coordinated behavior of hyenas mobbing lions.**. In this behavior, hyenas form a mob that attacks a group of lions, gaining possession of their kill. (*a*) A screen capture of a video documenting a mobbing event. Lions are much stronger than hyenas, but if the hyenas are much more numerous and coordinate their attack well, they can drive the lions away from the kill. This behavior is more complex than others that hyenas exhibit, largely hereditary, and may represent an evolutionary breakthrough. (*b*) A simulation of mobbing. A lion and several hyenas are placed in a 100×100 grid world. If four or more hyenas enter the interaction circle simultaneously, they get a high reward; if fewer than four, they get killed. Neuroevolution simulations suggest that mobbing can arise from the simpler stepping stones of attacking, waiting at a distance, and waiting at the circle. These behaviors persist even in prolonged evolution, making the mobbing behaviors more robust. Figure *b* from Rajagopalan, Holekamp, and Miikkulainen (2020). For videos of these behaviors, see `https://neuroevolutionbook.com/demos`.

2. Risk-evaders-outside-circle hung back and approached the lion only after it had been killed, receiving lower rewards with little risk, but also sometimes running out of time and not receiving any rewards.

3. Risk-evaders-at-circle approached the lion but stopped at the circle, and stepped in only after the lion had been killed, receiving low rewards reliably.

4. Mobbers behaved successfully as described previously.

At the start of the simulation, the networks were random, and their actions were random as well, which amounted to imperfect and inconsistent risk-taking and risk-evasion. Both of these behaviors quickly became more consistent. The number of risk-takers increased quickly because such a rushing behavior is easy to construct. On the other hand, risk-evading hyenas are more likely to survive, and they thus persisted in the population as well, establishing the opposite behavior (i.e., waiting). These two behaviors constituted the first two **stepping stones**.

Over a few generations, mobbing events started to happen by accident, and such events increased gradually with an increasing number of risk-takers. Risk-takers were occasionally recombined with risk-evaders, bringing them closer to the circle without crossing it. This progress led to the discovery of the circle, and thus the third stepping stone of risk-evaders-at-circle. Mobbing was happening still largely by accident, but frequently enough so eventually, it was possible for evolution to discover precise timing for it. As a result, in approximately 10 generations, 90% of the hyenas were mobbers, and they succeeded 90% of the time.

Thus, each of the stepping stones played a role in discovering mobbing behavior. Because of them, it was possible to overcome the **deceptive fitness landscape** and develop the precise coordination required. Interestingly, even in prolonged evolution over 1,000 generations, these stepping stones still existed in the population in low numbers. Evolution reached a dynamic equilibrium where some of the mobbers had risk-taker or risk-evader offspring, who again may have mobber offspring. The teams were robust enough to tolerate such diversity: so long as at least six of the 10 hyenas were mobbers, they successfully mobbed most of the time. However, the teams were even more successful with more mobbers, so why did such diversity persist?

As has been observed in prolonged evolution experiments in general, if evolution continues after solutions have been discovered, the solutions often become more robustly encoded and less likely to break in crossover and mutation (Rajagopalan, Holekamp, and Miikkulainen, 2014; Watson, Palmius, Mills, et al., 2011). However, the behavior itself may become more robust as well: In this case, the mobbers can be successful with more challenging initial states and be able to work with teammates with more varied behavior. Thus, diversity is important not only in discovering novel solutions, but also in refining the solutions so they are more effective in complex, uncertain environments; that is, in the real world. It is interesting that in such environments, evolutionary pressures exist that promote diversity automatically.

Thus, the simulation demonstrated how the mobbing behavior could have emerged, and in particular, the stepping stones that were required. A most interesting observation is that it does require individuals who are extremely bold, even to their own detriment. If some of them survive and reproduce, the offspring may discover a moderation that succeeds in a surprising way. There has, of course, been a long debate on the role of such behaviors in evolutionary biology, and many efforts to explain things like altruism (where individuals sacrifice themselves for the common good) have been developed (Kay, Keller, and Lehmann, 2020). The simulation suggests that altruism may not be necessary, but instead it is simply a variation in how bold the individuals are in trying to achieve their goals. Such a variation may be implemented through a different emotional balance, such as less fear and more affiliation and aggression.

In a broader sense, such variations in boldness may be crucial for innovation more generally. Even in humans, there are always individuals who are willing to take more risks, and it is often those individuals who drive innovation. Indeed, individuals may simply wonder what's on the other side of those mountains or what's on the other side of the ocean, and such somewhat irrational wanderlust may have allowed humans to spread over the entire globe. Even today, thousands of people have already signed up for the chance to get a one-way ticket to Mars, even though colonies or even the technology to get there do not yet exist. Such individuals are fascinated by the novelty and the unknown. Being the first one to get somewhere is a reward in itself. We still share a lot of the boldness of the first hyenas who wondered, "What happens if I just ignore the lions and run straight toward the kill?"

Further, such simulations may be a way to look into the future as well–that is, to predict how the hyenas are likely to evolve from their current state. Could this synchronized cooperative behavior serve as a foundation for developing more sophisticated communication? Or perhaps higher functions that could be useful in it as well, such as learning and memory? Other simulations suggest that discovering such functions requires overcoming deceptive fitness (Lehman and Miikkulainen, 2014)—very much like the immediate disadvantage of being too bold in the kill capture. Eventually, it may be possible to simulate **major transitions** as well, as discussed in section 9.1.5. One of them is the evolution of language, which may already be within reach of neuroevolution simulations, as will be discussed next.

14.8 Evolution of Language

The last major transition in biology is the **evolution of language** (Maynard Smith and Szathmáry, 1997; Szathmáry, 2015). It made cooperation possible more broadly and at a more sophisticated level: It allowed individuals to define roles and make them flexible, reason with hypotheticals and counterfactuals, and ultimately record knowledge and build on prior knowledge. Language is the ingredient that made it possible to construct complex societies. After a brief review of biological theory of language, neuroevolution approaches to evolving communication and structured language are reviewed in this section.

14.8.1 Biology of Language

Language can be defined as the ability to generate an unlimited number of meanings from a finite set of symbols using grammatical rules. Although many animal species communicate using signals (essentially single words), language is unique to humans; therefore, some crucial aspects of the language ability must be genetically encoded. However, all humans still need to learn the specifics of their language through interaction with the environment. Such interactions also need to take place at a precise time during development (Friedmann and Rusou, 2015). If children do not get proper linguistic input when they are one to five years old, they do not develop full language abilities. The urge to develop language at that age is so great that groups of children in a linguistically poor environment may develop their own language systems or enhance existing ones. For instance, pidgin languages, or incomplete communication systems between adults who do not share a common language, become creole languages; that is, fully formed languages of the next generation. It is also not tied to the verbal modality: Deaf children of hearing parents can develop a fully formed sign-language system (Singleton and Newport, 2004). Language learning is thus biologically programmed into humans. It can be seen as an example of both **expressive encoding** and **synergistic development** (sections 9.1.4 and 14.4): Evolution specifies a learning mechanism that constructs the final complex system.

The degree of **genetic determination** has been up for debate for decades. Chomsky and others have argued that the entire structure of language, a **universal grammar**, is genetically coded, and language learning consists of simply observing and setting the parameters of the grammar to obtain any specific language (Chomsky, 1986). On the other hand, there are now **large language models** (LLMs) that learn perfectly good language simply by observing large amounts of text (Ouyang, Wu, Jiang, et al., 2022). If the model is large enough, and there's enough data to train it, the simple task of predicting the next word results in a model that can generate grammatical and even meaningful text.

LLMs still need to see many more language examples than humans do during development. It is thus likely that genetic influences play a larger role in biasing the learning system toward the right kind of structures. What exactly these constraints are and how evolution discovered them is a fascinating question. Given the progress in the evolution of cooperation and intelligent behavior described here, it may be a question that we may be able to answer soon with neuroevolution simulations.

There are also clues from biology beyond just observations of current language abilities in humans. Earlier hominid species such as *Homo erectus* are thought to have developed protolanguage abilities. They were able to cooperate more generally (e.g., in scavenging that required competing with other species), and such cooperation may have required rudimentary language (Bickerton and Szathmáry, 2011). Several current higher species, such as dolphins and apes, communicate regularly through vocalizations and gestures. Moreover, it is possible to train them to extend these abilities to structures similar to human language, even when they do not spontaneously use them in the wild (Bindra, Patterson, Terrace, et al., 1981; Herzing and Johnson, 2015). It is therefore possible to see these species as intermediate stages in the evolution of language, potentially constraining simulations.

In terms of circuitry, **Broca's area** is composed of **Brodmann's areas** 44 and 45; syntax is processed in area 44, and area 45 is involved in action imagination and imitation. In our closest relatives, chimpanzees, area 45 similarly represents actions, but area 44 is missing (Gallardo, Eichner, Sherwood, et al., 2023). It thus appears that language evolved by expanding and lateralizing action processing into the processing of syntax, suggesting a possible foundation for neuroevolution simulations.

The next two subsections review work done so far in this area, from the early emergence of a communication code to multitasking of codes and cultural transmission. They also outline possible avenues for evolving language and uncovering the ingredients that make it possible.

14.8.2 Evolving Communication

Communication in artificial agents has been an active area of research for a long time (Wagner, Reggia, Uriagereka, et al., 2003). Several experiments, many of them using neuroevolution, demonstrate the emergence of **communication codes** for fundamental tasks such as mating, hunting, herding, and fighting. They are usually composed of symbols with simple meaning, although sometimes contextualized, rather than full language systems with grammatical structure. Nevertheless, they help us understand some of the conditions for communication and language to emerge.

One challenge is that it is difficult for the population in evolutionary simulations to converge on a common code. It is more likely to emerge within genetically related groups where selection operates at the group level (Floreano, Mitri, Magnenat, et al., 2007). It may also emerge more readily when the population is asymmetric, with clearly delineated roles. For instance, an influential early experiment focused on the simple but compelling problem of evolving a code for a **cooperative task** (Werner and Dyer, 1992). In a simulated grid world, there were males and females, both controlled through neural networks. The females were stationary but could sense the males' location and emit 3-bit signals to them; the males could move and could perceive the signals, but could not see the females. If a male entered the same location as a female, the two of them would create offspring through **genetic algorithms** (GAs). Thus, to mate, the females needed to send instructions to the males, guiding them step by step to find them. Initially, the males would wander around randomly; however, guidance on their last step would soon emerge, and gradually the symbols and their interpretation from farther away. Eventually, a common code evolved that was effective and reliable in most situations. The simulation thus demonstrated that an effective communication code emerges when it enables effective evolution, and asymmetric roles can make it easier to discover.

Since mating is a fundamental constituent in evolution, an interesting question is whether it is indeed a possible origin for communication. In particular, proper **mate selection** may guide evolution toward more effective mating and higher-quality offspring. In the simplest case, mate selection may be based on visible features and displays such as size, color, or strength. In higher animals, it is often based on communication–vocalizations or ritualized movements and gestures. Such signals can be interpreted as indicators of traits, making it possible to decide whether the potential mate is compatible. Once communication evolved to serve mate selection, it may have been exapted, or reused and adapted, for other tasks, eventually forming a basis for protolanguage (Bickerton, 1990).

Such a possibility can be investigated in neuroevolution simulations (Rawal, Boughman, and Miikkulainen, 2014). In a simulated world, individuals were controlled by **neural networks**, and each had a 2-bit trait encoding that determined compatibility with other individuals (figure 14.9). The network outputs a 2-bit message, as well as a control signal on whether to mate or not, and whether to move or not. As their input, they received a 2-bit message, the distance to a prey, and a bit indicating whether they were in a mate or a hunt situation. They were then paired up in both of these tasks. In mating, they communicated their trait to their partner and, upon receiving the trait message from their partner, decided whether to mate; if they mated when the traits were compatible, they received a high fitness. In hunting, they had to move closer to the prey at each step, and also communicate to their partner whether they were one step away from the prey; if they entered the prey location at the same time, they received a high fitness.

In a series of experiments, it turned out that if mate selection was evolved first, and hunting was then added as a second task, the agents evolved successful behavior in both tasks much faster than when the tasks were introduced in the opposite order, or both at once. In other words, the code evolved for mate selection served as a better foundation for a code needed for hunting than the other way around. The mate-selection code was simpler, and it was possible to complexify it to add hunting. Such incremental evolution was also more efficient than trying to evolve both behaviors at once. The final code used fewer symbols, and for instance, the message to indicate readiness to mate was often reused to indicate readiness for prey capture. It thus served as an effective stepping stone for evolving complex behavior. The simulations thus suggest that communication may

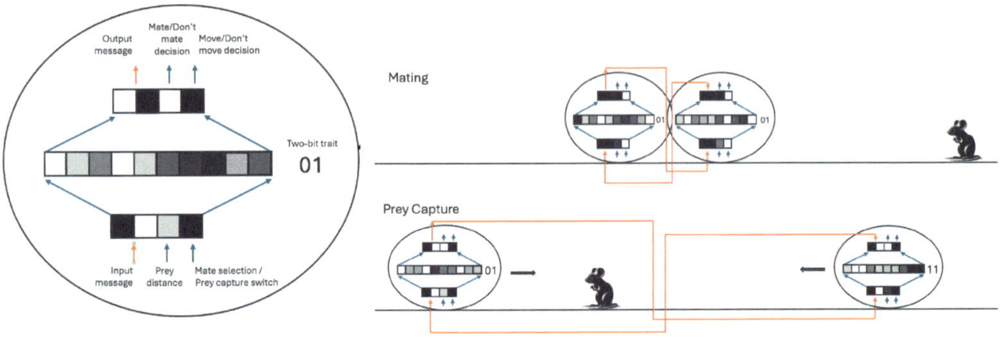

(*a*) Agent network (*b*) Mating and hunting tasks

Figure 14.9: **Evolution of communication code for mate selection and hunting.** The agents were able to move in a simulated one-dimensional world where their fitness depended on successful mating and hunting. (*a*) Each agent in the population is controlled by an evolved neural network that receives the current task (either mate selection or hunting), the distance to the prey, and the message from the other agent as its input. At its output, it decides to mate or move and generates a message that the other agents can use to decide whether to mate or whether to coordinate prey capture. (*b*) For mating to succeed, the agents need to be compatible; compatibility is determined by an inherited 2-bit trait. For prey capture to be successful, they need to step on it at the same time. Over evolution, the agents discover a messaging code that allows them to communicate their trait and current distance to the prey effectively to other agents. It turns out that if mate selection is evolved first, instead of evolving prey capture first or at the same time, the agents develop a more effective and parsimonious code for both tasks. This result suggests that communication may have originally evolved for mate selection, and later adapted to other uses.

have evolved incrementally through stepping stones, and mate selection is a plausible origin for that process.

One fundamental aspect that is missing from such simulations is that the communication codes in nature are usually not innate, but rather are learned during the early life of the individual. That is, it is the ability for learning the code that is evolved. It is possible to extend language evolution simulations to such a setting as well (Li and Miikkulainen, 2016). As in prior simulations, the agents were paired up in trials and had to cooperate to hunt or mate successfully. Each generation began with a **parenting phase**: The newly generated offspring were paired with their parents, and they learned to be successful in the necessary communication through **reinforcement learning**. Next, all agents were paired up randomly in a **socializing phase**, and their overall fitness was measured. Finally, the most successful agents became parents for the next generation. In this manner, it was possible to evolve successful behavior for both tasks through a communication code that was evolved over multiple generations and learned by each individual in each generation.

The simulation could then be used to further understand the pressures that cause communication to evolve. For the hunting and mating to succeed, both partners had to be ready for it. The agents could either sense that readiness directly or communicate it. By enabling and disabling such sensing and communication channels, it was possible to make communication necessary or optional.

It turned out that if the agents could sense readiness directly, communication did not evolve, even when communication channels were available. Evolution thus discovered the simplest and most reliable way to be successful. However, if one or both readiness senses were disabled, communication did evolve. This result makes sense: Without communication, they would succeed only randomly, and there was thus a strong pressure to take advantage of communication-based coordination. Most interestingly, if communication evolved for one of the tasks, it was also utilized in the other, even if it was not necessary for it. That is, if a communication ability is available, evolution will utilize it.

Evolution of communication and language may thus follow a similar process as many other innovations: Evolution is a tinkerer and will adapt whatever abilities exist to other uses. Communication may be one such general ability that originated from a fundamental need like for mate selection, and it was then exapted to others. Would it be possible to make the transition from signaling with single symbols to communication with linguistic structures in this way? The possibilities in this area are discussed in the next section.

14.8.3 Evolution of Structured Language

Evolution of language is difficult to study in biology because there is no fossil record and few other clues on how human ancestors communicated. Consequently, there are many theories about it, and they tend to be philosophical in nature. However, one significant tool that we have at our disposal is computational modeling. It may be possible to gain insight into the conditions under which language evolves by building simulations.

Many computational approaches have indeed been developed using different techniques (Wagner, Reggia, Uriagereka, et al., 2003). Rather than evolution, many of them focus on the emergence of language. That is, they do not aim to model multiple generations of agents, but rather how communication can emerge in small groups of agents—sometimes consisting of even just two members. They do, however, demonstrate discovery of some linguistic structure, not simply signaling between agents.

One approach is **agent-based modeling**, which may even involve physical robots (Kirby, Griffiths, and Smith, 2014; Steels, 2016). They take on the roles of a teacher and learner, and language emerges in order to perform a joint task. The signals not only combine into larger structures, but they also have a grounding; that is, a semantic system emerges. In a larger group, iterated learning may be established, where language is taught by individuals who learned it themselves earlier.

Mathematical modeling based on **game theory** has also provided interesting insights (Nowak and Krakauer, 1999). When the game focuses on establishing reliable computation, it turns out that words emerge from signaling, and grammar emerges from words, as a way to compensate for errors that are likely to arise in the communication medium.

Neural networks have also been used as an implementation for language agents in many studies (Batali, 1998; Galke, Ram, and Raviv, 2022). Most often, they use **recurrency** or **long short-term memory** (LSTM) to input and output language, and an **RL mechanism** such as **REINFORCE** to adapt. While compositional structures do emerge, they still do not match human languages well. It is possible that further cognitive constraints such as memory and alternation of speaker and listener roles are needed.

Evolutionary computing models constitute a fourth category of approaches. For instance, grammars can be evolved directly and compositionality discovered in service of a task (Zuidema and Hogeweg, 2000). It is also possible to apply evolution to neural networks that generate the language. This kind of approach fits the problem most naturally: The ability for language evolves over generations of a large number of individuals, and each individual learns the particular language during a lifetime.

While it is easy to discover communication through signaling in this manner (as was reviewed previously), it is much harder to discover **compositionality**; that is, linguistic structure. However, there has been some progress even early on. For instance, in an artificial environment with poisonous and edible mushrooms, neuroevolution discovered a signaling system that allowed the individuals to guide others to edible ones while avoiding poisonous ones (Cangelosi, 1999; Cangelosi and Parisi, 1998). Significantly, the system consisted of pairs of symbols signifying an action and an object. The offspring then learned the particular symbols through backpropagation. In this manner, a rudimentary grammatical structure evolved, and it is strikingly similar to the structures that can be taught to animals such as chimpanzees. Perhaps such a capability is the first step toward the evolution of human language?

From such a starting point, why did language evolve only in humans? It is possible that the origin of language is not in communication, but in cognition. That is, while it is possible to build such a simple action-object protolanguage by complexifying signaling, perhaps true linguistic structure was discovered as an exaptation of other cognitive functions.

One theory is that language emerged as a useful tool in society, making it possible to coordinate actions such as group hunting and group caring for the young when mothers were needed for foraging and other activities. As these activities became more sophisticated, it was necessary to understand that different individuals could take on different roles at different times, as well as how these roles might relate—in other words, flexible relational structures similar to grammatical structures. Once this structure was in place in the brain, it was exapted to enhance communication; and eventually, structured language emerged.

However, many other animals live in societies as well, and hunt in groups, and care for the young together (e.g., the hyenas discussed earlier in this chapter). There was something different about human societies that served as a stepping stone, and, again due to lack of any kind of direct evidence, there are many theories about what that might be (Bickerton, 2007; Corballis, 2011; Knight and Power, 2012). One theory is that as humans became the apex scavengers, they needed to communicate the type and location of their kills. First, this would be done iconically, but gradually with a displacement in time and space, which may have led to the abstraction that was needed for language. Another is that alliances and cliques formed in societies when members wanted to dominate other members, and their maintenance required language. Gossip has also been indicated as a potential source, replacing or adding to physical grooming. A plausible explanation is that language emerged as a result of (or together with) **symbolic culture**, for which there is some evidence in early objects and paintings (figure 14.10). As societies grew more complex, rules were established so they could function better; **symbolic representations** and displacement made them possible, forming an impetus for language.

Now the time may be right to start evaluating these hypotheses in computational neuroevolution simulations. There is enough computing power and sophistication to create virtual worlds where many of these conditions and constraints can be simulated. The neural networks would have to be much more complex and able to perform many

Figure 14.10: **A primary hypothesis is that language emerged at the same time as symbolic culture.** Then again, we don't really know. Figure by Essner (2021).

different tasks, but it is also an ability that is now emerging, as reviewed in this book. It is also possible to build up the simulations and hypotheses gradually from simple to more complex ones, and to gain insights along the way. Neuroevolution is uniquely well-suited to meeting these challenges, and it may form a crucial ingredient in developing a theory of how language evolved, which is one of the most fascinating and perplexing questions in science.

14.9 Chapter Review Questions

1. **Neural structure and evolutionary origins:** How can neuroevolution simulations help us understand the evolutionary origins of specific neural structures, such as command neurons, and their role in behaviors like navigation and foraging?

2. **Central pattern generators (CPGs):** What are CPGs, and how have neuroevolution experiments been used to model their role in controlling locomotion in animals, such as lampreys and salamanders?

3. **Modularity and wiring length:** How does the principle of minimizing wiring length contribute to the evolution of modular neural networks? Why does modularity lead to better performance and adaptability in evolving neural systems?

4. **Neuromodulation:** What role does neuromodulation play in adapting neural behavior? How does neuroevolution demonstrate its utility in tasks like the T-maze navigation?

5. **Synergistic development:** How does the concept of synergistic development explain the interplay between genetic biases and lifetime learning? How have neuroevolution experiments demonstrated this principle in tasks such as foraging or pattern recognition?

6. **Constrained evolution of behavior:** How do body and environmental constraints influence the evolution of believable and natural behaviors in simulated agents, as demonstrated in fight-or-flight behavior evolution?

7. **Human-like behavior in AI:** What role did performance constraints (e.g., limited accuracy, multitasking, and behavioral variability) play in evolving AI bots that were indistinguishable from human players in the Botprize competition?

8. **Evolutionary breakthroughs in social behavior:** How did neuroevolution simulations model the emergence of mobbing behavior in hyenas, and what stepping stones contributed to the evolution of this complex, coordinated strategy?

9. **Origins of communication:** In simulations of mate selection and hunting, how did evolving communication for one task (e.g., mating) serve as a foundation for communication in another task (e.g., hunting)?

10. **Evolution of language:** What theories exist about the origins of language, and how might neuroevolution simulations contribute to understanding the conditions and stepping stones that enabled its emergence?

Chapter 15

Epilogue

The last decade or so has seen an expansion of AI that was unexpected and unprecedented. Much of it was based on a few new neural network architectures, such as transformers, diffusion networks, and adversarial networks. But much of it was also based on old ideas that, with sufficient computation, started to work at a new scale. Despite all the progress in the past several decades, this success was hardly predictable or guaranteed. Indeed, scientific breakthroughs often emerge in unexpected areas.

Neuroevolution is closely related to these breakthrough areas, but it is also distinctly different. Indeed, it is in an interesting phase. As was the case with deep learning and generative AI, there is a long history of progress and success. Unlike in those other areas, there is also an existence proof that it can lead to tremendous success: After all, biological evolution successfully created complex and effective nervous systems. There are also indications that neuroevolution and biology are connected: Neuroevolution experiments have already replicated biological structures and biological behavior in many cases, giving computational explanations on how they may arise.

One aspect that neuroevolution still has not leveraged to its full extent is computational resources. To be sure, many experiments are run in parallel on hundreds of hosts, but that is still orders of magnitude less than the compute that made large language models (LLMs) and diffusion models work. Interestingly, unlike other creative AI methods such as reinforcement learning, neuroevolution is well-suited for such scale-up. Experiments can easily be parallelized over millions of hosts, allowing them to harness processes that so far have not been the mainstay of evolutionary computation but are fundamental in biology, such as large populations, weak selection, neutral mutations, and deep time. The scale-up, together with such untapped techniques, could lead to breakthroughs.

For such experiments to create intelligent agents, it will be necessary to create more complex and comprehensive virtual worlds than we have today. Such simulated environments play a role similar to the vast amounts of text that became available and made it possible to train LLMs with human knowledge. The simulations could be based on first principles of physics, but also include phenomenological components; that is, those that are trained with data from the real world. Such components may be necessary to simulate high-level behavior, phenomena, and societies, which do not readily arise from first principles. In particular, LLMs could be used to create a level of human-like agents for the environment, allowing neuroevolution to solve problems at the same level. Significant computation will be required, but it should become available in the near future, and we should be ready for it.

With such environments, it may be possible to use neuroevolution to create brain-like complexity. It could result in a runaway evolution not unlike that seen in actual brain evolution: Sufficient compute makes it possible to discover increasingly complex stepping stones, which then lead to a series of expansions in the capabilities of the agents. Such computational models may allow us to better understand biological evolution and the resulting complex brain structures and behaviors. It may also make it possible to construct agents with general, grounded intelligence, which can act as relatable, believable, and trustworthy assistants and companions to humans. With this approach, it may be possible to optimize AI construction, improving decision-making in society and quality of life in general.

As described in this book, the past three decades have led us to a striking distance from this goal. The next decade or so may allow us to realize it. Let's go do it!

References

Abelsson, Anna, and Anna Willman (2020). "Ethics and Aesthetics in Injection Treatments with Botox and Filler." *Journal of Women & Aging*, 1–13.

Achiam, Josh, Steven Adler, Sandhini Agarwal, et al. (2023). "GPT-4 Technical Report." *arXiv:2303.08774.*

Adami, Christoph, Jory Schossau, and Arend Hintze (2016). "Evolutionary Game Theory Using Agent-Based Methods." *Physics of Life Reviews* 19, 1–26.

Agogino, Adrian, Kenneth O. Stanley, and Risto Miikkulainen (2000). "Online Interactive Neuro-evolution." *Neural Processing Letters* 11, 29–38.

Agogino, Adrian, Kagan Tumer, and Risto Miikkulainen (2005). "Efficient Credit Assignment Through Evaluation Function Decomposition." In *GECCO'05: Proceedings of the 7th Annual Conference on Genetic and Evolutionary Computation*, 1309–1316.

Agüera y Arcas, Blaise (2025). *What Is Intelligence? Lessons from AI About Evolution, Computing, and Minds*. Cambridge, MA: MIT Press.

Agüera y Arcas, Blaise, Jyrki Alakuijala, James Evans, Ben Laurie, Alexander Mordvintsev, Eyvind Niklasson, Ettore Randazzo, and Luca Versari (2024). "Computational Life: How Well-formed, Self-replicating Programs Emerge from Simple Interaction." *arXiv:2406.19108.*

Aharonov-Barki, Ranit, Tuvik Beker, and Eytan Ruppin (2001). "Emergence of Memory-Driven Command Neurons in Evolved Artificial Agents." *Neural Computation* 13, 691–716.

Akiba, Takuya, Makoto Shing, Yujin Tang, Qi Sun, and David Ha (2025). "Evolutionary Optimization of Model Merging Recipes." *Nature Machine Intelligence* 7, 195–204.

Akopyan, Filipp, Jun Sawada, Andrew Cassidy, Rodrigo Alvarez-Icaza, John Arthur, Paul Merolla, Nabil Imam, Yutaka Nakamura, Pallab Datta, Gi-Joon Nam, Brian Taba, Michael Beakes, Bernard Brezzo, Jente B. Kuang, Rajit Manohar, William P. Risk, Bryan Jackson, and Dharmendra S. Modha (2015). "TrueNorth: Design and Tool Flow of a 65 mW 1 Million Neuron Programmable Neurosynaptic Chip." *IEEE Transactions on Computer-Aided Design of Integrated Circuits and Systems* 34, 1537–1557.

Alden, Matthew, Aard-Jan van Kesteren, and Risto Miikkulainen (2002). "Eugenic Evolution Utilizing a Domain Model." In *GECCO'02: Proceedings of the 4th Annual Conference on Genetic and Evolutionary Computation*, 279–286.

Alden, Matthew, and Risto Miikkulainen (2016). "MARLEDA: Effective Distribution Estimation Through Markov Random Fields." *Theoretical Computer Science* 633, 4–18.

Anil, Rohan, Sebastian Borgeaud, Jean-Baptiste Alayrac, et al. (2025). "Gemini: A Family of Highly Capable Multimodal Models." *arXiv:2312.11805*.

Anil, Rohan, Andrew M. Dai, Orhan Firat, et al. (2023). "PaLM 2 Technical Report." *arXiv:2305.10403*.

Anthropic (2025a). *System Card: Claude Opus 4 & Claude Sonnet 4*. https://www-cdn.anthropic.com/6be99a52cb68eb70eb9572b4cafad13df32ed995.pdf. Retrieved August 31, 2025.

Anthropic (2025b). *Introducing Claude 4*. https://www.anthropic.com/news/claude-4. Retrieved August 31, 2025.

Arjovsky, Martin, Soumith Chintala, and Léon Bottou (2017). "Wasserstein Generative Adversarial Networks." In *Proceedings of the 34th International Conference on Machine Learning*, 214–223.

Arsiwala, Shehnaz Z. (2018). "Trends for Facial Injectable Therapies in Medical Aesthetics." *Journal of Cutaneous and Aesthetic Surgery* 11, 45–46.

Assunção, Filipe, Nuno Lourenço, Bernardete Ribeiro, and Penousal Machado (2021). "Fast-DENSER: Fast Deep Evolutionary Network Structured Representation." *SoftwareX* 14, 100694.

Awad, Noor, Neeratyoy Mallik, and Frank Hutter (2020). "Differential Evolution for Neural Architecture Search." In *Proceedings of the Workshop on Neural Architecture Search, Eighth International Conference on Learning Representations*.

Bai, Jinze, Shuai Bai, Yunfei Chu, et al. (2023). "Qwen Technical Report." *arXiv:2309.16609*.

Baluja, Shumeet, and Rich A. Caruana (1995). "Removing the Genetics from the Standard Genetic Algorithm." In *Proceedings of the 12th International Conference on Machine Learning*, 38–46.

Banzhaf, Wolfgang, Peter Nordin, Robert E. Keller, and Frank D. Francone (1998). *Genetic Programming: An Introduction*. San Francisco, CA: Kaufmann.

Batali, John (1998). "Computational Simulations of the Emergence of Grammar." In *Approaches to the Evolution of Language: Social and Cognitive Bases*, edited by James R. Hurford, Michael Studdert-Kennedy and Chris Knight, 405–426. Cambridge, UK: Cambridge University Press.

Baxter, Jared A., Daniel A. Merced, Daniel J. Costinett, Leon M. Tolbert, and Burak Ozpineci (2018). "Review of Electrical Architectures and Power Requirements for Automated Vehicles." In *IEEE Transportation Electrification Conference and Expo*, 944–949.

Beane, Wendy Scott, Junji Morokuma, Joan M. Lemire, and Michael Levin (2013). "Bioelectric Signaling Regulates Head and Organ Size During Planarian Regeneration." *Development* 140, 313–322.

Beer, Randall D., Hillel J. Chiel, and John C. Gallagher (1999). "Evolution and Analysis of Model CPGs for Walking: II. General Principles and Individual Variability." *Journal of Computational Neuroscience* 7, 119–147.

Belew, Richard K. (1990). "Evolution, Learning and Culture: Computational Metaphors for Adaptive Algorithms." *Complex Systems* 4, 11–49.

Belew, Richard K., John McInerney, and Nicol N. Schraudolph (1992). "Evolving Networks: Using the Genetic Algorithm with Connectionist Learning." In *Artificial Life II*, edited by Christopher G. Langton, Charles Taylor, J. Doyne Farmer and Steen Rasmussen, 511–547. Redwood City, CA: Addison-Wesley.

Ben-Iwhiwhu, Eseoghene, Pawel Ladosz, Jeffery Dick, Wen-Hua Chen, Praveen K. Pilly, and Andrea Soltoggio (2020). "Evolving Inborn Knowledge for Fast Adaptation in Dynamic POMDP Problems." In *GECCO'20: Proceedings of the 2020 Genetic and Evolutionary Computation Conference*, 280–288.

Benson-Amram, Sarah, and Kay E. Holekamp (2012). "Innovative Problem Solving by Wild Spotted Hyenas." *Proceedings of the Royal Society of London B* 279, 4087–4095.

Bickerton, Derek (1990). *Language and Species*. Chicago, IL: The University of Chicago Press.

Bickerton, Derek (2007). "Language Evolution: A Brief Guide for Linguists." *Lingua* 117, 510–526.

Bickerton, Derek, and Eörs Szathmáry (2011). "Confrontational Scavenging as a Possible Source for Language and Cooperation." *BMC Evolutionary Biology* 11, 261.

Bindra, Dalbir, Francine G. Patterson, Herbert S. Terrace, Laura A. Petitto, Richard J. Sanders, and Thomas G. Bever (1981). "Ape Language." *Science* 211, 86–88.

Bingham, Garrett, William Macke, and Risto Miikkulainen (2020). "Evolutionary Optimization of Deep Learning Activation Functions." In *GECCO'20: Proceedings of the 2020 Genetic and Evolutionary Computation Conference*, 289–296.

Bingham, Garrett, and Risto Miikkulainen (2022). "Discovering Parametric Activation Functions." *Neural Networks* 148, 48–65.

Bingham, Garrett, and Risto Miikkulainen (2023a). "AutoInit: Analytic Signal-Preserving Weight Initialization for Neural Networks." In *Proceedings of the AAAI Conference on Artificial Intelligence, 37*, 6823–6833.

Bingham, Garrett, and Risto Miikkulainen (2023b). "Efficient Activation Function Optimization Through Surrogate Modeling." In *Advances in Neural Information Processing Systems 36*.

Bishop, Christopher M., and Hugh Bishop (2024). *Deep Learning: Foundations and Concepts*. New York, NY: Springer.

Blount, Zachary D., Christina Z. Borland, and Richard E. Lenski (2008). "Historical Contingency and the Evolution of a Key Innovation in an Experimental Population of *Escherichia Coli*." *Proceedings of the National Academy of Sciences* 105, 7899–7906.

Bongard, Josh C. (2011). "Morphological Change in Machines Accelerates the Evolution of Robust Behavior." *Proceedings of the National Academy of Sciences* 108, 1234–1239.

Bongard, Josh C. (2013). "Evolutionary Robotics." *Communications of the ACM* 56, 74–83.

Bongard, Josh C., and Rolf Pfeifer (2001). "Repeated Structure and Dissociation of Genotypic and Phenotypic Complexity in Artificial Ontogeny." In *GECCO'01: Proceedings of the 3rd Annual Conference on Genetic and Evolutionary Computation*, 829–836.

Bontrager, Philip, Wending Lin, Julian Togelius, and Sebastian Risi (2018). "Deep Interactive Evolution." In *Proceedings of the 7th International Conference on Computational Intelligence in Music, Sound, Art and Design*, 267–282.

Bontrager, Philip, Aditi Roy, Julian Togelius, Nasir Memon, and Arun Ross (2018). "DeepMasterPrints: Generating Masterprints for Dictionary Attacks via Latent Variable Evolution." In *IEEE International Conference on Biometrics Theory, Applications and Systems*, 1–9.

Brock, Andrew, Theodore Lim, James M. Ritchie, and Nick Weston (2018). "SMASH: One-Shot Model Architecture Search Through HyperNetworks." In *Proceedings of the Sixth International Conference on Learning Representations*, 2026–2047.

Brockman, Greg, Vicki Cheung, Ludwig Pettersson, Jonas Schneider, John Schulman, Jie Tang, and Wojciech Zaremba (2016). "OpenAI Gym." *arXiv:1606.01540.*

Bruce, Joseph, and Risto Miikkulainen (2001). "Evolving Populations of Expert Neural Networks." In *GECCO'01: Proceedings of the 3rd Annual Conference on Genetic and Evolutionary Computation*, 251–257.

Bryant, Bobby D., and Risto Miikkulainen (2006). "Evolving Stochastic Controller Networks for Intelligent Game Agents." In *Proceedings of the IEEE Congress on Evolutionary Computation*, 1007–1014.

Bryant, Bobby D., and Risto Miikkulainen (2007). "Acquiring Visibly Intelligent Behavior with Example-Guided Neuroevolution." In *Proceedings of the AAAI Conference on Artificial Intelligence, 22*, 801–808.

Bryant, Bobby D., and Risto Miikkulainen (2018). "A Neuroevolutionary Approach to Adaptive Multi-agent Teams." In *Foundations of Trusted Autonomy*, edited by Hussein A. Abbass, Jason Scholz and Darry J. Reid, 87–114. New York, NY: Springer.

Buccino, Alessio P., Tanguy Damart, Julian Bartram, Darshan Mandge, Xiaohan Xue, Mickael Zbili, Tobias Gänswein, Aurélien Jaquier, Vishalini Emmenegger, Henry Markram, Andreas Hierlemann, and Werner Van Geit (2024). "A Multimodal Fitting Approach to Construct Single-Neuron Models with Patch Clamp and High-Density Microelectrode Arrays." *Neural Computation* 36, 1286–1331.

Burt, D. Michael, and David I. Perrett (1995). "Perception of Age in Adult Caucasian Male Faces: Computer Graphic Manipulation of Shape and Colour Information." *Proceedings of the Royal Society of London. Series B: Biological Sciences* 259, 137–143.

Busoniu, Lucian, Robert Babuska, and Bart De Schutter (2008). "A Comprehensive Survey of Multiagent Reinforcement Learning." *IEEE Transactions on Systems, Man, and Cybernetics, Part C (Applications and Reviews)* 38, 156–172.

Buzsáki, György (2006). *Rhythms of the Brain*. Oxford, UK: Oxford University Press.

Cangelosi, Angelo (1999). "Evolution of Communication Using Symbol Combination in Populations of Neural Networks." In *Proceedings of the International Joint Conference on Neural Networks*, 4365–4368.

Cangelosi, Angelo, and Domenico Parisi (1998). "The Emergence of a 'Language' in an Evolving Population of Neural Networks." *Connection Science* 10, 83–97.

Cardamone, Luigi, Daniele Loiacono, and Pier L. Lanzi (2009). "On-line Neuroevolution Applied to the Open Racing Car Simulator." In *Proceedings of the IEEE Congress on Evolutionary Computation*, 2622–2629.

Caruana, Rich A. (1997). "Multitask Learning." *Machine Learning* 28, 41–75.

Centers for Disease Control and Prevention (2023). *COVID-19 Data Sources*. https://archive.cdc.gov/#/details?url=https://www.cdc.gov/coronavirus/2019-ncov/covid-data/covid-19-data-sources.html. Retrieved August 31, 2025.

Cha, Stephen, Taehyeon Kim, Hayeon Lee, and Se-Young Yun (2023). "A Survey of Supernet Optimization and Its Applications: Spatial and Temporal Optimization for Neural Architecture Search." *arXiv:2204.03916*.

Chankong, Vira, and Yacov Y. Haimes (2008). *Multiobjective Decision Making: Theory and Methodology*. Mineola, NY: Courier Dover Publications.

Chebykin, Alexander, Tanja Alderliesten, and Peter A. N. Bosman (2022). "Evolutionary Neural Cascade Search Across Supernetworks." In *GECCO'22: Proceedings of the Genetic and Evolutionary Computation Conference*, 1038–1047.

Chellapilla, Kumar, and David B. Fogel (1999). "Evolution, Neural Networks, Games, and Intelligence." *Proceedings of the IEEE* 87, 1471–1496.

Chemla, Sandrine, and Frédéric Chavane (2010). "Voltage-Sensitive Dye Imaging: Technique Review and Models." *Journal of Physiology-Paris* 104, 40–50.

Chen, Lili, Kevin Lu, Aravind Rajeswaran, Kimin Lee, Aditya Grover, Misha Laskin, Pieter Abbeel, Aravind Srinivas, and Igor Mordatch (2021). "Decision Transformer: Reinforcement Learning via Sequence Modeling." In *Advances in Neural Information Processing Systems 34*, 15084–15097.

Cheney, Nick, Josh C. Bongard, Vytas SunSpiral, and Hod Lipson (2018). "Scalable Co-optimization of Morphology and Control in Embodied Machines." *Journal of the Royal Society Interface* 15, 20170937.

Cheney, Nick, Robert MacCurdy, Jeff Clune, and Hod Lipson (2014). "Unshackling Evolution: Evolving Soft Robots with Multiple Materials and a Powerful Generative Encoding." *ACM SIGEVOlution* 7, 11–23.

Chevalier-Boisvert, Maxime, Dzmitry Bahdanau, Salem Lahlou, Lucas Willems, Chitwan Saharia, Thien H. Nguyen, and Yoshua Bengio (2019). "BabyAI: A Platform to Study the Sample Efficiency of Grounded Language Learning." In *Proceedings of the Seventh International Conference on Learning Representations*, 4429–4447.

Chiel, Hillel J., Randall D. Beer, and John C. Gallagher (1999). "Evolution and Analysis of Model CPGs for Walking: I. Dynamical Modules." *Journal of Computational Neuroscience* 7, 99–118.

Chomsky, Noam (1986). *Knowledge of Language: Its Nature, Origin, and Use*. Westport, CT: Greenwood Publishing Group.

Chung, Junyoung, Caglar Gulcehre, KyungHyun Cho, and Yoshua Bengio (2014). "Empirical Evaluation of Gated Recurrent Neural Networks on Sequence Modeling." In *Deep Learning Workshop, 28th Annual Conference on Neural Information Processing Systems*.

Cliff, Dave, Inman Harvey, and Philip Husbands (1993). "Explorations in Evolutionary Robotics." *Adaptive Behavior* 2, 73–110.

Clune, Jeff, Benjamin E. Beckmann, Robert T. Pennock, and Charles Ofria (2011). "HybrID: A Hybridization of Indirect and Direct Encodings for Evolutionary Computation." In *Advances in Artificial Life: Darwin Meets von Neumann, 10th European Conference,* edited by George Kampis, István Karsai and Eörs Szathmáry, 134–141. New York, NY: Springer.

Clune, Jeff, and Hod Lipson (2011). "Evolving Three-Dimensional Objects with a Generative Encoding Inspired by Developmental Biology." In *ECAL 2011: The 11th European Conference on Artificial Life*, 24.

Clune, Jeff, Jean-Baptiste Mouret, and Hod Lipson (2013). "The Evolutionary Origins of Modularity." *Proceedings of the Royal Society B: Biological Sciences* 280, 20122863.

Clune, Jeff, Kenneth O. Stanley, Robert T. Pennock, and Charles Ofria (2011). "On the Performance of Indirect Encoding Across the Continuum of Regularity." *IEEE Transactions on Evolutionary Computation* 15, 346–367.

Coello Coello, Carlos A., David A. Van Veldhuizen, and Gary B. Lamont (2007). *Evolutionary Algorithms for Solving Multi-objective Problems*. New York, NY: Springer.

Cognizant AI Lab (2023). *Pandemic Response Challenge: Technical Setup, Assessment, and Results*. https://evolution.ml/xprize/. Retrieved August 31, 2025.

Colas, Cédric, Vashisht Madhavan, Joost Huizinga, and Jeff Clune (2020). "Scaling MAP-Elites to Deep Neuroevolution." In *GECCO'20: Proceedings of the 2020 Genetic and Evolutionary Computation Conference*, 67–75.

Coleman, Kristen (2019). *Lophius Piscatorius, ADW*. https://animaldiversity.org/accounts/Lophius_piscatorius/. Retrieved August 31, 2025.

Collins, Francis S., Mark S. Guyer, and Aravinda Chakravarti (1997). "Variations on a Theme: Cataloging Human DNA Sequence Variation." *Science* 278, 1580–1581.

Combes, Dominique, Pierre Meyrand, and John Simmers (1999). "Motor Pattern Specification by Dual Descending Pathways to a Lobster Rhythm-Generating Network." *Journal of Neuroscience* 19, 2610–2619.

Confavreux, Basile, Friedemann Zenke, Everton Agnes, Timothy Lillicrap, and Tim Vogels (2020). "A Meta-learning Approach to (Re)discover Plasticity Rules That Carve a Desired Function into a Neural Network." In *Advances in Neural Information Processing Systems 33*, 16398–16408.

Corballis, Michael C. (2011). *The Recursive Mind: The Origins of Human Language, Thought, and Civilization*. Princeton, NJ: Princeton University Press.

Cully, Antoine, Jeff Clune, Danesh Tarapore, and Jean-Baptiste Mouret (2015). "Robots That Can Adapt Like Animals." *Nature* 521, 503–507.

Cussat-Blanc, Sylvain, Kyle Harrington, and Wolfgang Banzhaf (2019). "Artificial Gene Regulatory Networks—A Review." *Artificial Life* 24, 296–328.

Cybenko, George (1989). "Approximation by Superpositions of a Sigmoidal Function." *Mathematics of Control, Signals, and Systems* 2, 303–314.

D'Ambrosio, David B., Joel Lehman, Sebastian Risi, and Kenneth O. Stanley (2010). "Evolving Policy Geometry for Scalable Multiagent Learning." In *Proceedings of the 9th International Conference on Autonomous Agents and Multiagent Systems*, 731–738.

D'Ambrosio, David B., and Kenneth O. Stanley (2008). "Generative encoding for Multiagent Learning." In *GECCO'08: Proceedings of the 10th Annual Conference on Genetic and Evolutionary Computation*, 819–826.

Dai, Zihang, Hanxiao Liu, Quoc V. Le, and Mingxing Tan (2021). "CoAtNet: Marrying Convolution and Attention for All Data Sizes." In *Advances in Neural Information Processing Systems 34*, 3965–3977.

Dasgupta, Dipankar, and Douglas R. McGregor (1992). "Designing Application-Specific Neural Networks Using the Structured Genetic Algorithm." In *Proceedings of the International Workshop on Combinations of Genetic Algorithms and Neural Networks*, 87–96.

Davies, Mike, Narayan Srinivasa, Tsung-Han Lin, Gautham Chinya, Yongqiang Cao, Sri Harsha Choday, Georgios Dimou, Prasad Joshi, Nabil Imam, Shweta Jain, Yuyun Liao, Chit-Kwan Lin, Andrew Lines, Ruokun Liu, Deepak Mathaikutty, Steven McCoy, Arnab Paul, Jonathan Tse, Guruguhanathan Venkataramanan, Yi-Hsin Weng, Andreas Wild, Yoonseok Yang, and Hong Wang (2018). "Loihi: A Neuromorphic Manycore Processor with On-Chip Learning." *IEEE Micro* 38, 82–99.

de Jong, Edwin D., and Jordan B. Pollack (2004). "Ideal Evaluation from Coevolution." *Evolutionary Computation* 12, 159–192.

De Jong, Kenneth A. (1975). "Analysis of the Behavior of a Class of Genetic Adaptive Systems." PhD thesis. Ann Arbor, MI: The University of Michigan.

De Jong, Kenneth A. (2020). "Evolutionary Computation: A Unified Approach." In *GECCO'20: Proceedings of the 2020 Genetic and Evolutionary Computation Conference Companion*, 327–342.

Deb, Kalyanmoy, and Himanshu Jain (2014). "An Evolutionary Many-Objective Optimization Algorithm Using Reference-Point-Based Nondominated Sorting Approach, Part I: Solving Problems with Box Constraints." *IEEE Transactions on Evolutionary Computation* 18, 577–601.

Deb, Kalyanmoy, and Christie Myburgh (2017). "A Population-Based Fast Algorithm for a Billion-Dimensional Resource Allocation Problem with Integer Variables." *European Journal of Operational Research* 261, 460–474.

Deb, Kalyanmoy, Amrit Pratap, Sameer Agarwal, and T. Meyarivan (2002). "A Fast and Elitist Multiobjective Genetic Algorithm: NSGA-II." *IEEE Transactions on Evolutionary Computation* 6, 182–197.

Dellaert, Frank, and Randall D. Beer (1994). "Toward an Evolvable Model of Development for Autonomous Agent Synthesis." In *Artificial Life IV: Proceedings of the Fourth International Workshop on the Synthesis and Simulation of Living Systems*, edited by Rodney A. Brooks and Pattie Maes, 246–257. Cambridge, MA: MIT Press.

DiCaprio, Ralph A. (1990). "An Interneurone Mediating Motor Programme Switching in the Ventilatory System of the Crab." *Journal of Experimental Biology* 154, 517–535.

Dietterich, Thomas G. (2002). "Ensemble Learning." In *The Handbook of Brain Theory and Neural Networks*, edited by Michael A. Arbib, 110–125. Cambridge, MA: MIT Press.

Doncieux, Stéphane, Nicolas Bredeche, Jean-Baptiste Mouret, and Agoston E. Eiben (2015). "Evolutionary Robotics: What, Why, and Where To." *Frontiers in Robotics and AI* 2, Article 4, 1–18.

Dong, Xuanyi, and Yi Yang (2020). "NAS-Bench-201: Extending the Scope of Reproducible Neural Architecture Search." In *Proceedings of the Eighth International Conference on Learning Representations*, 11287–11302.

Dorigo, Marco, Vittorio Maniezzo, and Alberto Colorni (1996). "Ant System: Optimization by a Colony of Cooperating Agents." *IEEE Transactions on Systems, Man, and Cybernetics, Part B (Cybernetics)* 26, 29–41.

Dorigo, Marco, and Thomas Stützle (2010). "Ant Colony Optimization: Overview and Recent Advances." In *Handbook of Metaheuristics*, edited by Michel Gendreau and Jean-Yves Potvin, 227–263. New York, NY: Springer.

Dorigo, Marco, Guy Theraulaz, and Vittorio Trianni (2021). "Swarm Robotics: Past, Present, and Future." *Proceedings of the IEEE* 109, 1152–1165.

Doursat, René, Hiroki Sayama, and Olivier Michel (2013). "A Review of Morphogenetic Engineering." *Natural Computing* 12, 517–535.

Druckmann, Shaul, Yoav Banitt, Albert Gidon, Felix Schürmann, Henry Markram, and Idan Segev (2007). "A Novel Multiple Objective Optimization Framework for Constraining Conductance-Based Neuron Models by Experimental Data." *Frontiers of Neuroscience* 1, 7–18.

Earle, Sam, Justin Snider, Matthew C. Fontaine, Stefanos Nikolaidis, and Julian Togelius (2022). "Illuminating Diverse Neural Cellular Automata for Level Generation." In *GECCO'22: Proceedings of the Genetic and Evolutionary Computation Conference*, 68–76.

Edwards, Donald H., William J. Heitler, and Franklin B. Krasne (1999). "Fifty Years of a Command Neuron: The Neurobiology of Escape Behavior in the Crayfish." *Trends in Neuroscience* 22, 153–161.

Eiben, Agoston E., and Selmar K. Smit (2011). "Parameter Tuning for Configuring and Analyzing Evolutionary Algorithms." *Swarm and Evolutionary Computation* 1, 19–31.

Eiben, Agoston E., and James E. Smith (2015). *Introduction to Evolutionary Computing*. New York, NY: Springer.

Ellefsen, Kai Olav, Jean-Baptiste Mouret, and Jeff Clune (2015). "Neural Modularity Helps Organisms Evolve to Learn New Skills Without Forgetting Old Skills." *PLoS Computational Biology* 11, e1004128.

Elman, Jeffrey L., Elizabeth A. Bates, Mark H. Johnson, Annette Karmiloff-Smith, Domenico Parisi, and Kim Plunkett (1996). *Rethinking Innateness: A Connectionist Perspective on Development*. Cambridge, MA: MIT Press.

ElSaid, AbdElRahman, Karl Ricanek, Zimeng Lyu, Alexander Ororbia, and Travis Desell (2023). "Backpropagation-Free 4D Continuous Ant-Based Neural Topology Search." *Applied Soft Computing* 147, 110737.

Elsken, Thomas, Jan H. Metzen, and Frank Hutter (2019). "Neural Architecture Search: A Survey." *Journal of Machine Learning Research* 20, 1–21.

Essner, Timo (2021). *Emojis*. https://cartoonmovement.com/cartoon/emojis-0. Retrieved August 31, 2025.

Fairey, Jason, and Terence Soule (2014). "Evolution of Communication and Cooperation." In *GECCO'14: Proceedings of the 2014 Annual Conference on Genetic and Evolutionary Computation*, 169–176.

Faldor, Maxence, Jenny Zhang, Antoine Cully, and Jeff Clune (2025). "OMNI-EPIC: Open-Endedness via Models of Human Notions of Interestingness with Environments Programmed in Code." In *Proceedings of the Thirteenth International Conference on Learning Representations*, 97357–97482.

Fan, James, Raymond Lau, and Risto Miikkulainen (2003). "Utilizing Domain Knowledge in Neuroevolution." In *Proceedings of the 20th International Conference on Machine Learning*, 170–177.

Fernando, Chrisantha, Dylan Banarse, Charles Blundell, Yori Zwols, David Ha, Andrei A. Rusu, Alexander Pritzel, and Daan Wierstra (2017). "PathNet: Evolution Channels Gradient Descent in Super Neural Networks." *arXiv:1701.08734*.

Fernando, Chrisantha, Dylan Banarse, Henryk Michalewski, Simon Osindero, and Tim Rocktäschel (2024). "Promptbreeder: Self-referential Self-improvement via Prompt Evolution." In *Proceedings of the 41st International Conference on Machine Learning*, 13481–13544.

Fernando, Chrisantha, Dylan Banarse, Malcolm Reynolds, Frederic Besse, David Pfau, Max Jaderberg, Marc Lanctot, and Daan Wierstra (2016). "Convolution by Evolution: Differentiable Pattern Producing Networks." In *GECCO'16: Proceedings of the Genetic and Evolutionary Computation Conference 2016*, 109–116.

Fernando, Chrisantha, Jakub Sygnowski, Simon Osindero, Jane X. Wang, Tom Schaul, Denis Teplyashin, Pablo Sprechmann, Alexander Pritzel, and Andrei A. Rusu (2018). "Meta-learning by the Baldwin Effect." In *GECCO'18: Proceedings of the Genetic and Evolutionary Computation Conference Companion*, 1313–1320.

Ficici, Sevan G., and Jordan B. Pollack (2001). "Pareto Optimality in Coevolutionary Learning." In *Advances in Artificial Life: 6th European Conference*, edited by Jozef Kelemen and Petr Sosík, 316–325. New York, NY: Springer.

Figueira Pujol, Joao Carlos, and Riccardo Poli (1998). "Evolving the Topology and the Weights of Neural Networks Using a Dual Representation." *Applied Intelligence* 8, 73–84.

Finn, Chelsea, Pieter Abbeel, and Sergey Levine (2017). "Model-Agnostic Meta-learning for Fast Adaptation of Deep Networks." In *Proceedings of the 34th International Conference on Machine Learning*, 1126–1135.

Floreano, Dario, Peter Dürr, and Claudio Mattiussi (2008). "Neuroevolution: From Architectures to Learning." *Evolutionary Intelligence* 1, 47–62.

Floreano, Dario, Sara Mitri, Stéphane Magnenat, and Laurent Keller (2007). "Evolutionary Conditions for the Emergence of Communication in Robots." *Current Biology* 17, 514–519.

Floreano, Dario, and Francesco Mondada (1996a). "Evolution of Homing Navigation in a Real Mobile Robot." *IEEE Transactions on Systems, Man, and Cybernetics* 26, 396–407.

Floreano, Dario, and Francesco Mondada (1996b). "Evolution of Plastic Neurocontrollers for Situated Agents." In *From Animals to Animats 4: Proceedings of the International Conference on Simulation of Adaptive Behavior*, 402–410.

Floreano, Dario, and Joseba Urzelai (1999). "Evolution of Neural Controllers with Adaptive Synapses and Compact Genetic Encoding." In *Advances in Artificial Life: 5th*

European Conference, edited by Dario Floreano, Jean-Daniel Nicoud and Francesco Mondada, 183–194. New York, NY: Springer.

Floreano, Dario, and Joseba Urzelai (2000). "Evolutionary Robots with On-line Self-Organization and Behavioral Fitness." *Neural Networks* 13, 431–4434.

Floreano, Dario, and Joseba Urzelai (2001). "Evolution of Plastic Control Networks." *Autonomous Robots* 11, 311–317.

Floridi, Luciano, and Massimo Chiriatti (2020). "GPT-3: Its Nature, Scope, Limits, and Consequences." *Minds and Machines* 30, 681–694.

Fogel, David B. (1992). "Evolving Artificial Intelligence." PhD thesis. San Diego, CA: University of California, San Diego.

Fogel, David B. (2001). *Blondie24: Playing at the Edge of AI.* San Francisco, CA: Kaufmann.

Fogel, David B. (2006). *Evolutionary Computation: Toward a New Philosophy of Machine Intelligence*. 3rd ed. Piscataway, NJ: IEEE Press.

Fogel, David B., Lawrence J. Fogel, and Vincent W. Porto (1990). "Evolving Neural Networks." *Biological Cybernetics* 63, 487–493.

Fogel, David B., Timothy J. Hays, Sarah L. Hahn, and James Quon (2004). "A Self-Learning Evolutionary Chess Program." *Proceedings of the IEEE* 92, 1947–1954.

Fogel, Lawrence J., Alvin J. Owens, and Michael J. Walsh (1966). *Artificial Intelligence Through Simulated Evolution*. New York, NY: Wiley.

Fontaine, Matthew C., and Stefanos Nikolaidis (2021). "Differentiable Quality Diversity." In *Advances in Neural Information Processing Systems 34*, 10040–10052.

Fontaine, Matthew C., and Stefanos Nikolaidis (2023). "Covariance Matrix Adaptation MAP-Annealing." In *GECCO'23: Proceedings of the Genetic and Evolutionary Computation Conference*, 456–465.

Fontaine, Matthew C., Julian Togelius, Stefanos Nikolaidis, and Amy K. Hoover (2020). "Covariance Matrix Adaptation for the Rapid Illumination of Behavior Space." In *GECCO'20: Proceedings of the 2020 Genetic and Evolutionary Computation Conference*, 94–102.

Fox, Spencer J., Michael Lachmann, Mauricio Tec, Remy Pasco, Spencer Woody, Zhanwei Du, Xutong Wang, Tanvi A. Ingle, Emily Javan, Maytal Dahan, Kelly Gaither, Mark E. Escott, Stephen I. Adler, S. Claiborne Johnston, James G. Scott, and Lauren A. Meyers (2022). "Real-Time Pandemic Surveillance Using Hospital Admissions and Mobility Data." *Proceedings of the National Academy of Sciences* 119, e2111870119.

Francon, Olivier (2025). *Project Resilience Platform*. https://github.com/Project-Resilience/platform. Retrieved August 31, 2025.

Francon, Olivier, Santiago Gonzalez, Babak Hodjat, Elliot Meyerson, Risto Miikkulainen, Xin Qiu, and Hormoz Shahrzad (2020). "Effective Reinforcement Learning Through Evolutionary Surrogate-Assisted Prescription." In *GECCO'20: Proceedings of the 2020 Genetic and Evolutionary Computation Conference*, 814–822.

Frankle, Jonathan, and Michael Carbin (2019). "The Lottery Ticket Hypothesis: Finding Sparse, Trainable Neural Networks." In *Proceedings of the Seventh International Conference on Learning Representations*, 8954–8995.

Friedlingstein, Pierre, Michael O'Sullivan, Matthew W. Jones, et al. (2023). "Global Carbon Budget 2023." *Earth System Science Data* 15, 5301–5369.

Friedmann, Naama, and Dana Rusou (2015). "Critical Period for First Language: The Crucial Role of Language Input During the First Year of Life." *Current Opinion in Neurobiology* 35, 27–34.

Fukushima, Kunihiko (1980). "Neocognitron: A Self-organizing Neural Network Model for a Mechanism of Pattern Recognition Unaffected by Shift in Position." *Biological Cybernetics* 36, 193–202.

Fullmer, Brad, and Risto Miikkulainen (1992). "Using Marker-Based Genetic Encoding of Neural Networks to Evolve Finite-State Behaviour." In *Toward a Practice of Autonomous Systems: Proceedings of the First European Conference on Artificial Life*, edited by Francisco J. Varela and Paul Bourgine, 255–262. Cambridge, MA: MIT Press.

Gad, Ahmed G. (2022). "Particle Swarm Optimization Algorithm and Its Applications: A Systematic Review." *Archives of Computational Methods in Engineering* 29, 2531–2561.

Gaier, Adam, and David Ha (2019). "Weight Agnostic Neural Networks." In *Advances in Neural Information Processing Systems 32*, 5365–5379.

Galke, Lukas, Yoav Ram, and Limor Raviv (2022). "Emergent Communication for Understanding Human Language Evolution: What's Missing?" In *Workshop on Emergent Communication: New Frontiers, Tenth International Conference on Learning Representations*.

Gallardo, Guillermo, Cornelius Eichner, Chet C. Sherwood, William D. Hopkins, Alfred Anwander, and Angela D. Friederici (2023). "Morphological Evolution of Language-Relevant Brain Areas." *PLoS Biology* 21, e3002266.

Ganon, Zohar, Alon Keinan, and Eytan Ruppin (2003). "Evolutionary Network Minimization: Adaptive Implicit Pruning of Successful Agents." In *Advances in Artificial Life: 7th European Conference*, edited by Wolfgang Banzhaf, Jens Ziegler, Thomas Christaller, Peter Dittrich and Jan T. Kim, 319–327. New York, NY: Springer.

Gao, Boyan, Henry Gouk, and Timothy M. Hospedales (2021). "Searching for Robustness: Loss Learning for Noisy Classification Tasks." *2021 IEEE/CVF International Conference on Computer Vision*, 6650–6659.

García-Pedrajas, Nicolás E., César Hervás-Martínez, and Domingo Ortíz-Boyer (2005). "Cooperative Coevolution of Artificial Neural Network Ensembles for Pattern Classification." *IEEE Transactions on Evolutionary Computation* 9, 271–302.

Gauci, Jason, and Kenneth O. Stanley (2010). "Autonomous Evolution of Topographic Regularities in Artificial Neural Networks." *Neural Computation* 22, 1860–1898.

Gemini Team (2025). *Gemini 2.5: Pushing the Frontier with Advanced Reasoning, Multimodality, Long Context, and Next-Generation Agentic Capabilities*. Technical Report, Google DeepMind.

Ghawaly, James, Aaron Young, Dan Archer, Nick Prins, Brett Witherspoon, and Catherine Schuman (2022). "A Neuromorphic Algorithm for Radiation Anomaly Detection." In *Proceedings of International Conference on Neuromorphic Systems*. Article 22.

Ghawaly, James, Aaron Young, Andrew Nicholson, Brett Witherspoon, Nick Prins, Mathew Swinney, Cihangir Celik, Catherine Schuman, and Karan Patel (2023). "Performance Optimization Study of the Neuromorphic Radiation Anomaly Detector." In *Proceedings of International Conference on Neuromorphic Systems*. Article 13.

Giacomello, Edoardo, Pier L. Lanzi, and Daniele Loiacono (2019). "Searching the Latent Space of a Generative Adversarial Network to Generate DOOM Levels." In *Proceedings of the IEEE Conference on Games*, 1–8.

Giles, C. Lee, Clifford B. Miller, Dong Chen, Guo-Zheng Sun, Hsing-Hen Chen, and Yee-Chun Lee (1991). "Extracting and Learning an Unknown Grammar with Recurrent Neural Networks." In *Advances in Neural Information Processing Systems 4*, 317–324.

Gilpin, William (2019). "Cellular Automata as Convolutional Neural Networks." *Physical Review E* 100, 032402.

Global Partnership on Artificial Intelligence (GPAI) (2024). *Pandemic Resilience: Case Studies of an AI-Calibrated Ensemble of Models to Inform Decision Making*. Technical Report,

Glorot, Xavier, and Yoshua Bengio (2010). "Understanding the Difficulty of Training Deep Feedforward Neural Networks." In *Proceedings of the Thirteenth International Conference on Artificial Intelligence and Statistics*, 249–256.

Goldberg, David E., and Jon Richardson (1987). "Genetic Algorithms with Sharing for Multimodal Function Optimization." In *Proceedings of the Second International Conference on Genetic Algorithms and Their Application*, 414–425.

Gomes, Jorge, Paulo Urbano, and Anders L. Christensen (2013). "Evolution of Swarm Robotics Systems with Novelty Search." *Swarm Intelligence* 7, 115–144.

Gomez, Faustino (2003). "Robust Non-linear Control Through Neuroevolution." PhD thesis. Austin, TX: Department of Computer Sciences, The University of Texas at Austin.

Gomez, Faustino, and Risto Miikkulainen (1997). "Incremental Evolution of Complex General Behavior." *Adaptive Behavior* 5, 317–342.

Gomez, Faustino, and Risto Miikkulainen (2003). "Active Guidance for a Finless Rocket Using Neuroevolution." In *Genetic and Evolutionary Computation—GECCO 2003*, 2084–2095.

Gomez, Faustino, and Risto Miikkulainen (2004). "Transfer of Neuroevolved Controllers in Unstable Domains." In *Genetic and Evolutionary Computation Conference—GECCO 2004*, 957–968.

Gomez, Faustino, Jürgen Schmidhuber, and Risto Miikkulainen (2008). "Accelerated Neural Evolution Through Cooperatively Coevolved Synapses." *Journal of Machine Learning Research* 9, 937–965.

Gonzalez, Santiago, Mohak Kant, and Risto Miikkulainen (2023). "Evolving GAN Formulations for Higher Quality Image Synthesis." In *Artificial Intelligence in the Age of Neural Networks and Brain Computing,* 2nd ed., edited by Robert Kozma, Cesare Alippi, Yoonsuck Choe and Francesco C. Morabito, 289–305. Amsterdam, the Netherlands: Elsevier.

Gonzalez, Santiago, Joshua Landgraf, and Risto Miikkulainen (2019). "Faster Training by Selecting Samples Using Embeddings." In *Proceedings of the International Joint Conference on Neural Networks*, 4982–4988.

Gonzalez, Santiago, and Risto Miikkulainen (2020). "Improved Training Speed, Accuracy, and Data Utilization Through Loss Function Optimization." In *Proceedings of the IEEE Congress on Evolutionary Computation*, 289–296.

Gonzalez, Santiago, and Risto Miikkulainen (2021). "Optimizing Loss Functions Through Multivariate Taylor Polynomial Parameterization." In *GECCO'21: Proceedings of the Genetic and Evolutionary Computation Conference*, 305–313.

Gonzalez, Santiago, Xin Qiu, and Risto Miikkulainen (2025). "Effective Regularization Through Evolutionary Loss-Function Metalearning." In *Proceedings of the IEEE Congress on Evolutionary Computation*, 1–9.

Goodfellow, Ian, Jean Pouget-Abadie, Mehdi Mirza, Bing Xu, David Warde-Farley, Sherjil Ozair, Aaron Courville, and Yoshua Bengio (2014). "Generative Adversarial Nets." In *Advances in Neural Information Processing Systems 27*, 2672–2680.

Goodfellow, Ian, Jean Pouget-Abadie, Mehdi Mirza, Bing Xu, David Warde-Farley, Sherjil Ozair, Aaron Courville, and Yoshua Bengio (2020). "Generative Adversarial Networks." *Communications of the ACM* 63, 139–144.

Goodman, Erik (2025). *Annual Humies Awards For Human-Competitive Results*. https://human-competitive.org. Retrieved August 31, 2025.

Grattafiori, Aaron, Abhimanyu Dubey, Abhinav Jauhri, et al. (2024). "The Llama 3 Herd of Models." *arXiv:2407.21783*.

Grattarola, Daniele, Lorenzo Livi, and Cesare Alippi (2021). "Learning Graph Cellular Automata." *Advances in Neural Information Processing Systems 34*, 20983–20994.

Graves, Alex, Greg Wayne, and Ivo Danihelka (2014). "Neural Turing Machines." *arXiv:1410.5401*.

Grefenstette, John J. (1986). "Optimization of Control Parameters for Genetic Algorithms." *IEEE Transactions on Systems, Man, and Cybernetics* 16, 122–128.

Greff, Klaus, Rupesh K. Srivastava, Jan Koutník, Bas R. Steunebrink, and Jürgen Schmidhuber (2016). "LSTM: A Search Space Odyssey." *IEEE Transactions on Neural Networks and Learning Systems* 28, 2222–2232.

Greve, Rasmus B., Emil J. Jacobsen, and Sebastian Risi (2016). "Evolving Neural Turing Machines for Reward-Based Learning." In *GECCO'16: Proceedings of the Genetic and Evolutionary Computation Conference 2016*, 117–124.

Grillotti, Luca, and Antoine Cully (2022). "Unsupervised Behavior Discovery with Quality-Diversity Optimization." *IEEE Transactions on Evolutionary Computation* 26, 1539–1552.

Gruau, Frederic (1994). "Automatic Definition of Modular Neural Networks." *Adaptive Behavior* 3, 151–183.

Gruau, Frederic, and Darrell Whitley (1993). "Adding Learning to the Cellular Development of Neural Networks: Evolution and the Baldwin Effect." *Evolutionary Computation* 1, 213–233.

Gruau, Frederic, Darrell Whitley, and Larry Pyeatt (1996). "A Comparison Between Cellular Encoding and Direct Encoding for Genetic Neural Networks." In *Genetic*

Programming 1996: Proceedings of the First Annual Conference, edited by John R. Koza, David E. Goldberg, David B. Fogel and Rick L. Riolo, 81–89. Cambridge, MA: MIT Press.

Guo, Daya, Dejian Yang, Haowei Zhang, et al. (2025). "DeepSeek-R1: Incentivizing Reasoning Capability in LLMs via Reinforcement Learning." *arXiv:2501.12948.*

Guo, Qingyan, Rui Wang, Junliang Guo, Bei Li, Kaitao Song, Xu Tan, Guoqing Liu, Jiang Bian, and Yujiu Yang (2024). "Connecting Large Language Models with Evolutionary Algorithms Yields Powerful Prompt Optimizers." In *Proceedings of the Twelfth International Conference on Learning Representations*, 29890–29913.

Gupta, Agrim, Silvio Savarese, Surya Ganguli, and Fei-Fei Li (2021). "Embodied Intelligence via Learning and Evolution." *Nature Communications* 12, 5721.

Ha, David (2019). "Reinforcement Learning for Improving Agent Design." *Artificial Life* 25, 352–365.

Ha, David, Andrew Dai, and Quoc V. Le (2017). "HyperNetworks." In *Proceedings of the Fifth International Conference on Learning Representations*, 103–120.

Ha, David, and Jürgen Schmidhuber (2018a). "Recurrent World Models Facilitate Policy Evolution." In *Advances in Neural Information Processing Systems 31*, 2451–2463.

Ha, David, and Jürgen Schmidhuber (2018b). "World Models." *arXiv:1803.10122.*

Hadi, Muhammad U., Qasem Al-Tashi, Rizwan Qureshi, Abbas Shah, Amgad Muneer, Muhammad Irfan, Anas Zafar, Muhammad B. Shaikh, Naveed Akhtar, Syed Z. Hassan, Maged Shoman, Jia Wu, Seyedali Mirjalili, and Mubarak Shah (2025). "Large Language Models: A Comprehensive Survey of its Applications, Challenges, Limitations, and Future Prospects." *TechRxiv,* February 10.

Hadjiivanov, Alexander, and Alan Blair (2019). "Epigenetic Evolution of Deep Convolutional Models." In *Proceedings of the IEEE Congress on Evolutionary Computation*, 1478–1486.

Hafner, Danijar (2022). "Benchmarking the Spectrum of Agent Capabilities." In *Proceedings of the Tenth International Conference on Learning Representations*, 24538–24558.

Hale, Thomas, Sam Webster, Anna Petherick, Toby Phillips, and Beatriz Kira (2020). *Oxford COVID-19 Government Response Tracker.* https://www.bsg.ox.ac.uk/research/covid-19-government-response-tracker. Retrieved August 31, 2025.

Hansen, Nikolaus (2016). "The CMA Evolution Strategy: A Tutorial." *arXiv:1604.00772.*

Hansen, Nikolaus, Anne Auger, Steffen Finck, and Raymond Ros (2010). *Real-Parameter Black-Box Optimization Benchmarking 2010: Experimental Setup.* Technical Report, Institut national de recherche en sciences et technologies du numérique (INRIA).

Hansen, Nikolaus, and Andreas Ostermeier (1996). "Adapting Arbitrary Normal Mutation Distributions in Evolution Strategies: The Covariance Matrix Adaptation." In *Proceedings of IEEE International Conference on Evolutionary Computation*, 312–317.

Hansen, Nikolaus, and Andreas Ostermeier (2001). "Completely Derandomized Self-adaptation in Evolution Strategies." *Evolutionary Computation* 9, 159–195.

Hansis, Eberhard, Steven J. Davis, and Julia Pongratz (2015). "Relevance of Methodological Choices for Accounting of Land Use Change Carbon Fluxes." *Global Biogeochemical Cycles* 29, 1230–1246.

Hanson, Stephen J., and Lorien Y. Pratt (1988). "Comparing Biases for Minimal Network Construction with Back-propagation." In *NIPS'87: Proceedings of the 1st International Conference on Neural Information Processing Systems*, 177–185.

Hardison, Ross C. (2003). "Comparative Genomics." *PLoS Biology* 1, e58.

Harp, Steven A., Tariq Samad, and Aloke Guha (1989). "Towards the Genetic Synthesis of Neural Networks." In *Proceedings of the Third International Conference on Genetic Algorithms*, 391–396.

Hastings, Erin J., Ratan K. Guha, and Kenneth O. Stanley (2009). "Automatic Content Generation in the Galactic Arms Race Video Game." *IEEE Transactions on Computational Intelligence and AI in Games* 1, 245–263.

Hausknecht, Matthew, Joel Lehman, Risto Miikkulainen, and Peter Stone (2014). "A Neuroevolution Approach to General Atari Game Playing." *IEEE Transactions on Computational Intelligence and AI in Games* 6, 355–366.

Hawkins, Jeff, and Subutai Ahmad (2016). "Why Neurons Have Thousands of Synapses, a Theory of Sequence Memory in Neocortex." *Frontiers in Neural Circuits* 10, Article 23, 1–13.

Hawkins, Jeff, and Sandra Blakeslee (2004). *On Intelligence*. New York, NY: Times Books.

He, Kaiming, Xiangyu Zhang, Shaoqing Ren, and Jian Sun (2016). "Deep Residual Learning for Image Recognition." In *Proceedings of the IEEE Conference on Computer Vision and Pattern Recognition*, 770–778.

He, Xin, Kaiyong Zhao, and Xiaowen Chu (2021). "AutoML: A Survey of the State-of-the-Art." *Knowledge-Based Systems* 212, 106622.

Hemberg, Erik, Jamal Toutouh, Abdullah Al-Dujaili, Tom Schmiedlechner, and Una-May O'Reilly (2021). "Spatial Coevolution for Generative Adversarial Network Training." *ACM Transactions on Evolutionary Learning and Optimization* 1, 1–28.

Herzing, Denise L., and Christine M. Johnson (2015). *Dolphin Communication and Cognition: Past, Present, and Future*. Cambridge, MA: MIT Press.

Hingston, Phil, ed. (2012). *Believable Bots*. New York, NY: Springer.

Hinton, Geoffrey E., James L. McClelland, and David E. Rumelhart (1986). "Distributed Representations." In *Parallel Distributed Processing: Explorations in the Microstructure of Cognition, Vol. 1: Foundations*, edited by David E. Rumelhart, James L. McClelland and PDP Research Group, 77–109. Cambridge, MA: MIT Press.

Hinton, Geoffrey E., and Steven J. Nowlan (1987). "How Learning Can Guide Evolution." *Complex Systems* 1, 495–502.

Hinton, Geoffrey E., and Ruslan R. Salakhutdinov (2006). "Reducing the Dimensionality of Data with Neural Networks." *Science* 313, 504–507.

Hintze, Arend, Jeffrey A. Edlund, Randal S. Olson, David B. Knoester, Jory Schossau, Larissa Albantakis, Ali Tehrani-Saleh, Peter Kvam, Leigh Sheneman, Heather Goldsby, Clifford Bohm, and Christoph Adami (2017). "Markov Brains: A Technical Introduction." *arXiv:1709.05601*.

Ho, Jonathan, Ajay Jain, and Pieter Abbeel (2020). "Denoising Diffusion Probabilistic Models." In *Advances in Neural Information Processing Systems 33*, 6840–6851.

Hochreiter, Sepp, and Jürgen Schmidhuber (1997). "Long Short-Term Memory." *Neural Computation* 9, 1735–1780.

Holland, John H., and J. S. Reitman (1978). "Cognitive Systems Based on Adaptive Algorithms." In *Pattern-Directed Inference Systems*, edited by D. A. Waterman and Frederick Hayes-Roth, 313–329. San Diego, CA: Academic Press.

Hoover, Amy K., Michael P. Rosario, and Kenneth O. Stanley (2008). "Scaffolding for Interactively Evolving Novel Drum Tracks for Existing Songs." In *Applications of Evolutionary Computing*, edited by Mario Giacobini, Anthony Brabazon, Stefano Cagnoni, et al., 412–422. New York, NY: Springer.

Hoover, Amy K., Paul A. Szerlip, and Kenneth O. Stanley (2014). "Functional Scaffolding for Composing Additional Musical Voices." *Computer Music Journal* 38, 80–99.

Horibe, Kazuya, Kathryn Walker, Rasmus Berg Palm, Shyam Sudhakaran, and Sebastian Risi (2022). "Severe Damage Recovery in Evolving Soft Robots Through Differentiable Programming." *Genetic Programming and Evolvable Machines* 23, 405–426.

Horibe, Kazuya, Kathryn Walker, and Sebastian Risi (2021). "Regenerating Soft Robots Through Neural Cellular Automata." In *Genetic Programming: 24th European Conference*, edited by Ting Hu, Nuno Lourenço and Eric Medvet, 36–50. New York, NY: Springer.

Hornby, Gregory S., and Jordan B. Pollack (2001a). "The Advantages of Generative Grammatical Encodings for Physical Design." In *Proceedings of the IEEE Congress on Evolutionary Computation*, 600–607.

Hornby, Gregory S., and Jordan B. Pollack (2001b). "Body-Brain Co-evolution Using L-Systems as a Generative Encoding." In *GECCO'01 Proceedings of the 3rd Annual Conference on Genetic and Evolutionary Computation*, 868–875.

Hornby, Gregory S., and Jordan B. Pollack (2002). "Creating High-Level Components with a Generative Representation for Body-Brain Evolution." *Artificial Life* 8, 223–246.

Hornik, Kurt, Maxwell Stinchcombe, and Halbert White (1989). "Multilayer Feedforward Networks Are Universal Approximators." *Neural Networks* 2, 359–366.

Horvát, Szabolcs, Răzvan Gămănuț, Mária Ercsey-Ravasz, Loïc Magrou, Bianca Gămănuț, David C. Van Essen, Andreas Burkhalter, Kenneth Knoblauch, Zoltán Toroczkai, and Henry Kennedy (2016). "Spatial Embedding and Wiring Cost Constrain the Functional Layout of the Cortical Network of Rodents and Primates." *PLOS Biology* 14, e1002512.

Hougen, Dean F., and Syed N. H. Shah (2019). "The Evolution of Reinforcement Learning." In *2019 IEEE Symposium Series on Computational Intelligence*, 1457–1464.

Huang, Gao, Zhuang Liu, Laurens van der Maaten, and Kilian Q. Weinberger (2017). "Densely Connected Convolutional Networks." In *Proceedings of the IEEE Conference on Computer Vision and Pattern Recognition*, 4700–4708.

Huang, Jia-Bin (2021). *Types of Computer Vision Paper*. https://x.com/jbhuang0604/status/1388577506253475849. Retrieved August 31, 2025.

Huang, Pei-Chi, Luis Sentis, Joel Lehman, Chien-Liang Fok, Aloysius K. Mok, and Risto Miikkulainen (2019). "Tradeoffs in Neuroevolutionary Learning-Based Real-Time

Robotic Task Design in the Imprecise Computation Framework." *ACM Transactions on Cyber-Physical Systems* 3, 14:1–14:29.

Hubel, David H., and Torsten N. Wiesel (1968). "Receptive Fields and Functional Architecture of Monkey Striate Cortex." *The Journal of Physiology* 195, 215–243.

Huizinga, Joost, Kenneth O. Stanley, and Jeff Clune (2018). "The Emergence of Canalization and Evolvability in an Open-Ended, Interactive Evolutionary System." *Artificial Life* 24, 157–181.

Hurtt, George C., Louise Chini, Ritvik Sahajpal, et al. (2020). "Harmonization of Global Land-Use Change and Management for the Period 850-2100 (LUH2) for CMIP6." *Geoscientific Model Development* 13, 5425–5464.

Husbands, Philip, and Frank Mill (1991). "Simulated Co-evolution as the Mechanism for Emergent Planning and Scheduling." In *Proceedings of the Fourth International Conference on Genetic Algorithms*, 264–270.

Iacca, Giuseppe, Fabio Caraffini, and Ferrante Neri (2020). "Differential Evolution for Neural Networks Optimization." *Mathematics* 8, 69.

Iba, Hitoshi and Nasimul Noman, eds. (2016). *Evolutionary Computation in Gene Regulatory Network Research*. New York, NY: Wiley.

Ijspeert, Auke J. (2008). "Central Pattern Generators for Locomotion Control in Animals and Robots: A Review." *Neural Networks* 21, 642–653.

Ijspeert, Auke J., Alessandro Crespi, Dimitri Ryczko, and Jean-Marie Cabelguen (2007). "From Swimming to Walking with a Salamander Robot Driven by a Spinal Cord Model." *Science* 315, 1416–1420.

International Human Genome Sequencing Consortium (2004). "Finishing the Euchromatic Sequence of the Human Genome." *Nature* 431, 931–945.

International Telecommunication Union (ITU) (2023). *Project Resilience*. https://www.itu.int/en/ITU-T/extcoop/ai-data-commons/Pages/project-resilience.aspx. Retrieved August 31, 2025.

Iranmehr, Ensieh, Saeed B. Shouraki, Mohammad M. Faraji, Nassim Bagheri, and Bernabé Linares-Barranco (2019). "Bio-Inspired Evolutionary Model of Spiking Neural Networks in Ionic Liquid Space." *Frontiers in Neuroscience* 13, 1085.

Ishibuchi, Hisao, Noritaka Tsukamoto, and Yusuke Nojima (2008). "Evolutionary Many-Objective Optimization: A Short Review." In *Proceedings of the IEEE Congress on Evolutionary Computation*, 2419–2426.

Ishida Lab (2018). *The N700 Series Shinkansen (Bullet Train)*. https://www.sys.cs.tut.ac.jp/en/research-activities/research-introduction/what-is-a-genetic-algorithm/2/. Retrieved September 29, 2018.

Islam, Md. Monirul, and Xin Yao (2008). "Evolving Artificial Neural Network Ensembles." In *Computational Intelligence: A Compendium*, edited by John Fulcher and Lakhmi C. Jain, 851–880. New York, NY: Springer.

Jacob, François (1977). "Evolution and Tinkering." *Science* 196, 1161–1166.

Jaderberg, Max, Valentin Dalibard, Simon Osindero, Wojciech M. Czarnecki, Jeff Donahue, Ali Razavi, Oriol Vinyals, Tim Green, Iain Dunning, Karen Simonyan, Chrisantha Fernando, and Koray Kavukcuoglu (2017). "Population Based Training of Neural Networks." *arXiv:1711.09846*.

Jahns, James, and Arend Hintze (2018). "How the Integration of Group and Individual Level Selection Affects the Evolution of Cooperation." In *ALIFE 2018: The 2018 Conference on Artificial Life*, 530–535.

Jain, Ashish, Anand Subramoney, and Risto Miikkulainen (2012). "Task Decomposition with Neuroevolution in Extended Predator-Prey Domain." In *Artificial Life 13: Proceedings of Thirteenth International Conference on the Synthesis and Simulation of Living Systems*, 341–348.

James, Conrad D., James B. Aimone, Nadine E. Miner, Craig M. Vineyard, Fredrick H. Rothganger, Kristofor D. Carlson, Samuel A. Mulder, Timothy J. Draelos, Aleksandra Faust, Matthew J. Marinella, John H. Naegle, and Steven J. Plimpton (2017). "A Historical Survey of Algorithms and Hardware Architectures for Neural-Inspired and Neuromorphic Computing Applications." *Biologically Inspired Cognitive Architectures* 19, 49–64.

Jastrzebski, Stanislaw, Devansh Arpit, Oliver Astrand, Giancarlo B. Kerg, Huan Wang, Caiming Xiong, Richard Socher, KyungHyun Cho, and Krzysztof J. Geras (2021). "Catastrophic Fisher Explosion: Early Phase Fisher Matrix Impacts Generalization." In *Proceedings of the 38th International Conference on Machine Learning*, 4772–4784.

Jiang, Albert Q., Alexandre Sablayrolles, Arthur Mensch, et al. (2023). "Mistral 7B." *arXiv:2310.06825*.

Jiang, Shen, Zipeng Ji, Guanghui Zhu, Chunfeng Yuan, and Yihua Huang (2023). "Operation-Level Early Stopping for Robustifying Differentiable NAS." In *Advances in Neural Information Processing Systems 35*, 70983–71007.

Jordan, Jacob, Maximilian Schmidt, Walter Senn, and Mihai A. Petrovici (2021). "Evolving Interpretable Plasticity for Spiking Networks." *eLife* 10, e66273.

Kang, Hongwei, Fengfan Bei, Yong Shen, Xingping Sun, and Qingyi Chen (2021). "A Diversity Model Based on Dimension Entropy and Its Application to Swarm Intelligence Algorithm." *Entropy* 23, 397.

Kaplan, Jared D., Sam McCandlish, Tom Henighan, Tom B. Brown, Benjamin Chess, Rewon Child, Scott Gray, Alec Radford, Jeffrey Wu, and Dario Amodei (2020). "Scaling Laws for Neural Language Models." *arXiv:2001.08361*.

Karakida, Ryo, Shotaro Akaho, and Shun-ichi Amari (2019). "Universal Statistics of Fisher Information in Deep Neural Networks: Mean Field Approach." In *The 22nd International Conference on Artificial Intelligence and Statistics*, 1032–1041.

Karpov, Igor V., Leif M. Johnson, and Risto Miikkulainen (2015). "Evaluating Team Behaviors Constructed with Human-Guided Machine Learning." In *Proceedings of the IEEE Conference on Computational Intelligence in Games*, 292–298.

Karpov, Igor V., Leif M. Johnson, Vinod Valsalam, and Risto Miikkulainen (2012). "Evaluation Methods for Human-Guided Neuroevolution in Games." In *Proceedings of the AAAI Fall Symposium on Robots That Learn Interactively from Human Teachers*.

Karpov, Igor V., Jacob Schrum, and Risto Miikkulainen (2012). "Believable Bot Navigation via Playback of Human Traces." In *Believable Bots*, edited by Philip Hingston, 151–170. New York, NY: Springer.

Karpov, Igor V., Vinod Valsalam, and Risto Miikkulainen (2011). "Human-Assisted Neuroevolution Through Shaping, Advice and Examples." In *GECCO'11: Proceedings of the 13th Annual Conference on Genetic and Evolutionary Computation*, 371–378.

Kashtan, Nir, and Uri Alon (2005). "Spontaneous Evolution of Modularity and Network Motifs." *Proceedings of the National Academy of Sciences* 102, 13773–13778.

Kashtan, Nir, Shalev Itzkovitz, Ron Milo, and Uri Alon (2004). "Efficient Sampling Algorithm for Estimating Subgraph Concentrations and Detecting Network Motifs." *Bioinformatics* 20, 1746–1758.

Kay, Tomas, Laurent Keller, and Laurent Lehmann (2020). "The Evolution of Altruism and the Serial Rediscovery of the Role of Relatedness." *Proceedings of the National Academy of Sciences* 117, 28894–28898.

Keinan, Alon, Ben Sandbank, Claus C. Hilgetag, Isaac Meilijson, and Eytan Ruppin (2006). "Axiomatic Scalable Neurocontroller Analysis via the Shapley Value." *Artificial Life* 12, 333–352.

Kempka, Michael, Marek Wydmuch, Grzegorz Runc, Jakub Toczek, and Wojciech Jaskowski (2016). "ViZDoom: A Doom-Based AI Research Platform for Visual Reinforcement Learning." In *IEEE Conference on Computational Intelligence and Games*, 341–348.

Kennedy, James, and Russell C. Eberhart (1995). "Particle Swarm Optimization." In *Proceedings of the International Conference on Neural Networks*, 1942–1948.

Kennedy, James, Russell C. Eberhart, and Yuhui Shi (2001). *Swarm Intelligence*. San Francisco, CA: Kaufmann.

Kermack, William O., and Anderson G. McKendrick (1927). "A Contribution to the Mathematical Theory of Epidemics." *Proceedings of the Royal Society of London Series A* 115, 700–721.

Khadka, Shauharda, Jen J. Chung, and Kagan Tumer (2019). "Neuroevolution of a Modular Memory-Augmented Neural Network for Deep Memory Problems." *Evolutionary Computation* 27, 639–664.

Khadka, Shauharda, and Kagan Tumer (2018). "Evolution-Guided Policy Gradient in Reinforcement Learning." In *Advances in Neural Information Processing Systems 31*, 1196–1208.

Kingma, Diederik P., and Max Welling (2014). "Auto-Encoding Variational Bayes." In *Proceedings of the Second International Conference on Learning Representations.*

Kirby, Simon, Tom Griffiths, and Kenny Smith (2014). "Iterated Learning and the Evolution of Language." *Current Opinion in Neurobiology* 28, 108–114.

Kirschner, Marc, and John Gerhart (1998). "Evolvability." *Proceedings of the National Academy of Sciences* 95, 8420–8427.

Kitano, Hiroaki (1990). "Designing Neural Networks Using Genetic Algorithms with Graph Generation System." *Complex Systems* 4, 461–476.

Knight, Chris, and Camilla Power (2012). "Social Conditions for the Evolutionary Emergence of Language." In *The Oxford Handbook of Language Evolution*, edited by Maggie Tallerman and Kathleen R. Gibson, 346–349. Oxford, UK: Oxford University Press.

Kohl, Nate, and Risto Miikkulainen (2012). "An Integrated Neuroevolutionary Approach to Reactive Control and High-Level Strategy." *IEEE Transactions on Evolutionary Computation* 16, 472–488.

Koppejan, Rogier, and Shimon Whiteson (2011). "Neuroevolutionary Reinforcement Learning for Generalized Control of Simulated Helicopters." *Evolutionary Intelligence* 4, 219–241.

Korshunova, Maria, Niles Huang, Stephen Capuzzi, Dmytro S. Radchenko, Olena Savych, Yuriy S. Moroz, Carrow I. Wells, Timothy M. Willson, Alexander Tropsha, and Olexandr Isayev (2022). "Generative and Reinforcement Learning Approaches for the Automated de Novo Design of Bioactive Compounds." *Communications Chemistry* 5, 129.

Kotyan, Shashank, and Danilo Vasconcellos Vargas (2020). "Towards Evolving Robust Neural Architectures to Defend from Adversarial Attacks." In *GECCO'20: Proceedings of the 2020 Genetic and Evolutionary Computation Conference Companion*, 135–136.

Koutník, Jan, Giuseppe Cuccu, Jürgen Schmidhuber, and Faustino Gomez (2013). "Evolving Large-Scale Neural Networks for Vision-Based Reinforcement Learning." In *GECCO'13: Proceedings of the 15th Annual Conference on Genetic and Evolutionary Computation*, 1061–1068.

Koutník, Jan, Faustino Gomez, and Jürgen Schmidhuber (2010). "Evolving Neural Networks in Compressed Weight Space." In *Proceedings of the 12th Annual Conference on Genetic and Evolutionary Computation*, 619–626.

Koza, John R. (1992). *Genetic Programming: On the Programming of Computers by Means of Natural Selection*. Cambridge, MA: MIT Press.

Koza, John R. (1994). "Genetic Programming as a Means for Programming Computers by Natural Selection." *Statistics and Computing* 4, 87–112.

Kramer, Oliver (2010). "Evolutionary Self-adaptation: A Survey of Operators and Strategy Parameters." *Evolutionary Intelligence* 3, 51–65.

Krizhevsky, Alex, Ilya Sutskever, and Geoffrey E. Hinton (2012). "Imagenet Classification with Deep Convolutional Neural Networks." In *Advances in Neural Information Processing Systems 25*, 1106–1114.

Kudithipudi, Dhireesha, Mario Aguilar-Simon, Jonathan Babb, Maxim Bazhenov, Douglas Blackiston, Josh C. Bongard, Andrew P. Brna, Suraj Chakravarthi Raja, Nick Cheney, Jeff Clune, Anurag Daram, Stefano Fusi, Peter Helfer, Leslie Kay, Nicholas Ketz, Zsolt Kira, Soheil Kolouri, Jeffrey L. Krichmar, Sam Kriegman, Michael Levin, Sandeep Madireddy, Santosh Manicka, Ali Marjaninejad, Bruce McNaughton, Risto Miikkulainen, Zaneta Navratilova, Tej Pandit, Alice Parker, Praveen K. Pilly, Sebastian Risi, Terrence J. Sejnowski, Andrea Soltoggio, Nicholas Soures, Andreas S. Tolias, Darío Urbina-Meléndez, Francisco J. Valero-Cuevas, Gido M. van de Ven, Joshua T. Vogelstein, Felix Wang, Ron Weiss, Angel Yanguas-Gil, Xinyun Zou, and Hava Siegelmann (2022). "Biological Underpinnings for Lifelong Learning Machines." *Nature Machine Intelligence* 4, 196–210.

Kumar, Akarsh, Jeff Clune, Joel Lehman, and Kenneth O. Stanley (2025). "Questioning Representational Optimism in Deep Learning: The Fractured Entangled Representation Hypothesis." *arXiv:2505.11581*.

Kumar, Akarsh, Bo Liu, Risto Miikkulainen, and Peter Stone (2022). "Effective Mutation Rate Adaptation Through Group Elite Selection." In *GECCO'22: Proceedings of the Genetic and Evolutionary Computation Conference*, 712–720.

Kumar, Akarsh, Chris Lu, Louis Kirsch, Yujin Tang, Kenneth O. Stanley, Phillip Isola, and David Ha (2024). "Automating the Search for Artificial Life with Foundation Models." *arXiv:2412.17799*.

Kwon, Jaerock, and Yoonsuck Choe (2009). "Facilitating Neural Dynamics for Delay Compensation: A Road to Predictive Neural Dynamics?" *Neural Networks* 22, 267–276.

La Cava, William, Bogdan Burlacu, Marco Virgolin, Michael Kommenda, Patryk Orzechowski, Fabrício Olivetti de França, Ying Jin, and Jason H. Moore (2021). "Contemporary Symbolic Regression Methods and Their Relative Performance." In *NeurIPS Datasets and Benchmarks 2021*, 695–710.

Lacal, Irene, and Rossella Ventura (2018). "Epigenetic Inheritance: Concepts, Mechanisms and Perspectives." *Frontiers of Molecular Neuroscience* 11, Article 292, 1–13.

Lake, Brenden M., Ruslan R. Salakhutdinov, and Joshua B. Tenenbaum (2015). "Human-Level Concept Learning Through Probabilistic Program Induction." *Science* 350, 1332–1338.

Lamarck, Jean-Baptiste (1809). *Zoological Philosophy: An Exposition with Regard to the Natural History of Animals*. Translated by Hugh Elliot, 1914. Chicago, IL: The University of Chicago Press.

Lange, Robert T. (2023). "Evosax: JAX-Based Evolution Strategies." In *GECCO'23 Companion: Proceedings of the Companion Conference on Genetic and Evolutionary Computation*, 659–662.

Lange, Robert T., Yingtao Tian, and Yujin Tang (2024a). "Evolution Transformer: In-Context Evolutionary Optimization." In *GECCO'24: Proceedings of the Genetic and Evolutionary Computation Conference Companion*, 575–578.

Lange, Robert T., Yingtao Tian, and Yujin Tang (2024b). "Large Language Models as Evolution Strategies." In *GECCO'24: Proceedings of the Genetic and Evolutionary Computation Conference Companion*, 579–582.

Larrañaga, Pedro and Jose Lozano, eds. (2002). *Estimation of Distribution Algorithms: A New Tool for Evolutionary Computation*. Dordrecht, the Netherlands: Kluwer.

LeCun, Yann, Yoshua Bengio, and Geoffrey E. Hinton (2015). "Deep Learning." *Nature* 521, 436–444.

Lehman, Joel, Jeff Clune, Dusan Misevic, Christoph Adami, Julie Beaulieu, Peter J. Bentley, Samuel Bernard, Guillaume Beslon, David M. Bryson, Patryk Chrabaszcz, Nick Cheney, Antoine Cully, Stéphane Doncieux, Fred C. Dyer, Kai O. Ellefsen, Robert Feldt, Stephan Fischer, Stephanie Forrest, Antoine Frénoy, Christian Gagné, Leni K. Le Goff, Laura M. Grabowski, Babak Hodjat, Frank Hutter, Laurent Keller, Carole Knibbe, Peter Krcah, Richard E. Lenski, Hod Lipson, Robert MacCurdy, Carlos Maestre, Risto Miikkulainen, Sara Mitri, David E. Moriarty, Jean-Baptiste Mouret, Anh M. Nguyen, Charles Ofria, Marc Parizeau, David P. Parsons, Robert T. Pennock, William F. Punch, Thomas S. Ray, Marc Schoenauer, Eric Shulte, Karl Sims, Kenneth O. Stanley, François Taddei, Danesh Tarapore, Simon Thibault, Westley

Weimer, Richard A. Watson, and Jason Yosinski (2020). "The Surprising Creativity of Digital Evolution: A Collection of Anecdotes from the Evolutionary Computation and Artificial Life Research Communities." *Artificial Life* 26, 274–306.

Lehman, Joel, Jonathan Gordon, Shawn Jain, Kamal Ndousse, Cathy Yeh, and Kenneth O. Stanley (2023). "Evolution Through Large Models." In *Handbook of Evolutionary Machine Learning*, edited by Wolfgang Banzhaf, Penousal Machado and Mengjie Zhang, 331–366. New York, NY: Springer.

Lehman, Joel, and Risto Miikkulainen (2013). "Boosting Interactive Evolution Using Human Computation Markets." In *Proceedings of the 2nd International Conference on the Theory and Practice of Natural Computation*, 1–18.

Lehman, Joel, and Risto Miikkulainen (2014). "Overcoming Deception in Evolution of Cognitive Behaviors." In *GECCO'14: Proceedings of the 2014 Annual Conference on Genetic and Evolutionary Computation*, 185–192.

Lehman, Joel, and Risto Miikkulainen (2015). "Extinction Events Can Accelerate Evolution." *PLoS ONE* 10, e0132886.

Lehman, Joel, and Kenneth O. Stanley (2008). "Exploiting Open-Endedness to Solve Problems Through the Search for Novelty." In *Artificial Life XI: Proceedings of the Eleventh International Conference on the Synthesis and Simulation of Living Systems*, edited by Seth Bullock, Jason Noble, Richard A. Watson and Mark A. Bedau, 329–336. Cambridge, MA: MIT Press.

Lehman, Joel, and Kenneth O. Stanley (2011a). "Abandoning Objectives: Evolution Through the Search for Novelty Alone." *Evolutionary Computation* 19, 189–223.

Lehman, Joel, and Kenneth O. Stanley (2011b). "Evolving a Diversity of Virtual Creatures Through Novelty Search and Local Competition." In *GECCO'11: Proceedings of the 13th Annual Conference on Genetic and Evolutionary Computation*, 211–218.

Lehman, Joel, and Kenneth O. Stanley (2012). "Beyond Open-Endedness: Quantifying Impressiveness." In *Artificial Life 13: Proceedings of the Thirteenth International Conference on the Synthesis and Simulation of Living Systems*, 75–82.

Lehmann, Kenna D. S., Tracy M. Montgomery, Sarah M. MacLachlan, Jenna M. Parker, Olivia S. Spagnuolo, Kelsey J. VandeWetering, Patrick S. Bills, and Kay E. Holekamp (2016). "Lions, Hyenas and Mobs (Oh My!)" *Current Zoology* 63, 313–322.

Lenartowicz, Agatha, and Russell A. Poldrack (2010). "Brain Imaging." In *Encyclopedia of Behavioral Neuroscience*, edited by George F. Koob, Michel Le Moal and Richard F. Thompson, 187–193. Oxford, UK: Academic Press.

Lessin, Dan, Don Fussell, and Risto Miikkulainen (2013). "Open-Ended Behavioral Complexity for Evolved Virtual Creatures." In *GECCO'13: Proceedings of the 15th Annual Conference on Genetic and Evolutionary Computation*, 335–342.

Lessin, Dan, Don Fussell, and Risto Miikkulainen (2014). "Adapting Morphology to Multiple Tasks in Evolved Virtual Creatures." In *Artificial Life 14: Proceedings of the Fourteenth International Conference on the Synthesis and Simulation of Living Systems.*

Lettvin, Jerome Y., Humberto R. Maturana, Warren S. McCulloch, and Walter H. Pitts (1959). "What the Frog's Eye Tells the Frog's Brain." *Proceedings of the IRE* 47, 1940–1951.

Leung, Binggwong, Worasuchad Haomachai, Joachim Winther Pedersen, Sebastian Risi, and Poramate Manoonpong (2025). "Bio-Inspired Plastic Neural Networks for Zero-Shot Out-of-Distribution Generalization in Complex Animal-Inspired Robots." *arXiv:2503.12406.*

Li, Hui, Xuesong Wang, and Shifei Ding (2018). "Research and Development of Neural Network Ensembles: A Survey." *Artificial Intelligence Review* 49, 455–479.

Li, Liam, and Ameet Talwalkar (2020). "Random Search and Reproducibility for Neural Architecture Search." In *Proceedings of the 36th Conference on Uncertainty in Artificial Intelligence*, 367–377.

Li, Xun, and Risto Miikkulainen (2016). "Evolving Artificial Language Through Evolutionary Reinforcement Learning." In *ALIFE 2016, the Fifteenth International Conference on the Synthesis and Simulation of Living Systems*, edited by Carlos Gershenson, Tom Froese, Jesus M. Siqueiros, Wendy Aguilar, Eduardo J. Izquierdo and Hiroki Sayama, 484–491. Cambridge, MA: MIT Press.

Li, Xun, and Risto Miikkulainen (2018). "Opponent Modeling and Exploitation in Poker Using Evolved Recurrent Neural Networks." In *GECCO'18: Proceedings of the Genetic and Evolutionary Computation Conference*, 189–196.

Liang, Jason, Santiago Gonzalez, Hormoz Shahrzad, and Risto Miikkulainen (2021). "Regularized Evolutionary Population-Based Training." In *GECCO'21: Proceedings of the Genetic and Evolutionary Computation Conference*, 323–331.

Liang, Jason, Elliot Meyerson, Babak Hodjat, Dan Fink, Karl Mutch, and Risto Miikkulainen (2019). "Evolutionary Neural AutoML for Deep Learning." In *GECCO'19: Proceedings of the Genetic and Evolutionary Computation Conference*, 401–409.

Liang, Jason, Elliot Meyerson, and Risto Miikkulainen (2018). "Evolutionary Architecture Search for Deep Multitask Networks." In *GECCO'18: Proceedings of the Genetic and Evolutionary Computation Conference*, 466–473.

Liang, Jason, and Risto Miikkulainen (2015). "Evolutionary Bilevel Optimization for Complex Control Tasks." In *GECCO'15: Proceedings of the 2015 Annual Conference on Genetic and Evolutionary Computation*, 833–839.

Liang, Jason, Hormoz Shahrzad, and Risto Miikkulainen (2023). "Asynchronous Evolution of Deep Neural Network Architectures." *Applied Soft Computing* 152, 111209.

Liang, Tengyuan, Tomaso Poggio, Alexander Rakhlin, and James Stokes (2019). "Fisher-Rao Metric, Geometry, and Complexity of Neural Networks." In *The 22nd International Conference on Artificial Intelligence and Statistics*, 888–896.

Liao, Zhibin, Tom Drummond, Ian Reid, and Gustavo Carneiro (2018). "Approximate Fisher Information Matrix to Characterize the Training of Deep Neural Networks." *IEEE Transactions on Pattern Analysis and Machine Intelligence* 42, 15–26.

Liapis, Antonios, Georgios N. Yannakakis, and Julian Togelius (2011). "Neuroevolutionary Constrained Optimization for Content Creation." In *Proceedings of the IEEE Conference on Computational Intelligence and Games*, 71–78.

Light, Will (1993). "Ridge Functions, Sigmoidal Functions and Neural Networks." In *Approximation Theory VII*, edited by Elliot W. Cheney, Charles K. Cui and Larry L. Schumaker, 158–201. Boston, MA: Academic Press.

Lim, Heejin, and Yoonsuck Choe (2006). "Facilitating Neural Dynamics for Delay Compensation and Prediction in Evolutionary Neural Networks." In *GECCO'06: Proceedings of the 8th Annual Conference on Genetic and Evolutionary Computation*, 167–174.

Lindenmayer, Aristid (1968a). "Mathematical Models for Cellular Interactions in Development. I. Filaments with One-Sided Inputs." *Journal of Theoretical Biology* 18, 280–299.

Lindenmayer, Aristid (1968b). "Mathematical Models for Cellular Interactions in Development. II. Simple and Branching Filaments with Two-Sided Inputs." *Journal of Theoretical Biology* 18, 300–315.

Lipson, Hod, and Jordan B. Pollack (2000). "Automatic Design and Manufacture of Robotic Lifeforms." *Nature* 406, 974–978.

Liu, Aixin, Bei Feng, Bing Xue, et al. (2024). "DeepSeek-V3 Technical Report." *arXiv:2412.19437.*

Liu, Rosanne, Joel Lehman, Piero Molino, Felipe Petroski Such, Eric Frank, Alex Sergeev, and Jason Yosinski (2018). "An Intriguing Failing of Convolutional Neural Networks and the Coordconv Solution." *Advances in Neural Information Processing Systems 31*, 9605–9616.

Liu, Yuqiao, Yanan Sun, Bing Xue, Mengjie Zhang, Gary G. Yen, and Kay C. Tan (2021). "A Survey on Evolutionary Neural Architecture Search." *IEEE Transactions on Neural Networks and Learning Systems* 34, 550–570.

Liu, Zhenhua, Xinfeng Zhang, Shanshe Wang, Siwei Ma, and Wen Gao (2021). "Evolutionary Quantization of Neural Networks with Mixed-Precision." In *Proceedings of the IEEE International Conference on Acoustics, Speech and Signal Processing*, 2785–2789.

Liu, Ziming, Yixuan Wang, Sachin Vaidya, Fabian Ruehle, James Halverson, Marin Soljačić, Thomas Y. Hou, and Max Tegmark (2025). "KAN: Kolmogorov-Arnold Networks." In *Proceedings of the Thirteenth International Conference on Learning Representations*, 66342–66388.

Lockett, Alan, and Risto Miikkulainen (2013). "Neuroannealing: Martingale-Driven Learning for Neural Network." In *GECCO'13: Proceedings of the 15th Annual Conference on Genetic and Evolutionary Computation*, 711–718.

Lorenzo, Pablo Ribalta, Jakub Nalepa, Michal Kawulok, Luciano Sanchez Ramos, and José Ranilla Pastor (2017). "Particle Swarm Optimization for Hyper-parameter Selection in Deep Neural Networks." In *GECCO'17: Proceedings of the Genetic and Evolutionary Computation Conference*, 481–488.

Lozano, Jose A., Pedro Larrañaga, Iñaki Inza, and Endika Bengoetxea (2006). *Towards a New Evolutionary Computation: Advances on Estimation of Distribution Algorithms.* New York, NY: Springer.

Lu, Sen, and Abhronil Sengupta (2022). "Neuroevolution Guided Hybrid Spiking Neural Network Training." *Frontiers in Neuroscience* 16, 838523.

Lu, Zhichao, Kalyanmoy Deb, Erik Goodman, Wolfgang Banzhaf, and Vishnu N. Boddeti (2020). "NSGANetV2: Evolutionary Multi-objective Surrogate-Assisted Neural Architecture Search." In *Computer Vision—ECCV 2020.* Vol. 12346, 35–51.

Lüders, Benno, Mikkel Schläger, and Sebastian Risi (2016). "Continual Learning Through Evolvable Neural Turing Machines." In *Workshop on Continual Learning and Deep Networks, Neural Information Processing Systems Conference*.

Luke, Sean, and Lee Spector (1996). "Evolving Graphs and Networks with Edge Encoding: Preliminary Report." In *Late-Breaking Papers at the Genetic Programming 1996 Conference*, 117–124.

Luo, Calvin (2022). "Understanding Diffusion Models: A Unified Perspective." *arXiv:2208.11970*.

Lynch, Michael (2007). "The Frailty of Adaptive Hypotheses for the Origins of Organismal Complexity." *Proceedings of the National Acadademy of Sciences* 104, 8597–8604.

MacNeilage, Peter F. (1998). "The Frame/Content Theory of Evolution of Speech Production." *Behavioral and Brain Sciences* 21, 499–511.

Maheri, Alireza, Shahin Jalili, Yousef Hosseinzadeh, Reza Khani, and Mirreza Miryahyavi (2021). "A Comprehensive Survey on Cultural Algorithms." *Swarm and Evolutionary Computation* 62, 100846.

Makoviychuk, Viktor, Lukasz Wawrzyniak, Yunrong Guo, Michelle Lu, Kier Storey, Miles Macklin, David Hoeller, Nikita Rudin, Arthur Allshire, Ankur Handa, and Gavriel State (2021). "Isaac Gym: High Performance GPU Based Physics Simulation For Robot Learning." In *NeurIPS Datasets and Benchmarks 2021*, 1186–1198.

Mańdziuk, Jacek, and Piotr Rajkiewicz (2016). "Neuro-evolutionary System for FOREX Trading." In *Proceedings of the IEEE Congress on Evolutionary Computation*, 4654–4661.

Mańdziuk, Jacek, and Adam Żychowski (2023). "Duel-Based Neuroevolutionary Method for Stackelberg Security Games with Boundedly Rational Attacker." *Applied Soft Computing* 146, 110673.

Mao, Xudong, Qing Li, Haoran Xie, Raymond Y. K. Lau, Zhen Wang, and Stephen P. Smolley (2017). "Least Squares Generative Adversarial Networks." In *Proceedings of the IEEE International Conference on Computer Vision*, 2813–2821.

Markram, Henry, Yun Wang, and Michail Tsodyks (1998). "Differential Signaling via the Same Axon of Neocortical Pyramidal Neurons." *Proceedings of the National Academy of Sciences of the United States of America* 95, 5323–5328.

Masoudnia, Saeed, and Reza Ebrahimpour (2014). "Mixture of Experts: A Literature Survey." *Artificial Intelligence Review* 42, 275.

Mattiussi, Claudio, and Dario Floreano (2007). "Analog Genetic Encoding for the Evolution of Circuits and Networks." *IEEE Transactions on Evolutionary Computation* 11, 596–607.

Maynard Smith, J., and Eörs Szathmáry (1997). *The Major Transitions in Evolution*. Oxford, UK: Oxford University Press.

McQuesten, Paul (2002). "Cultural Enhancement of Neuroevolution." PhD thesis. Austin, TX: Department of Computer Sciences, The University of Texas at Austin.

McQuesten, Paul, and Risto Miikkulainen (1997). "Culling and Teaching in Neuro-evolution." In *Proceedings of the Seventh International Conference on Genetic Algorithms*, 760–767.

Meoded, Avner, Andrea Poretti, Susumu Mori, and Jiangyang Zhang (2016). "Diffusion Tensor Imaging (DTI)." In *The Curated Reference Collection in Neuroscience and Biobehavioral Psychology*. Amsterdam, the Netherlands: Elsevier.

Meredith, Robert W., Jan E. Janečka, John Gatesy, Oliver A. Ryder, Colleen A. Fisher, Emma C. Teeling, Alisha Goodbla, Eduardo Eizirik, Taiz L. L. Simão, Tanja Stadler, Daniel L. Rabosky, Rodney L. Honeycutt, John J. Flynn, Colleen M. Ingram, Cynthia Steiner, Tiffani L. Williams, Terence J. Robinson, Angela Burk-Herrick, Michael Westerman, Nadia A. Ayoub, Mark S. Springer, and William J. Murphy (2011). "Impacts of the Cretaceous Terrestrial Revolution and KPg Extinction on Mammal Diversification." *Science* 334, 521–524.

Metzen, Jan H., Frank Kirchner, Mark Edgington, and Yohannes Kassahun (2008). "Towards Efficient Online Reinforcement Learning Using Neuroevolution." In *GECCO'08: Proceedings of the 10th Annual Conference on Genetic and Evolutionary Computation*, 1425–1426.

Meyerson, Elliot, Olivier Francon, Darren Sargent, Babak Hodjat, and Risto Miikkulainen (2024). "Unlocking the Potential of Global Human Expertise." In *Advances in Neural Information Processing Systems 37*, 119227–119259.

Meyerson, Elliot, Joel Lehman, and Risto Miikkulainen (2016). "Learning Behavior Characterizations for Novelty Search." In *GECCO'16: Proceedings of the Genetic and Evolutionary Computation Conference 2016*, 149–156.

Meyerson, Elliot, and Risto Miikkulainen (2017). "Discovering Evolutionary Stepping Stones Through Behavior Domination." In *GECCO'17: Proceedings of the Genetic and Evolutionary Computation Conference*, 139–146.

Meyerson, Elliot, and Risto Miikkulainen (2018a). "Beyond Shared Hierarchies: Deep Multitask Learning Through Soft Layer Ordering." In *Proceedings of the Sixth International Conference on Learning Representations*, 1401–1414.

Meyerson, Elliot, and Risto Miikkulainen (2018b). "Pseudo-task Augmentation: From Deep Multitask Learning to Intratask Sharing—and Back." In *Proceedings of the 35th International Conference on Machine Learning*, 739–748.

Meyerson, Elliot, and Risto Miikkulainen (2019). "Modular Universal Reparameterization: Deep Multi-task Learning Across Diverse Domains." In *Advances in Neural Information Processing Systems 32*, 7901–7912.

Meyerson, Elliot, and Risto Miikkulainen (2021). "The Traveling Observer Model: Multi-task Learning Through Spatial Variable Embeddings." In *Proceedings of the Ninth International Conference on Learning Representations*, 2706–2722.

Meyerson, Elliot, Mark J. Nelson, Herbie Bradley, Adam Gaier, Arash Moradi, Amy K. Hoover, and Joel Lehman (2024). "Language Model Crossover: Variation Through Few-Shot Prompting." *ACM Transactions on Evolutionary Learning and Optimization* 4, Article 27, 1–40.

Meyerson, Elliot, Xin Qiu, and Risto Miikkulainen (2022). "Simple Genetic Operators Are Universal Approximators of Probability Distributions (and Other Advantages of Expressive Encodings)." In *GECCO'22: Proceedings of the Genetic and Evolutionary Computation Conference*, 739–748.

Miconi, Thomas (2008). "In Silicon No One Can Hear You Scream: Evolving Fighting Creatures." In *Genetic Programming: 11th European Conference*, edited by Michael O'Neill, Leonardo Vanneschi, Steven Gustafson, Anna I. Esparcia Alcázar, Ivanoe De Falco, Antonio Della Cioppa and Ernesto Tarantino, 25–36. New York, NY: Springer.

Miconi, Thomas (2009). "Why Coevolution Doesn't 'Work': Superiority and Progress in Coevolution." In *Genetic Programming: 12th European Conference*, edited by Leonardo Vanneschi, Steven Gustafson, Alberto Moraglio, Ivanoe de Falco and Marc Ebner, 49–60. New York, NY: Springer.

Miikkulainen, Risto (2021). "Creative AI Through Evolutionary Computation: Principles and Examples." *SN Computer Science* 2, 163.

Miikkulainen, Risto (2024). "Generative AI: An AI Paradigm Shift in the Making?" *AI Magazine*, 165–167.

Miikkulainen, Risto (2025). "Neuroevolution Insights into Biological Neural Computation." *Science*, eadp7478.

Miikkulainen, Risto, James A. Bednar, Yoonsuck Choe, and Joseph Sirosh (2005). *Computational Maps in the Visual Cortex*. New York, NY: Springer.

Miikkulainen, Risto, Myles Brundage, Jonathan Epstein, Tyler Foster, Babak Hodjat, Neil Iscoe, Jingbo Jiang, Diego Legrand, Sam Nazari, Xin Qiu, Michael Scharff, Cory Schoolland, Robert Severn, and Aaron Shagrin (2020). "Ascend by Evolv: AI-Based Massively Multivariate Conversion Rate Optimization." *AI Magazine* 42, 44–60.

Miikkulainen, Risto, and Michael G. Dyer (1991). "Natural Language Processing with Modular PDP Networks and Distributed Lexicon." *Cognitive Science* 15, 343–399.

Miikkulainen, Risto, Dan Fink, Olivier Francon, Babak Hodjat, Noravee Kanchanavatee, Elliot Meyerson, Xin Qiu, Darren Sargent, Hormoz Shahrzad, Deepak Singh, Jean Celestin Yamegni Noubeyo, and Daniel Young (2025). *NeuroSAN+NeuroAI: AI-assisted Decision-making Through a Synergy of Technologies*. Technical Report 2025-01, Cognizant AI Lab.

Miikkulainen, Risto, and Stephanie Forrest (2021). "A Biological Perspective on Evolutionary Computation." *Nature Machine Intelligence* 3, 9–15.

Miikkulainen, Risto, Olivier Francon, Elliot Meyerson, Xin Qiu, Darren Sargent, Elisa Canzani, and Babak Hodjat (2021). "From Prediction to Prescription: Evolutionary Optimization of Non-pharmaceutical Interventions in the COVID-19 Pandemic." *IEEE Transactions on Evolutionary Computation* 25, 386–401.

Miikkulainen, Risto, Jason Liang, Elliot Meyerson, Aditya Rawal, Dan Fink, Olivier Francon, Bala Raju, Hormoz Shahrzad, Arshak Navruzyan, Nigel Duffy, and Babak Hodjat (2023). "Evolving Deep Neural Networks." In *Artificial Intelligence in the Age of Neural Networks and Brain Computing*, 2nd ed., edited by Robert Kozma, Cesare Alippi, Yoonsuck Choe and Francesco C. Morabito, 269–287. Amsterdam, the Netherlands: Elsevier.

Miikkulainen, Risto, Elliot Meyerson, Xin Qiu, Ujjayant Sinha, Raghav Kumar, Karen Hofmann, Yiyang M. Yan, Michael Ye, Jingyan Yang, Damon Caiazza, and Stephanie Manson Brown (2021). "Evaluating Medical Aesthetics Treatments Through Evolved Age-Estimation Models." In *GECCO'21: Proceedings of the Genetic and Evolutionary Computation Conference*, 1009–1017.

Miller, Geoffrey F., Peter Todd, and Shailesh Hedge (1989). "Designing Neural Networks Using Genetic Algorithm." In *Proceedings of the Third International Conference on Genetic Algorithms*, 391–396.

Miller, Julian F. (2004). "Evolving a Self-Repairing, Self-Regulating, French Flag Organism." In *Genetic and Evolutionary Computation–GECCO 2004*, 129–139.

Miller, Julian F., ed. (2011). *Cartesian Genetic Programming*. New York, NY: Springer.

Miller, Julian F. (2020). "Cartesian Genetic Programming: Its Status and Future." *Genetic Programming and Evolvable Machines* 21, 129–168.

Miller, Julian F., and Andrew Turner (2015). "Cartesian Genetic Programming." In *GECCO Companion '15: Proceedings of the Companion Publication of the 2015 Annual Conference on Genetic and Evolutionary Computation*, 179–198.

Min, Bonan, Hayley Ross, Elior Sulem, Amir P. B. Veyseh, Thien H. Nguyen, Oscar Sainz, Eneko Agirre, Ilana Heintz, and Dan Roth (2024). "Recent Advances in Natural Language Processing via Large Pre-trained Language Models: A Survey." *ACM Computing Surveys* 56, 30:1–30:40.

Mistral AI (2024). *Models Overview*. https://docs.mistral.ai/getting-started/models/models_overview/. Retrieved August 31, 2025.

Mitchell, Melanie (2006). "Coevolutionary Learning with Spatially Distributed Populations." In *Computational Intelligence: Principles and Practice*, edited by Gary Y. Yen and David B. Fogel, 137–154. Piscataway, NJ: IEEE Computational Intelligence Society.

Mitchell, Melanie, James P. Crutchfield, and Rajarshi Das (1996). "Evolving Cellular Automata with Genetic Algorithms: A Review of Recent Work." In *Proceedings of the First International Conference on Evolutionary Computation and Its Applications*, 42–55.

Mjolsness, Eric, David H. Sharp, and Bradley K. Alpert (1989). "Scaling, Machine Learning, and Genetic Neural Nets." *Advances in Applied Mathematics* 10, 137–163.

Mnih, Volodymyr, Koray Kavukcuoglu, David Silver, Andrei A. Rusu, Joel Veness, Marc G. Bellemare, Alex Graves, Martin Riedmiller, Andreas K. Fidjeland, Georg Ostrovski, Stig Petersen, Charles Beattie, Amir Sadik, Ioannis Antonoglou, Helen King, Dharshan Kumaran, Daan Wierstra, Shane Legg, and Demis Hassabis (2015). "Human-Level Control Through Deep Reinforcement Learning." *Nature* 518, 529–533.

Montana, David J., and Lawrence Davis (1989). "Training Feedforward Neural Networks Using Genetic Algorithms." In *Proceedings of the 11th International Joint Conference on Artificial Intelligence*, 762–767.

Mordvintsev, Alexander, Ettore Randazzo, Eyvind Niklasson, and Michael Levin (2020). "Growing Neural Cellular Automata." *Distill* 5, e23.

Morgan, Nelson, and Hervé Bourlard (1990). "Generalization and Parameter Estimation in Feedforward Nets: Some Experiments." In *Advances in Neural Information Processing Systems 3*, 630–637.

Moriarty, David E., and Pat Langley (1998). "Learning Cooperative Lane Selection Strategies for Highways." In *Proceedings of the AAAI Conference on Artificial Intelligence, 15*, 684–691.

Moriarty, David E., and Risto Miikkulainen (1996). "Evolving Obstacle Avoidance Behavior in a Robot Arm." In *From Animals to Animats 4: Proceedings of the Fourth International Conference on Simulation of Adaptive Behavior*, edited by Pattie Maes, Maja J. Mataric, Jean-Arcady Meyer, Jordan Pollack and Stewart W. Wilson, 468–475. Cambridge, MA: MIT Press.
Moriarty, David E., and Risto Miikkulainen (1997). "Forming Neural Networks Through Efficient and Adaptive Coevolution." *Evolutionary Computation* 5, 373–399.
Mouret, Jean-Baptiste, and Jeff Clune (2015). "Illuminating Search Spaces by Mapping Elites." *arXiv:1504.04909*.
Mouret, Jean-Baptiste, and Stéphane Doncieux (2009). "Overcoming the Bootstrap Problem in Evolutionary Robotics Using Behavioral Diversity." In *Proceedings of the IEEE Congress on Evolutionary Computation*, 1161–1168.
Mouret, Jean-Baptiste, and Stéphane Doncieux (2012). "Encouraging Behavioral Diversity in Evolutionary Robotics: An Empirical Study." *Evolutionary Computation* 20, 91–133.
Mousavirad, Seyed J., Seyyed M. Tabatabaei, Davood Zabihzadeh, Mahshid H. Moghadam, Mehran Pourvahab, and Diego Oliva (2025). "Enhancing Neural Network Generalisation with Improved Differential Evolution." In *Advances in Optimization Algorithms for Multidisciplinary Engineering Applications: From Classical Methods to AI-Enhanced Solutions*, edited by Diego Oliva, Arturo Valdivia, Seyed J. Mousavirad and Kanak Kalita, 455–470. New York, NY: Springer.
Mühlenbein, Heinz, and Jörg Kindermann (1989). "The Dynamics of Evolution and Learning: Towards Genetic Neural Networks." In *Connectionism in Perspective*, edited by Rolf Pfeifer, Zoltan Schreter, Françoise Fogelman Soulié and Luc Steels, 301–308. Amsterdam, the Netherlands: Elsevier.
Müller, Gerd B. (2014). "EvoDevo Shapes the Extended Synthesis." *Biological Theory* 9, 119–121.
Nair, Vinod, and Geoffrey E. Hinton (2010). "Rectified Linear Units Improve Restricted Boltzmann Machines." In *Proceedings of the 27th International Conference on Machine Learning*, 807–814.
Najarro, Elias, and Sebastian Risi (2020). "Meta-Learning Through Hebbian Plasticity in Random Networks." *Advances in Neural Information Processing Systems 33*, 20719–20731.
Najarro, Elias, Shyam Sudhakaran, Claire Glanois, and Sebastian Risi (2022). "HyperNCA: Growing Developmental Networks with Neural Cellular Automata." In *Workshop on From Cells to Societies: Collective Learning Across Scales, Tenth International Conference on Learning Representations*.
Najarro, Elias, Shyam Sudhakaran, and Sebastian Risi (2023). "Towards Self-Assembling Artificial Neural Networks Through Neural Developmental Programs." In *ALIFE 2023: Ghost in the Machine: Proceedings of the 2023 Artificial Life Conference*, 80.
Newman, Mark E. J. (2002). "Spread of Epidemic Disease on Networks." *Physical Review E* 66, 016128.
Newman, Mark E. J. (2006). "Modularity and Community Structure in Networks." *Proceedings of the National Academy of Sciences* 103, 8577–8582.

Nguyen, Anh M., Jason Yosinski, and Jeff Clune (2015a). "Deep Neural Networks Are Easily Fooled: High Confidence Predictions for Unrecognizable Images." In *Proceedings of the IEEE Conference on Computer Vision and Pattern Recognition*, 427–436.

Nguyen, Anh M., Jason Yosinski, and Jeff Clune (2015b). "Innovation Engines: Automated Creativity and Improved Stochastic Optimization via Deep Learning." In *GECCO'15: Proceedings of the 2015 Annual Conference on Genetic and Evolutionary Computation*, 959–966.

Nichele, Stefano, Mathias B. Ose, Sebastian Risi, and Gunnar Tufte (2017). "CA-NEAT: Evolved Compositional Pattern Producing Networks for Cellular Automata Morphogenesis and Replication." *IEEE Transactions on Cognitive and Developmental Systems* 10, 687–700.

Nisioti, Eleni, Erwan Plantec, Milton Montero, Joachim Winther Pedersen, and Sebastian Risi (2024). "Growing Artificial Neural Networks for Control: The Role of Neuronal Diversity." In *GECCO'24 Companion: Proceedings of the Genetic and Evolutionary Computation Conference Companion*, 175–178.

Nolfi, Stefano (2011). "Behavior and Cognition as a Complex Adaptive System: Insights from Robotic Experiments." In *Philosophy of Complex Systems*, edited by Cliff Hooker, 443–463. Amsterdam, the Netherlands: North-Holland.

Nolfi, Stefano, Jeffrey L. Elman, and Domenico Parisi (1994). "Learning and Evolution in Neural Networks." *Adaptive Behavior* 2, 5–28.

Nolfi, Stefano, and Dario Floreano (2000). *Evolutionary Robotics: The Biology, Intelligence, and Technology of Self-Organizing Machines*. Cambridge, MA: MIT Press.

Nolfi, Stefano, and Paolo Pagliuca (2025). "Global Progress in Competitive Co-evolution: A Systematic Comparison of Alternative Methods." *Frontiers in Robotics and AI* 11, Article 1470886, 1–19.

Nolfi, Stefano, and Domenico Parisi (1992). "Growing Neural Networks." In *Artificial Life II: Proceedings of the Workshop on Artificial Life*, edited by Christopher G. Langton. Reading, MA: Addison-Wesley.

Nolfi, Stefano, and Domenico Parisi (1994). "Desired Answers Do Not Correspond to Good Teaching Inputs in Ecological Neural Networks." *Neural Processing Letters* 1, 1–5.

Nordin, Peter, and Wolfgang Banzhaf (1995). "Complexity Compression and Evolution." In *Proceedings of the Sixth International Conference on Genetic Algorithms*, 310–317.

Novikov, Alexander, Ngân Vũ, Marvin Eisenberger, Emilien Dupont, Po-Sen Huang, Adam Z. Wagner, Sergey Shirobokov, Borislav Kozlovskii, Francisco J. R. Ruiz, Abbas Mehrabian, M. Pawan Kumar, Abigail See, Swarat Chaudhuri, George Holland, Alex Davies, Sebastian Nowozin, Pushmeet Kohli, and Matej Balog (2025). "AlphaEvolve: A Coding Agent for Scientific and Algorithmic Discovery." *arXiv:2506.13131*.

Nowak, Martin A., and David C. Krakauer (1999). "The Evolution of Language." *Proceedings of the National Acadeny of Sciences* 96, 8028–8033.

Ochoa, Gabriela (1998). "On Genetic Algorithms and Lindenmayer Systems." In *Parallel Problem Solving from Nature—PPSN V*, 335–344.

Ochoa, Gabriela, Katherine M Malan, and Christian Blum (2021). "Search Trajectory Networks: A Tool for Analysing and Visualising the Behaviour of Metaheuristics." *Applied Soft Computing* 109, 107492.

Ollion, Charles, Tony Pinville, and Stéphane Doncieux (2012). "With a Little Help from Selection Pressures: Evolution of Memory in Robot Controllers." In *Artificial Life 13: Proceedings of the Thirteenth International Conference on the Synthesis and Simulation of Living Systems*, 407–414.

Olson, Randal S., Arend Hintze, Fred C. Dyer, David B. Knoester, and Christoph Adami (2013). "Predator Confusion Is Sufficient to Evolve Swarming Behaviour." *Journal of The Royal Society Interface* 10, 20130305.

OpenAI (2025). *GPT-5 System Card.* Technical Report, OpenAI.

Ororbia, Alexander, AbdElRahman ElSaid, and Travis Desell (2019). "Investigating Recurrent Neural Network Memory Structures Using Neuro-evolution." In *GECCO'19: Proceedings of the Genetic and Evolutionary Computation Conference*, 446–455.

Ouyang, Long, Jeff Wu, Xu Jiang, Diogo Almeida, Carroll L. Wainwright, Pamela Mishkin, Chong Zhang, Sandhini Agarwal, Katarina Slama, Alex Ray, John Schulman, Jacob Hilton, Fraser Kelton, Luke Miller, Maddie Simens, Amanda Askell, Peter Welinder, Paul Christiano, Jan Leike, and Ryan Lowe (2022). "Training Language Models to Follow Instructions with Human Feedback." In *Advances in Neural Information Processing Systems 35*, 27730–27744.

Oymak, Samet (2018). "Learning Compact Neural Networks with Regularization." In *Proceedings of the 35th International Conference on Machine Learning*, 3963–3972.

Papavasileiou, Evgenia, Jan Cornelis, and Bart Jansen (2021). "A Systematic Literature Review of the Successors of 'NeuroEvolution of Augmenting Topologies'." *Evolutionary Computation* 29, 1–73.

Papavasileiou, Evgenia, and Bart Jansen (2017). "An Investigation of Topological Choices in FS-NEAT and FD-NEAT on XOR-Based Problems of Increased Complexity." In *GECCO'17: Proceedings of the Genetic and Evolutionary Computation Conference Companion*, 1431–1434.

Pardoe, David, Michael Ryoo, and Risto Miikkulainen (2005). "Evolving Neural Network Ensembles for Control Problems." In *GECCO'05: Proceedings of the 7th Annual Conference on Genetic and Evolutionary Computation*, 1379–1384.

Park, J., and Irwin W. Sandberg (1991). "Universal Approximation Using Radial-Basis-Function Networks." *Neural Computation* 3, 246–257.

Pedersen, Joachim Winther, and Sebastian Risi (2021). "Evolving and Merging Hebbian Learning Rules: Increasing Generalization by Decreasing the Number of Rules." In *GECCO'21: Proceedings of the Genetic and Evolutionary Computation Conference*, 892–900.

Pelikan, Martin, David E. Goldberg, and Erick Cantú-Paz (1999). "BOA: The Bayesian Optimization Algorithm." In *GECCO'99: Proceedings of the 1st Annual Conference on Genetic and Evolutionary Computation*, 525–532.

Petroski Such, Felipe, Vashisht Madhavan, Edoardo Conti, Joel Lehman, Kenneth O. Stanley, and Jeff Clune (2017). "Deep Neuroevolution: Genetic Algorithms Are a Competitive Alternative for Training Deep Neural Networks for Reinforcement Learning." *arXiv:1712.06567*.

Pham, Hieu, Melody Guan, Barret Zoph, Quoc V. Le, and Jeff Dean (2018). "Efficient Neural Architecture Search via Parameter Sharing." In *Proceedings of the 35th International Conference on Machine Learning*, 4095–4104.

Pilat, Martin L., and Christian Jacob (2010). "Evolution of Vision Capabilities in Embodied Virtual Creatures." In *GECCO'10: Proceedings of the 12th Annual Conference on Genetic and Evolutionary Computation*, 95–102.

Plantec, Erwan, Joachim Winther Pedersen, Milton Montero, Eleni Nisioti, and Sebastian Risi (2024). "Evolving Self-Assembling Neural Networks: From Spontaneous Activity to Experience-Dependent Learning." In *ALIFE 2024: Proceedings of the 2024 Artificial Life Conference*. Article 37.

Polani, Daniel, and Risto Miikkulainen (2000). "Eugenic Neuro-evolution for Reinforcement Learning." In *GECCO'00: Proceedings of the 2nd Annual Conference on Genetic and Evolutionary Computation*, 1041–1046.

Poli, Riccardo, William B. Langdon, and Nicholas F. McPhee (2008). *A Field Guide to Genetic Programming*. Egham, UK: Lulu Enterprises.

Pollack, Jordan B. (1987). "Cascaded Back-propagation on Dynamic Connectionist Networks." In *Proceedings of the 10th Annual Conference of the Cognitive Science Society*, 391–404.

Popovici, Elena, Anthony Bucci, R. Paul Wiegand, and Edwin D. de Jong (2012). "Coevolutionary Principles." In *Handbook of Natural Computing*, edited by Grzegorz Rozenberg, Thomas Bäck and Joost N. Kok, 987–1033. New York, NY: Springer.

Potter, Mitchell A., and Kenneth A. De Jong (2000). "Cooperative Coevolution: An Architecture for Evolving Coadapted Subcomponents." *Evolutionary Computation* 8, 1–29.

Prellberg, Jonas, and Oliver Kramer (2018). "Lamarckian Evolution of Convolutional Neural Networks." In *Parallel Problem Solving from Nature—PPSN XV*, edited by Anne Auger, Carlos M. Fonseca, Nuno Lourenço, Penousal Machado, Luís Paquete and Darrell Whitley, 424–435. New York, NY: Springer.

Price, Kenneth V., Rainer M. Storn, and Jouni A. Lampinen (2005). *Differential Evolution: A Practical Approach to Global Optimization*. New York, NY: Springer.

Prior, John (1998). "Eugenic Evolution for Combinatorial Optimization." MA thesis. Austin, TX: Department of Computer Sciences, The University of Texas at Austin.

Prusinkiewicz, Przemyslaw, Mark Hammel, Jim Hanan, and Radomir Mech (1996). "L-Systems: From the Theory to Visual Models of Plants." In *Proceedings of the CSIRO Symposium on Computational Challenges in Life Sciences*, 1–32.

Pugh, Justin K., Lisa B. Soros, and Kenneth O. Stanley (2016). "Quality Diversity: A New Frontier for Evolutionary Computation." *Frontiers in Robotics and AI* 3, 40.

Qiu, Xin, Yulu Gan, Conor F. Hayes, Qiyao Liang, Elliot Meyerson, Babak Hodjat, and Risto Miikkulainen (2025). "Evolution Strategies at Scale: LLM Fine-Tuning Beyond Reinforcement Learning." *arXiv:2509.24372*.

Qiu, Xin, Elliot Meyerson, and Risto Miikkulainen (2020). "Quantifying Point-Prediction Uncertainty in Neural Networks via Residual Estimation with an I/O Kernel." In

Proceedings of the Eighth International Conference on Learning Representations, 2146–2180.

Qiu, Xin, and Risto Miikkulainen (2023). "Shortest Edit Path Crossover: A Theory-Driven Solution to the Permutation Problem in Evolutionary Neural Architecture Search." In *Proceedings of the 40th International Conference on Machine Learning*, 28422–28447.

Radcliffe, Nicholas J. (1993). "Genetic Set Recombination and Its Application to Neural Network Topology Optimisation." *Neural Computing & Applications* 1, 67–90.

Rafailov, Rafael, Archit Sharma, Eric Mitchell, Stefano Ermon, Christopher D. Manning, and Chelsea Finn (2023). "Direct Preference Optimization: Your Language Model Is Secretly a Reward Model." In *Advances in Neural Information Processing Systems 35*, 53728–53741.

Rajagopalan, Padmini, Kay E. Holekamp, and Risto Miikkulainen (2014). "The Evolution of General Intelligence." In *Artificial Life 14: Proceedings of the Fourteenth International Conference on the Synthesis and Simulation of Living Systems*, 63–70.

Rajagopalan, Padmini, Kay E. Holekamp, and Risto Miikkulainen (2019). "Factors That Affect the Evolution of Complex Cooperative Behavior." In *ALIFE 2019: The 2019 Conference on Artificial Life*, 333–340.

Rajagopalan, Padmini, Kay E. Holekamp, and Risto Miikkulainen (2020). "Evolution of Complex Coordinated Behavior." In *Proceedings of the IEEE Congress on Evolutionary Computation*, 3098–3105.

Rajagopalan, Padmini, Aditya Rawal, Risto Miikkulainen, Marc A. Wiseman, and Kay E. Holekamp (2011). "The Role of Reward Structure, Coordination Mechanism and Net Return in the Evolution of Cooperation." In *Proceedings of the IEEE Conference on Computational Intelligence and Games*, 258–265.

Ramachandran, Prajit, Barret Zoph, and Quoc V. Le (2018). "Searching for Activation Functions." In *Workshop Track, Sixth International Conference on Learning Representations*.

Rasmussen, Carl E., and Christopher K. I. Williams (2006). *Gaussian Processes for Machine Learning*. Cambridge, MA: MIT Press.

Raup, David M. (1986). "Biological Extinction in Earth History." *Science* 231, 1528–1533.

Rawal, Aditya, Janette Boughman, and Risto Miikkulainen (2014). "Evolution of Communication in Mate Selection." In *Artificial Life 14: Proceedings of the Fourteenth International Conference on the Synthesis and Simulation of Living Systems*, 16–22.

Rawal, Aditya, and Risto Miikkulainen (2020). "From Nodes to Networks: Evolving Recurrent Neural Networks." In *Deep Neural Evolution: Deep Learning with Evolutionary Computation*, edited by Hitoshi Iba and Nasimul Noman, 233–251. New York, NY: Springer.

Rawal, Aditya, Padmini Rajagopalan, and Risto Miikkulainen (2010). "Constructing Competitive and Cooperative Agent Behavior Using Coevolution." In *Proceedings of the IEEE Conference on Computational Intelligence and Games*, 107–114.

Real, Esteban, Alok Aggarwal, Yanping Huang, and Quoc V. Le (2019). "Regularized Evolution for Image Classifier Architecture Search." In *Proceedings of the AAAI Conference on Artificial Intelligence, 33*, 4780–4789.

Real, Esteban, Chen Liang, David So, and Quoc V. Le (2020). "AutoML-Zero: Evolving Machine Learning Algorithms from Scratch." In *Proceedings of the 37th International Conference on Machine Learning*, 8007–8019.

Real, Esteban, Sherry Moore, Andrew Selle, Saurabh Saxena, Yutaka L. Suematsu, Jie Tan, Quoc V. Le, and Alexey Kurakin (2017). "Large-Scale Evolution of Image Classifiers." In *Proceedings of the 34th International Conference on Machine Learning*, 2902–2911.

Rechenberg, Ingo (1973). *Evolutionsstrategie: Optimierung technischer Systeme nach Prinzipien der biologischen Evolution.* [Evolution strategy: Optimization of technical systems according to the principles of biological evolution]. Stuttgart, Germany: Frommann-Holzboog Verlag.

Reed, Russell (1993). "Pruning Algorithms—A Survey." *IEEE Transactions on Neural Networks* 4, 740–747.

Reisinger, Joseph, and Risto Miikkulainen (2006). "Selecting for Evolvable Representations." In *GECCO'06: Proceedings of the 8th Annual Conference on Genetic and Evolutionary Computation*, 1297–1304.

Reisinger, Joseph, and Risto Miikkulainen (2007). "Acquiring Evolvability Through Adaptive Representations." In *GECCO'07: Proceeedings of the 9th Annual Conference on Genetic and Evolutionary Computation*, 1045–1052.

Reynolds, John, James S. Plank, and Catherine Schuman (2019). "Intelligent Reservoir Generation for Liquid State Machines Using Evolutionary Optimization." In *Proceedings of the International Joint Conference on Neural Networks*, 3992–3999.

Reynolds, Robert G., Zbigniew Michalewicz, and Michael J. Cavaretta (1995). "Using Cultural Algorithms for Constraint Handling in GENOCOP." In *Evolutionary Programming IV: Proceedings of the Fourth Annual Conference on Evolutionary Programming*, edited by John. R. McDonnell, Robert. G. Reynolds and David B. Fogel, 289–305. Cambridge, MA: MIT Press.

Ribalta Lorenzo, Pablo, and Jakub Nalepa (2018). "Memetic Evolution of Deep Neural Networks." In *GECCO'18: Proceedings of the Genetic and Evolutionary Computation Conference*, 505–512.

Risi, Sebastian, Charles E. Hughes, and Kenneth O. Stanley (2010). "Evolving Plastic Neural Networks with Novelty Search." *Adaptive Behavior* 18, 470–491.

Risi, Sebastian, Joel Lehman, David B. D'Ambrosio, Ryan Hall, and Kenneth O. Stanley (2016). "Petalz: Search-Based Procedural Content Generation for the Casual Gamer." *IEEE Transactions on Computational Intelligence and AI in Games* 8, 244–255.

Risi, Sebastian, and Kenneth O. Stanley (2010). "Indirectly Encoding Neural Plasticity as a Pattern of Local Rules." In *From Animals to Animats 11: 11th International Conference on Simulation of Adaptive Behavior*, 533–543.

Risi, Sebastian, and Kenneth O. Stanley (2012a). "An Enhanced Hypercube-Based Encoding for Evolving the Placement, Density, and Connectivity of Neurons." *Artificial Life* 18, 331–363.

Risi, Sebastian, and Kenneth O. Stanley (2012b). "A Unified Approach to Evolving Plasticity and Neural Geometry." In *Proceedings of the International Joint Conference on Neural Networks*, 1–8.

Risi, Sebastian, and Kenneth O. Stanley (2019). "Deep Neuroevolution of Recurrent and Discrete World Models." In *GECCO'19: Proceedings of the Genetic and Evolutionary Computation Conference*, 456–462.

Risi, Sebastian, and Kenneth O. Stanley (2021). "Deep Innovation Protection: Confronting the Credit Assignment Problem in Training Heterogeneous Neural Architectures." In *Proceedings of the AAAI Conference on Artificial Intelligence, 35*, 12391–12399.

Risi, Sebastian, and Julian Togelius (2015). "Neuroevolution in Games: State of the Art and Open Challenges." *IEEE Transactions on Computational Intelligence and AI in Games* 9, 25–41.

Robson, Ann L. (2023). *Critical/Sensitive Periods*. https://www.encyclopedia.com/children/applied-and-social-sciences-magazines/criticalsensitive-periods. Retrieved August 31, 2025.

Rock, David, and Heidi Grant (2016). *Why Diverse Teams Are Smarter*. https://vcportal.ventura.org/committees/di/HBR._Why_diverse_teams_are_smarter.PDF. Retrieved August 31, 2025.

Rothe, Rasmus, Radu Timofte, and Luc Van Gool (2018). "Deep Expectation of Real and Apparent Age from a Single Image Without Facial Landmarks." *International Journal of Computer Vision* 126, 144–157.

Routley, Nick (2017). *Visualizing the Trillion-Fold Increase in Computing Power*. https://www.visualcapitalist.com/visualizing-trillion-fold-increase-computing-power/. Retrieved August 31, 2025.

Rumelhart, David E., Geoffrey E. Hinton, and Ronald J. Williams (1986). "Learning Internal Representations by Error Propagation." In *Parallel Distributed Processing: Explorations in the Microstructure of Cognition, Vol. 1: Foundations*, edited by David E. Rumelhart, James L. McClelland and PDP Research Group, 318–362. Cambridge, MA: MIT Press.

Ruppin, Eytan (2002). "Evolutionary Autonomous Agents: A Neuroscience Perspective." *Nature Reviews Neuroscience* 3, 132–141.

Russakovsky, Olga, Jia Deng, Hao Su, Jonathan Krause, Sanjeev Satheesh, Sean Ma, Zhiheng Huang, Andrej Karpathy, Aditya Khosla, Michael Bernstein, Alexander C. Berg, and Fei-Fei Li (2015). "ImageNet Large Scale Visual Recognition Challenge." *International Journal of Computer Vision* 115, 211–252.

Ryan Ruggiero, Vincent (2012). *Beyond Feelings: A Guide to Critical Thinking*. New York, NY: McGraw-Hill.

Salge, Christoph, Cornelius Glackin, and Daniel Polani (2014). "Empowerment–An Introduction." In *Guided Self-Organization: Inception*, edited by Mikhail Prokopenko, 67–114. New York, NY: Springer.

Salih, Adham, and Amiram Moshaiov (2022). "Evolving Topology and Weights of Specialized and Non-specialized Neuro-controllers for Robot Motion in Various Environments." *Neural Computing and Applications* 34, 17071–17086.

Salih, Adham, and Amiram Moshaiov (2023a). "Neuro-evolution-Based Generic Missile Guidance Law for Many-Scenarios." *Applied Soft Computing* 152, 111210.

Salih, Adham, and Amiram Moshaiov (2023b). "Promoting Transfer of Robot Neuromotion-Controllers by Many-Objective Topology and Weight Evolution." *IEEE Transactions on Evolutionary Computation* 27, 385–395.

Salimans, Tim, Jonathan Ho, Xi Chen, Szymon Sidor, and Ilya Sutskever (2017). "Evolution Strategies as a Scalable Alternative to Reinforcement Learning." *arXiv:1703.03864*.

Samet, Hanan (1984). "The Quadtree and Related Hierarchical Data Structures." *ACM Computing Surveys* 16, 187–260.

Samuel, Arthur L. (1959). "Some Studies in Machine Learning Using the Game of Checkers." *IBM Journal of Research and Development* 3, 210–229.

Sandler, Mark, Andrew Howard, Menglong Zhu, Andrey Zhmoginov, and Liang-Chieh Chen (2018). "MobileNetV2: Inverted Residuals and Linear Bottlenecks." In *Proceedings of the IEEE/CVF Conference on Computer Vision and Pattern Recognition*, 4510–4520.

Sarti, Stefano, and Gabriela Ochoa (2021). "A NEAT Visualisation of Neuroevolution Trajectories." In *Applications of Evolutionary Computation—24th International Conference*, 714–728.

Saunders, Gregory M., and Jordan B. Pollack (1996). "The Evolution of Communication Schemes over Continuous Channels." In *From Animals to Animats 4: Proceedings of the Fourth International Conference on Simulation of Adaptive Behavior*, edited by Pattie Maes, Maja J. Mataric, Jean-Arcady Meyer, Jordan Pollack and S. W. Wilson, 580–589. Cambridge, MA: MIT Press.

Schaffer, J. David, Rich A. Caruana, and Larry J. Eshelman (1990). "Using Genetic Search to Exploit the Emergent Behavior of Neural Networks." *Physica D: Nonlinear Phenomena*, 244–248.

Schaffer, J. David, Darrell Whitley, and Larry J. Eshelman (1992). "Combinations of Genetic Algorithms and Neural Networks: A Survey of the State of the Art." In *COGANN-92: International Workshop on Combinations of Genetic Algorithms and Neural Networks*, 1–37. Los Alamitos, CA: IEEE Computer Society Press.

Schmidhuber, Jürgen (1992). "Learning to Control Fast-Weight Memories: An Alternative to Dynamic Recurrent Networks." *Neural Computation* 4, 131–139.

Schmidhuber, Jürgen, Daan Wierstra, Matteo Gagliolo, and Faustino Gomez (2007). "Training Recurrent Networks by Evolino." *Neural Computation* 19, 757–779.

Schrum, Jacob, Igor V. Karpov, and Risto Miikkulainen (2011). "UT^2: Human-like Behavior via Neuroevolution of Combat Behavior and Replay of Human Traces." In *Proceedings of the IEEE Conference on Computational Intelligence and Games*, 329–336.

Schrum, Jacob, Igor V. Karpov, and Risto Miikkulainen (2012). "Humanlike Combat Behavior via Multiobjective Neuroevolution." In *Believable Bots*, edited by Philip Hingston, 119–150. New York, NY: Springer.

Schrum, Jacob, and Risto Miikkulainen (2016a). "Discovering Multimodal Behavior in Ms. Pac-Man Through Evolution of Modular Neural Networks." *IEEE Transactions on Computational Intelligence and AI in Games* 8, 67–81.

Schrum, Jacob, and Risto Miikkulainen (2016b). "Solving Multiple Isolated, Interleaved, and Blended Tasks Through Modular Neuroevolution." *Evolutionary Computation* 24, 459–490.

Schulman, John, Filip Wolski, Prafulla Dhariwal, Alec Radford, and Oleg Klimov (2017). "Proximal Policy Optimization Algorithms." *arXiv:1707.06347*.

Schultz, Wolfram (2024). "A Dopamine Mechanism for Reward Maximization." *Proceedings of the National Academy of Sciences* 121, e2316658121.

Schuman, Catherine, J. Parker Mitchell, Robert M. Patton, Thomas E. Potok, and James S. Plank (2020). "Evolutionary Optimization for Neuromorphic Systems." In *NICE'20: Proceedings of the 2020 Annual Neuro-Inspired Computational Elements Workshop*, 2:1–2:9.

Schuman, Catherine, Robert M. Patton, Shruti Kulkarni, Maryam Parsa, Christopher Stahl, N. Quentin Haas, J. Parker Mitchell, Shay Snyder, Amelie Nagle, Alexandra Shanafield, and Thomas E. Potok (2022). "Evolutionary vs. Imitation Learning for Neuromorphic Control at the Edge." *Neuromorphic Computing and Engineering* 2, 014002.

Schuman, Catherine, Thomas E. Potok, Robert M. Patton, J. Douglas Birdwell, Mark E. Dean, Garrett S. Rose, and James S. Plank (2017). "A Survey of Neuromorphic Computing and Neural Networks in Hardware." *arXiv:1705.06963*.

Schwefel, Hans-Paul (1977). *Numerische Optimierung von Computer-Modellen mittels der Evolutionsstrategie: mit einer vergleichenden Einführung in die Hill-Climbing- und Zufallsstrategie*. Basel, Switzerland: Birkhäuser.

Secretan, Jimmy, Nicholas Beato, David B. D'Ambrosio, Adelein Rodriguez, Adam Campbell, J. T. Folsom-Kovarik, and Kenneth O. Stanley (2011). "Picbreeder: A Case Study in Collaborative Evolutionary Exploration of Design Space." *Evolutionary Computation* 19, 345–371.

Sehnke, Frank, Christian Osendorfer, Thomas Rückstieß, Alex Graves, Jan Peters, and Jürgen Schmidhuber (2010). "Parameter-Exploring Policy Gradients." *Neural Networks* 23, 551–559.

Shahrzad, Hormoz, Babak Hodjat, and Risto Miikkulainen (2024). "EVOTER: Evolution of Transparent Explainable Rule-Sets." *ACM Transactions on Evolutionary Learning and Optimization* 5, Article 11, 1–30.

Shami, Tareq M., Ayman A. El-Saleh, Mohammed Alswaitti, Qasem Al-Tashi, Mhd A. Summakieh, and Seyedali Mirjalili (2022). "Particle Swarm Optimization: A Comprehensive Survey." *IEEE Access* 10, 10031–10061.

Sharma, Shubham, Jette Henderson, and Joydeep Ghosh (2020). "CERTIFAI: A Common Framework to Provide Explanations and Analyse the Fairness and Robustness of Black-Box Models." In *Proceedings of the AAAI/ACM Conference on AI, Ethics, and Society*, 166–172. New York, NY: Association for Computing Machinery.

Shayani, Hooman, Peter J. Bentley, and Andy Tyrrell (2008). "An FPGA-Based Model Suitable for Evolution and Development of Spiking Neural Networks." In *Proceedings of the European Symposium on Artificial Neural Networks*, 197–202.

Shim, Yoonsik, Sanghyun Kim, and Chiwook Kim (2004). "Evolving Flying Creatures with Path-Following Behavior." In *ALife IX: Proceedings of the 9th International Conference on the Simulation and Synthesis of Living Systems*, 125–132.

Silva, Filipe, Paulo Urbano, Luis C. Correia, and Anders L. Christensen (2015). "odNEAT: An Algorithm for Decentralised Online Evolution of Robotic Controllers." *Evolutionary Computation* 23, 421–449.

Silver, David, Thomas Hubert, Julian Schrittwieser, Ioannis Antonoglou, Matthew Lai, Arthur Guez, Marc Lanctot, Laurent Sifre, Dharshan Kumaran, Thore Graepel, Timothy Lillicrap, Karen Simonyan, and Demis Hassabis (2018). "A General Reinforcement Learning Algorithm That Masters Chess, Shogi, and Go Through Self-play." *Science* 362, 1140–1144.

Simione, Luca, and Stefano Nolfi (2020). "Long-Term Progress and Behavior Complexification in Competitive Coevolution." *Artificial Life* 26, 1–22.

Simon, Herbert A. (1969). *The Sciences of the Artificial*. Cambridge, MA: MIT Press.

Simon, Joel (2018). *Artbreeder*. https://www.artbreeder.com/. Retrieved August 31, 2025.

Simonyan, Karen, and Andrew Zisserman (2015). "Very Deep Convolutional Networks for Large-Scale Image Recognition." In *Proceedings of the Third International Conference on Learning Representations*.

Sims, Karl (1991). "Artificial Evolution for Computer Graphics." In *Proceedings of the Annual Conference on Computer Graphics and Interactive Techniques*, 319–328.

Sims, Karl (1994). "Evolving 3D Morphology and Behavior by Competition." In *Artificial Life IV: Proceedings of the Fourth International Workshop on the Synthesis and Simulation of Living Systems*, edited by Rodney A. Brooks and Pattie Maes, 28–39. Cambridge, MA: MIT Press.

Singleton, Jenny L., and Elissa L. Newport (2004). "When Learners Surpass Their Models: The Acquisition of American Sign Language from Inconsistent Input." *Cognitive Psychology* 49, 370–407.

Sinha, Ankur, Pekka Malo, Peng Xu, and Kalyanmoy Deb (2014). "A Bilevel Optimization Approach to Automated Parameter Tuning." In *GECCO'14: Proceedings of the 2014 Annual Conference on Genetic and Evolutionary Computation*, 847–854.

Sipper, Moshe, Jason H. Moore, and Ryan J. Urbanowicz (2019). "Solution and Fitness Evolution (SAFE): Coevolving Solutions and Their Objective Functions." In *Genetic Programming: 22nd European Conference*, edited by Lukas Sekanina, Ting Hu, Nuno Lourenço, Hendrik Richter and Pablo García-Sánchez, 146–161. New York, NY: Springer.

Sit, Yiu Fai, and Risto Miikkulainen (2005). "Learning Basic Navigation for Personal Satellite Assistant Using Neuroevolution." In *GECCO'05: Proceedings of the 7th Annual Conference on Genetic and Evolutionary Computation*, 1913–1920.

Smith, Jennifer E., Kenna D. S. Lehmann, Tracy M. Montgomery, Eli D. Strauss, and Kay E. Holekamp (2017). "Insights from Long-Term Field Studies of Mammalian Carnivores." *Journal of Mammalogy* 98, 631–641.

So, David, Quoc V. Le, and Chen Liang (2019). "The Evolved Transformer." In *Proceedings of the 36th International Conference on Machine Learning*, 5877–5886.

Sohl-Dickstein, Jascha, Eric Weiss, Niru Maheswaranathan, and Surya Ganguli (2015). "Deep Unsupervised Learning Using Nonequilibrium Thermodynamics." In *Proceedings of the 32nd International Conference on Machine Learning*, 2256–2265.

Solé, Ricard (2016). "The Major Synthetic Evolutionary Transitions." *Philosophical Transactions of the Royal Society B: Biological Sciences* 371, 20160175.

Solkoll (2005). *Dragon Trees*. https://commons.wikimedia.org/wiki/File:Dragon_trees.jpg. Retrieved January 17, 2026.

Solomon, Matthew, Terence Soule, and Robert B. Heckendorn (2012). "A Comparison of a Communication Strategies in Cooperative Learning." In *GECCO'12: Proceedings of the 14th Annual Conference on Genetic and Evolutionary Computation*, 153–160.

Soltoggio, Andrea, John A. Bullinaria, Claudio Mattiussi, Peter Dürr, and Dario Floreano (2008). "Evolutionary Advantages of Neuromodulated Plasticity in Dynamic, Reward-Based Scenarios." In *Artificial Life XI: Proceedings of the Eleventh International Conference on the Simulation and Synthesis of Living Systems*, edited by Seth Bullock, Jason Noble, Richard Watson and Mark A. Bedau, 569–576. Cambridge, MA: MIT Press.

Soltoggio, Andrea, Peter Dürr, Claudio Mattiussi, and Dario Floreano (2007). "Evolving Neuromodulatory Topologies for Reinforcement Learning-like Problems." In *Proceedings of the IEEE Congress on Evolutionary Computation*, 2471–2478.

Soltoggio, Andrea, Kenneth O. Stanley, and Sebastian Risi (2018). "Born to Learn: The Inspiration, Progress, and Future of Evolved Plastic Artificial Neural Networks." *Neural Networks* 108, 48–67.

Song, Sen, Kenneth D. Miller, and Larry F. Abbott (2000). "Competitive Hebbian Learning Through Spike-Timing-Dependent Synaptic Plasticity." *Nature Neuroscience* 3, 919–926.

Song, Xingyou, Wenbo Gao, Yuxiang Yang, Krzysztof Choromanski, Aldo Pacchiano, and Yunhao Tang (2020). "ES-MAML: Simple Hessian-Free Meta Learning." In *Proceedings of the Eighth International Conference on Learning Representations*, 9392–9410.

Song, Xingyou, Yuxiang Yang, Krzysztof Choromanski, Ken Caluwaerts, Wenbo Gao, Chelsea Finn, and Jie Tan (2020). "Rapidly Adaptable Legged Robots via Evolutionary Meta-learning." In *Proceedings of the IEEE/RSJ International Conference on Intelligent Robots and Systems*, 3769–3776.

Spector, Lee, and Sean Luke (1996). "Cultural Transmission of Information in Genetic Programming." In *Genetic Programming 1996: Proceedings of the First Annual Conference*, edited by John R Koza, David E Goldberg, David B. Fogel and L. R. Riolo, 209–214. Cambridge, MA: MIT Press.

Sporns, Olaf, and Richard F. Betzel (2016). "Modular Brain Networks." *Annual Reviews of Psychology* 67, 613–640.

Srivastava, Nitish, Geoffrey E. Hinton, Alex Krizhevsky, Ilya Sutskever, and Ruslan R. Salakhutdinov (2014). "Dropout: A Simple Way to Prevent Neural Networks from Overfitting." *Journal of Machine Learning Research* 15, 1929–1958.

Srivastava, Rupesh K., Klaus Greff, and Jürgen Schmidhuber (2015). "Highway Networks." In *Deep Learning Workshop, 32nd International Conference on Machine Learning*.

Stanley, Kenneth O. (2003). "Efficient Evolution of Neural Networks Through Complexification." PhD thesis. Austin, TX: Department of Computer Sciences, The University of Texas at Austin.

Stanley, Kenneth O. (2007). "Compositional Pattern Producing Networks: A Novel Abstraction of Development." *Genetic Programming and Evolvable Machines* 8, 131–162.

Stanley, Kenneth O., Bobby D. Bryant, and Risto Miikkulainen (2003). "Evolving Adaptive Neural Networks with and Without Adaptive Synapses." In *Proceedings of the IEEE Congress on Evolutionary Computation*, 2557–2564.

Stanley, Kenneth O., Bobby D. Bryant, and Risto Miikkulainen (2005). "Real-Time Neuroevolution in the NERO Video Game." *IEEE Transactions on Evolutionary Computation* 9, 653–668.

Stanley, Kenneth O., Jeff Clune, Joel Lehman, and Risto Miikkulainen (2019). "Designing Neural Networks Through Evolutionary Algorithms." *Nature Machine Intelligence* 1, 24–35.

Stanley, Kenneth O., David B. D'Ambrosio, and Jason Gauci (2009). "A Hypercube-Based Encoding for Evolving Large-scale Neural Networks." *Artificial Life* 15, 185–212.

Stanley, Kenneth O., and Joel Lehman (2015). *Why Greatness Cannot Be Planned: The Myth of the Objective.* New York, NY: Springer.

Stanley, Kenneth O., and Risto Miikkulainen (2002). "Evolving Neural Networks Through Augmenting Topologies." *Evolutionary Computation* 10, 99–127.

Stanley, Kenneth O., and Risto Miikkulainen (2003). "A Taxonomy for Artificial Embryogeny." *Artificial Life* 9, 93–130.

Stanley, Kenneth O., and Risto Miikkulainen (2004). "Competitive Coevolution Through Evolutionary Complexification." *Journal of Artificial Intelligence Research* 21, 63–100.

Steels, Luc L. (2016). "Agent-Based Models for the Emergence and Evolution of Grammar." *Philosophical Transactions of the Royal Society B: Biological Sciences* 371, 20150447.

Steuer, Inge, and Pierre A. Guertin (2019). "Central Pattern Generators in the Brainstem and Spinal Cord: An Overview of Basic Principles, Similarities and Differences." *Reviews in the Neurosciences* 30, 107–164.

Storn, Rainer M., and Kenneth V. Price (1997). "Differential Evolution—A Simple and Efficient Heuristic for Global Optimization over Continuous Spaces." *Journal of Global Optimization* 11, 341–359.

Strassen, Volker (1969). "Gaussian Elimination Is Not Optimal." *Numerische Mathematik* 13, 354–356.

Sudhakaran, Shyam, Miguel González-Duque, Matthias Freiberger, Claire Glanois, Elias Najarro, and Sebastian Risi (2023). "MarioGPT: Open-Ended Text2Level Generation Through Large Language Models." In *Advances in Neural Information Processing Systems 36*, 54213–54227.

Sudhakaran, Shyam, Djordje Grbic, Siyan Li, Adam Katona, Elias Najarro, Claire Glanois, and Sebastian Risi (2021). "Growing 3D Artefacts and Functional Machines with Neural Cellular Automata." In *ALIFE 2021: The 2021 Conference on Artificial Life*, 108–116.

Sun, Yanan, Bing Xue, Mengjie Zhang, and Gary G. Yen (2020). "Evolving Deep Convolutional Neural Networks for Image Classification." *IEEE Transactions on Evolutionary Computation* 24, 394–407.

Szathmáry, Eörs (2015). "Toward Major Evolutionary Transitions Theory 2.0." *Proceedings of the National Academy of Sciences* 112, 10104–10111.

Szegedy, Christian, Vincent Vanhoucke, Sergey Ioffe, Jonathon Shlens, and Zbigniew Wojna (2016). "Rethinking the Inception Architecture for Computer Vision." In *Proceedings of the IEEE Conference on Computer Vision and Pattern Recognition*, 2818–2826.

Takagi, Hideyuki (2001). "Interactive Evolutionary Computation: Fusion of the Capabilities of EC Optimization and Human Evaluation." *Proceedings of the IEEE* 89, 1275–1296.

Tan, James (2017). *Investing in ICOS: Results May Vary*. https://akaidotto.blogspot.com/. Retrieved August 31, 2017.

Tan, Mingxing, and Quoc V. Le (2019). "EfficientNet: Rethinking Model Scaling for Convolutional Neural Networks." In *Proceedings of the 36th International Conference on Machine Learning*, 6105–6114.

Tan, Mingxing, and Quoc V. Le (2021). "EfficientNetV2: Smaller Models and Faster Training." In *Proceedings of the 38th International Conference on Machine Learning*, 10096–10106.

Tang, Yujin, Duong Nguyen, and David Ha (2020). "Neuroevolution of Self-Interpretable Agents." In *GECCO'20: Proceedings of the 2020 Genetic and Evolutionary Computation Conference*, 414–424.

Tang, Yujin, Jie Tan, and Tatsuya Harada (2020). "Learning Agile Locomotion via Adversarial Training." In *Proceedings of the IEEE/RSJ International Conference On Intelligent Robots and Systems*, 6098–6105.

Tang, Yujin, Yingtao Tian, and David Ha (2022). "EvoJAX: Hardware-Accelerated Neuroevolution." In *GECCO'22: Proceedings of the Genetic and Evolutionary Computation Conference Companion*, 308–311.

Tansey, Wesley, Eliana Feasley, and Risto Miikkulainen (2012). "Accelerating Evolution via Egalitarian Social Learning." In *GECCO'12: Proceedings of the 14th Annual Conference on Genetic and Evolutionary Computation*, 919–926.

Taylor, Ross, Marcin Kardas, Guillem Cucurull, Thomas Scialom, Anthony Hartshorn, Elvis Saravia, Andrew Poulton, Viktor Kerkez, and Robert Stojnic (2022). "Galactica: A Large Language Model for Science." *arXiv:2211.09085*.

Templier, Paul, Emmanuel Rachelson, and Dennis G Wilson (2021). "A Geometric Encoding for Neural Network Evolution." In *GECCO'21: Proceedings of the Genetic and Evolutionary Computation Conference*, 919–927.

Teyke, Thomas, Klaudiusz R. Weiss, and Irving Kupfermann (1990). "An Identified Neuron (CPR) Evokes Neuronal Responses Reflecting Food Arousal in Aplysia." *Science* 247, 85–87.

Todd, Graham, Sam Earle, Muhammad U. Nasir, Michael C. Green, and Julian Togelius (2023). "Level Generation Through Large Language Models." In *Proceedings of the 18th International Conference on the Foundations of Digital Games*, 1–8.

Togelius, Julian, Georgios N. Yannakakis, Kenneth O. Stanley, and Cameron Browne (2011). "Search-Based Procedural Content Generation: A Taxonomy and Survey." *IEEE Transactions on Computational Intelligence and AI in Games* 3, 172–186.

Tonelli, Paul, and Jean-Baptiste Mouret (2013). "On the Relationships Between Generative Encodings, Regularity, and Learning Abilities When Evolving Plastic Artificial Neural Networks." *PloS One* 8, e79138.

Toutouh, Jamal, Erik Hemberg, and Una-May O'Reilly (2019). "Spatial Evolutionary Generative Adversarial Networks." In *GECCO'19: Proceedings of the Genetic and Evolutionary Computation Conference*, 472–480.

Touvron, Hugo, Louis Martin, Kevin Stone, et al. (2023). "Llama 2: Open Foundation and Fine-Tuned Chat Models." *arXiv:2307.09288.*

Towell, Geoffrey G., and Jude W. Shavlik (1994). "Knowledge-Based Artificial Neural Networks." *Artificial Intelligence* 70, 119–165.

Trianni, Vittorio, Elio Tuci, Christos Ampatzis, and Marco Dorigo (2014). "Evolutionary Swarm Robotics: A Theoretical and Methodological Itinerary from Individual Neuro-Controllers to Collective Behaviors." In *Horizons of Evolutionary Robotics*, edited by Patricia A. Vargas, Ezequiel A. Di Paolo, Inman Harvey and Phil Husbands, 153–178. Cambridge, MA: MIT Press.

Turing, Alan (1952). "The Chemical Basis of Morphogenesis." *Philosophical Transactions of the Royal Society B* 237, 37–72.

Turney, Peter D. (2020). "Symbiosis Promotes Fitness Improvements in the Game of Life." *Artificial Life* 26, 338–365.

Tutum, Cem C., Suhaib Abdulquddos, and Risto Miikkulainen (2021). "Generalization of Agent Behavior Through Explicit Representation of Context." In *Proceedings of the IEEE Conference on Games*, 95–101.

Tyulmankov, Danil, Guangyu R. Yang, and Larry F. Abbott (2022). "Meta-learning Synaptic Plasticity and Memory Addressing for Continual Familiarity Detection." *Neuron* 110, 544–557.e8.

Ulyanov, Dmitry, Andrea Vedaldi, and Victor Lempitsky (2018). "Deep Image Prior." In *Proceedings of the IEEE/CVF Conference on Computer Vision and Pattern Recognition*, 9446–9454.

US Department of Energy (2019). *Detecting Radiological Threats in Urban Areas.* https://www.topcoder.com/challenges/30085346. Retrieved August 31, 2025.

Valsalam, Vinod, James A. Bednar, and Risto Miikkulainen (2005). "Constructing Good Learners Using Evolved Pattern Generators." In *GECCO'05: Proceedings of the 7th Annual Conference on Genetic and Evolutionary Computation*, 11–18.

Valsalam, Vinod, James A. Bednar, and Risto Miikkulainen (2007). "Developing Complex Systems Using Evolved Pattern Generators." *IEEE Transactions on Evolutionary Computation* 11, 181–198.

Valsalam, Vinod, Jonathan Hiller, Robert MacCurdy, Hod Lipson, and Risto Miikkulainen (2013). "Constructing Controllers for Physical Multilegged Robots Using the ENSO Neuroevolution Approach." *Evolutionary Intelligence* 14, 303–331.

Valsalam, Vinod, and Risto Miikkulainen (2011). "Evolving Symmetry for Modular System Design." *IEEE Transactions on Evolutionary Computation* 15, 368–386.

van Eck Conradie, Alex, Risto Miikkulainen, and Christiaan Aldrich (2002a). "Adaptive Control Utilising Neural Swarming." In *GECCO'02: Proceedings of the 4th Annual Conference on Genetic and Evolutionary Computation*, 60–67.

van Eck Conradie, Alex, Risto Miikkulainen, and Christiaan Aldrich (2002b). "Intelligent Process Control Utilizing Symbiotic Memetic Neuro-evolution." In *Proceedings of the IEEE Congress on Evolutionary Computation*, 623–628.

Vargas, Patricia A., Ezequiel Di Paolo, Inman Harvey and Philip Husbands, eds. (2014). *The Horizons of Evolutionary Robotics*. Cambridge, MA: MIT Press.

Vassiliades, Vassilis, Konstantinos Chatzilygeroudis, and Jean-Baptiste Mouret (2017). "Using Centroidal Voronoi Tessellations to Scale up the Multidimensional Archive of Phenotypic Elites Algorithm." *IEEE Transactions on Evolutionary Computation* 22, 623–630.

Vaswani, Ashish, Noam Shazeer, Niki Parmar, Jakob Uszkoreit, Llion Jones, Aidan N. Gomez, Lukasz Kaiser, and Illia Polosukhin (2017). "Attention Is All You Need." In *Advances in Neural Information Processing Systems 30*, 5999–6009.

Venkadesh, Siva, Alexander O. Komendantov, Stanislav Listopad, Eric O. Scott, Kenneth A. De Jong, Jeffrey L. Krichmar, and Giorgio A. Ascoli (2018). "Evolving Simple Models of Diverse Intrinsic Dynamics in Hippocampal Neuron Types." *Frontiers of Neuroinformatics* 12, Article 8.

Venkatramanan, Srinivasan, Bryan Lewis, Jiangzhuo Chen, Dave Higdon, Anil Vullikanti, and Madhav Marathe (2018). "Using Data-Driven Agent-Based Models for Forecasting Emerging Infectious Diseases." *Epidemics* 22, 43–49.

Verbancsics, Phillip, and Kenneth O. Stanley (2011). "Constraining Connectivity to Encourage Modularity in HyperNEAT." In *GECCO'11: Proceedings of the 13th Annual Conference on Genetic and Evolutionary Computation*, 1483–1490.

Verel, Sébastien, Gabriela Ochoa, and Marco Tomassini (2010). "Local Optima Networks of NK Landscapes with Neutrality." *IEEE Transactions on Evolutionary Computation* 15, 783–797.

Versace, Elisabetta, Antone Martinho-Truswell, Alex Kacelnik, and Giorgio Vallortigara (2018). "Priors in Animal and Artificial Intelligence: Where Does Learning Begin?" *Trends in Cognitive Sciences* 22, 963–965.

Vinyals, Oriol, Alexander Toshev, Samy Bengio, and Dumitru Erhan (2015). "Show and tell: A Neural Image Caption Generator." In *Proceedings of the IEEE Conference on Computer Vision and Pattern Recognition*, 3156–3164.

Voelkle, Manuel C., Natalie C. Ebner, Ulman Lindenberger, and Michaela Riediger (2012). "Let Me Guess How Old You Are: Effects of Age, Gender, and Facial Expression on Perceptions of Age." *Psychology and Aging* 27, 265.

Volz, Vanessa, Jacob Schrum, Jialin Liu, Simon M. Lucas, Adam Smith, and Sebastian Risi (2018). "Evolving Mario Levels in the Latent Space of a Deep Convolutional Generative Adversarial Network." In *GECCO'18: Proceedings of the Genetic and Evolutionary Computation Conference*, 221–228.

Wagner, Andreas (2005). *Robustness and Evolvability in Living Systems*. Princeton, NJ: Princeton University Press.

Wagner, Kyle, James A. Reggia, Juan Uriagereka, and Gerald S. Wilkinson (2003). "Progress in the Simulation of Emergent Communication and Language." *Adaptive Behavior* 11, 37–69.

Wang, Bin, Yanan Sun, Bing Xue, and Mengjie Zhang (2018). "A Hybrid Differential Evolution Approach to Designing Deep Convolutional Neural Networks for Image Classification." In *Advances in Artificial Intelligence*, edited by Tanja Mitrovic, Bing Xue and Xiaodong Li, 237–250. New York, NY: Springer.

Wang, Chao, Jiaxuan Zhao, Licheng Jiao, Lingling Li, Fang Liu, and Shuyuan Yang (2025). "When Large Language Models Meet Evolutionary Algorithms: Potential Enhancements and Challenges." *Research* 8, Article 0646.

Wang, Jane X., Zeb Kurth-Nelson, Dhruva Tirumala, Hubert Soyer, Joel Z. Leibo, Remi Munos, Charles Blundell, Dharshan Kumaran, and Matt Botvinick (2016). "Learning to Reinforcement Learn." *arXiv:1611.05763*.

Wang, Lishuang, Mengfei Zhao, Enyu Liu, Kebin Sun, and Ran Cheng (2024). "Tensorized Neuroevolution of Augmenting Topologies for GPU Acceleration." In *GECCO'24: Proceedings of the Genetic and Evolutionary Computation Conference*, 1156–1164.

Wang, Rui, Joel Lehman, Jeff Clune, and Kenneth O. Stanley (2019). "POET: Open-Ended Coevolution of Environments and Their Optimized Solutions." In *GECCO'19: Proceedings of the Genetic and Evolutionary Computation Conference*, 142–151.

Wang, Rui, Joel Lehman, Aditya Rawal, Jiale Zhi, Yulun Li, Jeff Clune, and Kenneth O. Stanley (2020). "Enhanced POET: Open-ended Reinforcement Learning Through Unbounded Invention of Learning Challenges and Their Solutions." In *Proceedings of the 37th International Conference on Machine Learning*, 9940–9951.

Wang, Yong (2013). "Gene Regulatory Networks." In *Encyclopedia of Systems Biology*, edited by Werner Dubitzky, Olaf Wolkenhauer, Kwang-Hyun Cho and Hiroki Yokota, 801–805. New York, NY: Springer.

Warner, Jamieson, Ashwin Devaraj, and Risto Miikkulainen (2024). "Using Context to Adapt to Sensor Drift." In *Proceedings of the International Conference on Development and Learning*, 184–190.

Watson, Richard A., Niclas Palmius, Rob Mills, Simon T. Powers, and Alexandra Penn (2011). "Can Selfish Symbioses Effect Higher-Level Selection?" In *Advances in Artificial Life: Darwin Meets von Neumann, 10th European Conference*, edited by George Kampis, István Karsai and Eörs Szathmáry, 27–36. New York, NY: Springer.

Watson, Richard A., and Jordan B. Pollack (2003). "A Computational Model of Symbiotic Composition in Evolutionary Transitions." *Biosystems* 69, 187–209.

Werner, Gregory M., and Michael G. Dyer (1992). "Evolution of Communication in Artificial Organisms." In *Artificial Life II: Proceedings of the Workshop on Artificial Life*, edited by Christopher G. Langton, Charles Taylor, J. Doyne Farmer and Steen Rasmussen, 659–687. Reading, MA: Addison-Wesley.

West-Eberhard, Mary-Jane (2003). *Developmental Plasticity and Evolution*. Oxford, UK: Oxford University Press.

White, Colin, Mahmoud Safari, Rhea Sukthanker, Binxin Ru, Thomas Elsken, Arber Zela, Debadeepta Dey, and Frank Hutter (2023). "Neural Architecture Search: Insights from 1000 Papers." *arXiv:2301.08727*.

Whiteson, Shimon (2006). "Evolutionary Function Approximation for Reinforcement Learning." *Journal of Machine Learning Research* 7, 877–917.

Whiteson, Shimon, Peter Stone, Kenneth O. Stanley, Risto Miikkulainen, and Nate Kohl (2005). "Automatic Feature Selection in Neuroevolution." In *GECCO'05: Proceedings of the 7th Annual Conference on Genetic and Evolutionary Computation*, 1225–1232.

Whitley, Darrell, Stephen Dominic, and Rajarshi Das (1991). "Genetic Reinforcement Learning with Multilayer Neural Networks." In *Proceedings of the Fourth International Conference on Genetic Algorithms*, 562–569.

Whitley, Darrell, Stephen Dominic, Rajarshi Das, and Charles W. Anderson (1993). "Genetic Reinforcement Learning for Neurocontrol Problems." *Machine Learning* 13, 259–284.

Whitley, Darrell, and Thomas Hanson (1989). "Optimizing Neural Networks Using Faster, More Accurate Genetic Search." In *Proceedings of the Third International Conference on Genetic Algorithms*, 391–396.

Whitley, Darrell, Keith E. Mathias, and Patrick A. Fitzhorn (1991). "Delta-Coding: An Iterative Search Strategy for Genetic Algorithms." In *Proceedings of the Fourth International Conference on Genetic Algorithms*, 77–84.

Whitley, Derek (2024a). "The Intrinsic Evolution of Reconfigurable Electronic Circuitry." PhD thesis. Bloomington, IN: School of Informatics, Computing, Engineering, and Cognitive Science Program, Indiana University.

Whitley, Derek (2024b). "Neuroevolving Electronic Dynamical Networks." *arXiv preprint arXiv:2404.04587.*

Widrow, Bernard, Youngsik Kim, Dookun Park, and Jose Krause Perin (2023). "Nature's Learning Rule: The Hebbian-LMS Algorithm." In *Artificial Intelligence in the Age of Neural Networks and Brain Computing (second edition)*, edited by Robert Kozma, Cesare Alippi, Yoonsuck Choe and Francesco C. Morabito, 11–40. Amsterdam, the Netherlands: Elsevier.

Wiegand, R. Paul (2003). "An Analysis of Cooperative Coevolutionary Algorithms." PhD thesis. Fairfax, VA: George Mason University.

Williams, Ronald J. (1992). "Simple Statistical Gradient-Following Algorithms for Connectionist Reinforcement Learning." *Machine Learning* 8, 229–256.

Wissner-Gross, Alexander D., and Cameron E. Freer (2013). "Causal Entropic Forces." *Physical Review Letters* 110, 168702.

Wolpert, Lewis, Cheryll Tickle, and Alfonso Martinez Arias (2015). *Principles of Development.* Oxford, UK: Oxford University Press.

Woolley, Brian G., and Kenneth O. Stanley (2011). "On the Deleterious Effects of A Priori Objectives on Evolution and Representation." In *GECCO'11: Proceedings of the 13th Annual Conference on Genetic and Evolutionary Computation*, 957–964.

Wu, Xingyu, Sheng-hao Wu, Jibin Wu, Liang Feng, and Kay C. Tan (2024). "Evolutionary Computation in the Era of Large Language Model: Survey and Roadmap." *arXiv:2401.10034.*

Wulff, Niels H., and John A. Hertz (1992). "Learning Cellular Automaton Dynamics with Neural Networks." In *Advances in Neural Information Processing Systems 5*, 631–638.

Wurman, Peter R., Samuel Barrett, Kenta Kawamoto, James MacGlashan, Kaushik Subramanian, Thomas J. Walsh, Roberto Capobianco, Alisa Devlic, Franziska Eckert, Florian Fuchs, Leilani Gilpin, Varun Kompella, Piyush Khandelwal, HaoChih Lin,

Patrick MacAlpine, Declan Oller, Craig Sherstan, Takuma Seno, Michael D. Thomure, Houmehr Aghabozorgi, Leon Barrett, Rory Douglas, Dion Whitehead, Peter Dürr, Peter Stone, Michael Spranger, and Hiroaki Kitano (2022). "Outracing Champion Gran Turismo Drivers with Deep Reinforcement Learning." *Nature* 62, 223–228.

XPRIZE (2023). *Pandemic Response Challenge.* https://www.xprize.org/challenge/pandemicresponse. Retrieved August 31, 2025.

Yamauchi, Brian M., and Randall D. Beer (1993). "Sequential Behavior and Learning in Evolved Dynamical Neural Networks." *Adaptive Behavior* 2, 219–246.

Yang, An, Anfeng Li, Baosong Yang, et al. (2025). "Qwen3 Technical Report." *arXiv:2505.09388.*

Yang, Tsun-Yi, Yi-Hsuan Huang, Yen-Yu Lin, Pi-Cheng Hsiu, and Yung-Yu Chuang (2018). "SSR-Net: A Compact Soft Stagewise Regression Network for Age Estimation." In *Proceedings of the 27th International Joint Conference on Artificial Intelligence*, 1078–1084.

Yannakakis, Georgios N., and Julian Togelius (2018). *Artificial Intelligence and Games.* 2nd ed. New York, NY: Springer.

Yao, Xin (1999). "Evolving Artificial Neural Networks." *Proceedings of the IEEE* 87, 1423–1447.

Ying, Chris, Aaron Klein, Eric Christiansen, Esteban Real, Kevin Murphy, and Frank Hutter (2019). "NAS-Bench-101: Towards Reproducible Neural Architecture Search." In *Proceedings of the 36th International Conference on Machine Learning*, 7105–7114.

Yong, Chern H., and Risto Miikkulainen (2010). "Coevolution of Role-Based Cooperation in Multi-agent Systems." *IEEE Transactions on Autonomous Mental Development* 1, 170–186.

Yong, Chern H., Kenneth O. Stanley, Risto Miikkulainen, and Igor V. Karpov (2006). "Incorporating Advice into Neuroevolution of Adaptive Agents." In *Proceedings of the Second Artificial Intelligence and Interactive Digital Entertainment Conference*, 98–104.

Young, Daniel, Olivier Francon, Elliot Meyerson, Clemens Schwingshackl, Jacob Bieker, Hugo Cunha, Babak Hodjat, and Risto Miikkulainen (2025). "Discovering Effective Policies for Land-Use Planning with Neuroevolution." *Environmental Data Science* 4, e30.

Zador, Anthony M. (2019). "A Critique of Pure Learning and What Artificial Neural Networks Can Learn from Animal Brains." *Nature Communications* 10, 3770.

Zela, Arber, Julien N. Siems, Lucas Zimmer, Jovita Lukasik, Margret Keuper, and Frank Hutter (2022). "Surrogate NAS Benchmarks: Going Beyond the Limited Search Spaces of Tabular NAS Benchmarks." In *Proceedings of the Tenth International Conference on Learning Representations*, 7294–7329.

Zhang, Aston, Zachary C. Lipton, Mu Li, and Alexander J. Smola (2023). *Dive into Deep Learning.* Cambridge, UK: Cambridge University Press.

Zhang, Jenny, Joel Lehman, Kenneth O. Stanley, and Jeff Clune (2024). "OMNI: Open-Endedness via Models of Human Notions of Interestingness." In *Proceedings of the Twelfth International Conference on Learning Representations*, 17745–17791.

Zhang, Qingfu, and Hui Li (2007). "MOEA/D: A Multiobjective Evolutionary Algorithm Based on Decomposition." *IEEE Transactions on Evolutionary Computation* 11, 712–731.

Zoph, Barret, and Quoc V. Le (2017). "Neural Architecture Search with Reinforcement Learning." In *Proceedings of the Fifth International Conference on Learning Representations*, 2841–2856.

Zoph, Barret, Vijay Vasudevan, Jonathon Shlens, and Quoc V. Le (2018). "Learning Transferable Architectures for Scalable Image Recognition." In *Proceedings of the IEEE/CVF Conference on Computer Vision and Pattern Recognition*, 8697–8710.

Zuidema, Willem, and Paulien Hogeweg (2000). "Social Patterns Guide Evolving Grammars." In *Proceedings of the Evolution of Language Conference*, 274–279.

Subject Index

*Entries in **bold** indicate the most comprehensive explanations,*

Author Index

Publisher contact:
The MIT Press
Massachusetts Institute of Technology
77 Massachusetts Avenue, Cambridge, MA 02139
mitpress.mit.edu

EU Authorised Representative:
Easy Access System Europe, Mustamäe tee 50,
10621 Tallinn, Estonia
gpsr.requests@easproject.com

Printed by Integrated Books International,
United States of America